KU-755-052

THE COMPLETE MANUAL OF

Edited by

Basil Caplan

Editor of

HEADLINE

Copyright © 1992 Basil Caplan

The right of Basil Caplan to be identified as the editor of the work
has been asserted by him in accordance with the
Copyright, Designs and Patents Act 1988

First published in 1992
by HEADLINE BOOK PUBLISHING PLC

10 9 8 7 6 5 4 3 2 1

All rights reserved. No part of this publication may be reproduced, stored in a
retrieval system, or transmitted in any form or by any means without the prior
written permission of the publisher, nor be otherwise circulated in any form of
binding or cover other than that in which it is published and without a similar
condition being imposed on the subsequent purchaser.

British Library Cataloguing in Publication Data

Caplan, Basil
    Complete Manual of Organic Gardening
    I. Title
    635. 0484

ISBN 0 – 7472 – 0515 – 9

Design and computer page make up by Penny Mills

Colour reproduction by Koford, Singapore

Printed and bound in Great Britain by
Butler and Tanner Limited, Frome

HEADLINE BOOK PUBLISHING PLC
Headline House
79 Great Titchfield Street
London W1P 7FN

THE COMPLETE MANUAL OF

Organic

GARDENING

LEARNING ZONE
Welsh College Of Horticulture
NORTHOP COLLEGE
Learning Resources
Centre

107352

Northop College

N00225

Welsh College Of Horticulture
Learning Resources
Centre

TYNNWYD O STOC
WITHDRAWN
FROM STOCK

LEARNING ZONE
NORTHOP COLLEGE

FIRE DAMAGE
SEEN AT

CONTENTS

THE CONTRIBUTORS

Jean Andrews – Specialist in old cottage garden plants, member of National Council for the Conservation of Plants and Gardens. Holder of the National Collection of *Bellis perennis* cultivars.

Basil Caplan– Former journalist and an organic gardener for the past fifteen years, is the founder and editor of the UK magazine *Organic Gardening*.

Ben Davidson – Botanist and MSc in horticulture, has managed tree and wildlife gardens, and is now a professional landscaper.

Charles Dowding – Of farming stock, dedicated Somerset organic farmer.

Bob Flowerdew – Author, broadcaster, lecturer, horticultural journalist in UK and overseas; gardens in Norfolk.

Dr Bob Gibbons – Writer and photographer specializing in natural history and countryside topics. Co-author with wife Liz Gibbons of *Creating a Wildlife Garden*.

Geoff Hamilton – Presenter of BBC TV's 'Gardener's World', author and distinguished gardening editor, is the creator of the notable Barnsdale ornamental kitchen garden.

Jim Hay – A northern gardener (Wigan), obliged for health reasons to avoid chemicals in his diet, turned to organic methods fifteen years ago. Author of several books on organic cultivation including organic methods of pest and disease control.

Patrick Hughes – Head Gardener at the Henry Doubleday Research Association for seven years, now produces wildflower seed organically, in Suffolk.

Richard Hutson – Meteorologist and geographer, maintains his own weather station in the island of Anglesey. Special interest: gardener's weather.

Roy Lacey – Author, broadcaster, lecturer on organic gardening, has managed trial plots for the BBC and has been a practising organic gardener since 1950.

Joy Larkcom – Author, broadcaster, lecturer, a leading authority on vegetable cultivation, is widely known for her popularization of little-known salad vegetables from continental Europe and the Far East.

John Lewis, M. (Hort) RHS – For four years supervisor of the Propagation Department of the Royal Botanic Gardens, Edinburgh, lecturer and landscape designer.

Dr Fred McPherson – Biologist, has worked for the Plant Breeding Institute in Cambridge, now conducts experiments in new ideas and techniques relevant to organic gardening on a three-acre allotment.

John Stevens – Author of *National Trust Book of Wildflower Gardening*, expert on herbs and wild flowers, founder of Suffolk Herbs nursery.

Dr Bill Symondson – Doctoral studies at University of Wales on carabid beetles as biological control agents for the control of slugs; part-time presenter and pest control adviser to BBC 'Gardener's World' programme; member of the HDRA Research Committee.

Michael Walton – Aberdeenshire gardener of twenty-eight years' standing.

EDITOR'S ACKNOWLEDGEMENTS

May I express my keen appreciation of the dedicated efforts of the contributors with whom it has been my privilege to work. An especial thanks to Elisabeth Ingles for her splendidly rigorous, always calming, approach to editing the typescript in detail, to the team at Headline, notably Celia Kent, and to Mat Coward for compiling the index .

INTRODUCTION

Organic gardening can best be understood by considering its place in the history of horticulture. Nowadays, it is all too easy to imagine that chemical-based horticulture is the norm, that the organic alternative is something new, perhaps a trifle cranky to boot. This is not how it happened. Chemicals began to be deployed only in the 1930s, and the massive proliferation of pesticides and herbicides with which we are all familiar is even more recent. The organic alternative has been, essentially, a reaction to these developments. In this sense, organic methods are part of the mainstream; chemicals, an aberration.

Between the two, there is a profound difference in outlook, relating both to how we feed plants and how we protect them from pests and diseases. In nature, nutrients are made available to plants by the action of soil microlife on organic matter. The chemical approach to feeding is that of the laboratory; it relies on synthetic fertilizers, primarily nitrates, which are delivered directly to the plant in soluble form, which, so the reasoning goes, will do the job just as well as the real thing. The soil is little more than a containing environment. Pests tend to be treated in isolation, to be eliminated with appropriate poisons; the causes of the one and the effects of the other are of secondary importance.

To the organic gardener, chemical-dependent cultivation has taken a dangerously wrong turn. Synthetic nitrate fertilizers, pesticides and herbicides are environmentally harmful at many levels. Food containing excessive quantities of nitrates is unhealthy. Even more so is the seepage of nitrates into ground-water. Cultivation on this basis, albeit offering quick, short-term returns, by neglecting and impoverishing the soil may ultimately be unsustainable. Herbicides and pesticides turn gardens into battlegrounds where the drifts are not those of dandelion seed but of hazardous chemicals. They are a danger to the direct users and those in their vicinity, as well as to any hapless wildlife that happens to get in their way; their residues, finding their way into ground-water and the food chain, put at risk the community at large.

Despite the withdrawal of some of the most dangerous pesticides, what may be termed chemical abuse is widespread. Twenty years ago, the World Health Organization estimated that there were half a million pesticide accidents a year, over 9,000 of them fatal, most of them in Third World countries; recent estimates suggest that those numbers will now have doubled. These figures take no account of the unknown, long-term damage that may be caused by carcinogenic and mutagenic pesticides, in Third World and Western countries alike.

Environmental considerations apart, these methods, far from being necessary, are antagonistic to a healthy and productive garden. Nature is best enlisted as an ally in the garden, rather than treated as something to be circumvented. This not a matter of sentimentality. There are indeed no 'goodies' and 'baddies' in the natural world. Preservation of wildlife is not simply a question of high regard for these creatures. The beautifully patterned ladybird is everyone's delight, but to the aphid it preys on, it is a ruthless and dangerous killer. How are we to regard the predatory testacella slug, which cannibalizes other slugs? In encouraging those forms of wildlife which help keep down our garden pests, we become highly partial referees. We have our favourites and we can ensure that they usually score most points! The rules, however, are those of the players. Few pests need to be entirely eliminated. A garden without slugs would not necessarily be the better for it; slugs play an important part in disposing of waste vegetation. The organic approach is to maintain a balance between pests and predators compatible with our needs as cultivators. Similarly, companion planting is not just a question of 'muck and magic'. Plants are self-regarding. They co-exist only with those plants that, coincidentally, support their own existence. Those that compete for shared, but limited, nutrients will strive to win at each other's expense.

Other things equal, nature ensures that the soil is constantly regenerated, and plant life sustained, by the recycling of decaying matter. It also establishes a balance between rival life forms. The diversity of plant life resulting from the time, the place, and the competition will ensure myriad forms of insect wildlife, living and feeding on one another, ensuring that none becomes rampant.

Other things are not equal, however. And the big unequalizers are ourselves. Cultivation of the earth is not part of nature's design. When we cultivate a garden, when we decide that here we shall grow dahlias, there brassicas, here we shall root out undesirable plants, we are interrupting what would have been, but for our intervention. Especially when we are growing food crops, the normal cycle of vegetation being returned to the earth is interrupted. We have to take steps to restore the soil's fertility.

The starting point for organic methods is our relationship with the soil. Without a supply of humus-creating organic matter, soil life will be impoverished. Without an active soil life, nutrients will not be made available, and plants cannot be fed. The business of tending the soil is therefore one of replicating nature's way of recycling by ensuring that we provide the earth with an adequate supply of organic matter. Hence the emphasis on compost and manure. It is this condition, healthy, organically rich soil, that ensures healthy, pest- and disease-resistant plants.

Most important of all for pest control is to allow nature to continue to maintain its own 'balance of forces' between species. This means leaving it to natural predators to keep pests within limits. Pesticides, by indiscriminately killing predator and pest alike, make this impossible. If you wipe out aphids and, at the same time, eliminate the ladybirds, hover-flies, lacewings and other predators, the end result may be only to perpetuate the use of pesticides. The higher up the predator/pest scale you go, the slower is life to replicate itself. Long before their predators have succeeded in regenerating themselves after a pesticide campaign, the aphids will be back with a vengeance, this time without their natural foes. Birds, further up the scale, can be destroyed as the pesticide residues move up the food chain. It will be longer still before they are back. So the chemically reliant gardener finds himself on a treadmill. The next year, an even heavier chemical drenching will be indicated because the aphids, without their predators, are now running amok! But even more of the same may suddenly cease to be effective, because there is another, more sinister factor at work with chemical poisons: resistance. Before the direct dangers of DDT to human health had become established and its use was banned, the scientists were busily hunting for other pesticides. The reason? Pest strains had evolved that were resistant to DDT.

Thirty years ago, Rachel Carson in her seminal work, *Silent Spring*, warned of the Pandora's box opened up by the use of pesticides, citing the sudden emergence of the spider mite as a global pest after DDT had killed off its predators. DDT was replaced by various other persistent organochlorines, and, subsequently, by a new generation of organophosphates. But with each successive development, the time-lag for the emergence of resistant strains has shortened: it took six and a third years for a doubling of the number of DDT-resistant species, four years for those resistant to organophosphates, and by the time the pyrethroids came along, the number of resistant pests was doubling every two years, according to findings cited by the British Medical Association. A further complicating factor is that the elimination of one pest often serves only to make space for the proliferation of another. Indeed, all the indications are that pest problems have become far more widespread since the coming of the pesticide age.

Besides encouraging predators, organic gardeners place strong emphasis on adapting to their geographic, climatic and soil conditions and, within a garden, to the micro-climate of each area. Half the gallant failures of gardening stem from efforts to cultivate plants that have no business in the place they find themselves. Acid-loving plants belong in an acid soil; moisture-loving plants in a suitably damp site, not in hot, dry conditions. Once again, it is a question of understanding nature's imperatives in order to raise healthy, pest-resistant plants. All good gardeners are aware of these, but they are central to the organic way of thinking.

With plant diseases, the emphasis is, even more so, on prevention. A large number of common garden diseases are, in fact, not curable, whether by the use of organically acceptable sprays or synthetic fungicides, once they have taken a hold. As any medical doctor knows, his most effective tool is preventive medicine, and the same applies to plants. The starting point is to give the plant a robust constitution by raising it in soil of good heart and then following the best principles of garden hygiene.

How does this scheme of things fit in with the needs of the gardener? When gardening is prefaced by the word 'organic' it does not become something apart. Whether you are an organic, non-organic, or partly organic gardener, the rules of sound garden management still apply. Gardening excellence is no one's monopoly. There are very well managed gardens that would not claim to be organic and there are some organic gardens that are anything but well managed. Too, that elusive quality, the 'green thumb', is not the exclusive property of one gardener or the other. In practice, nowadays, many gardeners fall into that partly organic category, adopting some, if not all, organic methods.

Best of all is a mature organic garden, cared for by a gardener who is a master of the gardening craft, and who also happens to have that green thumb. To the organic gardener, organic methods are, indeed, an essential element of gardening excellence. Without them, however fastidiously a garden may be managed, no matter how carefully the best sowing and propagating techniques are practised, however expertly a garden is maintained, the result will be compromised in the absence of the organic approach to plant feeding, pest and disease control.

Gardeners converting to organic methods, or taking over a garden where the soil has been starved of organic material and heavily impregnated with chemicals, will not be able to reap instant benefits. Chemical spraying may have deprived the garden of its balancing predatory population, and residues may remain in the soil for some time. Soil fertility, the rejection of synthetic chemical feeds, the avoidance of pesticides and herbicides are very much interrelated, and the cumulative effects take time. Gradual adoption of organic methods will yield partial results. Suppose you incorporate lots of organic material into the beds but retain the use of herbicides and pesticides. The improved soil structure will certainly give you some benefits, but less than could be hoped for. Chemicals do not just kill their targets. They can also damage soil life, earthworms, essential microbial bacteria and fungi, without which the organic material you have incorporated will remain 'undigested'. Or, you may take a different approach and throw away the spray can, but continue to rely on synthetic nitrates. At least beneficial predators will have a chance, but while superficially fit for the show bench, your plants will be far more vulnerable to disease; their lush foliage will also offer a gourmet meal to aphid and slug.

Whether you opt for a partial or an all-at-once approach is a matter for personal choice, perhaps of temperament. However, once established, a mature organic garden will have no need of inorganic feeds, herbicides or pesticides and that desired goal may in the end be reached most speedily by commencing as you intend to proceed.

As already noted, many of the methods used by organic gardeners are as old as time. Frequently, *Organic Gardening*'s postbag contains a letter from a venerable gardener who points out that he has been using the methods we advocate for the past fifty years. He is right. Reliance on organically enriched soil was, of course, the norm before the age of fast plant food. Many of the companion planting antidotes to various pests and diseases have their roots in ancient folklore. With some of their techniques, such as intensive raised beds for vegetable cultivation, organic gardeners have brought back into use methods which are

centuries old and are still widely used in China.

Organic gardening, however, is not simply a matter of getting back to the pre-chemical days. Contemporary scientific enquiry has much to contribute. Organic cultivators have an urgent interest in the contemporary development of pest- and disease-resistant varieties. Equally promising are biological pest-control methods. Properly based verification of companion planting claims is to be welcomed, whether it be to validate them, to turn up new applications, or simply to conclude with a negative, in which case a lot of wasted time and energy can be avoided. Improved methods of cultivation are an ongoing process. So, too, are investigation of the leaching problems which can also occur in an organic setting, the relative merits of compost and manure, the search for viable alternatives to peat, the use of green manures in a garden context, and the role of compost in disease resistance.

Technology, too, has its role to play. Some organic gardeners are reluctant to embrace the use of plastic mulches because they depend on non-renewable resources and because, too often, the materials are a non-biodegradable source of pollution. The use of electric or petrol-driven shredders to turn woody waste into readily compostible material is rejected by some on the grounds that they are highly energy-intensive. Nonetheless, both plastic mulches and shredders have become valuable and effective aids to organic cultivation. Plastic materials, at least some of them, can be made biodegradable. Given the ubiquity of plastic bottles, the organic gardener's recycling of them to form slug-defeating mini-cloches, and hence a non-chemical way of controlling one of the gardener's most intractable pests, has surely to be weighed against other considerations. Similarly, the energy consumption involved in the use of shredders is compensated by the great gain in recycling organic matter that would otherwise be largely lost in polluting bonfires. At a more basic level, the organic gardener is especially interested in the perfection of hoes and other weeding tools. Because organic methods eschew the 'quick-fix' results obtainable with synthetic fertilizers, there is also keen interest in growing under cover, whether in greenhouses, cold frames or under cloches.

I hope that these brief observations will provide a pointer to the order and priority of chapters in this Manual. Given the central importance of the soil and its organic structure, the early chapters cover soil, compost, and related cultivation methods.

The gardener who does not use herbicides needs to deploy considerable expertise when it comes to dealing with weeds, and organics has developed a range of effective methods of weed suppression. First, though, it is helpful to be able to identify them and understand their growth patterns. In some cases, and at certain times, weeds can even be beneficial. For this reason, it was deemed appropriate to devote a lengthy chapter to the subject, together with an extensive table accompanied by photographs.

Two major chapters are given to the recognition of pests and diseases, and their control without synthetic chemicals. The organic gardener needs to know more than is contained on the outside of a spray can if he is to cope knowledgeably and effectively with these garden problems, and these topics are dealt with in considerably more detail than may be found in most general gardening books. Prevention is all-important. For this reason, these chapters should not be read in isolation. The starting point for prevention is the nurturing of healthy plants and the starting point for good health is the fundamental importance of the soil.

Because organic methods are deeply concerned with the preservation of wildlife and genetic variety, wildlife gardening and old cottage garden flowers are given chapters of their own, while the chapter on lawns shows how to combine them with wild flowers.

A large section of the Manual is devoted to fruit and vegetables. Commercial priorities such as mechanical harvesting and long shelf-life make for varietal standardization, often at the expense of flavour and other qualities. Too, supermarket pesticide-free organic produce is often patchily and expensively available. We have therefore attempted to do full justice to the widening interest in 'growing-your-own'.

However, it would be misleading to conclude that organic gardening is all to do with food crops. Too little attention has been given, in the past, to the ornamental garden. The Manual seeks to remedy this neglect. It is sometimes thought that when it comes to flowers, it does not really matter all that much whether or not synthetic fertilizers and chemical pesticides and herbicides are used – after all, we do not propose to eat the products of our flower beds. There are a number of reasons why this is wide of the mark. In point of fact, organic methods are as relevant to the ornamental as to the vegetable garden. For one thing, pesticides are hazardous to the user wherever they may be. The risk of seepage of pesticide residues and nitrates into ground-water is every bit as great. And when it comes to the protection of garden wildlife, warning 'Keep Off' notices cannot be installed to prevent the residents of the vegetable garden from visiting the herbaceous beds across the lawn.

Far from seeking to segregate the ornamental and the vegetable gardens, organic gardeners plan, in various ways, to bring the two into close contact. A factor which makes plants highly vulnerable to specific pest and disease attack in farming is the practice of monoculture. This is easily avoided in a garden setting by choosing a fine diversity of plants. Too, appropriate flowers act as a magnet for valuable predators. It is a good notion to have them growing around the vegetable beds. There are those who choose to go all the way, with a completely integrated ornamental/vegetable garden. Besides being a valuable means of pest control, it can also add a pleasing aesthetic dimension to vegetable plants. For this reason, the Manual discusses this approach in a separate chapter, while the extended chapter on vegetables also indicates those which are especially suited to growing in ornamental beds. Above all, perhaps, the underlying case for growing flowers organically is as valid as that for vegetables. If vegetables grow more healthily from a rich, well structured soil, and are more pest- and disease-resistant, then the best and loveliest flowers can be grown in the same way. In summary, the Manual seeks to cover every aspect of gardening from an organic viewpoint, including much detailed horticultural information not usually within the reach of the layman. As such, we hope that it will be of interest to all gardeners, with or without a prior knowledge of organics. Because this is a team-authored work, the reader will encounter variations in detail. In gardening there are too many variables – local climate, soil, site, etc. – for there to be a single correct answer. Rather than impose an artificial uniformity, these variations have been left in place. The reader's own experience will be the best guide as to which suit his circumstances.

We trust that the Manual reflects the extent to which organic horticulture is now involved in a period of exciting and rapid development. Today, it deploys an extensive body of expertise on the techniques of organic husbandry. Much derives from the spread of organic farming, providing a beneficial spin-off for gardeners. Important research is now undertaken by organizations such as the Henry Doubleday Research Association and the Soil Association in Britain, the Rodale Institute in the United States, by universities and even government-funded organizations in many countries. Distinctive contributions are being made by the biodynamics and permaculture movements – fascinating subjects in their own right.

Among those who do not wish to dispense with chemicals altogether, there is a growing acceptance that pesticide and herbicide use is best restricted. Integrated pest management, as it is called, seeks to harness other methods, including those used by organic cultivators. In many laboratories, the emphasis is shifting to genetic engineering, building pest-deterring toxins into plants as an alternative to pesticides. Attractive in principle, the implications call for as much scrutiny as the pesticides they may replace.

Over the garden fence, there is a growing

community of interest between organic gardeners and their neighbours. Most gardeners today seek at least to minimize their use of chemicals. Others are discovering the satisfaction of recycling their kitchen waste and lawn clippings, turning them into valuable compost to enrich their soil as an alternative to inorganic (and expensive) fertilizers. In so doing, incidentally, they are performing a valuable service in reducing the pressures on scarce landfill sites.

Gardening is above all a personal point of contact between the gardener, usually urban nowadays, and nature. The organic gardener does more than cultivate plants; highly practical, he also becomes something of a naturalist, aware of his garden as a mini-universe teeming with interrelated life. Taking part in that life, understanding and nurturing it, is an infinitely rewarding adventure. It gives to gardening an even more special lustre.

Guide to seasons

Seasons	Southern UK 50°–53°N	Northern UK 53°N+	Southern Europe 30°–45°N	USA 30°–45°N	Canada and northern US 45°N+	Australia and New Zealand 30°–45°S
Early spring	March	April	February	February–March	April	September
Mid-spring	April	May	March	March–April	May	October
Late spring	May	May–June	April	April–May	June	November
Early summer	June	June–July	May–June	June	July	December
Mid-summer	July	July	July–August	July–August	July–August	January
Late summer	August	August	September	August–September	August	February
Early autumn	September	August–September	October	September–October	September	March
Mid-autumn	October	October	November	October–November	October	April
Late autumn	November	November	November–December	November	November	May
Early winter	December	December	December	December	December	June
Mid-winter	January	January	January	January–February	January–February	July
Late winter	February	February–March	February	February March	March	August

Notes
Rather than use calendar months as guides to sowing, planting and pruning times throughout the Manual, wherever possible we have broken down the seasons into early, mid-, late spring, summer, autumn and winter categories. Reference to this Table will indicate the corresponding months in some of the principal temperate areas of the world. The reader will make his own modifications depending on local factors such as height above sea level, maritime or inland location, and other conditions which can have significant effects.

Broadly speaking, northern and central European growing seasons approximate to those of the UK.

1

CLIMATE AND WEATHER

The average conditions of a region form that region's climate. The significance of climate to gardeners lies in the range of plants which may be grown with some likelihood of success. It is generally accepted that crops will cease to grow when the temperature falls below 43°F (6°C). The climate of certain regions is so favourable to the growth of particular crops that famous associations of one with another have evolved: the vineyards of France, the citrus groves of Florida, the early potatoes and tomatoes of the Channel Islands and the orchards of Kent.

Three factors are important in forming the climate of a region. The first is latitude or distance north or south of the equator. Latitude, combined with the seasonal range of the sun due to the tilt of the earth's axis, influences temperature and sunshine in a garden. The second factor is the position of the garden relative to the sea or other large bodies of water such as the Great Lakes of North America. This factor influences temperature and rainfall as well as wind and storms. Third is the altitude of the garden and its position in the local landscape. These can influence temperature, sunshine and frost.

LATITUDE AND SUNLIGHT

All life on earth depends upon the sun, but most of the sun's rays which are intercepted by planet Earth are lost to us, some in passing through the atmosphere and some by scattering among the clouds. Reflection accounts for many more, especially from snow and ice. Still more are expended in the process of evaporation.

Of that proportion of the sun's energy received on earth much is of little use to the gardener, because it falls in high latitudes or desert areas where cultivation is impossible. Much falls above the treeline at altitudes where gardening, if possible at all, must be problematical. To all these must be added the greatest expenditure of all, that which takes place

OPPOSITE: **Every gardener's constant companion** (*Richard Hutson*)

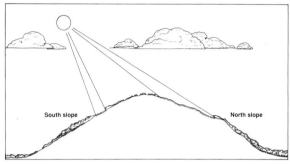

Effect of sun's rays on slopes (*Richard Hutson / Rob Dalton*)

over the oceans. The sea absorbs some radiation, reflects some back to the atmosphere and accounts for much more by evaporation.

The greatest concentration of the sun's rays is between the two tropics, where the sun is overhead at noon and the rays fall at right angles to the earth's surface. As the earth curves away from the tropical latitudes towards the poles a given ray of sunlight has to spread itself over an ever-increasing area. In the Land of the Midnight Sun there may be continuous daylight in summer, but the Laplanders are not notable gardeners. The rays are intercepted at too low an angle for gardening to be practicable. At the other extreme the searing, vertical rays of the tropical sun create desert conditions, burning up all hope of gardening. For most of us, latitude limits the scope of our gardening activities.

The intensity of the sun's rays also varies with the slope of the land. In the northern hemisphere a south-facing slope will receive a high concentration. The greatest input of energy to the garden is where the slope is at right angles to the rays.

INFLUENCE OF THE SEA

Britain, enjoying a mild, temperate climate, is in the same latitude as Labrador whose inhabitants experience winters of arctic severity. This fact and many other similarly startling climatic contrasts result from the influence of ocean currents on the temperature and humidity of the air masses which drift across them. The Atlantic coasts of western Europe are washed by the North Atlantic Drift, an extension of the Gulf Stream. The heat which maintains the comfortable existence of western Europeans was introduced into the ocean waters many months earlier in a long, slow drift under a tropical sun which began off west Africa, continued through the Caribbean and Gulf of Mexico and ended in Europe.

Atlantic air masses transport this heat from the ocean to the continent in a succession of weather systems which are vitally important to the climate of western Europe, but which have little influence on that of North America. On the coastal fringe of the Gulf of Mexico and of the Atlantic states of Georgia, the Carolinas and Virginia the Gulf Stream exercises some influence but it is limited in extent; even the violent hurricanes of the region rarely reach inland, for they depend upon the sea for their energy. Florida, however, bounded on both sides of the peninsula by warm waters, has the most equable climate in all of North America. The citrus plantations, frost-free and with adequate rainfall, need no irrigation as do those in southern California and, hurricanes apart, gardeners in this State have little to complain about.

In Europe the climates of the Mediterranean and Baltic regions do not benefit directly from the North Atlantic Drift, but the warm, humid air which is drawn occasionally into these landlocked basins from the Atlantic modifies the extremes of heat and cold which they would otherwise experience. The countries of Mediterranean Europe would suffer a desert climate if it were nòt for the winter rains which arrive with the Atlantic depressions, while those of the Baltic would have to endure even more severe winter weather than they do now.

Elsewhere in Europe distance from the sea leads increasingly to more extreme conditions in which hot summers and cold winters replace the warm, wet, temperate weather so characteristic of the west.

ALTITUDE AND LANDSCAPE

The third factor determining the climate of a region is the influence of altitude or height above sea level. The British Isles, although comparatively small in area, provide an exceptional variety of climatic conditions which reflect contrasts in the country's structure and relief. A line drawn from the Exe in Devon to the Tees at Middlesbrough divides Britain into an upland region in the north and west and a lowland country to south and east. Temperature usually falls with height at the rate of 1°F (0·5°C) for every 270 ft (82 m), while rainfall tends to increase.

In the mountainous regions of western Europe, in the Pyrenees and the Alps for example, it is

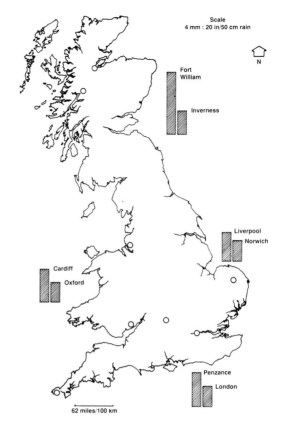

Annual rainfall comparisons (*Richard Hutson / Rob Dalton*)

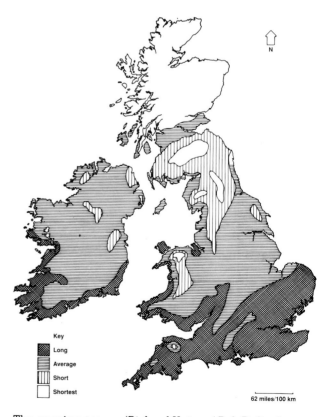

The growing season (*Richard Hutson / Rob Dalton*) (*After S. Gregory*)

Highland Britain is generally wet, windy and, on the mountains, cold, but within the upland zone there are many exceptions. Along the coasts of north and west Wales – Anglesey, Lleyn and Pembroke – the climate is so mild that early crops of vegetables can be first on the market, while the rich pasture produces the famous early Welsh lamb from these coastal regions. The Isle of Wight, the Isles of Scilly and the south-west of England also enjoy these favourable conditions.

In Scotland the northern highlands provide a rain shadow for the Moray Firth, so that crops may be successfully grown which are more typical of eastern England. On the west coast of Scotland the islands and peninsulas at sea level also experience much milder conditions than those on the higher ground, or even much further south in parts of lowland Britain, but gardens suffer badly from storms.

still possible to witness the migration of stock to and from the uplands as the seasons change. In the British mountains sheep which have wintered in the lowlands make use of the rising temperatures of springtime in similar fashion. Gardeners, unlike pastoralists, have no such freedom of movement unless, like the Norwegians, they maintain a summer garden in the mountains and another on the coast. The long, mountainous coastline of Norway presents a barrier against the Atlantic weather systems which greatly influences the climate of Sweden and neighbouring Baltic countries.

LOCAL CLIMATE

The position of a garden in the landscape, that is to say its site and situation, is important in defining the local climate. A valley site may increase the risk of frost, since cold air, like water, will flow downhill and collect at the bottom in a frost pocket. The aspect of garden features, that is to say their position in relation to a particular direction, influences light and shade, rain, wind and frost. A judicious arrangement of hedges, walls and fences enables gardeners to influence the climate of their plots to an important degree. A situation in the lee of mountains will give shelter from wind and a reduction in rainfall.

In cities and other extensively built-up areas gardeners can enjoy higher temperatures than in rural situations, sometimes by as much as 10°F (6°C). When flocks of starlings, wagtails and other birds fly in from the country to roost among the buildings they are doing so to keep warm. Plants in city gardens bloom early, while snow and ice melt more quickly. On the other hand there may be more air pollution and consequently less sunshine;

small country towns and villages where the smoke abatement laws may be ignored are often foul with chimney smoke in winter, especially during cold, calm evenings, when the warm smoke will not rise but will lie between the buildings to cause smog.

Large woods and plantations influence the local climate in several ways, particularly by providing shelter from wind. Tree roots impede the flow of rainwater and discourage flash floods.

Proximity to the sea not only modifies the climate but can have significant local effects, mainly related to the flow of air to and from the sea surface. The same is true to a lesser degree on lakesides. Gardeners on the coast are often grateful for the sea breeze which cools their gardens in the afternoons. Holidaymakers are less appreciative, for what promises to be a fine day in the morning so often clouds over and becomes cooler later in the day. These changes occur because water, unlike land, is slow to heat and equally slow to cool. As the day advances the sun heats the land quickly while the sea remains cool. The hot air rises and draws in a cold sea breeze. In addition the rising air cools and condenses into cloud, giving relief to the gardener but disappointment to visitors.

Often on summer mornings before the sea breeze sets in, warm air from the land will drift over the cool sea and create a sea mist. Such a mist or fog may then drift back over the gardens to condense on the leaves of the plants, where it can only do good.

MICROCLIMATES

It is beyond the power of man to control the weather, but by using our knowledge of principles gardeners can make the best use of what the weather has to offer. In small areas of the garden, by artificial means, they can control temperature, humidity, sunshine and wind. They can store rain when it is plentiful and irrigate in times of drought. Over these limited areas gardeners can create microclimates: one of the most obvious ways to do this is by the use of glass or some other transparent material.

The principal purpose of a greenhouse is not, as one might at first suppose, to attract the maximum amount of heat. Indeed, for most of the summer we try to exclude the sun's rays by shading the house. The heat we are hoping to trap is that which radiates at night from the ground at a time when external temperatures are falling. See *Growing Under Cover* (page 334) for more information.

Winds can have a very harmful effect on plant growth – the more so when drying winds evaporate the plant's moisture to cause desiccation. But the impact of winds in particular parts of the garden can be greatly modified by the presence of walls, hedges or specially built windbreaks. When using fences as windbreaks

In recent years polythene sheeting has become a useful method of heating the soil. Black is the best colour to use because it absorbs more sunlight than lighter colours. Several other products such as bubble plastic and fleece blankets aid in the creation of microclimates.

they should be no higher than 3 ft (1 m) and of a slatted design which allows some of the wind to pass through the fence. This reduces the tendency for a vacuum to develop. Gardeners might with advantage consider using temporary windbreaks such as Jerusalem artichokes or tall, strong annual flowers which would not permanently shade a plot as a fence will do.

Microclimates can be created in frames and under cloches. The problem here is to maintain the right degree of humidity. When Victorian gardeners built hotbeds, with their ample supplies of fresh manure, they were able to introduce both heat and humidity into the frame to create a healthy growing climate. The modern glass cloche will create some moisture by condensation on the cool glass but polythene is less likely to do so. Both types will draw moisture from the surrounding soil by capillary attraction.

South-facing borders can attract more energy from the sun if the soil can be drawn up to a slope. Building walls and terraces will also trap more heat, even if they are only inches high, and barn cloches will make the maximum use of the sun if they are aligned from west to east. If laid from north to south the sloping glass roofs will reflect too much of the light. On the other hand plants in rows not under glass will benefit from a north-south alignment because each side of the row will have an equal share of the sun's rays. Plants in rows also gain benefit from earthing-up so as to increase the angle of incidence of the ray.

WEATHER FORECASTING

Television weather forecasts cover too large an area to be of much help to gardeners. Moreover, they display the weather as seen from satellites far above the earth, whereas gardeners with their feet on the ground have to watch the weather changing from below. Only if they make their own forecasts can they be prepared for what is to come in their own immediate locality, but it is rarely possible for gardeners to forecast weather changes more than six hours in advance.

Professional forecasters receive numerous reports from around the world on which to base their forecasts, but the amateur observer has no such help. Nevertheless, with a little knowledge of the principles involved and a willingness to keep a continuous watch on the sky, gardeners can develop a useful technique. With practice they can forecast the more significant changes with some accuracy.

WILL IT RAIN?

It is a fact of nature that warm air has a greater capacity to hold water vapour than colder air. If for one reason or another the temperature continues to fall, then sooner or later the air will be unable to contain the water vapour and it will be precipitated as rain, snow, dew, mist or frost. There are four reasons why the air may be cooled. It may be forced to rise by crossing high ground; it may be undercut by a wedge of colder air; it may move across a cold surface of land or sea; or it may rise by means of heat convection.

Most of the rainfall in western Europe, for instance, is associated with the passage of weather fronts during which relatively warm air is forced to rise over colder air. In rising the air is cooled and when the water vapour can no longer be contained it condenses. Deciding when this process is likely to occur is important to gardeners who wish to take advantage of such advance information.

In the USA and Canada, gardeners on the west coast experience a similar rainfall to that of the western Mediterranean, while in southern California and the arid south-west gardens depend upon irrigation.

East of the Rockies the rains are light over the High Plains, but there is an imaginary line down the middle of the continent through the Dakotas, to the east of which gardeners can rely on adequate summer rains with 20 to 40 in (50–100 cm) annually. Much of it falls from thunderstorms.

In New England and the other Atlantic states the rainfall is adequate and favourable for gardening, well spread through the year with an autumn maximum, while gardens in the Mississippi Basin enjoy an early summer maximum.

Although much of the Australian continent is too arid for gardening without irrigation, most Australians live on or near the coast where rainfall is more favourable. There are monsoon rains and cyclones in the north, but the populous south-east coast receives a more regular rainfall. Gardens in Sydney have 40 in (100 cm) with an autumn maximum. Melbourne gardeners are fortunate to have a good proportion of their 25 in (63 cm) in the spring. The gardens of Adelaide and Perth experience a Mediterranean-type climate.

The climate of New Zealand's North Island is also similar to that of the Mediterranean, while the South Island is less favourable, being mountainous and with heavy rain and lower temperatures.

The name *front*, derived from the First World War, describes the zone of conflict which exists

Cirrus clouds (*Richard Hutson*)

Altostratus and altocumulus clouds (*Richard Hutson*)

BELOW: Dynamics of a depression. A cold front arrives and shunts warm air forward and up (*Richard Hutson / Rob Dalton*)

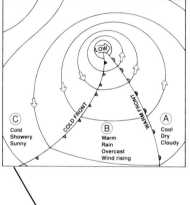

when air masses of differing characteristics come into contact. Warmer air will rise and colder air will undercut to create instability along the front. The rotation of the earth adds spin to the disturbance and the result of these various forces is the area of low pressure with which we are all familiar from television and radio forecasts. Such a depression is illustrated here.

At Position A in the diagram the observer is in the path of the depression. As the warm front approaches the clouds begin to form at a high level. These are the cirrus clouds. They represent the condensation of water vapour high overhead. As the front continues to advance the clouds increase and form at the intermediate height. These are the middle clouds altostratus and altocumulus. The observer on the ground is still unaffected by these changes but with the further advance of the front the cloud base continues to descend. The observer now notices that the wind is rising. If a barometer is available the pressure will be seen to be falling and the temperature will rise as the warm front crosses over. Rain will probably fall.

At Position B the observer is in the warm sector. Clouds are low and may be moving fast in a rising wind. The sky is heavily overcast with nimbostratus cloud and temperatures are relatively high. Humidity is high and rain may be falling.

With the passage of the cold front all this changes. Cold air from the rear of the depression is undercutting the warmer air and forcing it to rise. This causes heavy rain to fall along the front but it soon passes and at Position C the skies are clearing. In the cold air the thermometer is falling but the barometer rises to reflect the passage of the depression. All the heavy cloud is now replaced by fair weather cumulus and the sun is shining.

Because the cold front is moving more rapidly than the warm front it eventually undercuts it and forces the whole disturbance off the ground. It is now said to be occluded and at this stage in the development of the depression it is more difficult to forecast. Nevertheless the sequence of cloud types and the increasing heaviness of the sky will remain as guides to the weather.

The amateur observer in the garden will now appreciate why, with increasing humidity in advance of the disturbance, plants such as the scarlet pimpernel close their petals before rain and why the sun or moon may display a halo as they shine through the thin upper clouds and warn of worse to come. There are many such signs and sayings which, today, with our reliance on instruments,

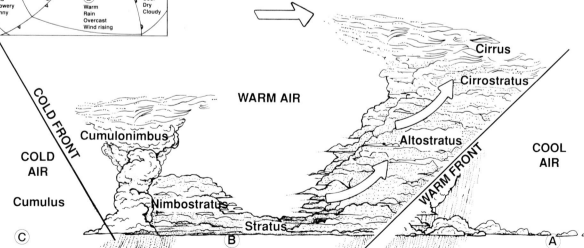

Cumulus clouds (*Richard Hutson*)

Sun reflected on storm clouds
(*Richard Hutson*)

have been all but forgotten but which gardeners can resurrect for their advantage and enjoyment. Probably the best known of these half–remembered sayings is that a 'red sky in the morning is the shepherd's warning'. This should be used with caution. The drawing explains how the verse is only true if the red sky is reflected from the rising sun on storm clouds in the west.

WILL IT BLOW?

Disturbances at the earth's surface are often influenced by fast-moving currents of air high overhead. These so-called jet streams may be recognized by bands of cirrus cloud moving across the sky. A useful forecast can be made by relating the direction of the wind at ground level with that in the jet stream (see diagram right). Face the surface wind. If the jet stream is from the right (A) the weather will worsen. At (B) it will improve, while if at (C) or (D) there will be no change. It is apparent from the diagram that winds circulating around a centre of low pressure do so in an anti-clockwise direction. This is invariably the case in the northern hemisphere, but the opposite is true for the southern hemisphere. These jet stream clouds often appear to be radiating from a point on the horizon but this is an illusion due to perspective. Nevertheless the disturbance may well come from that quarter.

WILL IT FREEZE?

The fact that water expands when it freezes explains why ice has such power to shatter objects which, in themselves, have great

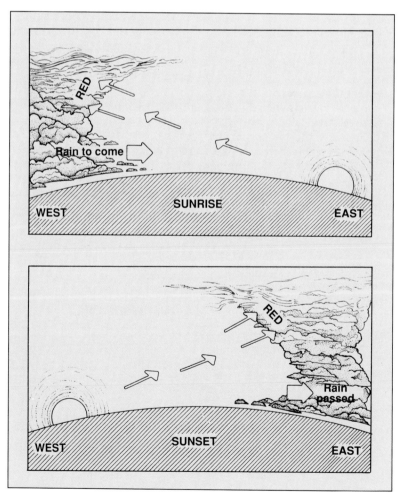

Shepherd's warning (*Richard Hutson / Rob Dalton*)

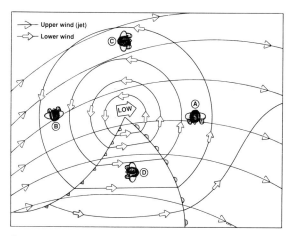

Crossing winds (*Richard Hutson / Rob Dalton*)

strength. In the garden it is a mixed blessing, being good for soil texture and the control of pests but damaging to tender plants. Either way it is important that gardeners should be able to anticipate it.

They will recognize two kinds of frost, ground and air frost. Ground frosts can occur when the air temperature is still above freezing point but the ground temperature, owing to the radiation of heat during the night hours, reaches 32°F (0°C). These conditions are unlikely to occur if the air is moist or turbulent but a clear sky, no wind, and a high barometric pressure with a slowly descending air flow will encourage the process. On contact with the ground the air is cooled and its moisture condenses as frost.

Air frost exists when the air temperature falls below freezing. This occurs when the cold ground is influencing the lower layers of the air up to a height of several feet. From this it is clear that while a ground frost will affect only plants at ground level, others such as fruit trees may not be touched. An air frost, however, may reach the blossom.

Gardeners have little practical interest in average temperatures, realizing that it is the extremes which threaten their plants. The chilling effect of the wind is a case in point. We know that there is a relationship between the force of the wind and the air temperature because we can feel the effect on our skins, resulting not only from wind speed and temperature but such factors as relative humidity and body temperature. Plants, which do not generate their own heat, are not affected in the same way.

Nevertheless, the damage done to plants by significant winds at any temperature is real enough and the accompanying table of equivalent wind-chill temperatures will serve as a guide to gardeners whose own discomfort due to wind-chill is a warning to protect their plants from physical damage.

WILL THERE BE DEW?

Old-timers in the garden used to argue as to whether dew came down from above or up from below, but the value to plants of this natural gift was never disputed. Dew can be formed from above when warm air condenses on cold ground and also from below when moist heat radiating from the ground is cooled by cold air.

When we step out into the garden early in the morning and observe the lawn bejewelled with moisture and the spiders' glistening webs the chances are that the night has been calm and cloudless. On such a night the heat that was poured into the ground by yesterday's sunshine quickly radiates back into the atmosphere. By morning the soil surface is colder than the air above so that water vapour in the air condenses, but for this to happen the air must already be humid with a high water vapour content.

Not all the moisture that is seen on vegetation in a summer garden is dew. Some is exuded from the leaves as the sap rises during the night hours. These droplets are not dew and they have not been condensed from the air.

The influence of soil texture on temperature is well known. Soils heavy with clay are said to be cold and slow to heat but equally slow to lose their heat. Sands and gravels are light and quickly heated but also quick to cool. If there is a variety of soil textures in the garden the ground temperatures will vary. Once they have got to know their soil gardeners can turn this knowledge to advantage.

Wind-chill				
WIND MPH	AIR TEMPERATURE (°F)			
0	45°	40°	35°	30°
10	34°	28°	22°	16°
20	26°	19°	12°	4°
30	21°	13°	6°	-2°
40	19°	11°	3°	-5°

It is important for the gardener to realize that not all parts of the garden radiate heat at the same rate. For example, soil covered with vegetation will cool more slowly than bare ground. Air trapped between the leaves acts as a blanket, retaining heat in the soil while allowing the leaves to cool more rapidly. Bare ground, on the other hand, has no such protection. If heat and dew are to be retained then successional crops, intercrops and mulches are recommended.

2 SOIL

Soil is more than an inert medium for roots to feed in: it has a life of its own. The breathing skin of the earth, it both gives us food to eat and nourishes us in a deeper way with beautiful plants and trees. How you treat your soil will ultimately decide whether or not your garden flourishes.

The practice which I recommend is to increase the amount of life in your soil, namely worms, insects such as beetles and centipedes, and all the invisible micro-organisms which promote plant growth. First of all, however, you have to start by seeing what your soil is like.

WHAT IS SOIL?

Within your soil there will, with luck, be a good balance of biology and chemistry. Soil is a collection of minerals such as calcium and silica which are continually in the process of being rendered soluble and available to plant roots, depending on the amount of 'soil life'. The latter lives off organic matter, which is vegetation in various stages of decomposition – leaves in the forest, compost and old roots in the garden. The percentage of organic matter or humus is often 3–5% in an arable (continually cropped) soil, rising to 8–10% in a healthy pasture and 25% or more in peaty soils. The organic matter is dark in colour and occurs mostly near the surface in the 'topsoil'; this is the zone we work with from day to day and is the most easily alterable.

To best understand the soil in your garden dig a hole 18 in (45 cm) square and 2 ft (60 cm) deep. Keep the zones of different-coloured soil separate so you can put them back in the same order. The lighter soil at the bottom has too little soil life to sustain all the little roots which a plant needs; it will also dry out and crack very quickly. If builders have been in your garden you may have some of this on top and the soil may also vary a lot from place to place.

OPPOSITE: The breathing skin of the earth (*David Woodfall*)

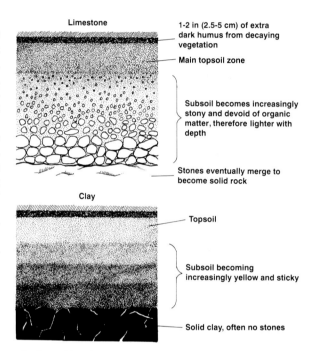

Limestone

1-2 in (2.5-5 cm) of extra dark humus from decaying vegetation

Main topsoil zone

Subsoil becomes increasingly stony and devoid of organic matter, therefore lighter with depth

Stones eventually merge to become solid rock

Clay

Topsoil

Subsoil becoming increasingly yellow and sticky

Solid clay, often no stones

Soil profiles (*Elizabeth Douglass*)

TOPSOIL

What should be on top is the topsoil, the darkest soil due to the presence of humus; it has a high carbon content, hence its deep colour. It is the main food for the various soil populations which convert it into plant nutrients. So if you have a dark topsoil you can probably expect good growth – but do not take it for granted. Some black soils in Britain are the poorest of all, the peaty covering of heath and moor, usually due to a combination of acidity and leaching (see page 14) and consequent lack of soil life.

SUBSOIL

If your surface soil is not at all dark it may be that the next zone down, the subsoil, has been exposed for one reason or another. This means a lot of effort to put matters right because the subsoil is, if you like, for reserves, not immediate nourishment. There is the potential for growth in terms of minerals and nutrients, but the life-

Soil changes: topsoil ⇒ subsoil ⇒ stones (*Charles Dowding*)

mechanisms which unlock these are present only in small degree: yet a subsoil is very necessary for holding reserves of goodness and moisture. It also forms the topsoil over a long time-scale.

BEDROCK

Finally there is bedrock, the underlying geology such as granite, limestone or sandstone. This may begin at almost any depth, and can have quite an effect on the soil above. Limestone, for instance, gives a soil the basic qualities of alkalinity, free drainage and stoniness. The connection may be less obvious or non-existent, as where wind- or water-borne deposits are very deep and give the topsoil their character, often a very fertile one due to the quantity of loose matter.

THE RANGE OF SOIL TYPES

Just as we can choose our friends but not our family, so we tend to choose a house and not the soil. What you have you are stuck with. Soils can often be considerably improved but will always retain certain basic qualities. Many soils are a mixture of extremes; all are better understood by knowing something about the various types.

Tilth

The common terms for describing soil relate essentially to the size of its principal constituent particles, from microscopic in clay to ½ in (1·25 cm) or more in gravel. Few soils contain only one size of particle, so the word 'loam' is used to indicate the presence of a mixture and is prefixed by 'clay', 'sand' etc. to say which quality is predominant. A 'medium' loam is possibly the most balanced and easily worked soil, being a mixture of clay, silt, sand and often small stones as well.

This balance together with the organic matter present will give rise to a 'tilth', which describes the soil's characteristics in the top few inches. A 'good tilth' means a collection of millions of small crumbs, large enough to sustain the presence of air in between and to admit the passage of water, while small enough to pack down firmly (not to a hard or rocklike surface) and to present a large surface area for roots to feed from. A tilth can be created mechanically, by a rotovator, as well as occurring naturally where there is sufficient organic matter to sustain the crumbliness of the soil, but if 'artificial' it will disappear through the effect of rain and treading on the soil.

You can assess the natural tilth of your soil when it is moist by picking some up between thumb and finger. If your soil is clay or silt you will be able to make a ball of it, but if the ball is not too sticky and will crumble apart there should be a reasonable quantity of organic matter. If on the other hand the soil trickles away before you can shape it you have sand predominating; if it nonetheless feels soft and looks dark you also have plenty of organic matter. Look especially to see whether the soil collapses to a solid mass under pressure or whether some element of crumb remains. The latter is a good sign of organic matter and arises principally through the action of worms.

Imagine a soil with no life or organisms, many particles of even size, perhaps some stones. Such soil tends to compact, leaving little space for roots

With the presence of living organisms, especially worms and their casts, the soil is opened up forming friable, slightly 'gluey' crumbs, $1/16$ - $3/8$ in (2-10 mm) in size, with space between for air and moisture, and roots to penetrate

However, a crumb is not an impermeable solid. Roots can penetrate to obtain the goodness within, where there will also be a big range of soil life as well as air and moisture

Soil structure (*Elizabeth Douglass*)

Clay is a common ingredient in all soils; where it predominates it is potentially fertile but in need of a careful approach. Your soil is clay if it is yellowish in colour, if it really sticks to your boots, and if when moist it will mould into a ball or even a 'worm' under slight pressure. These soils dry like a brick or go as hard as rock in the summer, and this can happen very quickly from when they were wet and pudding-like. This is a vital clue to successful handling: be ready for the right moment, as the French say 'when the soil flowers'. Too early and you squash the life and air out, making a mud-bath; too late and it goes hard and knobbly, making it difficult to achieve a tilth. Luckily the flowering of the soil should in fact happen more than once in the spring, after some dry warm weather and before the next lot of rain.

The essential quality of a clay soil is the smallness of its constituent particles – hence the air spaces are also small and vulnerable, prone to compaction. On the other hand this characteristic is a key to abundant growth because the surface area available to roots is so much greater. It may be more work but can be very worthwhile. An approach I would recommend is not to dig the soil at all, rather apply a good quantity every year of well-rotted organic matter to the surface, thus creating a shallow, easily worked topsoil. Plants should establish well in this, and be in a position to explore the goodness and moisture below. But since you are not digging, be extra careful not to compact the soil in wet conditions. If you have inherited an abused soil which looks solid and lifeless, digging *will* be necessary in the first year, preferably also incorporating some compost. The aim is to reach a point where nature can take over.

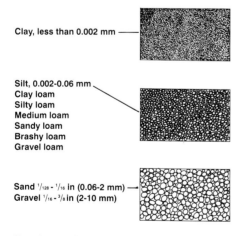

Clay, less than 0.002 mm

Silt, 0.002-0.06 mm
Clay loam
Silty loam
Medium loam
Sandy loam
Brashy loam
Gravel loam

Sand ¹/₁₂₈ - ¹/₁₆ in (0.06-2 mm)
Gravel ¹/₁₆ - ³/₈ in (2-10 mm)

Note: Loam soils contain a mixture of sand, silt and clay. The ideal medium loam is made up about 50% sand, 50% silt and clay and, perhaps, some small stones. Other loams are characterized by a higher proportion of one or other of these, or of gravel

Soil types (*Elizabeth Douglass*)

Silt is akin to clay, but the particles are a little larger so the difficulties are less acute, while there is still great fertility. Soils of pure silt are rare – usually silt is a minor ingredient in other soils.

Sand is approaching the other end of the spectrum, with large particles resulting in often low fertility, almost too good drainage (leaching nutrients away) and poor anchoring qualities for plant roots, e.g. brassicas tend to rock a lot in the wind. Such soils are often referred to as 'hungry'; they demand a lot of compost and organic matter and sometimes a lot of watering. Their advantages are earliness of cropping, as the soil dries out and warms up quickly; ease of access all through the year, as they do not compact to mud in wet weather; and excellent conditions for root vegetables. Carrots especially like a sandy soil.

Gravel is often present in soils, especially lower down. If there is much of it, the same hungry, free-draining qualities will be apparent as in sand.

Brashy soils have many small stones among even the topsoil. Do not be alarmed at this. Stones offer nutrients to soil as they weather, they assist in drainage and in dry weather they can act as a valuable mulch, preventing drying of the soil. If you really feel you have too many the no-dig approach can again be valuable in eventually creating a less stony top 2 in (5 cm); even so, heavy frost tends to push stones upwards and it might be worth picking them up – certainly the larger ones.

Medium loams are close to the ideal, being a composition of sand, silt and clay. Even if you have a friendly soil such as this, do not neglect its long-term fertility by skimping on organic matter. If you spread an inch or two of compost every year, almost any soil can become of a 'good' loamy type, particularly where digging is not practised.

SOIL QUALITIES

What is a good soil? Few questions have so many answers, the most important of which I now examine.

Air. To some extent a soil must have openness and aeration so that organisms and roots can move and breathe within it. In so doing they tend to sustain this very openness; for example, the excretion of worms ('casts') has a very stable crumb-like structure, which in a physical sense stops the soil slumping in on itself when saturated. From this the vital necessity for soil life is obvious. Clearly this may be difficult to sustain where air is in shortage: large quantities of compost and organic matter will be needed. On the other hand, an already animated soil needs fewer additions but careful maintenance to ensure that good aeration continues. Do not, for instance, move around on bare soil when it is very wet. If you do have to, try putting down some planking to spread your weight. This applies to all soils, but particularly those of a high clay content. This is in my view one of the very few rules of gardening. It is less of a problem in the wild, on uncultivated ground or even on a lawn, due to the presence of roots which anchor the soil.

Drainage. If rainfall cannot run away then the air spaces will fill with water, resulting in a swamp. Fortunately this is not common, but there are many soils in which drainage is slow, especially clays and silts where the lack of large particles or objects results in a compactness which water can penetrate only slowly. In moderation this can be an excellent attribute, preventing too rapid drying out in dry weather; or it can be a problem in areas of high rainfall and short summers.

The principal symptom of waterlogging, apart from the obvious one of lying water, is discoloration to a blue-grey metallic shade, often in pockets rather than affecting the whole soil. The cause is either insufficient organic matter (and thus air) in a heavy clay or silt soil, or the presence of a 'pan' of impenetrable material, often not far below the topsoil, a discernible layer which is hard to dig into; it can arise from always cultivating to the same depth as well as from frequent venturing on to the soil in wet conditions and, probably, again a lack of organic matter.

Break the pan by double digging (see page 58) to a depth sufficient to penetrate it fully. Mix in some compost or even strawy manure at this deep level to prevent the pan re-forming before a season's growth and composting of the topsoil will have encouraged enough roots and worms to stabilize the subsoil. This should also restore health to the soil with insufficient organic matter.

If you are unlucky enough to have a truly impenetrable subsoil of some depth (a natural occurrence as opposed to a manmade pan), some kind of drainage system will be worthwhile. It is a lot of work so do not undertake it unless absolutely necessary, and if only a small part of your garden is water-logged I suggest turning it into a bog garden (see

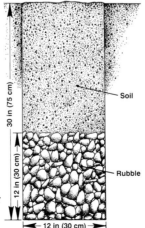

Trench drain to rectify poor drainage (*Joy Larkcom / Elizabeth Douglass*)

page 215) and growing normal plants elsewhere. If necessary, make trench drains to soak up the water. Site them across the lower levels of a sloping site, or at intervals across a level site. Make the trenches about 1 ft (30 cm) wide and about 30 in (75 cm) deep, and fill the lower 1 ft (30 cm) with stones and clinkers, even brushwood, before replacing the soil. In very serious situations it may be necessary to lay an interconnecting system of piped drains, leading to a ditch or soakaway. Consult the experts before embarking on this.

At the other extreme is too rapid drainage and consequent drying out, usually in sandy and gravelly soils. Again there will be insufficient organic matter, since it is primarily this which acts as a sponge and soaks up moisture for later use by plants. Most organic matter and good compost also has the ability to hold on to its nutrients in winter when rain is percolating through the soil and might otherwise cause leaching, or washing away of these nutrients. When the soil temperature rises above 43°F (6°C) they start to become soluble, just when plants start growing and need food. Our main role is to enhance nature's methods rather than imposing our own, as in the case of applying artificial fertilizers, which are soluble at low temperatures when plants cannot use them, creating a risk of leaching. Raw or fresh manure is also unstable in the same way, which is why it is recommended to compost it first and cover the compost heap. Similarly it is best to avoid large patches of bare soil during the growing season when the soil is warm and many nutrients soluble. If the area is beyond your immediate requirements, it is best to sow a green manure (see pages 21–5) .

Soil depth. A perfect topsoil is of little use if there is only an inch of it; there will be insufficient moisture and goodness to support worthwhile crops. In a well-managed organic garden sufficient depth and quality of soil, subsoil and even rock or stones in which roots can forage for water is maintained to make irrigation largely unnecessary. After all, at least in temperate climates, a lot of rain falls in wintertime and nearly all of this is surplus to plants' requirements at the time. Most of it disappears into streams and underground aquifers, but we should strive to retain as much as possible through the depth and quality of our soils.

Proportion of humus. This significantly affects the first three qualities: indeed it is hard to consider in isolation. As we have seen, humus or organic matter has the highly desirable ability to soak up water when there is an excess and then release it to roots in a drought. So it can save you a lot of watering. Sadly, many soils nowadays have an organic matter content of 2 to 3%, whereas a more desirable level is a minimum of 5%. Good compost and peat contain a minimum 15% organic matter, and can hold water to the extent of 90% of their own weight. Unfortunately, the use of peat is less desirable from an ecological point of view but the use of compost is wholly desirable.

Colour. Again, this is significantly related to humus, the absence of which will result in a colour similar to what lies below – white soil above chalk, yellow above clay, red above some sandstones. A darker soil is preferable as it soaks up more of the sun's rays and thus warms up earlier in the spring.

Fertility. As well as referring to good aspects in the other five, this quality also embraces the chemical composition of soil and the presence of all kinds of nutrients.

NUTRIENTS

There are two ways of looking at nutrients. One is the formal scientific approach which examines the NPK (nitrogen/phosphorus/potassium) reading on a piece of ground and decides whether or not there is a deficit of one or the other which must be rectified by the application of fertilizers. This approach regards the soil as a bank in which deposits must match withdrawals to prevent an overdraft/deficit. But can a soil 'run out' of nutrients? The other approach maintains that nutrients, as opposed to added fertilizers, are always to be found in the earth. In short, it may be argued, a healthy soil can, in a sense, recreate itself, roots penetrating deeply even to bedrock, introducing air and organic substances to these regions so that a little bit of rock converts to subsoil and a little bit of subsoil converts to topsoil. In a lifeless soil, however, nutrients can be 'locked up' and become unavailable to plant roots. The key to their release is the presence of vigorous micro-organisms in the soil and this is assured by the incorporation of good organic matter such as compost or manure.

While there is a degree of validity in this view, the analogy should not be taken too far. For three good reasons, we do need to influence the soil in certain ways. First, we are imposing a very particular range of vegetation and plant growth, whereas in nature there would be wild plants which exactly suited the soil and climatic conditions. Secondly, in the case of fruit and vegetables we are removing large quantities of matter without making a corresponding return. Thirdly, there is the question of areas of bare soil lying idle, which is not natural and can promote loss of nutrients through leaching and lack of photosynthesis.

While the incorporation of organic matter – compost or manure – will go most of the way to ensure that your soil makes available adequate nutrients, use of organic fertilizers and liquid feeds will often be indicated as well. And if you are converting your garden to organic cultivation for the first time, fertilizers and feeds can play a particularly important part, while you are building up the soil's organic content.

If in doubt about the suitability of your soil for the garden you desire, first take a look at the health and variety of surrounding vegetation. A soil-testing kit will enable you to check on your soil's acid/alkaline composition and on its nutrient requirements. A full picture of the trace elements may require a more expensive laboratory test.

As a starting point it is essential to check the pH, which means your soil's acidity or alkalinity. The preferred state is a slightly acid 6·5 (neutral, 7·0), a pH level suitable for most plants and one which lends itself to a rotation plan. A well-composted and well-looked-after soil will stay close to this value, except where there are special local conditions.

If the soil is allowed to become too acid (below 4·5 pH) a number of minerals will be locked up or washed out, the vital soil micro-organisms will become inactive, earthworms will disappear, and some nutrients will be released in toxic quantities. It is important to avoid over-liming, however (over 6·5 pH and it will not be called for), since this can lock up most of the nutrients. When needed, it is best applied in the winter. It should never be combined with manure or compost (allow an interval of several months) as

pH factor		
pH	Rating	Plant suitability
4·0	Extreme acid	Few plants survive below this level
4·5–5·5	Acid	Excellent for azaleas, rhododendrons, heathers, blueberries, cranberries
5·5–6·0		(Most top and soft fruit, potatoes, lawns
6·5	Preferred state	Most vegetables and flowers
7·0	Neutral	
7·5–8·0	Alkaline	Brassicas, spinach, clematis, dianthus
9·0	Extreme alkaline	Most plants will fail

Nutrients

The three main plant foods

Nitrogen (N): the most important plant nutrient, needed by all, derives mainly from decaying organic matter, but also from the air via root nodules on legumes. Responsible for shoot and leaf growth, it is the most likely of the main plant nutrients to become deficient, due to leaching. Plants respond most rapidly to applications of it, hence the widespread use of soluble nitrogen in conventional gardening – excess can result in too much lush foliage development at the expense of flowering and fruit quality. It is also available in organic form, released by the action of soil bacteria, in well-rotted manures (rabbit, poultry, goat, horse, cow in that order), compost, grass cuttings which add humus content at the same time, as well as from legumes which make it available to other plants, green manures, and some of the organic fertilizers.

Phosphorus (phosphate, P_2O_5): needed by all plants, important to root growth and germination. Available in soil organic matter, also in rock phosphate and phosphorus-rich organic fertilizers. Deficiency more frequent in acid soils.

Potash (potassium, K_2O): especially important for fruit crops, tomatoes and potatoes, and flowers. Soil K occurs almost entirely in mineral form, unavailable to plants. It is released by organic matter and is also available in very slow-acting rock potash and in the less delayed seaweed fertilizers and feeds. Deficiency more frequent in sandy soils. The faster-acting and highly soluble chemical forms of K can cause excess uptake, resulting in calcium and magnesium being locked up.

Other plant foods (needed in small quantities)

Calcium: important for plant protein formation and cell structure. Available in organic matter, ground limestone and dolomite, gypsum, mushroom compost, comfrey, and some organic fertilizers.

Magnesium: essential to plant development, responsible for putting the green (chlorophyll) into plants and needed for plant uptake of other nutrients. It is available in organic matter and in seaweed. Deficiency can also be overcome with dolomite liming.

Sulphur: important to plant growth, particularly brassicas and legumes. Present in all soils, also seaweed and gypsum. Rarely deficient.

Trace elements (micronutrients): iron (Fe), manganese (Mn), molybdenum (Mo), boron (B), zinc (Zn), copper (Cu), chlorine (Cl) in minute quantities. Most are available in adequate amounts in organically rich soil. Seaweed meal is rich in trace elements and specific deficiencies can also be remedied with liquid feeds. Excessive amounts can cause toxic conditions and trace minerals should never be added in chemical form.

---

this will cause the manure's nitrogen to escape in the form of ammonia.

Some peat and clay soils tend to acidity. Often this is related to poor drainage and correcting this will be effective in the long term. Some lime will be needed in the meantime, either slow release dolomite lime or ground limestone which will also supply calcium. Avoid slaked lime, which can scorch you and your plants. Clay soil will require at least twice as much lime as sandy soil (see table below).

Special situation

Lime can rejuvenate old garden soil by stimulating the release of nitrates and potash as well as inhibiting the activity of harmful insects in the soil. As much as 1½ lb/sq yd (680 gm/sq m) can be applied. This should be repeated every two or three years while limiting the application of animal manure.

Lime* requirements for acid soils
oz/sq yd (gr/sq m)

Original pH	Clay	Loam	Sand
6·0	10 (280)	7 (196)	4 (112)
5·0	25(700)+	20 (560)	10 (280)

* Using ground limestone. If you buy from a builder, this will be the stronger hydrated lime and should be used at ½ to ¾ of these rates.

+ This will not bring your soil up to the desired 6·5 pH level but it is safest not to apply more than this at one time. A soil of pH 5·0 or less may need liming again the following year.

Mineral deficiencies

A. MAJOR MINERALS

Nitrogen

Symptoms – plants lack vigour, leaves small and pale-coloured, sometimes even yellow or reddish-tinted. Growth is weak and plant stunted. Leafy vegetables fail to produce an edible heart, while fruit trees produce a poor crop, maturing late in the season

Nitrogen deficiency in chrysanthemums (*Horticulture Research International*)

Treatment – maintain an organically rich soil, use crop rotation to avoid depleting the soil. Ensure adequate drainage to prevent soil becoming water-logged and sour. Do not dig in fresh straw. Apply a nitrogen-rich organic fertilizer to correct deficiency, then a balanced one as a further dressing

Susceptible plants – many, particularly the leafy vegetables

Phosphorus

Symptoms – similar to nitrogen with weak growth, smaller than normal leaves, the older leaves showing a blue-green colour and falling prematurely. Flowering and fruiting later in the season. Roots are poorly developed. Occurs frequently on acid soils and those in poor condition

Phosphorus deficiency in cucumbers (*Horticulture Research International*)

Treatment – maintain an organically rich soil; correct the soil acidity with ground limestone. Apply a dressing of rock phosphate

Susceptible plants – many, particularly the brassica family

Potassium

Symptoms – shows on the older leaves which turn a blue-green with browning or scorching of the leaf margins and shoot tips, brown spotting of the leaf underside, interveinal yellowing and premature leaf-fall. General growth is checked: the plant can be stunted and in severe cases die-back of the shoots can occur. Fruits are affected, lacking in colour and failing to ripen correctly

Potassium deficiency in tomatoes (*Photos Horticultural*)

Treatment – apply rock phosphate, mulch plants with wilted comfrey leaves or seaweed, or foliar feed with comfrey or seaweed liquid

Susceptible plants – tomatoes: causes greenback and hollow fruit
- potatoes: turn black when cooked
- leafy vegetables, beans and fruits

Calcium

Symptoms – tips of young leaves become ragged, scorched and die off

Treatment – in acid soils apply ground limestone to correct pH level. Ensure there is not an excess of potassium or nitrogen in the soil by doing a soil test. An excess will cause calcium to be 'locked up' in the soil and be unavailable to the plants

Calcium deficiency in apples (linked to bitter pit) (*Holt Studios*)

Susceptible plants
- apple: linked to bitter pit
- brassicas: club root prevalent in acid soils
- Brussels sprouts: browning of the internals of the buttons
- lettuces: tip burn
- potatoes: multitude of small tubers
- tomatoes: blossom end rot
- many others

Magnesium

Symptoms – yellowing between leaf veins, the veins still remaining green, the effect showing on the older leaves first

Treatment – apply dolomite limestone; maintain an organically rich soil

Susceptible plants – many, particularly lettuce, potatoes, tomatoes, apples (reducing crop yield), bush fruit

Magnesium deficiency in tomatoes (*Photos Horticultural*)

Table prepared by Jim Hay

Mineral deficiencies

B. TRACE ELEMENTS

Boron
Symptoms – similar to calcium, scorching of tips of young shoots with subsequent death; root system fails to develop fully; plants commonly stunted and susceptible to disease

Treatment – immediate correction by an application of borax; long-term use of balanced seaweed fertilizers. Do not over–lime or apply excess nitrogen

Susceptible plants – apples: corky areas develop on leaves and within flesh of fruit
- beetroot: causes heart rots
- cauliflower: stunted leaves, brown patches on curds
- celery: cracking of stalks, usually on inner side
- swede/turnip: heart rots
- many others

Copper
Symptoms – young leaves turn blue-green colour, later yellow and showing signs of wilting

Treatment – as this is mainly caused by excess nitrogen in

Copper deficiency in cucumbers (*Horticulture Research International*)

highly organic soils, use seaweed-extract foliar feeds and avoid high-nitrogen fertilizers

Susceptible plants – many, including beans, peas, tomatoes, onions and tree fruits

Iron
Symptoms – loss of colouring on young leaves, yellowing

Iron deficiency in raspberries (*Holt Studios*)

between the veins while veins still remain green, plants generally unhealthy. Can fail to set flower or fruit and may eventually die

Treatment – caused mainly by being 'locked up' in alkaline soils. Increase organic matter content to reduce pH level. Do not over-lime

Susceptible plants – many including azaleas, hydrangeas, rhododendrons, roses, tree fruits and bush fruits, strawberries and raspberries

Manganese
Symptoms – older leaves lose their colour, turning pale green or yellow between the veins

Treatment – as associated with poorly drained alkaline soils, rich in organic matter, avoid over-liming and improve soil structure

Susceptible plants – peas: brown spots inside seed (marsh spot)
- potatoes: black spots develop along leaf veins, leaves turning inwards
- many others including beetroot, brassicas, tree fruits and bush fruits

Table prepared by Jim Hay

SOIL LIFE

Darwin gave much credence to soil biologists, and his study of earthworms pioneered an appreciation of these vital members of the biosphere: 'It may be doubted whether there are many other animals which have played so important a part in the history of the world.'

He discovered that over a span of ten years 2–3 in (5–7·5 cm) of fresh soil is commonly brought to the surface of a pasture by worms, amounting to as much as 20 tons per acre (10 tonnes per hectare) per year, achieved by a population of about 30,000 individuals (now it is estimated that there could sometimes be up to 3,000,000 per acre), who continually eat soil both in order to move through it and to extract some of its organic matter and living organisms as food. Leaves and even stones are ingested with the soil and worms 'mingle the whole intimately together, like a gardener who prepares fine soil for his choicest plants'.

In damp, mild weather worm casts are always visible on healthy soil. Research shows that they contain five to ten times the nutrients of the surrounding soil (how this is achieved is not known). Gum-producing bacteria in the worms' intestines give a stable structure with a crumb-like texture, which is vital in maintaining soil health. This structure allows the presence of air, vital to many useful bacteria (see page 27), and the rapid passage of developing roots which in fact often pass along worm burrows. The burrows may be 3, 4 or even 6 ft deep (90-180 cm) and at the bottom will be a small chamber for hibernation during spells of frost or drought.

Worms love warmth and moisture and are most active therefore in spring and autumn. They cover their burrows with leaves and any handy debris including stones up to 2 in (5 cm) in diameter, mainly to keep their homes warm, moist and safe from predators. The action of their pancreatic juices and their constant mingling of everything between a few inches and 3 ft (90 cm) deep are major factors in the creation of soil from stones and raw organic material.

Clearly worms are an invaluable ally, and they

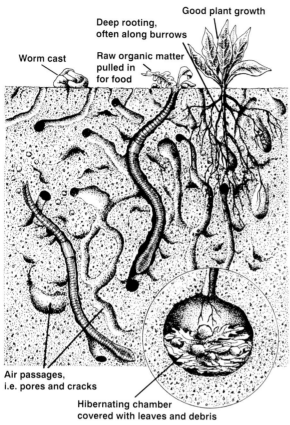

Worm activities (*Elizabeth Douglass*)

are encouraged by regular additions of compost, which is a favourite food and which they prefer to be placed on the surface of the soil.

Another vital attribute of compost is its encouragement of fungi in the soil, particularly those called mycorrhiza, whose presence is necessary for many plants as a 'bridge' for the passage of nutrients from soil to plant. This is particularly the case with 80% of flowering plants, including many trees, all the leguminosae, strawberries, potatoes, tomatoes, cucumber and lettuce. If you examine the roots of these plants in a healthy soil it will be evident that there are lots of little furry white hairs, the mycelium or roots of the mycorrhizae. They actually feed on

Earthworms (*Chris Algar*)

carbohydrate from the plant but are tolerated because they provide nitrogen and other nutrients in return.

Comparative trials have shown that many plants grow much more strongly when mycorrhizae are present and that the presence of a healthy living fraction in the soil, especially through the addition of compost, is a major factor in encouraging their effectiveness. This again emphasizes that compost is less valuable for the (nonetheless useful) nutrients it contains than for its ability to stimulate soil life and hence release previously locked up nutrients. At the same time there is an increased resistance to pests and disease, a better quality of growth, which also appears related to the presence of a thriving fungal population.

Clearly not all fungi are helpful to the gardener but we should encourage those that are, and bacteria, which are instrumental in making food available to plant roots. The best known is the *Bacillus radicicola*, which lives on roots of leguminous plants and feeds them with nitrogen taken from the air, providing a surplus visible as pinky-white spheres attached to the roots.

The microscopic size of bacteria should not cause us to underestimate them. Mostly they propagate by division: only one can become sixteen million in twenty-four hours. One gram of healthy soil contains many million, including (with luck) *Azotobacter chroococum*, free-living bacteria which also convert nitrogen from the air into nitrates which plants can use for growth – up to 25 lb (11 kg) per acre annually. Clearly, to achieve this there must be air in the soil, which brings us back to the usefulness of compost, worms and the interrelation of all aspects of soil life and plant growth.

The beneficial power of bacteria was emphasized eighty years ago by Professor W. Bottomley, who inoculated peat with both *B. radicicola* and *A. chroococum* (whose efficacy is increased by so combining) and transformed it from an inert acidic material to a rich alkaline fertilizer. The amount of soluble nitrogen increased from 0·2 to 2·7%, most of the humus content became soluble and even small quantities of this treated peat had a remarkable effect on plant growth.

Unfortunately many of the conditions which encourage worms, fungi and bacteria also favour the presence of slugs and snails – namely moisture, organic matter and surface debris. Some slugs should nonetheless be tolerated, as they help to decompose old leaves and convert them into plant food. Likewise the presence of moles is not necessarily a disaster, as they help to aerate the soil and will keep to existing runs if the soil is not cultivated.

Soil life

	Diet	Size	Good and/or bad	Remarks
Bacteria	decomposing plant matter	microscopic	G	A healthy soil will achieve its own balance of these largely underground inhabitants, who work ceaselessly, principally to make available old plant matter as food for new vegetative growth. Only a few kinds of nematodes and some fungi, e.g. honey fungus, are potentially troublesome and are also uncommon
Bristletails	decomposing plant matter	¼ in (0·5 cm)	G	
Earthworms	decomposing plant matter + soil and small stones	up to 6 in (15 cm) long	G	
False scorpions	decomposing plant matter	¼ in (0·5 cm)	G	
Fungi	decomposing plant matter + symbiotic relationship with plant roots	variable	G/B	
Nematodes	decomposing plant matter; a few eat living roots	microscopic up to ⅓ in (0·8 cm)	G/B	
Potworms	decomposing plant matter	½–1 in (1·25–2·5 cm)	G	
Protura	decomposing plant matter	microscopic	G	
Springtails	decomposing plant matter	¼–½ in (0·5–1·25 cm)	G	
Symphyla	decomposing plant matter	¼–½ in (0·5–1·25 cm)	G/B	

Nematode, *Meloidogyne spp.* (magnified x 175) (*Holt Studios*)

Springtail, *Onychiurus spp.* (*Holt Studios*)

Symphalid, *Scutigerella immaculata* (*Holt Studios*)

SOIL IMPROVEMENT

Nowadays most gardeners are aware of the value of peat, because it is porous, moisture-retentive, dark, of neutral pH, free of weed seeds and cheap. In fact we are using so much that, especially in the UK, the habitats of its origin are being destroyed. Recommended are various alternatives with similar qualities, bearing in mind the following aims in adding organic matter to the soil:

Aeration – by means of its fibrous nature.

Moisture retention – due to its sponge-like qualities.

Warming effect – from its dark colour.

Protection – of the soil (especially when applied as a mulch) from weather extremes.

Nutrients – not always present in large quantities, but all organic matter is valuable food for worms and other soil life, thus potentially making available those nutrients already in the soil. In some ways this last is the most critical. Some materials have so much carbon in proportion to nitrogen that they cause 'nitrogen robbery' if incorporated into the soil, so are best used as a surface mulch (see page 37).

TYPES

The most carboniferous materials are straw, bark, sawdust, cardboard or paper and leaves. These all benefit from stacking in a heap for a year before use so that breakdown has already begun.

The cheapest and most satisfying soil improver must be home-made compost (see next chapter). How you use it will depend on the results, and if you achieve an almost peat-like compost the uses are unlimited. The same applies to well-rotted cow and horse manure, but if these are fresh and strawy they should be used on the surface or, better still, stacked in a heap to rot down. Mushroom compost has an ideal peaty nature and nutrients to boot, but may have insecticidal and fungicidal residues (see page 45). Lastly, there are proprietary brands of animal compost for sale, which are undoubtedly effective but rather expensive, especially if you can make your own.

QUALITIES OF MANURES AND COMPOSTS

To state exact nutrient quantities is not possible, since these vary with the animals' diet and subsequent handling of the manure – whether mixed with straw, sawdust or paper, rained upon, or heated up in a heap. All animal manures contain some N, P and K plus other useful elements.

The figures given below (as percentages) should be taken as a rough guide only to their relative nutrient values.

Poultry manure should be used with caution as it is especially high in nitrogen and phosphates; but it is also a useful source of sulphur, magnesium and lime. The nitrogen is often volatile (making a smell of ammonia) and is best conserved by adding the manure to the compost heap or blending with other manures, or by making a liquid feed (put a sackful of droppings in a barrel of water for five days); when applied direct to the soil use very sparingly, ½–1 lb/sq yd (220–440 gm/sq m). [N 1·7; P 0·6; K 1·2]

Pig manure is also rich but not volatile, so may be applied in a fresher state, preferably in spring and early summer. It is excellent for the onion family, but again caution must be used: nowadays pig diets are rich in copper and this can be present in the manure at toxic levels, or at least will lock up nutrients – check out the source. [N 0·5; P 0·2; K 0·5]

Horse manure is the best all-rounder: it activates compost heaps, makes hot-beds and lightens heavy soils (if your soil is already light, cow manure is 'heavier' and will serve you better). Always compost it before spreading. Some gypsum mixed with the heap will help to lock in volatile ammonia and thus conserve the nitrogen. [N 0·6; P 0·4; K 0·7]

Cow manure is the least rich in terms of NPK and is usually not volatile; again, it is best composted before application and is most suitable for light soils whose water retention will be considerably increased. [N 0·4; P 0·2; K 0·4]

Proprietary brands of composted animal manure can be used where the original manures are in short supply. They are concentrated and expensive, so use sparingly. Do not use them as potting composts even if this is recommended – the levels of NPK can be too high and/or imbalanced for seedling plants.

Sewage sludge can be rich in nutrients (up to 3% N) and benefits leafy crops in particular; check that the level of heavy metals is acceptable. Using your own 'nightsoil' is quite possible, especially if you are a vegetarian. One way is to blend in an equal quantity of earth, gypsum and wood ash, which removes any smell. I often add it when making a hot aerobic compost heap. Do not put it directly on to the soil.

Mushroom compost is usually simply straw which has been thoroughly composted; as such the nutritive analysis is not impressive but I have witnessed amazing effects on plant growth. [N 0·7; P 0·4; K 0·5]

Garden compost may often be only 0·5% N, 0·3% P and no more than 0·6% K, figures which do not impress the chemists, but its ability to enhance the size and health of plants suggests that the chemical analysis of a manure may be only a small part of the story (see page 34).

GREEN MANURE

This is a further option besides importing organic materials or making a compost heap. Usually green manures are fast-growing catch crops like mustard and rye, longer-term fertility builders such as lucerne, or even intercrops like clover.

Green manure cut down and left to wilt before being dug in (*Joy Larkcom*)

Green manures

Plant	Fix* nitrogen	Time in ground	Possible sowing dates	Effect of frost
Alfalfa (*Medicago sativa*)	✓	3–24 months P	Mid-spring to mid-summer ⅛ oz/sq yd (4 gm/sq m)	Very hardy
Beans, winter field (*Vicia faba*)	✓	5–6 months A	Mid–late autumn 6 in/15 cm apart	Kills plant only if too precocious (i.e. sown too early) or if early frost very severe
Buckwheat (*Fagopyrum esculentum*)	✗	3 months A	Early spring to early autumn 1 oz/sq yd (30 gm/sq m)	Susceptible
Clover, alsike (*Trifolium hybridum*)	✓	3–24 months P	Mid-spring to early autumn, slow to get away as seeds are very small ⅛ oz/sq yd (4 gm/sq m)	Very hardy
Clover, crimson (*Trifolium incarnatum*)	✓	2–5 months A	Early spring to early autumn ⅛ oz/sq yd (4 gm/sq m)	Susceptible, survives mild winter
Clover, Essex red (*Trifolium pratense*)	✓	3–24 months P	As clover, crimson	Hardy, rarely killed
Fenugreek (*Trigonella foenum graecum*)	✗	2–3 months A	Early spring to early autumn ⅛ oz/sq yd (4 gm/sq m)	Fair frost will kill
Grazing (Hungarian) Rye (*Secale cereale*)	✗	6–8 months A	Early–mid-autumn 1 oz/sq yd (30 gm/sq m)	Very hardy
Lupin, bitter (*Lupinus angustifolius*)	✓	3 months A	Early–late-spring 2 in/5cm apart	Susceptible, can survive light frost
+Mustard (*Sinapis alba*)	✗	1–2 months A	Late summer–early autumn or early spring ⅛ oz/sq yd (4 gm/sq m)	Dies at ground temperature 19°F (–7°C)
+Phacelia (Californian Bluebell) (*Phacelia tanacetifolia*)	✗	2–6 months A	Early spring – early autumn ⅛ oz/sq yd (4 gm/sq m)	Dies at ground temperature 25°F (–4°C)
+Ryegrass (*Lolium italicum*)	✗	7 months A	As grazing rye	Very hardy
Trefoil (*Medicago lupulina*)	✓	3–12 months A/B	As clover, crimson	Severe frost will kill
Vetches and Tares (*Vicia sativa*)	✓	As grazing rye	As clover, crimson ¼ oz/sq yd (8 gm/sq m) or 6 in (15cm) apart	Very hardy

* nitrogen fixation does not occur until plants are well established
+ sowing is most effective by broadcasting then raking in the seed

Ease/difficulty of establishment	Ease/difficulty of killing	Special remarks	
As clover	As grazing rye	Long tap root ideal for penetrating compact subsoil, especially if left 2–3 years; can be hard to get rid of	Winter field beans, *Vicia faba* (Joy Larkcom)
As clover	Stems can be woody, sometimes the roots stimulate a regrowth	Best cleared by chopping at ground level and composting whole plant if allowed to grow until summer	
Relatively quick to establish	Tends to regrow so incorporate carefully		
Can suffer from weed competition in first two months, possibly sow in drills and hoe between	Regrows tenaciously so incorporate thoroughly	White flowers, height 2 in–1 ft (5–30 cm), flowering possible even in winter; sought after by bees. Tolerates being trampled on	Crimson clover, *Trifolium incarnatum* (Joy Larkcom)
		Purple flowers, early–mid-summer	
		Most common clover, red flowers, height 4 in–2 ft (10–60 cm), flowers very attractive to many insects, regrows well in a cold wet spring	
Relatively quick to establish	No problem unless left a whole season	1–2 ft (30–60 cm) white flowers, vigorous tap root	Essex red clover, *Trifolium pratense* (Joy Larkcom)
Thick leaf and tillers well so good against weeds; pigeons and rooks may eat the seeds	Needs thorough and careful incorporation	Especially useful for the last sowing of the year (mid-autumn) enabling a worthwhile amount of green matter even by early–mid-spring if mild	
Worth sowing in drills and hoeing	No problems	Superb flowers, need time to develop	
Fast and easy, smothers weeds especially if sown thickly	Simple to hoe off if frost is lacking	Simplest green manure, especially for autumn use and against weeds; no use in club-root-infected soil as it is a brassica	Phacelia (Californian bluebell), *Phacelia tanacetifolia* (Joy Larkcom)
Rapid and simple	Hoe just before flowering	Extremely fast and sappy; seed may be hard to find in quantity, rapidly seeds itself	
Can be invaded by weeds and mowing is good against this	As grazing rye	As for grazing rye but a little slower; seed should be cheaper	
Slow growth initially and weeds can smother it	Fairly difficult	Prefers chalky, limestone soils; like white clover is tolerant of being walked over so useful for intercropping	Trefoil, *Medicago lupulina* (Joy Larkcom)
As clover	No problems	Slow growth in the winter, often no bulk to incorporate until flowering commences in late spring	

A : annual; B : biennial; P : perennial

Winter tares, *Vicia sativa* (Joy Larkcom)

Organic fertilizers, minerals and liquid feeds

	Nutrients (percentage)				Application
	N	P	K	Others	
Blood, fish and bone	3·5	8·0	0·0	–	Quick release N source, plus useful source of P, 4–6 oz/sq yd (120–180 gm/sq m)
Bonemeal	3–3·5	20–30·0	–	calcium	Slow-acting source of phosphorus, good for root growth, strawberries, roses, 4 oz/sq yd (120 gm/sq m)
Calcified seaweed	–	–		50% calcium, 5% magnesium and trace elements	Will also raise pH, 4 oz/sq yd (120 gm/sq m)
Dried blood	10–15	0·8	–	–	Fast-acting N source, useful to add to a fibrous compost heap, 2–4 oz/sq yd (60–120 gm/sq m)
Fishmeal	5–10·0	5–10·0	–	many trace elements	N and P vary considerably; commercial brands sometimes add soluble, non-organic K, 3 oz/sq yd (85 gm/sq m)
Gypsum	–	–	–	calcium sulphate	Supplies sulphur, soil conditioner for clay soils, 8 oz/sq yd (240 gm/sq m)
Hoof and horn	13·5	–	–	–	Slow-release (depending on fineness) source of N, 2–4 oz/sq yd (60–120 gm/sq m)
Rock potash	–	–	10·0	–	From natural rock, very slow release, 8 oz/sq yd (225 gm/sq m)
Rock phosphate	–	26·0	–	–	Source of P for long-term soil improvement, 8 oz/sq yd (225 gm/sq m)
Seaweed meal	2·8	0·3	2·6	numerous trace elements	Slow-release, valuable soil feed and conditioner, rare among organic fertilizers in having meaningful quantity of K in addition to N and some P, 4–6 oz/sq yd (120–180 gm/sq m)
Soot	4·0	0·2–0·5	–	–	Fast-acting, 4 oz/sq yd (120 gm/sq m), also deters slugs, can scorch foliage and kill small plants
Wood ash	0·5–1	2–5·0	5·0–15·0	calcium	Good source of K, but highly soluble, so needs dry storage, 4 oz/sq yd (120 gm/sq m); can also deter slugs

Liquid feeds (ratios, not absolute quantities or percentages)

							Application
Comfrey	2	:	3	:	5		Foliar and liquid feed, benefits soil structure, K especially good for fruiting crops
Manure	4	:	2	:	5		Useful for fruit crops, tomatoes, potatoes
Nettle	3	:	2	:	3	calcium, iron, silicon	
Seaweed	2–5	:	0·5	:	2·5	trace elements	Foliar feed, useful to remedy trace element deficiencies; contains plant growth hormones assisting rooting and giving pest and disease resistance

Try them whenever your garden has a bare space which is not needed for a certain time during the growing season. Benefits are: suppression of most weeds which otherwise would have thrived in the absence of competition; reduction and even prevention of possible leaching of nutrients, especially in a wet autumn when the soil is still warm; creation of humus from the ultimately decaying plants and thus long-term enrichment of your soil; provision of nutrients.

Why it works. The major difference between bare and cropped soil is that the plants on the latter are photosynthesizing light from the sun, together with carbon dioxide from the atmosphere, and converting these to starches and sugars. When the plants die these are converted by worms and micro-organisms into food for the next generation of plants. The speed of this process is important for the success of subsequent crops, since decaying vegetation in the soil will use nitrogen and this stunts new growth until it is broken down. So if your green manure at maturity is thick and bulky it may be best to cut or mow it for the compost heap. Should you not need the ground for a while then certainly dig it in (called sheet composting) or even leave it on the surface as a mulch. Every situation is different: much depends on the liveliness of your soil, its temperature and moisture level, the type of green manure grown and how mature it is when cut down.

Check the table to see which green manure is best suited to each situation. Remember that any green manure will become stemmy during and after flowering and thus harder for the soil to digest, so either incorporate it before this happens or sow late enough that flowering barely begins before the onset of winter. Sometimes it is hard to judge the latest possible sowing date because winters can vary so much – grazing rye may grow 6 in (15 cm) between late autumn and early spring or else hardly at all; mustard may or may not be killed by frost.

The simplest green manure is of course weeds, and by all means let them grow if the soil is free of crops. But it is never long before they seed – three weeks for groundsel and four weeks for annual meadow grass – so they are a risky and only a short-term option (see *Weeds*, page 257).

AN ALTERNATIVE APPROACH

Intercropping is a possibility where space is short, growing certain green manures among your crops. It needs careful planning. In the USA Eliot Coleman has been successful at this, and emphasizes the importance of good timing – the crop must be well established before the green manure is sown, but not so dominant as to prevent its growth. Two combinations I have tried (in southern Britain) are planting sweetcorn on 12 May (or sowing on 1 May) then sowing clover in the first week of July after hoeing off all weeds. Later on I hand-weeded groundsel from the developing sward of clover which I had broadcast and raked into damp soil. In another bed I planted cos lettuce (big plants) and sowed red clover at the same time. Both experiments gave a worthwhile crop to eat, for me and for the soil organisms. White clover is probably better at smothering weeds. This method needs a relatively weed-free soil and dedication from the gardener.

ORGANIC FERTILIZERS

In contrast to soluble fertilizers, organic fertilizers do not feed directly to the plant, but require the action of soil bacteria to make them available. For this reason they are usually slower-acting and require earlier application. Where a more immediate response is required, they are best applied as liquid soil or foliar feeds.

3 COMPOSTS

Production of compost is at the heart of the organic method. Indeed, it is also at the heart of nature's way of renewal and life. Dying and decaying matter, whether the falling leaves of the forest or the decaying bodies of more complex life forms, is constantly being used as the raw material of new life. In nature, the forest floor is the 'workshop' for a continuous compost production operation. In our gardens, we interrupt this normal cycle by taking out some of the organic material produced. In setting up a compost-making operation, we are restoring the cycle and returning to the soil the humus which is the single most important element in its fertility.

This process of life renewal is achieved by a remarkably complex interaction of billions of microscopic life forms and is one in which we participate when we load up a compost bin at the bottom of the garden.

If we view, for a moment, our compost bin as a factory, the raw materials should comprise a suitable mixture of carbonaceous and nitrogenous materials, and the workforce is supplied by an army of bacteria, fungi, and various other microscopic life forms. The end product will be the desired, sweet-smelling, brown crumbly compost that will enrich the soil. To carry out this transformation, the 'workforce' requires moisture, heat and, depending on the type of production operation chosen, air. A single gramme of compost will contain up to a billion bacteria, 100 million actinomycetes, a million fungi, algae, pistozoae and others in their hundreds of thousands. Moreover, different bacteria with differing skills take over, depending on whether the heap is an aerobic (air-using) or anaerobic (airless) production line, the temperature, the pH level and the mineral content. The job of the bacteria is to utilize nitrogen to break down the carbon materials and form compost.

Our 'factory' is capable of making the end-product by two processes: one hot and quick, the other warm and slow. The hot method is the

The compost bin, as central to the organic garden as a cooker in the kitchen (*Roy Lacey*)

aerobic one in which, all other conditions being met, there will be a rapid rise in temperature, possibly to 140°F (60°C), within four days (a hot bath is about 110°F or 40°C), declining over the next fortnight or so. The bacteria which thrive at these temperatures get through a lot of decomposing work, so that, after two to four weeks, you already have a rough sort of compost. To improve on this quickly, you could then turn the heap (see below), introducing a fresh supply of air to stimulate the bacteria once more so that a second heating is achieved.

The slower method is the anaerobic, relatively cool one. Oxygen is not introduced, and a different set of bacteria take over, producing decomposition and the resulting compost at a much more leisurely pace. Within around twelve months you should have a dark, crumbly compost. The tendency among gardeners is to opt for the aerobic method, but before deciding which method to adopt it is worth considering which will suit you best. Both have their advantages and these are set out in the table overleaf.

When considering what to put in your heap, ask yourself if the proposed materials are of biological origin. Practically anything that is can be included.

OPPOSITE: Nature's way of composting: dead birch tree and vegetation in ancient woodland (*David Woodfall*)

The compost factory (*Elizabeth Douglass*)

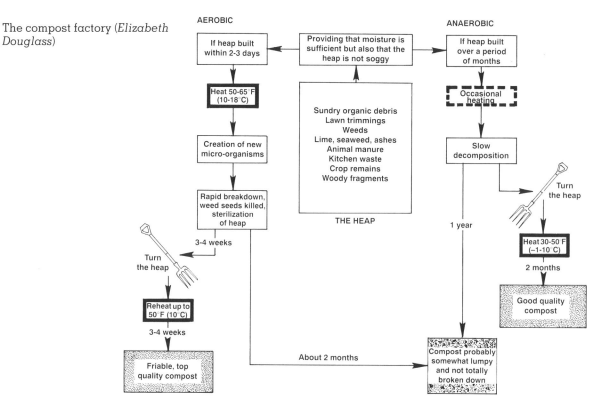

For example, cardboard, woollen carpets and ash all pass this test (see table of materials). Having established this, it is essential to ensure that the materials present the right mix of carbon and nitrogen. The former is associated with woody, fibrous material – hard stalks, roots; the latter with grass, kitchen waste, etc. Too much carbon, and the heap will remain 'cold' and the decomposition process will be

The look of good compost, dark, friable, soil-like texture (*Charles Dowding*)

Aerobic or anaerobic?

Advantages	Disadvantages
An aerobic heap	
Fast	More demanding, calling for continued attention
More likely to destroy weed seeds	May require turning to maintain heat
More likely to destroy disease spores	Requires more precise carbon/nitrogen mix
More complete decomposition	Usually needs insulation and a minimum size
An anaerobic heap	
Less demanding, not needing to be turned	Longer wait for compost
Need not be boxed (insulated)	Will not destroy weed seeds
Not depending on bulk, can be any size	Perennial weeds must be excluded
Can get by, albeit slowly, with less nitrogen	Diseased material must be excluded
	May not break down hard material
	More likely to require liming

protracted. Too much nitrogen, and the heat will be rapidly dissipated and you will be left with a treacly mass. The ideal ratio between the two is 30 parts carbon to 1 part nitrogen, which reduces to 10–15:1 when turned into mature compost. Alongside a correct moisture content, the art of making successful compost is largely associated with achieving a correct C:N balance. Fine grass mowings on their own will produce a treacly mass result, so straw, leaves or, possibly, cardboard would be good companions. If you include too much woody material such as bark and prunings without balancing this with sufficient green matter,

the pile may not heat up at all. Above all, it is not wise to include too much tree material except as a base. A lot of precious goodness is needed to complete its breakdown. You could 'mineralize' it instead on the bonfire, and then put the potash-rich ash into your heap. It is worth bearing in mind, however, that this potash is highly soluble, so, except when you are using it around vigorously growing plants, it will mostly be leached away. One alternative is to put this woody material aside, leaving it to rot quietly for two or three years before incorporation into the compost heap. Another is to shred the material so that the surface

Materials for the compost bin

Material	Carbon/nitrogen ratio	Comments
Urine	2:1	Excellent activator and source of potash; ideally mix it with water before putting on heap
Dried blood	4:1	Highly effective activator
Pig manure	5:1	
Poultry manure	10:1	Use sparingly; a powerful activator. Also source of phosphates
Comfrey	10:1	Rich in many nutrients, especially potash. Almost no fibre
Lawn trimmings	12:1	Too nitrogenous to use on their own, especially if soggy. Mix with damp straw, weeds or leaves
Kitchen waste	12:1	Ideal, balanced ingredients. Exclude meat and bones which may rot and attract rodents
Farmyard manure	14:1	e.g. animal excretions plus straw. Almost a balanced compost in itself after decomposition. Used fresh, when the straw is still quite yellow, it makes a good activator
Seaweed	19:1	Superb source of trace elements; no fibre or structure
Garden waste	20:1	Pea, bean, tomato, potato haulms provide valuable nutrients, also useful for holding air in the heap
Coffee grounds	20:1	
Horse manure	25:1	See farmyard manure
Weeds	30:1	Can range from sappy to fibrous, good source of nutrients. Avoid pernicious perennials. Note: stinging nettles are high in nitrogen and make an effective activator. If used in quantity, best treated in same way as lawn trimmings
Bracken	48:1	High in potash if used when green. Avoid handling when it is producing spores (health risk)
Straw	80:1	Must be damp before use and, preferably, part-rotted to avoid robbing too many nutrients from heap
Woody prunings	100:1	Shred first, or else use as mulch
Bark	100:1	See woody prunings
Newspaper, cardboard	200–500:1	Use sparingly, shredded or torn up. Dampen before use; avoid materials with coloured inks
Sawdust	500:1	Too demanding of nutrients in their breakdown and too slow, unless first stacked for two to three years

Note: C:N values should be regarded only as approximations and will vary according to age, precise make-up, etc. They are best used for comparative purposes to balance high C:N and low C:N materials at opposite ends of the table. A wide range of ingredients is the safest bet and will ensure a nutrient-rich compost, especially if seaweed and comfrey are added, even in small amounts. Wood ash, supplying potash and lime, may also be used. Lime need not normally be added to the compost pile, unless you have an acid soil.

Care should be taken with pet manure: cat and dog faeces can sometimes be hazardous if handled.

area is increased, allowing rapid oxidation and breakdown. It can then be mixed straight into your compost heap. Either way, you can avoid the necessity of a bonfire, whose heat destroys a lot of nutrients and whose smoke can be antisocial.

A compost heap, in fact, is somewhere between a bonfire and nature's own method of decomposition, which is a slow rotting process culminating in incorporation by worms into the soil when breakdown is completed. By speeding up the decomposition process we can increase a soil's fertility very quickly, especially by making a well aerated heap where oxygen-loving organisms can flourish.

THE AEROBIC HEAP

One main factor is speed of compiling the heap, to ensure a large enough bulk of food for the heat-loving bacteria to 'eat'; another is the retention of enough of this heat for them to thrive and multiply. If the pile is too small, there will be insufficient heat build-up. To obtain a suitable C:N mix on a garden scale, the materials may first need to be assembled over a period of time. This can best be achieved by creating a preliminary stockpile. Garden debris, mowings, weeds and so forth can be loosely stacked and covered in one pile or placed in plastic bags; likewise kitchen waste.

TEMPERATURE

It is worth bearing in mind that a well compiled heap will need sufficient air to sustain the temperature build-up. However, there should be no need to create special air channels. Simply

ensure that the material does not get compacted by forking through it and that grass mowings or the like, which are prone to settle into a solid, airless mass, are mixed with woody materials.

The question of temperature also relates to the weather and composting is more reliable in summertime. Luckily this is when you have most materials. Compost which may be ready in two summer months may require six months in winter.

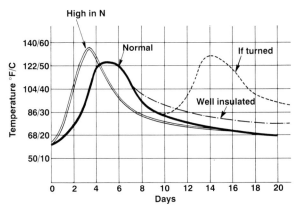

Possible temperature progression in an aerobic bin (*Elizabeth Douglass*)

MOISTURE

After warmth comes the necessity of the right amounts of water. In a dry summer the heap will definitely need some, preferably added every so often while you are constructing it. Ingredients need to look and feel pretty damp. When you dig into the heap later on you will know if they were too dry as they will be still identifiable in their original form. This can be corrected when turning the heap. Too much moisture is unlikely at the time of making the heap, but it should be protected from rain with polythene on top.

INGREDIENTS

The final consideration in making quick compost is the right mixture of ingredients. There are many variations (see table on page 29).

Most gardens have lawn mowings – unless you leave them on the lawn for worms to deal with. (The turf will improve from this.) Most mowings are soft and nitrogenous and these need the most care in balancing with carboniferous materials. Sometimes, however, they may contain a lot of twigs and leaves, which makes them suitable as they are. A good balancing material is straw. It is best to leave this outside first to get wet and begin the rotting process on its own, so that when you include it in your heap you will not need to wet it and it will already be a much richer plant food, with more nitrogen (from the air) and proportionately less carbon. If you want to compost sawdust I recommend as much as two years' pre-composting; ensure it is wet at the beginning.

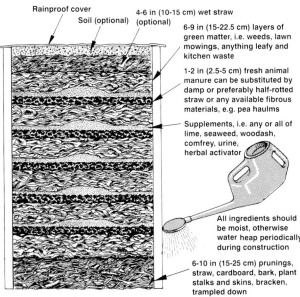

Compost bin built up in layer system. Alternatively the layers can be mixed together (*Elizabeth Douglass*)

Alternative use of compost bin. Unrotted manure mixed with straw can be quickly readied for use by composting (*Chris Algar*)

INGREDIENTS TO AVOID

Paratoxics: materials which definitely should not find their way into your heap include all metals, rubbers, glass and plastics – even so-called 'biodegradable' plastic will endure for many years. Large quantities of newspaper and cardboard will greatly slow the rotting process. Also inadvisable is diseased plant material, such as brassica stalks infected with club root, or white rot on onions, leeks or garlic. Both of these will almost certainly survive in some form to reinfect your soil when the compost is spread. Potato blight, however, can be safely composted. Other diseases are less perennial and a hot aerobic heap which is also thoroughly turned will neutralize them. If your heap does not meet these criteria it is safest to burn suspicious material.

ACTIVATORS

Some animal manure is a good idea to speed up the heating process; it must be fresh rather than already rotted. Should you keep a few hens you are well placed here. Fresh manure 'activates' by seeding the heap with bacteria, not unlike the leavening of bread. If enough is added it will also bring a lot of heat into the compost heap, enough to raise the temperature above the threshold where the heap generates its own heat by subsequent decomposition. This can be very useful in winter when it is cold and there is a shortage of green matter to engender heat.

The right bacteria can also be introduced by adding some of last time's compost as the heap is constructed. Commercial activators are unnecessary if the above conditions are met, but you might find it interesting to experiment with herbal products, which definitely make a difference. Packaged bacterial activators are also available but since the types of bacteria at work vary with the temperature, air conditions and other factors, these may be of limited use.

WASTES AND WEEDS

An ideal use for your more fibrous wastes, such as brassica stalks, tomato haulms and prunings, is to make a base of 6–10 in (15–25 cm) for the heap. This helps to keep warmth in and water out and provides an extra reservoir of oxygen. Another waste that can be problematical is perennial and seeding weeds – will the roots of the former and the seeds of the latter survive to grow again? The answer is yes and no: an aerobic heap should kill everything except at its extremities, but any heap made over a long period will not be hot enough for this. If this is the case it may be best to burn such weeds. See the chapter on *Weeds* (page 257) for ways to manage them.

SHREDDERS

Shredding machines, albeit energy-intensive, give great flexibility in dealing with woody and highly fibrous material. Once it is chopped up the process of decomposition becomes months rather than years and a bonfire can be avoided. Small amounts of woody material are useful, unshredded, for making a base to the heap.

TURNING

One way of speeding up the process is to turn the heap, ensuring that all the outside edges now find themselves in the middle where they receive a proper heating in their turn. This should ensure a compost free of weed seeds and roots. Other advantages are that the compost will become more tilth-like and nutritious due to the second heating (see below); there is the opportunity to break up any lumps of raw material; water can be added where the first heating has been fierce, resulting in white ashy substances; you can see how well all the ingredients have rotted (or not!).

A well-made heap which heats up rapidly can be turned after as little as ten days. Cooler heaps may also benefit from this, as the introduction of fresh oxygen will give a boost to the heating process, so in some sense turning is an 'activator' itself. The temperature to aim for is 120–150°F (50–65°C), at which higher point weed seeds are killed and decomposition is rapid. Available oxygen is fast used up and the bacteria which need it thus decline, until the heap is turned and the outer material starts to rot, when a second peak of 120–140°F (50–60°C) can be achieved. You can tell if your heap is this hot because you will not be able to hold your hand in there. If the heap is not turned, the outer 6 in (15 cm) of the heap will not decompose, and should be sliced off and put into the succeeding bin charge.

If within a week of making the heap there is no warmth then you will have to introduce whatever must be lacking, whether it be moisture, fresh green matter or (most helpful in this situation) some fresh animal manure. If the heap is very soggy you need to improve drainage at the base and to introduce some fibrous material as well as ensuring that it is covered against the rain.

A point to note regarding aerobic heaps is that it is not essential to 'layer' ingredients in the classical sense. Provided you have a proper balance of materials, composting will be that much more effective when mixed. Yet layering can be a useful way of structuring the heap at the start: for example, grass mowings followed by wet straw followed by weeds followed by manure and even a little old compost and soil, in thicknesses of about 6 in (15 cm), as if making a multi-decker sandwich. These will then be mixed when turning the heap.

THE ANAEROBIC HEAP

Anaerobic, 'no-air', describes the kind of process at work in many gardens where there is a pile of old vegetation rotting in the corner. Eventually a compost of sorts will be achieved, usually after a year. Ways to improve the quality of this are here presented.

It pays to consider the balance of ingredients, as for an aerobic heap, and the same principles apply. In fact the main element which is different is that the heap is constructed over weeks and months rather than in a day. This means that the same level of heat is never achieved, except in small pockets where a large amount of fresh matter is put in at one time. Hence be aware that weed seeds and the roots of perennial weeds will probably survive (unless you first dry the latter in the sun, worth the effort as they are mineral-rich). One solution is to blend a half-finished anaerobic heap with a large batch of new ingredients, particularly including a good activator (e.g. fresh animal manure), thus creating an aerobic heap which should quickly become hot enough to sterilize the unwanted elements.

An anaerobic heap can become very untidy, so some kind of enclosure, though not essential, is recommended. Some woody matter is good at the base to help in drainage. Thereafter simply keep an eye on it, balancing sappy greenstuff with more fibrous material, all moist rather than dry or wet. An activator is not necessary to trigger heat, but some old compost near the beginning is helpful to introduce plenty of good bacteria.

Building such a heap may last as long as six months. When the bin is full or the heap reaches a height of 6 ft (2 m) you need to start again. Cover the finished heap to keep the rain out and leave it, preferably for another six months; generally anaerobic heaps benefit from a year's cycle between starting and spreading, whether you make them in summer or in winter. The only way to speed this up is by turning the heap as well as mixing in fresh nitrogenous ingredients, thus making aerobic conditions and rapid breakdown. In practice a little of this will be happening in an anaerobic heap – we are simply delineating the two extreme possibilities to understand better what we are doing.

LEAF-MOULD

Leaf-mould comes under the category of anaerobic decomposition because leaves at the high end of the C:N spectrum are highly fibrous and rot very slowly. If you have a lot, rather than put them in the main compost heap where they will slow the whole process, it is worthwhile storing them in a wire mesh cage or in plastic bags in an obscure part of the garden. About two years will be needed (somewhat less if the leaves are pre-shredded) for satisfactory decomposition. At the end of that time you will have an ideal mulching material which worms love and slugs do not. Besides being a valuable resource for improving soil structure they can provide a peat substitute in potting compost. The rotting leaves should be kept moist. Any leaf variety can be used, although conifer and evergreen leaves will tend to be acidic (good for acid-loving azaleas, blueberries, and so on).

BINS

Making a compost bin is a good chance to use up bits of old wood and sheeting. Wood is the best, albeit expensive, since it acts as an insulator as well as a container. The classic design is what is known as a New Zealand box. Removable slats at the front give ready access for charging, turning and discharging. It incorporates two bays, enabling one of the bays to be loaded while the contents of the other are 'cooking'. It also provides the option of decanting the contents of one bay into the other, when turning. This will help you ensure that a good mixing of the materials is achieved. A minimum size is necessary to ensure enough 'middle' in the heap for the composting process to work well. To this end too, a square is better than a rectangle since the ratio of surface area to volume is lower. A minimum bin size for an aerobic heap is one cubic yard (or metre) for each bay: smaller, and the heap will have difficulty achieving the desired heat level. It is important to provide the bin with a cover, both to prevent excessive wetting from rain and also excessive drying. Black polythene or corrugated iron work well and may be

New Zealand compost bin (*Elizabeth Douglass*)

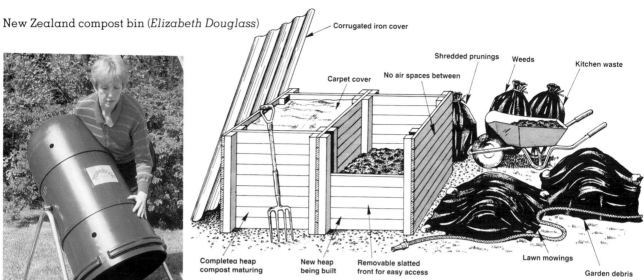

Corrugated iron cover

Carpet cover

No air spaces between

Shredded prunings

Weeds

Kitchen waste

Completea heap compost maturing

New heap being built

Removable slatted front for easy access

Lawn mowings

Garden debris

Ideal for the small garden, compost tumblers rapidly produce a rough, usable compost (*Blackwall Products*)

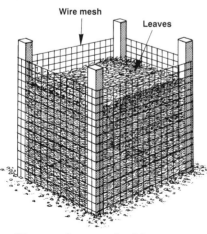

Classic, compact, conical shaped bin turns out useful quantities of compost (*Original Organics*)

Wire mesh

Leaves

Wire mesh cage, ideal for making leaf-mould (*Elizabeth Douglass*)

supplemented by a piece of old carpet to keep in the heat. It is worthwhile leaving a liberal space around the bin, to bring in a wheelbarrow and also for stacking materials and emptying.

An alternative, sometimes used, comprises walls made up of spaced slats. This may prevent the necessary heat build-up, however, and if used, is best lined with cardboard or other insulating material.

For the small garden, in particular, there are various types of plastic bins which are more economical in terms of space. Compost tumblers have become very popular in the last few years. These comprise a plastic barrel pivoted on a metal frame to enable regular rotation. This speeds up the composting process, and with daily turning can produce a rough but usable compost after about three weeks. Another plastic bin available in the UK is the conical type which has been found to make a very effective box for turning out useful small quantities of compost, and is easily located outside a kitchen door.

Wire mesh cages. These are simply made but rather flimsy, and are best reserved for the production of leaf-mould. You should again think in terms of a cubic yard (metre) in order to assist moisture retention, bearing in mind that the bulk of leaves will diminish to a fraction of their starting point.

SITING

Beholders seldom see beauty in the compost heap, so a secluded corner is best. If you live in a fairly warm area, moisture conservation may be the main consideration, in which case a shady spot, sheltered from the wind, should be selected. If heat is needed, it may be better to choose a sunny spot. It is sometimes suggested that certain trees are better 'compost companions' than others through secretions from their roots, and conifers are not recommended, but I have made excellent compost in heaps adjacent to Thuja trees.

Wherever it is sited, it is best stood on the bare ground to give access to worms as the compost matures. The most important consideration is drainage. If your garden lies very wet it is vital that you have about 1 ft (30 cm) of woody material at the bottom of the heap. In hot countries, where moisture conservation has priority, the opposite is true: hence the Indore method in India, where the bin consists of a pit dug into the ground. Wherever you are, it will be

The healing power of compost

The important healing power of compost, applied in the form of a spray, has recently been demonstrated at research stations in Germany. Compost is soaked for a week to ten days in five to ten times its volume of water, the liquid then strained off. Mildew on potatoes has been reduced from 70% to 20% of the leaves affected. Care needs to be taken to spray the tops and bottoms of the leaves, as success comes from direct contact of the abundant micro-organisms in the liquid (more than a million per cubic millimetre) with the disease. Similar results with powdery mildew on cucumbers seem to be achieved in a different way, by boosting the health and resistance of the plant itself. A further trial of cucumbers grown simply in soil compared with those grown in three parts compost to one part soil showed the latter to suffer 40% fewer attacks of fungi on their leaves.

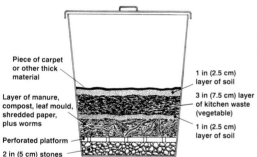

Piece of carpet or other thick material

Layer of manure, compost, leaf mould, shredded paper, plus worms

Perforated platform

2 in (5 cm) stones

1 in (2.5 cm) layer of soil

3 in (7.5 cm) layer of kitchen waste (vegetable)

1 in (2.5 cm) layer of soil

Worm compost bin (*Elizabeth Douglass*)

Worms at work, turning kitchen waste into compost (*Chris Algar*)

useful if the heap is accessible to a hosepipe which may be needed during dry spells.

TRENCHES

Compost trenches are especially good for runner beans and potatoes. Dig a trench in early spring about 18 in (45 cm) wide and deep and put in 12 in (30 cm) of green or partly rotted matter, kitchen scraps, not too much coarse or woody material, then replace the soil on top and tread down at all stages. Initially, growth will be helped by the heat generated, later by the nutrients as they become available.

WORM COMPOSTING

If you are prepared to give them care and attention, worms will produce for you a super-rich and fine compost, which in fact is their combined excretions from eating the wastes you give them. This is an ideal way of using up your kitchen scraps (of vegetable origin), leaves, old straw, and a few (non-perennial, non-seeding) weeds. Provided you take care about any weed material included, the end-product will be a fine potting compost base.

This can be achieved inexpensively, in a container, conveniently placed to receive kitchen waste. A plastic dustbin is easily converted for this purpose. Viewed in cross-section, the bin will comprise three levels – a drainage area at the bottom, topped by the worms' bedding, in turn topped by the worms' food supplies. One way of creating the drainage system is to place a 2–3 in (5–7.5 cm) layer of stones in the bottom of the bin and cover them with a perforated wooden platform. On the platform put a layer of well-rotted compost or manure, perhaps some leaf-mould and shredded newspaper. This can be topped with some dry soil (as an alternative to peat) to provide the necessary open, moisture-absorbing texture. It is important to ensure that the bedding is kept moist. The worms' food is best supplied regularly, in not too large a quantity. This can be covered with a piece of old carpet or thick material, which serves a dual purpose – keeping the moisture in, and ensuring that the worms, who are most comfortable in darkness, will come right to the top to feed.

The worms' needs are specific and must be seen to. They cannot stand either waterlogging or drought. They can live only within a given temperature range. Below 41°F (5°C) their activity ceases, and they die if they freeze. Activity increases with warmth, until 104°F (40°C) is reached. Above this, and they will also die. Hence the need to add small amounts of food regularly: a lot at once might cause heat from composting, which would put an end to the worms.

The more worms in the bin, the faster you will get compost. They will breed rapidly, but aim to start with at least fifty. These are not the ordinary earthworm, but brandling worms (*Eisenia foetida*). Smaller than earthworms and of a strong red colour, they can be found in manure heaps, purchased in fish-tackle shops, or their eggs can be bought in capsule form by mail order.

When the container is full of good compost, empty it on to a hard surface in a tidy heap. Wait a little for the worms to retreat to the middle, and scoop away the outside material, which is your usable compost. At the same time, the liquid which has drained to the bottom of the bin should be poured off. This can be used as a liquid manure, diluted about 10:1. Finally, replace the heap's centre, with all the worms, in the container, and you are ready to start the next cycle. There should be many more worms than when you started, so the compost should be ready more quickly the second time round.

Brandlings, smaller than earthworms, distinguished by a strong reddish colour (*Chris Algar*)

Other things equal, room temperature is ideal for the container and it is best located in a sheltered part of the garden. You should consider bringing it inside in the severest winter weather, in case the worms freeze. Provided the worms can be kept warm, there is no reason why your compost bin should not continue to produce all year round. If emptying the bin completely, it is well to remember that brandling worms do not survive in ordinary soil so there is no point in spreading them around the garden.

SHEET COMPOSTING

When there are plenty of worms in the soil you have the scope to try mulching (see page 36) and also 'sheet composting', which means leaving fresh green matter such as green manure to rot where it falls, worms then pulling it into the soil. Once I sowed mustard in early spring, and hoed it off as a thick sward in late spring, mixed a little with the topsoil, which speeded things up. I covered it with a paper mulch, which prevented regrowth as well as making conditions dark and moist underneath. The worms came right to the top, and within three weeks a peep under the paper revealed...simply soil. All the mustard had rotted or been pulled under by worms. The next step was to plant cabbages through holes in the paper and an excellent crop resulted. You could try many variations here, using green manure (see *Soil*, page 21), weeds or mulching materials.

USING THE COMPOST

Finally, here are some hints on using your compost. While it is waiting to be used, keep it covered. If all went well you will have something of a peaty nature. You can incorporate it into the topsoil or, preferably, use it as a mulch, spreading it 1–2 in (2·5–5 cm) deep over the surface. By all means use it as an ingredient in a sowing and potting medium. It may need sieving first: chicken netting nailed to a wooden rectangular frame makes a good sieve. Uses for your compost are unlimited – put it at the bottom of a good hole when planting trees and shrubs, use it to line the drills for your seeds so they start well, make growing bags for your tomatoes.

If the compost is very fibrous, sticky, lumpy and perhaps not sweet-smelling, you need to consider why, so that you know for next time. Think over the mix of ingredients or whether the heap got waterlogged, the two most likely causes of trouble; also remember that a heap made in winter will take much longer to decompose and needs rather more nitrogenous material to compensate. You have to be careful how you use this imperfect product. It still contains lots of goodness and food for soil life, only in less assimilable form. Surface mulching is the best option; worms will take it in eventually. Spread it on top of the soil in late autumn after clearing the ground; worms are breeding and growing at this time and will appreciate it. Any hard frosts will break up the lumps so that a little raking in the spring will produce a fine tilth.

A great virtue of well-made compost is its nutrient-stability. While it contains less 'plant-food' than synthetic fertilizers, such goodness as it has is water-soluble only in conditions of warmth, that is, when plants are growing and positively need it. You will not lose nutrients by spreading it in the winter, as the goodness is all locked up by cold – the possible danger time is a warm wet autumn. Note that this is not true for uncomposted animal manure, which often contains soluble nutrients, so if you have any of this put it in your compost heap; good organic gardening does not pollute the groundwater.

Raised beds cleared and covered with nutrient-stable compost (*Charles Dowding*)

4 MULCHES

WHAT IS A MULCH?

A mulch is any material that is applied on top of the soil. The usual mulching materials are straw, compost, manure, chipped bark and plastic sheets but there are many other highly effective materials which are sometimes overlooked.

Depending on what kind is used, however, its function can vary considerably. The two primary uses that spring to mind are soil enrichment and weed suppression. But mulching also offers a number of secondary and important benefits relating to moisture retention, temperature modification above and below ground level, soil texture, pest and disease protection and appearance.

SOIL ENRICHMENT AND PLANT FEEDING

These are among the commonest reasons for mulching, especially with manures or composts, although to a lesser degree with many other materials. The inherent value of these enriching materials is dealt with in the previous chapter.

When manure or compost is incorporated into the soil the stimulated microlife breaks down the material and releases much of its nutrient value. This provides perfect conditions for a newly planted tree or a heavily feeding vegetable during the growing season, but at other times fertility may be leached away, especially in wet weather and whenever there are insufficient active root systems to absorb it. A mulch using the same material is likely to break down more slowly, and any leaching has to pass through the entire depth of the soil, thus considerably reducing the chance of its being lost.

The presence of a mulch increases microlife activity in the soil by providing warmth and moisture. As the surface is less accessible to predators like birds, so the worms and other creatures can work the soil thoroughly without

OPPOSITE: Mulches for all seasons: hay and grass mulch for no-dig potatoes (foreground), black polythene mulch to make a new weed-free bed (rear) (*Chris Algar*)

In the last century so much horse manure was used for hotbeds before being disposed of on the adjacent ground that such gardens were inadvertently and exceptionally well mulched. French market gardeners even had clauses in their leases requiring them, on quitting, to reduce the soil to its original level. This involved the annual removal of about 500 tons per acre, or about 2 cwt (100 kg) per square yard!

Dangers of nitrogen robbery

High-carbon, low-nitrogen materials such as straw, sawdust, paper waste, dry grass clippings, mature green manures and leaves will rob plants of nitrogen while they are decomposing if they are mixed into the soil. Used as mulches this is unlikely, but you can spread first with a high-nitrogen material such as dried poultry manure and this will counteract any robbery.

being spotted. The increased activity then enriches the soil as the microbial biomass leaves more by-products and unlocks nutrients bound into soil particles; in particular the amount of exchangeable potassium in the soil is increased. Each year of mulching increases the depth of soil enriched.

The burgeoning life is easily seen when a mulch is removed: the numerous earthworm holes and droppings testify to their activity. These animals improve the drainage and aeration with their system of burrows, and so further aid other microlife and fertility. Worms work up into the mulch and leave many droppings, often deposited on top, especially on sand mulches. These casts are extremely rich in nutrients and have a water-stable texture which gives that sought-after 'brown sugar' feel to it.

WEED SUPPRESSION

Mulches are useful for suppressing weeds, but care must be taken not merely to aggravate the problem. Putting a shallow mulch on top of established weeds may look neat immediately, but after a very short time they will have grown through. Worse, they will be even more vigorous, as the mulch will suit them and eliminate a few of their weaker competitors. For specific ways to control them see the chapter on *Weeds* (page 240).

If the weeds are small, low-growing and do not include vigorous spreaders like ground ivy, nettles, thistles, *Equisetum* (horsetail) or bindweed then thick mulches will kill them. The easiest to apply in bulk and the cheapest is straw. Spread at least 1ft (30 cm) thick in spring it will eradicate many of the weeds, but any that do emerge must be pulled and destroyed straight away to prevent them rampaging. Extra layers of mulch applied every time the weeds reappear will be effective at suppressing them, but may require enormous amounts of material. Impenetrable mulches are much easier.

As all plants need light to survive, even tough, established weeds can be suppressed provided they are covered *completely* by impenetrable sheets of plastic, woven fabric or old carpet. Anything less sturdy will allow these weeds to romp through even immense thicknesses of loose mulch. It helps to surround the area with a narrow trench of about a spade-spit wide and deep, to prevent reinforcements, though this may not work with *Equisetum* and bindweed, which are pervasive and deep-rooted.

The best time to apply an impenetrable sheet mulch is in early spring, when it flattens the weeds which have just started to grow. Earlier and it has to cope with harsh weather; later and there is a chance that some early weeds such as celandines may return to dormancy for a year.

In late spring holes can be cut through and crops such as courgettes, sweetcorn, tomatoes or brassicas planted into the soil underneath. Even ornamental shrubs can be planted like this if they are pot-grown, but they will need copious watering all summer, as they are so much less vigorous than vegetables.

Provided no weed is allowed to reach the light the area will be cleared of all weeds by the autumn, when the sheets should be removed for soil cultivation. Organic materials can be left to rot in situ, but plastic and long-lasting woven sheets will degrade eventually and their removal then becomes tedious, particularly if weeds are ever allowed to grow through them. If the sheets are laid to kill weeds in paths or drives, on the other hand, they can be gravelled over and left. They could also remain under trees or shrubs but will look unsightly; a skim of shredded bark or other loose mulch will dramatically improve their appearance.

If the intention thereafter is to mulch the area with organic matter, obviously an impermeable

A generous straw mulch will eradicate most weeds (*Chris Algar*)

Clear ground after removal of impenetrable carpet mulch contrasts with adjoining weed-mass (*Bob Flowerdew*)

sheet must be removed or all the benefits will be lost; but if the mulch is solely for aesthetic reasons, the sheet can be left, though holes should be made with a fork to allow air (rather than water) to reach the soil.

Once the established weeds have gone, any mulch will help control new ones by preventing seed germination. For this either an opaque fabric sheet or a loose mulch at least 2–3 in (5–7.5 cm) deep is necessary. If the mulch is disturbed and the soil brought to the surface, weed seeds will rapidly germinate. A deeper mulch is therefore more effective than a shallow one: anything less than 1–2 in (2.5–5 cm) thick is completely wasted from the point of view of weed control.

Birds are the main cause of mulch disturbance (other than a careless gardener), and anyone who has used a bark mulch will know how they spread it over adjacent paths and lawns. Observe them and you will see that birds kick the mulch

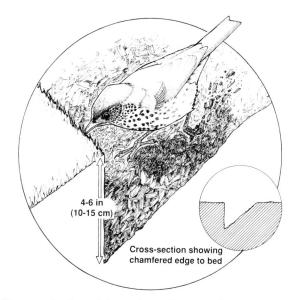

Keeping bark mulch in place. Correct edging discourages birds from spreading mulch onto adjacent lawn (*Rob Dalton*)

backwards and work towards obstacles. If the edge of the path or lawn is made 4–6 in (10–15 cm) deep and the bed is chamfered away from it the birds will face the perpendicular surface, kicking the mulch up onto the bed.

Soon after being laid most loose mulches will settle. Organic mulches will continue to do so as they break down and are absorbed into the soil. Thick layers settle more than thin ones, and heavy rain may beat them down considerably. New layers will need to be added quite often initially to maintain the depth, but the requirement will become less with time.

Loose non-organic mulches do not settle or become incorporated as much, though the finer-textured ones can become degraded by worm casts. These are usually deposited in or under organic mulches and on top of non-organic ones, especially sands, causing no problem in themselves, but containing weed seeds and providing suitable conditions for germination.

If weeds do germinate in a loose mulch they are initially easy to pluck out but rapidly become established, and then much of the mulch is dragged up with them when they are removed. In cases like this it is best to cut them off rather than pull them – hoeing may be possible, but is often difficult through a mulch. Flame-gunning will work well unless the mulch is dry! See the chapter on *Weeds* (page 255) for more on this.

MOISTURE RETENTION

This is one of the most valuable effects of a mulch. The increasing frequency of summer droughts and dry winters means that mulches are being used more and more to ensure that as little water as possible is lost. Without them, water is continually pulled from the subsoil by capillary action and evaporates from the surface. The mulch interrupts the flow by hindering the evaporation, trapping the water in its air spaces. This ensures that the soil remains moist all the way to the surface, thus increasing the volume available for microlife and plant activity. The rough surface of a mulch further reduces evaporation by breaking up the airflow, in the same way as a hedge does on a larger scale.

The water saving is great: where bare soil will take three to five days to evaporate ½ in (1 cm) of water, a mulched soil takes six weeks. Further, as the mulch breaks the impact of heavy rain and then allows it to percolate, it prevents soil impaction and keeps the surface permeable, preventing excessive run-off and soil erosion. If an absorbent mulch has dried out, of course, it will absorb some rain before allowing any to reach the soil. There is thus a danger that mulches can keep the soil dry if there are long arid spells with rain coming only in brief showers. If there is heavy rain there is little problem, as it will quickly drive through many mulches, but when brief showers predominate it is necessary to rake the mulch aside and allow the rain to reach the soil.

Impenetrable sheets such as plastic are first-rate for water retention, but a few points for their use must be noted (see page 46).

Gravel and stone mulches can actually increase the water available and so tend to be used more in hotter climates. The stones get hot on top during the day, expanding and driving out the air from underneath; in the night, they cool rapidly,

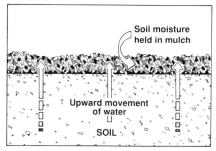
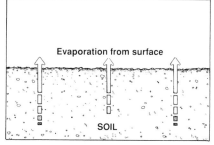
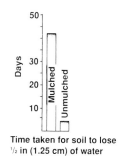

Water-holding mulch (*Rob Dalton*)

In order to save most, mulches for water retention should be in place before the end of the rainy season, which in the UK means by the end of March. Drying winds in April and May will otherwise rapidly deplete the water store.

sucking the air back into the spaces where the dew condenses on the cool underside of the stones and runs down into the soil.

TEMPERATURE CONTROL

Control of temperature above and below mulches is often overlooked but can have a critical effect, especially on plants in the early part of the year. As an insulating blanket, a mulch plays an important role.

Soil under a mulch has a more even temperature range and is warmer for most of the year. This insulation limits heat loss at night and keeps the average soil *minimum* temperature slightly higher than in unmulched soil throughout most of the year. At the same time, the average soil *maximum* temperature remains lower, especially through the heat of summer, thus creating those more stable conditions of warmer soil at night and cooler during the day which most plants require.

Because of their insulating effect mulches are very good at protecting roots in the soil from frost. Where bare soil will freeze to a depth of 2 in (5 cm), the same thickness of mulch will prevent freezing entirely – even a thin layer of litter gives considerable protection.

The converse is that as the heat is retained in the soil by the mulch, it is not available to warm the air around the plants' top growth during cold nights. For example, on a clear spring night the difference in temperature above and below a straw mulch can be as much as 13°F, 7°C, and the minimum air temperature over the mulch can be 7°F, 4°C, less than over adjoining bare soil.

Mulches, therefore, are good at protecting roots from frosts but may prove fatal to top growth. An understanding of this heat exchange process enables you to devise your own permutations (see table below).

The temperature effect of mulches

Effect	Gain or loss and reason	Winners and [losers]
More stable temperature under mulch	+ plants do not like big fluctuations	everything
Frost protection by mulch for soil	+ roots protected from freezing	bulbs, root vegetables, herbaceous and tender shrubs that regrow from below ground such as fuchsias
	– colder above mulch as less heat radiated from soil	[plants that cannot regrow from the roots, such as grafted plants] [blossoms lost which would have been protected by bare soil warmth, especially strawberries]
Slower warming of soil in spring	– cooler soil holds back early crops	[potatoes, peas and most crops sown before mid-spring outside]
	+ retarded crops may avoid late frosts	strawberries and other fruits especially
Slower cooling of soil in autumn	+ root activity continues longer	everything
Less cooling from evaporation of water	+ warmer soil plus water retention	everything
Higher night-time temperature in soil during growing seasons	+ increased temperature promotes more root and microlife activity	everything
Lower daytime temperature in soil during growing seasons	+ top layer of soil not baked, so promoting root and microlife activity	everything, especially crops that depend on both
	– less heat radiating back holds back ripening	[low-growing fruits, especially grapes]

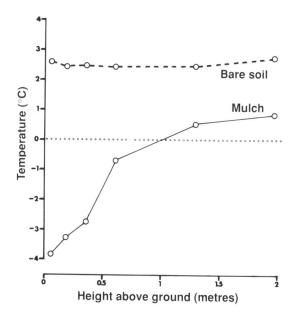

Mulch cools air temperature above ground (*Rob Dalton*). From *Trees and Weeds*, R.T.Davies, The Forestry Commission

SOIL TEXTURE

After a mulch is removed the soil will be in a much better condition than if it had been left bare. The combination of worm and other activity, favourable physical conditions and a lack of rain impaction gives most soils that crumbly brown-sugar texture beloved by gardeners and plants. Mulches on empty ground as a winter cover against soil erosion and leaching will also produce a good tilth without the digging and raking otherwise required.

Mulches protect the soil against erosion in several ways. They break the impact of heavy rain and prevent drying, stopping the granular soil that has formed being broken down into finer particles which would be more easily washed away. While the mulch remains the soil cannot be blown about or form a crust. It also helps prevent the formation

Repeated mulching over several years yields deep, rich soil (*Bob Flowerdew*)

of rivulets, which would cause further erosion.

The texture of soil is improved more deeply as mulching continues over several years and as more material breaks down and becomes incorporated. Even inorganic mulches such as sharp sand can improve texture.

PEST AND DISEASE CONTROL

Mulches provide extra benefits in disease prevention. Many diseases such as rose blackspot overwinter on leaves, plant debris and in the soil. If a new layer of mulch is applied on top of this infective material after leaf-fall it is sealed in and cannot be splashed back onto the plant to restart the cycle in spring. The warm moist conditions under the mulch also break down many of the dormant overwintering organisms.

Thus disease prevention may be an unnoticed side-effect, as when horse manure is applied to roses, and when strawberries and gooseberries are strawed.

Mulching can also protect indirectly against mildews, which are often aggravated, if not caused, by insufficient water; a moisture-retaining mulch will reduce attacks. Roses on walls, clematis and most soft fruit will benefit immensely from

Soil texture: crumbly brown-sugar texture beloved of gardeners and plants (*Bob Flowerdew*)

Mulch over diseased rose leaves can prevent blackspot reinfection (*John Walker*)

this, as they all suffer without a cool moist root-run. They are all woodland plants, and it may be safely assumed that most other such plants will enjoy a similar mulching, as it occurs naturally.

Apart from encouraging the soil microlife with nutrients, warmth and moisture a mulch also forms a good home for many larger creatures. Woodlice, for example, process the material and break it down; they then provide a basic food source for shrews, birds and hedgehogs, which help to control other more harmful bugs.

Mulches will further assist in the control of some pests such as pear midge, gooseberry sawfly and raspberry beetle. Their pupae form in the mulch, which is far more accessible to bird investigation than are most soils throughout the winter.

Sheets of impenetrable mulch can be even more effective. If they are put down before the pupae emerge, the pests are trapped underneath, die and are converted to soil fertility. In this way many pests in new ground are eliminated at the same time as weeds (described above, page 41), particularly wire-worms (the larvae of click beetles, *Agriotes spp.*) and leatherjackets (larvae of cranefly, *Tipula oleracea*), endemic in sward or weedy ground. Many pests such as these can be brought to the surface to be picked off or left for the birds, if the area is well watered and then covered overnight with a sheet of black plastic or old carpet. Be careful not to leave the sheet on sward the next day, especially in hot conditions, unless you wish to kill the grass as well.

APPEARANCE

Many people use a mulch for its appearance. An attractive covering is certainly pleasing to the eye and acts as an excellent foil to plants. If a mulch is less attractive, such as straw, it is usually confined to productive areas; conversely, the agreeable appearance of bark is offset by its cost, so it tends to be restricted to the ornamental garden.

The problem of cost against aesthetic value can be answered by using a thin layer of an attractive mulch on top of a cheaper or more effective kind. This works best where the under-layer is difficult for birds to pull up, such as straw, hay or sheets of fabric or plastic.

Mulches also come into their own where it is desirable to keep plants clean. Thin fabric or horticultural paper laid on the ground are excellent materials to protect saladings, especially spinach, from soil splash. Gravel can also be used for this purpose.

PROBLEMS

Apart from those already mentioned, mulches do have a few drawbacks. Not only beneficial forms of life but some pernicious ones are found in the

Horticultural paper mulch around sprouts and beetroot (*Charles Dowding*)

mulch habitat. Slugs and snails like the moist conditions beneath, though they are reluctant to move around on top of a dry mulch. Many bugs are a mixed blessing, such as woodlice and millipedes, which attack crops as well as processing dead material.

Care must be taken not to let the graft of a plant be covered by a mulch, or it may start to root from the scion. Warm moist conditions may encourage fungal or other diseases, so that the crowns of herbaceous plants rot or the emergent growths suffer from damping off or a neck rot. This tends to be worst with mulches containing manures or badly made compost, which can also introduce harmful organisms. To prevent neck or crown rot in susceptible plants leave a clear space free of mulch about the plant. To prevent the mulch encroaching on a valued plant use a ring of wire netting as a miniature snow fence.

Too thick or unperforated an impermeable mulch may restrict soil aeration; while this may not damage established plants during dry periods, wet anaerobic (oxygen-starved) conditions during the dormant season can rapidly cause root die-back and death. Anaerobic conditions can also change the composition of the soil microlife, leading to decreased beneficial activity and reduction of fertility.

The most direct damage to plants from mulches generally comes from birds spreading them on top of low-growing thymes and other susceptible carpeting plants. A hidden danger is where the sites of dormant plants are not marked and shoots might unwittingly be trodden on.

TYPES OF MULCH

There are two basic types: loose organic and non-organic, such as peat or gravel; and impenetrable or impermeable sheet types such as carpet or plastic. The mulches in these two groups are listed below alphabetically, with notes about advantages or problems specific to each.

LOOSE ORGANIC AND NON-ORGANIC MULCHES

Bark products are rapidly replacing peat for ornamental mulches, mainly because they are a sustainable resource, whereas peat is not. Bark is processed into different grades, from a powder replacing peat in compost to large pieces the size of two fingers.

The larger-textured bark chips are very long-lasting, provide plentiful holes for creatures to live in and allow aeration of the soil underneath more than do the finer grades. As some light will get through a thin layer, a greater depth of coarse bark is needed than of fine to prevent weed seeds germinating, unless a layer of loose mulch or plastic, newspaper or cardboard is laid first.

The greatest problem, other than cost, is that bark products contain phytotoxic oils that poison many plants, and these have to be removed by careful composting before application. Bark removed in the winter is more toxic than summer bark and softwood bark more than hardwood.

Commercial bagged bark products are already treated, but cheap bulk offers may well be in the raw state and will be a threat to plants, especially bark from white pine, silver maple, walnut, sitka spruce and Douglas fir. Added dangers from raw bark are animal pests and honey fungus (*Armillaria*), which is destroyed by shredding and composting. Bark products contain some nutrients, less nitrogen and magnesium but more calcium than sphagnum peat; the hardwood barks contain more nutrients than softwood. Softwoods are more acidic than hardwoods: both are in the range 3·5 to 6·5 pH, but the hardwoods require no lime when composted, as the pH rises, while the softwoods require the addition of chalk at 6 lb (3 kg) per cubic yard/metre.

The short-term effect of composted bark pH and nutrients on the soil is slight where the pieces are large, but with the finer grades the breakdown is rapid enough to add fertility, and also to incur some nitrogen robbery if the bark is mixed into the soil. As bark is relatively slow to break down and fairly expensive, it is best for the permanent mulching of ornamental areas. It is more effective and visually pleasing if a layer of a fine grade is covered with a thin scattering of coarser pieces: this prevents the finer stuff being blown about or used by birds for dust bathing.

For pathways bark provides a long-lasting, attractive surface that is pleasant to walk on, especially as it remains dry most of the time. It is hard to run narrow wheels over, though, and birds will tend to scatter the pieces about as well as taking some for nesting.

Bracken (Pteris aquilinum) A suppressant of other weeds, it is not dissimilar to hay or straw, though the midrib may persist for longer unless chopped. There is a danger of bracken establishing itself if any bits of root are introduced, or it may grow from spores. These are believed to be carcinogenic, so bracken should not be gathered on hot dry summer days when it is sporulating.

Cut young green bracken has considerable fertility value, adding about 2% nitrogen and almost 3% potassium; later in the season these levels drop, leaving a high cellulose content which resists breakdown. Because of the high level of potash, a bracken mulch is most suitable for potatoes, as a substitute for earthing up, and for soft fruit. Bracken discourages slugs and snails, making it especially useful for strawberries.

The open, airy quality of bracken makes it an excellent overwintering mulch for tender and herbaceous plants that may not be completely dormant, such as fuchsias and especially globe artichokes.

Cocoa bean shells are very expensive and have much the same use as coarse-textured bark, being most suited to undisturbed ornamental areas. In wet climates they can cake and become covered with mould, so may not be as attractive after a few weeks, though it helps to mix them half and half with bark of the same grade.

Coffee grounds and tea leaves are both unavailable in quantity except near factories. They dry out quickly, are similar to peat in appearance, acidic and with higher levels of nutrients. Coffee grounds contain up to 3% nitrogen and 1% potassium, tea leaves contain over 4% nitrogen, so they break down very rapidly. They can be used around most plants at an inch or so thick and incorporated afterwards, where they will be loved by the worms. Tea leaves contain high levels of aluminium, traditionally utilized for blueing hydrangeas.

Coarse bark over a layer of fine grade makes a visually pleasing mulch (*Chris Algar*)

Dust mulches are the top layer of the soil, frequently and thoroughly hoed to produce a powdery surface. You should make sure that all cracks and crevices are filled. These mulches are primarily intended to keep the soil moist by preventing evaporation; weed control comes from the hoeing. Though they cost nothing, dust mulches can be labour-intensive and rain will cause crusting of the surface, requiring more hoeing. They are very useful for early crops such as asparagus. Other mulches will slow down the warmth reaching the crowns and cause later cropping than a dust mulch, which will allow the sun to warm them quickly. Once the asparagus has finished cropping, other mulches will be more beneficial.

Feather waste is an unusual material, available only near poultry-processing farms, though small quantities can be obtained from recycled bedding. It contains 14% nitrogen in a fairly slow-release form, which can be beneficial but may overstimulate some plants. It blows about badly and needs to be sprayed with water to settle it. The worst problem is the horrible smell from wet feathers in hot weather.

Feather waste smothers most weeds. Because of its high nitrogen content it is too rich for low-growing herbaceous plants and should be used only on hungry crops such as peaches, plums, blackcurrants or globe artichokes. The white surface (which greens after a time) reflects heat, making for later crops and helping them avoid the effects of frost. It is good mixed with other mulches: once wetted it acts like glue to hold them in place, and both smell and nitrogen content are less fierce.

Feather waste may cause disease problems: if packed up in a wet state against bark or stems it can cause rotting.

Flax. An alternative to peat, the fibrous straw is ground and composted with bark to produce a relatively sterile material, pleasant to handle, with a pH of 6·5. Nutrient levels are not high but the amount of potassium is significant and may make this material of use for vegetable-bed mulching and under soft fruit.

Garden compost. See preceding chapter, page 35 and table, page 50.

Grass clippings are one of the most easily available mulches, underrated principally because of people's experience with smelly rotting masses when clippings are continually dumped in one spot. If they are put down in thin layers they form not this black ooze, but a loose friable soil with a dry, chopped-hay effect on top, as there is aerobic rather than anaerobic breakdown. The release of

CO_2 and plant nutrients provides a valuable addition to soil fertility. Layers an inch or so thick can be added once a fortnight to build up the depth without encouraging anaerobic conditions, as long as there is not also heavy rain.

Grass clippings can be used satisfactorily in most areas of the garden. They provide their own nitrogen if incorporated fresh, but may cause nitrogen robbery after long drying. They contain some weed seeds, but these should prove little problem where the area is continually mulched. Do not pile them deep about soft growth as they may then cause heating or rotting. They are especially useful as a sowing mulch for strongly-growing seeds such as the legumes. A layer about 1 in (2·5cm) thick spread on the soil after sowing keeps in moisture.

Gravel is pleasant to look at, easy to apply, long-lasting, cheap, and less prone to bird disturbance than many other materials. It may contain lime or even salt, so check this before applying it to sensitive plants. It allows drainage and plentiful aeration, so can benefit plants that hate damp conditions around their top-growth or crown, which is why it is so good for alpines. It reflects heat during hot weather while keeping the soil cool, so has been used to aid the ripening of grapes and benefit Mediterranean herbs.

Gravel is most suitable as a permanent rather than a temporary cover. It is excellent for most ornamental areas with permanent plantings. Fertilizing matter must be spread first and the gravel placed on top. Sheets of fabric, plastic or newspaper laid between the two will prevent intermingling and keep the gravel cleaner. As with any loose mulch care must be taken if you have to plant through it, and if it does get dirty it has to be raked and the soil washed out of it.

Anywhere, but especially on paths and drives, gravel must be at least 2 in (5 cm) thick. This is deep enough to suppress weed seeds and to enable raking without drawing up soil or seed. Even more than for most mulches a thin layer is a false economy. However, plastic sheeting is sometimes used underneath to prevent established weeds suckering, and this means a thinner layer of gravel can be used, but care is needed to ensure that water runs off properly.

Gravel is surprisingly good at germinating seeds that fall on to it. Once they emerge as weedlings they should be flame-gunned or raked; left longer, they will be harder to eradicate.

Green manures. See chapter on *Soil* (pages 21–5) and table, page 50.

Hop waste can be used as an attractive mulch resembling a finer grade of bark. As it dries quickly and is then light it may be kept in place with some chipped bark. The waste does not contain much intrinsic nutrient value, though its protein and carbohydrate content means it rapidly decays and adds greatly to the microbial biomass. If stacked for a year it breaks down to a fine 'leaf-mould' which is excellent round vegetables and free of weed seeds. Where available in quantity it can be used up to 1 ft (30 cm) thick around fruit trees, especially plums.

Leaves and leaf-mould   should be secured as much as possible. Where supplies are limited the productive garden will benefit the most.

Leaves make good mulches but blow around, so they need anchoring with grass clippings, sand or chipped bark, or must be covered with a net or some form of sheet mulch. They are probably the best mulch for protecting dormant plants through the winter, keeping them warm and dry. But if they blow on to low-growing evergreens or carpeting plants like thyme they will kill them. Leaf-mould resembles peat and is very pleasing; it contains many plant foods in the most nutritious form for mulching. To turn leaves into leaf-mould merely requires storing them outside for a year or so (see *Composts* page 32). Care should be taken with street sweepings, as they may contain salt or weedkillers as well as rubbish, but much is available for the asking.

Different leaves have different value. Oak and beech are excellent at adding nutrients, though oak leaves soon make soil more acid and need liming. Beech leaves contain almost 2% calcium and maple leaves are high in potassium. Chestnut, plane and sycamore are slow to break down and leave skeletons, making them more suited to permanent mulching in the fruit cage or shrub border than for vegetables.

Evergreen leaves, which are resistant to decay, can be used as a mulch, though as they often have phytotoxic effects (see page 43) they are best used under their own kind in the shrub border. Holly leaves are supposed to repel moles and mice, but will also repel fingers for many years. Yew is so poisonous that it should not be left where children may pick it up.

Leaf-mould may introduce weed seeds even after it has been stacked for years.

Manures   are best used in the spring, as when spread in the autumn they lose nutrients through leaching. Covering the mulch with plastic sheet will prevent this and aid its breakdown. Putting the garden to bed in the autumn like this gives good soil conditions for the spring but precludes green manuring.

The high nutrient level means it is possible to overfeed the crop, so manures may be better combined with materials of lower value such as straw. Orchard trees, asparagus, blackcurrants

Putting the garden 'to bed' in autumn: seaweed meal followed by cardboard, topped by manure, all tucked in with black polythene sheet (*Jim Hay*)

and raspberries, leeks and potatoes will gain most from these rich mulches. See also the chapter on *Soil*, page 21.

Mushroom compost   can be used in all areas of the garden and is probably the most practical all-round mulch. It is widely available, usually free of weed seeds, inexpensive, visually not unappealing and pleasant to handle. As lime and gypsum are added during mushroom-growing it may vary from an acid to a very alkaline pH. Care needs also to be taken against the risk of pesticide residues, as many chemicals are used against mushroom flies.

Peat   has little nutrient value but is an effective soil conditioner and has good moisture-holding properties. The finer-textured sedge peat is less acidic than sphagnum or moss peat. Neither can be recommended, because of the environmental cost. Moreover, as there are so many viable alternatives there is no case for using them for mulch purposes.

Pine needles   are often recommended for use with strawberries, as they reputedly improve the flavour and may discourage slugs and snails. They hinder the germination of seeds, so should be kept away from the vegetable area. They make good path coverings.

Sand   is one of the cheapest mulches, though rarely used. Sharp sand is preferable to the finer builder's sand, as it allows more aeration. In many ways sand is similar to gravel, with no nutrient value and little effect on pH unless it contains some chalk. It may contain salt if it comes from a coastal region.

Sand can be used to great advantage as a hoeing mulch or mixed with leaf-mould as a sowing mulch. The sand can be incorporated after use and will improve the texture of most soils except very light ones.

Earthworm casts will slowly accumulate on top of sand; these should be gathered up, otherwise weeds will gain a foothold. A sprinkling of soot to darken the sand helps it to absorb more warmth, as its light colour does tend to reflect heat and light. It is ideal for mulching herbaceous plants, as it keeps the crowns protected from the weather but allows them aeration while discouraging pests like slugs and snails.

Sawdust contains only half the nutrients of straw, is slow to break down and causes nitrogen robbery, so should not be incorporated into the soil unless and until it has broken down to a brown 'soil' and worms are found in it. Softwood sawdusts take longer than hardwoods to decompose and care must be taken to ensure that the dust comes from untreated wood. Thin layers break down much more quickly than thick ones, which form a skin.

Because of the nitrogen robbery raw sawdust is unsuitable in the vegetable garden. If sawdust is to be used amongst trees or shrubs, some high-nitrogen material must be spread first or mixed in. If thoroughly composted with animal manures it can be used in the same way as garden compost. As it is acid it will need the addition of some lime for all except acid-lovers.

Wood shavings are similar to sawdust, but as they come from planed wood they are more likely to contain chemical preservatives. They should be composted in the same way as sawdust before use. Shavings used as bedding will be easier to compost because of the manure content.

Once broken down the composted material is suitable for mulching most permanent crops except raspberries. As it resembles peat it can be used in ornamental areas. If the material is not fully decomposed it should not be applied until the autumn, which gives time for further breakdown and any robbery to take place before growth restarts.

Shredded prunings are an ecologically valuable way of recovering nutrient-rich organic materials and returning them to the soil. As a mulch they are weed-suppressing as well as soil-conditioning.

Stones are used like gravel. They are more effective at condensing dew and throwing up heat. If the stone is crushed and has sharp surfaces then it will discourage slugs and snails. The larger the stones the less effective they are at stopping weeds, unless there is a thick layer.

Stone chippings are used for mulching around alpines, where the drainage and appearance they afford is particularly suitable. For lime-loving plants crushed limestone is good, but may be too much for other plants especially if it is of a fine grade that readily leaches.

Another type of stone mulch consists of permanent flat stones or, preferably, brick, laid over the paths between the rows. They are effective at conserving moisture in the soil and also as heat absorbers. They are especially useful around ornamentals.

Straw (and hay) is the commonest bulk mulching material, especially for soft fruit, and for keeping strawberries clean. Straw is low in nutrient value but does not cause nitrogen robbery until dug in; the long stems and resistant waxy varnish prevent it breaking down while it lies as a mulch. If it is dug in then one third its weight of poultry manure must be added to prevent months of nitrogen robbery and poor soil.

There used to be a problem with hormone growth-regulating residues on wheat straw, which caused deformation and death to tomatoes, cucumbers and other plants, but newer hybrids have removed this danger.

Straw makes an excellent quick-drying pathway and is useful as a mulch in most parts of the productive garden, though its appearance is against it for ornamental areas. Where it is to be used as a permanent mulch, although not much nitrogen robbery will take place, some nitrogenous material should be spread first: if spread on the straw it will interact with it and be wasted.

In the vegetable garden it is more suitable for larger transplants, as the birds move it around and it can smother seedlings.

When used as a temporary mulch it causes a weed problem afterwards. Straw is invariably full of weed seeds (hay even more so), and it is only practical to use it permanently and keep topping up, or be prepared to deal with the following flushes of weeds.

IMPERMEABLE AND/OR IMPENETRABLE MULCHES

While there is no nutrient value or addition to the soil organic content, these offer similar physical benefits to loose mulches. One thin sheet of old carpet or plastic can replicate the water retention of several inches of a loose mulch. There is an insulation effect, but this is much less than for loose mulches; the weed control is far superior and the cost can be lower. They all benefit from camouflaging with a sprinkling of something like bark.

Old carpet is usually available free, but not all types are suitable. Foam and rubber backings have a tendency to flake off in bits which spread, and these may contain undesirable chemicals. Old natural-fibre carpets are the best as they eventually rot, so can be left in place. All synthetic carpets last for years, making them excellent for mulching pathways. Mixed-fibre carpets partially rot, leaving stringy pieces that take time to extricate.

Carpets are best used upside down. A thin layer of shredded bark can improve the appearance for the ornamental garden, but too thick a layer will cause premature rotting.

They are superb for eradicating established weeds and suppressing annual ones, and they retain moisture well. The woven texture allows air to penetrate as easily as rain. Underfelt is not quite as resistant to strongly-growing weeds as carpet, but can be used in the same way.

Newspaper and cardboard are impractical on their own, as they are too prone to blow away and once wet are soon broken up or penetrated by weeds. They can be useful underneath loose mulches, as they stop the soil being mixed in with the mulch and thus allow a thinner layer. Commercial papers are available, though expensive. They are most effective at keeping saladings clean. Rolls of plain wallpaper can be as effective. Take care not to use waxed or coloured paper as these may be contaminated with chemicals. Newspaper is now mostly chlorine-free and there is no danger of lead from the ink any more.

Plastic sheets are becoming available in rapidly increasing variety to meet different requirements, the main ones being weed suppression, moisture retention and soil warming.

Impermeable clear plastic (polythene) is primarily a soil warmer. As such, it will also encourage weeds unless covered by a loose mulch.

Impermeable opaque plastic (polythene), usually black, functions much like carpet, effective at stopping light, tough enough to stop weeds. But it is important that it be sufficiently thick – if you can hold it up and detect light, one thickness will be insufficient. Because black is a heat absorber, it will draw heat away from plants growing through. This can be overcome with sheet that is black on one side, turned face downwards to act as a weed suppressor, and white on the other (face up) to reflect light and warmth onto the plants.

Impermeable sheet, while excluding air, can still allow the entry of water, which can be sucked in under the plastic from the surrounding soil. Large areas of plastic may thus produce anaerobic conditions and a loss of favourable microlife.

Puncturing plastic sheets with a fork (both opaque and clear plastic can be obtained ready perforated) will allow air through but may also encourage weeds. For this reason as well as for aesthetic appeal it is a good idea to cover plastic sheets with a thin layer of a loose mulch.

Plastic sheets are especially useful for establishing trees and shrubs, as they provide the ideal moist, weed-free conditions for the first few years before breaking down. Voles and other rodents may hide underneath, causing pursuing predators to shred the plastic, but a layer of straw will stop this and protect the plastic from ultra-violet degradation.

Vegetables can be transplanted through slits in plastic sheets, reducing weeding and watering. This is especially beneficial to leafy types that are easily spoiled by dirt such as lettuce and spinach. The sheets are effective and last longer with fewest slits cut in them, so widely spaced crops such as courgettes are more economic.

Strawberries are worth planting straight through plastic but should be along pre-formed ridges to prevent water drowning the crowns, and drainage slits should be cut in the troughs.

Life expectancy can vary considerably, and it is worthwhile to obtain one of the heavier gauges. An environmental concern, however, is to ensure that after use the plastic will eventually degrade, and harmlessly. Almost all plastics are bio-degradable but take a long time. Most have to be exposed to strong sunlight to break down, and they do not rot if put in a compost heap or buried. Damaged plastic sheets should never be burnt, as this produces highly toxic substances. They are best deeply buried or added to the dustbin. Work on more effectively degradable plastics is proceeding.

Permeable plastic (woven polypropylene) membrane can last eight years, and has good porosity, allowing rain to penetrate. It is mostly used as an underlay to bark or other top mulch, assisting weed suppression and permitting a reduction in thickness of expensive bark or other mulches.

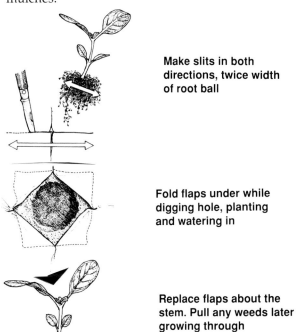

Make slits in both directions, twice width of root ball

Fold flaps under while digging hole, planting and watering in

Replace flaps about the stem. Pull any weeds later growing through

How to plant through plastic mulch (*Rob Dalton*)

Types and uses of mulches

A Loose Organic and Non-Organic*

Type	Uses	Pro and Con	Suited for
BARK	moisture retention soil enrichment weed control frost protection (roots) pest deterrence appearance	+ sterile – expensive + attractive	ornamental beds; paths; vegetable blanching
BRACKEN	moisture retention soil enrichment weed control frost protection (roots) pest deterrence	+ inexpensive – unattractive – weed problems	tender and herbaceous – winter protection; tomatoes, potatoes; strawberries; pathways
COCOA SHELL	moisture retention soil enrichment weed control frost protection (roots)	+ sterile – expensive	ornamental beds (best mixed 50:50 with bark)
COFFEE GROUNDS, TEA LEAVES	moisture retention soil enrichment weed control frost protection (roots) appearance	+ sterile + attractive + adds fertility rapidly	ornamental beds; vegetable beds (tea leaves for hydrangeas)
DUST	moisture retention weed control pest deterrence appearance	+ inexpensive + attractive	all areas; best for protecting early blossoms and young tender growth
FEATHER	moisture retention soil enrichment weed control frost protection (roots)	+ sterile – unattractive – disease problems + adds fertility rapidly	fallows and overwintering; under blackcurrants, globe artichokes, comfrey (best mixed with other mulches)
FLAX	soil enrichment	+ attractive	vegetable and ornamental beds

Apply

[keep depth topped up for all loose mulches]

*

All these types last longer if used over a mulch of plastic sheet (except where soil conditioning is intended), cardboard or newspaper. **Note:** some mulches, although effective weed suppressants, can also introduce fresh weed problems. These are indicated in both capacities.

2–3 in (5–7·5 cm) deep with coarse layer on top

Thinner, and more economical, layer of bark can suppress weeds when combined with porous plastic underlay (*Chris Algar*)

---

6 in (15 cm) thick of dry fronds

3 in (7·5 cm) thick of green fronds
3–4 in (7·5–10 cm) thick of dry fronds

Bracken (*Chris Algar*)

2–3 in (5–7·5 cm) deep
(goes mouldy in wet climate)

2–3 in (5–7·5 cm) deep

Cocoa shell (*John Walker*)

Tea leaves (*John Walker*)

---

hoe at least fortnightly
and after every rainfall

Feathers (*John Walker*)

2–3 in (5–7·5 cm) deep;
water down the layer

Flax (*Organico Ltd*)

2–3 in (5–7·5 cm) deep

Types and uses of mulches

Type	Uses	Pro and Con	Suited for
A Loose Organic and Non-Organic*			
GARDEN COMPOST	moisture retention soil enrichment frost protection (roots)	+ inexpensive – weed problems + adds fertility rapidly	vegetable beds; around fruit trees and bushes; winter 'bedding-down'
GRASS CLIPPINGS	moisture retention soil enrichment weed control frost protection (roots)	+ inexpensive – weed problems + adds fertility rapidly	vegetable beds; ornamental beds; around fruit trees and bushes
GRAVEL	moisture retention weed control pest deterrence appearance	+ sterile + inexpensive + attractive	ornamental beds; paths and drives; under grapevines around Mediterranean herbs Alpine and raised beds
GREEN MANURES	moisture retention soil enrichment weed control frost protection (roots)	+ inexpensive + adds fertility rapidly – weed problems	vegetable beds; around fruit trees and bushes
HOP WASTE	moisture retention soil enrichment weed control frost protection (roots) appearance	+ sterile + attractive + adds fertility rapidly	vegetable beds; ornamental beds; around fruit trees and bushes, especially plums
LEAVES AND LEAF-MOULD	moisture retention soil enrichment weed control frost protection (roots)	+ inexpensive + add fertility rapidly – weed problems – pest problems	vegetable beds; ornamental beds; around fruit trees and bushes
MANURES	moisture retention soil enrichment weed control frost protection (roots)	+ inexpensive – unattractive – weed problems – disease problems – pest problems + add fertility rapidly	vegetable beds; around fruit trees and bushes; winter 'bedding-down'

*All these types last longer if used over a mulch of plastic sheet (except where soil conditioning is intended), cardboard or newspaper.
Note: some mulches, although effective weed suppressants, can also introduce fresh weed problems. These are indicated in both capacities.

Apply

[keep depth topped up for all loose mulches]

2–3 in (5–7·5 cm) deep as available

Garden compost (*Chris Algar*)

1 in (2·5 cm) per week, in dry weather

Grass clippings (*Chris Algar*)

2–3 in (5–7·5 cm) deep

Gravel (*Chris Algar*)

as available

2–3 in (5–7·5 cm) deep

2–3 in (5–7·5 cm) deep

Hop waste (*John Walker*)

Leaves (*Chris Algar*)

Manure (*John Walker*)

2–3 in (5–7·5 cm) after stacking or composting

Types and uses of mulches

Type	Uses	Pro and Con	Suited for
A Loose Organic and Non-Organic*			
MUSHROOM COMPOST	moisture retention soil enrichment weed control frost protection (roots) appearance	+ sterile + inexpensive + attractive + adds fertility rapidly	best all-round mulch
PEAT	moisture retention soil enrichment weed control frost protection (roots) pest deterrence appearance	+ sterile + attractive – ecological cost of extraction	good all-round mulch
PINE NEEDLES	moisture retention soil enrichment frost protection (roots) pest deterrence appearance	+ sterile + attractive	supposedly add flavour to strawberries; good for paths
SAND	moisture retention weed control appearance pest deterrence	+ sterile + inexpensive	sowing mulch; herbaceous plants, especially asparagus; for heavy clay soils
SAWDUST	moisture retention soil enrichment weed control frost protection (roots) pest deterrence	+ sterile – disease problems + inexpensive – unattractive	vegetable beds; around fruit trees and bushes – not raspberries
SHREDDED PRUNINGS	moisture retention soil enrichment weed control frost protection (roots) appearance pest deterrence	+ sterile + inexpensive + attractive	soil-conditioning and weed-suppressing for ornamental beds; good for paths; provides valuable carbon balance in compost bins
STONES	moisture retention weed control appearance	+ sterile + inexpensive + attractive	ornamental areas, especially alpine and rock gardens; under grapevines
STRAW AND HAY	moisture retention soil enrichment weed control frost protection (roots)	+ inexpensive – unattractive – weed problems	fruit trees and bushes; rhubarb, potatoes and strawberries; winter 'bedding- down'; paths

Apply

[keep depth topped up for all loose mulches]

* All these types last longer if used over a mulch of plastic sheet (except where soil conditioning is intended), cardboard or newspaper. **Note:** some mulches, although effective weed suppressants, can also introduce fresh weed problems. These are indicated in both capacities.

2–3 in (5–7·5 cm) deep

2–3 in (5–7·5 cm) deep

Mushroom compost (*John Walker*)

2–3 in (5–7·5 cm) deep

2–3 in (5–7·5 cm) deep

Pine needles (*John Walker*)

Sharp sand (*Chris Algar*)

only if well mixed and composted, preferably with manure

2–3 in (5–7·5 cm) deep, or mixed with soft material (e.g. grass cuttings) in compost

Sawdust (*Chris Algar*)

Shredded prunings (*John Walker*)

2–3 in (5–7·5 cm) deep for fine grade; more for larger stones

4–6 in (10–15 cm) deep, spreading high-nitrogen material first

Stones (*John Walker*)

Straw and comfrey (*Chris Algar*)

Types and uses of mulches

B Sheet and Impenetrable**

Type	Uses	Pro and Con	Suited for
NEWSPAPER AND CARDBOARD	moisture retention weed control soil enrichment	+ inexpensive – short-lived	best for making loose mulches last longer; temporary weed suppression
PLASTIC SHEET (clear, impermeable polythene)	moisture retention warming soil	+ relatively inexpensive – weed problems	vegetable beds; under loose mulches for weed suppression; under paths
PLASTIC SHEET (opaque, impermeable polythene)	moisture retention weed control	+ relatively inexpensive	beds before/between crops; establishing trees, shrubs and hedges and for planting vegetables through; for winter 'bedding-down'; weed control between trees, shrubs and under paths
PLASTIC SHEET – HEAVYWEIGHT, PUNCTURED OR WOVEN POLYPROPYLENE (opaque, permeable) AND CARPET	moisture retention weed control pest deterrence	+ long-lasting + relatively inexpensive	laying as paths between soft fruit; planting valuable crops through; on ornamental beds under a top mulch

New infra-red-transmitting plastic is being developed which combines the soil-warming ability of the clear type with the weed suppression of the black. Experiments are also being undertaken in the United States with different, multi-coloured sheets for their effectiveness in raising yields and deterring pests.

Apply

** These are all good for moisture retention and weed control; all look better covered by a thin layer of coarse bark or similar. They are expensive in ecological resources (except for old carpet and newspaper), so use sparingly

lay under loose
mulch

Newspaper below loose mulch (*Chris Algar*)

lay at end of winter
as needed and tie down

lay and cover

Plastic sheet (left to right): black impermeable, white perforated, clear impermeable, black perforated, woven permeable polypropylene, black-and-white impermeable (*John Walker*)

lay as needed (after
rain)
lay and plant through

lay after crops removed
lay and cover with
bark, straw or gravel

Growing through plastic sheet (*John Walker*)

lay as required

Carpet around fruit tree (*Bob Flowerdew*)

5 METHODS OF CULTIVATION

Gardeners, in common with most of society, can be slaves to tradition. In preparing the soil for sowings and plantings we tend to follow time-honoured ways regardless of altered circumstances. But it often pays to ask 'Why am I doing this?' This question cries out for an answer in the matter of digging, since this is the most arduous and labour-intensive gardening task that any of us face. If, indeed, we do not have to dig – if even better results can be obtained without doing so – then clearly this must be a major consideration. Let us first take a look at the four main reasons why digging is traditionally considered necessary, and their counter-arguments.

TO DIG OR NOT TO DIG?

Burying debris and weeds. The necessity for this originates with the farmer, who mostly turns the soil over before cropping his fields. However, he is operating on a quite different scale, and ploughing is often the most straightforward way to accomplish this. On a garden scale, it is entirely feasible to pull or rake off brassica stalks, bean haulms, courgette plants and so on, and put them on the compost heap. It is also possible to keep the ground clear of weeds with amazingly little effort if one is well organized.

Aerating the soil. What is required here is faith in the soil organisms, worms in particular. A healthy soil contains enough of these to keep it wonderfully open without our help. In fact, interference may result in the killing of worms and general disturbance of soil life, which is otherwise carefully structured layer by layer.

Incorporating compost. The traditional idea is to 'put the goodness where the roots can get at it'. This sometimes makes sense. If your soil has been walked all over when it is wet, compacted by builders, for instance, and is more dead than

OPPOSITE: The making of a raised bed system (*Charles Dowding*)

alive, an initial digging and even double digging may be needed. In this event, certainly, you would be well advised to incorporate compost without stint, so as to ensure that you will not need to repeat the chore. Except in such special circumstances, however, this is an unsound proposition because compost is not a fertilizer. It is primarily a soil activator, bringing microlife into action to release the soil's nutrients (see *Soil,* page 19). It is, if you like, a kind of super topsoil, replacing the annual leaf-fall of the forest. As such, it should be placed where the leaves fall – on the surface. And in this too, we can rely on the worms to finish the job in their own good time, as and where it is needed.

Ensuring a frost tilth. I consider this to be an even less valid argument for digging. Creating a tilth becomes necessary only because the soil has been dug and made lumpy. Healthy, well composted soil has a pleasant tilth all the time – even clay, if it is well managed. Following a frosty winter, this is especially the case, if the soil has been spared a digging.

DIGGING

If you need – or want – to dig, first consider the type of soil that you have. If it is clay, digging is best undertaken in the autumn, leaving it exposed to the winter frosts to break up the heavy clay sods. Light soils should be left until the early spring. If the soil has become hard and compacted, a fork may be the most useful tool. It is easier to insert into the ground than a spade and is effective at breaking up lumps and clods. You can opt for either a single or a double dig.

Single dig: this means taking out a single spit (spade's depth) of soil. A single dig will be sufficient if the soil compaction is confined to the topsoil. Proceed as follows:
1. Lay a string line across the width of the area to be dug, giving you a 1 ft (30 cm) wide strip. Take out a spit of soil from one end, and place it in the corner diagonally opposite.

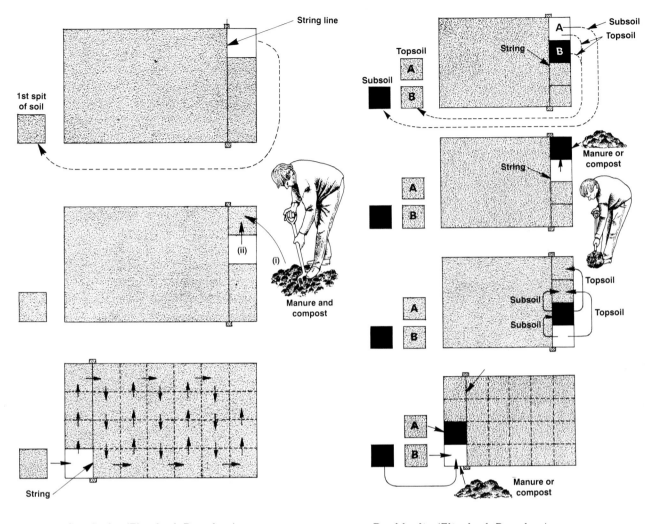

Single dig (*Elizabeth Douglass*)   Double dig (*Elizabeth Douglass*)

2. Facing this hole, and working backwards from it, drop a forkful of compost or well-rotted manure into the hole. Take out a spit of soil from the next 1 ft (30 cm) of earth in your strip and drop this on top of the organic material. Continue in this manner until you reach the end of the line and have dug a strip the width of your fork; you are left with a hole 1 ft (30 cm) square.

3. Move the string on a spade's width. Drop some organic material into the remaining hole in the first line. Take a spit of earth from the second line and drop it into the remaining hole in the first line. Continue in this manner along line two, and repeat until you have reached the end of the last line, dropping a forkful of organic material into each hole, until you reach the original spit of earth which will be waiting to be dropped into the last hole.

If you are using fine-quality, tilth-like compost, this is best reserved for the surface. If the soil is poor, you could incorporate some, and leave the rest for the surface.

Double dig: this involves taking out or working on two spits of soil, down to the subsoil level. If you are breaking in new ground, or if the soil is in a poor state or overgrown with weeds, you may decide to undertake this arduous task. It will certainly be necessary if compaction has formed a hard pan at subsoil level. You will have a tough job ahead of you, but the reward will be that you will also be improving the structure of the subsoil. It is important, however, to take care that you do not allow the subsoil to be mixed with your topsoil.

There are two ways to do a double dig. The first is to take out your spit of topsoil as with a single dig. Then, before dropping in organic matter and filling the hole up with topsoil, use your fork to loosen the subsoil. This will help break up the compaction and aerate the subsoil. The second method is more thorough, and even more arduous. It requires a spit of subsoil to be excavated, after you have taken out the spit of topsoil. The technique is as follows:

1. Proceed as for the single dig but start by

Slugs

The advantages of not digging do not extend to slugs, which tend to suffer when soil is moved and when they are exposed to predators. It may be worth raking beds to 2 in (5 cm) depth in the spring, to knock out any lumps of compost and expose some of the slugs.

removing two spits of topsoil to the far diagonal corner and also one spit of subsoil.
2. Turn the exposed subsoil from hole two into hole one. Incorporate organic matter.
3. Start hole three, taking a spit of topsoil and dropping it into hole one, over the organic matter. Take a spit of subsoil from hole three and drop it into hole two.
4. Proceed right through the area until the last two holes are reached.

If weeds are being incorporated, take care to turn the topsoil spit over when incorporating so that any perennial weeds are buried at least 6 in (15 cm) deep.

Clearly, digging, and especially double digging, is hard work. In subsequent years, it should not be necessary if, first, you maintain the organic matter with enough compost to encourage the presence of worms, whose movements have the same effect as your digging, and secondly, you take care not to trample the soil when it is wet, thus squeezing out the air and preventing water from draining away. In that event, you can look on it as a one-off tonic for poorly soil.

NO-DIG

The no-dig method relies on the application of organic mulch to the soil surface, leaving it to the worms, in effect, to do your digging for you. This may be regarded simply as a labour-saving device. But it is also, in my view, a superior method of soil management since it avoids disturbance to its structure and microlife. For it to be successful, a continued and generous application of organic matter to the surface is essential.

BEDS

The no-dig method usually goes hand-in-hand with the bed system of cultivation, the normal rectangular vegetable plot being broken up into a series of narrow beds, set between access paths. As we have already noted, digging may be needed to break up soil compaction. A key consideration in adopting the bed system (see below) is that it enables you to avoid this and to maintain a good soil structure.

The beds can be anywhere from 3 to 5 ft (90 to 150 cm) wide, to suit the individual. The guiding principle is a width that enables you to reach all parts of the bed comfortably when sowing, tending or harvesting the crops. Most people find a width of 3½ to 4 ft (105 to 120 cm) is adequate for their reach. The paths between can be narrow, to avoid undue waste of productive ground, but preferably of sufficient width to accommodate a wheelbarrow: 18 in (45 cm) is normally sufficient.

The beds can be any length, but it is convenient to break them up with crosspaths to facilitate access – and to avoid the temptation to walk across them. In this way, each bed will be accessible from a path on all four sides. This also provides a *cordon sanitaire* between the beds and any encroaching vegetation. They are best aligned north to south so that tall crops do not shade out lower, adjacent plants. Beds tend to be straight, but there is no reason why they should not be curved for aesthetic or other reasons.

FLAT OR RAISED BEDS?

If you opt for growing on beds, there is the further choice of having them on the flat, or raised. Flat beds simply involve putting the organic matter on a strip the width of a bed, leaving path spaces between. In a dry area, or with dry soil, this has the advantage that less surface area is exposed to wind and sun, and the moisture will not drain down from the beds. Flat beds may also be preferred for certain crops, such as potatoes, which benefit from earthing up and then being dug out.

The raised bed is built up higher than the surrounding paths. In many ways this is a logical progression from the decision to go for no-dig cultivation. It is often referred to as *intensive* raised bed gardening, because it can result in significantly higher yields. Far from there being anything new about the system, it is a return to practices reaching back to the ancient Chinese. It

Traditional flat beds in a Victorian walled kitchen garden (*Natural Image*)

Intensive raised bed gardening (John Walker)

Low-rise beds

Another, less common variant is what may be called a 'low-rise bed'. This works on the opposite principle to the raised bed in that the cultivated area is below the level of the surrounding paths. This can be worth considering if you have a light soil which easily dries out and may not keep its shape as a raised bed.

was also common practice in the West until the horse-drawn hoe came into use for weed control and dictated the adoption of wide spacing between the rows on big farm fields. Gardeners adopted this spacing too, quite inappropriately, and it became the yardstick – witness the standard instructions on most seed packets.

Advantages of the bed system

Raised beds
- Deeper layer of topsoil, open but firm
- Compost and manure reserved exclusively for growing area
- Better drainage
- Beds warm up more quickly, allowing earlier spring sowing
- Rotation management made easier

Access to all parts of the bed from paths
- Beds never walked on, protecting soil structure and soil life, raising fertility
- Weeding done without standing on soil
- Access to beds for cultivation during wet weather

Close, equidistant spacing
- Higher yields
- Light, moisture, nutrients distributed to maximum advantage between plants
- Greater control of plant size
- Less weed germination
- Foliage cover with leaf vegetables helps moisture retention
- Foliage cover protects soil surface from heavy rain damage

There are two reasons for the higher yields on the bed system – raised beds in particular. First, the ability to carry out weeding from the adjacent paths makes wide spacing between rows redundant. It has been established that optimum yields can, in fact, be obtained if closer spacings, based on grid patterns (see below), are employed. Secondly, the raised bed is usually associated with a higher level of fertility as a result of the application of regular and substantial amounts of organic material and the excellent soil structure and soil life that is maintained. It should be noted, too, that the overall increase in yield will more than compensate for the loss of ground given over to the paths.

Making a raised bed. The best time to do this is when the soil is neither soggy – especially important with a heavy soil – nor too dry. At this point, you have the option whether to go for a no-dig system from scratch, or first to dig and incorporate manure or compost. Some raised bed practitioners strike a compromise, starting the bed off with a double dig and lavish incorp-oration of organic matter, and subsequently relying on a no-dig annual mulch. Others choose to dig every four or five years, relying on mulches in between. The decision must be yours, and will be taken in the light of your specific soil conditions, the extent of weeds, stones and so on. If you decide to dig, then refer to the diagrams on page 58, and apply these to the following method for creating a raised bed.

The soil in the bed may first be loosened with a fork, as a one-off cultivation. At the same time remove any large stones. Remember, the aim is to clear the topsoil only. There is no need to worry about stones below 6 in (15 cm), as these assist drainage. The same applies to old roots.

The paths around the bed are now created, defined with a string line attached to wooden stakes. Dig out 6–8 in (15–20 cm) of soil and drop this on to the bed, which is thereby raised (especially useful if your topsoil is not very deep). As you do so, break this soil into a reasonable tilth. Do not dig the path too deeply, as this will make a trench which will be difficult to work in and

Making raised beds
(*Elizabeth Douglass*)

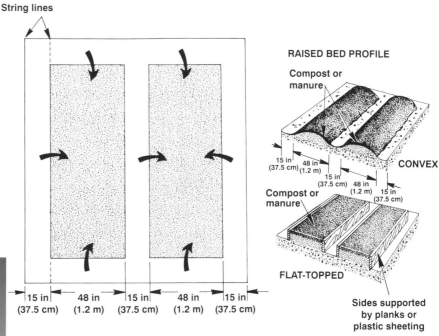

String lines

RAISED BED PROFILE

Compost or manure

CONVEX

15 in (37.5 cm) 48 in (1.2 m) 15 in (37.5 cm) 48 in (1.2 m) 15 in (37.5 cm)

Compost or manure

FLAT-TOPPED

Sides supported by planks or plastic sheeting

15 in (37.5 cm) 48 in (1.2 m) 15 in (37.5 cm) 48 in (1.2 m) 15 in (37.5 cm)

Compost goes further with bed system, being confined to intensively cultivated area instead of whole vegetable plot (*Charles Dowding*)

Paths between beds can be kept tidy and weed-free with bark chippings (*John Walker*)

maintain. A vigorous raking is a good idea at this point to level off the bed and make more of a tilth. The beds can be given a convex slope or can be flat, but I would recommend a flat-topped bed because this will reduce moisture loss by limiting the surface area and will also make for ease of working and spreading of compost or manure. Sloping sides tend always to be falling into the pathways. To achieve a flat top, however, you will need to support the sides with planks or other suitable material. The ends of the beds will be slightly higher due to the extra soil from the end paths: this can be eliminated by raking. Similarly, where you are creating a row of beds, the last one will tend to be higher because the soil of two side paths will have been deposited on it. If you prefer, this extra soil can be reserved for other uses.

Finally, spread your organic matter over the bed. With the bed system this will go further, since it is being confined to the intensively cultivated bed surfaces alone, not spread over the whole vegetable plot.

As the creation of raised beds is quite time consuming, it may be worth making just one or two each winter, gradually increasing the total. You may find it suitable, in fact, to combine a group of raised beds with a permanent flat area for potatoes and perhaps one or two other crops, such as runner beans, which can be rather wasteful of space on a narrow bed.

In time the beds will slump a little, but you will never 'lose' them, and they will, of course, be raised annually by the application of organic mulch. If necessary, they can be periodically reshaped.

The paths need to be covered to prevent weeds settling in and spreading to the beds. They can be turfed over, which will certainly look attractive, but they will require mowing, necessitating perhaps that they be wider than otherwise necessary. Besides, the sward may compete with the plants. Wood chips make an attractive covering and are, on balance, more suitable. They can be laid on old carpeting or other material, to extend their life.

If your soil is a truly sticky, yellow viscous clay with little dark topsoil, you may find it exceedingly difficult to create paths as

Mounds and hot-beds

On a small scale, it can be highly rewarding to make 'super-beds' of high fertility. You will need lots of the material specified below. Dig out the topsoil over an area about 5 ft (150 cm) wide and as long as the bed will be.

Create five layers, each about 6 in (15 cm) thick, as follows: twigs or prunings, leaves, fresh manure, well-rotted compost, and the original soil on top.

The resulting fertility will sustain multi-cropping for four or five years. During the first year, you can expect an early crop due to the heat from the composting manure and leaves. The more fibrous organic matter at the bottom will rot slowly and become available as nutrients only after two or three years, by which time the original dome shape will be much flatter.

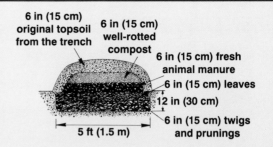

6 in (15 cm) original topsoil from the trench
6 in (15 cm) well-rotted compost
6 in (15 cm) fresh animal manure
6 in (15 cm) leaves
12 in (30 cm)
6 in (15 cm) twigs and prunings
5 ft (1.5 m)

Raised mound super-fertility bed (*Elizabeth Douglass*)

This was the principle of hot-beds, much favoured in Victorian kitchen gardens, when horse manure was abundant. A hot-bed can be made in a similar manner to a mound, using only fresh, preferably horse, manure, which heats more readily (see *Growing Under Cover*, page 370).

---

described or to create a tilth on the bed. In that case the only alternative is to import large quantities of compost or even topsoil to make the beds, in effect making your existing topsoil a subsoil.

SPACING

The spacing given to plants determines as much as any other factor how they develop. By varying spacings we have a better chance to obtain the kind of growth we want. For instance, closer spacing of lettuce gives more leaf and less heart; it also follows the golden rule of less space, smaller plants, though not necessarily lower yield. The *overall* yield can still be greater, because of the larger numbers of lettuces grown in a given space. Indeed, unless you want to grow mammoth vegetables for show purposes – often good for no other – small individual vegetables may be more useful for the average family. The spacings you choose will reflect your needs and also the layout of your garden. To a considerable extent, you can pre-programme the vegetable sizes of your choice. And when you are working with beds, quite different considerations apply, since there is no need to leave access space between the rows.

Instead of the conventional rows, plants are located equidistant from each other 'on the square'. Using this system, the actual 'rows' can be closer. For example, to achieve equidistant spacing of 6 in (15 cm), the distance between the rows will need to be only 5 in (12·5 cm) – see drawing. This will also ensure that all the plants benefit equally from the available moisture, light and nutrients. Envisage a circle around each plant from which these essentials are drawn. Now translate this into a hexagon and see how the plants fit together most efficiently, as in a honeycomb. With the closer

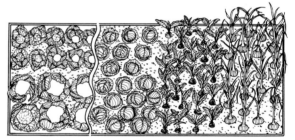

Cauliflowers and cabbages large size standard space (front); close-spaced mini-size (back)

Beetroot and onions plants 'on the square' for maximum overall yields

Using 'on the square' system for maximum results (*Rob Dalton*)

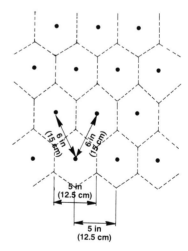

6 in (15 cm)
6 in (15 cm)
5 in (12.5 cm)
5 in (12.5 cm)

Equidistant spacing ensures all the plants benefit equally from available moisture, light and nutrients and reduces area required (*Elizabeth Douglass*)

spacing, the vegetable foliage should just about touch, so that this pattern is also the best way to achieve weed suppression.

Spacing

Crop	Spacing for beds* in(cm)		Comments	Conventional rows in(cm)	
	On the square	Rows			
Lettuce –early	8x8 (20x20)		Cos and iceberg 12x12	15x5	(38x12·5)
–main	12x12 (30x30)		(30x30) minimum for a	15x12	(38x30)
–small, leafy	3x2 (7·5x5)		good heart, Little Gem 6x6 (15x15)	12x1	(30x2·5)
Radishes	U	4x½ (10x1)	Leaves only if too close	12x⅓	(30x0.8)
Spring greens	6x6 (15x15)	12x3 (30x7·5)	Thin to 12x12 (30x30) for hearted cabbage	15x4	(38x10)
Summer cabbage	15x15 (38x38)		Smaller heads	18x12	(45x30)
	18x18 (45x45)		Larger heads	18x18	(45x45)
Winter cabbage	18x18 (45x45)			18x18	(45x45)
	21x21 (53x53)		For savoys	24x18	(60x45)
Brussels sprouts	24x24 (60x60)		One or two harvests of small sprouts	24x24	(60x60)
	36x36 (90x90)		Successional picking through the winter	36x36	(90x90)
Cauliflowers	8x8 (20x20)		Mini-curds	15x6	(38x15)
	21x21 (53x53)		Early harvest 'normal' size	24x18	(60x45)
	30x30 (75x75)		Late harvest	30x30	(75x75)
Calabrese	9x9 (23x23)		Early harvest, 4–6 weeks' picking	15x6	(38x15)
	15x15 (38x38)		Up to three months' picking of sideshoots		
Carrots	U	6x¼ (15x0·5)	Early baby carrots	12x¼	(30x0·5)
	U	10x½ (25x1)	Larger storable carrots	15x½	(38x1)
Parsnips	U	10x1 (25x2·5)	Small roots	15x1	(38x2·5)
	U	12x2 (30x5)	Large roots	15x2	(38x5)
Beetroot	12x12 (30x30)	U	For blocks presow 4–6 plants in each		
	U	12x2 (30x5)	Early and medium roots	15x2	(38x5)
	U	12x4 (30x10)	Large maincrop	15x3	(38x7·5)
Onions –bulb	12x12 (30x30)	U	For blocks presow 4–6 plants in each	15x10	(38x25)
	3x3 (7·5x7·5)	8x2 (20x5)	Medium single bulbs, seed or set	15x1	(38x2·5)
–salad	6x6 (15x15)	U	For block presow 8–10 plants in each	15x3	(38x7·5)
	U	6x½ (15x1)	Direct sown	15x¼	(38x0·5)
Leeks	10x10 (25x25)		For blocks presow 3–4 plants in each	15x8	(38x20)
	5x5(12·5x12·5)	12x2 (30x5)	For early and small leeks	15x2	(38x5)
	8x8 (20x20)	12x5 (30x12·5)	Large leeks	15x4	(38x10)
Garlic	6x6 (15x15)	12x3 (30x7·5)	Large bulbs	15x3	(38x7·5)
Peas (inc. mangetout)	U	12x½ (30x1)	Conventional row can be sown double	20x½	(50x1)

Cont.

Spacing

Crop	Spacing for beds* in(cm)		Comments	Conventional rows in(cm)	
	On the square	Rows			
Broad beans	6x6 (15x15)	15x3 (38x7·5)	One plant often produces many stems	18x2	(45x5)
Runner beans	One row along each side of the bed		12 in (30 cm) between plants	24x12	(60x30)
French beans	8x8 (20x20) 13x13 (32x32)		Early crop Long-season picking	15x4 15x10	(38x10) (38x25)
Celery	8x8 (20x20) 13x13 (32x32)		Small thin heads Large mature stems	12x8 18x12	(30x20) (45x30)
Celeriac	16x16 (40x40)		Large roots; closer spacing risks setting leaves only	24x12	(60x30)
Swedes	U	15x4 (38x10)	Large roots; closer spacing risks setting leaves only	18x3	(45x7·5)
Turnips	U U	8x2 (20x5) 12x3 (30x7·5)	Early baby roots Maincrop medium size	12x2 12x3	(30x5) (30x7·5)
Tomatoes	18x18 (45x45)	U	Bush and stem varieties	18x18	(45x45)
Cucumbers	24x24 (60x60)	U	Could be less for early production	30x30	(75x75)
Courgettes/marrows	24x24 (60x60)	U	Could be less for early production	30x30	(75x75)
Squashes/pumpkins	24x24 (60x60)	U		30x30	(75x75)
Parsley	4x4 (10x10)	8x2 (20x5)		12x2	(30x5)
Sweetcorn	8x8 (20x20) 12x12 (30x30)		Early small cobs Later large cobs	15x4 15x8	(38x10) (38x20)
Jerusalem artichokes	15x15 (38x38)			24x12	(60x30)
Bulb fennel	U	12x8 (30x20)		18x6	(45x15)

* Two spacings given for beds, where you may prefer to use rows
U = unsuitable: some vegetables, less flexible than others, are best grown 'on the square' or in rows

ROTATION

Rotating means growing specific groups of plants in a different place each season. This may not be feasible in a very small garden. Moreover, there are a number of reasons why rotation is undertaken and some of them, such as supply of nutrients, may be less important with a compost-rich organic system. On the other hand, pest and disease prevention is an important consideration.

Diseases. Crop families can be vulnerable to specific soil-borne diseases. The alliums – onions, leeks, garlic – are susceptible to white rot, a disease which, once present, will remain in the soil for many years. Root crops share many disease problems. Rotation can avoid the build-up of such diseases by depriving them of their host plants (see *Disease Prevention*, page 260).

Pests. Monoculture is one of the prime causes of pest build-up and, as with diseases, some pests are specific to plants of the same botanical family. They can proliferate rapidly where a plant group is cultivated year after year in the same place (see *Pest Control*, page 290).

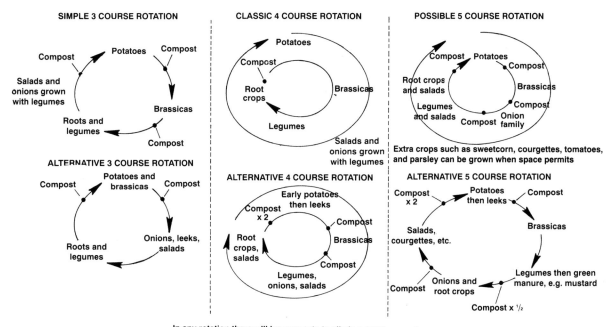

SIMPLE 3 COURSE ROTATION

ALTERNATIVE 3 COURSE ROTATION

CLASSIC 4 COURSE ROTATION

ALTERNATIVE 4 COURSE ROTATION

POSSIBLE 5 COURSE ROTATION

Extra crops such as sweetcorn, courgettes, tomatoes, and parsley can be grown when space permits

ALTERNATIVE 5 COURSE ROTATION

In any rotation there will be moments to slip in a catch crop of salads. As these are short-lived they need not be counted on a full cropping year. This also applies to a catch crop of mustard which, although a brassica, need not be counted as such.

Guide to possible
rotation plans
(*Elizabeth Douglass*)

Weeds. 'Cleaning' crops, such as potatoes, can help clear an area for their successor crop.

Nutrients. Even though organically rich soil can be relied on to make its abundant nutrients available, crops complement each other in their food needs. So it makes good sense to follow legumes, which take in nitrogen from the atmosphere and make it available through the soil, by other plants which will benefit. Likewise, plants seek out their food at different soil depths, a fact which can be taken into account when planning rotation of root crops.

Manuring. This can be concentrated, in the rotation sequence, on the plants such as potatoes that need it most, avoiding putting fresh manure on beds earmarked for root crops. Likewise, liming can be scheduled to avoid simultaneous manuring and liming, perhaps concentrating on the brassica beds, where it can help avert club root.

Green manuring: this can also be worked into a rotation plan, to improve fertility and avoid leaching of nutrients by keeping the ground covered.

There are many rotation patterns, varying from simple three-year plans to four-, five-, six- and even elaborate eight-year programmes, depending on what you want to grow, soil conditions, the terrain you have available, its siting, and so on (see *The Vegetable Garden,* page 88, for a detailed rotation plan). Too, you will need to take account of perennial crops such as asparagus, artichokes and herbs. The possibilities for intercropping, which may cut across the rotation plan, also need to be considered.

An understanding of the main principles involved, rather than following a rigid formula, is your best approach.

6 PROPAGATION

PROPAGATION BY SEED

The simple seed is one of nature's most extraordinary accomplishments. Apparently lifeless, each seed is a plant in waiting. Seeds can survive forest fires, freezing temperatures, burial, or even ingestion by man, beast or bird, and can turn these hazards to their own advantage. They come in all shapes and sizes: the largest seed most people will have seen is the coconut, while the dust-like seeds of trailing lobelia and begonia must be among the smallest. Some, like the field poppy, can remain viable for decades, while others die within weeks. Some of the oddest seeds come from the orchid – they are very small and light and are produced by the thousand, but they lack sufficient food reserves, and rely upon certain fungi which actually enter the seed and provide the necessary nourishment for germination to occur. Other seed oddities include the peanut and the animated oat. These actually sow themselves: the peanut pod forms on a stem above ground, then before it ripens it is pushed by its parent plant into the soil. The oat seed is equipped with a twitching whisker which makes it jump about until it falls into a crack in the soil.

A careful perusal of the seed catalogues reveals thousands of different sorts of seed. Growing from seed is reasonably cheap, and is often the only way of obtaining certain plants or

The animated oat (Rob Dalton)

OPPOSITE: Mixed seeds under magnification in all their extraordinary variety (Sawyers Farm)

varieties. Because nature has provided most plants with systems that protect their seeds from disease, seed-grown plants (unlike cuttings) will usually be free of viral or other sap-borne disease.

INORGANIC AND ORGANIC SEED

Some seed companies are now offering 'chemical-free' seed or 'organic seed'. The seed offered is not organically grown, but merely has not been treated with chemicals after harvest. The practice of coating seeds with chemicals, usually fungicides, is called dressing, and is demanded by inorganic vegetable producers. It must be clearly indicated under UK law. Sweetcorn and celery are particularly likely to have been treated, because the biggest market for them is with these large producers. The fungicides help prevent poor-quality seeds from rotting in the soil and can protect against seed-borne and seedling diseases. The process is not necessary if the seed is disease-free and of reasonable quality. Pelleted seed, enclosed in a clay pellet to make it easier to handle, is not necessarily chemically treated, but often germinates poorly, even under ideal conditions, and is best avoided.

F1 hybrids are steadily replacing many of the ordinary (open-pollinated) seeds. They are the result of crossing two inbred varieties, and the plants they produce are vigorous and uniform.

In the case of some vegetables, notably sweetcorn and green peppers, F1 hybrid varieties are significantly better than ordinary ones. However, most gardeners prefer flavour to yield and do not want the whole crop to ripen at once. F1 hybrids are liked by seed companies because farmers, gardeners and rival companies cannot produce seed from them, as it will not breed true.

Seed taken from organically grown, healthy, vigorous plants is clearly more desirable than inorganic, but practically the only way to obtain truly organic seed is to grow it yourself. This is often quite easy. Many plants produce perfectly good seeds without any help or interference. Sometimes, as with tomatoes, the seed is produced as part of the harvest; in other cases such as peas and beans the seed is the harvest, and merely needs to be left on the plant to mature. Many bedding plants such as French marigolds, sweet alyssum, pansies and nemesias will produce very good seed if they are allowed to, which means not dead-heading every flower but leaving some to do the job that nature intended.

Biennials, such as parsley, onions and parsnips, need to be kept through the winter before they will flower and set seed. Do not save seed from plants that seed in their first year or the offspring may also tend to bolt.

Some plants such as sweet peas, tomatoes and lettuces are fertilized by their own pollen and so will breed true. Others like radishes, wallflowers and sweetcorn prefer to cross-pollinate. This need not be a concern: a cross-pollinated vegetable will still produce good seed. The only plants not really worth collecting seed from are the brassicas (cabbage family), as they all interbreed very freely and home-saved seed is likely to be a mix of Brussels sprouts and broccoli. F1 hybrid seed can be saved: the offspring will be a little mixed but it will still be good.

Seed-saving is basically simple. In most cases the only task is to catch the seed before it is dispersed. If there is a risk of losing the seed before it is fully ripe cut the seed heads (with as much stalk as possible) and lay them out on a tray, or tie the heads up in a paper bag. The seed will continue to ripen and will fall out when ready. All that is required is a few paper bags, some common sense and, most important of all, some confidence; remember that seed does not have to come out of a prettily coloured packet before it will grow. Cleaning the seed is not always easy, though a kitchen sieve and a little gentle puffing can do a lot. Often it is best not to bother very much as the seeds will grow even if they are accompanied by a bit of rubbish. The one important fact to remember is that seeds will quickly go mouldy and spoil if allowed to become damp. Seeds and seed heads should therefore never be put into plastic bags: always use paper bags or paper envelopes. Organic home-grown seeds will often out-perform packet seeds both in germination and vigour, though the resultant plants may vary a bit in size and shape.

Most seeds will last from one year to the next, as long as they are properly stored (see table). The greenhouse is the worst place possible: the warm, moist atmosphere spoils seed very quickly. It requires somewhere cool and dry, conditions which are not immediately available in most houses. A good place is in a sock drawer or under the bed in a cool bedroom. The very best way to store seed is to put it in a self-sealing container, such as an ice-cream tub or a plastic

Seed head in bag

Sieve

Gentle blowing

Silica gel

Seeds

Seed saving
(Rob Dalton)

food box, along with a bag of silica gel and an indicator paper. Silica gel is a desiccant or drying agent which will absorb moisture and keep the seeds bone-dry. It is sold by good chemists and comes with an indicator paper which is blue when dry and turns pink when the gel needs drying out (just leave it on a warm radiator overnight, and then put in a plastic bag to cool before returning it to the seed box). Silica gel is non-poisonous and little packets are often put into the packets of expensive dried foods – it looks like chunky rock salt.

To test the viability of seed sprinkle a dozen or so on to some damp kitchen roll at the bottom of a plastic snap-top tub. Place the tub in the airing cupboard and check the seed daily. Good seed germinates evenly and has healthy-looking roots.

SUCCESSFUL SOWING

The careful preparation of a seed bed is the key to successful sowing. This usually means breaking the soil into particles small enough to enclose the seed fully and so provide it with water through capillary action while also protecting it from birds and drying winds. A quick raking will suffice on light or sandy soils, but a clay soil will

The life expectancy of vegetable and herb seeds

Vegetables	Years	Vegetables	Years	Herbs	Years
Aubergine	5	Kale	6	Balm, lemon	3
Beans, broad	4	Kohl rabi	5	Basil	8
Beans, French	4	Leek	3	Borage	7
Beans, runner	5	Lettuce	5	Caraway	3
Beet, leaf or chard	6	Marrow	6	Catmint	5
Beetroot	6	Okra	3	Chervil	1
Broccoli	5	Onion	3	Coriander	6
Cabbage (all kinds)	6	Parsnip	2	Elecampane	9
Calabrese	5	Pea	3	Fennel	4
Capsicum	4	Radish	5	Hyssop	3
Carrot	3	Rocket salad	4	Marjoram	4
Cauliflower	5	Salsify	2	Parsley	3
Chicory	8	Scorzonera	2	Rosemary	4
Corn salad	4	Spinach (both kinds)	5	Rue	2
Cress (land cress)	3	Swede	5	Sage	3
Cucumber	9	Sweetcorn	2	Summer savory	3
Endive	9	Tomato	4	Thyme	3
Florence fennel	4	Turnip	5		

need to be worked at. Clay dries out slowly in the spring, then sets like concrete. Hard work with forks, hoes and rakes will break up the lumps into a manageable size eventually. Aim to get a soil that will flow freely through the teeth of a rake, but do not over-rake. If a heavy soil is made too fine and dust-like it takes on the qualities of cement: a shower followed by a dry spell will give the soil a hard crust, which may prevent the seeds from emerging.

Heavy soils will sometimes refuse to crumble into a good seed bed. One solution is to take a rake and use it to draw out a rough furrow some 3 in (7·5 cm) deep and wide, and fill it up with sieved earth or compost. Then make your drill in this long strip of fine soil and sow into it in the normal way.

Vegetables are best sown in rows that are as straight and uniform as possible. They are a lot easier to hoe if you know exactly where they are supposed to be. Flowers usually look better and less regimented if sown in short, curved drills.

If there is not enough time both to prepare the seed bed and sow it, a large sheet of plastic (suitably weighed down) will protect the bed from being spoiled by rain.

To sow into the bed draw out a furrow or drill: this is best done boldly with a single flourish of the hoe or rake. However , if the seed bed is poor and lumpy, drawing out a straight line can be difficult. A plank laid down on the soil can help to produce a near-perfect drill. Run the hoe along its edge to get a furrow, then stand on the plank to sow the seeds. This also helps avoid compacting the soil, which can be important in

(ABOVE) A well-raked seed bed produces the fine tilth ideal for sowing (Chris Algar)

(TOP) Dried out clay soil can form a hard crusted surface (Chris Algar)

In heavy soils which will not crumble, fill a furrow with sieved earth. Plank minimizes soil compaction (*Chris Algar*)

RIGHT: Select the right sowing depths (*Rob Dalton*)

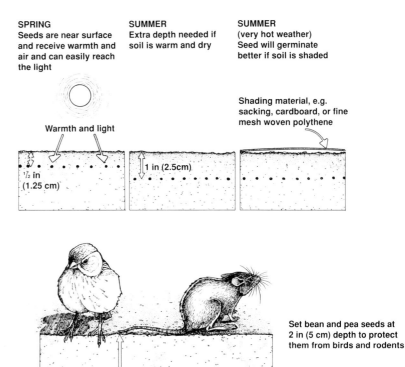

SPRING
Seeds are near surface and receive warmth and air and can easily reach the light

SUMMER
Extra depth needed if soil is warm and dry

SUMMER
(very hot weather)
Seed will germinate better if soil is shaded

Shading material, e.g. sacking, cardboard, or fine mesh woven polythene

Warmth and light

½ in (1.25 cm)

1 in (2.5cm)

Set bean and pea seeds at 2 in (5 cm) depth to protect them from birds and rodents

wet weather. A useful tip for sowing five or six fairly short rows is to sow the first while standing on a rake handle which has been laid down where the second row is to be. When the hoe is lifted it will give you a nice straight drill, and as you sow into it you again balance on the handle, making your third drill.

Seeds are often sown too deep. In the spring, on ordinary garden soils, ½ in (1·25 cm) is usually deep enough. By being near the soil surface they receive warmth and air and do not have far to grow before they meet the light. Only large seeds like peas and beans need be sown deeper, in order to protect them from birds and rodents.

During the summer when the soil is warm (perhaps hot) and dry, seeds need the protection of a greater covering of soil and should be sown at a depth of 1 in (2·5 cm) or so. In very hot, dry weather most seeds will germinate better if the soil is shaded. Anything that will keep it cool and moist will do, old sacking or opened-out cardboard boxes for instance. The woven green material sold in garden centres for shading is perfect, especially as it need not be removed before the seeds germinate.

The temptation to sow far too thickly is also difficult to resist. Crowded seedlings grow tall and weak-stemmed and need immediate thinning if they are to thrive. A handy guide is to sow some four times as many seeds as you want plants: one for the slug, one for the snail, one to thrive, and one to fail. If the eventual spacing is 6 in (15 cm) in the row, sow your seeds at about 1½ in (3–4 cm) apart, thin them to 3 in (7·5 cm), and again to 6 in (15 cm). Where slugs are a particular menace, double the number of seeds sown, but also provide an alternative diet of old cabbage or lettuce leaves, to tempt the slugs away.

An economical sowing method, useful when the final spacing is at least 6 in (15 cm), is station sowing. This involves making little groups of two or three seeds at their final spacings. When the

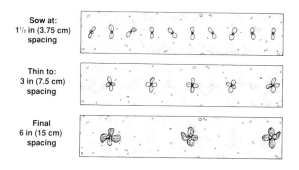

Basic sowing pattern (*Rob Dalton*)

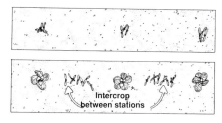

Station sowing (*Rob Dalton*)

seedlings emerge they are then thinned to just one. The gaps between the stations may be intersown with a quick-growing crop such as radishes.

Some people find the actual business of sowing the seed into the drill quite difficult. I find the best way is to take a pinch of seed with the right (or writing) hand between thumb and first finger, and by lightly twiddling the finger and thumb, the seeds can be made to fall one at a time into the drill. This may be difficult at first, but it is a skill worth acquiring. Once learnt it is much the easiest way of sowing, quicker than those little plastic devices which claim to be so easy to use, and safer than risking a major spillage by shaking the seed straight out of the packet.

When sowing a large area such as a lawn, or green manures, it is necessary to broadcast, as sowing in rows would be impractical. Prepare a good seed bed, and cast the seed with a sweep of the hand. To get the hang of this, practise with some sand. In order to ensure an even distribution it is a good idea to split the seed into four lots. Sow the whole area four times, using a quarter of the seed each time. Any discrepancies in the first sowings may be rectified using the remaining seed. Greater accuracy can be had by marking the ground into square yards/metres and weighing out the exact amount of seed. However, there is more room for error, and the result can look like a patchwork quilt. Once the seed is sown, lightly rake it in. Broadcasting is occasionally used for some vegetable crops, but they are difficult to

weed and thin. Its use is generally confined to cut-and-come-again types such as lamb's lettuce or mixed salad.

SPACING

Plant spacings are often a source of confusion. The notion may be made simpler if we use the terms 'density' and 'distribution'. Density is the number of plants per square foot, or metre, while distribution is the pattern in which they are arranged. Thus plants spaced at 2 x 12 in (5 x 30 cm) have the same density as those spaced at 6 x 6 in (15 x 15 cm), but have a different distribution. This may result in more small plants or fewer large ones, varying the overall yield.

Spacing to a grid system, where there is an exactly equal distance between plants, will often give high yields, but weeding and general access to the crop may be more difficult. The grid pattern is favoured by some people, especially for leaf crops such as lettuce. Rows for root vegetables are easier to sow and maintain. See *Methods of Cultivation* (page 62) and *The Vegetable Garden* (pages 82–127, under individual vegetables) for more details.

It is worth remembering that many gardening writers in the past had an eye on the show bench, and gave generous spacings in order to produce big plants rather than high yields.

Whatever sowing method you have used, cover the seeds with soil and lightly firm it by gently walking upon the rows. If the soil is too wet to trample on, press down on the drills with a rake held upright so that its teeth are flat. Firming ensures that seed and soil are in good contact, and by allowing moisture to be drawn up from below, it prevents the seed bed from rapidly drying out.

It is worth sprinkling a few radish seeds into the drills of such sowings as carrots and parsnips, which can take their time to germinate and may become lost in weeds by the time they emerge. The radishes will appear quickly and will mark the row so that it may be hoed with confidence, and they can be pulled for eating before they start

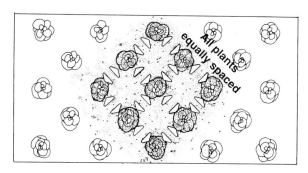

Grid system (*Rob Dalton*)

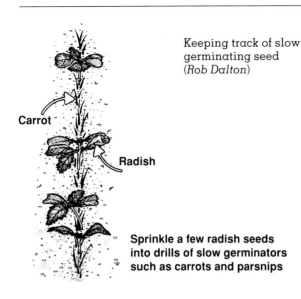

Keeping track of slow germinating seed (*Rob Dalton*)

Carrot

Radish

Sprinkle a few radish seeds into drills of slow germinators such as carrots and parsnips

Creating a no-go area (*Rob Dalton*)

Most plants are happy to be transplanted. The exceptions, which need careful treatment and the minimum of disturbance, are: The *cucurbita* family: melons, cucumbers, courgettes, pumpkins. Annual and biennial umbellifers, carrots, coriander, parsley and parsnips. Grasses and grains, such as sweetcorn.

Sweetcorn, here being planted through polythene mulch, is best germinated in individual pots to enable the undisturbed root ball to be transplanted (*Chris Algar*)

to interfere with the main crop. Sow the radishes at the same time as the other seeds, but very thinly indeed. About 6 in (15 cm) between radish seeds is quite close enough.

Unfortunately cats also appreciate a well-raked soil, and will often dig up the rows so painstakingly sown in order to make a dubious contribution to the fertility of the garden. They can be kept off long enough for the seedlings to emerge by spreading a few sticks and branches over the soil. Rose prunings work particularly well.

Many plants can be sown and raised in a seed bed, rather than in pots and trays in a greenhouse. Examples are brassicas, lettuces, leeks, onions and biennial flowers such as wallflowers, sweet williams and pansies. This is often a very good way to raise young plants as they do not require daily attention, but they will grow more slowly and must be kept free of weeds. Certain plants such as brassicas and leeks can be moved to a nursery bed to grow larger before they are planted into their final positions.

SEED TRAYS

Sometimes it is necessary to sow in seed trays indoors. Plants like capsicums, cucumbers and aubergines need the extra warmth of a sunny windowsill or heated propagator before they will germinate and grow in Britain. Without special conditions it would be impossible to produce these plants. Other plants such as runner beans, courgettes, and half-hardy annuals do not always need extra daytime warmth but do need protection from frost. By starting them off inside, it is possible to produce plants much earlier in the year.

It is usually easier to raise a tray or two of cabbage, lettuce or onion seedlings in a seed tray where they are safe and warm, rather than sow the seeds straight into a cold and inhospitable soil. When seed is expensive sowing into a tray can be much more economical, as germination will be better and each seedling should produce a plant. It is also a good idea to sow seeds that are very slow to germinate in a seed tray, where they will not be swamped by weeds or dug up by mistake. A further advantage is the protection offered to vulnerable seedlings from slugs and other pests.

Fill the tray with seed compost (see page 74) and lightly firm and flatten it, water it well and put aside for about ten minutes to drain. Scatter the seed thinly and evenly on to the surface and cover over with ¼ in (0·5 cm) of compost. The compost should not entirely fill the tray or it will be difficult to water: a lip of ½ in (1·25 cm) is ideal. Do not sow too thickly, or the tightly packed seedlings will grow tall, weak and spindly. To ensure that the seedlings have a good even distribution, mark out the tray with your fingers, making rows of shallow depressions with your fingertips as if playing chords on a piano. Sow two or three seeds in each depression and lightly cover with compost. When the seeds germinate thin to just one seedling. Using this method it is possible to sow for an exact number of plants.

Very small seeds such as lobelia germinate best when sown on the surface: cover with a sheet of glass which in turn should be covered with a sheet of paper. Water the compost well before you sow and do not use a watering can

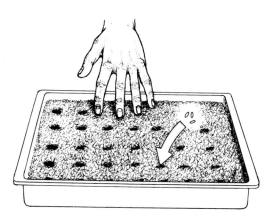

Four-finger exercise (Rob Dalton)

Types of tray

Old-fashioned wooden: looks nice but can harbour disease.

Flimsy plastic: cheap and reliable but a bit brittle; comes in a handy half-size.

Stout plastic: can be expensive and is not unbreakable; comes in a half-size.

Compartmental, made from expanded polystyrene or rigid plastic: divided into individual cells which facilitate easy removal with very little plant disturbance. However, they are more difficult to water evenly than an ordinary tray.

again until the seeds have germinated or you may wash them away. If necessary water from below by immersion. Do not leave the tray sitting in water or it may become soaked – few seeds germinate well in a marsh. Lift the glass occasionally to examine progress and let in some fresh air; when the seeds begin to grow, remove the glass altogether. Seeds such as those of nicotiana, impatiens and petunia, which germinate best in at least some light, also need to be sown on the surface. Some authorities recommend sowing on to a ¼ in (0·5 cm) layer of vermiculite or perlite which has been spread over the seed compost.

It is possible for seed trays on sunny windowsills or unshaded greenhouses to get too hot. A soil temperature of over 82°F (28°C) can halt germination altogether. It is worth buying a thermometer. During hot and sunny periods shade the compost with a sheet of newspaper, or shade the tray by taping the paper to the glass, until germination.

SEED AND POTTING COMPOST

These have nothing to do with the garden compost that all organic gardeners strive to produce. The job of this sort of compost is to support a plant in a pot or seed tray, an alien environment which requires a special sort of 'soil' with particular qualities.

A good growing medium must retain moisture and still drain freely, it should provide the seedlings with food, but encourage a good root system by keeping them a little hungry, it has to stay open to let in water and air and yet it should hold together. Finally, it should have stability and not decompose away, leaving pots and trays half empty. So it is not surprising that ordinary soil or garden compost are generally unsuited to this rather demanding role.

Most modern seed composts are based on peat mixed with sand and perhaps loam, together with fertilizers. They have replaced the loam-based (John Innes) composts largely because peat is not only cheap, but also weed- and disease-free, so does not need sterilizing. The advantage of loam-based composts is that they are very stable and are good for long-term pot plants. The biggest problem with loam is sterilizing it. Small amounts may be wrapped in a cloth and steamed like a Christmas pudding, or spread out in a tin and cooked for an hour; be warned, the smell is vile. In general the best idea is to leave it out of seedling composts and add it unsterilized to potting composts. In fact a totally sterile compost is not a good thing, because the ever-present damping off disease (and others) will not have any competition from the benign bacteria or fungi which can keep it in check.

Ingredients for home-made compost

Peat (moss): light in weight and colour, moisture-retentive and free-draining.

Peat (sedge): almost black, adds stability and substance.

Coir (pulverized coconut fibre): similar to moss peat; may be used to make up the bulk of the compost. For seed composts sieve out any long fibres.

Manure solids: composted manure which may be used on its own or added to a coir-based compost.

Pulverized bark: adds stability to coir-based composts, very good in potting composts for flower tubs or window boxes. It slowly decays and uses up nitrogen, so add an extra ounce of hoof and horn per two gallons. It is best when home-made with a shredder, as some commercial products contain a lot of sawdust, which consumes nitrogen and encourages fungus.

Sharp sand: opens and separates a compost, increases drainage and promotes a good root system. The best sharp sand feels rather like granules of glass.

Grit: used in potting composts, adds stability and promotes drainage.

Loam: adds stability and fertility but if not properly sterilized also adds weed seeds and diseases. Good in potting composts, best left out of those for seedlings.

Leaf-mould: varies a lot in quality; oak leaves are supposed to make the best. Good leaf-mould is similar to sedge peat and can be used as a substitute.

Comfrey and worm compost can also be included; they provide nutrients in an ideal form but may contain weed seeds and should be used for potting compost only. See pages 23, 24.

Recipe for home-made compost

This recipe has a higher fertilizer content than is normally recommended. For a simple seed compost reduce the amount of fertilizer by 50%. Ideally it should be left for a few weeks before using.

5 parts moss peat or coir
2 parts sedge peat or leaf-mould (optional)
1 part sharp sand
½ part well rotted garden compost (optional)
½ part good loam (optional)
½ part horticultural grit (optional)

Fertilizers per bushel (8 gal/36 l):
3 oz (85 gm) hoof and horn (finely sieved)
4 oz (110 gm) bone meal (finely sieved)
4 oz (110 gm) rock potash (finely sieved)
1 oz (30 gm) Dolomite limestone
2 oz (60 gm) calcified seaweed (optional)

Rub the various peats and coir through a garden sieve and mix them with the sharp sand and the fertilizers. Put the fertilizers through an old kitchen sieve so as to get very small particles – larger ones are released too slowly to provide any nutrients. You can if you like add garden loam, garden compost, and/or horticultural grit. Omitting the garden compost and loam ensures that the end product will be weed-free.

This compost will support the plants from germination until they are ready to plant out. Because the fertilizers are slow-release the compost can also be used for house plants.

Note: rock potash contains calcium as well as potassium, so this compost is not suitable for lime-hating plants. To make a lime-free compost leave out all the fertilizers except the bone meal, and use a good liquid plant food at least once a week (see page 24 for recipe).

Today, with increased concern over the destruction of diminishing peat-lands, good alternatives are being eagerly sought. The old-fashioned seed compost was almost devoid of plant nutrients and used solely for the germination of seeds. As soon as the seedlings emerged they were pricked out into a richer medium and later transplanted into a yet stronger potting compost. Today these mixtures have been largely replaced by the universal or all-purpose compost.

The normal seed and potting composts found in garden centres are not organic and contain chemical fertilizers, together with a chemical wetting agent which makes it easier to dampen the compost when it is dry. However, as far as I know they do not contain chemical fungicides or any other poison. There are a number of organic composts now on the market which are good, but you may wish to make your own. The best one to make is the peat-based, soil-less type (see recipe); the old loam-based home-made composts often give poor results.

DIFFICULT SEEDS

Most garden seeds germinate quickly and freely, but some require special treatment. Those which require a high germination temperature such as cucumbers, melons, and capsicums may be germinated before they are sown. This technique is called chitting, and is a useful alternative to using a heated propagator. It is best done by putting the seed upon a sheet of kitchen roll which has been dampened and folded so as to fit inside a margarine tub. Fit on the lid and place the tub somewhere warm and dark such as an airing cupboard: a temperature of 72°F (22°C) is ideal. Check the seeds every day and as soon as the roots start to emerge sow them into a seed tray or pot. Be careful when handling the seeds – a good way to pick them up is with the wetted point of a pencil.

Some seeds such as geraniums and sweet peas have a very hard seed-coat, which often needs to be abraded or softened before the seed can absorb water and germinate. In the case of sweet peas some people nick the backs of the seeds with a sharp knife, but a safer method is to rub the seeds between two sheets of coarse sandpaper. If this is not readily available try soaking the seed in a cupful of hot water – no more, or the water will stay hot for too long and may kill the seed. If soaked or rubbed seeds are chitted before they are sown; any which refuse to germinate may be removed for further attention.

Seeds of certain alpines, primulas and wild flowers either need or benefit from a period of intense cold or freezing before they will germinate. This is best done by sowing them in the autumn and exposing them to the winter frosts. You can mix the seeds with moist sand and after waiting a day for them to absorb a little water put them in the fridge for ten days. Aim for a temperature of just above freezing (see pages 209–10).

Occasionally there is nothing that can be done to hasten germination and the gardener just has to be patient. Seeds such as bluebell and wood anemone may take several years to grow. If seeds are sown in a clay pot which is

Seedlings being pricked out of multi-sowing plastic tray *(Chris Algar)*

then buried up to its neck outside in a suitable border the seeds may be almost forgotten about, except for careful weeding and occasional watering.

HANDLING THE SEEDLINGS

Where space is very limited sow into a 3 in (7·5 cm) pot and transfer the seedlings into a tray or pots. This transplanting of young seedlings is called pricking out. The seedlings should be newly emerged and must be handled with care. Using a good universal compost almost fill the trays or pots. Lift and separate the seedlings using a dibber – this can be an old knife, a teaspoon handle, even an ice-lolly stick, anything that will support them from underneath. Hold the seedling by a leaf and not by the stem, which is easily damaged. Replant the seedling just a little deeper than it was and carefully water it in.

POT SOWING

Some plants, notably the cucumber, do not like to have their roots disturbed. These are best sown not in a seed tray but in individual pots. Where seed is cheap sow two or three to a pot and pull out the weaker seedlings. If the plants have to be potted on to larger pots take care not to break the root ball or damage the roots. One way to reduce root disturbance is to use a bio-degradable pot. These may be planted straight into larger pots or into the ground. Some care has to be taken with watering, however, and many people prefer to tear off the bottom of the pot to allow the roots to grow freely into the soil.

POTTING ON

Fast-growing plants such as tomatoes and capsicums often grow too big for their first pots and need to be 'potted on' into larger ones before

This compartmental polystyrene tray enables individual sowings and avoids risk of root disturbance while pricking out (*Chris Algar*)

they are ready for planting out. This job can sometimes be avoided by pricking out into large pots to begin with, but plants often fail to thrive in pots which are too big. When potting on use a good potting compost (see recipe, page 74) which is damp but not wet and transfer the plants as carefully as possible, trying to keep any root disturbance to a minimum. Although some plants, such as the tomato, do not mind rough handling, others do. Firm the compost down gently around the roots and water well. Do not water again until the surface is obviously dry.

Before the advent of modern soil-less composts, bits of broken clay pots or crocks were put in the bottom of pots to provide extra drainage. With a good potting compost this is unnecessary, though a little stone or gravel in the bottom of big pots, tubs and window-boxes will help with drainage and save on compost.

WATERING

One of the major reasons for failure when raising seedlings and young plants is poor watering. When given too much water the roots stop working properly, the plant grows poorly, if at all, and is prone to botrytis, damping off and other fungal diseases. Most plants will die if consistently overwatered. Underwatering can cause slow growth, wilting and leaf scorch before the plant dies. There are no hard and fast rules. Different plants have different requirements, but in general most plants should be watered only when the surface of their compost has dried out. Never use green and stagnant water: it is a sure way to kill seedlings. If you are using rainwater, for example for lime-hating plants, make sure that the rain butt has a good lid which will keep out the light, and wash it out regularly or the

water will become stagnant and harm the plants. Most plants prefer water which has had the chill taken off. If a water barrel is kept in the greenhouse the water will be warmer than that straight from the tap, but it also must have a good lid and be washed out regularly. Ordinary mains water straight from the tap is good enough for most purposes: it is at least fresh.

Ideally, seed trays and pots should be watered in the morning, or at least the early afternoon. It is sometimes said that watering seedlings or plants in a greenhouse at midday can scorch foliage, but I have never found any problems even on the hottest days, although plants have suffered because they were not watered. If possible do not water young plants and seedlings in the evening , or they will stay damp all night and so risk problems such as damping off. One way to reduce problems caused by wet stems or foliage is to water from underneath. Plunge the pot or seed tray into a bowl of water until the surface of compost becomes damp.

DISEASES

Damping off. Seedlings keel over with shrivelled stems. This is the most common disease of greenhouse seedlings. Often caused by the inclusion of soil or leaf-mould in a seed compost, it is aggravated by warm days and cold moist nights. A dilute solution of a copper fungicide can help prevent it, but the best prevention is to water in moderation and if necessary, use a moss peat based compost.

Black leg is the name given to damping off when it attacks slightly older seedlings. The stem blackens and becomes brittle, but the plant may survive and may even recover full health.

PESTS

Slugs are always a problem with seedlings. Unlike older plants, seedlings cannot afford to lose a couple of leaves. See page 303 for treatments.

Woodlice. These will sometimes gnaw through the stems of certain greenhouse seedlings, especially lettuce. Woodlice are scavengers, and are not usually a problem in tidy greenhouses.

Flea beetles. These flea-like beetles attack brassica and crucifera seedlings, causing holes in the leaves. In severe cases spray with derris and/or pyrethrum, or better still with quassia.

TRANSPLANTING

Before transplanting vegetable or flower plants water them well, and while they are soaking work out the spacing or positions. Any plants which have been growing in the protective warmth of a greenhouse will need to be hardened off. This involves moving the trays or pots outside into a sheltered position for an increasing length of time each day. Tender plants will need to be hardened off gradually over several days. Tougher plants like cabbages and lettuces may be moved (still in their pots or trays) straight outside.

It is often a good idea to make all the holes before starting to plant. It helps to make sure that everything will fit, and during dry weather you can fill the hole with water which will soak into the soil at root level, where the plant needs it most. The best way to make the holes is to dig them with a good trowel, though on a light soil a dibber can be quicker. Try to disturb the plant roots as little as possible when transplanting, and (except for brassicas and tomatoes) do not bury them deeper than they were before. Firm the soil around the plants and water them in, then come back after twenty-four hours and water them again.

VEGETATIVE PROPAGATION

Being able to grow new plants from old is a very valuable skill. Vegetative propagation is a good and cheap way of stocking the garden and renewing plants such as thymes which grow old and straggly all too quickly. Growing just a few cuttings can often save a lot of money. For example, trailing verbenas, fuchsias and pelargoniums, which are quite expensive and are often used in large numbers for window-boxes and hanging baskets, are all easy to maintain and propagate. Instead of having to buy new plants each year, you can take cuttings from your old plants in late summer and keep them till spring.

A greenhouse is a very great help to the propagating gardener, but it is not essential. A north-facing windowsill or the bathroom shelf can be used to good effect. Most garden centres sell electric propagators, which work well but are expensive. Before buying one make sure that it will provide a steady 'bottom heat', as it is the soil or rooting medium that needs to be warmed, not the air above. The best temperature for quick rooting is 66°F (19°C). Any propagator with a soil heater should be thermostatically controlled, or it may get too hot and kill its contents. A little hand sprayer to give a fine mist of water is useful. The most important tool of all is a good sharp pair of secateurs.

LAYERING

This is a simple and reliable way of producing one or two young plants from an old favourite. Its particular advantage is that it is all done out of doors and requires neither trays of rooting compost nor careful watering.

Propagation by layering/cutting

Many plants may be propagated from either layering or cuttings. Plants which cannot be layered usually have no suitable stem to bend into the ground.

Plant	Layering	Cuttings
Buddleia	yes	hardwood or soft
Chrysanthemum	–	softwood
Currant	yes	hardwood
Fuchsia	yes	softwood
Geranium	–	softwood
Gooseberry	yes	hardwood
Lavender	yes	hardwood or semi-ripe
Magnolia	yes	no
Rhododendron	yes	difficult
Rosemary	yes	hardwood or soft
Sweet bay	yes	difficult

Branches or stems are carefully bent over to the ground and pegged down (with an old skewer, for instance) some 6 in (15 cm) from the tip. With a trowel dig a shallow hole around the peg, then lightly press the stem 2 or 3 in (5–7.5 cm) into the soil. Bury the pegged stem by covering it with soil, leaving 4 in (10 cm) of the

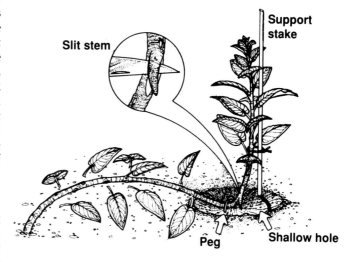

Layering (Rob Dalton)

stem tip above ground. To encourage rooting further the tip should then be pulled as upright as possible, perhaps by tying it to a stake.

If the stem you wish to layer is inflexible, do the bending, pegging and burying in weekly stages. Woody stems may be carefully broken, perhaps by cutting a slit, at the point of pegging. Rooting can be improved, especially on heavy clay, by first forking in a little sharp sand and leaf-mould. Many plants will respond well to a quite rough and ready layer: if soil is casually heaped over a low stem it will usually root. Layers are usually made in the spring, left alone all summer, and dug up as new plants in late autumn. But there are no hard and fast rules. A few plants will root easily and do not mind being transplanted immediately, while others root slowly and should be moved only when dormant. If a young layer is suffering from competition by surrounding plants it is usually best to move it as soon as it has rooted.

Layering may be seen as the rooting of a cutting before it is actually detached. It is often the only practicable way to propagate plants such as magnolia and sweet bay, which do not readily take from ordinary cuttings.

DIVISION

Many herbaceous plants form clumps: they produce several separate stems or crowns, each with their own roots. These may be propagated by division, splitting up one plant so that it becomes several, each with a root or roots and at least one stem or crown. Dig up the whole plant and discard any plant material that is decaying or old and woody, replanting with that which is young and healthy. When division involves cutting through a fleshy root, rhizome or crown the cut surface may be protected against rotting by a light dusting of sulphur. The best time to divide most plants is in late autumn or early spring. Many older plants are revitalized by being divided.

CUTTINGS

Often the best way to increase a plant fairly quickly or in large numbers is to take cuttings. Unlike layering and division it is not a foolproof method, but nor is it all that difficult. The cutting itself may be taken from various parts of the plant and from various types of growth. The different sorts of cuttings are:

Softwood cuttings: usually made in late spring/early summer; must be kept warm and moist; suitable for easily rooted plants such as fuchsias.

Semi-ripe cuttings: taken from early to late summer, using new shoots which have had a

chance to ripen and become a little woody. Cuttings of certain difficult shrubs must be taken during a specific month or week.

Hardwood cuttings: taken during autumn or winter, from fully ripened shoots of a pencil thickness. They do not normally require any special care or treatment.

Softwood semi-ripe and hardwood cuttings may be taken in the following ways:

Basal: cut off a side-shoot at its base, just where it joins the main branch or stem. Good for the more difficult subjects.

Heeled: pull off or cut a side-shoot so that an adjoining part of the main stem is left attached, and trim away any ragged bits. An old-fashioned sort of basal cutting, it may disfigure its parent plant.

Nodal: cut the shoot just below a node (a leaf-joint). Suitable for most subjects, though not quite as good as basal cuttings.

Internodal: cut the shoot between the nodes or leaf-joints. Only a few plants (such as clematis) require internodal cuttings, but they may be used for easily rooted plants.

Hardwood cuttings are simple and usually successful. They are taken in the autumn, and have all winter to establish before they produce their roots. Blackcurrants, gooseberries and many garden shrubs are best propagated from hardwood cuttings. After leaf-fall cut some vigorous and well-ripened one-year-old shoots of about pencil thickness. Trim off any soft growth at the tip, and

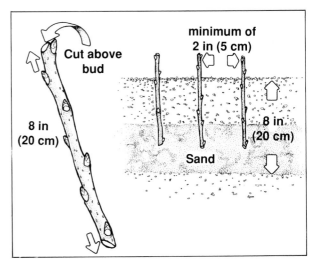

Hardwood cuttings: one-year-old blackcurrant shoots rooted outdoors in trench (*Rob Dalton*)

shorten the cutting to 8 in (20 cm). Ideally it should have a bud at its top end. Take basal cuttings from plants that do not root easily, or if this is not possible take nodal ones. Evergreen cuttings should have most of their leaves removed, leaving just a few at the top.

The cuttings should be rooted outdoors, and sheltered from strong sun and wind. Some garden soils are so light and free-draining that the cuttings may be just pushed straight in, but the more usual practice is to plant them in a narrow trench 8 in (20 cm) deep and half filled with sharp sand. Make the trench with a spade, pushing it in to its full depth and waggling it to and fro. Half fill with the sharp sand and insert your cuttings so that when the trench is filled they will be two thirds buried. Space the cuttings at least 2 in (5 cm) apart, then fill up the trench with some good soil and firm it down well. It is a good idea to label your cuttings fairly carefully, or you may forget what they are. Cover the cuttings in extremely cold weather – a cardboard box is ideal. A rapid increase in temperature during frosty weather, for instance from the morning sun, will do more harm than the cold itself.

Softwood and semi-ripe cuttings will not root well in ordinary soil but need to be stuck into pots or trays. These should be filled with a good rooting compost (see recipe right). Various sorts of pots or trays may be used. Normal seed trays will do, though they are a little shallow. Large margarine tubs and half-size ice-cream cartons, suitably perforated, are good, and so are those plastic hanging baskets that incorporate their own water saucer. Whichever container you choose it is a good idea to prepare it by filling and moistening it before you take the cuttings. Use a sharp pair of secateurs and remember, basal cuttings are best, though nodal ones are normally good enough. The cuttings should be put into the rooting medium without delay. If this is not possible put them into a bucket of water. Prepare the cutting by trimming off the lower leaves together with any damaged ones. If the tip is very soft it is a good idea to remove it, or it will almost certainly wilt and rot. Remove any flowers or flower buds. Large cut areas may be dusted with sulphur to help prevent fungal infection. If you wish to use a hormone rooting powder dip the bottom end of the cutting in it. But note that hormone rooting powders are not organic, and most brands contain a chemical fungicide; although they can assist root formation, they are far from essential. Make an appropriate hole in the rooting medium and insert the cutting.

When the tray or pot is filled cover it with some sort of clear lid. Shop-bought propagators come with a clear plastic cover, but you can make your own with some wire, a pair of pliers,

Cutting composts

There are various different types of cutting composts or rooting mediums. They must provide ample moisture together with free drainage and air. The compost should not contain any fertilizers, which tend to encourage fungal diseases; besides, the cuttings will grow better roots if kept hungry. Sharp silver sand is occasionally recommended as a compost, but I find it too heavy. A good mixture is two parts moss peat and one part sharp sand: the moss coir or peat lightens the mix and has proved to act as a natural disinfectant, significantly reducing disease. I use a rooting mix which contains perlite, a form of expanded volcanic rock: it is moisture-retentive and very free-draining, producing a well-aerated compost. Some gardeners prefer vermiculite, which has similar properties. Both may be used in almost any proportion with coir or peat and sharp sand. A good recipe is:

    4 parts perlite or vermiculite
    2 parts coir or moss peat
    1 part sedge peat (optional)
    1 part sharp sand

Coir (coconut husk) may be used instead of peat. It has similar physical qualities, but is not able to discourage fungal diseases.

a clear plastic bag and a bit of ingenuity. Put the cuttings somewhere cool and out of direct sunlight – a north-facing windowsill is ideal. If you have a greenhouse, either put cuttings under the staging or shade them with a sheet of newspaper. Leave them to make roots before potting them on.

The art of taking cuttings lies in preventing them from wilting and dying during the few weeks when they are without roots. This is done by preventing moisture loss and by the occasional use of a mist of water. When kept moist, the leaves can absorb enough water to keep the plant alive, but the damp makes them very prone to fungal or mould diseases. Because cutting composts do not contain any added nutrient, if potting up is delayed it can be advisable to give well-rooted cuttings a very dilute liquid feed.

ROOT CUTTINGS

Some plants, such as comfrey, sea kale and pulsatilla, are best propagated by root cuttings. Sometimes the ability of a plant to regenerate from bits of chopped root can be a thorough nuisance, as anyone who has tried to get rid of comfrey or horseradish will know only too well. This technique is generally used on plants which have insubstantial stems, but good fleshy roots.

Unless the plant grows vigorously from a cut root it is best to take the root cutting while it is dormant, usually in winter. However, some early flowering plants such as pulsatilla and certain alpines are just starting to wake up in midwinter, and are actually dormant during late summer and autumn. To take the cuttings either dig up the whole plant, or just expose a few roots. Using a good sharp pair of secateurs cut off a few young and healthy roots of about pencil thickness. Cut the roots into 3 in (7·5 cm) pieces and plant them right way up, and just buried, in a pot filled with cutting compost. If the plant has only thin roots cut them into 1 in (2·5 cm) lengths, lay them horizontally in a tray of cutting compost, and bury them ¼ in (0·5 cm) deep. If the plant does not seem to have any young roots but only old ones, cut them off and try them anyway. Return the plant to the garden and it will grow some nice new roots

Aphelandra being propagated by leaf cuttings
(RHS/Smith Collection)

by next year, which you can use if the old root cuttings fail.

LEAF CUTTINGS

Certain plants, notably begonias, may be propagated from plantlets produced by leaf cuttings. For simple leaf cuttings detach a young healthy leaf and trim its stalk to 2 in (5 cm). Insert the stalk at a very shallow angle into a tray of cutting compost, so that the leaf sticks out above the surface. The end of the stalk should be only just buried, as this is where the plantlets are produced. Cover the tray with a clear lid or plastic bag to keep in the moisture, and keep it warm and out of direct sunlight. The plantlets should form after three to five weeks. When they are large enough to handle, pot them on. The *Begonia rex* is usually propagated by slashed-leaf cuttings. Cut a healthy young leaf from the

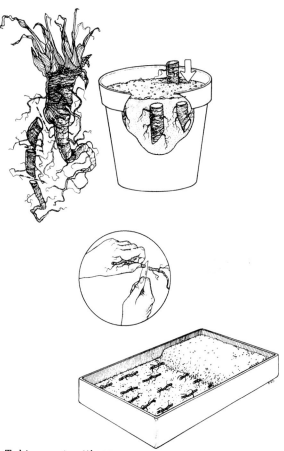

Taking root cuttings

Fleshy-rooted plants such as comfrey cut into 3 in (7·5 cm) pieces and planted upright in pot

Thin-rooted plants are laid horizontally in 1 in (2·5 cm) lengths (Rob Dalton)

Disease control

Inorganic gardeners rely upon chemical fungicides such as benomyl to protect their cuttings from rotting. Organic gardeners use the natural protection of hygiene, fresh air and sunshine. So remove any mouldy leaves, and allow the circulation of fresh air whenever possible. To ensure that the cuttings do not dry out, use a hand spray to give them a light mist of water. It is necessary to strike a balance between too much air and sun, which will make the cuttings wilt, and too much wet and stagnant air, which encourages mould.

A simple fungicide may be made by adding a couple of crushed cloves of garlic to a pint of water. This spray, which will help reduce the incidence of disease, may be made more effective by adding a teaspoon of sulphur and leaving it to brew for a couple of days. Strain the mixture through an old pair of tights before use.

parent plant and cut across the major veins on its underside with a safety razor. Do not make more than one cut per square inch. Bend a piece of wire into a staple and pin the leaf into a pot or tray of cutting compost, then treat as a simple leaf cutting. Organic gardeners may find this an unsatisfactory technique, as without the protection afforded by chemical fungicides the leaves may rot and die.

OTHER METHODS OF PROPAGATION

Bulbs and corms will increase in number quite naturally if left to their own devices. There are ways of propagating them artificially which rely upon cutting, scoring, or in some way mutilating the bulbs or corms. These techniques usually rely heavily upon artificial fungicides, which keep the damaged bulbs from rotting. Many bulbs and corms produce bulblets and cormlets from their bases which may be separated and grown on, but any kind of damage to the bulb is best avoided. Bulbs which form in clusters, like garlic, may be pulled apart, and each clove or scale potted up and grown on until it forms a little bulb of its own.

Some plants propagate themselves with overground or underground runners of various forms, for example mint, strawberry, soapwort, bramble. These plants usually produce a surplus which the gardener has to dig up or hoe out.

7 THE VEGETABLE GARDEN

PLANNING AND PLANTING

PLANNING THE GARDEN

Precisely where vegetables are grown is bound to be influenced by the size and character of the whole garden. The organic gardener has to decide essentially whether to concentrate all the vegetables in one plot (preferably laid out in the bed system), or to develop an integrated garden, with flowers, fruit, vegetables and herbs grown in close proximity. (See *The Ornamental Kitchen Garden*, page 196.)

The vegetable plot. The great advantage of a plot devoted to vegetables is that it is straight-forward, easily managed and, on balance, more productive than an integrated garden.

It is advisable to draw up a rough plan each year, even if uncontrollable circumstances, such as the weather, prevent it being followed slavishly. For information to help in planning see 'Plants for places' right, 'Groups for planning purposes', 'Vegetable crop planner', and the crop sequence chart (pages 84, 85–7, 88–9). Here is one approach.

1. Draw up a plan of the vegetable beds, numbering or naming them if necessary.
2. List the main annual vegetables to be grown (with an indication of the quantities required), broken down in rotation groups. List minor vegetables, where rotation is less important, in a miscellaneous category. Allocate a bed, or several beds if necessary, to each group.
3. List perennial vegetables separately, and allocate them to a bed where they can remain undisturbed for several years.
4. Beside each crop in the list indicate roughly the months it is normally in the ground. Remember this period can sometimes be shortened by raising plants under cover. Now use the list to devise the main sequences for each bed (or section of a bed) for Year 1, e.g.:

Plants for places

Tolerate damp soil

Note: they will not tolerate <u>waterlogged</u> conditions

Artichoke, Chinese; celery; celeriac; corn salad; dandelion; fennel; land cress; leeks; mizuna greens

Tolerate fairly dry conditions

Amaranthus; chicory, sugar loaf; iceplant; onions, pickling; purslane, summer and winter; spinach, New Zealand. Plus Mediterranean herbs, e.g. thyme, basil, marjoram, rosemary

Tolerate light shade

Note: The plants must of course have some water. Those that are low-growing can be used for inter- and undercropping

Amaranthus; artichoke, Jerusalem; basella; chicory, red and sugar loaf; chrysanthemum greens; corn salad; land cress; mizuna greens; oriental mustards; parsley, Hamburg; spinach

Tolerate light shade in mid-summer only

Chinese cabbage; endive; lettuce; pak choi; peas; spinach

Can be trained up supports

The correct cultivars must be chosen; in most cases there are dwarf or bush forms as well as climbing forms

Basella; beans, runner and French; cucumber; marrow

Can be used as ground cover

Artichoke, Chinese; marrow, trailing; pumpkin; rhubarb

Bed A (Onion group in 1992)

North end:
1 Early lettuce (early spring/early summer)
2 Leeks (early summer onwards)

South end:
1 Onion sets (early spring/late summer)
2 Green manure

5. Fit the minor plants and green manuring plans into gaps in each bed. Some minor crops can be grown as intercrops.

OPPOSITE: Raised beds and protective cover maximize vegetable garden potential (*John Walker*)

Groups for planning purposes

Fast-maturing (ready for use in eight weeks or less)

These can be used as 'catch crops' before or after a main crop is planted or lifted. They will only mature very rapidly in good growing conditions, and when sown at the correct season

Chrysanthemum greens; cut-and-come-again seedlings (see below); komatsuna; kohl rabi; land cress; texsel greens; turnip (young); Chinese cabbage (loose-headed); pak choi; radish

Cut-and-come-again seedlings

The following can be grown to maturity, or grown as cut-and-come-again seedlings

Chicory, sugar loaf; corn salad; cress, garden; endive; lettuce, cutting; mustard; oriental greens: loose Chinese cabbage, pak choi, komatsuna, mizuna, oriental saladini; purslane, summer and winter; seedling radish; salad rocket; salad rape; spinach; texsel greens; turnip tops

Perennial vegetables

Most of these will occupy the same ground for at least five years

Artichoke, globe; artichoke, Jerusalem (if not lifted); asparagus; cauliflower (a few years only); dandelion; onion, Welsh; rhubarb

Half-hardy crops

These cannot be sown or planted in the open until the risk of frost is over, and are normally destroyed by frost

Amaranthus; aubergine; basella; beans, French, runner and soya; cucumber; iceplant; marrow and courgette; melon; pepper; potato*; pumpkin; purslane, summer; tomato

* Tubers can be planted before the last frost

Vegetables in the ground all winter

*All can normally withstand at least 23°F (-5°C). Those marked * mature during the 'hungry gap' (see next column)*

*Artichoke, Jerusalem; beans, broad (autumn-sown); *broccoli, purple sprouting; *Brussels sprouts; *cabbage, spring and *savoy; *celeriac; *chicory (Italian red, hardy forms); *chrysanthemum greens; *corn salad; garlic; *kale; *komatsuna; *land cress; *leeks; *mizuna; onions (autumn-sown); *oriental mustards; *parsley, Hamburg; *parsnip; *peas (autumn-sown); *radish, winter; *purslane, winter (in well-drained soil); *salad rape; *salad rocket; *salsify; *scorzonera; *texsel greens; *turnip tops; *spinach (perpetual); *Swiss chard

Vegetables maturing in the 'hungry gap' (approximately late winter to late spring)

Crops marked * above; spring-sown cut-and-come-again seedling crops (see above); radish; carrots (early); lettuce

Vegetables suitable for containers

Amaranthus; asparagus pea; aubergine; bean, broad, French and soya; beetroot; carrot; chicory, red and sugar loaf; chrysanthemum greens; corn salad; courgette; endive; land cress; lettuce; mizuna greens; onions (spring); pak choi (small types); purslane, summer and winter; texsel greens; tomato (dwarf and bush types); turnip (early types); spinach; Swiss chard. Plus all cut-and-come-again seedling crops above and many herbs.

Main rotation groups

Brassicas (cabbage family)
Brussels sprouts; broccoli, purple sprouting; cabbage; calabrese; cauliflower; Chinese cabbage; kale; kohl rabi; komatsuna; mustard; oriental greens; pak choi; radish; salad rape; salad rocket; turnip; swede; texsel greens

Legumes (pea and bean family)
Beans (all types); peas

Solanaceae (potato family)
Aubergine; pepper; potato; tomato

Alliaceae (onion family)
Garlic; leek; onion; shallot

Umbellifer family
Carrot; celeriac; celery; parsley; parsnip

---

key to chart colours and symbols

	Actual period of growth in the cropping situation•	CC =	Can be grown using the cut-and-come-again technique
	Ground free for other crops/uses	H =	Plants raised in heat under protection prior to planting
	Crops maturing in approximately 8 weeks (suitable as catch crops)	HO =	Optional earlier sowing in heat under protection
	Crops maturing in approximately 12 weeks	SS =	Successional sowing for continuity of supply

Key continued on page 87

Vegetable crop planner

in (cm)
Average spread of plant ⟶
Average days to maturity ⟶

Crop		Average days to maturity	Average spread of plant in (cm)
AMARANTHUS	HO, CC, SS	42+	3–24 (7·5–60)
ARTICHOKE– Chinese		180	12 (30)
ASPARAGUS PEA	HO	75	18–24 (45–60)
AUBERGINE	H	150	24 (60)
BASELLA	H	30+	9–16 (23–40)
BROAD BEAN– Autumn Sown		210	15–18 (38–45)
BEAN–French or Kidney	HO	50–90	12 (30)
BEAN–Runner	HO	105	12 (30)
BEAN–Soya	HO	105	12–14 (30–35)
BEETROOT	SS, HO	77+	9–12 (23–30)
BROCCOLI– Sprouting		300	27 (68)
BRUSSELS SPROUT	HO	150+	24 (60)
CABBAGE–Spring	CC	255	12 (30)
CABBAGE– Summer/Autumn	HO	105	18 (45)
CABBAGE–Winter (Storage)		180	18–20 (45–50)
CABBAGE–Winter (Fresh)		210	18–20 (45–50))
CALABRESE– Summer Crop		70+	11 (28)
CARROT–Early	HO	84	9 (23)
CARROT– Maincrop	SS	150	9 (23)
CAULIFLOWER– Early Summer		240	21 (53)
CAULIFLOWER– Summer/Autumn		120+	24 (60)
CAULIFLOWER– Winter Heading		180+	28 (70)
CAULIFLOWER– Spring Heading		300	25 (63)
CELERIAC	H	180+	15–20 (38–50)
CELERY– Self-Blanching	H	150	12 (30)
CHICORY–Red	CC, SS	135	6–12 (15–30)
CHICORY–Sugar Loaf	CC, SS	135	6–12 (15–30)
CHICORY– Witloof in situ		180	10 (25)

Months columns: JAN FEB MAR APR MAY JUN JUL AUG SEP OCT NOV DEC

Vegetable crop planner

Average spread of plant
Average days to maturity
in (cm)

Crop		JAN FEB MAR APR MAY JUN JUL AUG SEP OCT NOV DEC	Days to maturity	Spread in (cm)
CHINESE CABBAGE	CC,SS		56	12–15 (30–38)
CHRYSANTHEMUM GREENS	CC,SS		42	6–8 (15–20)
CORN SALAD	CC		84+	4 (10)
CUCUMBER	H		84	18 (45)
ENDIVE	CC		90	12 (30)
FLORENCE FENNEL			60	12 (30)
GARLIC			300	6 (15)
ICEPLANT	H		75	8–12 (20–30)
KALE	CC		90+	15–24 (38–60)
KOHL RABI	SS,HO		49+	9–12 (23–30)
KOMATSUNA	CC,SS		20+	1–18 (2·5–45)
LAND CRESS	SS		60+	11 (28)
LEEK	HO		180+	6 (15)
LETTUCE–Summer Maincrop	CC,SS HO		120+	9–12 (23–30)
MARROW and COURGETTE	HO		90+	24 (60)
MIZUNA/MIBUNA GREENS	CC, SS		75	12 (30)
MUSTARD/CRESS, SEEDLING RADISH, SALAD RAPE	CC		10	xxx
ONION–Bulb Sown Spring	HO		180	4–6 (10–15)
ONION–Bulb Sown Autumn			210+	4–6 (10–15)
ONION–Bulb from sets (Spring planted)			180	4–6 (10–15)
ONION–Bulb from sets (Autumn planted)			210+	4–6 (10–15))
ONIONS–Spring/Bunch	SS		60	1 (2·5)
ORIENTAL MUSTARDS	CC		60+	12 (30)
ORIENTAL SALADINI	SS,CC, HO		21+	xxx
PAK CHOI	CC		30+	6–18 (15–45)
PARSLEY–Hamburg			150	9 (23)
PARSNIP	HO		210	10 (25)
PEA–Early, Spring Sown			77+	12 (30)

JAN FEB MAR APR MAY JUN JUL AUG SEP OCT NOV DEC

Vegetable crop planner

in (cm)
Average spread of plant →
Average days to maturity →

Crop		JAN	FEB	MAR	APR	MAY	JUN	JUL	AUG	SEP	OCT	NOV	DEC	Avg. days to maturity	Avg. spread of plant
PEA—Maincrop	SS													77+	12 (30)
PEPPER—Sweet	H													150	15 (38)
POTATO—Early														90+	15–18 (38–45)
POTATO—Maincrop														140+	15–30 (38–76)
PUMPKIN	HO													90	36 (90)
PURSLANE—Summer	CC, H													75+	6 (15)
PURSLANE—Winter	CC													56+	6 (15)
RADISH—Summer Types	SS													28+	3–6 (7–15)
RADISH—Large Overwintering Types	CC													60	7 (18)
RADISH—Leaf	CC													28	2–4 (5–10)
ROCKET—Salad	CC, SS													21+	xxx
SALSIFY														180	9–12 (23–30)
SCORZONERA														180	9–12 (23–30)
SHALLOT—Spring Planted														105	9 (23)
SPINACH—Ordinary, Summer Crop	CC,SS													75	6 (15)
SPINACH—Perpetual, Summer Crop	CC													75	6 (15)
SPINACH—New Zealand	H													56	18 (45)
SWEDE														161	15–18 (38–45)
SWEETCORN	HO													110	20 (50)
SWISS CHARD	CC													120	20 (50)
TEXSEL GREENS	CC,SS													20+	1–6 (2.5–15)
TOMATO—Outdoor Bush	H													150	20 (50)
TURNIP—Roots	SS													42+	15 (38)
		JAN	FEB	MAR	APR	MAY	JUN	JUL	AUG	SEP	OCT	NOV	DEC		

Months given for southern UK. Refer to chart on page xi for other area equivalents

Average days to maturity from sowing
Where '+' follows number, e.g. 42+, this indicates the earliest at which cropping can be expected to begin, depending on cultivar, season and local conditions.

Average spread of plants
(a) Where there can be wide variation, the smaller number refers to plants harvested at an early stage of growth, the larger to mature plants

(b) xxx indicates plants are usually grown as seedling crops

* Cropping situation
Cropping times should be treated as approximations. They are based on average outdoor conditions in a temperate climate. In practice cropping could be up to three weeks earlier in mild areas, and three weeks later in cold areas. Appropriate cultivars must be used for different sowings.

Chart compiled by John Walker

Planning the vegetable garden

Crop sequences for a single bed

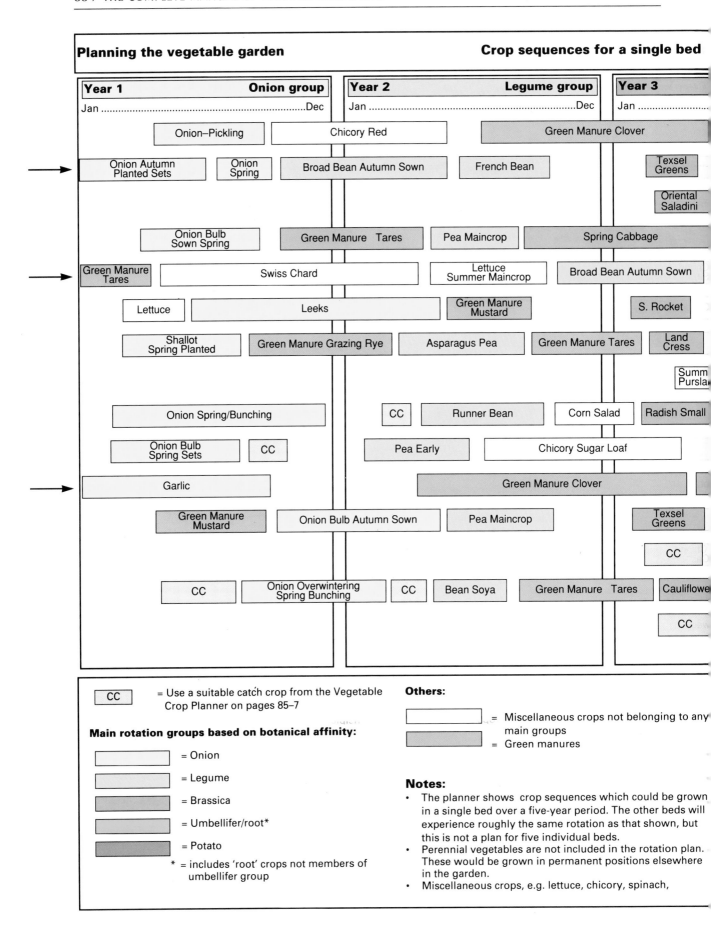

	Year 1	Onion group
Jan ....Dec

| | Year 2 | Legume group |
Jan ....Dec

Year 3
Jan ....

Onion–Pickling

Chicory Red

Green Manure Clover

Onion Autumn Planted Sets

Onion Spring

Broad Bean Autumn Sown

French Bean

Texsel Greens

Oriental Saladini

Onion Bulb Sown Spring

Green Manure Tares

Pea Maincrop

Spring Cabbage

Green Manure Tares

Swiss Chard

Lettuce Summer Maincrop

Broad Bean Autumn Sown

Lettuce

Leeks

Green Manure Mustard

S. Rocket

Shallot Spring Planted

Green Manure Grazing Rye

Asparagus Pea

Green Manure Tares

Land Cress

Summ Pursla●

Onion Spring/Bunching

CC

Runner Bean

Corn Salad

Radish Small

Onion Bulb Spring Sets

CC

Pea Early

Chicory Sugar Loaf

Garlic

Green Manure Clover

Texsel Greens

Green Manure Mustard

Onion Bulb Autumn Sown

Pea Maincrop

CC

CC

Onion Overwintering Spring Bunching

CC

Bean Soya

Green Manure Tares

Cauliflowe

CC

Legend

| CC | = Use a suitable catch crop from the Vegetable Crop Planner on pages 85–7 |

Main rotation groups based on botanical affinity:

	= Onion
	= Legume
	= Brassica
	= Umbellifer/root*
	= Potato

* = includes 'root' crops not members of umbellifer group

Others:

	= Miscellaneous crops not belonging to any main groups
	= Green manures

Notes:
- The planner shows crop sequences which could be grown in a single bed over a five-year period. The other beds will experience roughly the same rotation as that shown, but this is not a plan for five individual beds.
- Perennial vegetables are not included in the rotation plan. These would be grown in permanent positions elsewhere in the garden.
- Miscellaneous crops, e.g. lettuce, chicory, spinach,

in a five-year rotation plan for the main vegetable groups

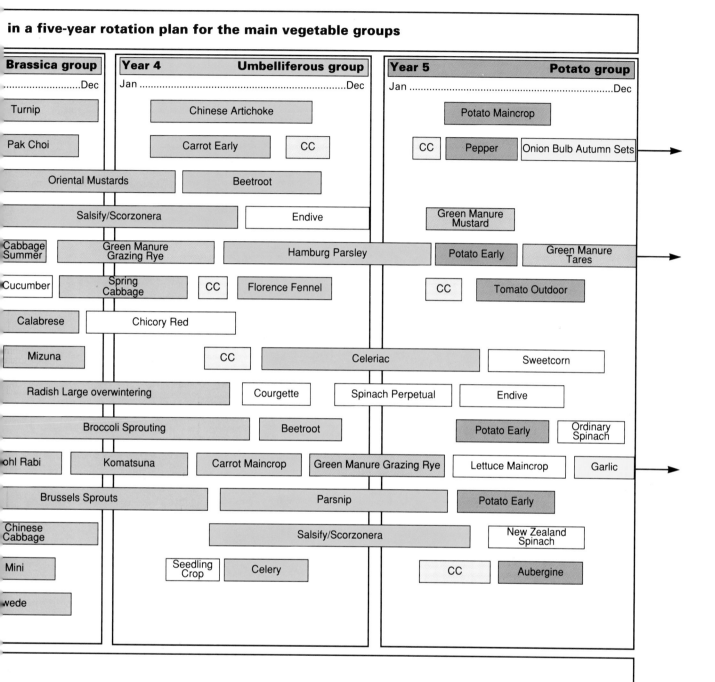

Brassica group
..........................Dec

Turnip

Pak Choi

Oriental Mustards

Salsify/Scorzonera

Cabbage Summer

Cucumber

Calabrese

Mizuna

Radish Large overwintering

Broccoli Sprouting

ohl Rabi

Brussels Sprouts

Chinese Cabbage

Mini

wede

Year 4   **Umbelliferous group**
Jan ....Dec

Chinese Artichoke

Carrot Early   CC

Beetroot

Endive

Green Manure Grazing Rye   Hamburg Parsley

Spring Cabbage   CC   Florence Fennel

Chicory Red

CC   Celeriac

Courgette   Spinach Perpetual

Beetroot

Komatsuna   Carrot Maincrop   Green Manure Grazing Rye

Parsnip

Salsify/Scorzonera

Seedling Crop   Celery

Year 5   **Potato group**
Jan ....Dec

Potato Maincrop

CC   Pepper   Onion Bulb Autumn Sets →

Green Manure Mustard

Potato Early   Green Manure Tares →

CC   Tomato Outdoor

Sweetcorn

Endive

Potato Early   Ordinary Spinach

Lettuce Maincrop   Garlic →

Potato Early

New Zealand Spinach

CC   Aubergine

sweetcorn, courgettes and other salad crops are not generally restricted to any particular group, but should not be grown continuously in the same spot.
- Where the crop or green manure 'overlaps' into the following year, this indicates it is overwintering.
- Each bar indicates roughly the average period in the cropping situation.
- Where appropriate, suitable combinations of follow-on crops are shown. Elsewhere the major crops in each rotation group are indicated for the appropriate year of the five-year plan.
- The planner is diagrammatic only and does not represent the actual arrangement of crops in the garden situation. It does, however, indicate a range of options within the framework of a rotation system. The basic rotation

principles and crop sequences illustrated could be adapted to a garden of any size.

- Months given for southern UK. Refer to chart on page xi for other area equivalents

Inter/Undercropping
Inter/Undercropping is not shown, e.g. undercropping of sweetcorn with maincrop summer lettuce. Choose suitable crops for this purpose from the Vegetable Crop Planner on pages 85–7, and work these in with the overall rotation plan.

Chart compiled by John Walker

If the plan works reasonably well in the first season, keep to it in subsequent years, making any minor adjustments necessary. Simply rotate it around the garden, so that the crops grown in Bed 1 in Year 1, will be grown in Bed 2 in Year 2, and so on.

GETTING THE BEST RETURNS

Most organic gardeners want the satisfaction of high returns from the vegetable plot, without, of course, using potent artificial fertilizers, excessive watering and the chemical pesticides the conventional gardener relies upon. While high productivity is largely the result of adopting the best organic practices, some special techniques have a role to play in getting the most from the garden.

CUT-AND-COME-AGAIN TECHNIQUES

This method relies on the fact that many leafy vegetables will re-sprout after being cut, to give further pickings, allowing them to be used over long periods without re-sowing. It is used for a wide range of salad crops including cresses, salad rape, salad rocket, endive, spinach and lettuce and for many oriental greens. This very productive system is particularly recommended for small gardens. It can be used at the 'large seedling' stage, and/or when plants are semi-mature or mature. In some cases – Salad Bowl lettuce is a good example – individual leaves can be picked as required, rather than cutting the whole plant. The plant will continue to grow.

Seedling stage.   For the best results sow seed fairly thinly (i.e. about ½ in/1·25 cm apart), in parallel, shallow drills 3–4 in (7·5–10 cm) wide. Make the drills as close together as possible. In very dry conditions water the bottom of the drill only, sow the seed on the moist base, and cover it with *dry* soil. This will prevent evaporation and help rapid germination. Make the first cut when the seedlings are anything from 1–3 in (2·5–7·5

Water bottom of parallel drills in dry conditions
(*Joy Larkcom*)

Sweetcorn, grown in block formation to assist pollination, undercropped with mizuna greens
(*Jacqui Hurst*)

cm) high, cutting at least ½ in (1·25 cm) above ground level. Depending on the crop and the time of year, they will normally re-sprout to give a second cutting within ten to fourteen days (and in some cases a third or fourth). The soil must be fertile and kept moist.

Semi-mature stage.   A number of plants including leaf spinach, Swiss chard, endives, sugar loaf chicory and various oriental greens can be cut when reasonably large but before they are fully mature. Cut about 1 in (2·5 cm) above the ground. This encourages them to put out a mass of fresh leaf, may prevent them from running to seed prematurely, and with plants on the borderline of winter hardiness, may increase resistance to low temperatures. (This fact can be utilized under cover. Plants that are trimmed back will survive winter, whereas a large leafy plant might be killed by frost.) Although it will probably cease growing in mid-winter, when temperatures rise in spring it will regenerate fresh leaf.

Mature stage.   Several vegetables, such as early spring cabbage, headed Chinese cabbage and winter lettuce, can be cut, rather than uprooted, when harvested. Cut about 1 in (2·5 cm) above the stump. Provided the soil is fertile and there is plenty of moisture, further heads may develop from the original stump.

INTERCROPPING

The space between widely spaced plants can often be used for a quick-growing 'catch crop'. Salad seedling crops and radishes are ideal for this purpose. Drills can be sown between and among brassicas such as cauliflowers. The intercrop must be cut or removed before the ground is required by the principal crop.

A fast and a slow-growing crop can be sown within the same row. The classic combination is parsnips, which are slow-growing, with radishes. 'Station sow' the parsnip seeds (see *Propagation*, page 70), and sow a few radish seeds between each group. The radishes will mature long before the space is required by the parsnips.

Some plants can be grown beneath the canopy of taller vegetables. Sweetcorn, for example, can be undercropped with a wide variety of plants, from salad seedlings to dwarf French beans, trailing marrows, or oriental brassicas such as mizuna greens. Small, undemanding salad plants such as corn salad or land cress can be grown under sweetcorn or among widely spaced winter brassicas such as cauliflower or purple sprouting broccoli.

GROWING IN CONTAINERS

The need to grow vegetables in containers arises in urban gardens, where there is little space other than patios, a flat roof or paved areas.

While in theory almost any vegetable can be grown in containers, they are most suited to quick-maturing, fairly compact, shallow-rooting vegetables (see 'Groups for planning purposes', page 84). In general avoid very deep-rooting vegetables such as parsnips, large vegetables such as globe artichokes, and heavy feeders such as cauliflowers and other brassicas grown to maturity.

All sorts of things can be used as containers – pots, boxes, old chimney-pots – but they should always be as large as possible. For medium to large plants they should be at least 10 in (25 cm) wide and deep. Lettuces and radishes can be grown in smaller containers, and salad seedlings can be grown in 1 in (2.5 cm) deep seed trays of light soil or good potting compost. In this case it would normally only be possible to take one cut.

Good drainage is most important. There should be several drainage holes of at least ½ in (1.25 cm) diameter in the base. Cover these with upturned broken crocks, and some fibrous material or dried leaves to facilitate drainage.

The soil or compost used must be rich, light and well drained, otherwise it soon becomes compacted with the constant watering necessary. Good potting compost, such as worm-based compost, is excellent in containers. Or use good-quality garden soil, mixing in several handfuls of garden compost and coarse sand or grit for each container.

Although containers must be well drained, measures should be taken to avoid excessive evaporation from both the sides and the top. Site them away from drying winds, bury them in the ground where feasible, and, once plants are established, keep the surface mulched to a depth of at least 2 or 3 in (5–7.5 cm). An organic mulch or stones or pebbles can be used.

Containers must be watered frequently – possibly twice a day in hot weather. As soon as growth seems to be slowing down, start feeding regularly with an organic liquid feed.

THE VEGETABLES

Rotation groups. For each vegetable, consult the table on page 84 for its rotation group. Where none is given treat it as 'miscellaneous'.

Recommended cultivars. There are many excellent cultivars available today. Those mentioned are notable for specific characteristics or purposes, but many others will be equally successful. ROG = recommended for organic growing, generally because of exceptional pest or disease resistance, or natural vigour, or a weed-suppressing habit. *DVG* = suitable for a decorative vegetable garden.

TERMS USED

Temperate/cool (climate): average UK climatic conditions, i.e. minimum winter temperatures of about 20°F (-7°C); mean temperature in the hottest month (July) about 60°F (15.5°C). Note that temperate-climate plants can be grown in the winter months in warm climates.

Warm (climate): frost-free winter, and longer, hotter summer temperatures than UK. Plants requiring a 'warm' climate can be grown in summer in the UK under cover.

Warm soil: above 50°F (10°C). (Soil temperature can be measured with an inexpensive soil thermometer.)

Gentle heat (in propagator): about 65°F (18°C).

Tender: killed by frost or near-freezing temperatures.

Moderately hardy: normally survives temperatures of 23°F to 14°F (-5° to -10°C). Hardiness is affected by the stage of the plant, the wind, and how well drained the soil is.

Hardy: normally survives temperatures below 14°F (-10°C).

AMARANTHUS *Amaranthus spp.*

Amaranthus is a very widespread family of productive, nutritious plants. The leaves and young stems are cooked like spinach, but can be eaten raw when young. Most types require a warm climate, and grow best in light, fertile, well-drained soil. They tolerate fairly dry conditions and fairly acid soil.

Sow in spring or summer either *in situ*, in warm soil, or in modules, transplanting young. Average spacing is 4 in (10 cm) apart each way. It can also be grown as a cut-and-come-again crop, harvested at any stage from seedlings to

Amaranthus: young leaves ready a few weeks from sowing; can be grown as cut-and-come-again crop (Jacqui Hurst)

Starting a globe artichoke bed (Elizabeth Douglass)

maturity. Young leaves and shoots may be ready a few weeks after sowing. Pick regularly to prevent toughening: remove any flowers which develop. Amaranthus can also be raised from soft cuttings.

ARTICHOKE, CHINESE Stachys affinis

Chinese artichoke is a temperate-climate, hardy annual with a rather sprawling habit and mint-like leaves. It is grown for its 2 in (5 cm) long, ¾ in (2 cm) wide, knobbly, nutty-flavoured, translucent tubers, which are used raw or cooked. The plants, which grow to about 2 ft 6 in (75 cm) high, do best in rich light soil in an open site, and need a reasonable amount of moisture throughout growth.

Plant tubers in spring 2 in (5 cm) deep and 12 in (30 cm) apart each way. They can be started earlier in pots, planting out when they have sprouted. When they are about 18 in (45 cm) high earth up the stems for about 3 in (7·5 cm). A liquid feed may be applied in mid-season.Trim back very straggly stems and remove any flowers which develop.Tubers are ready about six months after planting. Lift as required, as they shrivel rapidly once harvested. Cover the plants with straw in winter if very heavy frost is expected.

ARTICHOKE, GLOBE Cynara scolymus

This is a temperate-climate perennial of the thistle family, forming a large, handsome plant up to 3 ft (90 cm) high and with a similar spread. The bracts and 'choke' at the base of the flower

bud are a delicacy, and are normally cooked. It requires fertile, well-drained soil, rich in organic matter. It is moderately hardy, but should be protected from strong winds.

To start a bed of artichokes either buy good plants or take rooted suckers (offsets) from a friend's productive, established plants in spring. Slice them off with a spade so that each offset has a bud and a strong piece of root. Plant them 3 ft (90 cm) apart. Keep plants mulched, and water in dry conditions. A single flowerhead is normally produced in late summer. In subsequent years plants are more prolific and crop earlier. In cold areas protect the plants during winter with a loose layer of bracken, leaves or sacking. Plants generally start to deteriorate after about three years. Renew a few each year with offsets from the strongest plants. DVG

Globe artichokes can be raised from seed, but the plants will vary in quality. Sow indoors in early spring, planting out in early summer. After the second season take offsets from the most productive plants and discard the weakest.

ARTICHOKE, JERUSALEM Helianthus tuberosum

Jerusalem artichoke is a hardy member of the sunflower family, growing over 10 ft (3 m) high. The knobbly, distinctively flavoured tubers are normally cooked like potatoes. It is tolerant of a wide range of soils and site, and is excellent for breaking in heavy ground. Grow it on the edge of a garden as a windbreak, provided it does not shade small vegetables.

Plant egg-sized tubers in spring about 5 in (12·5 cm) deep, spaced 15 in (37·5 cm) apart. Large tubers can be cut into sections with at least three buds in each. Mulch plants once they are through the soil, and water in very dry weather. Earth up the stems when plants are about 12 in (30 cm) high, to make them more stable. Remove the

Jerusalem artichoke provides distinctive-tasting tubers and, growing over 10 ft (3 m) high, a useful windbreak (*Joy Larkcom*)

flower buds and cut the stems to about 5 ft (1·5 m) in late summer. In winter cut the stems just above ground level. Lay the stems over the stumps to help keep frost out of the soil so lifting is easier. Dig the tubers as required during winter, or store them in a clamp (see page 124). Retain a few to replant the following spring. Any left in the soil accidentally are apt to spread.

Recommended cultivar. Fuseau is relatively smooth, making for easier peeling

ASPARAGUS *Asparagus officinale*

Asparagus is a hardy perennial, grown for the delicious young shoots or 'spears' which emerge in spring, and are eaten cooked. It tolerates a wide range of soil types, provided there is good drainage. In wet areas it should be grown on raised beds. Very acid soils should be limed. Soil-borne root diseases develop over time, so never replant where asparagus was previously grown. Asparagus requires a lot of space and has a very

short season, so is best grown in large gardens, unless space between the plants is used to grow small salad plants. Avoid exposed sites. Male plants are more productive than the female (berried) plants, but as they are indistinguishable as seedlings, most old beds are a mixture of male and female. Where available, grow the recently developed all-male strains.

Prepare the ground thoroughly, working in organic matter and clearing it completely of perennial weeds. For a single row make a shallow trench about 12 in (30 cm) wide and 8 in (20 cm) deep. Fork the soil in the bottom of the trench into a 4 in (10 cm) high mound. Buy one-year-old asparagus crowns in spring and plant them immediately, laying the claw-like roots carefully over the mound about 18 in (45 cm) apart. (This wide spacing helps prevent root rots.) Cover with 2 in (5 cm) of fine soil, and earth around the stems as they develop until the trench is level. Where seedlings raised in modules are available, plant from spring to early summer, 4 in (10 cm) deep. With both these systems gentle cutting can start in the second season after planting, but plants must be allowed to build up to a reasonable size first. Cut spears with a sharp knife about 1·5 in (4 cm) below ground level, when about 6 in (15 cm) high. Only cut over six weeks initially, and over eight weeks when plants are established. Asparagus can be raised from seed but results are variable, unless modern F1 cultivars are used. Either sow in modules in early spring in gentle heat, planting out in early summer after hardening off, or sow *in situ* in spring, thin out to 3 in (7·5 cm), and plant out the largest plants the following spring.

Cut stems down to 2 in (5 cm) in autumn. Little other feeding or attention is required. Healthy beds may remain productive for twenty years.

Pests and diseases. Asparagus beetle; root rots
Recommended cultivars. Cito, Franklim, Lucullus (all F1 all-male hybrids)

ASPARAGUS PEA *Tetragonolobus purpurea*

Asparagus pea is a dainty, bushy, annual plant grown in temperate climates for its small, ridged pods which are cooked whole. (Do not confuse it with the nutritious tropical climbing bean, also known as asparagus pea.) Grow it in a sunny situation in rich, light soil.

Sow in spring, *in situ*, thinning plants to about 12 in (30 cm) apart. Use twigs to give the branches some support and protect them from pigeons where necessary. Pick pods small, less than 2 in (5 cm) long, or they become tough, and pick regularly so they keep cropping. *DVG*

AUBERGINE (Eggplant) *Solanum melongena*

Tropical in origin, the aubergine grows well

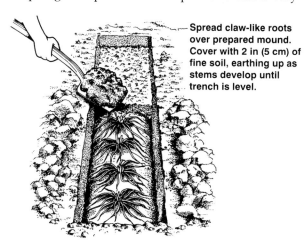

— Spread claw-like roots over prepared mound. Cover with 2 in (5 cm) of fine soil, earthing up as stems develop until trench is level.

Starting an asparagus bed (*Elizabeth Douglass*)

outdoors in temperate climates only in warm, sheltered situations or under cover. It is grown for its unusually flavoured purple or white fruits, which are cooked. It requires very fertile soil. Sow seed indoors in spring, prick out in stages into 3 in (7·5 cm) pots, and plant out after all risk of frost is past, at the stage when the first flowers are showing. For full cultivation details see *Growing Under Cover*, page 336.

BASELLA (Malabar spinach, Climbing spinach) *Basella spp.*

A climbing, perennial vine in tropical climates, basella can be grown as a half-hardy annual in warm areas (see page 91). Its glossy, fleshy leaves and young stems are cooked like spinach. It does best on rich, light soils, but needs plenty of moisture during growth.

Soak seed for twenty-four hours before sowing. Sow in a heated propagator in late spring, and prick out in stages into 3 in (7·5 cm) pots, maintaining a minimum temperature of 60°F (15°C) if possible. Plant when about 5 in (12·5 cm) high. Either grow as a climber, spacing plants 12 in (30 cm) apart and supporting them like climbing beans, or grow them as bushes spaced 16 in (40 cm) apart, nipping out the growing point when plants are 12 in (30 cm) high. Pick young shoots and individual leaves regularly, never stripping the plant entirely.

BEAN, BROAD (Fava bean) *Vicia faba*

A hardy annual bean, grown mainly for the large shelled beans (which must always be cooked), but also for the young leafy tips and the very young pods, which can be used sliced or whole. Broad beans can be deep-frozen or dried for winter. They grow best on well-dug, reasonably fertile, slightly acid soil. Their root nodules fix nitrogen, so they enrich the soil (see page 19). Generally speaking, the long-podded 'Seville' types are hardiest, and the broader, shorter-podded 'Windsor' types, which tend to be taller plants, are less hardy but better flavoured. The compact dwarf forms, most of which are very hardy, are recommended in small gardens.

Except in very cold areas sow *in situ* in autumn, using the hardier types. Sow seeds at least 1½ in (4 cm) deep, spacing them 9 in (23 cm) apart each way. They need to be no more than 1 in (2·5 cm) high before the onset of winter, or they may be damaged by severe frost. For a follow-on crop sow in early spring, as soon as the soil is workable. (Seed does not germinate well at high temperatures.) Medium and tall types require some support. Strings or wires can be attached to firmly anchored canes or posts at the corner of the plot. Alternatively, stretch standard bean or pea netting horizontally over the plot, attached to canes at the corners; raise it carefully

Compact, dwarf broad beans grow equally well in a container (*Joy Larkcom*)

Netting stretched across bed is raised to support broad beans as they grow (*Chris Algar*)

up the canes as the beans grow. Keep the ground mulched. In very dry weather water heavily when the beans start to flower and form pods, at the rate of 4 gal/sq yd (18 l/sq m) per week. Nip off the top 3 in (7·5 cm) of the stems when the plants are in flower, to encourage pod formation and discourage blackfly attacks. Autumn-sown crops are less likely to be attacked.

Mice often take overwintering bean seed. If this happens, sow beans indoors in mid-winter, widely spaced in 2 in (5 cm) deep seed trays or in modules, in garden soil or potting compost. Plant out in early spring after hardening off. Young plants are less vulnerable to mice than seed, but not immune. In cold areas broad beans may be protected with cloches or crop covers in spring. Autumn-sown beans are ready about seven months after sowing; spring-sown in about three months. After harvesting cut off stalks at ground level, and dig the roots into the soil as a source of nitrogen.

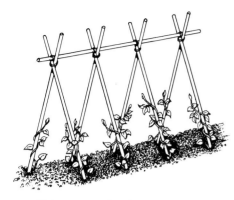

Criss-crossed pole supports

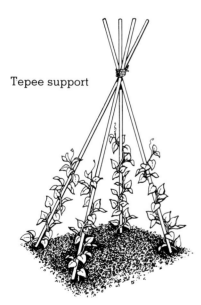

Method of growing beans against a house wall

Making use of an old hat stand (Maypole technique): strings are anchored to pegs in ground

Maypole support

Tepee support

Methods of supporting runner beans (*Elizabeth Douglass*)

Pests and diseases. Blackfly, mice, bean weevil; chocolate spot
Recommended cultivars. Autumn or spring sowing: Aquadulce, Express; Jubilee Hysor (Windsor type), Red Epicure (hardy, good-flavoured reddish seeds), The Sutton (hardy, dwarf)

BEAN, FRENCH (Kidney, snap, string) *Phaseolus vulgaris*

The French bean is a tender annual and in cool climates must be sheltered from cold winds and grown in a warm situation or under cover. It is mainly grown for the green, yellow, purple or flecked pods, but also for the immature beans ('flageolets') and for dried shelled beans. All must be cooked, as they can be toxic raw. There are many diverse cultivars. Most types are bush, but a few are climbers.

It requires rich, light, well-drained soil, into which manure has been dug the previous season. Seed will not germinate at soil temperatures below about 50°F (10°C) or grow well in cold soil, though dark-seeded cultivars are more resistant to cold. Never sow *in situ* outdoors until the soil has warmed up. In cool climates sow indoors (see Broad beans, opposite) two to three weeks before the last frost is expected. Plant out after any risk of frost, preferably under cloches or crop covers. Germination can also be speeded by pre-germinating seed indoors on moist paper towelling, then carefully sowing the sprouted seeds outdoors. Rhizobium granules can be scattered on the ground when sowing, or mixed with the seed, to improve the nitrogen-fixing properties of the root nodules and increase yields. (Consult organic seed catalogues for availability and details of use.) For maximum yields space plants in staggered rows 9 in (23 cm) apart each way.

Earth up the stems to keep the plants upright, and support them if necessary with twigs to keep them off the ground. Keep plants mulched. Grow climbing types like runner beans (below). The soil must be kept moist throughout growth. In very dry weather water as for broad beans when flowering starts. Beans are ready fifty to ninety days after sowing, depending on the cultivar. Where required for drying leave them on the plants until the pods are dry. In rainy conditions pull them up earlier and hang them in a greenhouse to dry. Shell them when the pods are crackly dry and store in jars.

Pests and diseases. Slugs, bean seed fly, aphids; anthracnose, foot and root rot, halo blight

Recommended cultivars. For flavour: Aramis (filet), Purple Queen (purple), Kinghorn Wax (yellow waxpod); for flageolets and drying: Chevrier Vert; for drying: Dutch Brown

BEAN, RUNNER (Scarlet runner) *Phaseolus coccineus*

This is naturally a tender, climbing plant, though some attractive but lower-yielding dwarf forms are available (which should be grown like French beans, above). The flat, well-flavoured pods must be cooked. Some modern cultivars are stringless. Shelled beans can be dried for winter use. It tolerates only slightly cooler conditions than the French bean and grows best in a sheltered situation, partly to attract pollinating insects. Being a vigorous plant, it needs plenty of moisture throughout growth and very fertile soil. Traditionally the ground was prepared by digging a trench at least 12 in (30 cm) deep and 24 in (60 cm) wide in autumn, working in plenty of organic matter. An alternative in well-drained soil is to make a trench in autumn, and during the winter months to fill it with household rubbish, mixed with soil. If prepared in spring line the trenches with a layer of very wet newspapers and/or comfrey.

Dwarf runner beans, useful in small gardens, can make an attractive border (Joy Larkcom)

Sow climbing runner beans as French beans, planting, after all risk of frost, at the base of supports. Standard spacing is 6 in (15 cm) apart in double rows 2 ft (60 cm) apart, but this can vary with the support system. Mature runner beans are a weighty crop and require very strong supports, at least 8 ft (2·4 m) high. The climbing shoots grip wooden poles, canes, strings, or nylon net but not plastic-coated netting. Various supporting structures can be erected - 'tepees', 'maypoles' and criss-crossed poles being the most common (see illustration, page 95). To convert climbing plants into dwarf, nip out the growing point when the plant is about 9 in (23 cm) high. Then nip off the growths that develop at the second joint.

Pollination and pod-setting may be a problem. White-flowered cultivars reputedly set more easily than red. Keep plants mulched and well watered, which has been shown to help pods set. (Sprinkling flowers with water has no effect.) Otherwise, critical times for watering are when the first buds appear and when the first flowers open. In dry areas water heavily twice weekly at these times with at least 1 gal/sq yd (5 l/sq m). The first beans are normally ready about three months after sowing. Keep picking young to encourage further cropping. *DVG*

Pests and diseases. See French bean. Pollen beetle and birds also attack flowers

Recommended cultivars. Stringless: Butler, Desiree (white-flowered); heavy-yielding: Enorma, Liberty; very decorative: Painted Lady ; naturally dwarf: Gulliver, Hammond's Dwarf, Pickwick

BEAN, SOYA *Glycine max*

Soya bean is a bushy, annual plant requiring a warm climate. However, watch out for new cultivars suited to cooler and northern climates. It is grown for the highly nutritious shelled beans, which are eaten cooked either at a semi-mature green stage or mature and dried. Temperature and day length are important factors in growing a successful crop, so consult local seed catalogues for cultivars suited to your area. It requires higher temperatures than French beans, but otherwise is grown similarly.

Recommended cultivars for cool, northern climates. Fiskeby V, Butterbean

BEETROOT *Beta vulgaris* var. *esculenta*
(for Leaf beet see Spinach leaf beet and Swiss chard)

Beetroot is a moderately hardy vegetable suited to temperate climates. It is grown mainly for its red-, yellow- or white-fleshed roots, which can be round, flat or cylindrical. The long types are considered sweetest. Beet is eaten raw or cooked; fresh, stored or pickled; hot or cold; and can be made into juice. The young leaves are also tasty cooked. It grows best in rich, light soil, preferably manured for the previous crop. Acid soils should be limed.

Beetroot is flexible in that it can be pulled at any size from about 1 to 3 in (2·5–7·5 cm) in diameter, depending on cultivar, and can be sown throughout the growing season. Seed may be soaked in warm water for half an hour before sowing to wash out a natural inhibitor which slows germination. Each seed contains several seedlings, so never sow thickly. Some 'single' seed forms, which require less thinning, are available. Beet does not germinate at soil temperatures below about 45°F (7°C), so in cool climates make the first sowings indoors in early spring. Round types of beet can be multi-sown in modules, sowing three seeds per module. Harden off well before planting outside when about 2 in (5 cm) high (see *Propagation*, page 76). These early sowings can be planted under cloches or crop covers.

Make the first outdoor sowings *in situ* once the soil is warm, or under cloches and so on. To encourage rapid growth, space early crops 6 in (15 cm) apart each way, or 12 in (30 cm) apart for modules. Pull the beet at any size from 1 in (2·5 cm) in diameter. They may be ready about eleven weeks after sowing. For all spring sowings use round, bolt-resistant cultivars.

For continuous supplies of young, fresh beet sow at monthly intervals until the end of summer, using any cultivar. For these mid-season sowings sow *in situ*, thinning plants to about 5 in (12·5 cm) apart each way. For small, pickling beet sow in rows 3 in (7·5 cm) apart, thinning to about 2½ in (6·5 cm) apart. Keep plants weed-free and mulched. Water moderately only if necessary to prevent the soil drying out. Overwatering results in leaf, rather than root development.

On well-drained soil, beet can be left in the soil

in winter, covered with at least 6 in (15 cm) of straw as protection against frost. But they gradually become woody and deteriorate, so storage indoors is advisable for use after mid-winter. For storage, use any reasonably sized beet sown mid-season. Lift them carefully in autumn and twist off the leaves leaving about 1 in (2·5 cm) of stem attached to the root. Layer them in boxes of moist peat or sand stored in a frost-free shed, with the top layer covered to retain moisture, or store them in clamps like swede (see page 124) with a 6 in (15 cm) thick layer of soil as extra insulation on top of the heap.

Pests and diseases. Birds (on seedlings), cutworm, black bean aphid; damping off, leaf spot

Recommended cultivars. Bolt-resistant: Boltardy, Regala; good flavour and novelty value: Burpee's Golden (yellow), Cheltenham Mono (long), Chioggia (white internal rings), Forono (long); DVG Bull's Blood (good beets and red leaves)

BRASSICAS (Crucifers) *Brassica spp.*

The brassicas (or crucifers), the members of the cabbage family, are important vegetables, but among the most difficult to grow organically until the soil has been brought into a fertile state. They include the large leafy greens: broccoli, Brussels sprout, cabbage, calabrese, cauliflower, kale, texsel greens; root vegetables: kohl rabi, swede, turnip; and the more recently introduced oriental greens like Chinese cabbage, komatsuna and mizuna greens. See under individual vegetables and Oriental Greens for detailed information. Some factors common to all brassicas are discussed here.

They are essentially cool-weather crops, several being very hardy. They are grown all year round in cool climates, but during the winter months in warm climates. Many brassicas are vulnerable to serious soil-borne diseases (e.g. club root) and pests (e.g. brassica cyst eelworm), so it is essential to rotate over at least a four-year cycle where feasible, to prevent their build-up. Club root can remain in the soil for twenty years, so adopt the measures described in *Disease Prevention* (page 267), or grow only fast-maturing brassicas such as texsel greens.

Soil. The large, slow-growing leafy brassicas may be in the soil for six months or more, and are greedy feeders requiring plenty of nitrogen and water throughout growth. So they require fertile soil with plenty of organic matter worked in. It is good practice to plant them after a nitrogenous green manure or broad beans (see pages 22–3, 88–9). Plenty of organic matter, good drainage, and a neutral soil (acid soils should be limed) all help prevent club root becoming established.

The large brassicas should be planted into firm rather than loose ground. For those planted in spring, prepare the ground the previous autumn, working in plenty of organic matter, and just rake it down before planting. For those planted in summer and autumn clear the previous crop and plant with no further digging. All brassicas must be grown in an open, unshaded site.

Plant-raising. Raising in modules or small pots is highly recommended to obtain good-quality, productive plants. Often only a few plants are required, so this is quite practical. Otherwise sow in seed beds and transplant carefully, or where appropriate, sow *in situ* and thin out.

Where club root is a problem, pot seedlings in stages into 4 in (10 cm) pots before planting out. Then plant in shallow trenches (see illustration), filled with potting soil or uncontaminated garden soil to postpone infection. These measures give a headstart so plants become productive before being infected with club root.

Large brassicas must be planted deeply and firmly, as they can become top-heavy and keel over when mature. On light soils plant in a shallow trench, earthing up the stems to ground level as they grow. The trench can be filled with well-rotted compost to increase fertility. This technique also helps to overcome cabbage root fly attacks, as secondary roots, which escape the initial attacks, develop from the earthed-up stem.

In heavy soils such trenches may become waterlogged, so it is preferable to plant on the level, earthing up the stems to about 4 in (10 cm) as they grow. In exposed situations tie large brassicas to strong stakes before winter sets in.

Widely spaced brassicas can be interplanted or intersown with small or fast-growing vegetables.

Watering. Water brassicas lightly after planting until well established, then mulch them. Growth

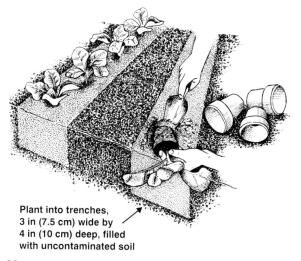

Plant into trenches, 3 in (7.5 cm) wide by 4 in (10 cm) deep, filled with uncontaminated soil

Minimizing effects of club root (*Elizabeth Douglass*)

should never be checked, so in dry conditions, the large brassicas especially should be watered weekly at the rate of 4 gal/sq yd (18 l/sq m). If water is scarce water at least once, very heavily, about two weeks before maturity.

Pests and diseases.   Other than club root (page 267), pests and diseases include flea beetle, cabbage root fly (page 314), caterpillars, mealy aphids and birds; damping off, mildew and leaf spots. Garden hygiene is important. Remove and burn diseased leaves and plants. Uproot and burn old stumps before late spring, as they harbour overwintering aphids.

BROCCOLI, SPROUTING *Brassica oleracea*
'Italica' group
(See also Brassicas)

Sprouting broccoli is a moderately hardy brassica, grown for its flowering shoots which are eaten cooked. They develop early in spring when choice of locally grown vegetables is limited. There are purple and white forms, the purple being the most prolific and the hardiest. A few plants are sufficient for most households. Sow in mid-to late spring, and plant firmly by mid-summer 2 ft (60 cm) apart each way. Stake if necessary. Snap off the flowering shoots in spring when about 6 in (15 cm) long, before the flowers open. If picked regularly they may crop over eight weeks. Broccoli is generally healthy, but may be attacked by birds in winter. There is little to choose between early and late forms.

BRUSSELS SPROUT *Brassica oleracea* Gemmifera group (See also Brassicas)

Brussels sprout is an invaluable winter vegetable, grown for the tight buds which develop up the stem. They are normally cooked, but can be eaten raw. Cultivars are divided loosely into early, mid-season and late types, the earlier ones being smaller, less prolific and less hardy. Where space allows grow a range to give a picking season from early autumn to late the following spring. The F1 hybrids are recommended, especially where the soil is fertile. Never plant on recently dug or manured soil, or the sprouts will be loose or 'blown'.

Sow in order of maturity from early to late spring, either in seed trays or in a seed bed. Unlike most brassicas, Brussels sprout does not normally respond well to being grown in modules. The earliest sowings can be started in gentle heat

Supports for tall Brussels sprout varieties (*Elizabeth Douglass*)

indoors. Plant out about a month after sowing, spacing early types about 18 in (45 cm) apart, tall types at least 2 ft (60 cm) apart. Closer spacing tends to give smaller sprouts. Plant tall types deeply and stake them. Due to the wide spacing, extra watering is rarely necessary. If plants are not thriving, give them a liquid feed in late summer. Remove dead and diseased leaves from the stems.

The first sprouts are ready about five months after sowing. The flavour is said to be best after exposure to frost. Pick from the bottom of the stem upwards. The plants are normally left in the ground, but in severe climates can be uprooted whole and hung in a cool shed, where they keep fresh for several weeks. With early types, if the top (crown) sprout is removed in late summer, the sprouts mature together rather than in succession. This is useful where sprouts are wanted for freezing. Sprout tops are well flavoured.

Recommended cultivars.   F1 hybrids in approximate order of maturity: Oliver, Peer Gynt, Cor Valiant (ROG), Mallard (ROG), Roger, Widgeon, Rampart, Lunet (ROG), Troika, Fortress, Rasmunde (ROG). Good-flavoured but low-yield, reddish sprout: Rubine

CABBAGE *Brassica oleracea* Capitata group (See also Brassicas)

Cabbage is grown for its compact heads (but see spring greens), which are eaten all year round, raw or cooked, fresh or stored. Heads can be near white, green or red in colour, smooth or crinkly-leaved (as in savoys), and rounded, flat or pointed. For soil see Brassicas. The winter storage types require somewhat less fertile soil than other types.

For a succession maturing from early spring to late winter, sow different cultivars at the correct times. For the main groups, sowing times and spacing, see accompanying chart. For preference, raise cabbage in modules, but otherwise sow in seed trays or in a seed bed. The standard spacing can be modified to determine the size of the cabbage: somewhat closer spacing will produce smaller cabbages; wider spacing, larger ones. Aim to grow sturdy plants, planting when 5-6 in (12·5-15 cm) high. This is generally about seven weeks after sowing for spring cabbages, and four to six weeks after sowing for other types. See pages 97 and 267 for measures to combat club root and cabbage root fly. Plant firmly.

Spring cabbage.   These sweetly flavoured cabbages are hardy, so in temperate climates can be overwintered outdoors. In cold and exposed areas grow them under cloches or crop covers.

Spring greens   are either loose-headed types, or standard spring cabbages harvested at an immature stage for earlier pickings. In the latter

Minicole, a summer cabbage that can be left to stand for several months, retaining good quality (*Chris Algar*)

Prosaic brassica in exotic mode: ornamental kale, Red Peacock, suitable for flower arrangement, garnish or salads (*John Walker*)

case, space plants in rows 10 in (25 cm) apart, 4 in (10 cm) apart in the rows. Leave every third plant to heart up, but harvest the intervening plants earlier for spring greens.

Summer and autumn cabbage. There are many cultivars, but some start to burst not long after maturing. Others, e.g. Minicole, stand for several months, remaining in good quality. Most survive only light frosts.

Winter cabbage. These vary in hardiness. The Dutch winter white storage types are the least hardy, and must be lifted and stored before severe frost. Hardiest of all are the winter savoys. The reddish-tinged January King types and some modern Dutch white/savoy hybrids are moderately hardy, and can be left outside in temperate climates most winters, or lifted and stored.

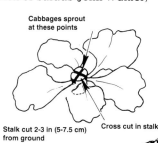

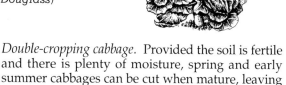

Double cropping cabbage (*Elizabeth Douglass*)

Double-cropping cabbage. Provided the soil is fertile and there is plenty of moisture, spring and early summer cabbages can be cut when mature, leaving the stump in the ground. Make a ¼ in (0·5 cm) deep

Main cabbage types			
Group according to maturity	Type	Main sowing	Standard spacing in (cm) apart each way
Spring	Small pointed or round heads	Late summer	12 (30)
	Loose-leaf 'greens'	Late summer	10 (25)
Early summer	Larger, mainly round heads	Very early spring (heat indoors)	14 (35)
Summer	Large round heads	Early spring	14 (35)
Autumn	Large round heads	Late spring	20 (50)
Winter storage	Smooth, white-leaved 'winter white' types	Spring	20 (50)
Winter fresh	Blue-green and savoy leaf types	Late spring	20 (50)

slit across the top of the stump. A second crop of four or five heads may develop for harvesting in late summer or early autumn.

Storage. Pull up cabbages for storage before severe frost. They store best with the root attached, but if that is inconvenient, trim so that at least 2 in (5 cm) of stem remains. Handle them gently so there is no bruising. Either hang them in nets or pile them on a layer of straw in a cool, frost-free shed. Inspect periodically during winter, and gently rub off any decaying outer leaves. Length of storage depends on the cultivar.

Pests and diseases. See Brassicas.

Recommended cultivars (all except the first are F1 hybrids). Spring: Offenham 1 – Myatt's Offenham Compacta (hearts and greens); summer: Castello (ROG), Hispi, Minicole, Stonehead, Ruby Ball (red); storage: Autoro (red), Hardoro (red), Jupiter; Savoy: Novusa (ROG), Wirosa

CALABRESE (Green or Italian sprouting broccoli)
Brassica oleracea 'Italica' group
(see also Brassicas)

A superbly flavoured brassica, calabrese is grown for its greenish-blue flowering head and side shoots, which are cooked. It does not grow well at high temperatures, but immature plants are moderately hardy, mature plants less so. As it tolerates less fertile soil than other large brassicas, is fast-maturing, and can be closely spaced, it is recommended for small gardens.

For crops from mid-summer to autumn, sow in succession from late spring to mid-summer. Calabrese does not transplant well, so either sow in modules or *in situ*, sowing two to three seeds per site, and thinning to one after germination. Average spacing is 9 in (23 cm) apart each way. Calabrese needs plenty of water: in dry conditions water at twice the rate recommended for brassicas. Cut the main head when still firm, before the flowers open, ten to thirteen weeks after sowing, depending on the cultivar. Liquid feed can be given at this stage. The side shoots then develop, and can be cut as ready over several weeks.

For a useful spring crop sow an early, fast-maturing cultivar in late summer or early autumn in modules, planting a few weeks later under cover or in a sheltered spot outdoors. Being no more than about 5 in (12·5 cm) high before winter, the plants survive low temperatures and grow rapidly in spring.

Pests and diseases. See Brassicas. Caterpillars can be damaging; pollen beetle may attack the curds

Recommended cultivars. F1 hybrids are generally

Calabrese, recommended for small gardens (John Walker)

recommended, e.g. Mercedes, Green Comet (early maturing)

CARROT *Daucus carota*

The carrot is a cool-season vegetable grown for its roots, eaten raw and cooked. The smaller, faster-growing types are used fresh for early crops; larger, slower-growing types are used fresh or stored for winter. Small round types are used for early crops and on shallow soils. Carrots do best on reasonably fertile, light, well-drained, stone-free soil. Heavy and compacted soils should be avoided. In many areas the main concern is avoiding carrot root fly, a low-flying insect with several generations each year, which disfigures and, in serious cases, destroys roots.

The standard method of growing carrots is to sow *in situ* (but see also below). Never sow until the soil temperature is above 45°F (7°C). As carrots are difficult to weed, it pays to warm the soil beforehand with cloches or transparent plastic film to encourage weeds to germinate; hoe these off before sowing. Always sow thinly to minimize the need for thinning, as the odour attracts carrot root fly. Thin in the evening, remove thinnings from the site, and firm any disturbed soil back around the roots. Weed carrots carefully in the early stages. Later their leaves form a canopy over the soil, suppressing weeds. Extra watering is necessary only in very dry weather. Water then at the rate of 3 to 4 gal/sq yd (14–18 l/sq m) every seventeen days or so, to maintain steady growth. Pull carrots when they reach the size required.

Early carrots. For very early carrots sow in gentle heat indoors, using round, Amsterdam or Nantes types. Sow in seed trays and transplant *before* any tap root develops. Plant under cover, or, to save space indoors, transplant about 3 in (7·5 cm) apart in 12 in (30 cm) deep boxes filled with potting compost or a light soil mixture.

Move the boxes outdoors when weather permits, and grow carrots in them to maturity. Deep boxes also give some protection against carrot fly, especially if placed 18 in (45 cm) or so above ground level. Another option, which can produce very good carrots, is to sow in modules and transplant outdoors. Round types only can be multi-sown, with four to five seeds per module, planting about 6 in (15 cm) apart.

Start outdoor sowings in spring as soon as the soil is workable, using the same types as above. In cold areas protect the first sowings with cloches or crop covers. Early spring sowings normally escape carrot fly attacks. Sow thinly in rows 6 in (15 cm) apart, thinning to 3 in (7·5 cm) apart. The wide spacing encourages the roots to grow rapidly, but may be unnecessary in very good carrot soils. Early carrots are ready about ten to twelve weeks after sowing.

Maincrop carrots. Sow from late spring to mid-summer, using mainly Chantenay, Berlicum and Autumn King types. In carrot fly areas delay sowing until early summer, to avoid the first carrot fly attack, or grow under nets. Sow in rows 6 in (15 cm) apart, thinning to about 2 in (5 cm) apart for large carrots, and somewhat closer for medium-sized. Maincrop carrots mature in about five months.

Carrot seed can be mixed with the seed of annual flowers and the two sown together. The carrots develop well among the flowers, and the flowers seem to deter the carrot fly.

In mild areas on well drained soil they can be left in the ground for winter. After the tops die down, and before heavy frost, cover them with a layer of straw or bracken at least 6 in (15 cm) deep, or spade extra soil over them. They retain their flavour well but may be damaged by slugs or mice. Otherwise lift them in autumn, twist off the foliage, and store healthy, undamaged roots in boxes or clamps as for beetroot or swede (see page 124). They normally keep until late spring.

Pests and diseases. For measures against carrot fly and partially resistant cultivars see *Pest Control*, page 312.

Recommended cultivars. (All ROG) Early: Nantes Tiptop, Nantucket; maincrop: Camus, Condor, Narman, Nantes Tiptop, Redca, Sytan, F1 Tamino

CAULIFLOWER *Brassica oleracea* Botrytis group (See also Brassicas)

Cauliflower is grown for its creamy white, green or purple head (curd), which is normally cooked. The coloured heads have notable flavour. Sowing the appropriate type at the correct time ensures that it is available fresh almost all year round in temperate climates (see chart overleaf). It needs moderately fertile soil, as on very rich soil it produces leaf rather than curds. Very acid soils should be avoided or limed, or mineral deficiencies may occur. Good curds develop only if growth is unchecked, such as by lack of moisture at any stage. For this reason spring-heading types are the most likely to succeed where summers are dry.

Sow in warm soil in modules, in a seed bed or *in situ* (see calabrese, opposite). Seed germinates poorly at temperatures below 70°F (21°C). Plant out about six weeks after sowing, at the spacing shown in the table. For early summer cauliflowers sow in modules or seed trays and pot up in small pots; keep plants in a cold frame during winter. Plant them out in spring. In dry weather water every two weeks at the rate given in Brassicas. Maturity rates depend on types: winter cauliflower at least ten months after sowing; early summer (autumn-sown) after eight months; autumn types after five. Cut heads when firm and tight. In hot summers bend a leaf over curds nearing maturity to prevent discoloration; in severe weather tie up the leaves to protect them from frosts.

Mini-cauliflower. For small curds 2 in (5 cm) in diameter maturing together (suitable for freezing or small portions), sow an early summer type in

Carrot seeds sown together with annual candytuft grow well: the flowers seem to deter carrot fly (*Joy Larkcom*)

Cauliflower Garant, produces small 2 in (5 cm) 'mini' curds suitable for freezing or small portions (*John Walker*)

Cauliflower types
(Temperate climate)

Group according to maturity	Sow	Plant	Space each way in (cm)
*Winter/very early spring	Late spring	Summer	28 (70)
Early spring	Late spring	Summer	25 (63)
Early to mid-summer	Autumn or early spring (in heat)	Spring	21 (53)
Late summer to late autumn	Mid- to late spring	Early summer	22–25 (55–63)
*frost-free zone only			

spring and early summer. Either sow *in situ* or in modules. Space plants 6 in (15 cm) apart each way. They mature about fifteen weeks later but deteriorate unless harvested when ready. This space-saving method suits small gardens.

Perennial cauliflower. A large, moderately hardy plant which may remain productive over three seasons, it produces a central curd and side shoots like sprouting broccoli. Grow it in very fertile soil. Sow in spring, spacing plants 3 ft (90 cm) apart. Harvest in spring and early summer like calabrese. Cut off straggly shoots when cropping is finished. Replace the plants when they start to deteriorate.

Pests and diseases. See Brassicas

Recommended cultivars. Winter, in frost-free areas only: Newton Seale; winter elsewhere: Walcheren Winter – Armada, April and Maystar; early summer: Alpha Paloma, White Summer; summer to autumn: Limelight (green), Plana, Violet Queen (purple), Romanesco (green); perennial: Nine Star Perennial

CELERIAC *Apium graveolens* var. *rapaceum*
Celeriac is a moderately hardy vegetable grown for its rough, celery-flavoured 'bulb'. This forms at ground level and is a most useful winter vegetable, cooked or raw. Leaves can be used for flavouring. It requires very fertile, moisture-retentive soil, rich in organic matter. It tolerates light shade.

Celeriac needs a six-month growing season, so sow indoors in spring, either in modules or in seed trays. Very early sowings can be made in gentle heat. Germination is often erratic. Plant out in spring after hardening off, spacing plants about 12 in (30 cm) apart. Water generously in dry spells and mulch after watering. A general-purpose liquid feed in mid-summer is beneficial. In autumn cover the ground between plants with

a thick layer of straw or bracken to protect against frost. Except in very severe climates, leave them in the soil for winter. Otherwise store indoors as for beet, leaving a central tuft of leaves attached to the bulb.

Pests and diseases. See celery, below. Celeriac is normally very healthy

Recommended cultivars. Snow White, Tellus

CELERY, Self-Blanching and 'Leaf' *Apium graveolens*
The easiest types of celery to grow are the fairly tender green or off-white 'self-blanching' kinds, grown for their stalks which are used cooked or raw, and 'leaf', 'cutting' or 'soup' celery, which is a much smaller, hardier and remarkably robust plant with fine leaves and stems used for seasoning, soup and salads, particularly in the winter months. The traditional English trench celery, in which the stems are earthed up as they grow in order to blanch them, requires a lot of

Celery-flavoured celeriac 'bulb' makes a most useful winter vegetable (*Joy Larkcom*)

space and labour. Celery does best in very fertile, moisture-retentive soil.

Self-blanching celery. Never hurry to sow celery, as it may bolt prematurely if the seedlings experience temperatures below 50°F (10°C) for more than twelve hours. Sow in spring in seed trays or modules, at a minimum temperature of 50°F (10°C). Sow on the surface or very shallowly; it needs light to germinate. Prick out seedlings at a young stage; harden off well before planting out in late spring/early summer after any risk of frost. Plant about 9 in (23 cm) apart each way. This fairly close spacing enables the stems to become slightly more blanched naturally. Plants can be protected with cloches or crop covers for the first four weeks or so. Remove any leaves which are blistered by celery fly maggots. Water and feed as for celeriac. Cut individual stems as required; they are usually ready about eight weeks after planting. Quality deteriorates severely after frost.

Pests and diseases. Celery fly (leaf miner), slugs; celery leaf spot

Recommended cultivars. Celebrity, Lathom Self-Blanching; for flavour: Greensleeves, Hopkins, Fenlander

Leaf celery. Make the main sowing in spring or early summer, either in a seed tray or modules for transplanting or *in situ*. Space plants about 5 in (12·5 cm) apart. In cold climates make a second sowing in mid- to late summer, and transplant under cover for a good-quality winter crop. Plants can be cut on reaching about 5 in (12·5 cm) high, and respond well to cut-and-come-again treatment.

The leaf normally remains green all winter. Allow a few plants to run to seed, and transplant the self-sown seedlings when young to where they are required.

Recommended cultivars. Dutch leaf celery, 'Parcel' (very curly decorative-leaved type) *DVG*

CHICORIES *Cichorium intybus*

The chicories are a group of vigorous, naturally healthy, leafy plants with a characteristic bitter flavour. Hardiness ranges from cultivars which stand only slight frost to the extremely hardy, non-hearting 'Treviso'. They are mainly used raw in autumn, winter and spring salads. The bitterness can be moderated in various ways, such as blanching in darkness, shredding the leaves before use, and mixing them with milder leaves. Plants seem to become less bitter on exposure to frost. Chicory grows on a wide range of soil types and tolerates light shade in the summer months. Greatly improved cultivars are gradually becoming available to gardeners.

Red chicory (radicchio): colours intensify in cold weather (*Joy Larkcom*)

Red chicory (radicchio). Red chicory plants bear some resemblance to the dandelion. Leaf colour ranges from green to variegated to red. With most types colours intensify in cold weather, and the leaves curl inwards to form a tight, crispy, red- and white-leaved heart. 'Treviso' is non-hearting, but its long, narrow leaves become deep red in winter, and, if blanched like Witloof chicory (see below), a superb pink and white. All can be treated as cut-and-come-again crops at the mature and semi-mature stage, and remain productive over many months.Less hardy and hardy types alike benefit in quality from being protected or grown under cover in winter.

For the main crop sow in early summer, either in seed trays and modules for transplanting, or *in situ*. Space plants on average 12 in (30 cm) apart. Sow a few more plants in late summer, to transplant under cover for a good quality mid-winter crop. Plants can be cut from early autumn onwards. Some new cultivars can be sown in late spring for a summer crop. 'Treviso' can also be sown broadcast, and thinned to about 5 in (12·5 cm) apart. Most chicories in the open benefit from some protection before heavy frost. Cover them with cloches or similar, or with about 3 in (7·5 cm) of straw or bracken. Remove rotting leaves as they develop during the winter. The plants often rejuvenate in spring. *DVG*

Recommended cultivars. Cesare (early sowing), Rossano, Verona Palla Rossa, Treviso

Sugar loaf chicory. Mature 'sugar loaf' chicory forms a conical green head of fairly tightly packed, crisp leaf, which is to some extent blanched naturally and so slightly sweeter than other chicories. It has better drought-resistance than most salad vegetables. It withstands only light frost, but is an excellent late summer and autumn salad vegetable outdoors, and can be very productive under cover in winter, responding well to cut-and-come-again treatment as semi-mature and mature plants. It can also be grown as a cut-and-come-again seedling crop.

For the main and protected crop sow as for red chicory in mid- to late summer, spacing plants 10 in (25 cm) apart. For cut-and-come-again seedling crops sow from early spring to autumn, making the first and last sowings under cover. Mid-summer sowings will prove less tender. After two or three seedling cuts the plants can be thinned in stages to about 10 in (25 cm) apart and remaining plants left to heart up. Protect outdoor plants as for red chicory: some may survive to spring, especially if cut back.

Recommended cultivars. For seedlings: Biondissima di Trieste; for heads: Crystal Head, F1 Jupiter, Poncho, Winter Fare

Witloof chicory (Belgian chicory). Witloof chicory is grown for the tight pointed 'bud' or 'chicon' of whitened leaves which develops when the roots are forced and blanched in the dark. It is very easy to grow. Sow seed in spring or early summer, either in seed trays or modules to transplant, or *in situ* in rows about 12 in (30 cm) apart, thinning to 8 in (20 cm) apart. Water only if the ground becomes very dry.

Forcing. Dig up the plants in late autumn, rejecting very thin roots of less than 1 in (2·5 cm)

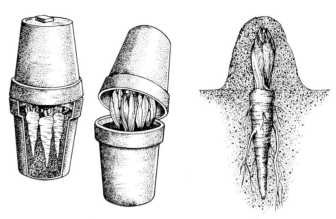

LEFT: Forcing Witloof 'chicons' in pots. RIGHT: Forcing chicory *in situ* can give better flavour (*Elizabeth Douglass*)

diameter at the top. Trim off the leaves to 1 in (2·5 cm) above the root. It is best to force a few at a time, so lay the remaining roots flat in layers in a box of sand in a cool place until required. To force, pot several roots close together in a large flowerpot or box, using ordinary garden soil. Trim off the root ends if necessary. Cover this with an inverted box or pot of the same size, with the drainage hole covered with tinfoil to exclude light. Put them in a room at a temperature between 50° and 65°F (10° and 18°C). Water if necessary to prevent the soil drying out. Within three to four weeks the chicons will have developed. Use them fairly soon, keeping them in the dark, or wrapped in tinfoil in a fridge, until required.

In areas with mild winters and on well-drained ground Witloof chicory can be blanched *in situ*. This may give a better flavour. Trim the leaves back to within an inch (2·5 cm) of the ground in autumn, and cover the stumps with soil to make a ridge about 6 in (15 cm) high. The shoots grow through during the winter months.

Recommended cultivars. F1 Normato, F1 Zoom

CHINESE CABBAGE *Brassica rapa* var. *pekinensis*
(See also Oriental Greens)

Chinese cabbage is pleasantly mild-flavoured, with a crisp texture. It stands only light frosts. There are two distinct types. The headed type (known as 'Chinese leaves') has either a compact barrel-shaped or a long, more pointed head. The leaves often have broad white midribs, outstanding white veins and a crinkled texture. The loose-headed types, which include the creamy-centred fluffy top cultivars, are less compact, somewhat easier to grow, and have some hardier forms. Most headed types have rough seedling leaves, so are unsuitable for cut-and-come-again seedlings.

Headed types. Delay the first sowing until early

Sugar loaf chicory has better drought resistance than most salad crops, F1 Jupiter shown here (*Joy Larkcom*)

Chinese cabbage: F1 Kasumi, headed type (*Joy Larkcom*)

Chinese cabbage: loose, fluffy top, Eskimo type, good in decorative vegetable garden (*Joy Larkcom*)

Chrysanthemum greens, distinctively flavoured, can be grown as a cut-and-come-again seedling crop cut over several weeks, or as single plants (*Joy Larkcom*)

to mid-summer. Sow in modules, or *in situ* to minimize the risk of bolting. Space plants about 14 in (35 cm) apart each way. The heads are ready on average two months after sowing. Cut the head, leaving the stalk to re-sprout. Make a second sowing in late summer. This may mature outside in mild areas; otherwise cover it with cloches in autumn or transplant module-raised plants under cover for a winter crop. If these late sowings fail to develop hearts, cut the immature leaves for tender greens, leaving the plants to re-sprout. If temperatures are not too low the cut plants may survive into spring, when they produce masses of tender flowering shoots which should be picked regularly.

Loose-headed. Unfortunately only a few of the many types of loose-headed Chinese cabbage are currently available. Most have the mild refreshing flavour typical of Chinese cabbage. They mature rapidly, often in less than eight weeks. They can be harvested at any stage from seedlings to mature head to flowering shoots. Some cultivars tolerate warmer and colder temperatures than headed Chinese cabbage.

Make the first sowings in late spring to early summer, either in modules for transplanting, or *in situ* for seedling crops. Avoid sowing in very hot weather, and make the last sowings under cover in late summer/early autumn for a winter crop. Space plants 8 in (20 cm) apart if harvesting at a semi-mature stage, or about 12 in (30 cm) apart if harvesting fully mature.

Recommended cultivars. Headed: F1 Kasumi, F1 Tip Top; loose-headed: Eskimo (fluffy top) (*DVG*), Santo

CHRYSANTHEMUM GREENS (Garland chrysanthemum, shungiku, chop suey greens) *Chrysanthemum coronarium*

The distinctively flavoured leaves of the edible annual chrysanthemum are usually cooked but can be used raw when young. It grows best in cool weather, withstands a few degrees of frost, and tolerates a wide range of soil types and light shade. It can be grown as a cut-and-come-again seedling crop, or as single plants, cut over several weeks. It can be cropped four to six weeks after sowing, but tends to run to seed rapidly in hot weather. The broad-leaved forms are the most prolific.

Sow from spring to late summer, except in very hot conditions, making early spring and late summer sowings under cover. Either sow in seed trays and transplant, or sow *in situ*, thinning to about 5 in (12·5 cm) apart each way if single plants are required. To keep plants productive pick regularly, nip out the growing point if plants are straggly, and remove any flowers which develop. Pull plants up when they start to become coarse.

They can be propagated from cuttings taken from side shoots before the plants run to seed. Water where necessary to prevent the soil drying out.

CORN SALAD (Lamb's lettuce) *Valerianella locusta*

Corn salad is a small, undemanding plant with

mild-flavoured leaves used raw in salads. Being hardy, it is mainly grown for winter and early spring use. The soft, large-leaved English or Dutch types are the most prolific, but the smaller-leaved French 'Verte' types are hardier. It is relatively slow-growing, and can be cultivated as a cut-and-come-again seedling crop or as single plants, which are either used whole or cut and left to re-sprout. It can be sown from early spring to late summer, either in seed trays and transplanting or *in situ*. Space plants about 4 in (10 cm) apart. Sow in mid-summer for the main winter crop, keeping the soil moist until the seed has germinated. Mature plants are ready about twelve weeks after sowing. Plants left to run to seed in spring often seed themselves.

COURGETTE (see Marrow)

CRESS (Garden cress, pepper cress) *Lepidium sativum*

Cress is a fast-growing, hot-flavoured salad plant. It is often grown on moist paper towelling on a saucer, and cut when about 1½ in (4 cm) high. It can also be sown in the ground as a cut-and-come-again seedling crop, in this case cutting it several times. It is best sown in cool weather, as it runs to seed rapidly in hot weather. Sow broadcast or in wide drills in spring and late summer to autumn, making the earliest and latest sowings under cover. A late autumn sowing under cover may give a cut or two before low winter temperatures stop growth, but the plants will re-grow on warm days in spring to give further cuts. The first cut can normally be made within ten days of sowing. 'Broad-leaved' and 'Greek' cress are very prolific types.

CUCUMBER *Cucumis sativus*

The long thin 'frame' cucumber is a warm-climate plant, and in cool climates must be grown indoors (see *Growing Under Cover*, page 338). The shorter, rougher, somewhat coarser 'ridge' cucumber is more tolerant of low temperatures, and can be grown outside in cool climates. Some improved hybrid types, many of Japanese origin, are longer and smoother, and have excellent disease resistance and cold tolerance. Grow outdoor cucumber in a sheltered site protected from strong winds, on fertile, well-drained but moisture-retentive soil with plenty of organic matter dug in beforehand. The plants can trail over the ground, but crop better if trained up strings, canes or a trellis. A few cultivars are compact bush types.

Sow seed indoors about four weeks before the last expected frost (see *Growing Under Cover*, page 338). Plant out after all risk of frost, taking care not to bury the neck of the plant. Space them 18 in (45 cm) apart if climbing, and 2½ ft (75 cm) if trailing. Protect them with cloches or covers in

their early stages. They can also be sown *in situ* after all risk of frost has passed, sowing individually under jam jars to give protection in the early stages. Tie plants to their supports where necessary, and nip out the growing point when the top of the support is reached. In dry conditions water regularly, especially once plants have started to flower and form fruits. The first fruits are usually ready about twelve weeks after sowing. Gherkins are grown in the same way, but usually trail over the ground. Pick at the size required for pickling, or allow them to grow larger and use as cucumbers. Outdoor cucumbers can be grown in greenhouses, but should never be mixed with all-female greenhouse types.

Pests and diseases. Aphids; cucumber mosaic virus, powdery mildew

Recommended cultivars. Hybrids: Burpee Hybrid, Burpless Tasty Green; bush: Patio Pik; Gherkin: Conda

DANDELION *Taraxacum officinale*

Dandelion is a hardy perennial. Leaves and roots (especially the root top) have long been cultivated for salads, although the flavour is slightly bitter. Use young leaves green. Older leaves can be blanched to tenderize them. Dandelion grows in most soil provided it is well drained. Sow in spring and early summer, either in seed trays and transplanting, or *in situ*. Space plants about 14 in (35 cm) apart. From late summer onwards plants can be blanched by covering, when the foliage is dry, with a light-proof bucket for ten days or so. This produces etiolated, whitened leaves. Plants die down in winter, but can be blanched after re-growth in spring. In very cold areas they can be lifted and forced indoors like Witloof chicory (above). Wild dandelions can be eaten, but cultivated strains are more prolific.

ENDIVE *Cichorium endivia*

Endive is a lettuce-like plant, grown mainly for use raw in salads. There are many cultivars, some moderately hardy, others adapted to high temperatures. Distinct types include the curly-leaved or *frisée* and the broad-leaved Batavian or *escarole,* but there are intermediate types. It is slightly bitter in flavour, and can be blanched to whiten and sweeten it, though many find this unnecessary. It responds well to cut-and-come-again treatment as seedlings (especially curly-leaved types) or as semi-mature and mature plants. Its main season of use is from summer to spring: it performs much better than lettuce in low winter light. It is important to sow the correct cultivar for each season. Endive grows on a wide range of moderately fertile soils.

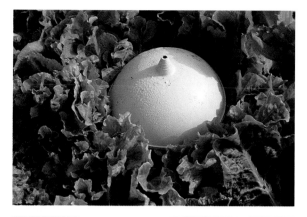

Purpose-made, lightweight endive blancher (Joy Larkcom)

Sow from late spring to mid-summer for the summer to autumn crop. (Earlier sowings may bolt prematurely if there is a cold spell.) Sow in seed trays for transplanting, or *in situ*, spacing plants 10 to 15 in (25–37·5cm) apart, depending on the cultivar. Make a late-summer sowing to transplant under cover for a winter crop, which may, with cut-and-come-again treatment, remain productive all winter into the following spring. Plants are normally ready about three months after sowing. To blanch, cover mature plants, when the foliage is dry, with a large bucket, or a purpose-made, lightweight blancher. Or place a dinner plate over the plant, which will blanch the central leaves. Blanching takes about ten days. Eat immediately, or the plants may start to deteriorate. Sow cut-and-come-again seedling crops from early spring to late summer, making the first and last sowings under cover. Curly types: *DVG*

Pests. Slugs

Recommended cultivars. Curled: Fine Maraîchère and Ione (summer), Pancalière (summer/ autumn), Ruffec and Wallonne (hardy); broad-leaved: Golda (all sowings), Full Heart Italian (hardy)

FLORENCE FENNEL *Foeniculum vulgare* var. *azoricum*

Florence fennel is a tender annual grown for the crisp, aniseed-flavoured 'bulb' at the base of the stem, used cooked or raw. The fern-like leaves and fine stems can also be used in salads and for seasoning (see *Herbs*, page 142). Warm, Mediterranean-type summers are ideal for fennel; it can withstand light frost once established. It requires reasonably fertile, well-drained but moisture-retentive soil, with plenty of organic matter worked in.

Fennel is not easy to grow well. It is likely to bolt prematurely, without forming a bulb, if sown in early spring, if subjected to fluctuating temperatures, if allowed to dry out or if seedlings are transplanted later than the three- to four-leaf stage. Make the main sowing in early to mid-summer, either in modules or *in situ*, spacing plants about 12 in (30 cm) apart. Earlier sowings, using bolt-resistant cultivars, *may* succeed: protect plants with cloches or covers after planting. A few plants sown in late summer can be transplanted under cover, to provide leaf in early winter, but they are unlikely to form bulbs.

Keep fennel mulched, and water generously in dry conditions. Once the bulb starts to swell it can be earthed up, to about half its height, to make it whiter and sweeter, but this is not essential. It will be ready to cut within twenty days. Cut just above ground level, leaving a small stump, which may re-sprout, producing more fern. *DVG*

Recommended cultivars. Perfection, Sirio, Sweet Florence; some bolt-resistance: Cantino, Zefa Fino

GARLIC *Allium sativum*

A hardy member of the onion family, garlic is grown for its bulb of pinkish or white cloves, used raw or cooked, fresh or stored. Garlic will grow in a wide range of climates, provided there is a cool, six-week winter period with temperatures between 32° and 50°F (0°–10°C). Soil must be well-drained: light sandy soils are ideal. On heavy soil it is sometimes grown on ridges to improve drainage. It has low nutrient requirements.

Where possible grow strains of garlic adapted to your climate, from healthy stock, guaranteed disease-free. Ideally the corms should be at least ½ in (1·25 cm) in diameter. To get a long growing season it is advisable to plant in the autumn. Plant with the flat base-plate downwards, to at least twice the clove's depth, spacing them about 7 in (18 cm) apart each way. On very heavy soil, or where winters are very severe, plant the cloves in modules in autumn, overwinter them in frames outdoors, and plant out in spring. To prevent the corms re-sprouting, garlic should be lifted as soon as the leaves start to fade in mid-summer. Garlic

After drying, hang garlic by the stems to keep it for winter (Joy Larkcom)

The unusual-looking iceplant sparkles in the sunshine. It needs warm summers (John Walker)

sometimes produces seedheads. This does not matter: just cut them off when the stems are paper-dry to facilitate bunching. Dry garlic like onions (see page 114), and store it in a dry place, ideally at a temperature of about 45°F (7°C). It often keeps up to ten months. If the corms look healthy, a few can be saved for future planting.

Pests and diseases. See onion (page 114). Garlic is normally a healthy crop.

ICEPLANT *Mesembryanthemum crystallinum*

An unusual-looking plant with fleshy leaves and stems covered in bladders, making it sparkle in sunshine, the edible iceplant is grown in warm climates for use raw in salads, or cooked as a spinach substitute. Grow it in a sunny, sheltered position on well-drained soil. It tolerates poor soil, but grows more lushly in fertile soil. The mature plants will survive very light frost.

In frost-free areas sow *in situ* outdoors in early summer. Otherwise sow indoors in gentle heat in late spring, four to five weeks before the last frost is expected. Plant out after hardening off, spacing plants about 12 in (30 cm) apart. Protect with cloches in the early stages if necessary. Start picking young leaves and stems about a month later, and pick regularly to encourage further growth. Remove any flowers which appear. Cover with cloches in early autumn to prolong the season. Iceplant can also be grown in greenhouses. Watch for slugs in the early stages.

KALE *Brassica oleracea* Acephala group
(See also Brassicas)

Kale is a very versatile brassica. Some are among the hardiest winter greens, but they also tolerate high temperatures. The loose-leaved American collards, and the very pretty, deeply curled kales, which have dwarf and tall forms, are grown mainly for the leaves. The broad-leaved and hybrid kales are grown mainly for the shoots which develop in spring. Both are cooked or used

raw when very young. Seed of a perennial type is sometimes available, though it is normally propagated by cuttings. The soil must be well drained; otherwise kale tolerates poorer soils than many brassicas, but responds well to rich soil.

Make the main sowing in late spring for the autumn/winter crop, and in early spring for a summer crop. Sow by any method. Space dwarf types 12 to 18 in (30–45 cm) apart each way; tall types about 27 in (68 cm) apart. Plant firmly. Staking is normally unnecessary. Curly types can be sown for a cut-and-come-again seedling crop, either in late summer or early spring outdoors, or early autumn or very early spring under cover.

The fastest-growing types are ready two months after sowing, but plants stand well over many months. Flavour is considered improved after frost. Pick the leaves of curly types as required, and the young shoots of other types in spring, when about 4 in (10 cm) long. Pick regularly to encourage further production. Liquid feed can be applied in spring to stimulate growth. Curly kale: *DVG*

Kale (foreground: curled Pentland Brig, background: broadleaf Thousandhead), among the hardiest of winter greens (Joy Larkcom)

Pests and diseases. See Brassicas. Kales tend to be more resistant to pests (even birds) and disease than most brassicas.

Recommended cultivars. Daubenton (perennial), F1 Fribor (curly), Pentland Brig (hybrid), Thousandhead (broadleaf)

KOHL RABI *Brassica oleracea* Gongylodes group
(See also Brassicas)

Kohl rabi forms a bizarre 'bulb' in the stem about 1 in (2·5 cm) above ground. Highly nutritious and well-flavoured, it is eaten cooked or raw. Although a cool-season vegetable, it may bolt prematurely at temperatures below 50°F (10°C). Purple-skinned forms are slightly hardier than green-skinned. It withstands drought reasonably well.

Sow outdoors from spring to late summer, *in situ*, thinning to about 10 in (25 cm) apart each way. Or sow in seed trays or modules and transplant young. Earlier sowings can be made under cover. In warm climates sow in spring and autumn only. Plants are ready on average seven weeks after sowing. Use traditional types at tennis-ball size, before they become woody, but good F1 hybrids may be eaten up to 4 in (10 cm) in diameter. Lift before heavy frost, and store in boxes (as for beetroot) with the leaves attached.

Recommended cultivars. F1 hybrids: Lanro, Kolpak, Rowel

KOMATSUNA (Spinach mustard) *Komatsuna rapa* var. *perviridis*
(See also Oriental Greens)

Komatsuna is one of the most robust and naturally healthy of the oriental greens, being more tolerant of extremes of heat, cold and

Komatsuna, one of the most robust and healthy oriental greens. After cutting, it resprouts to produce these edible flowering shoots (*Joy Larkcom*)

drought than most. Some cultivars are exceptionally hardy. The often glossy, deep green leaves can grow very large. They have a part-cabbage/part-spinach flavour, and are used raw or cooked.

Komatsuna is used at all stages (see Loose-headed Chinese cabbage, page 105), and is often grown close and harvested as whole young plants about 6 in (15 cm) high. It is an excellent winter vegetable. For cut-and-come-again seedling crops sow at monthly intervals from early spring to late summer, making the first and last sowings under cover. Make the main sowings for a winter crop, for use young or mature, in mid-summer. Either sow *in situ*, or in modules or seed trays for transplanting. Space plants 2 in (5 cm) apart for harvesting young, or about 12 in (30 cm) apart (depending on cultivar) if growing to maturity. Sow again in late summer to transplant under cover, for a highly productive winter and spring crop.

Recommended cultivars. F1 All Top, Komatsuna, Tendergreen (all very hardy)

LAND CRESS (American land cress) *Barbarea verna*

A very hardy plant with a strong watercress flavour, land cress is mainly grown for salads or as a watercress substitute for use in winter to spring. It needs fertile, moisture-retentive soil and, provided there is moisture, tolerates light shade. It can be grown in fairly damp corners. It tends to run to seed rapidly in hot weather and dry soil.

Sow in spring for a summer supply, and in summer for an autumn to spring crop. Either sow in seed trays and transplant, or sow *in situ*. Space plants about 5 in (12·5 cm) apart. Watch out for flea beetle attacks in the early stages. The first leaves can be picked two months after sowing. Cut them as required or cut across the plant a little above soil level, leaving it to re-sprout. Although very hardy, plants protected with cloches in winter, or grown under cover, will be more tender and lush. Leave a few plants to self-seed naturally.

LEEK *Allium porrum*

Leek is a hardy, cool-season crop in the onion family. It is grown for the thick white stem or shank, used cooked, mainly in the winter months. The earliest types, maturing in autumn, are tall, with long shanks and pale leaves. The hardier, later types, which can be harvested throughout winter and into spring, are shorter and stouter with darker, bluish foliage. Leeks require deep, fertile soil into which plenty of organic matter has been worked. They never do well on compacted soil. Including leeks in a rotation may help to overcome club root infection in the soil.

Sow early types first, progressing to later types. Leek seed germinates poorly at soil

Leeks are planted into 5-6 in (12·5-15 cm) deep holes to obtain a long white shank (Joy Larkcom)

Crisphead, iceberg type Saladin, mainly grown in summer (Joy Larkcom)

temperatures below 45°F (7°C). Make the first sowings indoors in gentle heat in early spring, in seed trays or modules, followed by late spring sowings without heat. Leeks respond well to multi-sowing, with three or four seeds per module. Transplant outside after hardening off, ideally when seedlings are about 8 in (20 cm) high, on average twelve weeks after sowing. Later sowings can be made *in situ* once the soil has warmed up. For average-sized leeks, space about 6 in (15 cm) apart each way, or 9 in (23 cm) for multi-sown leeks.

To get a long white shank, leeks are normally planted in smooth holes 5 to 6 in (12·5-15 cm) deep, made with a dibber. Drop in the leek (or group of leeks if multi-sown) and water gently. Soil will fall in around the stem in due course. Where leeks are sown *in situ* the stem can be blanched by drawing soil around it in stages as it grows. Leeks mature four to five months after sowing, and will stand for several months without deteriorating. Some people consider small, thin leeks better-flavoured than large mature ones. For small leeks, sow in drills in spring, using an early, long-shafted type. Pull them at the thickness required.

Once established, leeks require little further watering, except in very dry conditions or if outsize leeks are required. If the soil is not very fertile, apply liquid feeds during growth.

Pests and diseases. Stem and bulb eelworm; onion white rot, leek rust

Recommended cultivars. Early: King Richard, Genevilliers Splendid; late: Autumn Mammoth – Goliath, Walton Mammoth (ROG); Winterreuzen (ROG)

LETTUCE *Lactuca sativa*; Stem Lettuce *Lactuca sativa* var. *angustana*

The most widely grown salad vegetable, lettuce is a cool-season crop, apt to bolt prematurely in hot weather. If appropriate cultivars are chosen it can be harvested all year round. (For cultivation in winter and early spring under cover, see *Growing under Cover*, page 340.) Lettuce requires plenty of moisture throughout growth, and must be grown on fertile, well-drained but moisture-retentive soil.

Butterhead: smooth-leaved, hearted types grown in summer and winter, the fastest-growing type.

Crisphead: crunchier, curlier-leaved, hearted types. 'Iceberg' lettuce is a crisphead with the outer leaves removed for marketing. They are mainly grown in summer. Some will grow very large.

Cos and semi-cos: hardier, distinctively flavoured lettuce, with a looser heart, the true cos has long upright leaves and is fairly slow-growing. Semi-cos is shorter, more compact, and faster-growing. Both can be grown in summer and winter.

Loose-leaved ('Salad Bowl'): unhearted lettuces, much slower to bolt in summer, so grown mainly as cut-and-come-again crops. Many, notably the frilly-leaved 'Lollo' types, are very decorative, and make excellent edges to beds. The red-leaved forms include some of the hardiest lettuce. *DVG*

'Cutting': traditional types originally selected for growing in frames as early cut-and-come-again seedling crops. There are smooth and crispy-leaved forms.

Stem lettuce: a tall, oriental lettuce, grown for its succulent thick stem, which is sliced raw or cooked. The leaves are coarse unless used young.

Cultivation. Lettuce can be sown in seed trays or modules and transplanted, or sown *in situ*. For early outdoor lettuce sow in spring, under cover, for transplanting outdoors, after hardening off, as soon as the soil is workable. Plant out at the four- to five-leaf stage. Early outdoor plantings can be

Crisphead, red iceberg (*Joy Larkcom*)

Butterhead, Tom Thumb, under fleece cover (*Chris Algar*)

Cos, Lobjoits Green, hardy, summer and winter (*Joy Larkcom*)

Salad bowl, red and green Lollo varieties, ideal for cut-and-come-again, very good disease resistance (*Joy Larkcom*)

Marvel of Four Seasons, richly coloured loose-headed butterhead type (*John Walker*)

covered with cloches or protective films. For the main summer to autumn outdoor crop sow from late spring to mid-summer. For a continuous supply make the next sowing as soon as the previous one has germinated. Plant the last crop under cloches or covers in early autumn. As seedlings do not transplant well in hot weather, make mid-summer sowings *in situ* or in modules.

Germination, especially of butterhead types, is often erratic if soil temperatures above 77°F (25°C) occur several hours after sowing. This can happen in late spring and summer. Either water the soil before sowing to reduce the temperature, or sow in modules in the early afternoon, putting them somewhere cool to germinate.

Plant lettuce with the leaves just above soil level. Spacing depends on the cultivar. Plant small types such as 'Tom Thumb' 6 in (15 cm) apart; average butterheads 11 in (28 cm) apart; crispheads from 13 to 15 in (32–37·5 cm) apart; semi-cos 8 in (20 cm) apart; large cos, Salad Bowl and stem lettuce 14 in (35 cm) apart. Water and mulch after planting. Apply liquid feeds during growth if the soil is not very fertile.

For good-quality lettuce, water regularly in dry weather at a weekly rate of about 4 gal/sq yd (18 l/sq m). Most hearted types mature three to four months after sowing, but do not stand well. Harvest when the heads feel plump. Loose-leaved types can be treated as cut-and-come-again at any stage. Stem lettuce can be left until just before it runs to seed. Strip the leaves off the stem, and peel it if the skin is tough.

Cut-and-come-again seedling lettuce. Use cutting types, loose-headed Salad Bowl types and cos lettuce. The most useful sowings are in early spring, first under cover, followed by outdoor sowings, and again in late summer outdoors and early autumn under cover. The young leaves can often be cut within a few weeks of sowing, and then two or three more times. It is a productive method of growing lettuce in small areas.

Pests and diseases. Slugs, greenfly, root aphids, soil pests, birds; damping off in seedlings, grey mould, downy mildew, lettuce mosaic virus. Where available use cultivars with resistance to mildew and root aphid, and seed tested for lettuce mosaic virus

Recommended cultivars. Butterhead: Clarion (ROG), Musette (ROG), Sabine (ROG); crisphead: Kelvin (ROG), Minetto, Saladin (ROG); cos: Lobjoits Green Cos; semi-cos: Bubbles, Little Gem; loose-leaved: Red and Green Lollo, Red and Green Salad Bowl

MARROW (Summer squash, vegetable marrow) and COURGETTE (Zucchini) *Cucurbita pepo*

Marrows are warm-climate plants, grown for their fruits, which can be cylindrical, round, crook-necked, or flat and fluted – as in the 'custard' or 'patty pan' types. They are mainly used fresh, but some types can be stored. Courgettes are marrows which are eaten small and immature, when the flavour is more pronounced: cultivars with exceptionally tender skins are ideal for this purpose. The young leaves, shoot tips and flowers of marrows are also edible.

Most marrows are trailing plants, and can be grown flat, perhaps trained in circles (see pumpkin, page 120) or trained up or over very strong supports. A few, including most of the courgette types, make compact bushes. Marrows will not tolerate any frost. Grow them in an open site in rich, moisture-retentive but well-drained soil. To prepare the ground make individual holes about 12 in (30 cm) deep and 18 in (45 cm) wide, working in plenty of well-rotted manure, thoroughly mixed with the soil.

Either sow indoors, in individual pots or modules, about four weeks before the last frost is expected, or, after the risk of frost, *in situ* outdoors. Outdoor plants can be protected with cloches or fleecy films in the early stages. Space trailing types 4 ft (120 cm) apart, and bush types 3 ft (90 cm) apart. Never allow the soil to dry out completely. Once plants are established, and especially when fruits start to form, water regularly at the rate of 2 gal (9 l) per plant per week. Mulch heavily. The female flowers (distinguished by a tiny bump behind the petals) may need to be pollinated by hand in cold summers when few insects are about. Pick courgettes with the flowers still attached and fresh-looking, up to 4 in (10 cm) long for long types, or 3 in (7·5 cm) in diameter for flat and round types. They may be ready within three months of sowing. Marrows take a week or two longer. Pick mature marrows for storage in late summer, and store somewhere well ventilated at about 50°F (10°C).

Pests and diseases. Slugs; cucumber mosaic virus

Courgettes growing through white plastic mulch, reflecting light and warmth on to plants (*Natural Image*)

Recommended cultivars. For courgettes: F1 Ambassador, F1 Early Gem (dual purpose), F1 Gold Rush (yellow-skinned), F1 Supremo (ROG); for long marrow: All Green Bush and F1 Tiger Cross (ROG) (bush types); F1 Twickers (semi-trailing)

MIZUNA GREENS (Kyona) *Brassica rapa* var. *nipposinica*
(See also Oriental Greens)

The older types of mizuna have deeply serrated, shiny green leaves, while some of the modern

Mizuna greens with serrated leaves, used raw or cooked, with mild, mustard flavour (*Joy Larkcom*)

Mibuna greens, closely related to mizuna, distinguished by long, thin leaves (*Joy Larkcom*)

hybrids have broader, less serrated leaves. It is used raw or cooked, and has a mild mustard flavour. Although it grows best in cool weather, it tolerates both high and low temperatures reasonably well. It is moderately hardy, hardiness increasing when the plants are kept trimmed back (see page 90). It is a useful plant for edging beds or for undercropping, and responds very well to cut-and-come-again treatment at any stage. *DVG*

For sowing methods and times see Komatsuna (page 109). For small plants space 4 in (10 cm) apart; for medium plants 8 in (20 cm) apart; for large plants 14 in (35 cm) apart. Watch out for flea beetle attacks in hot-weather sowings.

Recommended cultivars. Mizuna Greens, F1 Tokyo Beau (very hardy)

Mibuna Greens. Very closely related to mizuna, mibuna forms a striking plant with deep green, long, thin leaves. Cultivation and use are as for mizuna. It is slightly less hardy.

MUSTARD *Sinapis alba*

The traditional partner to cress, mustard is milder-flavoured but faster-growing. For cultivation see Cress page 106), but sow two days later if the two are required together. It runs to seed faster than cress, so is less productive as a cut-and-come-again crop.

MUSTARDS, ORIENTAL (see *Oriental Mustards*)

ONION *Allium cepa* (Bulb onion, pickling onion, spring onion)

The many types of onion are used cooked and raw, fresh and stored, as a vegetable and for seasoning. Bulbing types include tiny pickling onions and spring onions, pulled young to use whole as tiny immature bulbs with green leaf. Also used green are Welsh and oriental bunching onion (see below).

Bulb onion. Of various shapes and white, yellow or reddish in colour, bulb onions tolerate light frost, grow best in cool climates, and require a cool period in the early stages of growth. Different types respond to different day lengths, so always grow cultivars recommended for the area. Only certain cultivars are suitable for storage. Onions need fertile, medium to light soil with good drainage, prepared by digging in well-rotted manure several months before planting. Avoid very heavy soils; lime very acid soil. It is important to rotate over at least a three-year cycle, preferably longer, to avoid the build-up of white rot disease in the soil. Onions are fiddly to weed and do not make a weed-suppressing canopy, so make sure the soil is weed-free. To keep down weeds, onions are sometimes grown successfully planted through black plastic film.

Bulb onions require a long growing season: the earlier they are sown the better. They can be raised from seed or from 'sets ' (specially raised small bulbs). These are easy to grow, mature fast, and often avoid onion fly attacks.

Maincrop and storage onions. From seed: make the earliest sowings indoors in gentle heat during winter or early spring. Sow in seed trays or in modules. These can be multi-sown with about five seeds per module. Harden off and plant out in early spring. Sow *in situ* outdoors as soon as the soil is warm and workable. The failure rate will be high in cold soil. Rake the soil smooth, and sow thinly in rows about 9 in (23 cm) apart.

From sets. Plant in early spring as soon as the soil is workable, except for sets which have been heat-treated to prevent premature sprouting. Plant these later, according to the supplier's instructions. Plant sets in a shallow furrow, with the tips just protruding, in rows about 9 in (23 cm) apart.

The eventual size of the onion is determined by spacing: the wider the spacing the larger the onion. For a good yield of medium-sized onions thin or plant to about 1½ in (4 cm) apart. Use thinnings as spring onions. Plant multi-sown modules about 8 in (20 cm) apart each way. Keep

Onions growing in multi-sown blocks *(John Walker)*

Bunching onion, Ishikuro *(Joy Larkcom)*

plants weed-free, especially in the early stages: little further attention is required, and extra watering is rarely necessary. Pull onions for use fresh when they reach a useful size, generally five to six months after sowing.

Harvesting and storage. Onions for storage should be allowed to die back naturally; the leaves should *not* be bent over, which may lead to disease in storage. Handle the onions gently, ease them out of the ground, and dry them as fast as possible, raised off the ground on boxes, or hanging on a wall, until the outer skins are paper-dry. In wet weather finish off the drying in a greenhouse. Store them in a frost-free, dry place, plaited, or loose in nets, or in single layers in boxes. Never store thick-necked or damaged bulbs. Depending on the cultivar, they will keep up to about six months.

Overwintering onions for early supplies. Very early onions can be grown to bridge the gap between the last of the stored onions in late spring, and the current season's onions reaching a usable size. Either plant sets of suitable hardy types (see recommended cultivars) in autumn or early winter, or sow the Japanese overwintering types in late summer. These must be neither too large nor too small at the onset of winter. The sowing date is critical: follow the supplier's recommendation for the area. Sow 1 in (2·5 cm) apart in rows 12 in (30 cm) apart. In spring thin them out, and give them a liquid feed. These types are unsuitable for storage.

Pickling onion. These do not require very fertile soil. Sow in spring broadcast or in 4 in (10 cm) wide bands, spacing seeds about ½ in (1·25 cm) apart. Do not thin them. Lift for pickling when about ¾ in (2cm) in diameter.

Spring onion. For soil see Bulb onion. Acid soils must be limed. For a continuous supply sow from early spring to the end of summer, making the first sowings under cover, and using hardy types for the last sowing. These can be protected with covers in mid-winter. Sow thinly in rows 4 in (10 cm) apart. Pull when they reach the size required.

Pests and diseases. Onion fly, stem and bulb eelworm; downy mildew, white rot, neck rot (in storage)

Recommended cultivars. Bulb (for use fresh or stored): F1 Caribo (ROG), F1 Hygro (ROG), Mammoth Red (red), Rijnsburger – Balstora (ROG) and Robusta, Southport Red Globe (red), Sturon, Stuttgarter Giant; overwintering Japanese: F1 Buffalo; autumn sets: Unwins First Early; pickling: Barletta, Paris Silver Skin; spring onion: White Lisbon, White Lisbon – Winter Hardy (hardiest)

ONION, WELSH AND ORIENTAL BUNCHING
Allium fistulosum

These types are grown mainly for the green leaf, used raw in salads or for seasoning.

Traditional Welsh Onion (Ciboule). A perennial plant, with hollow leaves which remain green all year round and a slightly thickened stem, Welsh onion makes a good semi-permanent edging. Sow *in situ* in spring or late summer, in rows about 10 in (25 cm) apart, thinning in stages to 8 in (20 cm) apart.

Start using spring-sown plants in autumn, either cutting leaves above soil level, or pulling up clumps whole. Summer-sown plants will be ready the following spring. Clumps should be lifted every two or three years and divided, replanting the younger outer sections in a fresh site.

Oriental bunching onion. In Asia many vigorous, high-yielding types have been developed from the Welsh onion. Depending on the cultivar, they can be used at all stages from very young, fine leaves to a strong leek-like stem with thick hollow leaves. Some types are very hardy. For soil requirements see Onion (above).

They can be grown as annuals or biennials. Most useful currently are the hardy types. Either sow indoors in early spring as for bulb onion, or sow *in situ* outdoors in spring as for Welsh onion. Sow or plant in rows about 12 in (30 cm) apart, spacing plants eventually about 3 in (7·5 cm) apart. Cut leaves when they reach a usable size, usually within about three months of sowing. With hardy types a second sowing can be made in late summer for use early the following year.

Recommended cultivars. Ishikuro, White Evergreen

ORIENTAL GREENS
(See also Brassicas)

This large group of brassicas is gradually becoming known in the West, with exciting new hybrids and cultivars being introduced. The F1 hybrids are of excellent quality. The oriental greens are generally cool-season crops, and do not grow well at very high temperatures. The types covered in this book – Chinese cabbage, Komatsuna, Mizuna and Mibuna greens, Oriental mustards, Oriental saladini and Pak choi – are among the easiest to grow and are exceptionally productive. They have several outstanding characteristics:

• They are naturally vigorous and fast-growing, often maturing six to eight weeks after sowing.
• They have a long season of use, especially if cut-and-come-again techniques are used.
• Most can be used at all stages: as seedlings, as

semi-mature or mature plants, at the flowering shoot stage when the plants bolt. They can be 'cut-and-come-again' at all these stages. The young flowering shoots, which are akin to broccoli spears, are in most cases very sweet and tender.

- They can be used cooked or raw, display an excellent range of flavours, and have attractive, healthy-looking leaves.
- Their main season of use is late summer into winter and early spring. The exceptionally hardy types are ideal winter and spring vegetables. Many can be grown outdoors, or, for improved quality, under cover.

Soil. To grow well, oriental greens must have very fertile, moisture-retentive soil into which plenty of organic matter has been worked. Because they grow very fast, they need plenty of moisture throughout growth. They tend to be shallow-rooted, so where extra watering is necessary, water frequently but moderately, unlike the recommended practice for western brassicas.

Sowing. Many of the oriental greens have a tendency to bolt prematurely if sown early in the year, due to factors such as day length, low temperatures and the bolting susceptibility of the cultivar. For this reason the main sowings are:

- Mid- to late summer for early autumn/winter crops. These can often be sown after early crops of peas, bean, potatoes, onions etc. are lifted.
- Early autumn for crops which will be grown under cover in winter.
- Spring, mainly for cut-and-come-again seedlings which can be cut a couple of times before running to seed, but also for quick crops of bolt-resistant types.

Best results are usually obtained by sowing in modules and transplanting. The main exception is cut-and-come-again seedling sowings *in situ*.

Pests and diseases. The oriental greens are susceptible to the same range as western brassicas. The very tender leaves of some types are especially vulnerable to slugs, flea beetle and caterpillars. Growing them under fine nets and fleecy films is highly recommended.

ORIENTAL MUSTARDS *Brassica juncea*
(See also Oriental Greens)

This is a very large and diverse group of plants, with coarser leaves than other oriental brassicas. They are hot-flavoured, and excellent cooked. Some types are adapted to high temperatures, others, including some beautiful purple-leaved and purple-tinged types, are exceptionally hardy. They are naturally healthy plants. They are slower-growing than the oriental greens, so are not generally suited to cut-and-come-again

Oriental red mustard, hot-flavoured, exceptionally hardy and healthy (*Joy Larkcom*)

treatment at the seedling stage, though semi-mature and mature plants respond well. The flowering shoots are edible, but can become extremely pungent.

The main sowing is in mid-summer for an autumn/winter crop. Either sow *in situ* and thin out, or in seed trays or modules for transplanting. Average spacing is about 12 in (30 cm) apart. Plants transplanted under cover in early autumn can be spaced up to 14 in (35 cm) apart, as growth is very vigorous under cover.

Recommended cultivars. Amsoi (moderately hardy), Green in the Snow (very hardy), Miike Giant and Osaka Purple (very hardy, reddish)

ORIENTAL SALADINI
(See also Oriental Greens)

The different types of oriental greens blend well together in cooking, and seed can be mixed and sown together. This can be cut young for salads, or, at a later stage, as greens for stir-frying and so on. Such mixtures have become known as 'oriental saladini'. Either buy commercial packets, or mix your own. A typical mixture would consist of 25% each of pak choi, mizuna,

Oriental saladini grown in a seed tray in potting compost (*Joy Larkcom*)

komatsuna and loose-headed Chinese cabbage; there is plenty of scope for experimenting. If sowing early, include bolt-resistant cultivars where possible. Measure the seeds in a teaspoon.

Sow very thinly as a cut-and-come-again seedling crop. Make the first sowings under cover in spring, followed by outdoor sowings. Continue sowing at roughly monthly intervals, except in very hot weather. The last sowings can be made in late summer or under cover in early autumn. Always sow in fertile soil and keep it well watered. In most cases the mixture can be cut once or twice as seedlings, and then left to develop into taller plants for use as greens. If sown thinly further thinning should be unnecessary. Plants remain productive over several weeks, but eventually run to seed, producing edible flowering shoots.

PAK CHOI *Brassica rapa* var. *chinensis* (See also Oriental Greens)

Pak choi is an attractive, smooth-leaved plant. In some types the leaf base broadens into a characteristic spoon-like shape; others have long slender leaf-stalks. Leaves, stems and flowering shoots can all be eaten at any stage, and have a refreshing, distinct flavour, somewhat stronger than Chinese cabbage. Pak choi ranges in size from small plants only 4 in (10 cm) high when mature to large, 24 in (60 cm) high plants. There are white- and green-stemmed forms, the latter considered superior in flavour. Mature plants survive light frosts, but immature and cut-and-come-again plants survive more severe weather. Cultivars vary in their resistance to bolting from

Pak choi: the whole plant is edible including leaves, stems and flowering shoots (*Jacqui Hurst*)

early sowings, and in their rate of growth. Some mature within six weeks of sowing.

For sowing times and methods see Loose-headed Chinese cabbage (page 105). Use bolt-resistant cultivars for the earliest sowings. Where mature plants are being grown, space them from 4 to 14 in (10–35 cm) apart, depending on the type. Early and late cut- and-come-again seedling crops are exceptionally good value.

Recommended cultivars. F1 hybrids with reasonable bolting resistance: Mei Ching Choi, Shanghai (both green-stemmed), Joi Choi (white-stemmed)

PARSLEY, HAMBURG (Turnip-rooted parsley) *Petroselinum crispum*

This is a very hardy, dual-purpose type of parsley. The leaves, which remain green and usable in winter, are like French or Italian parsley, and are used similarly. The smooth, well-flavoured root closely resembles parsnip and is used in the same way. It makes a useful winter edging. Grow Hamburg parsley like parsnip (below). It does not need as long a growing season, so can be sown in late spring and early summer. Pick the leaves from summer to the following spring. Lift roots as required.

PARSNIP *Pastinaca sativa*

Parsnip is a very hardy, cool-season crop, grown for its sweet-flavoured root, which is used cooked, mainly as a winter vegetable. It does not require very fertile soil but does best in deep, light, stone-free soils. On very shallow soil grow the shorter types.

Parsnip seed germinates slowly, and loses its viability fast, so never use seed more than two years old. Although parsnip requires a long growing season, delay sowing *in situ* outdoors until the soil is warm and in good condition. Sow evenly in rows about 12 in (30 cm) apart. Or station sow in groups of two to three seeds about 3 in (7·5 cm) apart, intersowing with a fast-growing crop like radish to mark the rows. Thin in stages to 6 in (15 cm) apart for very large roots, or 3 to 4 in (7·5–10 cm) apart for medium-sized roots. Parsnip can also be sown earlier indoors, in modules, provided it is planted out *before* the tap root has developed. Where it proves difficult to grow, this method is worth trying.

Parsnip is slow-growing, so must be kept weed-free or it will be smothered. Watering is necessary only in very dry conditions. Water then every eighteen days or so, at the rate of 2 gal/sq yd (9 l/sq m), to make the roots swell. Roots are normally ready about seven months after sowing. Except in very severe climates, leave the roots in the ground in winter, to conserve the flavour. Mark the ends of the rows so they can be found in snow. They may be covered with bracken or straw to make lifting easier in frosty conditions.

Pests and diseases. Celery fly, carrot fly, lettuce root aphid; parsnip canker

Recommended cultivars. All these have canker resistance: Avonresister, Cobham Improved Marrow, F1 Gladiator, White Gem, White Spear

PEAS *Pisum sativum*

Peas are cool-season crops, the plants tolerating frost in the early stages of growth. *Garden peas* are grown for the shelled peas, used fresh, dried or frozen. The edible podded *mangetout* or *sugar pea* types are grown for the flat or rounded pods, which have outstanding flavour and are highly productive. Peas cling to supports with tendrils, and range from dwarf bush types, requiring minimum support, to much higher-yielding types over 5 ft (150 cm) tall. In the 'semi-leafless' types leaves are modified into tendrils so plants cling to each other, becoming virtually self-supporting. The resulting 'airiness' makes them very disease-free. Peas are grouped into earlies and maincrop: the former mature faster but are lower-yielding.

Peas require reasonably fertile soil: the nodules on their roots fix soil nitrogen, so enriching the soil. Good soil drainage and plenty of moisture throughout growth are key requirements, both aided by working in plenty of organic matter. In summer peas can be grown in light shade.

Sowing times and methods. The main sowing for summer supplies is in spring, as peas do not grow well in hot weather. Sow *in situ* outdoors from early spring to early summer. Delay the first sowing until the soil is 50°F (10°C), as germination is poor in cold or wet soil. To

Mangetout, Bamby *(Joy Larkcom)*

overcome this seed can be pre-germinated indoors (see *Propagation* page 75), and sown carefully once sprouted. Early sowings can be made under cloches or protective films. To get a succession either sow at three-week intervals, starting with early types, or sow different types at the same time so they mature over several weeks. For an autumn crop, sow in late summer using an early type. In *mild* areas, hardy dwarf types can be sown outdoors in early winter to mature in spring, though losses from mice may be high. It is advisable to set mousetraps for several weeks before sowing to clear the mouse population.

Three ways to sow peas

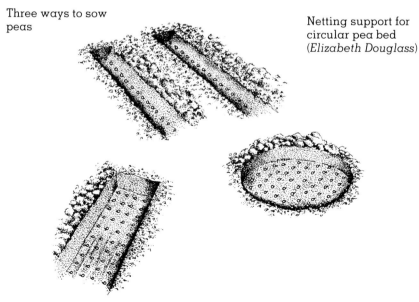

Netting support for circular pea bed *(Elizabeth Douglass)*

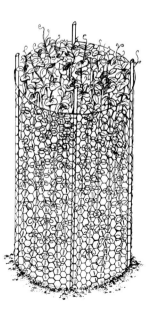

Stage at which peas should be supported using traditional twigs or pea netting (*Roy Lacey*)

Spacing. As a general rule, sow dwarf and semi-leafless types about 2 in (5 cm) apart, and taller types about 3 in (7·5 cm) apart. However, research has shown that peas spaced as much as 4·5 in (11 cm) apart each way have less competition and crop over a longer period. Peas can be sown in several ways: in pairs of drills 9 in (23 cm) apart; at equidistant spacing in flat-bottomed drills up to 8 in (20 cm) wide; spaced evenly across a bed or within a circular area.

Once they are about 3 in (7·5 cm) high and starting to develop tendrils, they should be supported. Use pea or bean netting, wire netting, or criss-crossed canes or twigs. Place them behind or down the centre of double rows or wide drills, or surrounding patches or circles.They should be at least 4 ft (120 cm) high for tall types.

Protect peas from birds in the early stages, and keep them mulched. Extra watering may be necessary in dry periods, but is most needed when flowers and pods are forming. Water weekly then at the rate of 4 gal/sq yd (18 l/sq m).

Peas mature eleven to fifteen weeks after sowing. Pick constantly to encourage production. Flat *mangetout* types are ready when the tiny peas are just visible within the pod; the rounded Sugar Snap type when plump. *Mangetout* peas can be left to grow larger and shelled like garden peas. To harvest dry peas, see Beans (page 95).

Pests and diseases. Birds, mice, pea moth, pea thrips; damping off, root rots, pea wilt

Recommended cultivars. Early: Hurst Beagle (hardy dwarf); maincrop: Dark-Skinned Perfection, Hurst Green Shaft, Tristar, Poppet (semi-leafless); *mangetout*: Oregon Sugarpod, Sugar Rae, Sugar Snap; drying: Maro, Progreta

PEPPER, SWEET *Capsicum annuum*
The pepper is a tender warm-season crop. It is less frost-tolerant than tomato and requires somewhat higher temperatures during growth. In cool climates grow it in the open in a warm, sheltered situation; otherwise grow it in a frame, or protected by cloches in the early stages. Grow only early fruiting F1 hybrid cultivars or compact dwarf types, in well-drained, moderately fertile soil.

For cultivation see *Growing Under Cover*, page 342. Sow about six weeks before the last frost is expected, prick out into 3 in (7·5 cm) pots, and plant out, after hardening off well, when the first flowers are visible. Space dwarf types 12 in (30 cm) apart, and others 16 in (40 cm) apart. Outdoor plants do not grow very tall, but can be supported with canes if necessary. If plants seem weak and spindly remove the first 'king fruit' on the main stem to encourage side shoots to develop. Nip off the ends of shoots once fruits start to form. Outdoor peppers usually have to be harvested immature, while still green. If frost threatens at the end of the season pull up the plants whole and hang them in a sunny place under cover. They may continue to ripen, and will keep in good condition for several months.

Recommended cultivars. Early F1 hybrids: Bendigo, Canape, New Ace, Early Prolific, Redskin (dwarf)

POTATO *Solanum tuberosum*
Potatoes are tender, cool-season crops. The many types range from the fastest-maturing but lower-yielding earlies, which require about ninety frost-free days before harvest, to the slower-maturing, heavier-yielding maincrops, which require up to 140 frost-free days. Potatoes must be rotated carefully. They are hungry feeders, requiring plenty of moisture during growth, and fertile, moisture -retentive, slightly acid soil into which plenty of manure has been worked. Soil fertility can be increased by lining the potato trenches with comfrey leaves or grass cuttings; the latter may help reduce the 'cosmetic' disease scab in dry seasons.

The main cultivars of potato vary in their resistance to pests and disease and suitability for different climates and soils. Try several until the most suitable are found for your conditions (see table). Earlies require less space and time and are healthier, so most worth growing in small gardens.

For planting buy certified, disease-free seed tubers of about the size of a hen's egg. Potatoes cannot be planted outside until the soil temperature is about 45°F (7°C) and the risk of heavy frost is past, but they can be 'chitted' or sprouted indoors beforehand to get growth started.

About six weeks before the last frost place them in shallow trays, out of direct sunlight, with the end where the 'eyes' or buds are visible uppermost. They can be planted when the

Potato varieties suitable for organic growing

| | Characteristics | | | Resistance to diseases and pests | | | | | | | |
	YIELD	FOLIAGE COVER	DROUGHT TOLERANCE	BLIGHT	BLACKLEG	COMMON SCAB	VIRUS Y (MOSAIC)	LEAF ROLL VIRUS	SPRAING	SLUG DAMAGE	GOLDEN POTATO CYST NEMATODE (PCN)
Early											
Maris Bard	***	**	**	**	**	**	***	**	*	–	*
Pentland Javelin	**	**	**	**	**	***	***	**	*	–	***
Premiere	***	**	–	**	–	**	**	**	–	–	***
Second early and maincrop											
Cara	***	***	***	***	**	**	**	***	**	*	***
Desiree	***	**	***	**	**	**	***	**	*	**	*
Estima	***	**	***	**	*	**	*	**	*	*	*
Pentland Crown	***	***	***	**	**	***	***	***	*	**	*
Pentland Squire	***	**	***	**	**	**	**	**	*	**	*
Romano	***	**	**	**	**	**	***	*	***	**	*
Sante	***	***	–	**	*	**	***	***	**	**	***
Stroma	***	**	**	**	***	***	***	**	**	*	**
Wilja	***	**	**	**	**	***	*	**	**	**	*

The varieties in the table are rated good for organic growing (National Institute of Agricultural Botany Potato Variety Handbook, 1992). They tend to bulk up reasonably early, so enabling the crop to escape blight, or to produce a good yield even when infected with blight or adverse growing conditions. Good foliage cover is an indication of general vigour, besides suppressing weeds. Choose varieties with resistance to the most prevalent pest or disease problems in your area, e.g. common scab on dry, chalky soils; golden potato eelworm on allotments or where rotation is impracticable; slug damage and blackleg in wet soils; blight in wet summers. (Most new varieties now have good resistance to blight, virus, and nematodes.) The performance of varieties varies widely according to local conditions.

Key
*** = high yield; dense foliage cover; high drought tolerance; good disease and pest resistance; resistant to golden potato cyst nematode
** = medium yield; medium foliage cover; medium drought tolerance; medium disease and pest resistance; partial resistance to golden potato cyst nematode
* = low yield; poor foliage cover; low drought tolerance; low disease or pest resistance; susceptible to golden potato cyst nematode
– = unknown

developing shoots are ¾ to 2 in (2–5 cm) long.

Plant potatoes upright in shallow trenches, deep drills or individual holes, so that the tuber is covered by at least 1 in (2.5 cm) of soil. Plant early potatoes about 14 in (35 cm) apart in rows about 17 in (42 cm) apart. Plant maincrops about 15 in (37.5 cm) apart in rows 30 in (75 cm) apart. After planting it is advisable to cover with a 6 in (15 cm) layer of straw or other organic mulch. This gives some frost protection, helps retain moisture, and benefits the soil. Early crops can also be covered with cloches or clear or fleecy films. Where potatoes are unprotected, cover them with newspaper at night if frost is forecast in the early stages. During growth potato tubers push above ground and become greened and poisonous. To prevent this earth up the stems when plants are about 9 in (23 cm) high, drawing soil from between the rows 4 in (10 cm) up the stems. Repeat if tubers reappear near the surface. Green potatoes should be peeled thickly and all green parts removed; likewise, in fresh or stored potatoes toxins can build up around bruises, diseased and damaged tissue, which should also be cut out before cooking.

Planting under black film. To avoid earthing up and to make lifting easy, potatoes can be planted

No-dig potatoes growing on surface under black polythene film (*Photos Horticultural*)

Potato crop after film is pulled aside (*Chris Algar*)

Cara, a high-yielding maincrop potato, enjoying top rating for most categories of pest and disease resistance, including blight (*Marshalls*)

under heavy black film. Plant on the surface, cover with film, anchoring the edges in the soil, and when the foliage presses against the film cut triangular holes to pull it through. Alternatively lay and anchor the film, make planting holes and push the tubers through. The film is simply lifted to pull up potatoes when required: they will be found on the surface. Unless maincrop potatoes are watered by hand, this method is suitable only for early potatoes.

In dry conditions yields of early potatoes will be increased by watering every two weeks at up to 4 gal/sq yd (18 l/sq m). Water maincrop potatoes after they reach marble size; one single watering at the above rate increases tuber size and yields. Scrape away the soil carefully to ascertain when this stage is reached.

Provided the plants are healthy, and there is not a serious slug problem, leave maincrop potatoes to develop into early autumn. If the potato haulm is diseased and infected with blight, cut it just above soil level in late summer, remove it and burn it, and lift the potatoes two weeks later after the skins have hardened. They are ready if the skin remains firm when rubbed. Otherwise cut the haulm and harvest before frost. After lifting, leave the tubers on the surface for no more than a couple of hours to dry off, reject damaged or unhealthy tubers, and store them in hessian or paper sacks in a cool, frost-free place.

Pests and diseases. Slugs, wireworm, cutworm, potato cyst eelworm; blight, blackleg, common scab, storage rots, various virus diseases

Recommended cultivars. See table, page 119

PUMPKIN (Winter squash) *Cucurbita maxima; C. moschata, C. pepo*

The diverse pumpkin group is characterized by gourds which can be eaten fresh or stored for up to six months. They can be long, round or onion-shaped; smooth or rough-skinned; almost any colour; and anything up to 70 lbs (30 kgs) in weight. Flowers, young shoot tips and leaves are also edible. For climate, soil, cultivation, pests and diseases see Marrows, page 112. As most grow into very large, trailing plants, prepare somewhat larger holes than for marrows.

Seed can be soaked overnight before sowing to hasten germination. Space plants 6 to 10 ft (1·8–3 m) apart, depending on the cultivar, and mulch heavily once established. Trailing types can be trained in circles so that they occupy less ground, by pinning the shoots with wooden or wire pegs. Extra roots often develop from the stems which help feed the plants.

Harvesting. Most pumpkins mature three to four months after planting. For storage cut before frost, when the stems have started to crack. Cut with a long stalk, and leave them in a dry sunny place for up to ten days so that the skins can harden, protecting against frost at night. Store in an airy place at about 50°F (10°C).

Recommended cultivars. Acorn, Buttercup, Butternut, Hubbard, Hundredweight, Red Kuri, Rouge Vif d'Etampes, Spaghetti marrow, Sweet Dumpling

PURSLANE, SUMMER *Portulaca oleracea*

Purslane is a tender, succulent-leaved, warmth-loving annual, grown for its leaves and stems, used mainly raw in salads. There are yellow- and green-leaved forms, the latter heavier-yielding, the former very decorative. Grow it in a sunny sheltered situation on light, well-drained soil. For climate, general cultivation and harvesting see Iceplant, page 108. Either grow as single plants spaced 6 in (15 cm) apart, or, for earlier pickings, grow as a cut-and-come-again seedling crop. Spring and late summer sowings can be made under cover. Watch out for slugs in the early stages.

PURSLANE, WINTER (Claytonia, Miner's lettuce) *Montia perfoliata*

Winter purslane is a moderately hardy, mild-flavoured salad plant which grows best in cool weather. The slightly succulent young pointed leaves and the mature, rounded leaves, as well as the stems and flowers, are edible raw. Provided the soil is well drained it tolerates all conditions from low fertility, to very sandy soil, to heavy clay. Once established, it self-seeds freely.

Sow in spring for summer use, or in summer for autumn to winter use. Make a late sowing at the end of summer to transplant under cover for a very productive winter to spring crop. Sow *in situ*, or in seed trays for transplanting. The seed is very small. Grow it either as single plants spaced about 6 in (15 cm) apart, or as a cut-and-come-again seedling crop. The first cuts can be made about eight weeks after sowing.

RADISH *Raphanus sativus*

With a few exceptions, radish is a cool-season crop, grown primarily for its root. The small salad radishes tolerate only light frost, but some of the larger types, which can also be cooked, are moderately hardy. The young leaves and immature seed-pods of some types are edible. Radishes need plenty of moisture throughout growth and grow best on rich, light soil; the large types, which can be up to 12 in (30 cm) long, require deep, stone-free soil. These should be rotated in the brassica group, as they are in the soil for several months.

Small types. Sow *in situ* from early spring to early autumn, either broadcast, or in drills about 5 in (12.5 cm) apart, or in bands about 4 in (10 cm) wide. Always sow very thinly; if seeds are spaced 1 in (2.5 cm) apart, no further thinning is necessary. Otherwise thin *early* (seedlings never recover if they become leggy) to at least 1 in (2.5 cm) apart. These types are ready to pull within four weeks of sowing. In dry weather water at the rate of 2 gal/sq yd (9 l/sq m) every week.

Large types. These can be divided into the long-rooted, usually white, oriental mooli (daikon), which are mainly summer radishes, and the large, round or long, black, red or violet-skinned hardy overwintering radishes. For the mooli type the main sowing is from early summer to early autumn; earlier sowings run the risk of bolting, except with a few bolt-resistant cultivars. Sow *in situ*, thinning to about 4 in (10 cm) apart depending on cultivar.

Sow the hardy, overwintering radishes from mid- to late summer, thinning early (see small types, above) to about 9 in (23 cm) apart. In most areas they can be left in the soil during winter and lifted as required. Mulch with straw to lessen frost penetration, and make lifting easier. Slugs may be a problem in heavy soil. In very cold areas lift in autumn, cut off the foliage, and store in boxes or straw-covered heaps in a cellar or frost-free shed. On average the large radishes are ready ten to twelve weeks after sowing. Water as for small radishes.

Winter purslane, tolerant of most soil conditions, makes a pleasant addition to the salad bowl (Joy Larkcom)

F1 April Cross, an oriental mooli variety for early summer to early autumn sowings
(Harry Smith)

Radish seed-pods. Young, crisp, green seed-pods have an excellent flavour and texture and can be used raw, cooked or pickled. The best pods are obtained from large mooli, overwintered radishes, and a few large-podded cultivars. Allow a plant to run to seed in late summer, or, for hardy types, in early spring.

Seedling radish. Most cultivars of small radish can be used for a cut-and-come-again seedling leaf crop, instead of for the roots. Mooli types such as Bisai have been selected for leaf and are high-yielding. The most useful sowings for seedling radish are in spring, late summer and autumn. Make the first and last sowings under cover. They can be cut three to four weeks after sowing. If Bisai is left beyond the seedling stages larger leaves develop which can be cooked.

Pests. Flea beetle, slugs, cabbage root fly

Recommended cultivars. Small types: Crystal Ball, French Breakfast, Pontvil, Red Prince, Sparkler; summer mooli: F1 April Cross, F1 Minowase Summer Cross No. 2; for seed-pods: Munchen Bier; for seedling leaves: Bisai

RAPE, SALAD *Brassica napus*

This mild-flavoured, fast-growing, very hardy plant is often substituted for mustard in 'mustard and cress'. For cultivation see Cress page 106. It responds very well to cut-and-come-again treatment, and if sown thinly, can often be left to grow into plants about 2 ft (60 cm) high and used for cooked greens.

RHUBARB *Rheum x cultorum*

Rhubarb is a large hardy perennial plant, grown for the leaf stalks, which are used cooked as a fruit. It grows best in cool climates, on well-drained, moisture-retentive, fertile soil. It tolerates acid soils. Before planting work in plenty of well-rotted manure or compost. Rhubarb must be grown in an open position. Its large leaves are poisonous if eaten, but make weed-suppressing ground cover.

Plant rhubarb when it is dormant, from early winter (preferably) to spring. For top-quality rhubarb plant 'sets' – pieces of root with a large bud – from a good strain guaranteed virus-free. Either purchase sets, or take them from a good established plant after the leaves have died down. Lift the plant (it can be replanted afterwards) and slice through the rootstock with a sharp spade, selecting pieces roughly 4 in (10 cm) in diameter. Plant at least 3 ft (90 cm) apart; on light soil plant with the buds just below ground level, but on heavy soil buds should be above ground.

Rhubarb after forcing (*Joy Larkcom*)

Rhubarb can be raised from seed, but this is slower and plants will be of variable quality. Sow in spring in an outdoor seed bed in rows 12 in (30 cm) apart. Thin to 15 cm (6 in) apart and plant the most vigorous in autumn or the following spring.

Keep rhubarb heavily mulched with manure or organic matter to maintain the soil fertility and moisture. The roots are deep, and it is necessary to water only in exceptionally dry weather. Cut off any flowering heads at the base. Plants can be given a liquid feed in spring if growth is weak. Rhubarb can last many years, but if the stems become spindly, lift and divide the crowns, replanting the younger outer parts in a fresh site.

To harvest rhubarb grasp the stem near the base and pull; it should not be cut. In the first year after planting sets, pull lightly in spring; with seed-raised plants, wait until the second year. Well-established plants can be pulled until the stems start to soften, usually in mid-summer.

Forcing. Rhubarb can be forced to get a very early, very tender crop. After the leaves have died back in winter cover the crowns with a 4 in (10 cm) layer of straw or dead leaves. Then exclude light by covering with a large upturned ashcan about 18 in (45 cm) high, or with a lidded, clay, rhubarb-blanching pot. The shoots are normally ready within about three weeks.

Diseases. Honey fungus, crown rot, virus diseases

Recommended cultivars. Champagne, Timperley Early, Victoria

SALAD, ROCKET (Rucola, Mediterranean rocket or cress) *Eruca vesicaria*

A moderately hardy, spicily flavoured plant, rocket is mainly used in salads though it can be cooked. It grows best in cool conditions; in very hot weather it runs to seed rapidly, becoming too hot-flavoured. It will grow on most soils provided they are well drained and retain some moisture.

It can be grown as single plants, or as a cut-and-come-again seedling crop. For a continuous supply, sow from early spring until autumn. Avoid mid-summer sowings in hot areas, or make them in light shade. The first and last sowings can be made under cover. Rocket is an excellent winter and spring salad. It is normally sown *in situ*. For single plants thin to 6 in (15 cm) apart. They respond well to cut-and-come-again treatment. Rocket germinates fast and seedling leaves may be ready within three weeks of sowing. It will often seed itself if a few plants are left to run to seed in late spring or autumn. Flea beetle is a common pest in the early stages.

SALSIFY (Oyster plant) *Tragopogon porrifolium*

Salsify is a hardy biennial grown mainly for its root, though the young shoots (chards) which develop in spring are blanched and used in salads; the flower buds are also edible. To get roots of a reasonable size, salsify must be grown on deep, light, stone-free soil. Avoid freshly manured soil.

Roots: sow *in situ* in spring, using fresh seed, in rows 6 in (15 cm) apart. Thin to 4 in (10 cm) apart. Little attention is required, other than keeping plants weed-free. Water only in very dry conditions. Roots are ready for lifting about six months after sowing. Except in very cold areas they can be left in the soil in winter. Otherwise store like winter radish (see page 121).

Chards: either cut back the stems and cover the roots in autumn (see Witloof chicory, page 104), or cover the plants with a 5 in (12·5 cm) layer of straw in spring. In both cases the young shoots push through, and can be cut and eaten raw when 4 to 6 in (10–15 cm) long.

Flower buds: leave a few plants in spring to produce flower stalks. Cut flowers in bud with at least 2 in (5 cm) of stem, which is also edible. They are excellent cooked and cooled. *DVG* in flower.

SCORZONERA *Scorzonera hispanica*

Scorzonera is very similar to salsify except that it is perennial, the root is black-skinned and probably better-flavoured, and the flowers are yellow instead of purple. Grow and use it as salsify, above. *DVG* in flower.

SHALLOT *Allium ascalonicum*

The shallot, which is used in cooking like the onion, is valued for its distinctive flavour and storage qualities. It can keep up to ten months after harvesting. For soil see Bulb onion, page 113. It is important to plant shallots which are guaranteed virus-free.

Plant single shallots of about ¾ in (2 cm) diameter; larger bulbs may bolt prematurely. In mild areas plant in winter, otherwise plant early in spring. Plant in shallow drills so that only the necks protrude above soil level, spacing them about 7 in (18 cm) apart. If they are uprooted by worms or birds, ease them out and replant, rather than pushing them back in, which may break the roots. In dry conditions they may need gentle watering in the early stages; otherwise little attention is required. They develop into a cluster, ready for lifting from mid-summer onwards, when the foliage has died down. Lift, dry and store as for onions. Provided bulbs are healthy, a few can be saved for planting the next season.

Pests and diseases. Although generally healthy, shallots are subject to the same problems as onions.

Recommended cultivars. Atlantic, Topper

SPINACH, Ordinary *Spinacea oleracea*

Spinach is a moderately hardy annual, very prone to premature bolting in hot weather and dry conditions. The leaves are used cooked and raw; they are probably the most nutritious and well-flavoured of the spinach-like plants. Spinach requires moderately fertile soil and plenty of moisture throughout growth. Most of the modern types are suitable for summer or winter crops.

Spinach can be grown as single plants or as a cut-and-come-again seedling crop. It is normally sown *in situ*, but can be sown in a seed tray and

Spinach as a cut-and-come-again seedling crop (Joy Larkcom)

transplanted. Seed germinates at low temperatures but not at soil temperatures above 86°F (30°C). For a continuous supply sow thinly from early spring (for summer supplies) to early autumn (for winter supplies) at roughly monthly intervals.

Omit mid-summer sowings in hot areas, or sow in light shade. Make the first and last sowings under cover. For single plants sow in rows about 12 in (30 cm) apart, thinning early to about 6 in (15 cm) apart. The first cut can usually be made within ten weeks of sowing; the plants can be treated as cut-and-come-again at any stage. Spring-sown plants generally run to seed fairly rapidly, but the summer crop may remain productive all winter and into the following spring, especially where protected.

Pests and diseases. Birds; downy mildew, leaf spot

Recommended cultivars. Medania, Norvak, Sigmaleaf

SPINACH, New Zealand *Tetragonia expansa*

This somewhat fleshy-leaved type of spinach is a half-hardy perennial, which sprawls over the ground. It is tolerant of high temperatures and dry conditions, so useful where ordinary spinach is hard to grow. It will produce a crop on fairly poor soil, but grows more lushly in fertile soil. Sow as for Iceplant (page 108), planting out after frost about 18 in (45 cm) apart. Plants can spread as much as 4 ft (120 cm). The tender shoots and young leaves can be picked from about eight weeks after sowing. Pick frequently to encourage further development of tender leaves.

SPINACH, Perpetual (Spinach Beet) *Beta vulgaris*

Similar to ordinary spinach in appearance but with larger leaves, perpetual spinach is a hardy biennial. It is more robust than spinach, and more tolerant of higher and lower temperatures and, to some extent, dry conditions. For soil, use, cultivation and pests and diseases see Spinach, above. As the plants can be cut over a longer period than spinach two sowings are sufficient: in spring for a summer crop, and in late summer for a winter/spring crop. Where grown as single plants space them 9 in (23 cm) apart. Perpetual spinach is a very useful winter crop under cover, grown either as single plants or as cut-and-come-again seedlings.

SWEDE *Brassica napus* Napobrassica group (See also Brassicas)

A moderately hardy brassica, swede is grown for its large, sweetly flavoured yellow- or (less commonly) white-fleshed roots, used cooked in winter. Soil must be well drained but water-retentive; swede does not withstand drought

Swede clamp (*Elizabeth Douglass*)

well. Sow in late spring *in situ*, thinning plants in stages until they are about 10 in (25 cm) apart. In dry conditions water occasionally at the rate of 2 gal/sq yd (9 l/sq m). Roots mature on average twenty-three weeks after sowing. They can be left in the ground until severe frost is likely, when they should be lifted to prevent deterioration. Cut off the leaves and store the roots in a clamp outdoors in a sheltered spot on well-drained ground. Put an 8 in (20 cm) layer of straw on the ground, pile the swedes on it in tapering layers (so rain will run off), and cover with a second layer of straw. They keep well until spring. Alternatively store in boxes like beetroot.

Pests and diseases. See Brassicas. Mildew is a common problem

Recommended cultivars. Marian (some resistance to mildew and club root)

SWEETCORN *Zea mais*

Sweetcorn is a tender plant grown for its cobs, which are usually cooked. Depending on the cultivar, it requires 70 to 110 frost-free days to mature, but it does not tolerate very high summer temperatures. In cool areas grow early, fast-maturing types. Grow sweetcorn in a sheltered site, on reasonably fertile, well-drained soil. As the leaves do not form a dense canopy it can be under-cropped with salad plants, dwarf beans, courgettes, etc. The new 'supersweet' types have exceptional flavour and keep sweet longer, but are harder to get going at low temperatures. Do not grow them in the same garden as ordinary types, as the sweetness will be lost with cross-pollination.

Sow sweetcorn *in situ*, after soil temperatures are above 50°F (10°C). To assist wind pollination, plants should be grown in a block formation, at least four plants deep, rather than in rows. Sow groups of three seeds, spaced about 12 in (30 cm) apart each way, thinning to one plant after germination. Or sow indoors in modules (to

Cobs are ready for picking when their silks turn deep brown (*Harry Smith*)

Texsel greens, a recently developed vegatable with an interesting flavour (*Horticulture Research International*)

avoid checking on planting) about six weeks before the last frost, and transplant. Sweetcorn can be sown *in situ* under small jam jars, or sown or planted under protective films or cloches, but remove films by the five-leaf stage. If sown under clear film or black plastic mulches, cut holes to pull the seedlings through after germination.

In windy areas earth up the stems of young plants to give extra support. Water is most needed when first the tassels, and later the cobs, develop: in dry areas water heavily at those stages. Cobs are ready for picking when their silks are turning deep brown, and juice exuded from a kernel punctured with a thumbnail is 'milky' rather than watery or 'doughy'.

Pests. Mice, birds, slugs, frit fly

Recommended cultivars (all F1 hybrids, in order of maturity). Pilot, Sunrise, Earlibelle; supersweet: Candle, Sweet Nugget, Conquest, Two's Sweeter (bi-colour)

SWISS CHARD (Silver or seakale beet) *Beta vulgaris* 'Cicla' group
Swiss chard is a very hardy biennial with large, glossy, spinach-like leaves and broad white or pinkish midribs and leaf stalks, which can be cooked and used as a separate vegetable. It is naturally vigorous and healthy and is more tolerant of high temperatures than spinach. It requires fertile, moisture-retentive soil with plenty of organic matter worked in. Very acid soils should be limed.

It is grown mainly as single plants, which however respond well to cut-and-come-again treatment as mature plants. It can remain productive over many months. Two sowings a

year ensure a continuous supply. Sow in spring for plants which will crop from summer until the following spring; sow in summer for plants which will crop from autumn through to the following summer. Plant a few under cover in late summer, for a top-quality winter to spring crop. Either sow *in situ*, or in seed trays or modules for transplanting. Sow thinly, as germination is usually very high. Space plants 12 in (30 cm) apart each way. Keep plants mulched. Apply a liquid feed if growth is not vigorous. *DVG*

Recommended cultivars. Fordhook Giant, Lucullus

TEXSEL GREENS *Brassica carinata* (See also Brassicas)
Texsel greens is a useful, recently developed brassica; it has nutritious, glossy leaves with an excellent spinach-like flavour, used raw and cooked. It matures very rapidly, so can be grown in soils with a club root problem, and harvested before it becomes infected. It is moderately hardy.

Grow it either to harvest as spring greens or as a cut-and-come-again seedling crop. It will normally give two cuts. For spring greens sow outdoors *in situ* at three-week intervals from early spring to late summer, in rows about 6 in (15 cm) apart, thinning to 2 in (5 cm) apart. Pull up plants when about 10 in (25 cm) high, or cut them 1 in (2·5 cm) above the ground, leaving them to re-sprout. Even when running to seed the small leaves on the flowering stems are edible. Keep plants well watered in dry conditions. Sow also in very early spring and late autumn under cover, for 'greens' or cut-and-come-again seedlings.

TOMATO *Lycopersicon esculentum*
The tomato is a warm-season plant, growing ideally at temperatures of 70° to 75°F (21°–24°C) and in high light intensity. Young plants can

Tomatoes display a large variety of colour, shape and size. Most tomatoes can be grown outside (*Joy Larkcom*)

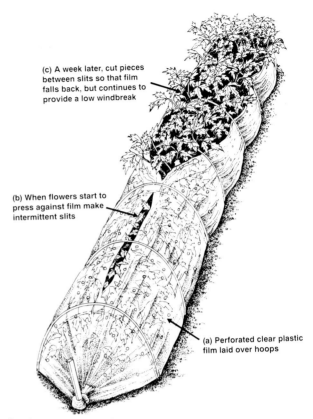

(c) A week later, cut pieces between slits so that film falls back, but continues to provide a low windbreak

(b) When flowers start to press against film make intermittent slits

(a) Perforated clear plastic film laid over hoops

Bush tomatoes under perforated film (*Elizabeth Douglass*)

stand very light frost. In cool climates grow tomatoes outdoors in a sheltered situation, such as against a south-facing wall. They will usually need some protection in the early stages, and may not ripen fully in poor summers. Outdoor tomatoes require well-drained, moderately fertile soil, and must be rotated carefully. Work in plenty of well-rotted manure or compost before planting. The ground can be prepared by making a trench 9 to 12 in (23–30 cm) deep, and lining it with comfrey leaves before refilling with soil.

Tall or cordon: this 'indeterminate' type grows several feet high on a main stem. The side shoots must be nipped out as they develop. When plants reach an appropriate height the tip is nipped out ('stopped') two leaves above a truss, to prevent further growth and concentrate energy on the maturing fruit.

Plants require staking or some kind of support such as wires stretched between poles. They can be grown outdoors under cloches or protective films in the early stages; when the cloches are outgrown they can be placed on their sides and 'wrapped around' the plants to give some shelter. 'Semi-determinate' types are tall types which 'stop' naturally when about 4 ft (120 cm) tall.

Bush: these are 'determinate' in that the main stem stops growing and develops into a number of branches which sprawl on the ground. The side shoots are not removed. Bush tomatoes are more suited to outdoor cropping, as they are easier to protect with cloches or films. A little support with twigs may be necessary to keep fruit off the ground.

Bush crops under perforated film. This method enables an earlier crop to be obtained in fairly cool areas. Raise bush cultivars in the normal way. Plant out, preferably through black and white film (see *Mulches*, page 47) and cover either with fleecy film laid directly over the plants, or with perforated clear plastic film laid over hoops. Unperforated film is unsuitable, as temperatures and humidity will rise too high. When the flowers start to press against the film make intermittent slits about 3 ft (90 cm) long down the centre to 'wean' them. Cut the pieces between slits a week later so the film falls back, but do not remove it completely, as the edges form a low windbreak.

Dwarf: these are naturally very small, compact bushes, which can be used in small containers or to edge beds, or protected as bush types, above. They are low-yielding, and often early-maturing. No support is necessary.

Raise plants as indoor tomatoes, sowing six to eight weeks before the last frost (see *Growing under Cover*, page 344). Harden off well before planting out. Plant when the first flower truss is visible, but delay planting if soil temperatures are below 50°F (10°C) or night temperatures below 45°F (7°C), unless plants are protected with covers. Planting through black and white mulching films is highly recommended. Average spacing for tall types is 16 in (40 cm) apart, bush types 21 in (53 cm), dwarf types 10 in (25 cm). Space somewhat closer for earlier crops and wider apart for higher yields. Mulching once the soil warms up is advisable. Bush and dwarf plants can be mulched with straw to keep the fruits clean, though this may attract slugs.

When flowers develop, slit or remove film mulches and ventilate or move cloches, to allow insect pollination. Remove side shoots on tall types and 'stop' them in mid-summer: in cool climates this will be after three to five trusses have developed. Avoid unnecessary watering, which can diminish flavour, but in dry weather water once flowering starts at a weekly rate of 2 gal/sq yd (9 l/sq m). Plants grown in dry situations, such as near walls, may need watering sooner. Supplementary feeding is normally unnecessary, except for plants grown in containers. Feed then as for indoor tomatoes. Remove and burn any dying or diseased leaves.

Fruits normally ripen about ten weeks after planting. They will be ruined by frost. If tall types seem unlikely to ripen before frost, spread straw on the ground in late summer, cut them down from their supports (but leaving the roots in the soil so they lie flat) and cover them with cloches or plastic film supported on low hoops to encourage ripening. Bush types can be covered similarly. Lift all plants before frost and hang them by the roots in a greenhouse or indoors to continue ripening. Individual green fruits can be wrapped loosely in paper and brought indoors, where they will colour up.

Pests and diseases. Birds, slugs, potato cyst eelworm; grey mould, stem rot, potato blight, potato mosaic virus

Recommended cultivars. Tall: Britain's Breakfast (solid, freeze well), Gardener's Delight (cherry), F1 Shirley, Supermarmande ('Marmande'type); bush (all hybrids): Alfresco, Pixie, Red Alert, Sleaford Abundance; dwarf: F1 Totem, Whippersnapper

TURNIP *Brassica campestris* Rapifera group
(See also Brassicas)

Although mainly grown for the root, turnip can also be grown for its leafy 'tops'. Both are normally cooked. Roots vary enormously in shape, skin and flesh colour. Early types are fast-maturing, less hardy and deteriorate fast on maturity; maincrop types are slower-maturing, stand longer, withstand light frost and are suitable for storage. Turnips grow best in fertile, moist, cool soil. The faster they grow, the better the quality.

Make the first sowings of early types in early spring under cover, followed by outdoor sowings. Make early sowings *in situ*, sowing thinly in rows about 6 in (15 cm) apart or in wide drills. Young turnips can usually be pulled without thinning; thin if necessary to about 3 in (7·5 cm) apart. They can be eaten as small as ¾ in (2 cm) in diameter, often five to six weeks after sowing. For a continuous supply sow every three weeks. Sow maincrop turnips in summer, thinly *in situ*; start thinning early, so that plants are eventually about 8 in (20 cm) apart each way. Water as for swedes if necessary. They take up to twelve weeks to mature. Use fresh, or lift and store before heavy frost as for swedes. If clamped, cover the clamp with 6 in (15 cm) of soil as frost protection.

Turnip tops. Grow as a cut-and-come-again crop. Sow in late summer and autumn, outdoors or under cover, using maincrop cultivars; in spring sow first under cover, then outdoors, using early types. Sow thinly, either broadcast, in drills, or in rows about 6 in (15 cm) apart. Cut as small seedlings, or wait until plants are about 6 in (15 cm) high. They grow fast and may be ready in a few weeks.

Pests and Diseases. See Brassicas

Recommended cultivars. Early: Hakutaka, Presto, Purple Top Milan; main-crop: Golden Ball (yellow flesh), Manchester Market (Green Top Stone)

8 COMPANION PLANTING

PRINCIPLES UNDERLYING COMPANION PLANTING

The effects of plants on one another have been observed since time immemorial. Yet companion planting, with its roots in folklore, is sometimes greeted with scepticism. It must be admitted that often scientific proof is lacking; however, the fact that plants do have an effect on each other for the better – sometimes, too, for the worse – cannot be denied, and in some cases scientific confirmation has begun to emerge. In other cases, plants may not actually influence one another, but having common 'tastes', they can grow well in each other's company.

Also, with the modern emphasis on monoculture, the age-old conviction that beneficial effects can be obtained by the judicious mixing and combination of plants takes on added significance. There is a growing recognition that diversification and variety can provide protection against massive increases in pest and disease populations. This general principle is no substitute for good husbandry, and many other variables have to be taken into account, especially the soil, positioning of intercropped plants and microclimate. Equally decisive can be the timing of sowings and plantings of companion plants for maximum effect, as well as their numbers; a token handful of scent-confusing chives, for example, will hardly ward off marauding carrot flies from a large bed of vulnerable carrots, while too many will start to choke the carrots.

Another problem is that we have not been breeding or selecting for 'companion' effects, and these may only exist with certain varieties. One experiment at the University of California apparently confounds the notion that *Tagetes* (the African marigold variety) keeps whitefly at bay in the greenhouse. I use the closely related French marigolds, and I suspect it is their strong smell that works. Yet many varieties have been bred for less smell, as some object to it, and it is possible that these may work less well.

These complex interactions can explain why one gardener may be successful and find that certain combinations work well, while others, with slight differences in their conditions or methods, may find the results less favourable. The best approach is to experiment and observe what works well for you.

In the past, as plants interacted, gardeners observed them and how they behaved in different ways, then adopted methods that took into account these effects. Nowadays the original effect may pass almost unrecognized as such. Thus weed control is necessary to prevent damage to yields by 'bad companions', and crops are rotated to overcome or utilize the conditions created by the previous occupants. Rotation prevents diseases such as onion white rot and brassica club root building up, and the changing crops each extract different nutrients in varying amounts, leaving many more useful residues themselves. 'Replant' disease is similarly another companion effect over time, with the last plant leaving conditions unsuitable for its own genus for many years. This is encountered most often with apple orchards and rosebeds, which should not be replanted in the same place but on fresh ground.

The many different companion effects of plants can be broken down into five groupings: those that help each other and work through the soil, those that help to suppress either pests or diseases, those that attract predators and pollinators, those that complement each other, and those that are bad companions and are best sited away from others.

COMPANION PLANTS AFFECTING OTHER PLANTS

All plants are in competition for air, light, water and nutrients; anything they can do to hinder others acts to their own advantage. Companion planting is about turning these effects to our own ends. Onions need weed-free conditions to prosper while young, but once they start to ripen

OPPOSITE: Marigold border alongside vegetable beds (*Natural Image*)

the weeds may be left to grow, taking up water and nutrients; the onions are then less inclined to produce secondary growth, and so ripen and keep much better. Ground-cover and weed-suppressant plants save weeding. The competition of a carefully selected sward is used to check growth and improve fruiting when a young orchard is grassed down.

Hindering seed germination with exudates from leaf litter is employed by many plants, particularly by the aromatic herbs such as rosemary, sage, rue and lavender. Because of this they should not be planted in areas that are to be sown, such as vegetable beds. When wanted nearby for their other beneficial effects, as masking plants (their strong aromas hide crop plant smells from their pests) or to encourage predators and pollinators, they should be confined to the borders and around edges. Pines and many other conifers are remarkably successful at preventing seeds germinating, as can be observed in any pinewood. Lupins have been noted for suppressing weeds, especially fat hen, since Classical times.

There are many physical interactions, such as when plants provide shelter from the wind or sun for more tender companions. Nurse crops of weeds can be as beneficial to little seedlings as hedges are to delicate shrubs. Tall crops provide summer shade and wind shelter, so the marrow family grow well under sweetcorn, and both go well together with runner beans. Ground cover plants give the cool moist root-runs needed by roses, clematis and others.

Support is given for climbers and scramblers by other plants, especially old trees, but for temporary use sunflowers can be sown *in situ* to form natural canes. Growing melons and cucumbers up them in a polythene tunnel works much better than using strings.

Underground companions aid other plants, as their old roots decay and leave channels for others to follow. Deep rooters such as alfalfa may penetrate difficult layers; when they are supplanted their pathways can be followed by less vigorous plants that would not otherwise root as deeply.

All plants guard the soil against erosion from wind and rain, and may slowly increase its depth by trapping wind-blown debris and dust as well as with their own remains. Those with sticky stems such as tobacco and *Lychnis viscaria* trap not only dust but also insects, and so their litter is rich in chitins, believed to give plants improved disease-resistance. Companions such as *Phacelia* and flax are of benefit by improving the texture of the soil; others such as spinach provide saponins, which help gel the humus fraction.

Many plants improve soil fertility by providing access to relatively unavailable nutrients for others – sometimes as green

Companion plants and their beneficial herbs

Plant (or position)	Good grown with
Apple	
Asparagus	tomatoes
Aubergines	beans, sweet peppers
Beans, broad	brassicas, carrots, celery, cucurbits, potatoes
Beans, French	celery, cucurbits, potatoes, strawberries, sweetcorn
Beans, runner	sweetcorn
Beetroot, chards	most beans, brassicas, onions, garlic, kohl rabi
Brassicas (cabbage family)	most beans, beetroot, chards, celery, onions, garlic, peas, potatoes
Carrots	leeks, lettuces, onions, garlic, peas, tomatoes
Celery and celeriac	brassicas, beans, leeks, tomatoes
Chrysanthemum greens (edible)	cabbages and generally
Cucurbits – cucumbers, courgettes, marrows, melons, pumpkins, squashes	beans, peas, radishes, sunflowers, sweetcorn
Gate corners and greenhouse doors	scented plants
Lawns and grass paths	clover
Leeks	carrots, celery, onions, garlic
Lettuce	carrots, cucurbits, radishes, strawberries
Onions and garlic	beetroot, chards, lettuces, strawberries, tomatoes
Orchard borders	brambles, nuts, stinging nettles
Pears	
Peas	beans, carrots, cucurbits, radishes,
Potatoes	beans, brassicas, peas, sweetcorn sweetcorn, turnips

Not good grown with	Beneficial herbs	Effect
	nasturtium, chives	nasturtiums deter woolly aphids, chives deter scab and aphids
	basil, parsley	considered generally beneficial
		aubergines like the same warm, moist conditions
onions and garlic	summer savory	broad beans are inhibited by alliums; they are protected by savory from black aphids
onions and garlic		considered generally beneficial (alliums generally harmful)
beetroot, chards, kohl rabi, sunflowers	summer savory, sweet peas	savory protects beans from aphids; sweet peas attract pollinators
runner beans		French beans generally make good intercrops, probably because they are leguminous; runner beans may make the soil too dry and shady
runner beans, strawberries, tomatoes	nasturtium, dill	dwarf French beans, sown three weeks after cabbages, confuse cabbage rootfly and aphids
	chives	chives, interplanted or around edges, deter rootfly
		celery shares with leeks a need for rich, moist conditions
		reported to deter cabbage white butterflies, while the roots deter pathogenic nematodes
potatoes	nasturtium, dill	considered generally beneficial (potatoes generally harmful). The marrow family appreciate light shade provided by runner beans, and the support of sunflowers or sweetcorn
thorny plants	southernwood, marigolds	confusing scents hide crops from pests
buttercups, thistles, plantains	chamomile, thyme	considered generally beneficial (buttercups, etc. harmful)
		see celery above
		among others, lettuces benefit from taller crops which provide light shade in summer
beans, peas	summer savory	summer savory may keep away onion fly
	all aromatic herbs	herbs deter disease and encourage predators and pollinators; stinging nettles deter disease and promote keeping qualities of fruit
grass	chives, catnip	chives and catnip make better ground cover than grass, which stunts pears
onions and garlic		peas appear to be inhibited by alliums
cucurbits, sunflowers, tomatoes	horseradish	considered generally beneficial (cucurbits etc harmful)

manures. Deep-rooting plants such as alfalfa, docks and thistles give access to nutrients such as zinc which may be unavailable to shallow rooters; they donate the material after use in their leaf litter and root residues.

Many plants store minerals in much greater proportions than would normally be available. Thorn-apple accumulates phosphorus, locust tree leaves calcium; potato plants build up magnesium in their leaves to a large proportion of the dry weight. These can then be composted for favoured plants or left *in situ* for widespread benefit. See the chapter on *Weeds*, page 239, for the most effective mineral accumulators.

The legumes (peas and beans) fix atmospheric nitrogen and make the surplus available to other plants; when they die, bacteria nodules on their root systems give up the bulk, which can amount to an annual production of about 200 lb (90 kg) per acre (0·4 hectare). Thus the addition of clover to a grass sward increases the production of clippings for use as mulch or fertility elsewhere.

Lupins, laburnums, sweet peas and other leguminous plants will similarly add nitrogen fertility to the ornamental areas.

Some plants excrete unwanted nutrients back into the soil. Cereals and tobacco excrete potassium as they mature, lupins produce acid secretions that liberate phosphates in the surrounding soil and the depth of available potassium increases annually under a grass sward. Dead flower and leaf litter soon return humus and minerals to the soil, and the more variety the greater the value.

Companion plants and their beneficial herbs	
Plant (or position)	*Good grown with*
Radishes	cucurbits, lettuces, peas
Roses	ground cover
Shrubs	bulbs, *Limnanthes douglasii*
Spinach	everything
Stone fruit	
Strawberries	beans, lettuces, spinach
Sweetcorn	beans, cucurbits, peas, potatoes, sunflowers
Sweet peppers	aubergines
Tomatoes	asparagus, carrots, onions, garlic
Turnips and swedes	peas
Vegetable plot	*Limnanthes douglasii*, alpine strawberries
Vegetable plot borders	

Legumes fix atmospheric nitrogen and make the surplus available to other plants through these bacterial nodules on their root system (*Natural Image*)

Companion plants also work by stimulating the soil microlife. Yarrow and valerian encourage earthworms, which are probably the most important factor in improving soil fertility. Elder and silver birch encourage decomposition of material by microlife and are thus especially useful planted next to compost areas, while pines have a pronounced negative effect on composting and should be avoided.

COMPANIONS VERSUS PESTS

Many exudates are used by plants against pests and diseases, and we can employ these by interplanting to protect crops. The pests are confused, discouraged or poisoned by the guard plants before they can do much damage. In the USA nightshade is used to poison Colorado beetles looking for potato and tomato plants. Nasturtiums grown up and over apple trees drive away woolly aphids; all alliums, especially garlic, are efficacious against aphids.

Asparagus is a good companion to tomatoes as it gives off an exudate that kills their eelworm pest *Trichodorus*, while tomatoes have been observed to discourage couch grass. The Mexican

Not good grown with	Beneficial herbs	Effect
	chervil	chervil is said to deter the flea beetle and make the radish less hot
	chives and garlic, thyme and catnip	chives and garlic said to discourage blackspot and mildew; thyme and catnip make good ground cover that encourages predators
Mediterranean plants		*Limnanthes douglasii* brings in and sustains predators and pollinators
		considered generally beneficial
brassicas	chives	chives said to discourage aphids
	borage	considered generally beneficial
		considered generally beneficial. runner beans provide welcome wind shelter
brassicas, kohl rabi	basil	basil prefers same conditions as these plants, and aphids appear to prefer basil
potatoes	basil, parsley, French marigolds	asparagus prevents *Trichodorus* attacks; basil will deflect aphids; French marigolds said to discourage whitefly
		considered generally beneficial
	marigolds, nasturtiums	all will attract predators and pollinators
	all the aromatic herbs	pest-confusing scents

Good companions in the vegetable bed – onions and carrots can confuse their respective flies (*Photos Horticultural*)

marigold (*Tagetes minuta*) gives off root exudates that kill eelworms and also inhibit herbaceous weeds.

Some plants give off alarm signals that warn others of imminent attack and initiate defensive action, causing them to produce increased levels of protective chemicals. Research at Washington State University has found that sagebrush, which has high levels of methyl jasmonate, initiates protective chemical production against pests in tomato plants within the space of a few hours.

Plants with strong scents confuse pests that locate their prey by smell. Moles have been said to be driven away by plantings of *Euphorbia lathyrus* or *E. lactea*, castor-oil plants and myriad others, but a truly effective mole repellent has yet to be found.

Cannabis plants were formerly used by Dutch cabbage-growers to drive away the white butterfly; mixing onions with carrots to confuse their respective flies is ancient practice. Intercropping similarly handicaps those seeking their prey by sight. French and broad beans, when intercropped with brassicas, can provide protection against cabbage root fly and mealy aphids.

A clump of marigolds among the vegetables attracts predators such as hover-fly, as well as pollinators (*Natural Image*)

The aromatic herbs are among the most effective for causing scent confusion, diverting pests from their targets. In some cases, too, they act as decoys. Basil is especially liked by aphids, and can be used to deflect them from neighbouring crops; also repels flies.

COMPANIONS VERSUS DISEASES

Stinging nettles have the effect of causing earlier ripening in fruit, yet they can prevent it going mouldy when used as packing. They are said to stimulate oil production in herbs and to protect nearby plants from fungal attack. Most companion gardeners encourage a few patches, especially as their aphids will feed many ladybirds for the benefit of the rest of the garden. A tea made from stinging nettles has often been used to discourage pest and disease attacks and garlic has been used likewise. Garlic has long been planted beneath roses with the aim of preventing blackspot, and all alliums, garlic in particular, are traditionally held to be effective against fungal diseases, especially on roses and fruit-trees. Some chilli pepper varieties give off an exudate that destroys the pathogenic fungus *Fusarium*. One fungus, *Trichoderma*, will live in plants and protect them from other fungus attacks.

COMPANIONS TO ENCOURAGE PREDATORS AND POLLINATORS

Companion plants such as dead nettles act as valuable cover for ground-dwelling predators like shrews, frogs and beetles. Intercrops can also perform this function. Other plants, especially dense-growing ones, evergreen trees and bushes, give them somewhere suitable to nest or hibernate and provide shelter, nest sites and food sources for birds and other creatures, which all help in controlling pests and creating greater fertility.

Many crops rely on pollination, and pollinators can be encouraged and maintained by growing companion plants to provide a longer season of nectar and pollen production. Bumble-bees are most important to early-flowering fruit, and they need the help of aubretia, flowering currants, dead-nettles and wallflowers. Flowers in among the fruit and vegetables attract the bees to the area so that the crop's flowers are more quickly spotted and pollinated. Brassicas, *Alliums* and root vegetables left to flower provide much nectar and pollen. There is little lost to the compost if they are chopped up before the seed forms.

In the same way flowering companions can increase the stock of predatory insects such as hover-flies: the poached-egg plant (*Limnanthes douglasii*) is one of the most effective. Buckwheat,

Convolvulus tricolor and pot marigold (*Calendula officinalis*) are nearly as beneficial, and alpine strawberries are useful as they flower from spring to winter unceasingly.

COMPLEMENTARY COMPANIONS

Many plants which have been found to be good companions derive their good neighbourliness from shared growing needs. Celery does well alongside leeks, both needing rich, moist soil. Aubergines are good companions for peppers because they share a liking for the same warm, moist conditions. The converse can also be the case. Runner beans will make the soil too dry and provide too much shade for beetroot to thrive alongside.

BAD COMPANIONS

Some plants have developed the ability to suppress other plants, not only by out-competing, outgrowing and shading them but also by giving off allelopathic chemicals that directly affect the other's growth. It was discovered that wormwood leaves give off an exudate that checks brassicas when the effect of wormwood on deterring cabbage caterpillars was investigated. Black walnut leaf exudates kill most plants under them; dandelions give off ethylene gas, which causes premature ripening in flowers and fruits and stunts other plants. Fennel, rue and wormwood are all considered to be generally detrimental and should be grown away from other plants. Beans do not grow well with onions; tomatoes and potatoes should be kept apart, as they may cross-infect each other with many diseases.

See also *The Ornamental Kitchen Garden* (page 196).

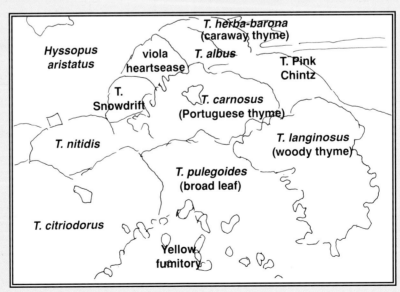

Hyssopus aristatus

T. herba-barona (caraway thyme)

viola heartsease

T. albus

T. Pink Chintz

T. Snowdrift

T. carnosus (Portuguese thyme)

T. nitidis

T. langinosus (woody thyme)

T. pulegoides (broad leaf)

T. citriodorus

Yellow fumitory

9 HERBS

It is difficult to define a herb precisely. From the very earliest times herbs were used as healing plants, being the only form of medicine, and magical and sacred properties were ascribed to them. Collections of useful plants or herbs must have been made thousands of years ago. We certainly know of records going back beyond 2000 BC in China and Egypt. In Europe the monasteries maintained herbal knowledge throughout the Dark Ages until the great revival of interest in the fourteenth century, when serious scientific study was applied to their medicinal use. With the advent of printing in the late fifteenth century many herbals were produced and circulated: plants could now be properly identified from accurate botanical illustrations. By this time exotic herbs from the East were available, although expensive.

The first physic garden was established in Italy at Padua University in 1545. By the next century the Chelsea physic garden was created, and still exists on the same site. Students could now study a large range of herbs from all over the world.

THE USES OF HERBS

Herbs could be defined today as plants useful to man in medicine, cookery, cosmetics, as natural dyestuffs and for their scent. When we consider their extensive uses it is clear how important they are to the life of our planet. It is known for certain that thousands of plants have not been recorded or investigated for medicinal and other properties, and that therefore the widespread destruction of habitat (especially rainforests, which are so tremendously rich in plant life) is disastrous. Plants with vital properties are being rapidly destroyed by ignorance, folly and greed.

The medicinal uses of herbs are extremely important but are outside the scope of this book. Many specialist manuals are available, but you are strongly advised to consult a qualified practitioner before treating any except the most minor

ailments. Essential oils derived from herbs have various healing properties; they can be vaporized in a fragrance burner and, suitably diluted, used to scent the body. Herbs used in skin and hair care products include marshmallow, chamomile, rosemary and lavender. Other herbs provide dyestuffs (see *The Dyer's Manual* by Jill Goodwin for an excellent treatment of this subject). Most people, however, grow them in the garden for culinary purposes, to provide scent, to attract beneficial insects and repel others, or for their decorative qualities.

CULINARY USE

Culinary herbs cover a wide range of plants. Most cooks have a favourite which they would never be without, but there are many which are worth experimenting with to add a new zest to food. There is a widespread misconception that herbs have to be dried to be used. This is quite wrong: there is nothing better than fresh-picked herbs from the garden. Some are not available all year, and can certainly be dried for out-of-season use.

Usually the leaves are used and this can include the young stems as well. Always pick young, healthy leaves. Flowers of many herbs can be added to salads – try borage, chives, nasturtiums and violas. Seeds of some herbs such as coriander, dill, caraway and cumin are valuable for flavouring. Herb teas can also be made from dried leaves and flowers: apart from offering a delightful fragrance and freshness all are beneficial and have some medicinal property.

SCENT

Most herbs have a strong scent which is very attractive. A jar or vase of cut herb flowers and foliage smells wonderful in the house, as well as being decorative – many herbs have beautiful foliage, especially the grey and silver varieties. Herbs are an important ingredient in pot pourri, a decorative and highly scented mixture of flower, leaf and bark which you can mix yourself according to personal taste and availability of material. Many herbs can be used together with other flowers, especially the old cottage-garden

OPPOSITE: Many herbs such as thymes are at home in a rock garden (*Sawyers Farm*)

varieties. Rosebuds, lavender, rosemary, thyme, lemon verbena are some of the most fragrant.

ATTRACTING/REPELLING INSECTS

Herb flowers are particularly attractive to butterflies and bees, and some herbs are worth planting for this purpose alone. The most valuable include clover, hyssop, scabious, thyme, marjoram and sage. Effective insect repellents include southernwood and santolina for moths, tansy for flies, and pyrethrum, used as a general insecticide. The tagetes are considered to have some protective action against whitefly. See *Companion Planting* (page 128) for a more extensive discussion.

DECORATION

Many herbs make a lovely edging or small hedge. Lavender in all its varieties is an obvious one, and cotton lavenders are also very attractive, including the bright green *Santolina viridis*. These can be clipped to size and shape. Other suitable plants include bushy thyme, decorative sage, marjoram, gold feverfew, winter savory and hyssop. Of the smaller plants violets make a decorative edging. For colourful, less formal edgings try pot marigold or catmint, chives and parsley.

The foliage of many herbs is a decorative feature, from the delicate lacy bright green chervil to the strong grey leaves of sage, for example decorative sage, tansy, artemisia, fennel (green and bronze), rosemary, lavender, savory and thyme.

PROPAGATION

The propagation of most herbs presents few problems to the gardener and good results can be achieved without special equipment. The basic methods of propagation are from seed, by cuttings or by division.

Seed Most herbs can be grown easily from seed, but with what are really more or less wild plants, do not expect in all cases the rapid and high germination you get from garden flowers and vegetables. Some herbs have notoriously erratic germination. Catnip is difficult and slow. Rosemary rarely germinates at a rate of more than 60%; it requires a temperature of over 70°F (21°C)and the seed should not be covered. Horehound, lavender and mint can also be tricky, and winter savory is slow and requires light. Lavender seems to germinate best if autumn-sown and left in the cold greenhouse. Sweet cicely will germinate in spring if seed is sown outside the previous summer.

If seed does not germinate within three weeks you may have given it the wrong conditions. If you have no result check that the seed is still firm and has not rotted: if it is healthy it should germinate when conditions are right. Do not throw seed trays away if you get no results: just leave them and you will almost certainly have a pleasant surprise, maybe months later!

Cuttings Some herbs cannot be grown from seed, either because they produce no seed (like French tarragon) or because they do not come true from seed (like mints and some coloured and variegated-leaved plants). The skill in taking cuttings is in judging what is good cutting material. Here are a few basic guidelines.

1. Cuttings are normally taken from soft non-flowering shoots of approximately 2–3½ in (5–9 cm) long. It is important that growth is not new and too soft but semi-mature or robust (not too thin and spindly or too floppy).
2. Take off the lower leaves so that leaves do not contact the cutting medium.
3. Cutting medium can be bought ready-made, or can be either pure sharp cutting sand (from garden centres) or sharp sand and peat (or preferably peat alternative), say 50:50.
   Another particularly good cutting medium is perlite (available from garden centres). This can be used alone or again mixed with peat or peat substitute. The great advantage of perlite is that it cannot be overwatered, stays moist a long time and contains plenty of air.
4. Cuttings should be covered with plastic to keep in the moisture and stop them wilting. For just a few cuttings this might be a plastic bag over a pot of cuttings. For larger quantities a simple frame can be made and placed over a bed of sand which is kept moist to maintain high humidity. It goes without saying that cuttings should be well shaded from the sun.
5. Cuttings are ready to prick out into small pots of potting compost when rooted. This can take from two to several weeks, according to type.
6. Difficult cuttings: sweet bay is very difficult to root and in normal conditions will take six months or more. This subject really needs mist and bottom heat; it will then root by autumn from cuttings taken between the fifth and seventh weeks after mid-summer (the last week of July or first week of August in the UK). This is the *only* time when cuttings can be taken successfully. Lemon verbena and tarragon are difficult to keep from wilting and are normally done under mist.
7. Woody cuttings. Cuttings from shrubby plants can be taken in autumn by pulling off a woody shoot with a heel (part of the main stem). Cuttings of rosemary and lavender, for instance, will root over winter without being covered. This method does not produce such good plants, however.

Division Many plants may be divided by pulling

away part of the plant with roots attached. Tarragon is easily divided this way, as are lemon balm, tansy and bergamot. Mints and other plants with creeping rootstocks are easily split up and every bit of root or runner will usually produce a plant – they are very invasive. Comfrey will grow from every piece of root and even from leaf stems, so be warned! Horseradish roots can be cut up to include a shoot on each piece; they will quickly put down more root and establish new plants.

SOIL AND SITE

Herbs include a very wide range of plants. Bear in mind that some naturally grow on hot rocky hillsides, others in woodlands and still others in damp situations. Rosemary and lavender, from Mediterranean hillsides, are not really going to enjoy your bog garden or a position under trees.

As a general rule most herbs thrive with good drainage and this is often vital in the dormant winter months. If drainage is a major problem then try a raised bed. They also enjoy alkaline conditions. Aim for a pH of 7, adding lime in the form of calcified seaweed, which breaks down slowly and lasts for years.

The main problem soils are heavy clay, where lack of drainage in a wet cold winter will finish many of the Mediterranean herbs, and very sandy soil which will get too dry in the summer to sustain growth. See the chapter on *Soil* (page 10) for ways to improve these types.

The ideal site for a herb garden is one which gets plenty of sun from late morning to evening. It should be reasonably sheltered from cold winds and gales, especially deadly east winds. It must, of course, be convenient for the kitchen. You are unlikely to use many herbs if you have to trudge to the bottom of the garden to pick your flavourings.

TYPE OF GARDEN

This will be very much related to the site. You do not have to have a formal herb garden, although these are most attractive. Herbs mixed in the border with cottage flowers look very good, and you can really make the most of the herbs with interesting foliage to show off the more colourful flowers. Another effective arrangement is an island bed cut into the lawn. This could be circular or perhaps an irregular shape.

Many herbs will fit well into a rock garden. If you have shady or moist sites there is a range of herbs that will enjoy these situations: sweet woodruff, wood avens and lungwort for shade; mints, valerian and wild garlic on moist soil. A gravel, limestone or chalk garden is worth considering as a surprising number of herbs will thrive in these habitats. Gravel bedded in hoggin over soil is particularly good and the

Brick paths outlining a herb garden are especially attractive (*Harry Smith*)

annuals seem to reseed themselves readily in it.

Many people prefer a formal herb garden and the secret here is to keep the layout simple and prepare your plan well. Apart from the complex traditional knot garden, which is hard work for most gardeners with all that clipping to do, the simplest and most effective form is the chequerboard – alternate flagstones and soil, each square planted with one type of herb. As with all hard-edge designs, once the plants are established and have flowered and sprawled over the edges there are few straight lines remaining. Brick paths outlining the herb garden are especially attractive. It can be expensive to purchase old mellow bricks, and time-consuming to lay them properly, but it is well worth the effort.

There is another possibility. In kitchen gardens there is still a tendency to go in for vegetable monoculture, which is rather boring to look at and is conducive to pests and diseases. Herbs, with their strong fragrances, are the ideal companions to vegetables, as are many flowers. See *Companion Planting* and *The Ornamental Kitchen Garden* (pages 128 and 196) for plentiful suggestions .

HERBS IN CONTAINERS

Herbs grow well and can look beautiful in containers of all sorts, especially terracotta, stoneware and wooden barrels. The same rules apply as for growing other plants in containers.

In small containers the larger shrubby herbs like rosemary will dwarf themselves (Bonsai are also possible with woody subjects). Herbs make lovely foliage displays, with a lot of flower colour in season. Annuals can be grown with perennials or on their own. Herb window-boxes and hanging baskets are most attractive, and here some of the lovely scented-leaved pelargoniums can be used to good effect. There are some herbs that are not suitable for mixed plantings: fennel, wormwood and mints should be kept separate. Angelica and lovage are too big to be suitable for containers.

Terracotta herb planter with dwarfing rosemary in the top, parsley and sage in the middle, tarragon and chives in the bottom pockets (J. Houdret)

NUTRIENTS AND MULCHES

Herbs require little feeding – in fact many thrive on a rather poor soil. The ones that require a richer situation are those constantly being cut, like parsley, chives and basil in summer. Manures are therefore not needed. Good compost, however, will help to retain moisture in light soils, break down heavy ones and give a good balance of nutrients.

Mulches are essential for suppressing weeds, keeping in moisture and stopping the soil from drying out in the summer. A good material is spent mushroom compost – cheap, low in nutrient and with some beneficial lime. Forest bark is attractive and a good weed suppressant. Stones and gravel are an excellent mulch, keeping the soil moist and cool. See the chapter on *Mulches* (page 46) for full information.

PESTS AND DISEASES

Luckily herbs are susceptible to very few pests and diseases. If grown well in a healthy soil and not put under undue stress, as might happen in a container, they will look after themselves.

Aphids will attack some herbs but are seldom a great problem. If you have some colourful nasturtiums in the herb garden they will be the first target. Red spider will attack lemon verbena, but only under cover. Cold water sprays tend to dampen their enthusiasm. If the problem is serious, an insect predator can be obtained.

Sweet bay sometimes suffers from scale, which manifests itself in the form of small waxy scabs on the underside of the leaves and on the stems. They can be rubbed off by hand. This is never serious out of doors.

Rust is the main problem. This is unsightly, and spreads on the wind. It can attack comfrey badly, as it can mints. Chives and hollyhocks are also affected. These are different rusts and do not pass from one plant species to another. Some strains of the Russian comfrey are reasonably rust-free, such as the Bocking 14 strain. The problem is only serious if the plants are under stress because of lack of moisture or nutrients (comfrey is a strong feeder). The best treatment is to cut off affected leaves and burn them. In bad cases cut the plant to the ground and flame-gun the remaining roots and surrounding soil to kill the spores. This treatment also holds good for mints, which do not suffer badly from rust unless growing in poor conditions. The general rule is to remove any infected part of the plant directly the red spots appear.

Other, more general diseases are dealt with in the chapter on *Disease Prevention* (page 258). Some of these are fungus diseases: damping off of seedlings, botrytis (or grey mould), root rots, powdery mildew and downy mildew. Powdery mildew is quite common in sage, mints (especially Bowles variety), and sometimes tarragon. Top watering on a regular basis helps to control it in hot dry weather.

HARVESTING

Herbs may be harvested to be used fresh at any time during the growing season. Always pick the younger, fresher leaves and shoots free from blemishes or disease. If you want to use flowers for seasoning and for decoration, they should be picked if possible when newly opened.

When harvesting for drying, cutting should be done at the point when the plants have maximum flavour. The best time for stem and leaf is just before the flowers open. Harvesting should be done when the plants are completely dry from overnight dew or rain.

Seed should be harvested when it is brown or black and is not full of moisture when squeezed. When the seed is ready, cut the flowers and hang them upside down over a tray, or place a paper bag over them and let seed drop off into the bag.

Green material should always be dried out of the sun to retain colour and essential oils. Hang the whole stems in a dark, airy dry place or dry the leaves in a low oven until crisp. If properly dried, leaf will retain a good green colour and strong aroma.

Storage should always be in the dark – use opaque or darkened glass jars or brown paper bags. In full light herbs will quickly lose their colour and flavour.

Balm, lemon
(Melissa officinalis)

Type	Perennial
Height	2 ft (60 cm)
Spread	16 in (40 cm)
Site	Full sun or part shade
Soil	Medium to poor
Flower	Pale yellow/white, sometimes pinkish, in summer
Scent	Lemon
Propagate	Soft stem cuttings, root division or seed in spring/late summer
Harvest	Younger leaves
Uses	With fish, poultry, stuffings. Melissa tea. Medicinal. Bee plant
Other varieties	Gold variegated form from plants only

Lemon balm *(Sawyers Farm)*

Basil, sweet
(Ocimum basilicum)

Type	Tender annual
Height	18 in (45 cm)
Spread	7 in (18 cm)
Site	Full sun
Soil	Good and well drained
Flower	White in summer
Scent	Very aromatic
Propagate	Seed, under glass mid–late spring; outside early summer
Harvest	Leaves
Uses	With tomatoes, pasta sauce, combines with garlic well. Insect deterrent
Other varieties	Dark Opal; Genovese (sweet, shiny rounded leaved); Lemon or Kemangie *(O.citriodorum)*; Green and Purple Ruffles; Horapha; Mammoth; Lettuce leaf *(O.neapolitanum)*; Holy or Sacred *(O. sanctum)*; Greek *(O.minimum)* miniature bush; Spice and others

Basil: Purple Ruffles *(Sawyers Farm)*

Chervil
(Anthriscus cerefolium)

Type	Annual/Biennial
Height	12–24 in (30–60 cm)
Spread	12 in (30 cm)
Site	Light shade
Soil	Moisture-retentive loam
Flower	White, spring to summer
Scent	Sweet scent
Propagate	By seed late summer or spring; allow to self-seed
Harvest	Young leaves
Uses	In *fines herbes* with soups and salads, vegetables, egg dishes. Medicinal
Other varieties	Brussels winter, plain and curled leaved varieties

Chervil *(Pat Brindley)*

Chives
(Allium schoenoprasum)

Type	Perennial
Height	9–12 in (23–30 cm)
Spread	9 in (23 cm)
Site	Sun or part shade
Soil	Rich moisture-retentive loam
Flower	Rose-purple in early summer
Scent	Mild onion

Chives *(Sawyers farm)*

Propagate	By seed in spring/early summer or division of rootstock in spring
Harvest	Leaves
Uses	Use as garnish on salads with potatoes and tomatoes, to flavour cheeses
Other varieties	Fine-leaved, giant, garlic or Chinese (*A. tuberosum*)

Coriander
(Coriandrum sativum)

Type	Hardy annual
Height	24 in (60 cm)
Spread	12 in (30 cm)
Site	Full sun, protected from wind
Soil	Fertile and well drained
Flower	Pinkish white, summer
Scent	Strong aromatic leaves. Seeds, sweet spicy
Propagate	By seed in spring or late summer
Harvest	Fresh leaves and seeds when ripe
Uses	Leaves with curries, salads and sauces. Seeds in curries, chutney, ratatouille and with cakes. Also medicinal
Other varieties	For leaf, Cilantro; for seed, Moroccan

Coriander *(Sawyers Farm)*

Dill
(Anethum graveolens)

Type	Hardy annual
Height	9 in–3 ft (23–90 cm)
Spread	6–12 in (15–30 cm)
Site	Full sun, protected from wind
Soil	Fertile
Flower	Yellow umbels in summer
Scent	Leaf and seed strongly aromatic
Propagate	By seed sown in spring/early summer. Readily self-seeds. Do not grow near fennel, as they cross-pollinate
Harvest	Fresh leaves and ripe seeds
Uses	Leaves added to salads, potatoes, cheese, raw fish. Seeds in pickles, fish dishes, with apples. Also a valuable medicinal
Other varieties	For leaf, Dukat; for seed, Mammoth

Dill *(Sawyers Farm)*

Fennel
(Foeniculum vulgare dulce)

Type	Perennial
Height	3–4 ft (90–120 cm)
Spread	2–3 ft (60–90 cm)
Site	Full sun, sheltered from wind
Soil	Loam, well drained
Flower	Yellow umbels in summer
Scent	Strongly aromatic, leaves and seeds
Propagate	By seed sown in spring/early summer
Harvest	Fresh leaves and ripe seed

Uses	Leaves used with fish, salads, soups. Seeds used with fish and bread
Other types	Wild, with thin stems; Sweet, with thick stems and ample leaf; Bronze, Florence or Finocchio with bulbous stems. For recommended cultivars see *The Vegetable Garden*, page 107)

Bronze fennel *(Sawyers Farm)*

Hyssop
(Hyssopus officinalis)

Type	Perennial sub-shrub
Height	12–18 in (30–45 cm)
Spread	12–18 in (30–45 cm)
Site	Full sun
Soil	Well-drained calcareous
Flower	Blue in early summer
Scent	Aromatic
Propagate	By seed sown in spring or late summer; by soft stem cuttings in spring or late summer
Harvest	Leaves

Uses	Grown for hedging and knot gardens. Culinary and medicinal. Bee plant
Other varieties	Pink, white and purple flower forms. Rock hyssop (*H. aristatus*), dwarf habit, flowering blue in August

Lavender
(Lavandula angustifolia)

Type	Perennial sub-shrub
Height	9 in–3 ft (23–90 cm)
Spread	12 in–3 ft (30–90 cm)
Site	Full sun
Soil	Well-drained calcareous
Flower	Mauve in summer
Scent	Very fragrant
Propagate	Seed sown in autumn or late summer. Will germinate at low temperatures. Soft stem cuttings in spring or late summer
Harvest	Flowers and leaves
Uses	Leaves used to stuff chicken. Flowers for flavouring, in pot pourri and lavender bags. Used in soaps, essential oil, perfume, etc. Also medicinal
Other varieties and species	Folgate, Hidcote, Munstead, Nana Alba (white flowered), Twickle Purple, Vera (Dutch) all (*L.angustifolia*); Old English, Grappenhall (large leaf), Seal, Loddon Pink all (*L. latifolia*); Woolly lavender (*L.lanata*); French lavender (*L.stoechas*); Spanish lavendar (*L.stoechas pedunculata*); L. dentata; L. viridis

Spanish lavender *(Sawyers Farm)*

Hyssop *(Harry Smith)*

Single marigold (*Sawyers Farm*)

Plain-leaved French parsley (*Sawyers Farm*)

Marigold, pot
(Calendula officinalis)

Type	Annual
Height	12–18 in (30–45 cm)
Spread	12 in (30 cm)
Site	Full sun
Soil	Moist, well drained
Flower	Pale to bright orange in summer. Single and double
Scent	Aromatic flowers
Propagate	Sow seed in spring. Self-seeds
Harvest	Flower petals
Uses	Valuable medicinal, antiseptic and healing. Use petals to give saffron colour to rice, cheese, yoghurts, cakes, etc. Distinct mild flavour
Other varieties	Many garden varieties, mainly double. Small single (orange/yellow)

Marjoram/oregano
(Origanum vulgare)

Type	Perennial
Height	12–24 in (30–60 cm)
Spread	12–18 in (30–45 cm)
Site	Full sun
Soil	Well-drained alkaline
Flower	Pink to white (some varieties deep red/purple bracts) in summer
Scent	Very aromatic
Propagate	Seed sown on surface (left uncovered) spring to late summer. Soft tip cutting of non-flowering shoots in spring and late summer
Harvest	Leaves and flowers in summer
Uses	Use to flavour pizza, tomatoes, meats, eggs and cheese. Also medicinal: aids digestion, antiseptic, respiratory disorders
Forms and species	Gold and variegated forms of *O. vulgare*; Greek oregano *(O.heracleoticum)* white flowers, very pungent; Sweet or knotted marjoram *(O.majorana)* half-hardy annual/perennial, sweet spicy scent, white flowers; *O.scabrum* from S. Greece, very decorative; Dwarf Winter marjoram and many others

Origanum scabrum (*Sawyers Farm*)

Parsley
(Petroselinum crispum)

Type	Biennial
Height	12–24 in (30–60 cm)
Spread	12 in (30 cm)
Site	Full sun or light shade
Soil	Rich and moisture-retentive
Flower	Yellow umbels
Scent	Aromatic
Propagate	Seed sown in spring or ideally late summer. Needs warm soil to germinate. Once established, best to leave one plant to self-seed
Harvest	Leaves
Uses	Most widely used herb. Use fresh on vegetables, egg dishes, soups, cheese, fish, etc. Medicinal, for digestion and stimulating appetite. Chew fresh leaf to destroy garlic odour
Other types	Many varieties of curled including Bravour, Darki, Moss Curled. Flat-leaved, French and Giant Italian have strongest flavour. Hamburg parsley *(P. tuberosum)* grown for its root

Rosemary
(Rosmarinus officinalis)

Type	Perennial shrub
Height	6 in–6 ft (15–180 cm)
Spread	2–4 ft (60–120 cm)
Site	Full sun, sheltered
Soil	Well-drained alkaline
Flower	Pale blue but some cultivars have deep blue flower in late spring. Also white- and pink-flowered forms
Scent	Very aromatic leaves
Propagate	Seed sown in mid–late summer or in seed trays at 70–80°F (21–26°C). Germination erratic. Named varieties from soft stem cuttings in spring and summer
Harvest	Leaves and young stems
Uses	Use to flavour meat, especially lamb, pork; potato dishes. Medicinal
Other varieties	Miss Jessopp's Upright, Severn Sea both *(R.officinalis)*; White flowered *(R.o. albus)*; Dwarf Blue Prostrate *(R.o.prostratus)*; Majorca Pink (half-hardy)

Rosemary *(Sawyers Farm)*

Sage
(Salvia officinalis)

Type	Perennial sub-shrub
Height	12–28 in (30–70 cm)
Spread	to 2 ft (60 cm)
Site	Full sun
Soil	Well-drained alkaline
Flower	Violet blue (sometimes pink or white) in summer
Scent	Very aromatic leaves
Propagate	Seed sown in spring or late summer. Soft stem cuttings taken in spring or summer
Harvest	Leaves
Uses	Used in stuffings, with pork and other rich fatty meats

White-flowered sage *(Sawyers Farm)*

Other varieties and species	Painted sage *(S.horminum)* annual with coloured bracts; Narrow-leaved sage *(S. lavendulifolia)* balsamic scent; Gold variegated *(S.o.icterina)*; Red or Purple sage *(S.o. purpurascens)*; *S.o. Tricolor* (half-hardy); Broad-leaved sage (seldom flowers); Prostrate sage *(S.o.prostratus)* balsamic scent; Pineapple sage *(S.rutilans)* half-hardy perennial, scarlet flowers in autumn; Clary sage *(S.sclarea)* biennial with very large leaves

Savory, winter
(Satureja montana)

Type	Perennial, low-growing, shrubby
Height	12–15 in (30–38 cm)
Spread	18 in (45 cm)
Site	Full sun
Soil	Well-drained alkaline
Flower	Tiny white/pinky white, early summer
Propagate	Seed sown in spring and late summer. Seed must be left uncovered. Erratic germination. Soft stem cuttings taken in spring
Harvest	Leaves any time and flowering tops
Uses	Used especially to flavour beans and salami. Medicinal for digestion and gastric complaints
Other species	Summer savory *(S. hortensis)* annual upright growing to 12 in (30 cm). Similar uses. Creeping savory *(S. repandra)* perennial,

Winter savory *(Sawyers Farm)*

low-growing with much finer leaves than winter savory. White flowers late summer. Very decorative. Similar uses

Sorrel
(Rumex acetosa) Broad-leaf sorrel

Type	Perennial
Height	2–5 ft (60–150 cm)
Spread	12 in (30 cm)
Site	Sun or light shade
Soil	Rich, moisture-retaining loam
Flower	Long spikes of tiny reddish flowers in summer
Propagate	From seed sown in spring or late summer. Will self-seed
Harvest	Younger leaves. Stop from flowering
Uses	Eaten raw in salads, made into soup with potatoes. Medicinal
Other varieties	Named varieties from France, e.g. Blond de Lyon
Other species	Buckler-leaved sorrel *(R. scutatus)* , also called French sorrel: low-growing, spreading with small silver-green leaves

Sorrel *(Sawyers Farm)*

Spearmint
(Mentha spicata)

Type	Perennial
Height	2 ft (60 cm)
Spread	Spreads by underground runners
Site	Sun or partial shade
Soil	Rich and moisture-retentive
Flower	Pale lilac to mauve in late summer
Scent	Strongly aromatic
Propagate	The smallest piece of underground runner will grow; normally 2 in (5 cm) sections covered in soil. Seed will not come true and produces inferior flavour
Harvest	Fresh leaves in season
Uses	To add minty flavour to vegetables, sweets, drinks. Mint sauce. Mint tea
Other varieties	Many forms, some with inferior scent, some prone to rust. Moroccan spearmint has best scent and vigour
Other mints	Peppermint, white, black and crisp black, Eau de cologne, red raripilla, curly mint, ginger mint, lemon mint, Bowles mint, applemint and variegated applemint, Corsican mint (*M. requienii*), pennyroyal (*M. pulegium*), upright and prostrate forms; many other hybrids and species

Peppermint (*Sawyers Farm*)

Tarragon, French
(Artemisia dracunculus)

Type	Perennial spreading rootstock
Height	to 3 ft (90 cm)
Spread	to 3 ft (90 cm)
Site	Full sun
Soil	Well-drained loam
Flower	Tiny insignificant white/green in summer
Propagate	Does not produce seed. From soft stem cuttings which need mist and bottom heat. Easiest by dividing rootstock in spring
Harvest	Young shoots or leaves
Uses	Indispensable in French cooking. Use with chicken, vegetables, sauces and tarragon vinegar. Use sparingly
Other species	Russian tarragon(*A. dracunculoides*), may be grown from seed. Has coarse and inferior flavour

French tarragon (*Sawyers Farm*)

Thyme, common
(Thymus vulgare)

Type	Perennial evergreen sub-shrub
Height	6–12 in (15–30 cm)
Spread	to 12 in (30 cm)
Site	Full sun
Soil	Well-drained, poorish
Flower	Lilac pink in early summer
Propagate	Seed sown in spring or late summer. Soft stem cuttings in spring
Harvest	Leaves, any time
Uses	Used extensively to flavour meats, poultry, game and in sauces
Other varieties and species	Culinary: Lemon thyme, wild thyme, broad-leaved thyme, orange thyme (*T. citriodorus*), caraway thyme (*T. herba-barona*), Silver thyme, Golden thyme;

many decorative carpeting thymes with red, pink/mauve to white flowers. Many decorative thymes do not come from seed

Common thyme (*Sawyers Farm*)

Verbena, lemon
(Alloysia triphylla)

Type	Half-hardy perennial shrub
Height	to 5 ft (150 cm)
Spread	4 ft (120 cm)
Site	Full sun and very sheltered. Will survive outside in mild-climate coastal regions
Soil	Well drained
Flower	Tiny white to pale lavender in late summer
Propagate	Stem cuttings in spring under mist and with bottom heat. Does not produce seed in UK
Harvest	Leaves in summer
Uses	Use where strong lemon fragrance is required. Verbena tea (called Vervaine in France) is popular and aids indigestion and nausea

Lemon verbena (*Sawyers Farm*)

10 FRUIT

TREE FRUIT

Planting. Winter is the best time for planting fruit trees, though if the soil is frozen, wait until it thaws. Container-grown plants may be planted throughout the year, but they will need to be watered during dry spells.

First dig a hole deep and wide enough for the roots to fit into with room to spare, then lightly fork over the soil in the bottom. If possible incorporate a bucket of well-rotted compost or a handful of bone-meal. Put the tree in the hole and spread out its roots, trimming off with secateurs any which are ragged or broken.

If you are going to use a stake now is the time to put it in. In a sheltered garden and for small trees with good roots they are usually unnecessary; often they can do more harm than good by rubbing against the tree or by being tied too tightly. Part the roots, position the stake about 9 in (23 cm) away from the tree's stem, and drive it firmly in. Where wind is a problem it should be placed on the windward side so that the tree is blown away from the stake and not into it. Unstaked trees should be supported by a bamboo cane pushed into the ground at an angle 2 to 3 ft (60–90 cm) away, then tied high up on the stem. This temporary support is to protect the roots from wind rock, and the bamboo may be untied after a few months.

The tree will have a soil mark on its stem, which shows how deep it should be planted. Always ensure that the join where the tree has been grafted on to its roots is well clear of the ground. Make a small mound in the bottom of the hole so that the tree sits on a firm base, and the roots spread out, down and away. Check that the tree is at the right height by laying a stick across the hole. If the soil mark on the stem does not coincide with the ground level, raise or lower the height of the mound.

The business of filling in the hole and firming down the soil is really a job for two people, one to

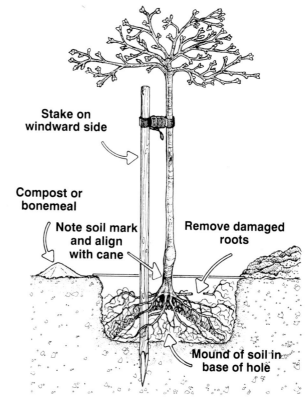

Stake on windward side

Compost or bonemeal

Note soil mark and align with cane

Remove damaged roots

Mound of soil in base of hole

Planting a fruit tree (*Rob Dalton*)

hold the tree and another to fill and firm. Tread the soil down firmly as you fill. In clay soils this can be awkward and messy, but if the roots are not in full contact with the soil the tree will not thrive. Bone-meal and compost can be added to the hole as you fill, but don't over do it. The soil immediately surrounding the roots should not be made too fertile, or the roots will lack the incentive to spread beyond the confines of the original hole. Without a good spread of roots the health of the tree will suffer, especially in times of drought. The best place for compost or manure is on the soil surface as a mulch – the worms will take it down and distribute it properly.

Culture. For the first decade of its life a fruit tree should grow in a weed-free and grass-free soil.

OPPOSITE: Sea Eagle peach growing against a wall (*Harry Smith*)

Elements of pruning

Many people are put off fruit-growing because pruning often seems, or is made to sound, so difficult. Pruning is actually quite easy, but it is difficult to describe. Details are given under specific crops, but the elements are as follows:

1. Have a good sharp pair of secateurs.
2. Cut to a bud.
3. Have a clear idea of the shape you are aiming for.
4. Know the best time to prune any particular tree.

Ideally it should stand in a circle of bare earth 6 ft (2 m) wide. This is not always easy to achieve. One solution is to sow nectar-rich but undemanding annual flowers around the base, such as nemophila, *Limnanthes douglasii* and nasturtiums. These will help keep the ground free of hungry weeds and will also attract predatory insects to prey upon aphids and other pests.

Frost. One of the greatest threats to fruit is a hard spring frost. If the blossom is frozen it is all too often ruined. When you know that a frost is expected, use old sheets (or, if necessary, newspaper) to cover over bushes or small trees, but be careful not to damage the blossom yourself.

If a frost strikes unexpectedly, get out there early and wash it off with cold water. A lot of frost damage is done by the sun defrosting the plant too rapidly. When white with frost the plant initially reflects the sun's rays, and so prevents the ice from melting until the sun has risen higher and become hotter. When the ice finally melts it does so quickly and the plant warms up much too fast. If the frost is washed off early enough the plant can warm up gradually. This is why a wall facing west or south-west is better for fruit than one which faces the rising sun.

There are varieties available which are to some extent frost-resistant, either because they flower late or because their blossom is particularly hardy. See under the specific fruit for details.

Pests and diseases. The best way to prevent disease is to encourage health. Ensure that the trees grow in a fertile soil, but do not overfeed them and so encourage lush soft growth. Be vigilant and give your trees an occasional inspection so that any problem can be caught early. A few diseased shoots may be pruned off, but once a whole tree is infected there may be no remedy. See the chapters on *Pest Control*, (page 290) and *Disease Prevention* (page 258) for full information on recognition, prevention and treatment for all the fruits discussed.

When choosing fruit varieties, do not buy just the well-known sorts, which all too often have poor disease resistance, not to mention second-rate flavour. There are thousands of different fruit varieties to choose from and it is important that they should be kept in cultivation, since they provide a wide genetic base, which is our best protection from pests and diseases. If just one or two varieties are grown, any diseases to which they are not fully resistant are liable to turn into epidemics. Moreover, the widespread planting of any variety exposes it to a greater risk of becoming susceptible to disease; this has been the fate of the popular Bramley Seedling apple and the Conference pear, once resistant to many of the more common diseases. Some of the finest varieties are also the oldest.

APPLES

Once upon a time apple trees were real trees which grew as tall as a house. Today, because they are grafted on to dwarfing root-stocks, they have become the same size as many shrubs, and can easily be kept to a manageable size. A new introduction are the ballerina and genetic dwarf types; these are very compact indeed and do not need pruning. However, apple trees as tiny as these are perhaps hardly worth growing.

Dwarfing root-stocks are really just roots with low vigour which have been specially bred to restrict (or stunt) the growth of the tree. Apples on very dwarfing root-stocks such as M27 and M9 will not do well in poor soils, and may suffer badly during a drought. Their roots also tend to be brittle and may snap in high winds – these very dwarf trees need to be staked throughout their life. M26 is more vigorous and does well on good soils and under good conditions, but it still needs a stake. The MM106 is the best all-round root-stock, strong enough to produce naturally healthy trees under less than perfect conditions, and also dwarf enough to be grown in a garden. For taller apple trees for planting in a paddock you will need the M25. Where you are growing two or more apple trees they should be planted at the distance apart that at least equals their likely eventual height. So trees on MM106 should be planted more than 12 ft (4 m) apart. If you are planting more than one row of trees they should be spaced at a minimum of one and a half times their eventual height.

Pruning. There are several different ways of pruning apple trees, but most of them use the same basic formula. This divides the tree into leaders, sub-leaders and laterals. The leaders and sub-leaders make up the framework of the tree, while the laterals provide branch space for the fruit.

The simplest form of tree (though not the

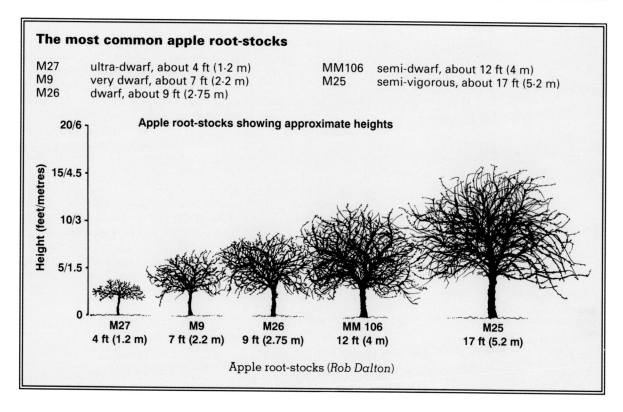

The most common apple root-stocks

M27   ultra-dwarf, about 4 ft (1·2 m)   MM106   semi-dwarf, about 12 ft (4 m)
M9   very dwarf, about 7 ft (2·2 m)   M25   semi-vigorous, about 17 ft (5·2 m)
M26   dwarf, about 9 ft (2·75 m)

Apple root-stocks showing approximate heights

Height (feet/metres)

20/6

15/4.5

10/3

5/1.5

0

| M27 | M9 | M26 | MM 106 | M25 |
| 4 ft (1.2 m) | 7 ft (2.2 m) | 9 ft (2.75 m) | 12 ft (4 m) | 17 ft (5.2 m) |

Apple root-stocks (*Rob Dalton*)

easiest to look after) is the cordon. It is very compact, so many different trees can be grown in a small space. It has just one leader, which is the stem, every other branch being a lateral. When it is pruned, which is usually done in the summer to restrict growth, the leader is pruned by a half, and the laterals are cut back to three leaves (about 1 in/2·5 cm). The espalier form is also space-saving, and is particularly suited to growing against a wall or fence. It is not as difficult to shape and prune as it may look. Just work out where the young branches should go, and push or pull them to fit. If done a little at a time and over several weeks, the young branches may be bent any way you like. Pruning is done in the same manner as for a cordon.

Perhaps the easiest and best tree shape for a

garden is the dwarf bush. The tree should look a bit like a goblet and have a stem of a clear 2 ft 6 in (75 cm), and a 'bowl' of five or six leader branches. It might be described as like a hand holding an invisible orange. The open centre allows all parts of the tree plenty of fresh air and sunlight, two of the greatest aids to health.

Each of the leaders may be treated as a cordon, with the main stem cut back by up to a half and the laterals pruned to three or four buds (about 1 in/2·5 cm). In order to make the best use of space, each branch may have one or two sub-leaders – laterals which should be treated as leaders and allowed to fill in any gaps between the branches.

Winter pruning encourages growth, so young trees are generally winter-pruned to speed them up. Do not prune in very severe frosts.

BELOW: Cordon
RIGHT: Espalier
(*Rob Dalton*)

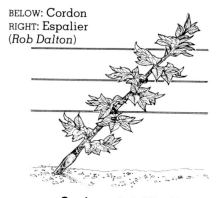

**Cordon set at 45° with
permanent wire supports**

**Can be trained against a wall or
fence to save space**

Shape like a goblet

Dwarf apple bush (*Rob Dalton*)

Summer pruning discourages growth, and is generally used on trees which must not grow too big, such as cordons or espaliers, in order to slow them down. This is best done in late summer, when the tree will have put on most of its growth. As a general rule prune back laterals to 2–3 in (5–7·5 cm), and if the tree has reached its desired height prune back the leading branches. If the tree responds by sending up new shoots pinch them out while they are still soft.

Tip-bearing varieties, such as the Worcester Pearmain, fruit only from new wood and so should not have the new growth shortened. Instead simply take out crossing (and rubbing) branches and any spindly stems.

Old trees. Neglected trees sometimes need more than just a light trim. Whole branches may have to be cut away to open up the middle or reduce the height. This is a job for the winter and not one to be rushed. Take plenty of time over deciding which branches need to be cut out. When sawing out large branches do it with two cuts: first reduce the weight on the branch by cutting off all but 2 ft (60 cm) or so. Then make a second, perfect cut. Do not cut out more than a

Apple varieties

There are several hundred varieties of apple, though many garden centres stock just five or six. The best choice is offered by the mail-order specialist fruit nurseries, whose catalogues give good descriptions and advice on pollination and pruning. (See page 152 for explanation of bracketed numbers.)

A. DESSERT (EATING) APPLES

Baker's Delicious: a second early, good-flavoured and juicy. Crops well on young trees. Resistant to scab and mildew (2)

Bess Pool (1874): a very late-flowering frost-proof apple; tip-bearing (6)

Cornish Aromatic (1813 or probably earlier): said to do well in wet climates; a good-keeping late variety (4)

Court Pendu Plat, an ancient variety (1613), generally healthy (*Crown copyright: Brogdale EHS*)

Discovery: well flavoured, generally disease-free (*Crown copyright: Brogdale EHS*)

Baker's Delicious: second early, crops well on young trees (*Crown copyright: Brogdale EHS*)

Court pendu plat (1613 or probably earlier): also called the wise apple, an ancient variety, frost- and scab-resistant and generally healthy; a smallish tree producing smallish apples; good on clay soils. A late-cropping keeper (5)

Cox's Orange Pippin (1825): the best apple of all, especially when grown well and not picked under-ripe; however, the tree is susceptible to most diseases and dislikes poor summers. Crops from mid-autumn (3)

sixth of the tree – if necessary wait until the next winter to complete the cutting out. Most trees will respond to heavy pruning by sending out a large number of rather vigorous shoots. If you want a replacement branch let one or two grow on unmolested, otherwise either rub out the shoots as they emerge or trim them right back in mid-summer. You may have to cut them back again during the winter. If you feel that all this sounds too much like hard work, leave the tree alone.

A poorly growing tree can often be revitalized by clearing the grass and weeds away from its trunk: like a young tree (page 148) it should ideally stand in a wide circle of bare ground. Once the ground has been weeded give the tree a good dressing of compost.

June drop. Sometimes, in mid-summer, a tree will start dropping its unripe fruit. This may be a welcome thinning of a heavy crop, but it is more often just a waste of fruit. A simple foliar feed applied in late spring to top up the tree's food reserves prevents any large-scale loss of fruit.

Biennial cropping can be a problem with certain varieties, such as Laxton's Fortune, Tydeman's Late Orange and Millar's Seedling. These can develop the habit of having a heavy crop one year and, consequently, a poor crop the next. The remedy is to thin the apples out during the good year. However, on a tree of any size apple-thinning is a tedious and time-consuming business, and you may prefer to put up with a bumper harvest every other year. If a heavy crop of apples does appear to be weakening a tree, it may be necessary to remove some of the young fruit. During the early summer and over a couple of weeks reduce the number of apples in each

---

Discovery: a well-flavoured early apple, widely grown, resistant to scab and generally disease-free. Fruits on both tips and spurs (3)

Egremont Russet (1872): excellent russeted apples cropping from late September. Disease-resistant and largely self-fertile; a good garden variety (2)

Ellinson's Orange: an excellent apple, rather like an early Cox, but without the problems. Good in dry areas and on light soils, tip-bearing (4)

Greensleeves: a hardy and frost-resistant, good garden variety, largely self-fertile, with a good flavour. Crops well on young trees (3)

Egremont Russet (1872): good garden variety (*Crown copyright: Brogdale EHS*)

Kidd's Orange Red: resistant to scab and mildew; Cox type (3)

Pitmaston's Pineapple (1785): a special apple, small but with a rich, distinctive flavour (4)

Redsleeves: a red sister to Greensleeves. Scab- and mildew-resistant, and heavy-cropping even when young, self-fertile and said to require little pruning; a good garden variety (3)

Suntan: a frost-resisting Cox-type apple (5)

White Transparent (introduced from St Petersburg c. 1750): the earliest apple, ripening in July; may also be used as a cooker. Usually scab-free (2)

Worcester Pearmain (1874): good flavour, especially if left to ripen on the tree. Its blossoms are very frost-resistant. Tip-bearing, best grown with little manuring and less pruning. Liable to scab (3)

B. CULINARY (COOKING) APPLES

Belle de Boskoop (1856): dual-purpose. A poor pollinator, but keeps well and has good scab and canker resistance (3)

Bramley seedling (c. 1810): the archetypal cooker; susceptible to scab (3)

Crawley Beauty (1870): the latest-flowering apple, self-fertile, with attractive blossom. May be eaten as a dessert apple. Scab-resistant (7)

French Crab (pre -1750): also called the two-year apple, notable for its ability to keep in storage for two years (5)

Golden Noble (1820): generally disease-free and very high in vitamin C; may be used as a dessert apple (4)

Norfolk Beauty: a very big, frothy cooker (3)

Woolbrook Russet: scab-resistant; large, deep green fruit, rich in vitamin C (5)

C. CRAB APPLES

The fruits of some crab apples are surprisingly pleasant.

Dartmouth and **John Downie** are both worth a taste.

cluster to one or two. This will also encourage the remaining apples to grow to a decent size.

Picking. Apples are ready to pick when they come away in the hand. Gently lift the fruit and give it a quarter twist. If it does not part easily from the tree, the apple is not ripe.

Storage. The simplest way to keep apples sound and crisp is to put them in ventilated freezer bags. Make four or five holes with a paper punch or knitting needle. Put in your apples (which should be a keeping variety) and tie up the bag. Check the bags occasionally and remove any rotting fruit. Store somewhere cool and dark. A steady temperature is best as it prevents condensation. Apples give off ethylene gas which, even in tiny quantities, will cause potatoes to sprout, so keep them apart. Also keep apples away from anything with a strong smell, like onions, creosote or paint, or they may take on a taint.

Pests and diseases. Apples can suffer from hundreds of different pests and diseases, but the good organic grower can forget most of them. A good mulch of compost is often the best medicine. Nectar-rich annual flowers (see page 134) sown around the base will encourage predatory insects and help reduce pest problems. A thin mulch of old straw will encourage the ever-hungry rove beetles, which eat the larvae of fruit-spoiling pests. One of the best organic controls is hygiene. Many diseases overwinter on fallen leaves, so collect the leaves up and compost them. If the trees are growing in grass use a lawn-mower to shred and collect them. Do not worry if some shredded leaves are left behind, as they will be pulled under by the worms. Fallen fruit will harbour both pests and diseases; it should be gathered up and put into the middle of a hot compost heap. The two most common diseases are scab and canker. If any tree continually suffers ill-health despite receiving the best care and attention it is probably badly situated, and needs to be either moved elsewhere or burned.

Pollinators. Most apple varieties need to be pollinated by another variety, which obviously must flower at the same time. Where several varieties are growing in the neighbourhood, pollination is usually not a problem. However, some varieties such as Blenheim's Orange, Bramley's Seedling and Ribston Pippin are poor pollinators, and yields can often be improved by providing at least two suitable pollinating partners. The varieties listed in the table have been categorized into seven numbered groups of flowering times (the number in brackets). Varieties in any one group will fertilize each other and also those in neighbouring groups:

Group 3, for instance, will pollinate and be pollinated by Groups 2, 3 and 4.

PEARS

Pears are not quite as hardy as apples, and need a sunny and sheltered site. They flower two weeks earlier than apples and so may suffer more from frost damage. A pear tree grown on its own roots would become a large and long-lived tree, able to thrive on poor soils, but likely to take fifteen years to fruit. In order to produce a more convenient, small and early-bearing tree, pears are now grafted onto a quince root-stock. These are shallow-rooting and so need a good fertile soil, which must be high in humus, and moist but free-draining.

Pruning. Pears should be pruned in the same manner as apples (see page 148), though pruning is often done in late summer to reduce vigour. Pears have an upright habit and are often grown with one central stem; each branch radiating off the stem is treated as a cordon. Each year the new growth on the leader is cut back by about a third and the laterals (side shoots) cut back to two or three leaves (1 in/2.5 cm). This is called the pyramid system and has the advantage that if a branch has to be removed it can be easily replaced. The goblet-shaped bush is an easier and more manageable shape. Because of its upright growth the first young leaders may need to be bent and tied downwards with a guy-line, to be released later. This is best done in late summer. Young pear branches are quite amenable to this; after a few weeks the branch will have settled into its new position and may be untied.

Pears are often grown as espaliers. Simply tie the young leading branches so that they run horizontally along the wall. Young branches, just

**Tie down leaders with
weights for a few weeks
to achieve shape**

Training a goblet-shaped pear tree (*Rob Dalton*)

Pear varieties

Beurre Hardy (c. 1840): scab-resistant and vigorous, one of the best-flavoured hardy pears. Dual-purpose and a good keeper. Sometimes slow to come into bearing but crops heavily thereafter

Beurre Superfin (c. 1844): very good flavour but requires good conditions, and is susceptible to scab. Crops from early autumn; the fruit does not keep

Catillac (1665): a very large cooking pear that keeps until spring. Immune to scab. Distinctive large flowers, but a poor pollinator

Catillac: ancient (1665), large cooking pear, immune to scab (*Crown copyright: Brogdale EHS*)

Concorde: a new dessert variety; crops early and heavily, and has a good flavour. Ripens to a pale yellow; keeps (unripe) until mid-winter

Conference (1855): a reliable cropper, but not particularly hardy or disease-resistant. It will set fruit unpollinated, but the quality is not as good. Cropping from mid-autumn, it is a good, if unexciting variety

Dr Jules Guyot: has the musky flavour of Williams Bon Chrétien, but resists scab and is semi-self-fertile. A good garden variety

Doyenne du Comice (1849): the queen of pears, a superb flavour but intolerant and fickle. Susceptible to disease, especially scab, and often an unreliable cropper; cropping in late autumn. A poor pollinator

Fertility Improved: hardy, heavily cropping and disease-resistant, semi-self-fertile. Cropping from mid-autumn, the smallish yellow , dual-purpose fruit is good rather than excellent. Attractive red foliage in autumn

Hessle (pre-1850): an old Yorkshire variety, hardy and disease-resistant, with small russeted fruit in early autumn

Jargonelle (pre-1600): an old variety, very early ripening, with smallish green/brown fruit. Tip-bearing, so prune on a renewal system. Hardy, suitable for cool climates. A poor pollinator

Williams Bon Chrétien (1750): excellent flavour but demands good conditions; susceptible to scab. Crops in early autumn. The variety Glow Red Williams is identical except that the fruit has a thicker, red skin which resists scab

Hessle: an old (pre-1850) Yorkshire variety, hardy and disease-resistant (*Crown copyright: Brogdale EHS*)

a few months old, are the most pliable, but even three-year-old wood can be pulled into a new position if the process is done gradually over several months.

Old trees. Old and poor-cropping trees may be reinvigorated by careful pruning, weeding and feeding. Any diseased branches should be cut back to healthy wood. Use a good sharp saw and leave a tidy cut that will heal easily. If the tree is overcrowded take out the middle branches, aiming to let in both light and air. Follow the same procedure as for apples (page 150).

Picking. Pears should be picked while still under-ripe; if left on the tree they can become disappointingly 'mealy' or 'sleepy'. Early and mid-season pears should be harvested before they turn from greenish to yellowish. When the fruit will come away cleanly from its branch it is

ready to harvest. Ripen the pears indoors – in a living-room temperature of 60°F (15·5°C) is ideal. To store pears put them, unripe and straight from the tree, somewhere cool and dark, bringing them into the warmth to ripen only when you wish to eat them, for ripe pears will not keep.

Propagation. This is inadvisable: pears will come readily from hardwood cuttings, but will grow large without the restraining influence of dwarfing root-stock and will take years to fruit. Producing fruit trees by grafting requires professional expertise.

Pollination. Pears are generally self-sterile and require another variety close by. Some varieties (such as Catillac) are poor pollinators and should be outnumbered by good pollinators by at least two to one.

The pear shares most of its pests and diseases

with the apple. Its foliage is also subject to attack by slugworms, shiny, slug-like sawfly larvae. Pear scab, which is similar to apple scab, is one of the commonest problems. See *Pest Control* (page 290) and *Disease Prevention* (page 258).

PLUMS, GAGES AND DAMSONS

The plum is always sweeter when eaten ripe and juicy straight from the tree. It produces the best fruit when grown in a sunny, sheltered spot. Plums and gages can do particularly well when grown as espaliers or fans against a south-facing wall.

Although the plum tree likes a hot summer it actually prefers a cold hard winter, which will keep it dormant. Mild winters may encourage early growth, which is then at risk from frost.

The plum, like all stone fruit, likes lime. If your soil is not naturally high in calcium, incorporate a few handfuls of dolomite lime or calcified seaweed in and around the planting hole. A light dressing of calcified seaweed or dolomite lime should then be given annually to maintain a good supply of calcium. Plums growing on light or sandy soils may benefit from an annual dressing of rock potash given in late winter. If there is compost to spare the plum will appreciate it.

Plums should be planted in the usual way (see page 147), and staked for at least the first nine months to prevent wind-rock damage to the roots. Tie the tree to its stake with care, making sure that the tree does not rub against it, as bark wounds in plums often heal poorly and sometimes not at all. It is often a good idea to spray the newly planted tree with an aphid killer to prevent leaf curl (see page 156).

Once established a standard plum tree can be grown with almost no pruning; all that is required is the removal of diseased or crossing branches. However, it is wise to spend a little time shaping the tree in its formative years. When growing an ordinary standard, the aim is to produce a goblet-shaped tree with five or six strong leader branches coming off the trunk at right angles. This shape is often the best for gardens as it gives a clear trunk of 4–5 ft (120–150 cm), and so the ground beneath may still be used in some way. Because plums are prone to silver leaf disease (see page 282), which can enter through pruning cuts or wounds, pruning is normally done in spring when the tree is beginning to grow strongly.

A method of pruning popular with fruit growers is the 'dwarf pyramid', a central trunk with branches radiating from it. It makes good use of the available space, and is easily managed and pruned once you get the hang of it. However, it does need proper pruning, both to establish the shape of the tree and to maintain it (see Pears, page 152, for details). Plums fruit on both old and new wood.

When fan-trained against a wall, plums are easier to net, take up less space and perhaps gain from an especially sunny site. Gages, a most superior form of plum, do well on a sunny wall. Fans are best bought ready-formed, and trained to fill the available space. Most pruning can be done by pinching out unwanted shoots. Espaliers may be formed from any one-year-old (maiden) tree by pulling and tying appropriate young branches into position. Unwanted branches should be pruned out. Trees on dwarfing root-stocks are much easier to train.

There is now a dwarfing root-stock, 'pixy', for

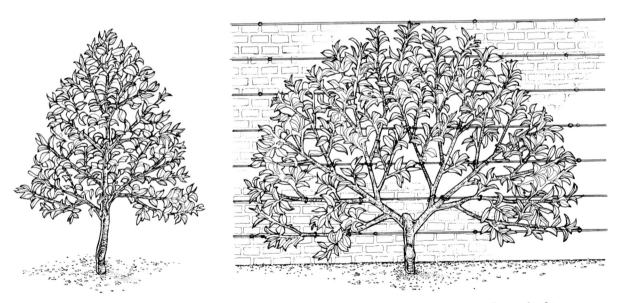

Easy to manage and prune, the dwarf pyramid makes good use of available space

Protective netting is more easily applied to a tree trained against a wall (*Rob Dalton*)

Plum varieties

A. DESSERT (EATING) PLUMS

Coe's Golden Drop (c. 1810): famously good fruits, but requires good conditions and even then is a shy cropper. Requires a pollinator

Early Laxton: the earliest plum, small and golden, but early flowering and so susceptible to spring frost. Requires a pollinator

Merton Gem: similar to Victoria but later, with better silver leaf resistance, and better flavour. Requires a pollinator

Opal: good-sized, early plums with a fine flavour, reliable and heavy-cropping. Requires a pollinator

Oullins Gage (c. 1860): not a true gage, but with very good quality gage-like plums. Mid-season and dual-purpose; flowers late and so may miss the frost. Self-fertile

Severn Cross: an autumn plum; large, juicy yellow fruits with a good flavour. Self-fertile

Victoria: the famous dual-purpose plum. Not really the best-quality fruit, and the tree is susceptible to silver leaf and canker and can look ungainly, yet it remains popular, especially where just one kind is grown. Self-fertile

Warwickshire Drooper: a pretty 'weeping' tree, producing large yellow plums for eating or cooking in late summer. Self-fertile

Early Laxton, frost susceptible but first out (*Crown copyright: Brogdale EHS*)

Pershore Yellow Egg: hardy, self-fertile, ideal garden variety (*Crown copyright: Brogdale EHS*)

B. CULINARY (COOKING) PLUMS

Black Prince: an early and good cooking plum, with some resistance to silver leaf and branch breakages; but it is early-flowering and so is susceptible to frost damage. Requires pollinators

Czar (pre-1880): the blossom is frost-resistant; self-fertile

Pershore Yellow Egg (1827): an ideal garden variety, especially when only one tree is grown. Disease-resistant, especially to canker, hardy and reliable; blossoms have some frost resistance. Mid-season, self-fertile

C. GAGES

Not as hardy as plums, but with a sweeter, more aromatic flavour

Cambridge Gage: a selection of the old greengage, tasting as good but fruiting much more reliably. Requires pollinating

Denniston's Superb (1835): the hardiest and most reliable gage, probably because, though it looks and tastes like and is categorized as a gage, it is really a plum. Self-fertile, very resistant to canker, and a good pollinator for other varieties

Early Transparent Gage: excellent flavour, perhaps the best variety to grow as a fan; self-fertile

Denniston's Superb (1835), hardiest and most reliable gage (*Crown copyright: Brogdale EHS*)

D. DAMSONS

They are the hardiest form of plum. The fruits are produced in autumn and are excellent when cooked. Damsons are often used as wind-breaks

Farleigh Damson: the heaviest cropper, but not fully self-fertile

Merryweather: a plum-like damson; the tree is much less upright than other damsons. Crops well and is self-fertile

Shropshire Damson (Shropshire Prune) (pre-1850): compact and upright, with good-quality fruit. A regular, but often light cropper. Self-fertile

E. OTHER TYPES

Mirabelle (French Cherry Plum): hardy and reliable, but not widely available. Small, round, dual-purpose plums with a good flavour. The Red and Yellow 'Nancy' varieties are generally considered the best

Myrobalan (Wild Cherry Plum): usually grown as a hedging tree; the fruits are quite pleasant

Quetsche produces long oval fruit in mid-autumn with an excellent flavour when cooked. Self-fertile plums and damsons; this produces an early-cropping tree, which if pruned can be kept to 8 ft (2·5 m) in height. However, the 'pixy' root-stock may not be suitable for poor or sandy soils, and the fruit will tend to be smaller than that produced from the more usual St Julien A. root-stock. If allowed to grow unchecked a tree on the latter will reach some 15 ft (4·5 m) in height. There are also vigorous stocks available, such as Brompton and Myrobalan, which produce a larger tree. Because they take up so much room these are now rather out of fashion, but if you have space, and patience, it is said they produce a more flavoursome fruit. When not on the dwarf stock, a young plum tree may grow rather too vigorously and put its energies into becoming bigger instead of producing flowers and fruit.

If you are impatient for fruit and do not mind the work, try root pruning. About 2 ft (60 cm) away from the trunk (3 ft/90 cm if the tree is more than seven years old) dig a semi-circular trench some 2 ft (60 cm) wide and deep, half-way round the tree, cutting through any roots thicker than a pencil. Any thin fibrous roots should, where possible, be left undamaged. If this process does not bear fruit it may be repeated the following year on the other side of the tree. Do not ring the tree by carving into the bark of the trunk. Another way to hasten cropping is to festoon the tree. This involves pulling the young supple branches into a downward curve, and tying them into position. The branch should be forced into as much of a bow as possible, though care should be taken not to break it. The more tension the branch is put under the more it will be inclined to stop growing and produce fruit buds. Festooned branches may be pruned back as for dwarf pyramids (see page 154), or, if they have helped to develop the shape of the tree, left alone.

Pollinating. If you are intending to grow only one plum tree it will have to be a self-fertile variety, such as Victoria, Czar or Denniston's Superb. These varieties also make the best pollinators for varieties that need them.

If the tree sets a very large number of small fruits it is a good idea to thin them out. The eventual harvest will not necessarily be lighter, but the plums will be heavier and the strain on the tree will be less because the tree has fewer plum stones to produce. A tree will sometimes produce such a heavy crop that the branches require propping up. Use anything which comes to hand to stop them from breaking, or the whole shape of the tree may be spoiled.

Picking. Plums and gages are best left on the tree until fully ripe, except perhaps when they are to be cooked. They do not ripen all at once so the tree will need to be picked over three or four times. Do not pull the stalks out of the fruit or they may quickly rot. Plums may be frozen straight from the tree without blanching or cooking.

Pests and diseases. Birds can be a real pest, pecking both the buds in spring and the fruit in summer. If fan-trained the plum can be netted, otherwise there is little that can be done.

Leaf-curl aphids can do a lot of damage, especially on young trees. They are particularly difficult to kill once they are enclosed within the curled leaves. They may be more easily destroyed by spraying the tree with derris or similar in early spring, before the leaves appear and the aphids have somewhere to hide.

Silver leaf can be particularly destructive with plums. There is a cure in the form of a fungus called *Tricoderma viride*. This was available some years ago and encouraging research is again underway to bring it back to the market for the benefit of gardeners. (See also page 261.)

False silver leaf, which is associated with over-feeding, does not stain the wood. It is not fatal, and does not require any particular action. Canker is another problem. See *Pest Control* (page 308) and *Disease Prevention* (pages 266, 282).

CHERRIES

The two types of cherry are the sweet, and the dark and sour Morello. They both produce sumptuous fruit. Formerly the sweet cherry grew too tall for the fruit to be protected from birds. Today, thanks to dwarfing root-stocks such as Inmil Colt and Camil, we can grow smaller, more easily managed trees.

The best way to grow a cherry is against a wall or garden fence, where it can be easily netted against birds. The espalier form is easiest. Simply train the appropriate branches sideways along a fence or wall. The young branches are quite flexible and may be pulled, pushed and tied to fit almost any shape. Prune out any unwanted branches in mid-summer.

Pruning. The pruning of sweet cherries begins in mid-spring, when unwanted side-shoots should be pinched out (with the fingernails) while they are still very young and soft. The new growth on leading branches should be tied in, either on to wires or supported bamboo canes. Ensure that old ties are constantly renewed or they may become tight and damage their branches. On the modern root-stocks the trees require very little pruning, and if grown as a free-standing tree, cherries can be left almost entirely unpruned except to remove any crossing branches. All pruning should be done during the summer to prevent silver leaf infection.

Pollination. Most varieties of sweet cherry

Nabella: a Morello type of cherry, resistant to die-back (*Crown copyright: Brogdale EHS*)

require another variety with which to swap pollen. These have to be carefully chosen, and the whole subject is rather complicated. Pollinators are given for the varieties described below. There are some garden varieties, most notably Stella, which are self-fertile and may be grown alone. The Morello cherry is also self-fertile, and both make excellent pollinating partners.

Morellos are hardier than sweet cherries and will crop successfully where other sorts will not. They produce an excellent sour fruit which freezes well and is most often used for cooking, though it is deliciously tart eaten raw when fully ripe. They require a different pruning regime, as they fruit only on young wood. The aim should be to build up a good framework whether the tree is grown free-standing or against a wall. Then keep encouraging new side-shoots. As they fruit only at their ends, the branches tend to become overlong, with most of the wood being unproductive. Each year about a quarter of the young branches should be pruned out, cutting back into three- or four-year-old wood. When pruning always cut back to a single bud; double ones are fruit buds and will not produce a shoot.

Pests and diseases include silver leaf; die-back, which can be a problem, especially with Morellos (often appears during flowering:

Cherry varieties

a. **Early Rivers** (pre-1881): very early, with delicious, large black fruit. Pollinate with d, h, m

b. **Merton Bigarreau:** early mid-season; purple-black cherries with the very best flavour. Vigorous and a heavy cropper. Pollinate with c, e, f, i, j

c. **Merton Glory:** early mid-season; yellowish-red fruit, not prone to cracking in wet weather. Pollinate with b, d, f, i, m

d. **Merton Heart:** early mid-season. Dark red with a good flavour. Pollinate with a, b, c, i

e. **Merton Late:** a very late cherry, but not otherwise outstanding. Pollinate with b

f. **Morello:** an excellent sour variety, most often used for cooking

g. **Napoleon Bigarreau** (pre-1791): a well-known variety with good fruit but susceptible to disease, so not really recommended. Pollinate with d, f, j

h. **Noir de Guben:** early mid-season, with good-quality, near-black fruit; canker-resistant. Pollinate with a, c, m

i. **Roundel:** mid-season dark red cherry, good quality and reliable. Pollinate with a, b, c, d, j, m

j. **Stella:** mid to late season. An ideal garden cherry, self-fertile so needs no partner; good grown as an espalier or fan. Perhaps not first-class cherries, but as good as those in the shops

New varieties that might be worth trying include:

k. **Cherokee:** self-fertile sweet cherry; yields well and unlike Stella is not prone to cracking

l. **Inga:** large, near-black fruit with resistance to canker. Pollinate with j, k

m. **Merchant:** good quality, dark red fruit with canker resistance. Pollinate with a, c, h, i

n. **Sunburst:** self-fertile, sweet black cherry

immediately remove any shoots that start to wilt); cherry leaf scorch. Cherry blackfly, a leaf-curling aphid is often farmed by ants, which will reintroduce the aphids after they have been dosed with derris or pyrethrum, and will also protect them from ladybirds – if possible kill off the ants (see page 318).

ABOVE: In cooler climates, peaches do best fan-trained against a wall (*Crown copyright: Brogdale EHS*)

RIGHT: Fan-trained peach tree (*Harry Smith*)

PEACHES, NECTARINES AND APRICOTS

There are several hardy varieties of peach, but their early blossom is very prone to frost damage, which is the major cause of peaches failing to fruit. The nectarine is not hardy, and its flowers are equally prone to frost damage. It is really little more than a smooth-skinned peach, and is treated in the same way.

Peaches demand good drainage, and prefer a good garden soil. They produce the best fruit when grown in a sunny site. In cooler climates they do best when fan-trained against a wall. This requires some skill and care. The hardier peaches will often grow and fruit successfully when given practically no attention at all, though they can become quite large bushes which may take up a lot of room. However, the newer dwarfing root-stocks offer the possibility of a low-maintenance dwarf tree. Another new development is the so-called 'genetic dwarf' type, which promises to produce a very compact, easily grown tree. When on semi-vigorous roots such as St Julien A., peaches may be kept to a quite manageable size by pruning. There are very vigorous root-stocks (such as Brompton) available which are not recommended.

As well as increasing the risk of frost damage (see page148 for precautions), early flowering can also produce pollination problems, as there may not be enough insects visiting the blossoms to ensure a good fruit set. Hand-pollination is quite easy: simply go from flower to flower, giving each one a gentle rub in its middle with a soft camel-hair brush, or even the traditional rabbit's tail. Where pollinating insects abound, peaches, nectarines and apricots are self-fertile and do not need a partner.

If the climate will allow, the easiest way to grow a peach is as a bush on a good dwarfing root-stock such as the 'pixy' type. Very little pruning is required. Crossing branches must be removed, and as the peach fruits only on last year's wood, care must be taken not to let all the branches get too long. Prune the bush on a renewal system, and when it begins to get too spindly simply cut back a branch or so in order to encourage new growth.

When grown against a sunny wall as a fan the peach has the

Peach, nectarine and apricot varieties

A. PEACHES

Duke of York: ready to eat in mid-summer; greenhouse variety

Dymond: ready in early/mid-autumn; greenhouse variety

Early Alexander: a hardy variety, producing an early crop of fruit

Peregrine: perhaps the best garden variety; also good in the greenhouse. Good-flavoured, crimson fruit, ripening in late summer

Robin Redbreast: said to have resistance to peach-leaf curl; not widely available

Rochester: hardy, and later flowering so often missing frost, but not such good flavour

Royal George: ready in late summer; greenhouse variety

Garden Lady, Bonanza: promising new dwarf varieties

B. NECTARINES

Early Rivers: fruits ripen in mid-summer; greenhouse variety

Humboldt: later-blossoming variety, capable of bearing very heavy crops

Lord Napier: a good garden variety, also good in the greenhouse; well-flavoured and a regular cropper

Pineapple: early autumn; perhaps the best-tasting nectarine, but not the most robust; good under glass

Dwarf Nectarine, Nectarella: promising new dwarf varieties

C. APRICOTS

These may be grown as peaches; they suffer from all the problems related to early flowering and so are best grown where they can be protected from frost, against a wall. Apricots can suffer from die-back, and affected branches should be cut out

Alfred: resists die-back

Early Moorpark: the most popular variety, commonly available; resists die-back

---

benefit of warmth and shelter. However, fan pruning is more difficult, though it is made easier by a dwarfing root-stock. Fans may be bought ready-formed; they are a little more expensive, but save some two years of pruning and are well worth the money. The wall should be fitted with a good system of support wires which should run parallel to the ground and be 6–8 in (15–20 cm) apart. The fixing hooks (called vine-eyes) come in two sorts, screw-tipped with a large eye, for fixing into wood or drilled holes; and the masonry nail type, which may be hammered into the cement mortar between bricks. Ideally a young fan should have eight main stems, four from each side. Plant the fan some 9-10 in (23-25 cm) from the wall at ground level and tie the stems, slanting towards the wall, on to bamboo canes, which themselves are tied to the wires. On semi-vigorous root-stocks such as St Julien A., prune back the last year's growth by a third.

Because peaches fruit on the last year's shoots the aim is to allow the fan to produce a number of new shoots along its stems every year. Unless it is required to be part of the fan's framework, once a shoot has blossomed and (with luck) fruited it is cut out. The old and unwanted shoots should be cut out in the autumn immediately after fruiting, and the new shoots should be tied in to the support wires. They should be spread out so as to make the best use of the wall space, but kept at least 5 in (12·5 cm) apart. In late winter pinch out the surplus shoots or any which are pointing in the wrong direction. If necessary continue to pinch out excess shoots through the spring and summer, but

do leave enough for next year's crop. When pruning a peach it is important to cut back to a wood bud, which is pointed, and not to a plump fruit bud which will never produce a shoot.

Pests and diseases. Peach-leaf curl is a universal problem; some gardeners find that garlic planted beneath the tree helps. Mildew can also be troublesome.

FIGS

The fresh fig is a delicious fruit, as different from the dried fig as the grape is from the sultana. Although it is really a Mediterranean fruit, the fig can be grown outside in mild climates such as southern England. Severe cold may kill parts of the tree: especially damaging are periods of sudden and intense frost during otherwise mild weather. A good position for a fig is against a south-facing wall, where it benefits from the extra protection and summer warmth. During spells of cold and snow, a south-facing wall can get quite warm. This winter warmth actually makes the effects of the cold much worse, and can harm the fig, so protect it through the day as well as during the night. I use an old flannelette sheet – heavier coverings such as blankets should be used with care , as they may break weaker branches.

When planting a fig it is most important to confine its roots. If they are allowed to grow unrestricted, the tree will be too vigorous and will fruit poorly or not at all. The best way to confine the roots is to dig a large square hole about 18 in

White Marseilles fig – not the hardiest, but the better fruit (*Harry Smith*)

(45 cm) deep and 30 in (75 cm) wide, and line its sides and bottom with paving slabs or bricks. Refill the hole with good soil mixed with 4 oz (120 gm) dolomite lime or a few handfuls of calcified seaweed, and plant the fig in the usual way. Alternatively, the fig may be planted in a paved area such as a patio. If you are planting against a wall, make sure that the tree is at least 9 in (23 cm) away, as the stem will eventually grow into a substantial trunk. Figs may also be grown in large pots and moved into a greenhouse to overwinter.

Pruning should be directed towards keeping the fig open and uncrowded. However, as any cutting back simply encourages more growth it should be kept to a minimum. Cut out any unwanted branches in the autumn, or, where winters are particularly harsh, prune in the spring and after bud-burst, when the extent of any frost damage may be ascertained. Do not trim back the shoots: they should be either cut out or left. In early summer pinch out the growing tips of side-shoots. Unwanted shoots should be rubbed out entirely.

The fig fruits upon matured one-year-old shoots, that is, those which grew the previous year, so the aim is to maintain a good supply of new fruiting wood, without crowding out the tree. In Mediterranean climates (or when grown in a greenhouse) the fig will produce a large early crop from the fruiting buds that form in the autumn. Outside, in more northern latitudes, this summer crop almost always fails to ripen.

The young tree may be given compost and liquid feeds to hasten its growth, but these should cease from the third year, when any feeding is best avoided or restricted to just foliar feeds. On a poor soil mulch around the tree with leaf-mould. The fig is a lime-lover and will benefit from an annual dose of a handful of crushed eggshells or calcified seaweed. If the roots have been properly confined it may be necessary to water the fig during a drought.

The main disease is canker.

QUINCES

Quinces have a wonderful rich, spicy flavour, but are too tough to be eaten uncooked. Use them in apple pies, or turn them into a distinctive jam. Quinces have a strong, pleasant scent. Many years ago they were carried in a jacket pocket like a personal pot pourri. The quince enjoys a wet soil, but it can be grown on any site that would suit a pear or apple. The tree is really no more than a large shrub, eventually growing to about 12 ft (4 m). The blossoms are very pretty. Unfortunately the tree has a straggly and ungainly habit, which can spoil its appearance. All too often branches will cross and rub one against another. Prune out the offenders in the winter, and leave the rest of the tree alone. Quinces are difficult to prune well and the gains of extensive pruning are not worth the trouble. They are usually disease-resistant, though they can share some problems of the apple and pear. Plant in the usual way (see page 147). Quinces are self-pollinating and will set good fruit without a partner. They may be propagated by layering or hardwood cuttings.

Fig varieties

Brown Turkey (pre-1850): hardy and widely available, but its figs are not the best

White Marseilles (pre-1525): produces a better fruit, but is not quite as hardy

Other varieties such as Rouge de Bordeaux have the very best fruit, but they are not hardy and do not fruit well in poor summers, so may need to be grown in a greenhouse.They are available only from specialist nurseries

---

Quince varieties

Champion: apple-shaped fruit

Meeches Prolific: crops well when young

Portugal: good quality fruit, but not very hardy

Vranja: large pear-shaped fruit

The ornamental **Japanese quince** (*Chaenomeles japonica*) produces edible fruits that are very similar to the true quince, and make a particularly good jam

Vranja, large, pear-shaped quince (*Crown copyright: Brogdale EHS*)

Medlar varieties

Dutch: produces the largest medlar, and has larger flowers

Nottingham: smaller, hardier, more prolific and more commonly found

---

Mulberry varieties

Morus alba: the white mulberry. Its foliage is the staple food of silkworms. The fruit is actually red-black. Specialist nurseries may have weeping and restricted forms of the white mulberry, which produce a smaller, garden-sized tree

Morus nigra: the black mulberry, large and long-lived; the best fruit

---

MEDLARS

The medlar is not to everyone's taste. Traditionally the small, brown and russet fruits are bletted (left to become very soft, almost rotten) before eating. They were often used to accompany sweet wines and liqueurs and served after dinner. A less adventurous way to enjoy these peculiar fruits is to sprinkle them with sugar and spice, bake them like small apples and serve with lashings of cream. The medlar tree requires very little attention; just prune out any crossing branches. They are normally quite quick to crop and will often produce fruit after just a couple of years. The medlar is self-fertile. The late spring blossom is most attractive – indeed, the tree is often grown purely for decoration. It is suitable for most gardens, as after a few years of steady growth it slows down and reaches a maximum of about 15 ft (5 m). Medlars are often grafted on to thorn root-stock.

MULBERRY

The common mulberry tree grows tall and is not suitable for small gardens. The fruit, which looks like a large raspberry, is produced only after some six or seven years. It requires almost no special attention, though it will grow much better if it is kept free from grass and weeds. The fruit, which should be totally ripe before it is eaten raw, is often used in puddings and pies, or in liqueurs such as mulberry gin. Different mulberries vary in their ability to produce fruit. If possible ensure that the tree is taken from a good early-fruiting parent. Mulberries may be grown as patio plants in pots or tubs; when so restricted they are supposed to produce a better-quality fruit.

SOFT FRUIT

Soil and preparation. All soft fruit prefer a good soil. The best is a moist but free-draining loam. Less than perfect soils such as light sands or heavy clays should be treated to copious quantities of compost or manure. Dig in as much as you can spare while the ground is unoccupied: once the bushes are planted it will be too late. Soft-fruit bushes are generally hungry for potassium, and will benefit from a generous application (up to 8 oz per sq yd/225 gm per sq m) of rock potash. This is especially beneficial on light sandy soils, which are naturally low in potassium. Do not use wood ashes as they make heavy soils sticky and wash out from light soils all too quickly; besides which, wood ashes are a product of the bonfire – environmentally and socially unsatisfactory. It is important to take the trouble to ensure that the soil is free from perennial weeds. Couch, docks, bindweed and thistles are difficult to eradicate at the best of times, but once they are entangled in the roots of young fruit bushes they become almost impossible to get rid of. Ideally the ground preparation should be done in the autumn, some seven or eight weeks before the bushes or canes are planted.

Planting. Young plants will establish themselves better than old ones. Largish plants which have spent a year or two in pots, sitting unsold in a garden centre, are not likely to do well. Soft-fruit bushes are subject to many virus diseases; where possible buy certified virus-free stock.

Plant them at any time during late autumn and winter when conditions are suitable. The bushes

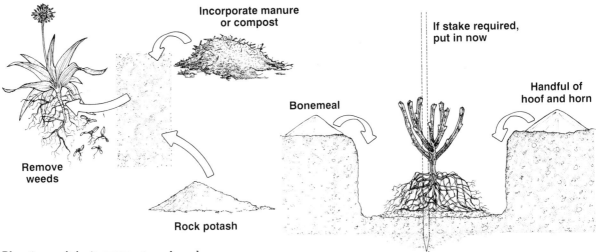

Incorporate manure or compost

Remove weeds

Rock potash

If stake required, put in now

Bonemeal

Handful of hoof and horn

Hole wider than root spread

Planting soft fruit ABOVE: stage 1 – advance, autumn preparations; RIGHT: stage 2 – eight weeks later (*Rob Dalton*)

or canes should always be given a hole larger than the spread of their roots. A handful of hoof and horn and another of bone-meal may be dug in at the bottom of the hole, but is not essential. Put the plant in its hole and carefully spread out the roots, trimming off any which have been damaged. If they are going to require staking put the stake in now, then refill the hole, perhaps incorporating another handful of hoof and horn and/or bone-meal, and firm down the soil.

The plants should now be pruned (unless this has already been done), which usually involves reducing the young bush or cane to a fraction of its former self. See under specific varieties for details. The prunings from these young bushes may be treated as cuttings; as they are certified disease-free it would be a shame to waste them.

Spacing. The spacings for soft fruit always look too wide at first, then after a few years they become a little cramped. With bush fruit, if a reasonable crop is wanted quickly, double up the number of plants within the row, and be prepared to dig them out after a few years to make more space. It is not a good idea to plant the rows closer together, or put extra rows in between, as it impedes access. The space can be better used for strawberries or vegetables.

Weeding. Young soft-fruit bushes might survive in weed-infested ground, but they will not thrive. During the first few years keep the soil well weeded. Hand-weeding is best, as soft fruits have shallow roots which are easily damaged by deep hoeing, or any close digging.

Straw mulches are very useful in suppressing weeds. They increase the moisture content of dry soils, and encourage earthworm activity, which helps the drainage. But they do cool the soil, and seem adversely to affect young bushes, which

will establish better and more quickly if grown in a clear soil.

Feeding and deficiencies. Soft fruit can be a hungry crop. Some sorts, for example raspberries, produce a lot of growth which is annually pruned away. This may lead to certain nutrients being used up and so cause mineral deficiencies, but when organically grown, soft fruits should be well supplied with all the nutrients they need. Every few years use a soil testing kit to determine the soil pH, and give an appropriate dressing of dolomite lime (see page 16). A foliar feed of comfrey or seaweed liquid fertilizer may be given in late spring and again a month later to help with fruit production.

Moving old bushes. It is possible to move established bushes quite successfully, but it takes both time and effort. The job is made easier if there are two of you, and if the plants are first pruned back ruthlessly. During the early winter, carefully dig up the plant with a fork, and try not to damage too many roots – be prepared to spend up to an hour per bush. Move the bush carefully to its new home and replant it. Later, trim away

Feeding soft fruits

Poor soils should be given an annual dressing of compost or well-rotted manure, and if the soil is especially prone to mineral deficiencies (if, for instance, it is sandy) also give the plants a winter dressing of seaweed meal (up to 3 oz per sq yd/85 gm per sq m) , together with a dose of rock potash. Rock potash also acts as a liming agent, containing calcium oxide, and also a useful amount of magnesium.

the blossom to prevent the bushes from fruiting during their first season, and be prepared to water them, especially during dry spells.

Birds such as bullfinches can be a major pest on soft fruit. In late winter they will happily peck out the buds and severely damage the bush. Where possible protect the bushes with nets. A fruit cage is ideal but expensive. Home-made temporary cages rigged up with bamboos as support can be just as effective. The best solution of all is to grow your soft fruits against a garden wall or fence, where they can be protected by a single draped net.

One way to reduce bird damage to buds is to delay pruning until the buds are beginning to open and are out of danger. The birds peck out the buds at the ends first, and these will often be pruned out anyway. This very late pruning is not particularly good for the fruit, and is really a last resort. In the summer birds will eat all the fruit they can, if it is unprotected.

Harvesting. The best time to pick soft fruit is early in the morning, just after the dew has lifted. If the fruit has to be picked wet, spread it out on trays to dry. Care should be taken not to bruise it, or it will quickly become mouldy. The refrigerator is the best place to keep soft fruit. Keep it covered or it may become tainted with other flavours. All fruit freezes well; only rhubarb, which is a stem, not a fruit, needs to be blanched.

Culinary and dessert. These terms are used to indicate whether the fruit is going to be cooked or not. Dessert fruit is eaten fresh and raw, while culinary fruit is cooked first.

GOOSEBERRY (*Ribes grossularia*)

The gooseberry is the first soft fruit of summer. It makes a superb jam and is especially welcome for early summer puddings and pies. A sprig of elder blossom added to stewing gooseberries imparts a delicate muscatel flavour.

The gooseberry plant is the most vigorous and hardy of soft fruits. It will grow in most sites and situations, thriving where other sorts might fail. It does not like dry, light soils, nor hot dry climates. The gooseberry fruits upon its old wood and has a permanent framework of branches; it may be trained into fans or cordons, and so may be grown up walls or fences, even north-facing ones. There are two ways to prune gooseberries. The easy way is, in the winter, to cut out any crossing branches and trim back spindly growth, trying to encourage an open-hearted bush by pruning out branches that are growing inwards. The proper, and more difficult, way is that described under red currants. Fan-trained and cordon gooseberries have to be pruned properly. It is best to plant two-year-olds; ideally they should have a stem to hold the branches above the ground. Half-standard

gooseberries are becoming popular. These are grown on a 3 ft (1 m) stem which makes picking and pruning a great deal easier, but they need to be well staked.

Most varieties of gooseberry are not covered by a health certification scheme, but it is still worth buying plants from a specialist fruit nursery.

Plant gooseberries during winter, and space them 5 ft (1.5 m) apart, with 6 ft (1.8 m) between the rows. This spacing always looks over-generous to start with. Double planting within the rows will give heavier yields earlier, but unless every other bush is taken out after three or four years the gooseberries will form an impenetrable hedge. Cordon bushes should be spaced at 1 ft (30 cm) apart, double cordons at 2 ft (60 cm) and triple cordons at 3 ft (90 cm). After planting, prune back the branches by a half: ideally cut to an outward-facing bud.

Picking. Gooseberries are often harvested for cooking before they are fully ripe, as they hold together better. Ripe fruit, though sweeter raw, may turn into a mush if stewed. Half the berries may be picked when under-ripe, for cooking, leaving the remainder to grow bigger and sweeter for dessert use. This is a useful way of thinning heavily-laden bushes.

Pests and diseases. Sawfly caterpillars are the major pest of gooseberries. Spray them with derris or pyrethrum, but watch out for their habit of

Planting

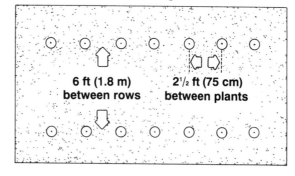

6 ft (1.8 m)
between rows

2½ ft (75 cm)
between plants

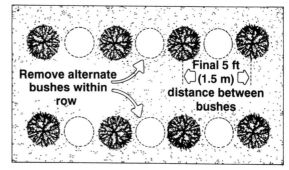

Remove alternate bushes within row

Final 5 ft (1.5 m) distance between bushes

Double planted gooseberry bushes (*Rob Dalton*)

Gooseberry varieties

Black Velvet: the result of a cross between a Worcester berry and a gooseberry, this new variety is completely immune to mildew. The dark red fruits are different, if not over-large

Captivator: a nearly thornless variety, though perhaps the better gooseberries are worth a few scratches

Careless (1851): reliable and popular where flavour is not the first consideration

Howard's Lancer: the best variety for light soils; high-yielding, with a first-class flavour and yellow-green fruit. Sulphur-shy

Invicta: an excellent new variety, remarkable for its very high resistance to mildew. High-yielding, with light green fruits, but not the best for flavour

Jostaberry: a cross between the gooseberry and the blackcurrant, vigorous and disease-resistant; the fruit is like a large, bland blackcurrant

Leveller (1851): superb flavour, but needs very good conditions. Sulphur-shy

Lord Derby (pre-1880): a very late variety with very large dark red berries of good flavour. Sulphur-shy

Invicta: excellent recent variety with high mildew resistance (*Crown copyright: Brogdale EHS*)

May Duke (1900): the young fruit can be picked for cooking very early, in late spring or sometimes early summer. But the ripe berries are not among the best

Whinham's Industry: vigorous and hardy, even in shade; good on heavy soils. Dark red fruit with a first-class flavour

Worcester Berry (Ribes divaricatum): a vigorous bush, which produces interestingly flavoured red-purple berries; immune to most gooseberry diseases

dropping off the bush, and so avoiding a fatal dose. American gooseberry mildew is the commonest disease, but varieties are now available which have considerable resistance to mildew.

Gooseberries are easy to propagate, and will root readily from hardwood cuttings taken in early winter (see page 78).

RED CURRANTS (*Ribes vulgare*) and WHITE CURRANTS (*Ribes vulgare album*)

The red currant is generally healthy and productive and it deserves to be more widely grown. The currants are high in vitamins, and can be picked quite quickly. When they first ripen, they are pleasantly sharp, while if left on the bush until late summer they lose their acidity and become quite sweet, delicious eaten raw.

Most varieties of red (and white) currants are not covered by a UK health certification scheme, so it is particularly important to buy new stock from a reputable nursery. Space new bushes at 5 ft (1·5 m) apart in rows 6 ft (1·8 m) apart. As with gooseberries, if new plants are double-planted within the row (and dug out when they get too large) early crops will be twice as heavy. The space between the rows may be used for strawberries or vegetables, but do not dig around the red currant roots.

Red and white currant varieties

There is not very much difference between either red currant or white currant varieties

A. RED CURRANTS

Jonkheer van Tets: the earliest

Laxton's No. 1: mid-season; very good quality fruit, early and heavy-cropping

Red Lake: ripens late; one of the best for flavour

Redstart: mid-season; a new variety with a strong, sharp flavour

Stanza: late-flowering and so avoids frost; high yields

B. WHITE CURRANTS

White Dutch (1831): mid-season; an old variety

White Versailles (1843): early; the colourless fruit does not look as nice as red currants but has an excellent, sweet flavour

Pruning. The red currant fruits on spurs which are formed on old wood, so the aim is to build up a framework of permanent branches to form an open-centred bush. Ideally the bush will have a short stem or leg of at least 4–6 in (10–15 cm), and then branch out, with six or seven main leaders forming a bowl. They should look rather like a hand that is holding an invisible ball. If the bowl of the bush is incomplete at any point, allow a side-shoot from a leader to fill in and become a leader too. During the winter these leaders should be pruned back by about a half. This will produce strong branches, able to bear the biggest crops. All the branches or shoots that are not leaders are laterals. Ideally these are first pruned in early summer, when they should be cut back to five or six leaves. Then in the winter they should be pruned back again, so as to leave just an inch (2·5 cm) of growth with two or three buds.

A cordon red currant is treated as a bush with just one leader, and double and triple cordons are treated accordingly. Other shapes such as fans are also possible. The art is to allow the leaders to make the best use of the space available.

Red currants are usually pest- and disease-free, though they can suffer from the same problems as gooseberries. They may easily be propagated from hardwood cuttings taken in early winter. Rub off all but the top buds so as to encourage a stem.

BLACKCURRANTS *(Ribes nigrum)*

Blackcurrants do best in a deep fertile loam, and respond to generous applications of compost, especially in their first few years.

They are hardy and will grow in most conditions.

Viral diseases are a major problem, and in the UK are covered by a ministry certification scheme. Buy only certified plants. Do not plant new clean stock near old (infected) bushes, or into soil recently inhabited by old plants.

Space the bushes at 3–4 ft (90–120 cm) apart, with 6 ft (1·8 m) between the rows. Blackcurrants grow quite quickly, so do not double up on the spacings. After planting cut back the shoots to 3 in (7·5 cm).

Pruning. Blackcurrants fruit on wood grown the previous year. This makes it necessary to take out the old wood and encourage new growth, so renewing the bush. Unlike the red currant and the gooseberry, the blackcurrant cannot be

---

Blackcurrant varieties

Baldwin: especially high in vitamin C

Ben Lomond: mildew- and frost-resistant

Ben Sarek: a small but very high-yielding new variety with large fruits borne on frost- and mildew-resistant bushes; unless it is encircled by twine, the heavy crop may break down the bush

Blackdown: very resistant to mildew

Boskoop Giant: the earliest-ripening variety, but only a moderate cropper and susceptible to frost

Jet: late-flowering (and ripening), so avoids frost; small-fruited but high-yielding

Laxton's Giant: the largest-berried blackcurrant; good flavour but requires good conditions

Seabrook's Black: resistant to big bud

Ben Sarek, high-yielding, mildew-resistant blackcurrant (*Crown copyright: Brogdale EHS*)

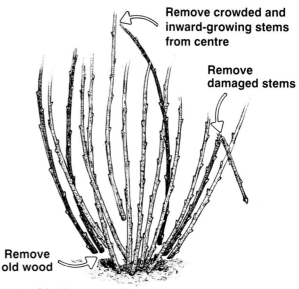

Remove crowded and inward-growing stems from centre

Remove damaged stems

Remove old wood

Pruning blackcurrants (*Rob Dalton*)

trained to a permanent shape. It forms a stool, which means that branches rise directly out of the ground. Prune out the older branches, which have already fruited, and encourage the younger stems, which will bear next year's fruit. Up to a third of the bush may be pruned away each year. If too many young stems are crowding together in the middle of the bush, cut out the weakest, to encourage the others.

Pests and diseases. The worst pest is big bud mite, which feeds and breeds within the buds, producing the typical swollen buds which never open to produce leaves. Bad infestations reduce yield, but the bigger threat comes from the fact that the mite transmits the reversion virus – the worst problem of all, which will eventually affect most bushes (see *Pest Control*, page 326, and *Disease Prevention*, page 288).

Propagation. Because blackcurrants are so prone to virus diseases, which are carried over in cuttings, it is usually better to buy in new healthy bushes. However, the first prunings (cut after planting) will root if treated as hardwood cuttings, and so a couple of new plants may eventually produce up to a dozen more.

RASPBERRIES (*Rubus idaeus*)

The raspberry is perhaps the best of all dessert soft fruit. The best raspberries have a rich, sweet, slightly musky flavour, together with a delicacy which makes the strawberry seem almost vulgar.

Raspberries prefer a good, free-draining soil which has a high content of organic matter. Like other soft fruits they are potash-hungry and respond well to generous applications of compost. Raspberries are (or should be) vigorous, and because they produce so much growth, annually renewed, they can run out of certain nutrients such as iron, potash, manganese and magnesium. Annual applications of compost together with a dressing of seaweed meal should prevent problems, but if the leaves look yellow or discoloured give the plant a good foliar feed (see page 24). Sadly, the canes inevitably become

---

Raspberry varieties

A. SUMMER-FRUITING

Glen Clova: early to ripen, with heavy yields of good-quality fruit produced over a very long picking period, but susceptible to die-back. To prevent infection do not plant with other varieties. Very good as the sole variety in a garden

Glen Moy: a new variety, virus-resistant, aphid-resistant and spine-free. Reasonable flavour and heavy yields, but has a short harvest period of just a couple of weeks

Golden Everest: the standard yellow-fruiting variety, preferred by some

Leo: the latest of the summer-fruiting varieties; its only real advantage is in extending the season

Malling Admiral: good flavour but not the highest yields. Strong-growing canes, with resistance to several viral diseases, spur blight and cane botrytis

Malling Jewel: not high yields, but good fruit, which keeps on the bush. It has some resistance to botrytis and flowers late, so misses frost. Tolerant to virus infection but may help spread it to nearby plants – do not plant with other varieties

Malling Joy: a new variety with good resistance to all the various aphids which attack raspberries and spread viral diseases. Good flavour, but the canes are very spiny

Yellow Antwerp (pre-1855): a very old variety, neither vigorous nor high-yielding (and not widely available), but with a good reputation for flavour

Malling Admiral, good flavoured, healthy raspberry (*Crown copyright: Brogdale EHS*)

B. AUTUMN-FRUITING

New varieties are being released all the time. They are much heavier-yielding and an improvement on the older autumn-fruiting sorts

Autumn Bliss: the heaviest-cropping of all autumn varieties, with reasonably good flavour. Short, sturdy canes

Fall Gold: yellow berries. Like all autumn-fruiting sorts can be rather weak-flavoured, especially in wet years, but also hates a late drought

Other names to look out for include **Heritage** and **Zeva**

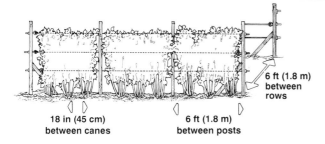

Raspberry cane spacing (*Rob Dalton*)

infected with viral diseases and plantings usually become unproductive after seven or eight years. Always buy in certified stock and plant well away from old infected canes. The ideal time to plant new stock is late autumn, as this gives them time to get well rooted before spring, but they may be planted at any time during the winter. When planting the canes the roots should be covered by at least 4 in (10 cm) of soil, even if the soil mark on the stem suggests that they were originally not so deep. Space the young canes at 18 in (45 cm) apart with at least 6 ft (1·8 m) between rows. Less vigorous varieties, such as Leo, may be planted at two plants per station. Once planted cut down the cane so it protrudes by no more than a foot. This is to prevent the canes from fruiting in their first year, which weakens them and prevents them from becoming well established.

Raspberries need a good supporting frame of stakes and wires if they are to do well. Where possible use good stout end posts, which should be strutted with angle braces; there should be middle posts every 6 ft (1·8 m). Strong galvanized wires should run across (parallel to the ground) at 2, 3½ and 5 ft (60, 100 and 150 cm). If the prospect of so much fencing work is too daunting, a satisfactory crop can be got by planting them against a sunny fence. Summer raspberries should be pruned straight after they have finished fruiting. Cut out the old canes which have just produced the crop, and tie in the new ones which will yield next year. Any canes which are much taller than the wires should be trimmed back to within a few inches of the top wire.

Autumn-fruiting raspberries are produced on shorter, sturdier canes, and are much easier to support. They do not need to be tied in, but may be kept together by stretching a line on either side of the row. The lines should be kept parallel by connecting them with string ties at intervals.

Pests and diseases. All raspberries will eventually become virus-ridden and unproductive. There is no cure and the plants should be dug up and burnt. A few other diseases which occasionally trouble raspberries include cane blight (withering from ground level), cane spot (purple spots turning to purple-edged blotches on canes and leaves), and spur blight (purple blotches, turning silver, around nodes on canes; affected buds and shoots die back). The main pest is the raspberry beetle, or rather its grub, which is all too often present in raspberries (and blackberries).

Propagation. It is worth propagating only from very healthy canes. Raspberries are easily propagated by digging up the suckers which spring up outside the row.

BLACKBERRIES AND HYBRID BERRIES

A good blackberry has a rich, sweet flavour, excellent eaten raw, delicious in puddings and pies; all varieties freeze well. Blackberries are hardy and easy to grow. They may be trained to a fence or a wire support or just left to ramble. The thorny varieties are ideal for keeping out unwelcome visitors. There are also several thorn-free varieties, but most lack flavour.

Blackberries are vigorous and need plenty of room. Space new plants at no less than 6 ft (1·8 m) apart, with 10 ft (3 m) or more between vigorous varieties. After planting prune the stems back to 9 in (23 cm). The blackberry produces fruit on last year's stems, so pruning should consist of cutting out, in early winter, the old wood which has fruited. When trained against wire or a fence, the stems should be carefully tied in, and a space should be left to receive the new young stems which grow from the base of the plant. These should be supported as they grow, and tied in when the old stems are pruned out.

In cold or exposed sites the new stems may be protected by tying them together in one large pillar-like bundle at the beginning of winter. Untie the stems and spread them out in very early spring.

Blackberries are generally healthy, though they can suffer from the raspberry beetle (see page 320). Hybrid berries are not quite so healthy, and may suffer from other raspberry problems.

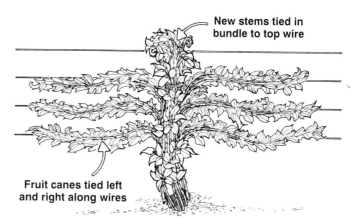

New stems tied in bundle to top wire

Fruit canes tied left and right along wires

Fan method of training blackberries and hybrid berries (*Rob Dalton*)

Blackberry and hybrid varieties

A. BLACKBERRIES

Ashton Cross: early to mid-season; vigorous and exceedingly high-yielding, medium-sized with a sharp flavour, ideal for culinary use

Bedford Giant: the earliest blackberry; heavy crops of large berries but rather weak flavour

Fantasia: mid-season; very large berries of good flavour

Loch Ness: a new thornless variety. Unlike other blackberries the canes are semi-erect, and should be tied upright and fanned out. Perhaps the only thornless variety with a reasonable flavour

Merton Thornless: not a very good flavour

B. HYBRID BERRIES

These may be described as a cross between a raspberry and a blackberry, both in taste and colour. They crop after raspberries but before blackberries

Black Raspberry (Starlight): grow like a raspberry; good-flavoured fruit, produced after ordinary raspberries have finished

Boysenberry: similar to a loganberry but sweeter; the stems can be killed by a hard winter

Fantasia yields large, good-flavoured berries (*Ken Muir*)

Japanese Wineberry (*Rubus phoenicolasius*): has bristles rather than thorns; quite an attractive plant, with sweet, well-flavoured fruit

Loganberry: dark red fruit, with a sharp flavour; good for culinary use

Tayberry: perhaps the best hybrid berry, sweet enough for dessert use

Tummelberry: similar to the tayberry but a little later and hardier; perhaps not such a good flavour

Propagation. Blackberries and hybrids are easily propagated by burying the end of a stem in the ground. Midsummer is a good time, when the stem will root quickly and produce a good plant for moving on in late autumn.

STRAWBERRIES

Strawberries grow best on slightly acid soil (pH 6·5). So hold back on the dolomite lime, and use rock potash with caution as it is a little alkaline. The best fertilizer for strawberries is compost. Before planting dig in as much as you can spare. On light sands which are naturally low in potash give the plants a comfrey liquid feed in late spring (see page 24).

Planting. Good strawberry plants are expensive, so it is worth planting them properly. New stock is best bought in from a reputable mail-order fruit nursery. Accept only plants which have been certified. Ordinary runners, which come freshly dug, are available from mid-autumn; some nurseries offer cold stored runners for dispatch in mid- to late summer, which is just about the ideal planting time in order to establish the plants for fruiting the next year. The more expensive pot-grown plants are available all year round. Plant the strawberries in rows 3 ft (90 cm) apart, with 12 in (30 cm) between plants. If this seems too far apart use the space between to catch a quick crop of lettuces or radishes. The new plants should go in at the correct depth. The crown should not be buried, nor the roots left exposed. Dig out a 6 in (15 cm) deep hole and place the crown in position against one side of the hole; spread out the roots, then fill in and firm down the soil. Water the plants in well, and keep them watered as necessary until they are established.

As long as newly planted strawberries are growing strongly they may be allowed to fruit as soon as they like. If the plants look a little puny, cut off the flower trusses as they appear. Strawberries may be grown as individuals or in matted rows.

Straw mulch keeps strawberries clean (*Bob Flowerdew*)

The separate plants are easier to keep weed-free and will produce bigger and better-looking fruit, but the matted row produces a bigger and better yield. To maintain a row of single plants cut off the runners as they appear; to get a matted row, don't.

A mulch of straw applied in spring, before the plants start to spread out, will help to keep the berries clean, but it can make the ground cold and delay ripening as well as giving the slugs somewhere to hide. The name 'strawberry', incidentally, has nothing to do with straw, but comes from the plant's habit of producing runners and 'strewing' itself about.

After fruiting trim back the old leaves and encourage new growth – this is the basis of next year's fruit. Even a good strawberry bed will last only five or six years, before the yield becomes disappointing. A good plan is to plant up a new patch every couple of years, so that you have one bed starting as the other finishes. Propagate new plants by allowing certain runners to grow unhindered, and transplant them to their final position in mid-autumn or, if you are prepared to look after them very carefully, in late summer. Don't propagate from poor-looking plants, but buy in good new stock.

Strawberries may be grown under cloches or in tunnels, and with the newer perpetual varieties an almost year-round harvest is in prospect. Ensure as much access by insects as possible, or poor pollination will lead to a low yield and distorted fruits.

Pests. The main pests of strawberries are birds

Strawberry varieties

Some varieties come rapidly in and out of fashion, while others cannot be improved on

A. STANDARD TYPES

Cambridge Favourite: the most widely grown, cropping well on most sites and soils, and suitable for the greenhouse; the fruit lasts well on the plant; moderate flavour. Resistant to mildew but susceptible to red spider mite

Cambridge Vigour: excellent flavour (especially from first-year plants) and flowers late to miss the frost, but susceptible to verticilium wilt and mildew

Marastar: resistant to mildew

Rabunda: perpetual variety, mid-summer to late autumn; suitable for the greenhouse

Red Gauntlet: heavily cropping, resistant to mildew and botrytis; suitable for the greenhouse. Often has a second crop in late summer, but not the best flavour

Royal Sovereign (1892): famous old variety, once claimed to have the very best flavour of all (though today not everyone agrees). But not a vigorous grower and susceptible to disease, especially mildew, although does well in the greenhouse

Saladin: strongly resistant to red core and mildew; some resistance to botrytis. Produces a high yield but has a second-best flavour. Does not like a drought

Shuskan: said to freeze better than any other; good yield and resistant to red core

Silver Jubilee: very good flavour, and resistant to red core, mildew and botrytis. Not an enormous yield but a good garden variety

Tantallon: a good yield of reasonable flavour, with resistance to red core, mildew and botrytis, but not drought-resistant

Cambridge Favourite crops well on most sites and soils (*Crown copyright: Brogdale EHS*)

Troubadour: good resistance to red core, mildew, and verticilium wilt. Crops late to extend the season and flowers late so usually misses any frost; does not like a drought

B. PERPETUAL-FRUITING AND DAY-NEUTRAL STRAWBERRIES

These will fruit all summer long, and most of the autumn too. In a heated greenhouse (minimum mean temperature 50°F/10°C) some varieties will continue almost all the year round. New varieties are not yet widely tested, but names to look out for are:

Honeoye: very long cropping

Tribute: reasonable flavour and disease resistance

Tristar: reasonable flavour and disease resistance

C. ALPINE VARIETIES

Alexander, Baron Solemacher, Red Wonder, Yellow Wonder, among others

and slugs, which will both eat the fruit, and the ubiquitous aphid (see *Pest Control*, page 308). Aphids and the red spider mite can be controlled by a good washing with a hosepipe, which will help reduce red spider mite numbers and also up-turn the leaves, which can then be sprayed with soft soap.

Diseases. Strawberries are prone to several diseases. Varieties which have resistance to disease are detailed above. Otherwise, hygiene is the best preventive. Clear away old leaves, picking up all those removed in the post-harvest trim. Keep the plants well hoed and weeded, and give an occasional dressing of compost or, better still, leaf-mould.

The main diseases are: mildew, which first affects the foliage, producing purple blotches, and then moves on to the fruit, giving it a dull appearance with protruding seeds; red core, which affects the roots, destroying the rootlets first, and giving the main roots a red core (it is more prevalent on ill-drained soils); grey mould or botrytis, at its worst in wet weather; verticilium wilt, which is often at its worst in the maiden year, causing the old leaves to turn reddish brown, the young leaves to yellow, and the plants to wilt.

Frost damages the blossoms, blackening their middles. If a late frost threatens, throw an old sheet over the plants at night.

Alpine strawberries are very hardy plants that will grow almost anywhere and still produce a summer-long supply of tiny, sweet strawberries. It takes patience to pick them, but just a few will perk up the morning muesli, or decorate a dessert such as cheesecake. Easily grown from seed, they do not produce runners.

GRAPES

Grape-vines can be very long-lived. The famous Black Hamburgh vine at Hampton Court was planted in 1769 and shows no sign of declining; indeed, in 1990 this vine produced 850 lb (385 kg) of grapes, its highest yield for at least a century.

Vines require a sunny and sheltered site, and need good drainage. The best dessert grapes require lots of warmth and sun: if possible the vines should be grown against a south-facing wall or fence. They may then be grown as a cordon or fan and treated and pruned like greenhouse grapes (see *Growing Under Cover*, page 351). Wine grapes are not so fussy and the hardy varieties may be grown in open ground almost anywhere in northern Europe.

They will need the support of a base wire running horizontally about 20 in (50 cm) off the ground. After planting, cut back the vine to three buds. In the spring select the strongest shoot and pinch out any others so as to produce one strong stem. During the winter cut the shoot back to 4 ft (1·2 m) and train it along the wire. If it has not grown well during its first year, cut the shoot right back to three buds as before and start again.

In its second year the shoots which arise from the horizontal stem should be supported with the help of two double lengths of twine strung above the wire, the first at 2½ and the other at 3½ft (75 and 105 cm). The twine should be stretched either side

---

Grape varieties

A. STANDARD TYPES

Brandt: a late, small black grape for dessert, hardy and reliable with attractive foliage

Glory of Boskoop: heavy-cropping, blue-black dessert variety, combining sweetness with hardiness

Himrod Seedless: a little flavourless, best on a wall

Leon Millot: black grapes for wine or dessert; prolific, with mildew-resistant foliage

Madeleine Sylvaner: early-ripening; heavy yields of small golden berries ideal for wine; good under cold conditions

Mueller-Thurgau: ideal for a moselle-type white wine; grow in a sheltered position, or against a wall

Sieve Villard: makes a delicate white wine; some resistance to mildew

Strawberry Grape: large dark red fruits with a flavour supposed to be like that of strawberries. Good resistance to mildew; best grown against a wall

B. GRAPES FOR THE GREENHOUSE OR WARMER CLIMATES

Black Corinth: a very old variety with small, seedless black fruit

Black Hamburgh: sweet and juicy dessert grapes, ripening early and well even in a sunless summer, high disease resistance

Foster's Seedling: good companion to Black Hamburgh for early forcing. White grapes, easy to grow in cold house

Muscat of Alexandria: among the very best white grapes for dessert. Requires a sunny autumn to develop its full flavour

Royal Muscadine: introduced in 1660, still one of the best varieties for pot culture. Early, sweet, rich white grapes

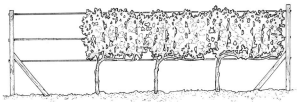

Vine holding frame (*Rob Dalton*)

should be cut back to two shoots. One should be tied to the wire as a replacement and if necessary pruned to 2 ft (60 cm).

The shoots which grow from it need to be supported as before, but this time they may be allowed to fruit. The other shoot is cut back to two or three buds, which are reduced to one strong shoot in early summer as before. During the following winter, this shoot is cut back to 2 ft (60 cm) and trained along the wire, but this time in the opposite direction. The stem which has fruited should be cut out, leaving just one shoot, which is pruned to two or three buds; these in turn are reduced to one strong shoot, which is then tied to the wire. The aim of this pruning is to have a stem producing fruiting shoots on one side of the plant, and a replacement growing on the other.

Grapes for dessert may be thinned out when the berries begin to swell. Use a sharp, pointed pair of scissors and cut away from the inside first. Harvest the fruit some four or five weeks after the grapes have coloured up, cutting the bunches with a sharp pair of secateurs.

Vines appreciate a dressing of compost in the winter, and monthly foliar feeds in the summer. They can fall prey to a host of pests and diseases, but the biggest problem is usually mildew.

Best harvested four to five weeks after the grapes have coloured (*Crown copyright: Brogdale EHS*)

of the shoots, which may be trimmed back after they have grown above the top string. Cut off the young grape bunches, as if the vine fruits while still so young it will be considerably weakened.

After its second summer the vine should be fairly well established. During the following winter the stem which was tied to the wire

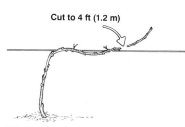

Vine training: first three years (*Rob Dalton*)

Cut to 4 ft (1.2 m)

Planting: prune to 3 buds

Early summer: pinch out all but one shoot

Winter: cut back to 4 ft (1.2 m) and tie to wire

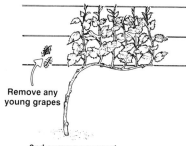

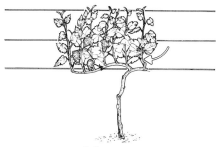

Remove any young grapes

2nd summer: support new growth with twine

Winter: tie in 1st shoot

3rd summer: next year's fruiting shoot

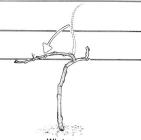

11 THE ORNAMENTAL GARDEN

The philosophy and practice of organic gardening can achieve their fullest potential in the ornamental garden. By using the widest range of plant types and varieties, as well as inert materials, we can create niches, microclimates and habitats – indeed a complete ecosystem. A new garden pond will be rapidly colonized by dragonflies and frogs, creatures that feed on many plant pests; flowers will provide energy-rich nectar for hover-flies and protein-rich pollen for bees; prostrate ground-cover plants trap leaves and conserve organic matter, moisture and nutrients; hedges provide nest sites for birds and green corridors for amphibians and invertebrates. Almost every ornamental feature brings benefits through species richness and habitat variety.

Soil cover. In a natural environment the soil may become uncovered through fire, landslip, tree fall or some other natural catastrophe, but this raw scar will be only temporary. Within days seedlings will emerge, and after a few weeks new and existing vegetation will begin to cover the ground. Plants protect the soil from many of the extremes of wind, water and temperature, conserving its structure and contents, while utilizing its goodness.

Gardening is not a completely natural process. Left to their own devices, gardens would gradually change and develop. Plants would come and go, following a natural progression leading ultimately to a stable vegetation type, such as oak forest or grassland. The form that this takes will depend upon latitude, topography, and soil type, and may last for thousands of years. The garden needs constant management if it is not to start reverting to nature in this way.

By carefully maintaining soil cover we follow a natural pattern which benefits our chosen plants and helps to conserve moisture, organic matter and plant nutrients. It also ensures that troublesome weeds do not become established.

OPPOSITE: Blaze of tulips for beds and borders
(*Photos Horticultural*)

> 1. Create or provide maximum soil cover at all times.
> 2. Use a balanced mix of plant types.
> 3. Grow the right plants in the right place.
> 4. Utilize fully the niches and microclimates created both by features and by plants within those features.

Plant types. A wide mix of plant types reduces the possibility of imbalance among the other creatures which share the garden, and avoids the pest and disease epidemics which are such a marked feature of monocropping systems. Wide species diversity ensures that pest populations will rarely build up to damaging numbers, as food sources and host plants will be scarce. Many garden pests are quite specific in their food requirements, unlike their natural predators which will be favoured by a range of food as well as egg-laying and overwintering sites. As they become available, choose cultivars which are resistant to their main pest and disease problems. Plant breeders have done wonders with pest- and disease-resistant vegetables, but much less work has been done with ornamentals, although this is slowly changing.

The right position. All plants have a range of basic needs, and some plants, like some humans, are particularly fussy. Soil type and pH, aspect, temperature and soil moisture can be critical. In order to grow healthy plants, free from stresses and checks, they should be carefully chosen to suit the available conditions. An acid-loving heather, for instance, planted into an alkaline soil, will suffer stress and become chlorotic due to iron deficiency. Shortage of iron will prevent it from manufacturing sufficient quantities of chlorophyll, which will weaken and expose it to other disorders and diseases. Many herbaceous plants suffer from root rots during winter if grown in poorly drained soils, while moisture-loving marginal plants will wither and die in hot, dry sites. Always ascertain the soil and exposure requirements of a new plant or feature before planting.

Rose border with standard and bush varieties
underplanted with violas (*Photos Horticultural*)

Utilize existing features and microclimates. It is
not often that a new garden is begun on a
completely virgin site – there are usually some
structures, plants or planting schemes which
have already modified the environment or
created a microclimate. A wall or hedge running
east to west, for instance, will create two very
different climates: on the south side it will be
hot and dry, suitable perhaps for bulbs or herbs,
while on the north side it will be cool and damp,
good for ferns or moisture-loving plants.
Similarly, a large shrub will create niches ideal
for smaller shade-loving plants at its base.

ANNUALS AND BIENNIALS

Annual and biennial plants are among the most
satisfying of ornamental plants to grow. The great
majority can be easily raised from seed, quickly
forming sturdy plants covered in bright flowers in
almost every colour of the spectrum. They are an
ideal group for children and novices to cut their
gardening teeth on, as well as being welcome
additions to spring and summer gardens.

Botanically, annuals are plants whose life
cycle, from seed to seed, is completed in one year,
usually one growing season. Hardy annuals can
be sown outside without protection in late winter
or early spring, while half-hardy annuals will
require protection from frost in the early part of
the year.

Biennials complete their life cycle, from seed to
seed, in two years, usually building up a sturdy
tap root or leafy rosette in the first season, and
sending up a flowering shoot in the second.

Horticulturally, an annual is simply a plant
which is given garden space for only one season,
and a biennial for two seasons. This is why you
may find some botanically perennial plants such
as wallflowers classed as biennials, and others,
such as petunias, classed as annuals.

HARDY ANNUALS

Many hardy annuals come from the South
African veldt or southern California, where the
summers are long and hot and the soils poor
and dry. For this reason gardeners are often
recommended to give them similar conditions,
but it is not really good advice. Most cultivated
plants grow better in soil which has been
improved with the addition of organic matter
such as manure, leaf-mould or compost, and
hardy annuals are no exception. In dry and
stony soils they will have a brilliant but
regrettably brief flowering period and will then
set seed and die. They certainly dislike heavy
wet soils, and will make foliage at the expense
of flower where nitrogen is over-plentiful, so
careful manuring is essential. Dig in well-rotted
organic matter in autumn, where space permits;
otherwise fork in leaf-mould or compost
between existing plants.

Where soils really are poor and very free-
draining, use varieties such as Californian poppy,
horned poppy or viper's-bugloss. The last is a real
bee's friend, with a stunning spike of blue flowers.

Propagation. Directly sown hardy annuals, and
some of the tougher half-hardies, will happily fill
in temporary gaps between larger plants to great
effect. Indeed, you may find yourself so
enamoured that you deliberately create areas to
fill with their cheerful presence. Many, such as
white alyssum, will self-seed and pop up here
and there, seldom being aggressive enough to
become a nuisance.

Sow seed into prepared outdoor seed beds
during the early spring and thin out in stages to
the required final spacing. Seed sown broadcast
will result in a less regimented stand of seedlings
than those sown in rows. However, I defy any-
body to distinguish between all the possible
weed seedlings and all the possible hardy annual
seedlings. Swallow your pride, sow in drills and
thin out to leave as near random a stand as
possible.

You can also sow in the same manner as for
half-hardy annuals.

HALF-HARDY ANNUALS

A widely varied group of plants, these are used
mainly as summer bedding displays in beds and
borders, or for planting into window-boxes, pots,
hanging baskets and every conceivable container.
They have in common a relatively short stature,

Annual bedding with hardy annuals (*Photos Horticultural*)

Viper's-bugloss (*Echium vulgare*). A nectar-rich, bee-attracting hardy plant for poor soils (*Sawyers Farm*)

Annuals for better soils

Love-lies-bleeding (*Amaranthus*)
Red orache (*Atriplex*)
Poached egg flower (*Limnanthes*)
Pot marigold (*Calendula*)
Cornflower (*Centaurea*)
Clarkia (*Clarkia*)
Larkspur (*Delphinium*)
Sunflower (*Helianthus*)
Strawflower (*Helichrysum*)
Bee's friend (*Phacelia*)

seldom exceeding 12 in (30 cm); a compact habit; and a succession of bright summer flowers of every hue imaginable. They seldom set viable seed, unlike many of the hardy annuals, and are usually killed outright by the autumn frosts.

Propagation. When you should start sowing depends very much upon where you live, what equipment you have and, perhaps most importantly, how much growing-on space you can provide for pricked-out seedlings. I would suggest that some time in mid-spring is quite early enough to begin, sowing small batches throughout the following six weeks or so.

Sow in pots or trays of seed compost in a frost-free environment (see *Propagation*, page 75 for full details). Prick out as soon as the cotyledons or seed leaves have expanded and before the first true leaf has appeared, as the shock of pricking out will be much less than

when the seedlings are several centimetres in height. Water with a dilute seaweed feed at each watering to build up sturdy plants. Harden off by gradually exposing the young plants to outside conditions before planting out once all danger of frost is past. This will seldom be before early summer.

Plant into moist, fertile soil with plenty of organic matter in it, water in and keep well watered in dry weather. Regular dead-heading, watering and liquid feeding will keep them healthy and flowering all through the summer.

For growing bedding plants in containers or hanging baskets, use a high-potash compost such as one suitable for tomatoes.

BIENNIALS

True biennial plants and perennials used for spring bedding should be sown outdoors in prepared seed beds. Choose an open, sheltered site in full sun or light shade with soil that is moisture-retentive and of reasonable fertility. Soil and seed bed preparations are much the same as for most vegetables – indeed, there is no reason why they should not share the same site.

Sow thinly into drills about 6 in (15 cm) apart from late spring to mid-summer and keep well watered during dry weather. Thin out to about 1–1½ in (2·5–4 cm) apart when the first true leaf appears so that they have plenty of room in which to develop. They will need to be transplanted into nursery rows once they have grown sufficiently and before they begin to encroach too much upon their neighbours. Water well before transplanting and lift gently with a fork in order to avoid damaging the root systems. Plant out the larger species, such as forget-me-nots and wallflowers, at 6–9 in (15–25 cm) apart and the smaller types, such as pansies and daisies, at 4–6 in (10–15 cm). Water in well and keep moist during dry spells. Plant out into their final positions in early autumn so that they are well established before the onset of winter.

Most will commence flowering in late winter or early spring, but the Universal pansies will

Common pests and diseases

Aphids	Slugs and snails
Caterpillars	Botrytis (Grey mould)
Cats	Damping off
Red spider mite	Powdery mildew

flower copiously from late summer onwards, with just a few weeks off in mid-winter.

Biennials can be viewed as entailing a lot of effort for little return, but they are very rewarding when they are well grown. (Leggy wallflowers and tired sweet williams are better on the compost heap.) Use sturdy plants of primulas, polyanthus, pansies, forget-me-nots and the like in a similar manner to hardy annuals, filling temporary spaces or reserved spaces among perennial plants or, if this is your taste, plant them out in formal bedding schemes after the half-hardies have given of their best.

HARDY PERENNIALS

These are among the most beautiful and versatile ornamental plants, with origins in almost every part of the globe. Some are straight species, little changed from their wild cousins, while others are the result of many centuries of selection and breeding.

I include in this group only plants which live for three years or more, survive outside without protection, and do not have woody stems. The great majority are herbaceous, that is, they die back each winter to a crown or rootstock, and most have fibrous root systems.

Herbaceous border (*Harry Smith*)

There are hardy perennials of almost every conceivable shape, size and colour, a cornucopia of form and hue, each with its particular soil and aspect preference. No garden should be without its complement of them to provide colour and interest in almost every month of the year, and no feature is so extreme that it cannot provide a home for some members of this tribe.

Traditionally, hardy perennials were grown in long borders backed by a hedge or wall. Plants at the back tended to become drawn, prone to attack by pests and diseases, and needing support or staking. After their heyday in Victorian times such features and their associated plants fell increasingly out of fashion, mainly because of the labour-intensive management involved. Recently there has been a tremendous reawakening of interest in them, thanks to the pioneering work of specialist nurserymen. Plant breeders have released smaller and more compact forms and many new and exciting species have been introduced.

What do hardy perennials have to offer to organic gardeners? First, they are excellent value for money, often tripling or quadrupling in size by the end of their first season. Secondly, many kinds have attractive foliage as well as beautiful flowers. Thirdly, their flowers are frequently visited by butterflies, bees, hover-flies and other gardeners' friends – the many members of the daisy family are especially favoured. Fourthly, if planted in association with other plant types such as trees, shrubs, and bulbs they can minimize pest and disease problems. And, as an added bonus, they are simplicity itself to propagate.

CULTIVATION

Site. The majority of hardy perennials prefer an open situation with plenty of light, air and sun. Many of the kinds which are quite happy in deep shade will be discussed in more detail in the section on ground-cover plants.

Soils. Because most hardy perennials die back in autumn and spend the dormant season below the ground, they are particularly prone to root rots in waterlogged soils. However, this can be minimized by careful selection, choosing only moisture-loving kinds for planting in heavy clay soils and drought-tolerant kinds for light dry sands.

Aspect. South and west aspects are both sunny and warm and will suit most species, although those with a preference for moist soils and light shade may be happier in a north or east aspect. Don't forget that proximity to a wall or hedge will always exaggerate the influence of a particular aspect – there are few positions more hot and dry than at the foot of a south-facing wall. Remember also that a shrub or rock creates its own aspects and microclimate.

Weed Control. Weed control should always be the first task to consider in the development of a new feature. This is particularly so if hardy perennials are to be used, as aggressive weeds such as bindweed (*Convolvulus arvensis*) and ground elder (*Aegopodium podagraria*) will quickly become entangled among their root systems and prove extremely difficult to eradicate. Small patches of perennial weeds may be dug out to prevent them from spreading, if there is room enough in the bed to wield a spade.

Annual weeds can be easily and successfully controlled by regular hoeing, or, preferably, by maintaining a thick mulch (3in/7·5 cm minimum) of a suitable organic material. Although this will not suppress perennial weeds completely, it will make them easier to pull out when they appear. If a bed becomes heavily infested with perennial weeds, then the only answer may be to dig up all the plants and pick out the weed rhizomes from the herbaceous root clumps; dig over the bed removing all weeds, or leave a carpet or sheet of black polythene on the bed for a good few months (see pages 46–7 and 241, for more details); then replant.

Soil Improvement. Hardy perennials make a tremendous amount of growth in a season and so make heavy demands upon a soil for both moisture and nitrogen. For this reason the addition of well-rotted farmyard manure will be beneficial, especially on light soils. To give a long and colourful display of flowers they will also benefit from frequent dressings of well-made compost and potash-rich fertilizer such as seaweed meal or wood ash. The soil pH is not so critical, although most kinds will thrive in a neutral to alkaline soil, so check the pH and apply lime, or better still calcified seaweed, if and when necessary.

Planting is best done with a trowel, although a spade may be needed for large clumps. Make sure that you do not plant too deeply – dormant perennials should generally have the top of their crowns just below the soil surface. If in active growth, plant so that the point where roots and shoots meet is at the soil surface. Firm well, but avoid over-compaction on heavy soils. Water in immediately, especially in dry weather.

Planting density. As a rough guide, the distance between plants should be no less than half their ultimate height.

Always plant in groups of odd numbers to avoid a regimented look. Groups of three or five which will form solid blocks of colour are more successful than single plants dotted about.

Lift and divide herbaceous plants every three to four years (*Harry Smith*)

Distance between groups should be greater than between plants within the group.

Maintenance. Keep on top of weeds, especially during the first year or two after planting. Remove dead flowerheads regularly to encourage further flowering, but do not forget to leave some, especially in late summer, to provide seed for wildlife in the winter. Cut back dead and dying foliage in late autumn to within about 4 in (10 cm) from soil level.

After cutting back and removing dead foliage, lightly fork (prick over) between plants to relieve compaction and improve aeration and drainage. Replenish or renew organic mulches regularly.

Plants will need to be lifted, divided and replanted every three to four years or so. Discard the older centre of each clump and replant the younger outer growths.

ROCK GARDEN PLANTS AND ALPINES

This is a very wide and varied group, with just about the only common feature a maximum size of 18 in (45 cm). The first alpines to be cultivated came, of course, from the European Alps, with later introductions from New Zealand, the Himalayas, China, Japan, Canada, the Andes – indeed from any part of the globe with temperate mountain regions. The group includes almost every plant type – trees, shrubs, herbaceous plants and bulbs – but only those of a dwarf or very slow-growing habit.

Life on a mountain can be tough, and only those with a hardy constitution will survive. Alpine plants spend the winter under a dry but cold blanket of snow. Spring is a brief period of melting snow and rushing waters, quickly followed by the long, baking hot months of summer. There is very little organic matter on the mountain slopes; rain and melt-waters drain away almost instantaneously and the winds blow strong and frequent. Rock gardens were first built in an

Perennials for damp and dry situations

All the plants in these lists prefer full sun; please refer to the table on ground cover for shade-loving hardy perennials, page 186.

Moisture and waterside	Hot and dry
Aruncus sylvester	Achillea in variety
Astilbe in variety	Acanthus in variety
Astrantia in variety	Centranthus in variety
Caltha in variety	Crocosmia in variety
Filipendula in variety	Erigeron in variety
Gentiana in variety	Eryngium in variety
Lythrum in variety	Gaillardia in variety
Monarda in variety	Gypsophila in variety
Polygonum in variety	Oenothera in variety
Rodgersia in variety	Pyrethrum in variety
Senecio przewalskii	Salvia in variety
Trollius in variety	Sedum in variety
	Yucca in variety

Mixed astilbes (Photos Horticultural)

Crocosmia, Lucifer (Photos Horticultural)

Pests and diseases to which these plants are prone include slugs and snails; aphids; caterpillars; powdery and downy mildew.

attempt to recreate, in the lowlands, a microcosm of the true alpine habitat. In a few famous botanic gardens the attempt has been very successful, but that is not often the case elsewhere.

In areas where there is no natural stone, or where space is limited, alpines can be grown to great effect in scree beds, sinks and walls. Dwarf plants which are not true alpines can be placed among stones and slabs, at border edges and in a host of other niches where they will not be swamped by their larger brethren.

GENERAL CULTIVATION

True alpines must have full sun and good drainage, especially during the winter. Cold and frost they can cope with, but they will quickly succumb to wet winter conditions.

A proposed rock garden site in heavy clay soil may require drainage installation before construction can begin, and all but the lightest soils will need the attention of leaf-mould, coarse sand and grit.

Growing media for containers should be made up from roughly 50% loam, 25% leaf-mould and 25% sharp sand or grit, plus a sprinkling of bonemeal. There are almost as many lime-haters as there are lime-lovers in this group, so choose plants or correct the pH accordingly.

Rich feeding is quite unnecessary – indeed, it may be positively harmful. Confine yourself to a little slow-release feed such as hoof and horn or bonemeal.

Mulch plants with gravel or stone chippings to conserve moisture, keep down weeds and prevent neck rots.

ALPINE FEATURES

There is not space here to go into the detailed construction of rock gardens and scree beds, but I would stress that the careful preparation of the site and the thoughtful positioning of a few large pieces of rock will always prove more effective than a huge jumble of boulders in an unsuitable site. Furthermore, the best place for that load of concrete chunks from the old drive is in a skip.

Choose a site that is well drained and in full sun. Select sandstone or limestone rocks which have some character to them, and ensure that any raw or dressed faces will be hidden. Identify the

Sink garden (Photos Horticultural)

strata within the rock and ensure that they run in a roughly horizontal line when positioned. Build up the rocks into outcrops, canyons or moraine, packing soil tightly between them and making sure that they are well anchored. It is essential that the soil in the planting pockets between rocks should connect with the earth beneath. If the soil or compost in the pockets is made to slope backwards and inwards into the crevices it will not be so readily washed out by rain.

Sinks and troughs are perhaps the most delightful way of using alpines in very small gardens, or in paved areas. Stone troughs are beyond the reach of most people's pockets, but you can do a lot with an old porcelain sink, hypertufa or simulated stone surfacing, and a fertile imagination. Create a miniature rock arrangement – just a few fairly large pieces are best – and top-dress with stone chippings after planting. Try a dwarf conifer or two, some creeping and mat-forming plants and miniature bulbs. Don't forget to spray the hypertufa with ricewater or milk to encourage mosses and algae.

ALPINE PLANTS

There is a wealth of beautiful plants to choose from, particularly if one includes those which are not true alpines but share with their mountain cousins a compact habit and slowness of growth.

The table gives a selection of plants which will grace any alpine garden or bed, but which are particularly suitable for growing in a sink or trough. Both groups will thrive in the standard alpine mix noted above, but the acid-lovers will require a pH of about 5 to 5·5.

BULBS

Bulbs are storage organs derived from modified stem and leaf bases. Plants from a number of different families and continents have developed bulbous 'rootstocks' in order to cope with broadly similar climatic conditions. By storing the products of summer's bounty in an underground bulb a plant is able to die back to this secure resting place during the harsh months of winter. In some parts of the world it is the summer, being extremely hot and dry, that is the dormant season.

The bulb is also an efficient means of vegetative reproduction, producing offsets which are capable of enlarging the plant colony considerably. This characteristic is a valuable one which can be utilized by gardeners.

Bulbs are one of the most under-used groups of garden plants. There are both tender and hardy types; they can be grown in pots and containers, troughs and sinks, rock gardens, beds and borders and also naturalized in grass; and, to cap it all, there are bulbs to give flower in all four seasons of the year.

Although bulbs contain an almost self-sufficient package of plant organs and stored food they are frequently neglected in the garden,

---

Plants particularly suitable for sinks or troughs

Lime-Lovers	Acid-Lovers
Androsace carnea	Arabis androsacea
Chamaecyparis obtusa Densa	Calluna vulgaris Tom Thumb
Erica cinerea Coccinea	Cryptomeria japonica Compressa
Gentiana saxosa	Edraianthus pumilio
Hedera helix Congesta	Erica cinerea Mrs Dill
Hypericum empetrifolium Prostratum	Erigeron aureus
Jovibarba sobolifera	Gentiana verna
Juniperus communis Compressa	Geranium celticum
Phlox douglasii May Snow	Linum Gemmell's Hybrid
Potentilla tabernaemontani Nana	Minuartia verna
Sagina boydii	Picea abies Doone Valley
Saxifraga caesia	Primula clarkei
Sedum sexangulare	Raoulia australis
Sempervivum arachnoideum	Saponaria x olivana
Thymus serpyllum	Sempervivum dolomiticum
	Silene acaulis
	Tsuga canadensis Minuta

Rhodohypoxis baurii (front), Saxifraga, Tumbling Waters (top right and left) (Pat Brindley)

Narcissus naturalized at random (*Photos Horticultural*)

Bulbs for naturalizing in grass

Autumn crocus
Colchicum
Snowdrop
Crocus
Winter aconite
Grape hyacinth
Snowflakes

Fritillary
Star of Bethlehem
Daffodils and
    narcissus
Allium (the larger
    species of the
    ornamental onion)

Bulbs for rock gardens

Arisaema
Asarum
Crocus
Cyclamen
Reticulate iris
Rhodohypoxis
Zigadenus

Miniature species of
tulip, allium, daffodil
and other narcissus

Anemone
Corydalis
Oxalis
Puschkinia

but this is a mistake. Like all plants they will repay a little care and attention many times over.

THE DORMANT PERIOD

Most bulbs change hands during the period of inactive growth, but they are living and breathing, so should be handled and stored carefully. Keep them dry and frost-free, checking them periodically for storage rots. Before planting, reject any which are damaged or diseased. Naked bulb species such as lilies and fritillaries should not be kept as dry as those, like daffodils and gladioli, which are covered with papery or fibrous coats.

Bulbs which are in large containers or planted in the soil will generally come to no harm over the winter, although in cooler zones it may be necessary to lift and store some of the marginally tender types like tulips and lilies. If left in the ground they should be marked with a stick to avoid being accidentally dug up. Keep the soil weed-free so that they gain full benefit from the sun's warmth.

CULTIVATION

There are very few bulbs that will tolerate wet or stagnant soils. In such anaerobic conditions they will quickly succumb to disease and rot. Most prefer a warm, well-drained site, so choose their positions carefully and improve conditions with sand or grit where necessary. Arum lilies are an exception, as are some of the rhizomatous iris species, liking nothing better than to stand with their feet in water.

Once in growth ensure that there is an adequate supply of moisture. Feed with a dry top-dressing of fish, blood and bone-meal, or liquid feed, a number of times during the season and keep weeds under control. Remove flowerheads as soon as they are spent, in order to divert goodness into next year's bulbs rather than seed formation.

Do not be in too much of a hurry to cut back the foliage after flowering, for this is the time when most bulbs prepare for winter by laying down stores. Offsets and new flower-buds for next season are also being formed at this time, so keep watering and feeding until the foliage has died right down.

Planting depth varies with species, but, as a very general rule of thumb, plant to twice the depth of the bulb. Thus a bulb 1 in (2·5 cm) in length will need to be covered by 2 in (5 cm) of soil.

NATURALIZING

Broad drifts of bright-flowered bulbs in grass are one of the great joys of springtime. There are many different bulbs which can be naturalized and the technique is of the simplest.

Most areas of grass or lawn are suitable, but avoid poorly drained sites and areas of very coarse grasses such as couch. The stronger species such as daffodils can compete with this, but not the smaller and more delicate types.

Planting should be done in such a way as to appear random and natural. The method often recommended is to put the bulbs in a bucket, sling them into the chosen area and plant them where they land. This works very well, but with a number of provisos. First, use only the larger bulbs such as daffodils and the more robust narcissi.

Bulbs for beds and borders

Allium	Glory of the	Lily
Anemone	Snow	Liriope
Crocus	Grape	Narcissus
Cyclamen	hyacinth	Scilla
Gladiolus	Hyacinth	Tulip
	Iris	

Crocus speciosus, autumn flowering (*Pat Brindley*)

Bulbs for hot, dry sites

Brodiaea	*Rhodohypoxis*
Iris unguicularis and	*Tigridia*
similar iris species	*Triteleia*
Nerine	*Zephyranthes*

Iris unguicularis for hot dry sites (*Photos Horticultural*)

Bulbs for moist sites

Arisaema	Bluebell
Arum lily	*Dierama*
Arum italicum	Dog's tooth violet

Secondly, make sure that the grass is cut short before commencing. Thirdly, throw gently. Small bulbs, long grass and wild throws are a recipe for disaster. Use a bulb planter or lift two sides of a turf sod with a spade, pop in the bulb, the correct way up, and firm down with your heel.

Alternatively, place and plant the bulbs in scattered groups across the chosen area.

Perhaps I could clarify here a matter which does seem to cause some confusion. Daffodils are members of the genus *Narcissus* and can therefore be called narcissi, but it seems to be a gardener's convention that the all-yellow narcissi are referred to as daffodils, hence many references to 'daffodils and narcissi'.

PERMANENT BEDS AND BORDERS

Bulbs will mix quite happily with most other plant types, and can be used with great effect to bring seasonal interest to many different garden features. Avoid associating them too closely with hardy herbaceous perennials, as many dislike disturbance. Heavy shade from trees and shrubs can also cause them problems, though dappled shade is fine.

ROCK GARDENS, SCREE BEDS, AND ALPINE TROUGHS

The dwarf bulb species are perfect companions for alpines; indeed, many of them are alpine in the true sense of the word. They will cope quite happily with gritty and free-draining soils, but like plenty of moisture in spring and early summer.

Plant bulbs anywhere else in the garden that has a little space or which could do with some added seasonal interest.

Pests and diseases which affect bulbs include slugs and snails, cutworms, lily beetles, vine weevils, especially in containers; botrytis, and viruses.

ROSES

No garden is complete without its complement of roses, perhaps the best-known and best-loved of flowering plants. There are numerous kinds of rose and thousands of different cultivars, reflecting both their ancient lineage and the tremendous amount of breeding work done with them.

SITE AND SOIL PREPARATION

There are many wild species of rose, with a multitude of homelands across the globe. Although many have been used in breeding work for their flower colour, they have retained their site preferences, so that it is now possible to choose a rose for any conceivable garden situation.

Just consider three roses native to Britain: *R. eglanteria* (*R. rubiginosa*, sweet-briar) is found growing in grassland and scrub on moist, alkaline soils; *R. tomentosa* (downy rose) prefers the dry, acid soils of heathland; while *R. pimpinellifolia* (*R. Spinossima*, burnet rose) is happiest growing on coastal sand dunes.

Aspect is not usually critical for roses, although some cultivars are more fussy than others. Remember, however, that south aspects will be warm, and if backed by a wall, may be exceptionally dry, which could cause powdery mildew problems or a very short flowering season. Taking another extreme, sites open to easterly winds may suffer from wind-rock problems or foliage scorch. Both scent and flower duration will be enhanced in a sheltered location.

Soil. Roses can be grown on all types of soil, from shallow chalks to heavy clays, but the more extreme types will benefit from improvement. It is probably fair to say that they do best on rich, moist soils which are slightly acid to neutral.

A well-structured soil with plenty of coarse organic matter added if necessary will ensure both the requisite summer moisture and winter drainage, as well as supplying adequate nutrients for healthy growth and flower production.

Soil Improvement. Roses have a long life and do not take kindly to disturbance, so thorough soil preparation is essential before planting.

Overly acid soils will need occasional dressings of lime or calcified seaweed, and shallow chalks will need regular dressings of organic matter. Use bone-meal as a slow-release source of phosphates for healthy root growth, and hoof and horn or fish, blood and bone-meal as a base dressing. Wood ash, seaweed meal, rock potash and seaweed extracts will all supply potash for flower production and healthy growth.

PLANTING

Most roses are purchased as bare-rooted plants in autumn. Being deciduous, they can be quite safely lifted and transplanted at this time provided that their root systems are constantly protected from frost and from drying out. Even a few minutes' exposure to drying winds and sunshine can be enough to kill the fragile root hairs on which the plant depends for moisture uptake.

Planting can take place at any time during the dormant period, although autumn is perhaps the ideal season. Do not attempt to plant when snow is lying or during periods of hard frost. Plunge the root systems into a bucket of water and leave to soak overnight if they appear at all dry, or if they have been stored for any time owing to inclement weather.

Excavate a hole wide and deep enough for the root system of your plant. The bud union of bush roses and some other types should be 1 in (2·5 cm) below the soil surface after planting, otherwise plant so that the planting mark is level with the soil surface. Backfill with added compost and bone-meal, firm well and water in.

Weed Control. Like most woody perennials, roses will compete quite successfully with most aggressive weeds, but are particularly vulnerable to competition in their first year or two. For this reason it makes sense to control perennial weeds before planting into new beds or borders. Annual weeds are a lesser problem, and can be much more easily controlled after planting. Regular applications of an organic mulch will control weeds, conserve moisture, and, if it is farmyard manure, supply nutrients as well.

PRUNING

Half prune the long shoots of bush roses in early autumn to prevent wind-rock during the winter.

More detailed pruning of all types can be done at any time during the dormant months between early winter and early spring, although periods of hard frost should be avoided. Pruning is easiest in early spring, as healthy buds are clearly visible then, although early winter pruning possibly results in better flowering.

Secateurs are the easiest and most efficient tool to use. The parrot-bill type is generally the best, but they must be sharp and well maintained. Ragged cuts and macerated tissues will allow the entry of disease. Always cut as close to a bud as possible without damaging it, making a cut which slopes gently away from the bud. The slope will prevent rainwater collecting behind the bud and rotting it.

Begin by cutting out all dead, diseased or damaged wood and any very spindly shoots. All of this material can harbour pests or disease. Make sure that you cut well below the dead or diseased area (6 in/15 cm below may not be excessive); there should be no discoloration of the tissues exposed by the cut.

Cut to outward-pointing buds only and remove completely any shoots growing into the centre of the bush (or, in the case of climbers, any shoots growing directly into the wall).

Prune hard on heavy, moist soils but much more lightly on dry sands. Always prune yellow varieties lightly.

Each kind of rose, whether bush, climber or miniature, will in addition need slightly more specific attention which will be detailed in the relevant sections below.

SHRUB ROSES

Nearly all of our modern roses are descended from the original shrubby species. Some are little changed, with single flowers and short flowering

R. Frau Dagmar Hastrup, a healthy rugosa type of shrub rose (*Harry Smith*)

R. Albertine, a vigorous, scented rambler with attractive salmon-pink flowers (*Pat Brindley*)

season, while others are changed almost beyond recognition.

A large collection of shrub roses is possible only in the most spacious of gardens, where their individual flowering seasons , scent, hips and vigorous growth can be enjoyed to the full. However, there are an increasing number of modern repeat-flowering and smaller shrubs suitable for the smaller garden.

Cultivars such as Cécile Brunner, Angèle Pernet, Salet, Souvenir de la Malmaison, Perle d'Or, Pompon de Bourgogne, Nestor, Ballerina, Joseph's Coat, Othello are worth seeking out from nurserymen, as well as the *Rugosa* types such as Frau Dagmar Hastrup, Roseraie de l'Hay, Blanc Double de Coubert and Sarah van Fleet. The *Rugosas* are among the healthiest of roses, with lovely bright green foliage and luscious fat red hips in autumn. Species such as *R. glauca (R. rubrifolia), R. virginiana, R. gallica* Versicolor *(Rosa mundi), R. pimpinellifolia* and *R. p. altaica* are also well worth considering.

Shrub roses require very little pruning – simply remove dead or diseased growth and occasionally remove one of the oldest branches right down to ground level in order to maintain vigour.

CLIMBING ROSES

Climbing roses are basically shrubs or bushes with very long stems. They need to be tied to and trained against a wall to be seen at their best. Plant at least 18 in (45 cm) from the base of the wall and incorporate well-rotted manure or compost to aid moisture retention and reduce the risk of powdery mildew attack.

Look for varieties such as Danse du Feu, Handel, Schoolgirl, Mrs Sam McGredy and Zéphirine Drouhin.

Pruning consists initially of training new growths to cover the available wall space, removing awkwardly growing shoots and pruning back weak shoots to encourage vigour. The short flowering shoots should be pruned back to a strong bud below the old flower stems in spring.

PILLAR ROSES

Essentially these are climbing roses which grow to no more than 8–10 ft (2·5–3 m) in height. They can be grown up a pillar or post to provide a most effective display where wall space is limited. Prune as for climbers.

Choose varieties such as Aloha, Compassion, Dortmund, White Cockade, or Swan Lake.

RAMBLER ROSES

Ramblers make more vigorous growth than climbers; their stems are longer and more flexible and carry large trusses of small flowers which have a single, short season.

As they are frequently prone to mildew, especially when trained against a wall, the rambler types are best grown on pillars or pergolas through which air can circulate. They can also be used most effectively as ground cover or allowed to romp up trees or over stumps or sheds.

Look for varieties such as Wedding Day, *Rosa Filipes* Kiftsgate (this one grows to 40 ft/12 m), New Dawn, Seagull, Crimson Shower.

Prune in late summer or autumn by cutting out down to ground level all shoots which have flowered and tying in the new stem which will flower next year. Some varieties will benefit from lighter pruning.

BUSH ROSES

I must confess that bush roses, the large-flowered

(Hybrid Tea) and cluster-flowered (Floribunda) types, are not my favourites. Their flowers are of course beautiful and frequently scented, but the plants themselves are fussy, do not mix well with other species, and are prone to pests and diseases. They exist only through the technique of plant-breeders, being weak-rooted cultivars budded on to highly-bred root-stocks, and their flowers are of little or no value to the other species which inhabit our gardens. Newer varieties tend to have greater resistance to diseases. Here is a brief selection:

Large-flowered: Pinta, Sweet Promise, Silver Jubilee, Mister Lincoln, Alec's Red, Fragrant Cloud.

Cluster-flowered: Norwich Union, Scarlet Queen Elizabeth, Zambra, Anne Cocker, Iceberg, Pink Wonder.

Prune shoots down to about half their un-

R. Trumpeter, bush rose grown as a standard (*Harry Smith*)

Roses as ground cover – often remarkably free of disease problems (*Harry Smith*)

pruned height in early spring. Harder pruning will result in fewer but larger flowers. Remove flowers as soon as they die off in order to encourage repeat flowering.

STANDARD ROSES

Cultivars of shrub, bush and rambling roses may all be budded on to the single, straight stem of a root-stock to form a standard rose. Stem length ranges from 2½ to 5 ft (0·75–1·5 m) depending on type. The root-stock can be a wild dog rose from the hedgerow, although commercial growers use one of the specially bred seedling root-stocks used for bush roses.

Hard pruning should be avoided, otherwise prune as above, depending upon type.

MINIATURE ROSES

This type of rose has become very popular of late, mainly due to mass production by micro-propagation.

Use as edging plants, in rock gardens, troughs and pots. Varieties range from 8 to 18 in (20–45 cm) in height. Pruning should consist of no more than a very light trim over after flowering. Here is a small selection: Cinderella, Red Ace, Josephine Wheat croft, Fire Princess, Magic Carousel.

GROUND-COVER ROSES

Roses such as Max Graf, Nozomi and *Rosa wichuriana* have been appreciated as ground cover for a very long time, but over the past few years there has been a succession of releases bred specifically for this purpose. Do not forget, though, that the ground must be free of perennial weeds such as ground elder, couch grass and bindweed before planting.

Many of the newer varieties are remarkably free from disease problems. Consider: Swany, Red Belle, Grouse, Rosy Cushion, The Fairy.

Pruning is usually unnecessary, but remove upright growing shoots which could alter the creeping habit.

PESTS AND DISEASES

Roses are chiefly affected by aphids, black spot and powdery mildew. See chapters on *Disease Prevention* and *Pest Control* (pages 268, 287, 308–10).

HEATHS AND HEATHERS

Strictly speaking, heathers are the many forms and cultivars of the Scottish heather or ling, *Calluna vulgaris*, which flowers in late summer and autumn. The heaths, *Erica* and *Daboecia* species, are related plants found in similar habitats both in the British Isles and other European countries. I shall use the term 'heather' in this section to denote all members of the group, whether *Calluna*, *Erica* or *Daboecia*.

Winter flowering heathers (*Harry Smith*)

The heathers are hardy evergreen shrubs or sub-shrubs with tiny leaves and whorls of bell-shaped flowers in terminal spikes. They range in height from under 4 in (10 cm) to over 16 ft (5 m), with an enormous range of foliage and flower colour. Several species are lime-tolerant, particularly those which flower during the winter, but most of the late summer and autumn flowerers will only grow happily in acid soils.

SITE AND SOIL

Heathers are found growing naturally on mountain slopes, moor and heathland, where exposure is extreme and the soil generally poor.

Their tough little leaves can cope with salt spray and low summer rainfall, and strong winds pose few problems for their wiry, flexible branches and sparse foliage. In addition, many have adopted a ground-hugging or hummock-forming habit in response to their harsh environment.

Some species, such as *Erica tetralix* and *E. ciliaris*, are happiest in moist sites or even bog, while the bell heather or *E. cinerea* will be found in even drier conditions than most. All the species and cultivars dislike heavy shade and will thrive best in an open, sunny site.

Soil. Almost every soil type will allow the cultivation of heathers, although heavy and poorly drained clays will probably need the most modification.Coarse leaf-mould, composted bracken or straw or garden compost are effective soil improvers. Although heathers are frequently found growing in very dry sites they will need plenty of moisture to aid establishment.

Most of the late summer and autumn-flowering heathers such as *Calluna, Daboecia, Erica ciliaris, E. cinerea* and *E. tetralix* will thrive only in acid soils, relishing heavy dressings of pine litter or acid leaf-mould.

The winter flowerers are less fussy about pH and will tolerate some lime, so if you garden on an alkaline soil, plant the cultivars of *Erica carnea, E. x darleyensis* and the slightly tender *E. arborea* and *E. lusitanica. Erica vagans*, although flowering in summer, will tolerate some lime.

Plant material grown on alkaline soils will make alkaline compost. Only sphagnum peat and pine litter can actually lower a soil's pH.

PLANTING

Ensure that root-balls are well moistened before planting. Soil should be a loose, friable tilth, firmed well after planting. The point where the stem bases emerge from the container compost should be buried about 1 in (2·5 cm) below the surface. This allows for settling, and the top of the root-ball will eventually come to just below the surface.

Heathers are possibly seen to best effect in a massed display, preferably on a sloping site, where careful positioning can form a rich tapestry of flower and foliage colour, shape and form. They associate well with conifers, Japanese maples, brooms and gorses, birch and dwarf rhododendrons, but they do need light.

Use them also in rockeries and borders, for edging beds, as bedding plants and even in winter hanging baskets and window-boxes.

Like herbaceous perennials, they are best planted in blocks or drifts of a single colour, or two or three contrasting colours, rather than single plants of a wide range of colours.

PRUNING

Summer-flowering types: prune lightly, cutting back the old flowerheads to a point just below the bottom flowers, in early spring.

Winter-flowering types: prune in the same way immediately after flowering, usually in early to mid-spring.

PESTS AND DISEASES

Rabbits can be a nuisance in the early years – protect the plants with wire netting.

Erica wilt causes shoot tips to wilt and within a few weeks whole shoots may die back (see *Disease Prevention* page 289). Feed plants with seaweed or comfrey liquid feed.

Calluna species are particularly susceptible to attack by honey fungus, which may kill plants outright. Dig out infected plants, including as much of the soil as is practicable, and burn them.

ORNAMENTAL GRASSES

Grasses, and grass-like plants – rushes, sedges, bamboos – are found in an astonishing variety of habit, form, colour and site preference. They are perfect foils to the broad, flat leaves and rounded shapes of herbaceous perennials and shrubs.

Mixed grasses border (*Harry Smith*)

Plant in spring into well-prepared soil, mulching those which prefer moist soil with well-rotted manure or compost, and those which prefer warm, dry soils with stones. Herbaceous types should be cut back to within 2 in (5 cm) of the ground after the foliage has died back. Top-dress annually with fish, blood and bone-meal or well-made compost.

The ubiquitous Pampas grass is well known, but there are many other tall and stately grasses which make excellent specimen plants. Whether in sun or shade, wet or dry conditions or even standing in water; as annuals or perennials, hardy or requiring protection, acid or alkaline; as hedges or screens, there are grasses to suit any position or use. Their most decorative role, if allowed to flower, is to toss their silken, restless plumes over the dullness of the garden in late autumn.

GROUND-COVER PLANTS

A soil which is not covered by vegetation is in a vulnerable state and will almost certainly become less fertile. As organic gardeners we must aim to improve the soil's fertility, and one of the finest ways of doing this is to maintain, as far as possible, a continuous soil cover. Obviously, this can be done with mulches and hard landscape materials, but there is a multitude of ornamental plants which can do the job better.

Ground-cover plants will conserve all the components of fertility and will control weeds, but, in addition, their use will knit together all the plants and features of a garden into a harmonious whole. Grass is, of course, the ground-cover plant *par excellence* – indeed, it is so ubiquitous that we tend to forget that it is ground cover!

What is a ground-cover plant? Simply one which makes most of its growth horizontally rather than vertically. One could argue that beech trees are excellent ground cover because they totally dominate their environment, allowing no

Shrubs for ground cover

Calluna vulgaris	Many cultivars with flower and foliage variation
Ceanothus thyrsiflorus repens	Prostrate Californian lilac with blu flowers and rich green foliage
Convolvulus cneorum	Slightly tender, but well worth the effort
Cotoneaster dammeri	One of a number of excellent cotoneasters for ground cover
Euonymus fortunei	There are a number of coloured foliage forms
Gaultheria procumbens	
Genista pilosa	
Hebe 'Carl Teschner'	
Hedera	A number of species and many cultivars of ivy are ideal ground cover
Lithospermum	
Pachysandra	Excellent, though slow to establish
Santolina	Clip annually for best results

Consider also the many prostrate conifers, especially

Hardy perennials for ground cover

Acanthus	Beautiful glossy foliage; will succeed in many different situations
Ajuga reptans	Blue-flowered bugle. Several coloured foliage forms
Brunnera macrophylla	Forget-me-not flowers
Ceratostigma plumbaginoides	Blue flowers and wonderful autumn colour
Epimedium	
Hosta	Many species and hybrids with a wide range of foliage shape and colour
Lamium	Dead nettle. Beware yellow archangel, sometimes sold as *Lamium*
Nepeta	Catmint, also loved by bumble-bees
Polygonum	There are a number of species with a great difference in height and invasiveness
Symphytum	Comfrey. There is an increasing number of ornamental forms

Deciduous/ Evergreen	Habit	Shade/Sun	Moist/ Dry	Acid/ Alkaline	Height	Planting distance
E	Clump	Sun	Dry	Acid	2 ft (60 cm)	18 in (45 cm)
E	Carpet	Sun	Dry	Either	2 ft (60 cm)	3 ft (90 cm)
E	Clump	Sun	Dry	Either	18 in (45 cm)	18 in (45 cm)
E	Carpet	Either	Either	Either	6 in (15 cm)	2 ft (60 cm)
E	Clump	Either	Either	Either	2 ft (60 cm)	18 in (45 cm)
E	Carpet	Shade	Either	Acid	6 in (15 cm)	18 in (45 cm)
D	Carpet	Sun	Dry	Alkaline	9 in (23 cm)	2 ft (60 cm)
E	Clump	Either	Either	Alkaline	9 in (23 cm)	18 in (45 cm)
E	Carpet	Either	Either	Either	9 in (23 cm)	18 in (45 cm)
E	Carpet	Sun	Dry	Acid	9 in (23 cm)	2 ft (60 cm)
E	Carpet	Shade	Either	Either	9 in (23 cm)	15 in (38 cm)
E	Clump	Sun	Dry	Either	18 in (45 cm)	2 ft (60 cm)

species and cultivars of *Juniperus*, and also ground-cover roses (see Roses, page 184)

Deciduous/ Evergreen	Habit	Shade/Sun	Moist/ Dry	Acid/ Alkaline	Height	Planting distance
D	Clump	Sun	Dry	Alkaline	3 ft (90 cm)	3 ft (90 cm)
E	Carpet	Either	Either	Alkaline	3 in (7·5 cm)	1 ft (30 cm)
D	Clump	Shade	Either	Alkaline	1 ft (30 cm)	2 ft (60 cm)
D	Clump	Sun	Dry	Either	1 ft (30 cm)	18 in (45 cm)
D and E	Carpet	Either	Either	Either	1 ft (30 cm)	18 in (45 cm)
D	Clump	Shade	Moist	Either	18 in (45 cm)	18 in (45 cm)
D and E	Carpet	Either	Either	Either	9 in (23 cm)	1 ft (30 cm)
D and E	Clump	Sun	Dry	Either	1 ft (30 cm)	18 in (45 cm)
D	Carpet	Either	Moist	Either	2 ft (60 cm)	4 ft (120 cm)
D	Clump	Either	Moist	Either	2 ft (60 cm)	2 ft (60 cm)

Gaultheria procumbens, shade-happy, for acid soils (Photos Horticultural)

Ajuga reptans, hardy perennial, evergreen (Photos Horticultural)

competition from any other species. Nettles, similarly, can out-compete most plants, but both these examples are extreme.

A useful ground-cover plant will spread, and will be quick to become established without being aggressive. It should be tolerant of most soil and site conditions and should be easy to propagate. Some types will have attractive flowers or fruits, but it is for the beauty of their foliage that this group is so rewarding. The bold, bright colours of bedding plants, for instance, are not exactly restful. Even colours of roses and hardy perennials, unless very cleverly used, can result in a garden that is a restless hotch-potch of colour. Use the wonderfully subtle shades and hues of green foliage to soften, tone down and tie together the main specimen plants.

WEED CONTROL

Ground-cover plants can control annual weeds

totally, once established, but flourishing perennial weeds must be eradicated prior to planting. Seedlings of both types will, of course, be easily suppressed by the established ground cover. The first priority must therefore be control of mature perennial weeds.

Ground cover will not give you instant weed control. Until the plants grow together and meet there will be bare soil which will almost certainly become colonized by weeds. Keep these down by hoeing or mulching until soil cover is complete. Obviously this time will vary with spacing, plant type and local conditions.

Once established, ground cover will need no more than a quick check once or twice a year to haul out the occasional tree seedling or grass plant which has managed to penetrate the defences.

SOIL PREPARATION AND PLANTING

Most ground-cover plants are either low-growing shrubs planted closely together, or spreading forms of shrubs and hardy perennials. Prepare soil and plant as for any perennial, long-term plant type, paying particular attention to coarse organic matter and slow-release organic fertilizers.

PROPAGATION

Propagate hardy perennials by division, replanting the younger outer portions of each clump.

Deciduous shrubs can be propagated from softwood or semi-ripe cuttings in summer.

Evergreen shrubs are best propagated by semi-ripe cuttings between mid-autumn and late winter.

A few species, such as privet, dogwood, shrubby willow and ornamental elder, can be very easily propagated by way of hardwood cuttings during the dormant season. Take 3 ft (1 m) lengths of stem and push them into the soil as far as they will go, making sure of course that they are the right way up. This type of ground cover will not mix so well with the other plant types unless planned on a larger scale.

PLANTS

Beware of Lamiastrum galeobdolen (yellow archangel), Vinca species (periwinkle), Petasites (winter heliotrope), and Trachystemon orientale. These are wonderful plants where they can be given space to romp, but they will very quickly

---

Uses of ground cover

Use ground-cover plants to clothe problem areas such as steep banks or areas of deep or dry shade; as an alternative to grass where even that cannot thrive; but most particularly between and among other plants such as shrubs, trees and hardy perennials.

smother any other garden plant. Established trees can cope with them, but otherwise use them with great care.

Bulbs can be planted among ground cover to great effect, but as a rule of thumb, the foliage of the ground cover should not exceed one third of the height of the bulb's foliage. Avoid those bulbous types which require a hot dry period after flowering, such as nerine and amaryllis.

GARDENING BY THE SEA

For gardeners, living in a coastal area is a mixed blessing. Proximity to the sea ensures that frosts are far less frequent than further inland, indeed almost non-existent. Cloud cover is generally less dense and light levels consistently higher, all of which allows the cultivation of many half-hardy or tender species.

Unfortunately, coastal regions may be exposed to both offshore and onshore winds, which can shred delicate leaves and break branches as well as sucking water from soil and foliage. In addition, the winds blowing off the sea carry sand and salt, which greatly exacerbate the problem. Wind-blown sand lacerates shoots and foliage and the salt draws moisture out of the exposed tissues, leaving them tattered and desiccated. Not many plants can put up with this sort of punishment for long unless they are protected in some way.

The keys to successful gardening by the sea are protection and careful choice of plants.

CHOICE OF PLANTS

Only tough plants will survive and flourish on the coast, those which can cope with the strong, frequent winds and the abrasive assaults of sand and salt. Suitable types will be those with thick leaves, covered by waxy cuticles or hairs, or those adapted in other ways to protecting their delicate water-rich tissues.

Evergreen trees and shrubs bear foliage which is notably tougher than that of their deciduous cousins. Hollies, holm oak and strawberry tree (*Arbutus*); escallonias, elaeagnus, euonymus, hebes, camellias and rhododendrons will all grow happily by the sea, provided that soil conditions are suitable.

Some conifers are especially well adapted to coastal conditions, as their foliage is not only tough but also much reduced, whether to needles like the pines, or scales like *Cupressus* and *Cupressocyparis*.

Shrubs like olearias, senecios, helianthemums and cistuses have the additional protection of hairs on their leaves, which gives them a silvery or felted look.

Reduction of foliage size and increased use of stem and shoot as the photosynthetically active part of the plant is a device used by many species to cope with harsh conditions. Shrubs such as the tamarisks, brooms and gorse are good examples.

Finally, a miscellany of tough and versatile types such as the palms, cordylines, yuccas, phormiums, heathers, pampas grasses, agaves, bamboos, mallows, and, perhaps surprisingly, sycamores and ash, will all cope admirably with life by the sea.

Genera which will thrive if given some protection from the wind include *Buddleia*, *Ceanothus*, *Fuchsia*, *Pelargonium*, *Griselinia*, *Hydrangea*, *Osteospermum*, *Penstemon*, *Pittosporum*, *Romneya*, *Salvia*, *Sedum*, poppies of all-kinds and the majority of bulbous plants.

PROTECTION

If a coastal garden could be protected from the excesses of wind, sand and salt, the plants within that garden would reap fully the benefits of mild climate, bright light and moist air.

Walls and fences can play a useful role here, but remember that impenetrable barriers can cause turbulence in moving air which can be as destructive, if not more so, than unimpeded wind. Permeable barriers, such as the many proprietary windbreak materials , are better, but the best is living material.

Use the tough and hardy plants mentioned to form a series of screens, to filter out wind and salt, and create a softer microclimate for more delicate subjects. Make full use of sheltered niches created by individual plants and be prepared to experiment, both with plant type and garden plans.

Spartium junceum, Spanish broom, is well adapted to demanding maritime conditions (*Photos Horticultural*)

12 COTTAGE GARDEN FLOWERS

Today we view the traditional English cottage garden with nostalgia. The Victorian flower painters depict picturesque thatched cottages merging into the landscape, the walls covered with roses and the front garden filled with a profusion of hollyhocks, delphiniums, lilies, sunflowers and daisies. However, life was hard and the gardens played a vital role in the lives of the cottage dwellers.

THE VICTORIAN COTTAGE GARDEN

The traditional cottage garden originally had to supply food and medicines for the family. The layout of the garden was strictly practical, with the need to get water from the well and visit the privy in all weathers making straight paths essential. Every nook and cranny was used to grow something. Lawns were not laid; they did not appear until much later in gardening history, when the middle class tried to copy the idea of a green landscaped park around the house in the style of the country stately home.

Hedges were very important to keep out passing herds of cows and other animals; hawthorn, blackthorn and holly made good deterrents. Birds and squirrels would help by unwittingly planting hazel, ash and other native trees, which the cottagers cut and laid to form a strong impenetrable barrier. Wild dog roses, honeysuckle, bryony, blackberries and ivy climbed through the branches to form a living tapestry of leaves intertwined with flowers and berries. Primroses, violets, periwinkles and other wild flowers grew among the roots in the hedge bottom, away from the churning hooves.

The cottage would be built of local materials: stone from a nearby quarry, bricks made in the area, thatched, shingle or slate roofs; so would the garden paths and outbuildings, making the garden and cottage an integral feature in the landscape. Many cottages have long thin gardens alongside lanes, because this land was regarded as unowned and could be adopted and built on by someone in need of a home.

The front garden, with its straight path up to the front door, was often planted with flowers just for the pleasure of them, but even so, many of them also had another use in the kitchen or medicine cupboard. The cottagers did not grow wild flowers in their gardens as there were plenty growing in the surrounding countryside, but unusual forms or colours of wild flowers, such as the hose-in-hose cowslips, double primroses, pink violets and the 'hen and chicks' daisy would find a home alongside the paths, to be admired and presented as gifts to friends and visitors who were also interested in these curiosities.

Scented flowers had a special place in the garden. Roses climbing up the walls helped overcome the musty smell of the cottage, which did not have drains and a damp course, and honeysuckle trained over the privy was intended to disguise odours and make a visit there more pleasant. Other fragrant flowers were grown for their scent in the evening. Sweet rocket, the evening primrose, the tobacco plant and night-scented stocks would all find a place near the garden bench.

Pinks and violets were grown for their perfumed flowers, which could be used to scent and flavour drinks and food, and lavender, with its aromatic leaves and flowers, was found alongside every cottage wall. Many of the herbs grown for preparing home-made remedies had scented flowers or leaves, which could be used in many ways for cooking, preserving and protecting clothes from moths and belongings from the damp.

Many of the flowers and shrubs found in the garden were grown because they had a traditional meaning to the cottagers. The myrtle bush was often from a wedding bouquet; the highly scented orange blossom and lily-of-the-valley were popular decorations for wedding feasts, snowdrops for Candlemas and madonna lilies for the church. Yew was planted to protect the building and often gave the cottage its name: Yew Tree Cottage instantly conjures up an image

OPPOSITE: *Papaver somniferum*, the opium poppy, at the outer edge of this cottage garden (*Jean Andrews*)

of a cottage nestling beside the protective bulk of a clipped dome of evergreen yew. Clipping box and yew into strange shapes and animals was a popular hobby, and provided the garden with a form of living statuary.

The walls of the cottage were the home of quite a number of plants. Roses around the door were very popular, but a plant that was introduced in 1840 from China soon found a place, with its bright yellow trumpet flowers seemingly impervious to the frosts and snow. The winter-flowering *Jasminum nudiflorum* was taken up as an ideal cottage garden plant, and was happy to sprawl in a tangled mass through a latticed porch over the front door. The summer-flowering jasmine, with its scented white flowers, was another popular wall climber in milder districts. The wide-scale brewing of home-made wine popularized the growing of vines on the south wall, and a vast range of different wines could be made from the surplus fruit and flowers produced in the garden or collected from the hedgerows and fields.

Lack of space made the practice of growing fruit trees up the cottage walls a sensible solution. Pear trees could be trained on wires along the walls, providing flowers in spring followed by fruit ripened by the reflected heat of the sun, and a cherry tree on the north wall was more easily protected from the attentions of birds with muslin or netting than one grown in the garden. Ornamental flowering trees that did not produce edible fruit would not be given space, the flowers of apple trees, damsons and plums being considered just as beautiful and productive too.

The back garden of the cottage would be given over largely to growing vegetables and fruit, but among the rows of food crops might be planted flowers that could be cut and sold, or flowers that were thought to be beneficial to bees or used as herbs. Most cottagers had a beehive, and a supply of nectar plants for the bees was important throughout their active season, when they would be making honey and fertilizing the fruit and vegetable crops.

Winter-flowering *Jasminum nudiflorum* (Jean Andrews)

These flowers would be planted in any available space in and among the cropping plants. Among the many good bee plants were, and are, *Limnanthes douglasii*, borage, lemon balm, sedum, echinops, teasel, lamium and foxglove. These also attract hover-flies, which lay their eggs on nearby plants so that the larvae will feed on aphids. The scent of some of the more pungent plants was thought to disguise the smell of the vegetables, and so garlic, marigolds and rue would be positioned to help confuse pests, such as carrot fly and aphids, looking for plants to lay their eggs on.

The cottage garden was less likely to be affected by the passing whims and fancies of more affluent householders. When the owners of large country houses swept away their formal beds, borders and topiary in favour of a naturalistic landscape, the cottagers carried on growing their herbs and curiosities and the yew peacock that decorated the front garden and gave the cottage its name.

Victorian plant hunters brought back many beautiful plants from countries around the world, and wealthy gardeners again made new gardens with long herbaceous borders and conservatories to house their new treasures. Eventually the fashion for carpet bedding meant that borders were again unfashionable, and a dearth of cheap labour after the world wars resulted in gardens having to be more labour-saving. Many of the previously treasured plants were again thrown on to the rubbish heap, to be rescued and planted in local gardens where they were allowed to remain, appreciated for their hardiness and beauty.

THE COTTAGE GARDEN TODAY

It is possible to make a modern cottage garden using the species and old varieties of flowers, vegetables and well trained fruit trees that our grandmothers used to grow. You can create either a traditional or an ornamental cottage garden, where the strictly practical features of the traditional garden are softened with curving paths, a grassed area, more flowers and fewer vegetables.

If the garden surrounds a period cottage or house, it is tempting to keep the garden in period, and grow only those plants that would have been available at the time that the garden was first made; it is also enjoyable to find out about and restore any period features, such as paths, arbours and pools, that may have been removed in subsequent years. Old photographs are very helpful in this case, and it is often worth talking to elderly neighbours who may remember what the garden looked like in earlier years.

To keep a garden strictly in period can become a little limiting, and most people settle for something that has the right feel. This can be achieved by keeping in mind the rules that governed the traditional cottage garden, building

ABOVE: Geraniums and oxeye daisies (*Jean Andrews*)

TOP RIGHT: Classic, early twentieth-century, cottage garden (*Natural Image*)

RIGHT: *Rosa* Madame Grégoire Staechelin, an early, scented climber (*Jean Andrews*)

paths and features of local stone or other materials, and planting productive trees such as apple, cherry, pear, damson and plum, rather than ornamental cherries, almonds, acers, willows, conifers and foliage shrubs that are grown for their looks alone.

Likewise the flowers should be herbs, old curiosities, hardy species and their varieties, cut-and-come-again hardy herbaceous border flowers, cheerful annuals, scented flowers, climbers, and old roses, not hybrid tea roses, bedding plants, zonal pelargoniums (commonly known as geraniums), or flowers that have been developed and bred over-large so that they cannot support themselves. Plants that would not normally grow in the local soil and need special beds of peat also look incongruous. Heathers, rhododendrons, azaleas and camellias are not really cottage plants. Alpines that are not content with a gravel path also look wrong; the Victorian rockery is not a cottage garden feature.

Victorian painters have been accused of romanticizing the gardens they depicted and filling them with flowers that were never really there. Obviously, every cottage garden was not a picture of riotous colour, just as they are not today, but keen gardeners will always make the best of their gardens, and as it is quite possible to have a garden just like the paintings, we must assume that they were real.

ROSES

Old varieties of plants that will recreate the painterly effect are still listed in nursery catalogues and cost no more than modern ones. The choice of roses for around the walls, over arbours, tied up rustic poles or scrambling through trees is vast. Life is made much easier if you take note how much the rose will grow, for many climbing roses will climb high into trees; trying to restrain them to grow around the door, while perfectly possible, is time-consuming.

Avoid the climbing hybrid tea roses with their large but often unscented flowers for around the door. Buy the old ones such as Etoile de Hollande, with its deep red, highly scented double flowers, Madame Alfred Carrière, with its fragrant white pink-flushed flowers, Zéphirine Drouhin, with its thornless stems, and its large pink flowers often late in the season, or Madame Grégoire Staechelin, a pink, early scented climber. Bear in mind the colour of the wall against which the rose will be flowering, so that the flowers will show up well but not clash.

For arbours and rustic poles the rambler roses can be trained over, as they send up new stems each year for the following year. Dorothy Perkins was a favourite rose for this purpose, with its rather strident pink trusses of double flowers, and Emily Gray with its rich gold, small, scented double flowers and almost evergreen glossy foliage. Intersperse with honeysuckle and clematis for a spectacular display most of the year. Roses and clematis both like plenty of compost and horse manure. The species roses for climbing really high up trees are *Rosa longicuspis*, with masses of single white flowers, *R. filipes* Kiftsgate, one of the tallest roses, again with white trusses of scented flowers, and Paul's Himalayan Climbing Musk, with highly scented, small, double, pale pink flowers.

Rose hedges can be planted to divide up the garden. *Rosa rugosa* and its hybrids make a trouble-free screen, with large scented purple, pink or white single or double flowers on and off all summer, colourful hips in the autumn and foliage resistant to mildew and blackspot. The old shrub roses can also be planted, to give a sensational show of highly perfumed blooms packed with petals that weigh the flowers down if they get too wet. The deep red Charles de Mills, with its huge flowers, opening flat, also provides plenty of perfumed petals for pot pourri. The practice was to underplant with garlic or ornamental onions to keep the bushes free of blackspot.

To control greenfly on roses it is possible to train bluetits to do the job for you. These little birds love to eat fat from the feeding bells that can be bought for this purpose. Provide one or more of these bells, keep them full of food most of the time, but move them about the garden, hanging from different branches of various shrubs and trees during the year. The birds will soon get used to this game of hide-and-seek and discover the bells wherever they are hanging. During the summer, when you notice an infestation of greenfly, hang up a bell nearby, and when they come to feed from it they will see and eat the greenfly too. When they find them they will completely clear the whole bush.

OTHER OLD PLANTS

Low-growing plants that form a tidy mound were often found growing alongside the paths. A very old one, used in the knot gardens of the sixteenth century, is *Armeria maritima*, commonly known as thrift, a native wild flower from the cliffs that has pink pompon flowers on sturdy stems. Pinks, hybrids of another wild flower, *Dianthus plumarius*, with their pretty clove-scented single and double pink and white flowers, have always earned their place in the garden, and can be used to make a trim border. There are many beautiful pinks for the garden, some very old, with attractive fringed and streaked petals and glorious scents, that are worth collecting and cosseting. They have intriguing names, such as Pheasant's Eye, Painted Lady or Paisley Gem. Sops in Wine is so called from the practice of scenting and flavouring drinks with the flowerheads.

Sweet William, *Dianthus barbatus*, a biennial relation of the pinks, will seed itself and grow happily among the hardy perennials, sending up stems topped with mopheads of flowers of all colours from white through speckled pink to deepest red. The gillyflower, an old name for wallflower, was another popular scented flower. It will look after itself if allowed to seed freely,

Dianthus barbatus or Sweet William with *Digitalis* and delphiniums *(Jean Andrews)*

growing into walls and on paths as well as in the border. When it is used in mass plantings as bedding it loses all its character, but growing on its own it reveals how attractive it really is, especially the double form *Cheiranthus* Bloody Warrior, with its rusty red flowers.

Other plants that are more usually used as bedding plants are snapdragons (antirrhinums) and daisies, but in a cottage garden they should be grown either on their own or in little groups, to give the right effect. Antirrhinums are happy in the border or can live in a wall and keep flowering for years until they succumb to rust disease. The popular little daisies, cultivars of our native lawn daisy *Bellis perennis*, are happiest where they have rich damp soil and shade from the sun during the summer. The older cultivars, such as the 'hen and chicks' daisy *B.p. Prolifera* and Parkinson's Double White, were some of the earliest garden flowers and were grown not for food or as a herb, but as a curiosity and to decorate the garden. The 'hen and chicks' daisy is so called because of the way the main flowerhead sends out miniature flowerheads from underneath the petals, like youngsters around their mother.

Other daisy-like flowers, but belonging to other families of plants, have always formed the bulk of cottage garden planting. They range from the huge sunflowers depicted nodding over the hedges to the tall, spreading, bright yellow *Helianthus* and the shorter heleniums and pyrethrums for the middle of the border; all of these give a good show and make fine cut flowers. Michaelmas daisies, *Aster novi-belgii* and other hybrids keep up the display right through to early winter.

The stately, tall delphiniums and hollyhocks, formerly the pride of the formal herbaceous

Digitalis Sutton's Apricot, an attractive old variety, but still available *(Jean Andrews)*

border, found a natural home, along with the phlox, in cottage gardens. These plants revel in compost-rich soil. They soon make large clumps that can be divided up, or from which cuttings may be taken if the roots become infested with eelworm. Hollyhocks are prone to rust in some areas and in this case are best grown from seed each year. The lupin, with its wide range of colours – although blue is the most traditional – can also easily be grown from seed. The iris is another plant that can be sited in the middle of the border or along the edge of a path, where its many varieties of beautiful flowers with their velvety throats can be admired, and their sword-like leaves provide a foil for other flowers.

The sweet pea, *Lathyrus odoratus*, was a popular cash-crop flower, bunches of the highly scented flowers being used as table centrepieces, set off by a few sprigs of asparagus fern. The hardy perennial pea, *Lathyrus latifolius*, with its magenta and pink flowers, makes a vivid display for many weeks, and the long penetrating roots enable it to endure the most inhospitable of positions, sometimes making it the sole survivor in old gardens. Unfortunately it is not scented, and so it is a good plan to plant some of the highly perfumed old varieties of the annual sweet pea among the roots of a perennial pea so that they can mingle their flowers and provide the fragrance that everyone expects.

Gaps among rows of vegetables traditionally provided space for annuals. Useful herbs, such as borage with its sky-blue flowers and *Satureja hortensis*, the summer savory, with tiny mauve flowers, are highly attractive to bees. *Calendula officinalis*, the pot marigold, with its bright golden petals that can be used in salads or stews, will also act as a deterrent to insects. Summer savory is traditionally planted alongside broad beans to repel aphids. Marigolds are used to repel eelworms and whitefly, and so have been considered ideal for planting alongside tomatoes, particularly the small *Tagetes patula*, with its pungent smell.

As well as creating a beautiful garden, the cottage garden owner can help to conserve our heritage of old garden plants, vegetables and fruit. There are societies and organizations now devoted to finding and conserving plants for the future, which can provide information. Mixed ornamental and vegetable cultivation (see next chapter) is nowadays an important consideration with organic gardeners, as is the value of diverse varieties. By growing the old plants that are not readily available commercially, the vegetables that have been superseded by more modern seed strains and the old varieties of fruit trees and bushes no longer grown for the retail trade, the keen gardener can make a very real contribution to keeping these historical plants a part of our horticultural future for generations to come.

13 THE ORNAMENTAL KITCHEN GARDEN

My own views on organic gardening differ fundamentally from those normally accepted. Many organic gardeners will disagree with them, and many more will consider me too optimistic. I leave you to make up your own mind.

I am convinced that gardeners have made one basic mistake over the past hundred years or more, and I am concerned to see that the new organic movement is tending to take that mistake on board too. I think we need to grasp the nettle and make a U-turn. I see nothing wrong with admitting to mistakes and correcting them.

Our basic error has been blindly to follow the growing practices of the commercial grower and the farmer, simply reducing the scale and applying them to gardening. Yet our method of growing is so fundamentally different that we find ourselves applying the same set of solutions to what should be completely different problems.

Farmers grow all their crops in straight lines and gardeners follow suit. But think back to the reason for growing in rows. It was for nothing more or less than the convenience of pulling the horse-hoe through the crop, reducing the work of hand-hoeing and so saving labour and money. Well, I don't know when you last put a horse-hoe through your plot.

If farmers spray everything that moves, so do we, yet I maintain that, in the properly managed garden, there is absolutely no need to resort to even the so-called 'organic' pesticides. Certainly, if a farmer grows twenty acres of cabbages, he is bound to attract all the cabbage white butterflies in the area. What an advertisement for a free meal that spread of grey-green foliage must be; perhaps he has to spray. But gardeners can simply hide the cabbages away and generally avoid an attack completely.

My way is to shun *all* chemicals and to rely on natural and physical methods of pest control. And the whole theory depends for its existence on doing away with monoculture.

OPPOSITE: Globe artichokes, instantly at home in an ornamental setting (*Stephen Hamilton*)

A QUESTION OF SCALE

As it happens, the need for a change of methods is necessary on another front too. Modern gardens are very much smaller than their pre-war counterparts and they are shrinking every year. New houses are now often built with plots measuring just 20 x 15 ft (7 x 4.5 m) – room to swing only the smallest cat.

The traditional advice, for example to grow your roses in beds set in grass, one variety per bed, is therefore outdated. The very thought of the herbaceous border, the orchard or indeed the vegetable plot is just not on in many modern gardens. There simply isn't the room.

Realistically, everything has to be grown in the same borders. But that is just the way the old cottagers used to do it – they would grow only useful plants that would supplement their meagre wages. There were vegetables, herbs and fruit as well as plants grown for curing ills both naturally and supernaturally. Flowers were certainly grown too, just because they gave a much-needed lift to the spirits and, let's not forget, helped to neutralize what must have been some pretty strong smells. Their plants were never sprayed with chemicals and their fertilizer came from the pig and the privy. There's a lot to be learnt from our country ancestors. (See *Cottage Garden Flowers*, page 190.)

So my 'new' methods are actually as old as the hills, but I believe they are just as applicable to today's gardens as they were then.

Many modern gardeners want to be self-sufficient, or nearly so, in vegetables and fruit while also growing a garden that looks, smells and feels wonderful. I maintain that it is not only possible, it is downright easy and it is far healthier, even, than traditional organic gardening.

FERTILITY

The basis of any organic garden is the maintenance of high fertility. Just as a child fed

Plan for a medium-size garden
(*Elizabeth Douglass*)

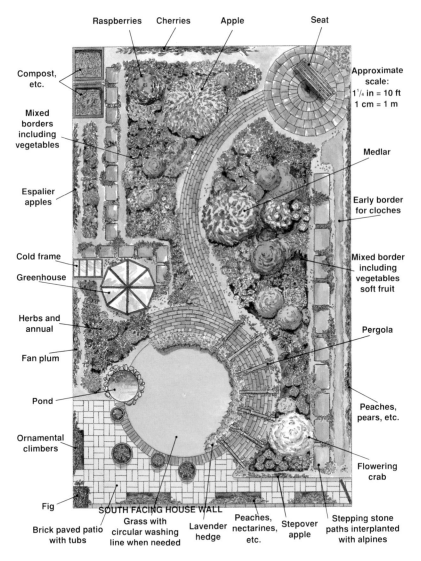

Raspberries   Cherries   Apple   Seat

Compost, etc.

Mixed borders including vegetables

Espalier apples

Cold frame

Greenhouse

Herbs and annual

Fan plum

Pond

Ornamental climbers

Fig

Brick paved patio with tubs

Grass with circular washing line when needed

Lavender hedge

SOUTH FACING HOUSE WALL

Peaches, nectarines, etc.

Stepover apple

Stepping stone paths interplanted with alpines

Approximate scale:
$1\frac{1}{4}$ in = 10 ft
1 cm = 1 m

Medlar

Early border for cloches

Mixed border including vegetables soft fruit

Pergola

Peaches, pears, etc.

Flowering crab

Runner beans and courgettes in a
border make the most of space in
a modern garden (*Joy Larkcom*)

on junk food is prone to every ill under the sun, so a force-fed plant is softer, weaker and more likely to succumb to pest and disease attack. But in my 'OK' garden there is another reason to maintain fertility at the highest level. The borders are so packed with plants, both productive and ornamental, that they need to be given the best possible chance to thrive.

I do this by growing everything on the 'deep bed' system (page 59). With this method, everything is sown or planted into deeply-dug 4 ft (120 cm) wide beds. The planting is closer than normal and the beds are not trodden on from one season's end to the next, all the work being done from the paths. Thus rooting depth is increased, soil structure is improved and plants can be grown much closer together. I have calculated that there is always a doubling of yield per square yard, and sometimes it triples.

But a garden divided into straight-up-and-down beds would not look that ornamental. It could defeat its own object. So, though my garden is divided into several beds, they are by no means formal. This creates two problems.

First of all, more paths than usual are required. But, rather than putting up with potentially ugly divisions, I have made all my paths attractive as well as functional.

Deep-dug, organically rich beds make possible a galaxy of close-planted ornamentals and vegetables (*Stephen Hamilton*)

Gentle curves lend the style and grace of the ornamental garden to vegetable beds (*Photos Horticultural*)

I started by putting in a 3 x 1 in (7·5 x 2·5 cm) wooden edging. Quite sharp curves can be negotiated by the simple expedient of making a series of saw-cuts on the inside edge of the bends. They go about two-thirds of the way through the wood, which then bends quite easily. Within the edging goes a bed of gritty compost on which slabs are laid stepping-stone fashion. A dressing of coarse gravel between the slabs and the wooden edges completes the job and has allowed me to put prostrate plants, mostly alpines, between the slabs. They will eventually creep over the slabs and turn even the paths into alpine scree borders. I have to say that they are not access routes for the gardener in a hurry, but sometimes it is an advantage to be forced to slow down.

With the paths down, the borders can then be double dug, incorporating manure, compost, composted straw or spent mushroom compost into the soil at all levels.

The second problem in my garden is that it is impossible to reach right across all the beds from the paths, thus defeating one of the main principles of the deep-bed system.

The answer is to plant taller permanent plants – shrubs, fruit trees and bushes and herbaceous

Coarse gravel between stepping stones provides for prostrate plants to turn paths into alpine scree borders (*Stephen Hamilton*)

plants – in the middle areas which cannot be reached, and to leave 'bays' at the front for growing annuals and vegetables.

Fertility is maintained with a very heavy input of bulky organic matter and organic fertilizer. Every time I harvest one crop and before I replace it with another, I incorporate a dressing of compost or manure and a light dusting of fertilizer.

This does disturb the roots of adjacent plants and that certainly will restrict their growth a little. I do not think that matters at all – in fact, I believe it is an advantage in a tiny garden.

SOWING AND PLANTING

Instead of sowing and planting in rows in the way that has become traditional, in the 'OK' garden it is all done in 'patches' within the bays near the front of the borders. I still actually sow in rows, but for a very different reason.

A crop like lettuce, for example, would be sown in shallow rows, scratched with the tip of a stick and about 6–9 in (15–23 cm) apart, depending on the variety. If weeds germinate at the same time as the lettuce, you will be able to recognize which is which because the lettuces are the ones growing in rows. When the plants are thinned to 6–9 in (15–23 cm) apart, of course, the rows disappear and you are left with an attractive patch.

And they do look attractive. In the next 'bay' you might be growing the poached egg plant or a patch of petunias, and believe me, they look very good together.

Planting is done in much the same way; indeed, I cheat a little in order to maintain a sure succession of harvesting. On my patio, I grow a number of plants, both vegetables and flowers, in pots and modules. That way, as soon as a place becomes available, the plants can be put in already half-grown, thus dramatically reducing the time before harvesting.

Some vegetables, of course, are not grown in this way. Those, like globe artichokes, that are attractive architectural plants in their own right, are given a more central place in the borders and are planted singly.

I do the same thing with early potatoes: I just put a single tuber here and there, planting with a trowel. Alone, they look very attractive in the border and you can harvest a meal for two or three by digging up just one plant at a time.

FRUIT

Fruit can take up a lot of room, but it need not. The first thing is to utilize every wall and fence space you have – all can be used, whatever the aspect.

On the south wall I grow peaches, nectarines, figs and even apricots. They are all grown fan-trained and are much easier to manage than you might think. Just buy a tree already trained and remember that peaches and nectarines fruit on wood made the previous year. See *Fruit*, pages 158–9, 160, for pruning details.

On the west wall, grow pears as espaliers or fans. Here you prune in mid- to late summer, simply cutting back the current season's growth to one or two buds. It really is that easy.

You prune apples in the same way which, together with plums and cherries, can be grown on the east-facing wall. Even the cold north wall can be used for cooking (Morello) cherries, which crop well and look good.

Gooseberries, red currants and white currants can be grown against a fence, this time as upright cordons. You can also grow gooseberries as standards, which consist simply of a bush on a 3–4 ft (90–120 cm) stem. They look good, they crop well and they enable you to grow something

The appearance of a gooseberry bush is transformed as a standard - leaving space for low growers at ground level (*Stephen Hamilton*)

underneath, so they take up virtually no space.

Blackcurrants are a bit more of a problem and my only space-saving solution here is to grow a compact variety like Ben Sarek. But the biggest headache of all is the invaluable raspberry. Wherever you put a row of raspberries it is in the way of the rest of the border, or is shading other crops. My solution is to grow them as a column rather than a row. I nail a couple of cross-pieces to a post and plant the canes around it. The canes are then tied to wires fixed to the cross-pieces. They crop well, and they look terrific.

Strawberries, of course, are no problem. Once you clear your mind of the idea that fruit and vegetable plants are ugly, you will realize how attractive these plants can look simply grown in the borders alongside the flowers.

CLIMBERS

Runner beans, trailing marrows, grapes and peas could present the same problems as raspberries. They are always in the way of something else. I solve this problem by growing them up a pergola.

Mine consists of a series of wooden posts at about 9 ft (2·75 m) intervals, with cross-pieces over the top. The posts are clothed with ornamental plants in the traditional way, but the spaces in between are certainly not wasted.

Here I grow runner beans up canes pushed into the ground and stapled to the cross-beams above. If you choose a red and white variety like Painted Lady or grow all red and all white varieties alternatively, they make superb ornamental climbers.

Peas are grown up netting fixed to the top beams. Here I again use attractive varieties like Carouby de Maussanne, which has marvellous purple flowers and delicious *mangetout* pods.

But it is the trailing marrows, cucumbers and squashes that really cause visitors to raise their eyebrows. Imagine huge green and yellow marrows or rugby-ball-sized vegetable spaghetti growing at eye level and you will see why. They make an attractive, interesting and novel feature and, again, they take up next to no growing room. Make sure, though, that you support large fruits with strong nylon twine. Tie it from the pergola to the neck of the fruit.

PEST AND DISEASE CONTROL

I have thrown my pesticide sprayer away. I still have one trusty old knapsack sprayer, but all that is ever in it is liquid seaweed, which I use as a foliar feed.

I first dabbled with organic gardening in the mid-1970s. I had been trained as a commercial grower, and that is how I spent my early career. So naturally, it was drummed into me that 'if it moves, you spray it'. Despite some unhappy

Plant diversity provides the best defence against pests and diseases in this potager *(John Walker)*

experiences (including a short spell in hospital with metasystox poisoning and seeing someone die from nicotine poisoning), I happily continued with this undeniably very successful method of pest control, and my first organic effort was an attempt to prove that organic methods did not work.

I set up four plots. One was entirely organic, one entirely chemical, the third a mixture of the two, which is how most traditional gardeners work, and finally a control plot with no additions at all. They all grew the same flowers and vegetables.

In the first year I was delighted to see the organic plot struggle to produce quite inferior crops, while the chemical plot romped away. But in the second and third years, there was a quite marked improvement in the organically grown plants, while the chemically grown ones seemed to slide a little. By the fifth year I was eating my words, as well as some of the best vegetables I had ever grown.

That amazed me, but not as much as the behaviour of the wildlife. The plots were actually adjacent to each other, separated only by a 3 ft (1 m) fence of plastic windbreak. But, while the chemically sprayed plot was almost

entirely devoid of insects, the organic area was buzzing. Somehow they seemed to know where they were well off. That got me thinking, investigating and carrying out trials.

The fact is that, once you fill your garden with a wide diversity of plants and do not spray them at all, you soon find your self surrounded by every kind of wildlife. My garden has seen all kinds of birds (even, thrillingly, a nightingale), butterflies, hover-flies, lacewings, bees, beetles, ladybirds, frogs, hedgehogs and shimmeringly beautiful dragonflies. This is another fascinating and exciting dimension to gardening, and I refuse to risk killing even the smallest hover-fly by dosing it with derris. But the great plus with what I call 'natural' gardening is that you do not need to.

Every one of the insects considered enemies has an enemy of its own, and if you leave nature to get on with it without interfering you will create a balance of wildlife, so that no one species ever builds up to unacceptable proportions.

You will get attacks of greenfly - but not for long. The birds, the hover-flies, the ladybirds and the lacewings will quickly polish them off. You will find the odd caterpillar hole in a lettuce - but not too many. The frogs, the birds and the ground beetles will quickly deal with them. It does pay to do a bit of picking off yourself, but not killing by spraying.

Certainly you will need to protect your fruit from your allies the birds. They get up earlier than you do and they like the fruit just as much, but a simple net will deter them.

You can cover some crops with spun polypropylene or perforated polythene to protect against flying insects, and use all the physical controls mentioned in *Pest Control* (page 290), *Disease Prevention* (page 258) and *Weeds* (page 234). They do no harm.

I would also encourage wildlife by providing the right conditions for it (see *The Wildlife Garden*, page 212). Ground beetles, for example, need cover to hide during the day, or they will be snaffled by the birds. Hover-flies like open-structured flowers to give them the feed of pollen they need before laying eggs to produce their greenfly-eating larvae. And all wildlife needs a drink from time to time, so water is essential. If you have little room for a pool, a 2 ft (60 cm) diameter half-barrel sunk into the ground will do.

I am very hopeful for the future of pest and disease control even in commercial growing.

Much chemical company research now is aimed at the breeding of plants that are resistant to or immune from pest and disease attack.

Many varieties of all kinds of plants resistant to pests or diseases are, of course, already available to gardeners. There is no need to grow roses that are a martyr to blackspot and mildew, and I would never, for example, grow Britain's favourite apple, Cox's Orange Pippin, because of its susceptibility to scab and particularly mildew.

Biological controls are also becoming available. But the main plank of organic pest control is to avoid monoculture by growing crops in patches rather than large blocks or straight lines; to grow as wide a diversity of plants as you can; and never to spray with pesticides that will kill indiscriminately.

Nature will then sort out the problem for you, at the same time providing you with the most glorious show of colour, perfume and interest. What is more, you will fill your patch with 'friends' and you will feel the beneficent glow of knowing that you are not deliberately killing anything.

And that is what gardening should be all about.

14

TREES, SHRUBS AND BUSHES

TREES FOR SEASONS

A good garden tree should 'earn its living', and, ideally, be of interest throughout the year. The first choice then should be something like the *Sorbus* species (rowans) or *Malus* (crab apples), which give blossom in the spring, followed by colourful fruit in the autumn, and attractive foliage into the bargain. The common red-berried rowan (*Sorbus aucuparia*) is beautiful enough, but there are now cultivated types, such as *Sorbus* Joseph Rock, which has good autumn foliage colour and yellow berries, or *Sorbus vilmorinii* with rose-white berries. Planted as a group, these three varieties look quite stunning.

Crab apples also give great value for money, with lovely displays of blossom in the spring followed by attractive crops of fruit in the autumn. The best varieties are John Downie, with scarlet-blushed crabs suitable for jelly-making, and Golden Hornet , which is covered in cherry-like yellow fruits. Again, the best effect is created if these are planted together, or they can be combined with some of the *Sorbus* varieties and *Acers* for a riot of autumn colour.

Many spring- and summer-flowering trees can be rather boring at other times of the year, so the best place for them is the back of a border or shrubbery. Such are laburnum, lilac and *Prunus*.

Laburnums are totally reliable and give a magnificent display of blossom in late spring or early summer. The variety *Laburnum x watereri* Vossii is the one to buy, as it has the longest racemes of flowers. The seeds are very poisonous, so carefully remove them if you have young children. Do not let this put you off: the laburnum is indisputably one of our most beautiful garden trees.

Lilacs are an old favourite, and there is nothing to beat the nostalgic fragrance of their flowers at the beginning of summer. The common lilac, *Syringa vulgaris*, is perfectly acceptable, but there

are double-flowered varieties available, and for sheer intensity of perfume go for the white-flowered Madame Lemoine.

The *Prunus* species are essential for late spring blossom, and there are now a bewildering number of varieties. You cannot go far wrong with *Prunus kanzan* (upright, 20 ft/7 m), *Prunus* Kiku-shidare Sakura or the Cheal's Weeping Cherry, and, for very small gardens, *Prunus* Amanogawa, which has a narrow, columnar growth habit.

The hawthorn of country hedgerows makes a fine ornamental tree, particularly suited to the wild garden or a rural situation. The tree is

Rowan tree (*Sorbus aucuparia*) combines spring blossom, autumn berries and attractive foliage (*Michael Walton*)

OPPOSITE: *Berberis darwinii*, essential for spring colour. Hardy, reliable and generally pest- and disease-free (*Michael Walton*)

Lilac (*Syringa vulgaris*) brings early summer fragrance (Michael Walton)

smothered in fragrant white blossom in late spring and early summer, and the red haws last well into the winter, giving plenty of colour. Because it is a wild species it is very hardy, and needs very little attention. In larger gardens it makes a fine hedge. More sophisticated are the beautiful cultivated varieties that bear pink or red flowers. *Crataegus* Paul's Scarlet and Rosea Flore Pleno are recommended.

Another wild tree that does well in gardens is the elder, *Sambucus nigra*. Trouble-free, it gives a good display of fragrant blossom in summer and a worthwhile crop of luscious berries in the autumn. (Puréed, with lemon juice and sugar added, they are as delicious as blackcurrants. Both flowers and berries also make superb wines.)

For a winter treat grow a witch hazel (*Hamamelis mollis*). This is completely hardy and its bare branches are covered in yellow, spidery, scented blossoms in mid-winter.

A few conifers are essential in every garden, but they should not be overdone. Small groups of various sizes and forms are better than single specimens dotted about like sentries. The one everyone knows is *Cupressocyparis leylandii*, which is so common that it is even sold in some supermarkets. The Leyland cypress is not, however, suitable for every situation; indeed, it can look dull and may be a bad choice if bought and planted on impulse. It is fast-growing and (eventually) very tall, so don't use it for a low front hedge. It can also grow very leggy and thin at the base.

Junipers are always a good choice as they are hardy, tolerant of dry conditions and poor soils, and have fragrant foliage. The choice of conifers is vast, from tiny dwarf forms that will grow in sink gardens to giant redwoods suitable only for

parks. One tip to remember is that the *Chamaecyparis* varieties are not as wind-hardy as the *Cupressocyparis* varieties, so choose the latter for exposed sites. However, most conifers are susceptible to wind scorch, especially while young, so if you want to use them for a windbreak they will themselves need protection from the wind for the first few years.

When buying conifers, always check the mature height and spread of each plant to be sure that it is right for its allotted space and will never outgrow its welcome. It is also wise to check the foliage colour, as yellow-foliaged types may be green when young.

HEDGES

Many gardens have at least one hedge. Hedges are better than solid fences in cold, windswept areas, as they will not trap cold air inside the garden as fences or walls do. Careful consideration should be given to choice of hedge, for it is planted only once. First of all ask yourself if you want it evergreen or deciduous. An evergreen hedge stays green all winter, but it may never do anything else. A deciduous hedge on the other hand will give you a display of flowers, berries, or both. If you want a clipped hedge evergreens are the usual choice, while flowering hedges are more informal. Other questions to consider are whether the hedge must serve as a windbreak, and if it should be thorny to keep children, dogs, or grazing animals in or out.

For a neat, clipped hedge of low to medium height, box is a good choice, although it has a smell which some people dislike. Privet is a good standby, but has the reputation of inhibiting the growth of plants near it. Yew is fine for a larger hedge, but is poisonous. Cotoneaster is probably the best choice. This is not evergreen, but in winter it is covered in scarlet berries, which the birds love.

If you want an informal hedge use roses or flowering shrubs. Honeysuckle will quickly clothe an unattractive wire fence. Broom or berberis can be used for low hedges, and the flowering currant, *Ribes sanguineum*, may also be used. Ring the changes by planting alternate colours such as red and yellow broom, or gold and green evergreens. Or use something that the neighbours do not have. Snowberry (*Symphoricarpos*) can make a very good low or medium hedge and is very hardy. In warmer areas fuchsias make attractive hedges.

In larger gardens, why not plant your own English hedgerow? This is basically hawthorn, with a few hazels, blackthorns, wild roses, and elders included. Such a hedge is a haven for wildlife and is virtually maintenance-free.

Another plant that can make an unusual informal hedge is the tree lupin, *Lupinus arboreus*.

ABOVE: Sunshine (*Senecio greyi*) thrives in poor soils and wind-swept locations (*Michael Walton*)
LEFT: The tree lupin (*Lupinus arboreus*) provides an unusual hedge, highly attractive to beneficial insects (*Michael Walton*)

In full flower it is a beautiful shrub, covered in candles of yellow blossom. These flowers are better for cutting than the ordinary border lupin, and have a superb scent. The plant is ideal for poor soils and hot, sandy banks, growing happily where nothing else would thrive, and it flowers freely without any feeding or attention. Give it plenty of sun and plenty of room (it will grow to a height and spread of 5 ft x 5 ft /1·5 x 1·5 m) and replace it every six or seven years. It is hardy, and remains evergreen in all but the coldest winter weather. Replacement and propagation could not be easier, as it can be grown from seed. Just sow like ordinary lupins, transfer the seedlings to a nursery bed when large enough, protect from slugs, and plant out when about knee-high – which can be as little as eight months from sowing. The only pest it is prone to is aphids, so keep a sharp look-out for these.

SHRUBS

There are shrubs to give pleasure in every season and any climate. Free-flowering, nectar-bearing shrubs like honeysuckles, buddleias and tree lupins attract a great many beneficial insects to the garden. Buddleias should be in every organic garden, for they bear an abundance of huge scented cones of blossom which are a magnet for bees and butterflies. Buddleias, like tree lupins, are easily raised from seed, but they require chilling or stratification for one month before they will germinate (see page 75).

Honeysuckles make excellent wall shrubs if given room to spread. As well as their scented flowers, they also provide a short display of scarlet berries later on in the season. Being tough, hardy, and usually disease-free, they make an ideal plant for the organic garden. Once you have one honeysuckle, you can easily propagate it by layering. Simply pin down a low hanging shoot, and cover the pin with earth. In a few months it will have rooted and can then be severed from the parent plant and moved elsewhere.

Another good wall shrub is the winter jasmine (*Jasminum nudiflorum*), which gives a reliable display of yellow blossom right through the winter. In warmer areas this could be grown along with the summer jasmine (*Jasminum officinale*) for year-round bloom. Also suitable for walls in mild areas is the Passion flower, *Passiflora caerulea*, which is really a lot hardier than many people imagine; it can be grown easily from seed.

Senecio greyi (or Sunshine) is a must in every garden. A hedge of this makes a magnificent sight in full bloom, and even when it is not flowering the attractive grey foliage always looks neat and fresh. This shrub seems happy anywhere provided it is in the sun, but it looks especially good in front of a dull stone wall. It thrives in poor soils and windswept locations, even by the sea.

Two essential shrubs for spring colour are forsythia and *Berberis darwinii*. Both are hardy and reliable, and appear to be generally pest- and disease-proof. *Berberis darwinii* can grow to tree size and is magnificent when in full flower.

Pernettya is an ideal winter shrub. An evergreen, it is covered in large, 'porcelain' berries, red, pink, or white, all through the depths of winter. To obtain these berries you must plant a group of two or three females with one male.

For shady places you cannot go far wrong with the Rose of Sharon (*Hypericum calycinum*), which will quickly spread, covering the ground with fragrant foliage and large, glistening yellow flowers. It is especially good for covering banks. Another variety of *Hypericum* well worth looking out for is the Tutsan, *Hypericum androsaemum*.

This has smaller flowers and is taller than the other variety, but in the autumn it is a mass of red berries which darken to black.

Other shrubs to be recommended are, from winter through to autumn: skimmia, aucuba, *Viburnum bodnantense* Dawn, red- and yellow-stemmed dogwood (*Cornus*), *Mahonia* Charity, holly, hazel, Japanese or ornamental quince (*Chaenomeles japonica*), gorse (*Ulex europaeus*), Broom (*Cytisus*), camellias (especially the hardy variety Donation), weigela, *Deutzia scabra*, philadelphus, hydrangeas, hebes, firethorn (*Pyracantha*) and *Stranvaesia davidiana*.

Less hardy, but recommended for milder climates or sheltered areas, are: wintersweet (*Chimonanthus praecox*), *Garrya elliptica*, winter hazel (*Corylopsis spicata* or *pauciflora*: *C. pauciflora* is more tender and will not survive in cold areas), magnolias (*M. stellata* is the hardiest), wisterias (try to avoid *W. sinesis* seedlings; *W. floribunda* is best, and better still is a grafted plant), osmanthus, ceanothus, summersweet (*Clethra alnifolia*), daisy bush (*Olearia*) and eucryphia. Many of these are 'borderline' shrubs that will grow in cooler areas if planted in a very sheltered spot or against a wall. They are often passed off as 'hardy', but gardeners in cold areas should be cautious, and think carefully before buying.

Japanese quince (*Chaenomeles japonica*), a fine wall shrub (*Michael Walton*)

CULTIVATION AND PROPAGATION

Get all your trees and shrubs off to a flying start by planting them properly. Prepare the site well beforehand – in fact, in colder areas, it is best to prepare the planting sites in the autumn, before the frosts.

Dig the ground thoroughly, taking care to incorporate plenty of well-rotted manure or compost. In heavy soils sand may be dug in. Calcified seaweed is a good soil dressing if lime-tolerant shrubs are to be planted, but never use this where ericaceous subjects are to go. Mark prepared sites with canes until plants arrive.

If the weather is unsuitable for planting when the plants are delivered, heel them in by digging a V-shaped trench in the vegetable plot or other vacant space and putting the plants in side by side. Fill in the trench and firm. The plants should keep in good condition like this for a week or two. If planting is going to be delayed for only a few hours, plunge the roots into pails of water as soon as possible – this is vital, for they may have dried out.

Dig a hole that is wide enough to allow the roots to be spread out in it, and deep enough to bring the 'soil mark' on the stem level with the soil surface. With grafted stock, the grafting point (the knobbly bit near the bottom of the stem) must be clear of the ground. Sprinkle in some general organic fertilizer, bone-meal, or rock phosphate, then place the plant in position and drive in the stake, if any. Water well, and begin to backfill, shaking the soil well down into the roots as you go. Finish by firming around the stem with your feet so there is no movement, but don't overdo it. If planting trees you must use a good tree tie.

Container-grown plants may be planted at any time of year, but if planting is done in summer they will need lots of water. In hot weather it is a good idea to wet the foliage every night as well as watering the roots, until the plant is settled in and growing. A few feeds with liquid manure during its first summer will help get the plant going and ensure strong, healthy growth. Always label well: it is prudent to note the name of the variety somewhere safe, for labels always seem to come adrift eventually.

Most of the varieties mentioned here are trouble-free, and rarely, if ever, suffer from pests or diseases. However, the *Prunus* varieties may be affected by silver leaf (see *Disease Prevention* (page 282) and die-back. Die-back, which is self-explanatory, is best treated by pruning back to healthy wood and spraying with Bordeaux mixture during the summer.

A common complaint is that a flowering shrub fails to flower. If soil and situation are correct, a

Planting times

Bare-rooted deciduous trees and shrubs
Mid-autumn to early spring

Bare-rooted evergreens
Early autumn or early spring

Container-grown deciduous trees and shrubs
Any time, but best to avoid mid-summer

Container-grown evergreens
Any time, but best planted in early autumn or early spring

Planting
(*Rob Dalton*)

Bare rooted plant   Container plant

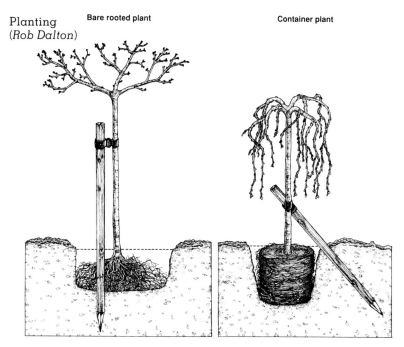

likely cause is an excess of nitrogenous feed (such as dried blood or manure) and/or a lack of potash in the soil. To correct this and stimulate flowering, give potash in the form of rock potash or wood ash, and reduce all other feeding for a while. Bear in mind, however, that many new shrubs and trees can take a year or two to establish themselves before they will flower, so do not be too impatient.

You can propagate a number of shrubs quite easily from semi-ripe wood cuttings or hardwood cuttings. Propagation techniques are given in detail elsewhere in this volume (see page 78); I will describe how the methods are applied to trees and shrubs.

Semi-ripe wood cuttings are taken in the summer or early autumn when the current year's growth is just starting to stiffen and strengthen. The wood must be 'ripe' or the cuttings will fail to root. Hardwood cuttings are taken in late autumn or winter, while the plant is dormant.

To take a semi-ripe wood cutting, pull off a shoot with a heel, or remove the tip of a suitable stem, cutting below a leaf node. Remove the lower leaves and insert into a 50:50 mixture of compost and sand; keep to the edge of the pot. The standard method is to place the cuttings in the humid environment of a plastic bag or propagator, with gentle bottom heat; but I have found that most cuttings root perfectly well if placed in a shady place outdoors, so long as they are kept moist. Indeed, I have successfully rooted cuttings outdoors which succumbed to rot in the pampered environment of the propagator. Outdoors there is always a free circulation of air, so rot is less likely. Another advantage is that, once the cuttings are rooted, no hardening off is necessary.

To take hardwood cuttings, select a suitable stem and make a straight cut below a bud, removing the shoot from the bush. Then make a second, sloping cut above another bud to leave about 12 in (30 cm) of stem. Insert this into a V-shaped trench in the garden with some sharp sand in the bottom, and rooting should take place in about six to eight months.

A great many trees and shrubs can be successfully raised from seed, but most hardy varieties need stratification. The purpose of stratification is to break the dormancy of the seed by fooling it into

Taking cuttings
(*Rob Dalton*)

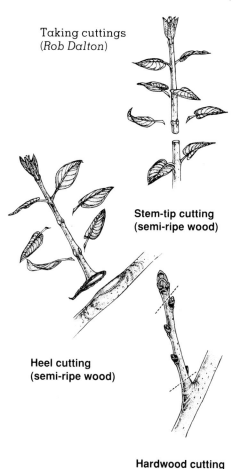

Stem-tip cutting
(semi-ripe wood)

Heel cutting
(semi-ripe wood)

Hardwood cutting
(dormant only)

Rooting cuttings
(Rob Dalton)

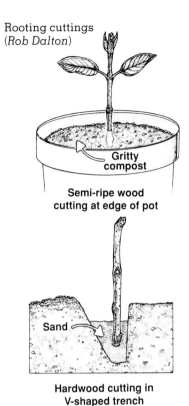

Gritty compost

Semi-ripe wood cutting at edge of pot

Sand

Hardwood cutting in V-shaped trench

BELOW: Spanish broom (Spartium), at home in dry soils or hot sunshine (Michael Walton)

thinking it has passed through the winter. You can sow seeds and place the pots outside over the winter – by a north wall, covered in netting to prevent mice getting them; but it is quicker and more reliable to 'fake' winter by putting the seed into the refrigerator (not the freezer).

Sow as usual but in a gritty compost and cover with a little sand. Label clearly, then place in the bottom of the refrigerator covered with a small sheet of glass. Note carefully the date they were put in and the date they must come out. Keep compost slightly moist and check once a week. After the required time remove the pots and place in warmth. The seeds should then germinate, but germination can sometimes be erratic. Stratification time varies, but on average one to two months should suffice.

Some seeds (such as peonies) are double dormant and need two three-month periods of chilling separated by a three-month period of warmth.

Start your stratification experiments with easy seed such as the buddleia mentioned earlier, and you will soon gain confidence.

Growing from seed is well worth the trouble as it allows you to obtain large numbers of plants or unusual varieties otherwise unavailable. Good seed-merchants produce useful guides to the germination of many species.

PRUNING

Most of the subjects covered need little or no pruning, other than the removal of dead or diseased branches. However, shrubs such as buddleia must be cut down quite hard each spring to encourage plenty of fresh young growth to come up from the base.

How a shrub is pruned depends on whether it flowers on the current year's growth or on older wood made last year. The buddleia

Climbers/wall shrubs

Winter jasmine
Pyracantha (firethorn)
Cotoneaster horizontalis
Honeysuckle
Forsythia
Wisteria
Clematis
Passiflora (passion flower)

Acid soils

Rhododendron
Azalea
Camellia
Magnolia
Pernettya
Pieris
Skimmia
Liquidambar (sweet gum)
Kalmia (calico bush)

Damp, boggy ground

Betula (birch)
Salix (willow)
Alder
Hawthorn
Liquidambar (sweet gum)
Enkianthus
Skimmia
Dipelta
Danae (Alexandrian laurel)
Clethra alnifolia

Alkaline soils (chalk)

Philadelphus
Buddleia
Caryopteris
Kolkwitzia (beauty bush)
Pyracantha (firethorn)
Senecio Sunshine
Syringa (lilac)
Viburnum
Lavender

Shade-lovers

Aucuba
Cherry laurel
Rhododendron
Box
Cotoneaster
Hypericum
Mahonia
Skimmia
Enkianthus (pagoda bush)
Fatsia japonica

Dry soils and/or hot sunshine

Santolina   *Helianthemum*
Lavender   Cistus (rock rose)
Tree lupin   Carpenteria
Ulex (gorse)   Caryopteris
Broom   Indigofera
Juniper   *Senecio* Sunshine
Rosemary   Yucca
Phlomis

Windbreaks

Hippophae (sea buckthorn)
Ribes (flowering currant)
Hawthorn
Box
Tamarix
Holly
Cupressocyparis leylandii

Specimen trees/shrubs

Ailanthus (tree of heaven)
Buddleia alternifolia
Camellia
Magnolia
Cordyline (Palm)
Cheal's Weeping Cherry
Fatsia japonica
Gleditsia (honey locust)

is one of the former, so the aim in pruning is to encourage plenty of new growth during the current season. In shrubs that flower on older wood, such as weigela, *Ribes* or deutzia, cut back the branches that have flowered to encourage the growth of new stems that will flower next year. Such pruning is done immediately after flowering.

Pruning frightens some people, but if you stand back and study the bush carefully, you should be able to see which group it belongs to, and therefore when and how it ought to be pruned.

The pruning cut should be just above an outward-facing bud, and sloping away from it. Larger stems require a good pair of loppers or a pruning saw, for a clean cut is essential. The aim is always to create an open-centred bush. If you remember that the bud immediately below the pruning cut is the one that will break and grow, you can ensure that your shrubs grow in exactly the way you want them to. Indeed, with expert pruning and training, all kinds of weird and wonderful shapes can be created. Pleaching was

common in the past, where beeches or limes were woven horizontally into each other to create green 'corridors', and espalier training is still popular for fruit trees on walls and fences. Standards and half-standards are usually bought ready-made, but you can, if you wish, create one yourself with a suitable maiden stock plant (which is best grown from seed to get a single straight stem).

VARIETIES FOR PARTICULAR SITUATIONS

In order to help you choose the best trees and shrubs for any situation and avoid expensive mistakes, the lists above are offered. These are by no means comprehensive, for the range of species available now is truly enormous, especially if you include those varieties offered only as seed.

The beauty of trees and shrubs is that they will last many years and, for very little care and attention, give an abundance of pleasure.

15 THE WILDLIFE GARDEN

WHY GARDEN FOR WILDLIFE?

There are two excellent reasons why you might consider gardening with wildlife in mind. The first is that by creating a wildlife garden successfully, you can make a very real contribution to the survival of some of the hard-pressed native wildlife (in the widest sense). The second reason is that a garden rich in wildlife gives great pleasure to those who use it. Gardens have an enormous amount to offer anyway, but the added dimension of numerous butterflies, dragonflies emerging from the pond, masses of tadpoles, and nesting birds is a wonderful bonus.

The countryside of Britain, and much of the rest of the world, has changed dramatically in the last few decades. Development has burgeoned over the countryside, and modern agricultural practices are hostile to most forms of wildlife. In your own garden, although you are obviously affected by what goes on in the countryside or other gardens around you, you can control so much of the environment that you can remain apart from this general pattern of homogenization of the countryside and create a small area of great beauty and diversity.

Another very worthwhile consideration is that wildlife plays a valuable role in maintaining the balance of nature, preventing pests from dominating in the garden. A wildlife garden is therefore organically very desirable.

The overriding principle of wildlife gardening is that you are attempting to create an environment, on however small a scale , that will be attractive to as wide a range of species as possible. Because the number of species that you might potentially attract is so huge, it is better to try to create broadly wildlife-friendly environments rather than just trying to attract a few individual species. For example, it is not much use putting up bat-boxes if there are no insects for the bats to feed on. The table on page 214

The table on page 214

OPPOSITE: Small tortoiseshells on iceplants (*Sedum spectabile*) (*Natural Image*)

Dragonfly, *Aeshna cyanea* (*Natural Image*)

gives an idea of what an average-sized garden, in a good area, managed for wildlife, might attract or support. The diversity is enormous , and the wider the range of species you attract, the better balanced your garden will be.

DESIGN PRINCIPLES

Design is important in the wildlife garden, for both practical and ecological reasons. Much depends on personal circumstances such as size of garden, presence of children and pets, other uses to which the garden is put, and finance, to name but a few; the garden has to be right for the circumstances. To achieve a balanced, successful wildlife garden, it is well worth starting out with a rough plan of the garden and giving some thought to the following: 1. How much of the garden you want to devote specifically to wildlife. 2. Whether you want the wildlife garden to spread throughout, or be confined to one area; if so, where. 3. The ecological principles that should guide any attempt at creating wildlife habitats in the garden (see below). The prevailing soil conditions will influence your choice of species,

Garden wildlife

- About 250 species or varieties of flowering plants

- About 50 species of bird, resident, visiting or passing through

- 15 or so butterfly species

- 5 or more dragonfly/damselfly species

- Hundreds, or possibly thousands, of different insects and other invertebrate species

- Occasional amphibians, reptiles, mammals, and lower plants like lichens and mosses

and you may have particular features (such as a boggy area, or an old chalk-pit) that you can make use of, though the general principles are the same whatever your soil is like.

THE ECOLOGICAL FRAMEWORK

Species of plant, insects, birds and other forms of life do not operate independently of each other. They form a complex interconnecting system, competing, preying on, being preyed on, being parasitized by and generally interacting with each other, and it is impossible to look at one species without considering others, if only indirectly. Not only do species interact, but they also use different ecological 'niches' at different stages or for different aspects of their life, and the wildlife gardener has to consider how best to provide these different 'niches' for a range of species.

Frogs, for example, need ponds in which to breed. But the spawn and tadpoles are highly vulnerable to predation, and they will not do well if there are fish in the pond; or they may do reasonably well if there is ample water-weed in which they can find cover. When the froglets emerge from the pond to disperse, they are also highly vulnerable to predation by birds and mammals. If the pond is surrounded by bare concrete or paving, they are almost certain to be seen and eaten; if, on the other hand, the pond has long grass, shrubby areas, and a bit of tangled vegetation around it, maybe in addition to the paving, then they have a much better hope of survival. Adult frogs need insects for food, so their survival depends on a good supply of these, which, in turn, depends on many factors. They also need places to shelter, hide and hibernate.

Butterflies are similarly complicated. A common suggestion for attracting butterflies is to plant a buddleia bush; this will certainly attract butterflies, but it is only providing a food source (nectar) for mid- to late summer adult individuals, many of which may have bred anyway by then. All the other requirements of butterflies – larval food plants for the caterpillars, safe pupation sites, overwintering places, warmth and shelter, nectar from flowers at all stages of their flight period, especially early on, and so on – are not met by the buddleia. Some butterflies, like the Holly Blue, need two different caterpillar food plants at different stages of their life-cycle – holly in spring and ivy in autumn.

Even the familiar hedgehog needs to be made to feel at home. It needs a good place to sleep during the day, a hibernation site such as deep leaf-litter (or a purpose-made dry box), and a supply of pesticide-free invertebrate food.

Ecologically, therefore, the keynote of the wildlife garden is variety, and sensible juxtaposition of the wilder habitats to allow species to move from one to the other as necessary. Overlying both of these is the need to refrain from poisoning large sections of the ecological community by careless or unnecessary application of pesticides, or by excessive tidiness that negates much of what you are trying to achieve.

CREATING MINIATURE HABITATS

The idea of creating miniature habitats may seem a daunting prospect, especially to the owners of small gardens, but in fact it is a flexible and valuable way of working that can introduce variety to any garden on almost any scale. Essentially, you are taking the key features of naturally-occurring habitats, and trying to recreate them on a small scale. The easiest ones to achieve success with are ponds and wetlands, a meadow, and a 'woodland' edge, though other possibilities include flowing water, heathland and coppice, which may be feasible, according to the characteristics of the site. If you can spare only a little space and time, put in a pond: this will dramatically increase the range of species visiting and living in the garden, and give great pleasure to owners and visitors (see page 220, *Water Gardening*).

There is not enough space here to give full constructional, planting and management aims for the habitats; this chapter is intended to stimulate ideas, and there are ample good books on wildlife gardening and habitat creation for those wishing to go further.

PONDS AND WETLANDS

A pond is the hub of a wildlife garden, providing food, shelter, drinking water, a bathing place and

Wildlife pond with purple
loosestrife (*Natural Image*)

Wetland and water plants

O = oxygenating plants
F = floating-leaved plants
E = emergent aquatic plants
W = wetland plants

Amphibious bistort	
Polygonum amphibium	F, W
Angelica	
Angelica sylvestris	W
Brooklime	
Veronica beccabunga	W
Cuckooflower	
Cardamine pratensis	W
Flowering rush	
Butomus umbellatus	E, W
Fringed water-lily	
Nymphoides peltata	F
Gipsywort	
Lycopus europaeus	W
Greater spearwort	
Ranunculus lingua	E, W
Hemp agrimony	
Eupatorium cannabinum	W
Marsh marigold	
Caltha palustris	W
Meadowsweet	
Filipendula ulmaria	W
Monkey-flower	
Mimulus guttatus	W
Pondweeds	
Potamogeton species	F
Purple loosestrife	
Lythrum salicaria	W
Ragged Robin	
Lychnis flos-cuculi	W
Royal fern	
Osmunda regalis	W
Water forget-me-not	
Myosotis scorpioides	W
Water milfoil	
Myriophyllum spicatum	O
Water mint	
Mentha aquatica	W
Water starwort	
Callitriche stagnalis	O, F
White water-lily	
Nymphaea alba	F
Yellow flag	
Iris pseudacorus	E, W
Yellow loosestrife	
Lysimachia vulgaris	W

much else to a wide range of plants and animals. Its site will depend on various factors such as the other uses of the garden. Points to consider include: putting the pond close to other wild areas, if these are planned; deciding whether you want to see the pond clearly from the house, or whether you prefer it to be secluded; and the position relative to trees and shade.

While constructing the pond, it is worth considering the idea of a wetland attached to it; this can be a simple shallow depression, connected to the main pond over a bar so that it gets the overflow water, then filled with soil or peat substitute and planted with marsh plants. Such areas look very attractive, and give a valuable added dimension to the pond. The pond itself should be well vegetated with both submerged oxygenating plants and with emergent and marginal plants. For other plants see the chapter on *Water Gardening* (page 220).

THE FLOWERY MEADOW

Flowery meadow areas are perhaps the most evocative and colourful of potential garden habitats. They are also one of the most threatened of our more natural habitats – virtually all rich flowery

Woodland edge in spring (Pat Brindley)

meadows, outside nature reserves, have disappeared from the countryside. A garden meadow will not have everything that a natural ancient meadow has – no centuries-old anthills, no long-established clumps of Dyer's greenweed, fewer soil invertebrates – but you can produce something that looks like a meadow, and which will attract insects like a meadow.

The 'meadow' area is best sited somewhere reasonably sunny (or you can use especially shade-tolerant species if necessary), with some shelter such as a hedge or shed, and preferably next to any other mini-habitat that you are planning. The best soil is the least fertile, since most meadow plants cannot tolerate the high nutrient levels of fertilized ground; if you only have highly fertilized soil, the process will take longer, and you will need to keep on removing the cuttings for many years.

It is best to prepare the ground thoroughly first, clearing out the perennial weeds like docks and thistles if possible. You can use an existing lawn, but it needs a different approach (see *Lawns*, page 232). If starting with a clear site, choose a meadow seed mixture that is right for your soil and situation (there are many types available from specialist suppliers), and sow it carefully as you would for a lawn, well dispersed onto a well-prepared soil. When the mixture is established, roll it lightly and mow it about twice, with a high cut, in its first year. After this, you can vary the mowing according to what species flower when, whether you are trying to attract breeding butterflies (such as Common Blues, Meadow Brown, or Gatekeepers), or whatever your requirements are. If starting with a lawn, assuming it has not been too well fertilized, a good technique is to plant in it clumps of more desirable meadow species, such as oxeye daisies and cowslips, and allow them to spread. They will look odd at first, but will soon appear more natural if they are right for the site. You will need to alter your mowing regime to a higher cut, less frequently.

Beware of buying mixtures of plants that are annuals only – these produce a super display in the first year, but will not survive in a closed sward, and need re-cultivating and re-sowing each year. Although many will set seed adequately, the proportion of perennial or aggressive weeds such as docks and thistles will rapidly increase, ousting the plants you want to keep. One other point: if you want it to look as though you have planned the meadow, and not just left the lawn unmown, it is worth having a more tightly mown area next to the meadow, to show the difference.

Conservation wood pile at woodland edge with holes and gaps for insect/small mammal habitat (*Natural Image*)

THE WOODLAND EDGE

Although the term 'woodland edge' sounds as though it must take up a lot of space, in reality this is more of a hybrid between a hedge and a woodland, and can be fitted into quite a small space. Most woodland species are actually best adapted to clearings, glades and coppiced areas, and by reproducing just the edge of the wood, you are actually re-creating its richest part.

The features of a woodland edge that you are attempting to bring into the garden are: dappled sun and shade, shelter, increased humidity, leaf-litter, and the structure of the plant layers. Obviously not all of this is possible in a tiny garden, but it is surprising what can be done.

Some plants for woodland and the woodland edge

Soil preference, if relevant: A = acid; N = neutral; C = alkaline;

Betony *Stachys officinalis*		
Bluebell *Hyacinthus non-scripta*	A–N	
Bugle *Ajuga reptans*		
Butcher's broom *Ruscus aculeatus*		
Columbine *Aquilegia vulgaris*	N–C	
Foxglove *Digitalis purpurea*	A–N	
Garlic mustard *Alliaria petiolata*		
Greater stitchwort *Stellaria holostea*		
Ground ivy *Glechoma hederacea*		
Lily-of-the-valley *Convallaria majalis*		
Lords and ladies *Arum maculatum*		
Lungwort *Pulmonaria officinalis* (and others)		
Nettle-leaved bellflower *Campanula trachelium*	N–C	
Primrose *Primula vulgaris*		
Solomon's seal *Polygonum multiflorum*		

Stinking hellebore *Helleborus foetidus*	N–C	
Stinking iris *Iris foetidissima*	N–C	
Sweet violet *Viola odorata*	N–C	
Wild daffodil *Narcissus pseudonarcissus*		
Wood anemone *Anemone nemorosa*		
Wood avens *Geum urbanum*		
Wood cranesbill *Geranium sylvaticum*		
Wood spurge *Euphorbia amygdaloides*		
Wood vetch *Vicia sylvatica*		
Woodruff *Galium odoratum*		
Yellow archangel *Lamiastrum galeobdolon*		

Redwing, *Turdus iliacus*, feeding on holly berries (*Natural Image*)

Food for birds

Bird cherry *Prunus padus*
Brambles *Rubus fruticosus* and other species
Cotoneasters especially *C. frigida, horizontalis,*
    and x *watereri*
Crab apple *Malus sylvestris*
Dog rose *Rosa canina* and others
Dogwood *Thelycrania sanguinea*
Elder *Sambucus nigra*
Fruit bushes, various
Guelder rose *Viburnum opulus*
Hawthorn *Crataegus monogyna*
Hogweed *Heracleum sphondylium*
Holly *Ilex aquifolium*

Ivy *Hedera helix*
Plantains *Plantago species*
Privet *Ligustrum vulgare*
Pyracantha coccinea, P. Mojave, *P.* Orange Glow
Red chokeberry *Aromia arbutifolia*
Rowan *Sorbus aucuparia*
Spindle *Euonymus europaeus*
Stinging nettle *Urtica dioica*
Sunflower *Helianthus annuus*
Teasel *Dipsacus sylvestris*
Thistles, various *Carduus* and *Cirsium* species
Vine (grape)
Wayfaring tree *Viburnum lantana*

Structure the planting so that the largest trees are at the back, perhaps next to an existing hedge, with smaller trees and then shrubs in front. The size of the larger trees will vary according to your space, from oaks through birches to rowans, or just larger native shrubs. It is best to bring some rough grass up to the edge of the planting, to allow an attractive and flowery gradation through from trees to grass, without a hard edge. This area should receive a reasonable amount of sun. Plant suitable shade-tolerant herbaceous plants into the wooded area (see list), bringing in leaf-mould if there is none, to speed up the process. This is also a good place to put a conservation wood pile (i.e. a pile of logs left for insects, fungi, small mammals and so on

Larval food plants for butterflies and moths

Alder buckthorn *Frangula alnus*

Bird's-foot trefoil *Lotus corniculatus*

Common sorrel *Rumex acetusa*

Cuckooflower *Cardamine pratensis*

Dame's violet *Hesperis matronalis*

Garlic mustard *Alliaria petiolata*

Holly *Ilex aquifolium* and Ivy *Hedera helix* (for Holly Blue)

Lime trees *Tilia* species

Privet *Ligustrum vulgare*

Rosebay willowherb *Epilobium angustifolium*

Stinging nettle *Urtica dioica*

Various soft grasses

to use, and not removed for burning), as these are most successful in the shade, and the rotted wood will eventually add to the forest-floor effect.

As the woody plants become established, the larger ones can be coppiced (cut back to ground level) or pollarded (cut off at head height) in rotation to prevent them from becoming too large and dominant, while still retaining the woodland atmosphere. Berry-bearing shrubs and small trees, such as guelder rose, wild red currant or rowan, are excellent for the edges, where they will produce most fruit.

PLANTS FOR THE WILDLIFE GARDEN

The range of possible species that can be planted in the wildlife garden is enormous, and we can pick out only a few possibilities for different purposes here. The wild flowers suggested in these lists are for the specific purpose of attracting other forms of wildlife. As a general principle, plants that are native to your region or country will attract the widest range of insects to feed on them as larvae, and these are a good general choice for the trees and shrubs of the wildlife garden. However, there are many exotic species that make excellent nectar sources for insects, and many others that produce fruit that is highly attractive to birds. Nesting birds are more affected by structure than species. Meadow plants are not covered since these are normally available in standard mixtures to suit different soil types.

Good nectar sources for insects

Applemint *Mentha x rotundifolia*

Aubretia

Blackthorn *Prunus spinosa*

Bramble *Rubus fruticosus*

Buddleia davidii in various forms

Caryopteris X clandonensis

Convolvulus tricolor Blue Ensign

Dame's violet *Hesperis matronalis*

Devil's bit scabious *Succisa pratensis*

Fleabane *Pulicaria dysenterica*

Globe thistle *Echinops ritro*

Golden rods *Solidago* species

Greater knapweed *Centaurea scabiosa*

Hebe, various species including *H. albicans*, *H. brachysiphon*

Hemp agrimony *Eupatorium cannabinum*

Honeysuckle *Lonicera periclymenum* and other species

Hyssop *Hyssopus officinalis*

Iceplant *Sedum spectabile*

Lavender 'Dwarf Munstead Blue'

Marigolds, all sorts

Marjoram *Origanum vulgare*

Michaelmas daisies *Aster* species, various

Night-scented stock *Mathiola longipetala bicornis*

Red valerian *Centranthus ruber*

Thyme *Thymus drucei*

Tobacco plant *Nicotiana* species

Verbena venosa

16 WATER GARDENING

A pond does many things for a garden. It brings beauty and tranquillity, colour, movement and reflected light with, perhaps, the gentle sound of water in motion. It provides a focal point for the smaller garden as much as the larger one, and gives the opportunity to grow and enjoy a new and exciting range of plants. Equally important for the organic gardener, a properly made and managed pond will provide a home for wildlife such as frogs, toads and hedgehogs, which, as well as being delightful creatures with which to share the garden, will also play a major role in keeping slugs and snails under control.

Thanks to the introduction of pre-formed plastic liners, the actual construction of the pond is within the capabilities of any able-bodied gardener. If the chore of digging out the hole for a large pond seems too daunting, hiring a mini-digger for a day could be the answer. If excavating a hole for a pond is out of the question, there is the attractive alternative of having a raised pond as a feature of the patio or garden, although this would mean sacrificing some of the planting schemes for a sunken pool.

Two important points should be emphasized at the outset. First, if you have a toddler in the family, ask yourself whether it would be better to wait a few years before embarking on pond installation. Water acts like a magnet to very young children and even a shallow garden pond can be lethally dangerous to them. Secondly, the location of the pond must be considered in relation to its surroundings. It should not be permanently in shade, nor should it be located under trees, where it would become congested with rotting leaves.

MAKING YOUR PLAN

Obviously, a feature as important as a pond needs careful planning before any of the manual work is undertaken. Although there is a sound principle that the larger the pool, the better will be the biological balance for the plants and, maybe, fish that will be a feature of the water garden, the depth of the pond is a particularly important factor. The water in a too-shallow pond heats up rapidly on a warm summer's day and, while this is tolerated by some plants such as water-lilies, for fish and the wildlife in the pond a rapid increase in water temperature can be fatal as the oxygen in the water is driven out. You should aim for a minimum depth of 18 in (45 cm) in a pond without fish, but a preferred depth of 30 in (75 cm) to ensure a frost-free winter home for fish, even deeper in areas of long, hard winters. Deep pools tend to accumulate mud which, in time, becomes stagnant and must be removed.

Other factors to consider in the planning stage: 1. If the pond is to have a fountain or waterfall, a pump will be necessary and an electricity supply to power it. That means laying a cable before the landscaping of the site is completed. 2. The surroundings of the pond will need to be planned at the same time as the layout of the pond itself. As well as making provision for the aquatic plants bordering the pond remember to include an area for sitting and enjoying the pleasures of pond ownership. (See also *The Wildlife Garden*, page 213.) 3. Don't forget that you will have to decide what you are going to do with the soil that is excavated. It is surprising how much space is needed to dispose of the spoil from the excavation of even a small pond. A good plan is to use it as the basis for a rockery bordering the pond, but this needs proper terracing and planting so that it becomes an integral part of the water garden. If the site of the pond is in the lawn, do not waste the turves. Stack them, grass side down, and after six months or so you will have valuable loam.

MAKING THE POND

Installing a ready-formed pond-liner made of resin-bonded glass fibre, of the type that can be bought at most garden centres, is a relatively simple operation; however, the resulting pond is

OPPOSITE: Conventional lawn and border is transformed by pond (*Roy Lacey*)

Water-lilies provide sub-surface shade for frogs (inset) in this large garden pool (*Natural Image*)

generally too small for fish to survive a warm summer or a hard winter and, of course, your choice of size and style is limited. With this type of liner you first dig the hole slightly larger than the pool, making sure the base is firm and level. Allow about a week for the soil to compact, then put down a layer of sand on which to bed the liner.

Place the liner in position and check that it is level, then fill the gap between the liner and the edge of the excavation using spoil from the hole. Next, slowly fill the pond with water and at the same time continue to fill the gap between the liner and the edge of the hole with spoil. Finally, cover the overlapping edge of the liner with paving stones or slabs of stone, large pebbles or whatever you like.

A pond lined with plastic sheeting is the easiest and least costly way of making one, and offers the opportunity of creating an individualistic design. Don't be too ambitious with the shape: sweeping curves are generally far more satisfactory than harsh angles. Use graph paper to plan your design

to scale, having first tried out the design on site using a length of rope or a hosepipe to mark out the shape.

When you have finalized the design, calculate the size of the lining sheet you will need (see formula). Do not be tempted to buy any old plastic sheeting for the lining. Thickness is no criterion of quality or longevity. Polythene is not a wise choice because it has a life of only three or four years. Nylon-reinforced PVC is better, with a lifespan of about five or six years. Best of all is butyl, universally used as a lining for reservoirs, far more expensive than polythene or PVC but with a life of at least fifty years.

You can, of course, make your pond a concrete one, although its construction becomes something of a civil engineering job and its cost is far greater than that of flexible liners.

Maintaining the shape of the pond while you are digging out the hole can be a bit tricky, because any marking can be obliterated by the spoil. Start by marking the shape with a trickle of sand or flour and at, say, 4 in (10 cm) outside this,

Outline the desired shape of the
pond with canes and string
(*Chris Algar*)

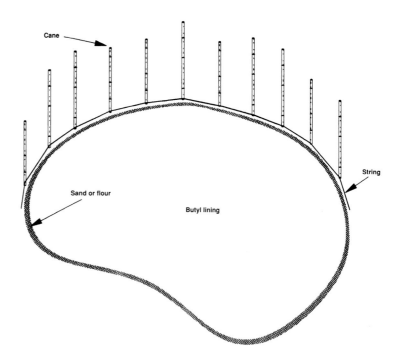

Cane

String

Sand or flour

Butyl lining

outline the shape with canes and plastic string. It is easier to
maintain a level surface for the lining if the excavated soil is thrown
well clear of the hole or removed in a barrow.

Remember that at the bottom of the hole you will need to allow
for a cushion for the lining, so dig about 1 in (2·5 cm) deeper to
allow for this. If your lining is to be reinforced PVC, the cushion
could be a thick layer of newspaper or old carpeting. If you are
using butyl, you will need a layer of fine sand.

When preparing the internal profile of the hole it is important to
terrace it with a ledge at about 6 in (15 cm) from the surface for the
marginal aquatic plants. It is also necessary to ensure that the
lining, once installed, is level at every point of the perimeter.

Laying the lining is the next stage of the operation and to
prepare for this it should be spread out for a day or two. If the
weather is cold, lay it out in a warm room. Getting the lining into
position is a job best done by two people, especially with a pool
larger than about 20 sq ft (6 sq m). Have large stones or lengths of
timber handy to lay on the 12 in (30 cm) edges of the lining to
prevent it slipping into the hole. Press the lining into the
extremities of the pond before filling with a hosepipe. As the pond
fills up, the lining will stretch to hug the contours of the hole.

When the pond is full, the next step is to lay the edging, allowing
an overhanging lip of about 1 in (2·5 cm), but always leaving a few
gaps so that small animals which fall in have an escape route. What
you use as edging is up to you. The important thing is that it
should be firm and, preferably, non-slippery when wet. If you use
paving stones, crazy paving or paving blocks, they should be
bedded on to a thick layer of sand.

For circulating the water through a fountain or water cascade
you will have to install a submersible pump fixed to a firm base on
the bottom of the pond. One pump can be used to operate both a
fountain and a waterfall, the waterfall pool and the main pond
being connected to the pump and fountain via a length of buried
hose with a 1 in (2·5 cm) internal diameter. This can be installed
while you wait a week or ten days for the pond liner to bed down.

**To calculate size of
lining sheet**
Length of pond + twice
deepest depth x widest
part of pond + twice the
average depth.
Add 2 ft (60 cm) to both
width and length to allow
for lining to be buried at
the edges.

Pump arrangement for fountain and waterfall. Note terraced ledge for marginal aquatic plants (*Chris Algar*)

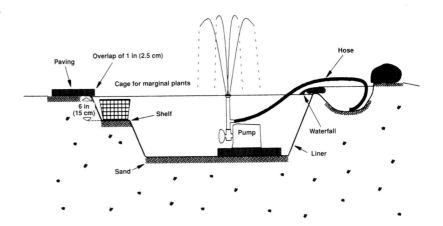

During this period the borders of the pond can be landscaped, using moisture-loving plants such as large and dwarf irises, hostas and ferns. Reeds and bulrushes should not be planted directly into the soil because their roots are very invasive. Plant them, instead, into suitable containers which can then be sunk into the borders.

THE PLANTS

With the pond full of water and the border planted up, you can now plan for the aquatic plants to go in the pond, but do not hurry: allow ten to fourteen days before visiting your local water-garden centre. You will find that plants for the pond are grouped into four types: the oxygenators or submerged aquatics; floating plants for the surface; marginal aquatics for shallow water; and deep-planted water lilies and other fixed floating aquatics.

Oxygenators: vital plants in keeping the water clear. They provide oxygen for the fish and absorb some of the carbon dioxide exhaled by them. They are suitable for water depths of 1–3 ft (30 cm–1 m) and include the commonest underwater plant, often sold with goldfish, Canadian pondweed (*Elodea canadensis*), very fast-growing; the water hyacinth (*Eichhornia crassipes*), with bright green glossy leaves and pale blue flowers; water chestnut (*Trapa natans*); water violet (*Hottonia palustris*); the submerged water soldier (*Stratiotes aloides*); hornwort (*Ceratophyllum*); and water crowfoot (*Ranunculus aquatilis*).

Free-floating waterfern (*Natural Image*)

Free-floating plants: these include bladderwort (*Utricularia vulgaris*), with tiny buoyancy pouches on the stems and, in summer, yellow orchid-like flowers; fairy floating moss (*Azolla caroliniana*), fast-growing and with foliage that turns pink, then red, in the autumn; and the beautiful miniature floater, frogbit (*Hydrocharis morsus-ranae*), with leaves like tiny water-lilies and white flowers in summer.

Nymphaea laydekeri, a lily for a medium-size pond /*Natural Image*)

Marginal plants: for the shallow water or marginal zone of the pond where the water depth is 2–6 in (5–15 cm) there are beautiful plants that thrive with their feet in the water. Having bought your stock plants, thereafter you can multiply this group by division in the spring. Choose from the golden marsh marigold (*Caltha palustris*), which grows 9–12 in (23–30 cm) tall; the water forget-me-not (*Myosotis scorpioides*), 9 in (23 cm); arrowhead (*Sagittaria sagittifolia*), with distinctive arrow-shaped leaves and handsome white flowers, growing to about 2 ft (60 cm); flowering rush (*Butomus umbellatus*), with pink flowerheads in late summer and early autumn, growing to about 3 ft (90 cm) tall.

Bulrush or reedmace (*Typha latifolia*), growing to 6 ft (180 cm), is rather too tall for a small pond, although there are smaller varieties, such as *T. minima*, 12–18 in (30–45 cm) and *T. stenophylla*, 3 ft (90 cm) tall.

Perhaps the loveliest of the marginal plants are the irises which flower in early summer and grow to about 2 ft (60 cm) tall. *I. laevigata*, a dwarf variety, is especially suitable for the smaller pond, while the sweet flag (*Acorus calamus variegatus*), about 3 ft (90 cm) tall, deserves a place for its attractive foliage.

Fixed floating aquatics: among these look for brandy bottle (*Nuphar lutea*), with leaves like the water-lily and bright golden urn-shaped flowers in summer; water hawthorn (*Aponogeton distachyus*), with flowers like the common hedgerow shrub but large oval leaves that float on the surface; and water fringe (*Villarsia nymphaeoides*), which has bright yellow trumpet-shaped flowers in summer and leaves like water-lily pads.

Water-lilies. The jewel in the crown of water-garden plants is undoubtedly the water-lily and, fortunately, there are colours and sizes to suit every type of pond. Because they are so attractive, it is very easy to overdo the stocking rate. Too vigorous a variety will quickly carpet the surface of a small pond, so always seek the advice of the experts at the water-garden centre before you buy. An average-sized water-lily will need about 8–12 sq ft (0·7–1·1 sq m) of water space to itself.

As a guide, choose from the varieties 'Aurora', 'Comanche', 'Froebeli' and 'Hermine' for small pools up to 72 sq ft (6·5 sq m) ; for medium-sized pools choose from the *Nymphaea laydekeri* hybrids, including 'William Falconer' and 'Rose Arey'; while for the larger pools with a water depth of 2 ft (60 cm) there are many excellent varieties, such as 'Crystal White', 'James Brydon', 'Escarboucle', 'René Gérard' and 'Mrs Richmond'.

Planting. Early spring is the best time for planting the water garden and the easiest of the groups to plant are the oxygenators. Simply make a bundle of a few stems and tie the bundle to a stone so that it sinks to the bottom of the pond. Allow two bundles to each square yard/metre of the surface of the pond. The surface-floating plants are placed on the surface of the water, while the marginal and the fixed floating plants, including water-lilies, are planted in special plastic baskets filled with ordinary garden soil. The method is to line the basket with old hessian sacking, felt carpet underlay or old carpet, then fill with the soil and set the plant into the top inch or two. Finally add a mulch of coarse gravel. Stocked with the appropriate plants, a garden pond needs little attention.

POND LIFE

If you decide to add fish to the pond, it is a sound idea to buy a handbook on their care and to buy the fish from a specialist supplier. Do not raid the village pond for sticklebacks: they are voracious predators and once in residence are difficult to get rid of. Common goldfish are deservedly the most popular fish for the garden pond. They are beautiful and undemanding. Golden orfe are another attractive proposition, but you will need at least twelve as they are a shoal fish.

Grass carp are not suitable for a small pond; they grow fairly large, and will also eat other creatures and just about every plant. Koi carp are very attractive but also very expensive, while golden tench are another popular fish for the garden pond, although they tend to stay near the bottom. You will need to allow a minimum of 1 sq ft (30 sq cm) of water area for each fish. In winter the fish will not need feeding, but they must have oxygen at all times, so if the pond freezes over, a hole should be made by placing a kettle or pan of boiling water on the surface – *not* pouring the water on! Do not break the ice by whacking it with a hammer, as this could create a pressure wave that might kill the fish. In rural areas, especially, herons and kingfishers can quickly rob a pond of its fish, and everywhere cats can be a nuisance. To stop them a mesh of nylon can be stretched just above the surface, although it looks unsightly.

In the autumn the surface of the pool should be kept scrupulously clear of fallen leaves and other debris. A bright, sunny summer will cause evaporation and you will have to top up the water from a hosepipe. If the pond has an electric pump, the filter should be cleaned regularly – how often will depend on the size of the pond and the clarity of the water.

In spring the phenomenon of 'green water' often occurs as the weather warms up, but this should quickly revert to normal as the oxygenating plants do their job and, perhaps, tadpoles appear to feed on the algae. Blanket weed may also put in an appearance, but can be removed without difficulty using an ordinary garden rake.

AMPHIBIANS

If you want to be sure of introducing frogs and toads to the pond, plan for this in early spring by

Medium-sized pond fed by waterfall in a suburban garden (*Chris Algar*)

contacting your local wildlife trust or similar organization, which should be able to tell you where to obtain spawn. But remember that fish and tadpoles do not co-exist. As soon as the spawn hatches, the fish will eat the emerging tadpoles.

Your pond may, with luck, attract amphibians without your having to find an initial stock of them. The natural environment of the great crested newt is disappearing all the time, so the garden pond offers an important refuge to this creature. The common toad and the frog each claim territorial rights, so the garden will not become over-populated with them and their service as slug and snail controllers is of great benefit to the organic gardener. These delightful creatures spend the winter under a pile of leaves , under the garden shed, in the crevices of the rockery or in some other sheltered place. They usually return to spawn to the pond where they were born: a journey that accounts for a great number of fatalities en route. Apart from road risks, they face many other traumas, and for every 2,000 eggs spawned only about five reach maturity. Frogs spawn near the surface of the pond, usually at about 3 am, and each female lays some 3,000 eggs. Toads spawn in deeper water with up to 2,500 eggs in strings.

The tadpoles of both toads and frogs suffer heavy predation. As well as being the prey of fish, they are eaten by water beetles, dragonfly nymphs and water-boatmen. But, happily, in a garden toads can live up to twenty years and frogs up to twelve years.

STREAMS

If you plan to have a pond fed from a stream, here are some points to bear in mind:
1. Water purity should be checked before work begins and monitored regularly thereafter. Determining whether there is run-off of pesticides or fertilizers from outside your domain calls for expert help and could, in the long term, prove expensive.

Algae control

A promising new approach to algae control is being pursued in the UK by the Aquatic Weeds Research Unit of Long Ashton Research Station, using barley straw to inhibit algae growth.

The straw works best in loose form and should be introduced at least a month before algal growth starts; it should remain in the water throughout the growing season.

The researchers warn, however, that too much straw could result in a drop in the level of dissolved oxygen, which could be harmful to fish and other wildlife.

2. Aquatic plants grow best in still water, so a stream-fed pond severely limits your choice of plants.

3. Stream-fed ponds are most effective if they incorporate a waterfall or series of falls over a rocky base or a focal feature such as stepping stones or a bridge. Before undertaking work of this sort you should consult the rivers authority (in the UK, the National Rivers Authority) on the viability of your plans. It might, for example, be illegal for you to extract water from your pond for any purpose except an emergency.

4. Remember that you will own the structure of the pond but not the contents. You could be legally liable if you accidentally contaminated the water on its way through your property or if your pond construction caused flooding or other damage to neighbouring land.

5. Check the seasonal changes in the water level. It might be a quiet stream in summer: in winter it could become a raging torrent. If you live near the coast, a stream could become brackish during spring tides.

17 LAWNS

CREATING A LAWN

When creating a lawn first ask yourself: what do I want? Need it resemble astroturf, or would a daisy-flecked football pitch suffice? Perfectly manicured lawns are difficult to maintain, and are therefore best restricted to small patches.

Steep slopes make troublesome lawns, drying out in summer and in winter losing nutrients which are leached away by rain, while mowers succumb to gravity. Other sites to avoid are waterlogged areas, which should be drained for a good-quality lawn.

Preparation depends on the standard required. Grass is shallow-rooting, so does not need a great depth of soil, but the finest lawns will require 6 in (15 cm) of topsoil. Variations in the quality of the soil, such as stony patches, should be evened to avoid a patchy lawn.

The finest lawns may require levelling of the subsoil in order that the topsoil thickness will not vary. Accurate levelling may be done using strings and wooden pegs, even a spirit level for a surface suitable for croquet and bowls. Merely eliminating bumps on which the mower might catch will suffice for rough lawns. Rotovating produces a tilth quickly, but on clay soils can leave a water-impermeable pan, making prior digging necessary.

The next question to arise is: to sow seed or plant turf? Turf is instant but hard work, cannot be stored for long, and generally comes only as one grade. Sowing is limited by season, which is early spring or early to mid-autumn, unless you water after sowing in summer. Autumn sowing is easiest, and ground prepared in early summer can be hoed regularly before sowing to reduce weeds.

TYPE OF GRASS

From hundreds of wild species of grass, mixtures are made from four main types. The rye-grasses (*Lolium perenne*) and meadow-grasses (*Poa*

OPPOSITE: This herb-rich lawn speckled with oxeye and common daisies, cowslips, clover and buttercups is an exciting counterpoint to its mown neighbour (*David Woodfall*)

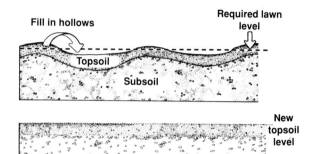

Levelling out the bumps: levelling out can be combined with top dressing in the autumn (*Rob Dalton*)

species) are harder-wearing, but also require the richest soils, while fescues (*Festuca* species) and bent-grasses (*Agrostis* species) are finer, slow-growing grasses, suitable for poorer soils. It is important to select the correct mixture for the soil and purpose at the outset, otherwise rogue grasses and weeds will replace the chosen varieties.

Rye-grass tolerates some clay, is quick to germinate and grow, but has a great need of frequent cutting and feeding. Some newer, more expensive varieties are finer and slow-growing, so may be used on a rich soil where a shorter, lower-maintenance lawn is required.

Meadow-grass needs a fine, rich soil to germinate and is shorter than rye-grass, being used at a high level in mixtures where a turf of less than ¾ in (20 mm) is desired. It is also tolerant of shade.

The finest lawns are composed of a mixture of the slow-growing grasses (Chewing's fescue 80%, Browntop bent-grass 20%). Such a lawn makes an excellent bowling green and will not require high fertility, but will demand frequent cutting, and any weeds will ruin its appearance. Bent-grasses are also used at a low percentage in most mixtures because of their ability to recolonize by rhizomes (underground runners) patches affected by drought or autumn leaves; they are, however, the slowest to germinate and establish.

For wildflower mixes and rough lawns, hard

Grass varieties

	Type of grass	Rate of growth	Grade	Wear	Soil and feeding
RYE GRASSES	Lolium perenne	quick	coarse	hard-wearing	rich soil, regular feeding
	Lolium perenne (rye) (newer varieties e.g. Loretta)	slow	fine	hard-wearing	as above
MEADOW GRASSES	Smooth-stalked meadow-grass, Poa pratensis	slow	fine	hard-wearing	fertile, light soil
	Wood meadow-grass, Poa nemoralis	slow	fine	hard-wearing	as above
	Reuben's flattened meadow-grass, Poa compressa	slow	fine	hard-wearing	poor soil
FESCUES	Chewing's fescue, Festuca rubra species commutata	slow	fine	poor	poor soil; less regular feeding than Lolium
	Hard fescue, Festuca longifolia	slow	fine	poor	poor
	Sheep's fescue, Festuca ovina	slow	very fine	poor	tolerant of very poor soil and high and low pH
	Creeping red fescue, Festuca rubra species litoralis	slow	fine	moderate	moderate
BENT GRASSES	Highland browntop bent-grass Agrostis tenuis (casellana)	slow	fine	moderate	poor
	Creeping bent-grass Agrostis stolonifera	slow	fine	poor	poor; tolerant to salt

fescue *(Festuca longifolia)* and sheep's fescue *(Festuca ovina)* make a good base, with the latter species also being the most tolerant of acid and alkaline soils. Such lawns, ideal for large areas, are low in maintenance and rich in their diversity of species.

For very poor soils, mixtures incorporating nitrogen-fixing legumes, such as clover, are available. Although garden centres usually stock only ready-made mixtures of grasses, it is important to be aware of the uses of different grass types. In this way you will avoid, for example, the common mistake of choosing rye-grass for its 'toughness', while overlooking its need for frequent cutting and feeding which, unless the soil is inherently very fertile, makes it the least suitable grass for most organic gardens.

Sow at a rate of about 1 oz per sq yd (30 g per sq m), unless taking a risk with a mid-autumn

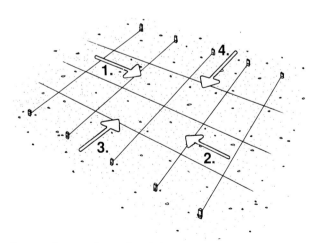

Sowing by numbers: the right way to sow grass – up, down, and across *(Rob Dalton)*

Rate of establishment	Other notes
quick	least suited to organic gardens due to feeding requirements
quick	expensive seed; still requires feeding
slow	re-colonizes by rhizomes after drought, so useful in most mixes
slow	as above, but more tolerant of shade
slow	good for use on poor soils and wildflower seed mixes
quick	all fescues useful in organic lawns due to low feeding requirement, but should be mixed with meadow and bent-grasses to improve wear
quick	good for wildflower mixes
quick	
quick	tolerant to drought; shortest fescue
low	base ingredient in most mixes; re-colonizes by rhizomes after drought
low	above-soil stolons make it less hard-wearing than A. tenuis, but new hard-wearing varieties are being developed

sowing, when this quantity should be doubled. Using string-marked yard/metre squares broadcast the seed first in one direction, then again at right angles for an even spread. Rake in the seed very lightly. Tinfoil deters few birds, neither are bird repellents effective against all species. The most effective, though expensive, solution is netting. A cheaper compromise is to sow at a higher rate where birds might present a problem.

LAWN MAINTENANCE

First set your standards. Following all the tips in this section should give you a bowls and croquet surface; sticking to only half of them will result in a presentable lawn.

Talk about lawn maintenance and you talk about weeds. Some may have to, quite simply, be pulled out, an arduous task when upgrading a lawn, but one which becomes easier after a couple of years' persistence. Other weeds may be controlled more easily with the correct mowing strategy (see chapter on *Weeds*, page 241). Central to organic lawn care is optimization of conditions: for example, drainage, soil (grass prefers slightly acid conditions) and feeding.

Dandelions are the lawn fanatic's pariah. They are rosette weeds, as are daisies, plantain and docks, which smother grass by forming a dense sheet beneath the level of the mower blades. Lower the blades, and these weeds simply lower their heads. All is not lost: if you persuade them to raise their heads a little (perhaps just once a year in spring) by omitting a few cuts, then chop the rosettes back down to the ground, you will deplete the energy reserves of such weeds.

The other group of lawn weeds are the creepers, such as clover and creeping buttercup. Tackle these by raking them above the grass before mowing to where they will be pruned by the blades. Don't forget that clover may serve a useful purpose. It is a nitrogen-fixing plant, and indicates soils that are low in nitrogen, so another way round the problem could be to feed the lawn with a top dressing of compost, or wait until the clover's own nitrogen-fixing root nodules have boosted the nitrogen in the soil. This may take several years, after which the clover will tend to die out. Creeping buttercup – incidentally an indicator of poor drainage – presents the dual problem of being both a rosette and a creeping weed. For this a combined technique is needed, utilizing the 'grow and chop' mowing strategy and improving soil conditions to make the soil more conducive to grass, rather than weeds.

The timing, frequency and height of cut will affect the quality of a lawn. In spring the first cut should not be too early, otherwise the grass may be weakened, allowing dandelions – which spring into growth before grass gets moving – a head start in forming their impenetrable rosettes. The first cut of the season should leave the grass at ¾ to 3 in (2–7·5 cm), depending on the grade of the lawn, subsequent cuts being to between ½ and 2¼ in (1·5 and 6 cm). Fine lawns may have to be cut as often as every four days during warm, wet summer weather in order to maintain a dense turf, while longer lawns can be left for two weeks. In dry weather, cuts can be less frequent.

On a rough lawn the clippings need not be collected, although spreading them with a brush prevents bare strips from developing. On finer lawns it is best to remove clippings, especially when a heavier cut is made which may smother the grass. Where clippings are left on the lawn, the need for feeding is reduced as nutrients are recycled. Lawn clippings tend to dry up in hot weather, so are better used as a thickly spread, weed-suppressing mulch around plants. A mulch mowing machine chops clippings very finely so that they are well incorporated into the lawn and do not dry on the surface (see page 388).

Autumn is a good time to rake out moss and thatch which will have built up during the year. Raking also encourages grass plants to tiller – that is, produce new plants from the old. Spiking a lawn in the autumn, either with a garden fork or a machine, will encourage deeper rooting of grass, reducing the need for irrigation the following summer.

Irrigation may be helped on very even lawns by drawing a string across the surface each morning during hot weather, knocking dew to the roots of the plants. The high total surface area of the grass blades makes this old gardener's trick remarkably effective.

Re-seeding a lawn in autumn or spring is an economical and easy way to ensure a good new crop of grass, and one that is often overlooked. Any bumps too large to be missed by the mower can be levelled at the same time by applying a top dressing mixture of loam, leaf-mould and sand. For all soil types two parts loam should be mixed with each part leaf-mould. On very sandy soils the sand may be omitted from the mix, while on heavy clays two parts sand should be added to the mix for each part of loam. Leaf-mould helps to acidify the soil, which promotes grass growth, and it will improve the soil texture, avoiding compaction.

Organic lawn feeding is easier than its chemical cousin, as it can be done less frequently, since organic composts and fertilizers are, in general, less soluble. The best material is sieved compost, which will increase the soil's acidity, improve the soil structure and feed the grass. Compost may be applied through a garden sieve and brushed in. Make sure that the compost has been produced in an efficient compost heap, otherwise you may give yourself a prize crop of weeds. Commercial organic lawn composts are also available. Spring is a suitable time to apply compost, although an autumn application will allow time for the compost to be incorporated into the soil by earthworms.

Additional feeding – in particular necessary where lawn clippings are removed – may be provided by applying a compound organic compost of blood, fish, bone and seaweed meal in spring. Organic liquid feeds are also useful.

For the difficult shaded spots where grass seems destined never to thrive, plant snowdrops and winter-flowering hardy cyclamen, which grow well in the rooty soil beneath trees and will brighten any gaps in the lawn.

Do not be tempted, in a moment of despair, to use a chemical weed and feed. These tend to produce sudden bursts of soft growth which rapidly weaken as the soluble nutrients are washed away, and the weedkiller usually only suppresses rosette weeds, which later return with renewed vigour.

WILDFLOWER LAWNS

The work involved and the often sterile appearance, particularly of large, flat lawns, has made the idea of wildflower meadows popular. They encourage wildlife and can be used to make a garden blend with a hedgerow, shrubs and trees or countryside beyond.

An existing lawn can be converted to a wildflower meadow, or an area of bare earth can be sown with a suitable seed mixture. The latter will produce a bright array of annuals, such as poppies, in the first season, which in subsequent years (unless dug over and re-sown each autumn) will tone down to the pastel shades of meadow flowers.

Successful wildflower meadows require low fertility, which can be achieved by cutting a lawn short (1 in/2·5 cm or less) at frequent intervals for a year, and removing the cuttings, or by growing a heavy feeding crop such as potatoes.

To convert an existing lawn, following one year of cutting short, cut to 4 in (10 cm) in mid-spring and subsequently every other month until mid-autumn. This will suppress grass growth, continue to lower fertility, but encourage the development of wild flowers. It is important always to remove the clippings, so that flowers will not be smothered. In subsequent years flowers for different seasons can be encouraged by different cutting programmes. To encourage spring flowers such as primroses, bugle (*Ajuga reptans*), bluebells (*Hyacinthoides non-scriptus*), violets (*Viola* species) and woodruff (*Asperula odorata*), start cutting in late spring when their flowering season is over, and continue cutting each month. Early summer flowers can be promoted by cutting only from late summer onwards. This will encourage species such as bird's-foot trefoil (*Lotus corniculatus*), yellow archangel (*Lamiastrum galeobdolon*), ragged Robin (*Lychnis flos-cuculi*), foxgloves (*Digitalis purpurea*), meadow crane's-bill (*Geranium pratense*) and oxeye daisy (*Leucanthemum vulgare*). For the development of late summer and autumn-flowering species such as yarrow (*Achillea millefolium*), bellflower (*Campanula* species), tansy (*Tanacetum vulgare*), St John's wort (*Hypericum perforatum*) and toadflax (*Linaria vulgaris*), the grass should be kept short in spring and left to grow between early summer and mid-autumn.

If the garden is not large enough for three such areas, the early summer to autumn-flowering species may be combined in one area by cutting once in mid-spring, then leaving it uncut until autumn. Keep to the same pattern of cutting each year to allow plants a chance to develop.

The cutting programmes are summarized in the table opposite.

A wildflower patch is at its best, defined(*Natural Image*)

For a spring flower lawn, defer cutting until late spring (*Harry Smith Collection*)

For early summer flowers, cut only from late summer onwards (*Harry Smith Collection*)

Cutting a path through long grass will make it more accessible, avoid trampling and give it a deliberate form rather than the appearance of an accidental mess. A sickle is an essential tool for a small garden, and a scythe for larger areas.

Grass left to grow long will not be at its best in the first year. You may end up with a lot of one plant, which may need to be thinned. Thistle seeds are good food for birds, but the wind-blown parachute seeds create weed problems elsewhere, so you may need to cut and compost them before they set seed.

You can add interesting perennials to a meadow, such as mallows (*Malva* species) and rock roses (*Helianthemum nummularium*), by sowing seed in autumn in compost sterilized to avoid weeds. Leave the pot outside during winter for the seeds to germinate in spring. Be patient; most wild species take a long time to germinate. Plant out your pot-grown specimens carefully, minimizing soil disturbance in order to avoid weed germination.

As wild flowers need cold conditions to spark them into germination, a meadow on bare earth will need to be sown in autumn. It is possible to buy mixtures of flowers for different soils, aspects and heights of plants.

Possibly the greatest obstacle you are likely to encounter will be the objections of fastidious neighbours. Do not aggravate them by allowing plants with wind-blown seeds (thistles and dandelions) to set seed, but do explain the benefits to them: that the grasses, poppies and teasels provide food for the birds, and almost all the wild flowers attract butterflies.

	Flowering time	Cutting schedule
Three different flowering areas are possible in a larger garden	Spring	Cut once a month from late spring
	Early summer	Cut once a month from late summer
	Late summer to autumn	Cut once a month until earlysummer, then leave uncut until mid-autumn
For the smaller garden	Early summer to autumn	Cut in mid-spring, then leave uncut until autumn

18 WEEDS

WEEDS AND THE NEED TO CONTROL THEM

To the gardener a weed, broadly, is a plant in the wrong place. It may be a common weed such as chickweed, bindweed or groundsel, or it may be an invasive garden plant. Any plant can be looked on as a weed when it detracts in some way from other, preferable plants. Generally herbaceous weeds cause most concern but brambles, seedling sycamores, even the neighbour's thirty-foot *leylandii* hedge can also be regarded as weeds in many ways and their detrimental effects should be borne in mind.

Weeds need to be controlled because they compete with both vegetables and flowers for air, space, light and water. They can be, though are not always, unattractive – daisies in the sward have more charm than groundsel in the asparagus bed. Some, such as nettles and thistles, can be physically deleterious. The greatest problem is the time and effort that have to be regularly devoted to preventing weeds taking over. The speed with which the most invasive kinds establish themselves and multiply is horrendous: dandelion and fat hen produce just a few thousand seeds, but scentless mayweed produces about 34,000 seeds per plant. All these seeds are designed not to germinate at once but to do so over several seasons – hence the old adage of one year's seeds giving seven years' weeds. Many weed seeds are still viable after twenty years of burial. Over half the seeds of docks (*Rumex*) and mulleins (*Verbascum*) have been shown to be viable after fifty years, while frozen seed from permafrost can germinate after thousands of years. This is why digging produces flushes of weeds. Burying seeding weeds is, therefore, just postponing the problem.

Weeds are, clearly, the plants most suited to their situation. There are many different weed seeds in each square inch of soil, but only some kinds germinate. They have chosen to grow exactly where they are because the conditions are exactly right for them – which is soon evident if they are left uncontrolled. Weeds of damp places do not germinate in dry spots, few acid-lovers reach maturity on limey soil, sun-lovers do not thrive in shade. They gain the advantage of germinating *in situ*, which is almost always best for the growth of any plant, and they germinate as soon as the conditions are suitable, thus getting established before more valued plants start into growth. They can then not only outperform crops and other plants, but may also have a direct, damaging effect, secreting allelopathic chemicals from their roots and leaves which stop rival seeds germinating or retard growth. Dandelions, for instance, give off ethylene gas, as do rotting dock leaves, which, although it helps to ripen fruit and tomatoes, prevents germination. Buttercups give off a toxin that eliminates clovers, and is poisonous to humans and livestock to boot.

Furthermore, if there is a deficiency in a particular area of any nutrient, the natural selection process ensures that the weeds flourishing there will be those most efficient at utilizing that scarce resource. They will rapidly compete for it with crops and ornamental plants, which will result in great detriment to growth and yield.

Because weeds produce rapid growth early they monopolize space underground even more than above it; their roots steal the supply of nutrients and moisture. Competition for light is often inconsequential (unless the weeds are allowed to overrun the crop), and for the CO_2 in the air unlikely if the soil is rich in organic material and microlife. Nutrients are important but water is by far the critical factor, as weeds not only lock it up internally but transpire it away rapidly from early in the year. Weed control is therefore especially

---

Some seeds can wait for many decades in the soil until the opportunity to germinate comes. The fields of Flanders turned red from long-buried poppy seed; the plant also spreads very rapidly once the first flowers set seed.

OPPOSITE: **Creeping thistle** *(Cirsium arvense) (Chris Algar)*

Mankind has made the problem worse over centuries of ineffective weeding: we have merely eliminated varieties that were slow to mature, while inadvertently selecting for rapid seed-setting. Some weeds like hairy bittercress, chickweed and groundsel can set seed in about six or seven weeks from germination. We continue to overlook this effect on weed selection, and the habit of not weeding after the end of summer produces strains of common weeds that go on growing even in the winter: annual meadow grass, cleavers, groundsel, ivy-leaved speedwell, parsley piert, shepherd's purse, stinging nettle are the main ones.

important in dry areas and at times of low rainfall, and when establishing new plants with necessarily small root systems.

The competition for other nutrients is fierce. Weeds will grab any available nitrogen as soon as it is released in spring, and this may severely set back less competitive crop plants. If the weeds are then allowed to set seed they are locking up the nutrients in an inaccessible form until the seeds germinate, compost or rot.

Apart from the direct competition with valuable plants, weeds also harbour pests and diseases. Pests may often be a relatively minor problem to the organic gardener, as they are needed to feed and maintain predator populations. Plentiful supplies on the weeds ensure a large resident population of parasites and predators to control later pest attacks on the crops. However, some pests, especially ground-dwelling ones, are more pernicious. For example *nematodes* (eelworms), which attack the beet family, are harboured by charlock, chickweed, docks, fat hen, hedge mustard, knotgrass and shepherd's purse, while chrysanthemum eelworm thrives on oxeye daisy and groundsel. Although pests such as aphids may be a relatively small problem in themselves, they also transmit diseases which may severely affect some crops. One of the commonest, the peach potato aphis, overwinters on black nightshade, charlock, shepherd's purse, stinging nettle and many others.

Diseases that are carried by the weeds themselves are even more of a problem, particularly the viruses. Weed populations will by natural selection develop a relative immunity to any disease, but crops remain far more susceptible and can be severely damaged. Some of the worst offenders are members of the *Cruciferae* family such as shepherd's purse and charlock, which can carry club root disease and ruin brassica crops. Many different weeds carry cucumber mosaic virus, which devastates the marrow family. Tomato spotted wilt is widely carried, particularly by bindweed and plantains.

TYPES AND IDENTIFICATION

Weeds can be dealt with according to type, even though there may be little or no botanical connection within the group. However, the most important difference between weeds is not what type they are but how well established.

In clean soil, such as a well-cultivated vegetable plot, all weeds that appear must come from seed. It does not matter initially whether they

BELOW: Tap root of the perennial dock

RIGHT: Growth of the stinging nettle is achieved by its extensive spreader root system as well as by seed (*John Walker*)

If annuals are left too long before being tackled not only may they recover but, worse, they may be able to set seed without recovering. Chickweed and groundsel in flower may have enough reserves to draw on to form viable seed while they lie uprooted on the soil.

are annuals, biennials or perennials: when they are little seedlings they are all equally vulnerable and easily killed. While the 'weedlings' are very small they can be treated as annuals; hoeing, flame-gunning, mulching on top of them will all be quick and easy ways of dispatch. Once they have formed three or four true leaves they become more vigorous and harder to eradicate. They may reroot after hoeing, recover after flame-gunning and grow up through a mulch, so it is always essential to hit them while they are small and tender.

Whereas true annuals are relatively easy to kill throughout their life the longer-lived plants soon become more difficult. As perennials become established their ability to recover from weeding treatments increases, and some such as *Convolvulus* and *Equisetum* become almost invincible.

Tap-rooted perennials are more difficult to kill than those with fibrous roots, as plants with fleshy roots can usually shoot from any piece of the root left in the ground. Both tap- and fibrous-rooted perennials tend like annuals, to spread more by seed than by root invasion, so they can be easily contained even if not quickly eliminated. Docks, for instance, may be a long time dying but they do not spread.

The spreaders are by far the worst weeds to contend with. Unless and until they are totally annihilated there is always the danger of them fully recovering, and very quickly. Weeds that spread by underground stolons will regrow from every tiny piece that is overlooked. Willowherb, ground elder, bindweed, *Equisetum*, creeping buttercup are the biggest menaces, and eradication takes persistent, regular hard work. *Never* let these gain or regain a foothold. Other weeds: cinquefoil, silverweed, tormentil may spread above ground in the manner of strawberries; or like brambles, which throw long arching stems which then root from the tip. These too must be severely dealt with.

Bulbous weeds such as oxalis and celandines are another difficult type to control, but fortunately are much rarer. Each little bulbil, as small as a seed, will form another cluster of plants and they are easily spread on tools and shoes. Care should be taken not to introduce these into the garden; as with most weeds, prevention is always much easier than cure.

Much effort should be made to ensure that you gain control initially, so that you only have to continue dealing with annuals. To have poor initial control and, worse still, to plant up perennial crops in ground with uncontrolled perennial weeds is just storing up immense difficulties for the future.

It is a good idea to get to recognize your native weed population, to make weeding easier. If you cannot tell the crop seedlings from the weedlings it is impossible to work quickly and effectively. Weed identification is easy with a trial plot. Simply clear a piece of ground and watch what starts to grow. Some weeds are very easy to identify from the seed leaves, and almost all are distinguishable by the time they have grown the first pair of true leaves. Eliminate most of the weedlings of each type, leaving a few to grow on until you can identify them by name if you wish, but what is most important is simply to learn to recognize them. Similarly, it is a good idea if you are growing a crop for the first time to sow a few seeds in a pot indoors just to get your eye in and be able to spot the seedlings when they appear out of doors.

It is possible to put soil in a tray and watch the weeds grow in comfort indoors, but there is a strong likelihood that those germinating in the warm will be a different selection from those in open ground. There is no shortage, as every cubic foot of soil will contain thousands or tens of thousands of seeds of many different species, transported by wind, animals and man. Once you recognize your allotted weeds and your crops, anything else is soon apparent and can be left to grow bigger. Many choice seedlings can be saved from the weeding this way: hollies, yews, lilacs and cotoneasters are useful findings. Raspberries, blackberries, strawberries and blackcurrants are common, but may not be good fruiters; however, many of today's favourites were themselves chance findings.

THE EFFECT OF CLIMATE AND SOIL CONDITIONS

Different varieties of weed flourish in different types and conditions of soil. They are not an exclusive class; any new plant you introduce to your garden that is immune to pests and disease, well suited to your soil and microclimate and produces plentiful viable seed will without much doubt very soon become a weed. Feverfew, poppies, foxgloves and honesty are among the most notorious for this.

The critical factors are the climate and soil. Hardiness is almost essential for a plant to become a weed, unless it is exceptionally fast to seed. Thus the Himalayan balsam is a rampant annual by river banks and is cut down by the first frost, but seeds during the brief British summer. The water hyacinth, a spreading perennial, is an uncontrollable weed in warmer climates but is prevented by frosts from becoming so in northern Europe. Some weeds are surprisingly recent: Buddleias, which have colonized bomb-sites in Britain since the last war, were introduced at the end of the last century.

Nature is extremely profligate with seed, and weeds are continually trying to colonize all bare soil; the majority fail while a few survive. Most remain dormant if conditions are unsuitable until they finally cease to be viable. A minority germinate and fail; a very few, the most nearly suitable, will grow and compete with each other until a still smaller number attain maturity. Annual weeds that manage to mature then set seed, and the following year this natural selection process ensures that many more of these suitable strains will flourish and fill a congenial space, such as your vegetable bed. As bare soil is rare in nature, to compete for space annuals make plentiful seed that is easily distributed. Perennial weeds, especially spreading perennials, will occupy an area more slowly but will gradually squeeze annuals out, as they are persistently more competitive.

Different degrees of fertility help select different forms of weed. The progression from annuals to perennials to trees is intrinsically connected with soil fertility. Each progressive type of weed cover, though initially well suited, slowly changes the fertility until it is itself no longer apt and is then supplanted. Shrubby perennials eventually prevail over herbaceous, and trees come to dominate. This process may take decades or even centuries to complete, but it is astonishing how rapidly it can take place . In only two or three years a neglected vegetable plot can be hidden under brambles and a forest of ash and sycamore saplings. Through the process of selection the weeds in the soil are thus not only the most suitable kinds but are exact indicators of the soil type and how it has been modified by its treatment and history.

Any human intervention changes soil conditions. The site of a bonfire or outbuilding can be deduced from the kinds of weeds growing there. Old privy pits and stables are frequently indicated by luxuriant stands of nettles; sewage sludge gives flushes of tomato seedlings (the seeds being undigested by humans); large numbers of docks probably indicate that horses were formerly kept.

It is not individual weeds but the mixture and the proportions that tell the story. If you find one weed that is indicative of, say, acid conditions it may give a false impression, but a majority of acid-lovers provides fairly conclusive evidence. (A note of caution: if the soil is compacted or badly damaged it may be that only the top layer is acid, with different conditions underneath. This is frequently the case with old grassland: the top inch becomes acid through the build-up of thatch, even with limier soil underneath.)

Weeds indicating soil type

Acid soil:	betony, black bindweed, cinquefoil, corn chamomile, cornflower, corn marigold, corn spurrey, daisy, foxglove, fumitory, harebell, heather, horsetail (marestail), lesser periwinkle, mercury, pansy, scabious, shepherd's cress, small nettle, sorrel, spurrey, tormentil
Limey soil:	bellflower, black medick, briar rose, candytuft, cat's-ear, cowslip, goat's-beard, greater hawkbit, horseshoe vetch, knapweed, lamb's lettuce, mignonette, oxeye daisy, penny cress, salad burnet, stonecrop, tansy, valerian, wallflower, white mustard, wild carrot, yarrow
Heavy moist clay:	annual meadow grass, cowslip, creeping buttercup, goosegrass, meadow crane's-bill, nipplewort, plantain, selfheal, silverweed
Light dry soil:	annual nettle, bramble, broad dock, bulbous buttercup, charlock, dandelion, groundsel, knotgrass, mouse-eared chickweed, poppy, red dead-nettle, rosebay willow-herb, shepherd's purse, speedwell, spurge, stinging nettle
Wet areas:	bugle, buttercup, comfrey, cuckoo flower, dock, great willow-herb, hemp agrimony, Himalayan balsam, loosestrife, meadowsweet, mints, primrose, ragged robin, sedge, stinging nettle, thistles

BENEFICIAL WEEDS

Weeds detract from other plants most of the time, but there are cases where they provide benefit. Once a crop of onions starts to mature, weeds can be left to grow – they take up any available water and nutrients, helping the onions ripen off and keep better. Similarly, orchard grass is allowed to grow long from late summer to help ripen and redden the apples. Stands of weeds protect the soil and act as miniature hedges, providing shelter for crop seedlings. Most importantly, weeds are useful as a source of compost material if they can be grown without detriment to crops.

'Weeds' you want to see on land you are thinking of cultivating as they show a balanced soil, fertile, in good heart: a dense mixed turf sward of chickweed, goosegrass, groundsel, stinging nettles, thistles, yarrow.

Weeds can overwinter when crops cannot, and the hardiest weeds will scavenge any nutrients that would otherwise leach out, and convert winter sunlight into biomass for later incorporation and fertility. They also act as ground cover and prevent soil erosion, capping and impaction.

The use of naturally occurring weeds, when carefully chosen and allowed to grow as green manures, is especially beneficial. Weeds, being the plants best adapted to the situation, are generally able to utilize the resources most effectively, and make superb mineral accumulators, correcting any soil deficiency. However, such a crop of green manure has to be carefully controlled or it can get out of hand.

Many plants accumulate minerals to high proportions of their dry weight; weeds excel at this. Thorn-apple (*Datura*) contains abundant phosphorus, nettles and *Equisetum* accumulate silica and comfrey is exceedingly good at concentrating potassium. It would, of course, be foolish ever to allow *Equisetum* or bindweed a foothold, but many weeds can be controlled by hoeing or mulching while still vulnerable. The scarce minerals they have accumulated can then be recycled to the crops as they are hoed in or composted.

It cannot be overstressed that this must be controlled, not uncontrolled weed cover. By choosing which weeds seed and 'weeding' the weedlings it is possible to avoid the problem of pernicious types becoming established, but great care is needed. Later the weeds must be incorporated while young and well before they seed.

Weeds can give other benefits. They may be companion plants to crops (see page 130), especially in small proportions. Legumes like the clovers improve the lawn. The odd clump of nettles improves the health and vigour of nearby plants, especially in orchards.

Those weeds that are allowed to flower provide food sources for predatory insects such as wasps and hoverflies and for pollinators like bees and butterflies. Weeds are now so scarce in intensively cultivated farmland that populations of wild bees have declined drastically, with the consequence of poor crop pollination. Bumble-bees are often more threatened than honey-bees, so leave a wild corner to feed them with: clovers, comfrey, dandelions, knapweed, mallows, thistles, white deadnettle, vetches. (Town

Minerals found in weeds

The following minerals are found in especially high quantities in these weeds, which are all relatively easy to keep under control.

Boron:	euphorbia or spurge family (irritant sap)
Calcium:	corn chamomile, corn marigold, daisy, dandelion, fat hen, goosegrass, purslane, scarlet pimpernel, shepherd's purse, silverweed
Cobalt:	ribbed plantain, rosebay willow-herb, vetch
Copper:	chickweed, dandelion, plantain, sowthistle, vetches, yarrow
Iron:	chickweed, dandelion, fat hen, foxglove, groundsel, silverweed
Magnesium:	chicory, daisy, plantain, salad burnet, silverweed, yarrow
Manganese:	chickweed
Nitrogen:	black nightshade, chickweed, clovers, dandelion, fat hen, groundsel, purslane, sowthistle, vetches, yarrow
Phosphorus:	corn marigold, fat hen, purslane, sheep sorrel, thorn-apple, vetch, yarrow
Potassium:	chickweed, chicory, corn chamomile, fat hen, goosegrass, plantain, purslane, tansy, thistle, thorn-apple, vetch, yarrow
Silica:	plantain, stinging nettle
Sulphur:	fat hen, purslane

beekeepers often have greater yields of honey than rural ones because of the greater number of cultivated flowers available.)

Weeds in hedge bases and untamed areas provide a store of pests, and thus keep alive populations of predators as well. Wild areas left at the edge of the garden are therefore of benefit, but care must be taken that they cannot spread or seed onto cultivated land or gravel paths.

The minerals accumulated by weeds can be made available to other plants after the weeds have been processed in the compost heap or have decomposed in the soil. They can also be applied as liquid feeds or 'teas'. As weeds are so good at collecting nutrients, it is surprising that so few

Edible weeds

Many weeds are edible, even tasty, and their young leaves could be added with benefit to our diet: cat's-ear, charlock, chickweed, chicory, comfrey, common penny, cresses, dandelion, deadnettle, fat hen, goosegrass, ground elder, hedge garlic, salad burnet, shepherd's purse, sorrel, sowthistle, stinging nettle. Some may be more palatable if lightly cooked (chickweed, dandelion, dock, fat hen, good King Henry, ground elder, nettle, shepherd's purse, sorrel).

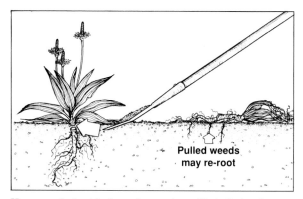

Pulled weeds may re-root

Hoe weeds just below the surface (*Rob Dalton*)

are used for making feeds – with the exception of comfrey, which is rotted in water and gives levels of nitrogen, potash and phosphorus that are ideal for tomato plants. Weeds such as dandelion, valerian, yarrow and stinging nettle not only add material to the compost heap but also are believed to stimulate it.

Some weeds are used for disease control. *Equisetum* contains much silica and its tea is used against mildew and other fungal attacks, especially by biodynamic gardeners. Similarly, stinging nettle and horseradish teas are sprayed for fungicidal protection of plants and fruits.

Those weeds with strong smells can be made into teas to 'disguise' plants from their pests. Tansy, mints and yarrow are useful, but there may be side-effects: wormwood is often recommended to drive away cabbage white butterflies, but it also decreases the yield of cabbages. Weeds with insecticidal properties such as elderberry leaves have been used as teas for killing pests, and many poisonous plants could probably be utilized, but this is potentially hazardous and illegal in the UK.

WEED CONTROL

The basic principle for killing weeds is to remove their leaves until they are dead. No plant can survive the frequent total removal of all top growth; even the worst expire eventually, and annuals do so with little resistance when attacked early. Where weeds are reinforced or replaced from beyond the area being weeded, however, there is no hope of a lasting clearance. If bindweed or *Equisetum* are killed in one garden but are not eradicated simultaneously in adjacent plots they will rapidly be back. The neighbours' cooperation must be sought!

The different ways of killing weeds are all based on this principle. Each time the top growth is removed the plant loses nutrients and stops receiving energy and new materials until the leaves are replaced. If the replacements are removed before they have replenished the

resources used to grow them the plant is badly weakened, and if this is done methodically the plant dies and the roots wither and rot – even bindweed. Once a week is the best interval.

The most vulnerable point in weeds is just below the soil surface. Cut off here, fewer regrow than if the cut is higher. Pulling weeds up can be less effective than cutting: if left to lie they may reroot in contact with the soil, since the complete plant has more resources than the severed parts.

ERADICATING ESTABLISHED WEEDS FROM NEW GROUND

The control of weeds must start with getting rid of all established weeds, so that from then on only annuals have to be suppressed or eliminated. Eradication is a one-off task which requires methodical and persistent work. If it is done well, maintaining weed-free conditions is relatively easy.

Where only a few perennials have had time to establish themselves and the root systems have not turned the soil into a tough mat, thorough hoeings at weekly intervals can return it to clean conditions. If it has been neglected for more than a season or two there will be many spreaders and deep rooters, and it will be much harder to make clean. Where the area is down to grass and has

Tougher weeds

These weeds are tough but expire after several attacks at a week apart:

brambles, coltsfoot, couch grass, creeping buttercup, docks, ground elder, knotweed, nettles, thistles

Weeds that take a lot of work and persistence to eradicate:

Equisetum, horseradish, Japanese knotweed, lesser celandine, oxalis, white-flowered bindweed, winter heliotrope

been cut regularly the weeds will mostly be surface rooters, which are easily skimmed off or possibly even dug in.

It is easier to eliminate everything in an area at one go than to work piecemeal. Make a realistic assessment of the area, and temporarily move or propagate any plants really worth saving as they will be a great handicap to work around. To recover an area containing valued plants that cannot be moved, see page 255.

GRASSING DOWN AND DIGGING UP

As it is easier to make a bed from cut sward than from uncontrolled growth, it is a good plan to spend the first growing season reducing rough weed growth with a tough mower. Regular grass-cutting once a week (slowly reduce the height of the blades and spread the cuttings) will eliminate most weeds and convert their biomass into fertility.

Start cutting from early in the year, when holes and junk can still be seen, and continue till autumn. Cutting alters the weed population, and low-growing plants with shallow root systems, especially grasses, are rapidly selected. Dock and nettle patches become grass and couch is replaced by better species.

Once a sward is established it is easy to mark out and slice off the turves and stack them, well limed, to rot down for re-incorporation or potting compost. (It is feasible to invert each spit of soil and bury the turf intact, but this can be recommended only with sward that is exceptionally free of weeds and weed seeds.) Late summer to early autumn is the time to start, as the turf peels and the soil can settle and become friable over winter. With the turf removed the soil can be dug over with little difficulty, as by now there should be few deep roots to pull out. Inevitably there will be some weeds missed, which will regrow rapidly and will need hoeing at regular weekly intervals until they expire. If the digging is done later than early autumn, regrowth will be in the spring, interfering with the crops. Spring digging has this drawback and is very hard work with heavy soil, because of the much higher water content. However, more fertility is saved as the broken soil has not been leached all winter.

Only for the largest areas does power assistance become useful. In an average-sized garden it is better to do without a rotovator, as it kills worms, can damage soil structure, especially if used on wet clays, and helps spreading weeds to proliferate.

Where there is a small area to clear, shortage of time or enough enthusiastic labour, weeds can be attacked immediately by hand. Each spit of earth must be grubbed up and the weed roots extracted. This is hard work and there is always more regrowth than from after a skimmed sward, but it does bring the bed into use quickly.

Covering the area with heavy mulches of straw or similar materials eliminates many weeds, but encourages any strong-growing spreaders. If such weeds as ground elder, bindweed, *Equisetum*, creeping thistle, nettles or brambles are not present, thick mulches will make the digging and cleaning of the ground much easier after the mulch is removed. A heavy impenetrable mulch such as old carpet or thick black plastic sheet can be used to prevent established weeds reaching the light. This method makes the least work and is very effective (see page 38).

Whatever method is used to break the ground the result will be flush after flush of weeds in the early years of cultivation. Most of these will be annuals from seed, but initially there may be perennials re-establishing themselves from pieces of root. These *must* be hoed, cultivated or flame-gunned at weekly intervals or the area will rapidly revert. The treatments must continue throughout the next growing season, for if any regain a foothold all the labour will have been wasted.

There is also a danger of weeds re-establishing themselves by encroachment: beds and borders made against weed-infested hedges are not going to stay clear for long! If your neighbours have ground elder it will continually grow through hedges and fences. A pathway next to the hedge makes a cordon sanitaire, reducing the likelihood of weeds entering. Solid paths stop the weeds encroaching, while on sward paths the weed topgrowth is removed when you cut. Either makes for easier hedge or fence maintenance and they are sited on impoverished soil from the hedge competition, so there is little loss of productive ground. The cordon sanitaire can be reinforced or replaced with a slit trench lined with impermeable plastic sheeting which the roots cannot penetrate.

Where the sward contains creeping weeds, rather than the usual 2 in (5 cm) drop from grass path to border soil make it 6 in (15 cm) and fewer weeds will encroach, saving time tidying the

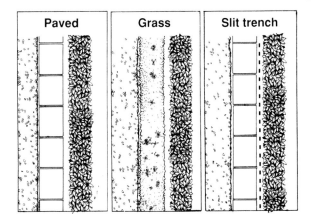

Cordon sanitaire to prevent weed encroachment
(Rob Dalton)

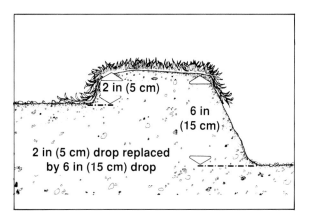

Barrier against creeping weeds (*Rob Dalton*)

edges. Give the edge a slope and it will last longer, or reinforce with continuous edging. Any edging with gaps where weeds can grow, such as bricks or tiles, makes more work.

SUPPRESSING WEED SEEDS

Having cleared established weeds from an area you now have the problem of preventing potential weeds ever germinating at all, killing any that do as early as possible and *never* letting any establish or seed.

Before attempting to prevent seeds germinating it is important to prevent the existing population being reinforced. Weeds that spread by seed should not be allowed near beds and borders, or they should be deadheaded. Most seeds are dropped close to the parent, even wind-blown ones, so the cleaner the immediate surroundings the fewer new seeds.

Hedges filter out seeds from the wind, while fences and walls cause them to be dropped in eddy pockets on either side. So hedges help reduce the number arriving but may prove a secondary source of infection.

A source of many weed seeds is farmyard manure, which should always be composted to

Spreading garden plants

Weeds may often be other garden plants. The following should be carefully deadheaded, or there will be great flushes of them: allium, bellflower, bluebell, euphorbia, feverfew, forget-me-not, foxglove, Himalayan balsam, honesty, *Iris foetidissima*, polemonium, poppy, pot marigold, sedum, sisyrinchium, sweet rocket, viola. Garden perennials that spread threaten other plants, so keep control of : ajuga, alstroemeria, celandine, grape hyacinth, hypericum, lamium, loosestrife, Michaelmas daisy, mint, oxalis, polygonum, shasta daisy, lemon balm, vinca.

kill as many as possible. Wherever straw is used, be prepared for flushes of weeds afterwards. Badly made garden compost, leaf-mould and cheap peat products similarly introduce many seeds. Weed seeds spread on wheels, feet and tools, and with the soil around living plants that are introduced. Not only seeds, but growing weeds: many a plant comes with several extra 'friends'! Without doubt the worst spreaders of weeds are garden centres. Almost every plant sold in a pot carries gratuitous weeds, particularly hairy bittercress.

STOPPING GERMINATION

Having ensured that the weed seeds in the soil are not being reinforced, eliminate as many as possible before your plants are introduced. There is little likelihood of eradicating all seeds from the full depth of the soil, but it is possible to deal with those most likely to germinate. Fortunately weed seeds have to be in the top inch of soil or less before they will germinate and grow. Light causes many to start into growth, and even if they are then buried they may still continue. Experiments show that far fewer weeds germinate from soil cultivated in the dark, but this is rather impractical for gardeners.

Minimal cultivation and no-dig methods: help weed control by not disturbing the deeper soil layers and, therefore, any deeply buried seeds, but confining all cultivation to the topmost inch. This becomes thoroughly scoured over a season or two, and few weeds then germinate, unless new seed is introduced.

Early seed-bed preparation: allows weeds to germinate and be hoed, raked or flame-gunned with minimum soil disturbance, so that new seeds are not uncovered. The next flush of weedlings is similarly treated, so that by the time the crop is sown there are few potential weeds left to compete. This preparation can be done early in the year with cloches or a sheet of clear plastic laid to warm the soil, when it is more effective.

Rotation: is practised for fertility and pest and disease control, but it also helps with weed control. As the crop changes each year the conditions change, and no particular weed is allowed to build up. It is easy to miss a weed growing amongst peas, but if it sets seed the weedlings may come up under, say, potatoes, where the soil disturbance from earthing up eliminates many, or brassicas, where the open conditions make it easy for them to be hoed.

Mulching. For weed control this is a simple extension of burying seed too deep to germinate.

In trials at the University of Erlangen in Germany, land cultivated in the light in September was 80% covered in weeds; ten months later cultivated in the dark, it was just 2%. Only a flash of light is needed to initiate germination in many weed seeds, on the surface and up to ½ in (1 cm) underneath as well. The effect of light on seeds appears to decrease as the seed ages. It is especially effective at stimulating the seeds of docks and mulleins, while chickweed germinates best of all in the light with the temperature varying from 68 to 86°F (20–30°C).

Similarly the effect of varying temperatures is greater on fresh seed than on that six months or more old. Initially many more weed seeds are started into germination by varying temperatures than by constant warmth, especially burdock, fat hen, plantain, purslane and sow thistle.

For a mulch to work it merely has to insulate the weed-seed-infested soil from light and air. It is very effective if used properly, but can cause problems. Mulches have many uses and effects other than for weed control: see the chapter on *Mulches* (page 36) for details on types, materials and how to use them. What is important is never to put loose mulches on the ground with established weeds as it only benefits the weeds; mulches are only good at preventing the seeds from germinating.

Sowing-mulches are very useful in weed-seed-infested soil. It is especially inconvenient having weeds right next to crop seedlings – they compete more, and weeding damage is likely. When sowing, cover the seed with sharp sand, old potting compost or similar seed-free material. This dramatically reduces the weeds germinating close by (for they will not mostly germinate more than ¼ in/0·5 cm from the surface) and it also marks the sites.

Ground cover, green manure and choke plants: help prevent weeds. Their cover stops light and air starting seeds into germination, and as the chosen plants already occupy the ground they outdo any weed trying to gain a foothold. They are really only of use out of season or under woody plants, as they compete too strongly to be used together with vegetables, herbs or most herbaceous ornamentals.

Under shrubs and trees the right ground cover is effective, but it must be carefully tended and weeded until well established and covering the area densely. For suitable plants see the chapter on *The Ornamental Garden* (page 186).

For temporary ground cover in the productive garden, green manures are most suitable as they enrich the soil while preventing weeds. See the chapter on *Soil* (page 22) for suitable ones and how to use them.

Under soft fruit the low-growing *Limnanthes douglasii* is easy to control and brings in many beneficial insects, although mulching produces better crops because of less competition. At edges and along borders herbs such as rosemary, thyme, sage and rue, grown as companion plants, also act as weed-suppressing ground cover. Mints grow too rampantly.

Choke plants are very vigorous growers that outperform even pernicious weeds, so they cannot be combined with cropping. Their establishment can be laborious and they are not as effective as regular cutting at reducing weed populations. *Tagetes minuta* is one of the best, as it kills nematodes at the same time, is believe to suppress herbaceous weeds and has less effect on woody plants. Potatoes are reputed to choke out weeds, but it is the earthing up and soil disturbance that does it, not the crop itself.

Intensive planting is a form of ground cover suited to the productive garden. The soil is hidden from the light by the crop foliage, inhibiting weeds from germinating and starving any that do. Close block planting with many even-sized plants is needed; this produces smaller specimens than wider spacing, but the total yield for the area is increased (see *Methods of Cultivation*, page 62)

Intensive planting is augmented by planting out crops from seedbeds, pots and multi-celled trays. It is quickest to weed empty beds and between established plants, as crop seedlings are hard to spot. If these are part-grown before planting out they will cover the bare, weeded soil more quickly. Planting out rather than sowing can also give more production from inter- and catch-cropping.

Biological control methods are still in their infancy. On a large scale 'green lawnmowers' such as geese, sheep and rabbits have their uses, but they are selective and will change weed populations rather than eradicate them. Goats will eliminate everything given the opportunity. It should be possible to train pigeons to eat brassica-related weeds such as shepherd's purse and charlock, as they are so partial to greens. There has been some success in eradicating weeds with their pests, such as with prickly pear and its moth in Australia. Although there is potential here there are no products yet available and much research is needed to prevent any biological control, especially those that arise from bio-engineering, becoming a pest, as so many weeds are closely related to cultivated plants. Fungal weedkillers have similar potential for good and bad: they have been used with some success to control dock, fat hen, creeping thistle and cleavers.

Common weeds

A = Annual   * Winter germination and growth   S = Seeder
B = Biennial   + Multiple generations per year   R = Roots/stolons/runners
P = Perennial   Bb= Bulb(il)s

Common name	Latin name (spp. = species)	Type of plant	Spreads by
Bent	*Agrostis spp.*	P	S/R
Bindweed, field	*Convolvulus arvensis*	P	S/R
hedge	*Calystegia sepium*	P	S/R
Black grass	*Alopecurus myosuroides* (*A. agrestis*)	A *	S
Black medick	*Medicago lupulina*	P	S
Bracken	*Pteridium aquilinum*	P	R
Bramble	*Rubus spp.*	P	S/R
Buttercup	*Ranunculus spp.*	P/A *	S/R
bulbous	*Ranunculus bulbosus*		
Canadian fleabane	*Conyza canadensis*	A	S
Cat's-ear	*Hypochaeris radicata*	P	S
Celandine	*Ranunculus ficaria*	P	Bb
Chamomile	*Anthemis* and *Matricaria spp.*	A	S
Charlock	*Sinapis arvensis*	A	S
Chickweed	*Stellaria media*	A +	S
Cinquefoil	*Potentilla reptans*	P	S/R
Cleavers (goosegrass)	*Galium aparine*	A *	S
Clover, white	*Trifolium repens* var. *sylvestre*	P	S/R
yellow suckling	*T. dubium*	A	S
Cocksfoot	*Dactylis glomerata*	P	S
Corncockle	*Agrostemma githago*	A	S

Black grass (*Alopecurus myosuroides*) (*Holt Studios*)

Black medick (*Medicago lupulina*) (*HRI*)

Bent, black (*Agrostis gigantea*) (*HRI*)

Bindweed, Field (*Convolvulus arvensis*) (*HRI*)

Bracken (*Chris Algar*)

Bindweed, Black (*Polygonum convolvulus*) (*HRI*)

Bramble (*Rubus species*) (*Chris Algar*)

Buttercup, bulbous (*Ranunculus bulbosus*) (*Natural Image*)

Stinking chamomile (*Anthemis cotula*) (*HRI*)

Cleavers or goosegrass (*Galium aparine*) (*Chris Algar*)

Canadian fleabane (*Conyza canadensis*) growing among onions (*HRI*)

Charlock (*Sinapsis arvensis*) (*HRI*)

Clover, white (*Trifolium repens var. sylvestre*) (*Chris Algar*)

Cat's-ear (*Hypochaeris radicata*) (*Harry Smith*)

Chickweed (*Stellaria media*) (*Chris Algar*)

Cocksfoot (*Dactylis glomerata*) (*Harry Smith*)

Lesser celandine (*Ranunculus ficaria*) (*HRI*)

Cinquefoil (*Potentilla reptans*) (*Harry Smith*)

Corncockle (*Agrostemma githago*) (*HRI*)

Common weeds

A = Annual   * Winter germination and growth   S = Seeder
B = Biennial   + Multiple generations per year   R = Roots/stolons/runners
P = Perennial   Bb = Bulb(il)s

Common name	Latin name (spp. = species)	Type of plant	Spreads by
Cornflower	*Centaurea cyanus*	A	S
Corn marigold	*Chrysanthemum segetum*	A	S
Couch	*Elymus repens (Agropyron r.)*	P	S/R
Cow parsley	*Anthriscus sylvestris*	P	S
Crane's-bill meadow	*Geranium spp.* *G. pratense*	A	S
Creeping soft grass	*Holcus mollis*	P	S/R
Crowfoot ivy-leaved	*Ranunculus spp.* *R. omiophyllus*	P	S/R
Daisy	*Bellis perennis*	P	S/R
Dandelion	*Taraxacum officinale*	P	S
Deadnettle henbit red	*Lamium spp.* *L. amplexicaule* *L. purpureum*	A *	S
Dock broad-leaved curled	*Rumex spp.* *R. obtusifolius* *R. crispus*	P P B/P	S S S
Fat hen	*Chenopodium album*	A	S
Fescue red sheep's	*Festuca spp.* *F. rubra* *F. ovina*	P	S/R
Field mint	*Mentha arvensis*	A	S
Field mouse-ear Chickweed	*Cerastium arvense*	A	S
Fool's parsley	*Aethusa cynapium*	A	S
Fumitory	*Fumaria officinalis*	A	S

Cow parsley (*Anthriscus sylvestris*) (*HRI*)

Crane's-bill, meadow (*Geranium pratense*) (*Sawyers Farm*)

Crowfoot, ivy-leaved (*Ranunculus omiophyllus*) (*Natural Image*)

Cornflower (*Centaurea cyanus*) (*Chris Algar*)

Corn Marigold (*Chrysanthemum segetum*) (*HRI*)

Couch (*Elymus repens*) (*Chris Algar*)

Daisy (*Bellis perennis*) (*Chris Algar*)

Dandelion (*Taraxacum officinale*) (*HRI*)

Deadnettle, red (*Lamium purpureum*) (*HRI*)

Fat hen (*Chenopodium album*) (*HRI*)

Field mouse-ear chickweed (*Cerastium arvense*) (*Harry Smith*)

Deadnettle, henbit (*Lamium amplexicaule*) (*HRI*)

Dock, broad-leaved (*Rumex obtusifolius*) (*Chris Algar*)

Fescue, sheep's (*Festuca ovina*) (*Harry Smith*)

Fool's parsley (*Aethusa cynapium*) (*Chris Algar*)

Dock, curled (*Rumex crispus*) (*Chris Algar*)

Field mint (*Mentha arvensis*) (*Holt Studios*)

Fumitory (*Fumaria officinalis*) (*Chris Algar*)

Common weeds

A = Annual   * Winter germination and growth   S = Seeder
B = Biennial   + Multiple generations per year   R = Roots/stolons/runners
P = Perennial   Bb = Bulb(il)s

Common name	Latin name (spp. = species)	Type of plant	Spreads by
Goosegrass (see cleavers)			
Greater celandine	*Chelidonium majus*	P	S
Ground elder	*Aegopodium podagraria*	P	S/R
Groundsel	*Senecio vulgaris*	A + *	S
Hairy bittercress	*Cardamine hirsuta*	A + *	S
Hawkbit rough	*Leontodon spp.* *L. hispidus*	P	S
Hawksbeard rough	*Crepis spp.* *C. biennis*	B/P	S
Hemlock, common	*Conium maculatum*	P	S
Hemp nettle downy large-flowered	*Galeopsis spp* *G. segetum* *G. speciosa*	A	S/R
Henbane, common	*Hyoscyamus niger*	A	S
Hoary pepperwort	*Cardaria draba*	P	S
Hogweed	*Heraclium sphondylium*	B/P	S
Horsetail, field giant	*Equisetum arvense* *E. telemateia*	P	R
Japanese knotweed	*Polygonum cuspidatum*	P	S/R
Knapweed greater	*Centaurea nigra* *C. scabiosa*	P	S
Knawel	*Scleranthus annuus*	A	S
Knotgrass	*Polygonum aviculare*	A	S

Hairy bittercress (*Cardamine hirsuta*) (*HRI*)

Hawkbit, rough (*Leontodon hispidus*) (*Harry Smith*)

Greater celandine (*Chelidonium majus*) (HRI)

Ground elder (*Aegopodium podagraria*) (HRI)

Groundsel (*Senecio vulgaris*) (*Chris Algar*)

Hawksbeard (*Crepis biennis*) (*Harry Smith*)

Hemlock, common (*Conium maculatum*) (*Harry Smith*)

Hoary pepperwort (*Cardaria draba*) (*Harry Smith*)

Greater knapweed (*Centaurea nigra*) (*Sawyers Farm*)

Japanese knotweed (*Polygonum cuspidatum*) (*Chris Algar*)

Hemp nettle *(Galeopsis spp.)* *(Harry Smith)*

Hogweed (*Heraclium sphondylium*) (*Harry Smith*)

Knawel (*Scleranthus annuus*) (*Harry Smith*)

Henbane (*Hyoscyamus niger*) (*HRI*)

Horsetail (*Equisetum arvense*) (*John Walker*)

Knotgrass (*Polygonum aviculare*) (*Chris Algar*)

Common weeds

A = Annual
B = Biennial
P = Perennial

* Winter germination and growth
+ Multiple generations per year

S = Seeder
R = Roots/stolons/runners
Bb = Bulb(il)s

Common name (spp. = species)	Latin name	Type of plant	Spreads by
Mallow	*Malva sylvestris*	A	S
Mayweed	*Anthemis* and *Matricaria spp.*	A	S
pineapple	*M. matricarioides*		
scented	*M. recutita*		
scentless	*Tripleurospermum inodorum*		
Meadow grass	*Poa spp.*	A/P*	S/R
annual	*P. annua*	A	S
Mouse-ear chickweed	*Cerastium vulgatum*	A	S
Mustard, black	*Brassica nigra*	A	S
white	*Sinapis alba*	A	S
Nettle, annual	*Urtica urens*	A	S
stinging	*U. dioica*	P *	S/R
Nightshade, black	*Solanum nigrum*	A	S
deadly	*Atropa belladonna*	P	S
woody	*Solanum dulcamara*	P	S
Oxeye daisy	*Chrysanthemum leucanthemum*	P	S
Parsley piert	*Aphanes arvensis*	A *	S
Pennycress	*Thlaspi arvense*	A	S
Persicaria	*Polygonum persicaria*	A	S
Plantain	*Plantago spp.*	P	S
broad-leaved	*P. major*	P	S
ribwort	*P. lanceolata*	P	
Poppy, corn	*Papaver rhoeas*	A *	S
Ragwort	*Senecio jacobea*	B/P	S
Runch	*Raphanus raphinistrum*	A	S

Mustard, black (*Brassica nigra*) (*Natural Image*)

Mustard, white (*Sinapis alba*) (*Harry Smith*)

Mallow (*Malva sylvestris*) (Chris Algar)

Mayweed, scented (*Matricaria recutita*) (*HRI*)

Mayweed, pineapple (*Matricaria matricarioides*) (Chris Algar)

Meadow grass, annual (*Poa annua*) (*HRI*)

Nettle, annual (*Urtica urens*) (*HRI*)

Nettle, stinging (*Urtica dioica*) (*Chris Algar*)

Nightshade, black (*Solanum nigrum*) (*HRI*)

Oxeye daisy (*Chrysanthemum leucanthemum*) (*Harry Smith*)

Parsley piert (*Aphenes arvensis*) (*HRI*)

Pennycress (*Thlaspi arvensis*) (*HRI*)

Plantain, ribwort (*Plantago lanceolata*) (*HRI*)

Poppy, corn (*Papaver rhoeas*) (*HRI*)

Ragwort (*Senecio jacobea*) (*HRI*)

Nightshade, deadly (*Atropa belladonna*) (*Harry Smith*)

Persicaria or redshank (*Polygonum persicaria*) (*HRI*)

Nightshade, woody (*Solanum dulcamara*) (*Chris Algar*)

Plantain, broad-leaved (*Plantago major*) (*Chris Algar*)

Runch or wild radish (*Raphanus rephanistrum*) (*HRI*)

Common weeds

A = Annual
B = Biennial
P = Perennial

* Winter germination and growth
+ Multiple generations per year

S = Seeder
R = Roots/stolons/runners
Bb = Bulb(il)s

Common name	Latin name (spp. = species)	Type of plant	Spreads by
Rush	*Juncus inflexus*	P	S/R
Ryegrass, perennial	*Lolium perenne*	P	S/R
Scarlet pimpernel	*Anagallis arvensis*	A/P	S
Sedge, great pond	*Carex riparia*	P	S/R
greater tussock	*C. paniculata*	P	S/R
Shepherd's needle	*Scandix pecten-veneris*	A	S
Shepherd's purse	*Capsella bursa-pastoris*	A *	S
Silverweed	*Potentilla anserina*	P	S/R
Soft brome	*Bromus mollis*	A/B	S
Sorrel	*Rumex spp.*	P	S
sheep's	*R. acetosella*	P	S
Speedwell	*Veronica spp.*	A*	S
Spurge, sun	*Euphorbia helioscopia*	A	S
Spurrey, corn	*Spergula arvensis*	A	S
Thistle	*Sonchus* and *Cirsium spp.*		
creeping	*C. arvense*	P	S/R
sow	*S. oleraceus*	A	S
spear	*C. vulgare*	B	S
Timothy	*Phleum pratense*	P	S/R
Treacle mustard	*Erysimum cheiranthoides*	A *	S
Vetch, common	*Vicia sativa*	A	S
Wild carrot	*Daucus carota*	B	S

Sedge, great pond (*Carex riparia*) (*Harry Smith*)

Shepherd's needle (*Scandix pecten-veneris*) (*HRI*)

Shepherd's purse (*Capsella bursa-pastoris*) (*Chris Algar*)

Rush (*Juncus inflexus*) (*Harry Smith*)

Ryegrass, perennial (*Lolium perenne*) (*Holt Studios*)

Scarlet pimpernel (*Anagallis arvensis*) (*Chris Algar*)

Silverweed (*Potentilla anserina*)
(*Harry.Smith*)

Speedwell (*Veronica species*)
(*Chris Algar*)

Timothy (*Phleum pratense*)
(*Natural Image*)

Soft brome (*Bromus mollis*) (*Harry Smith*)

Spurge, sun (*Euphorbia helioscopia*) (*HRI*)

Spurrey, corn (*Spergula arvensis*)
(*HRI*)

Treacle mustard (*Erysimum cheiranthoides*) (*Harry Smith*)

Thistle, smooth sow (*Sonchus oleraceus*) (*HRI*)

Vetch, common (*Vicia sativa*)
(*HRI*)

Sorrel (*Rumex acetosa*) (*John Walker*)

Thistle, spear (*Cirsium vulgare*)
(*Chris Algar*)

Wild carrot (*Daucus carota*)
(*HRI*)

Common weeds

A = Annual	* Winter germination and growth
B = Biennial	+ Multiple generations per year
P = Perennial	

S = Seeder	
R = Roots/stolons /runners	
Bb = Bulb(il)s	

Common name	Latin name (spp. = species)	Type of plant	Spreads by
Wild oat	Avena fatua, A. ludoviciana	A *	S
Wild onion	Allium vineale	P	Bb
Willow-herb rosebay	Epilobium spp. E. angustifolium	P	S/R
Yarrow	Achillea millefolium	P	S/R
Yorkshire fog	Holcus lanatus	P	S/R

Willow-herb, rosebay (Epilobium angustifolium) (HRI)

Yorkshire fog (Holcus lanatus) (Harry Smith)

Wild oat (Avena species) (Harry Smith)

Wild onion or crow Garlic (Allium vineale) (HRI)

Yarrow (Achillea millefolium) (HRI)

WEEDING TECHNIQUES

Despite all measures there will always be some weeds that germinate, especially during warm wet springs. Once you have eradicated established weeds with your weekly attacks, weed-free conditions can be maintained with a fortnightly routine. More frequent weeding bouts are beneficial, but a fortnightly session minimizes the total effort. Leaving a longer gap makes for more work, as each day a weed grows makes it tougher and harder to kill. As we have seen, weedlings with few leaves are killed by one hoeing, flame-gunning or swamping with a mulch. Once they get bigger they can regrow vigorously, when several attacks become necessary.

Hand-weeding: this must be resorted to when weeds are intertwined with valued plants, as in mixed borders. It is employed among onion and carrot seedlings, where more vigorous efforts may cause too much damage. Rather than pulling up weedlings and weeds it is better to cut them off just below ground level, minimizing soil disturbance. Old knives are ideal – I prefer them

cut to a chisel end. Scrapers and onion hoes are useful. No matter what is used it must be sharp.

Fingers are soon damaged so wear gloves; rolled-up newspaper or carpet make kneelers to protect the knees, and save your back. If the weeds are being collected then a trug or an old washing-up bowl is good, as it is shallow – to put each handful straight in the barrow takes more effort. Stepping-stones are useful to save treading on wide beds or borders, and planks make temporary paths to work from. Raised beds only a few inches high make hand-weeding easier and more comfortable, and the chore gets done more quickly.

Hoeing: this is in effect using a knife on a stick to save bending, so the hoe must be as sharp as a knife. Most hoes would not cut wet string. A hoe sharpened every twenty minutes with a whetstone makes the job easy. The type of hoe is not important, though Dutch ones may make a better soil mulch and disturb the soil less than a swan-necked or draw hoe. Many different patterns have been tried but few are made of the best metal. Thin, springy steel like an old scythe blade is best. The angle of the head to the shaft, the length and the user's height and arms interact, so change hoes about for convenience and comfort. Almost all are much better with a longer shaft!

Hoeing is easiest when the soil is moist but just dry on top, though there is rarely the luxury of choice. Strong sun and drying winds kill weeded plants rapidly, while warm wet conditions will allow them to survive and reroot. Some experts prefer to work backwards, as then weeds just hoed are not firmed in, but as it is easier to spot weeds when working forwards try treading carefully.

If the ground is frozen it is impossible to hoe, but if the surface has just defrosted in the sun it is amazingly quick and easy. In very wet conditions, with sticky soil, or with many stones, hoeing is difficult. It is made much easier with a hoeing mulch of ½ in (1 cm) of sharp sand.

When there are great flushes of weeds and the weather is drying, weedlings can be raked instead of hoed. This is quicker while they are tiny, but when they get too big hoeing becomes necessary – and arduous. As the worst flushes come in wet conditions when it is too difficult to hoe, they could be dug in as a green manure, but it is less work to use a sharp spade to lift and invert a thin slice of soil, which kills off most of them. The mat of dead weeds and any survivors gets chopped up when hoed the next time.

Mechanical cultivators are really only suited to commercial holdings: they are designed for coping with large areas of regularly spaced crops, and among mixed crops damage may easily happen by accident. They are better used several times prior to crop-sowing rather than later among the growing plants, but if they are used then it is critical that planning and spacing of the crops is adjusted to the particular machine and that it is set to run very shallow. In all other respects the advice for hoeing applies.

Flame-guns: these (see *Tools*, page 387) are a great aid to weed control. They kill weeds by just cooking the leaves. They work very rapidly and large areas can be covered with little time or cost, even in wet weather when other methods fail. The leaves are only lightly cooked and wither, weakening and desiccating the root system for days afterwards; slowly charring them to ash is less efficient.

Weedlings disappear with one pass but more established weeds may need several weekly attacks. As each pass burns the shrivelled leaves from the previous visit, it removes biomass from the soil. Flame-guns are therefore ecologically and organically expensive for removing long-established growth, but ideal at maintaining clean conditions on beds, gravel paths and drives. They are especially good on gravel, as all litter is burnt and there is no build-up of mould to encourage other weeds. They are of great use in combating flushes of weedlings in wet springs and

particularly cleaning early seedbeds, as there is no soil disturbance. A refinement is to treat the first flush or two, then to sow. If the seed has a minimum germination period of, say, twelve days, anything showing on the bed up to day eleven must be a weed, which can be flamed with no danger to the buried seed. The crop then emerges and is established and dominant before more weeds appear. Obviously, it is critical to be aware of the minimum germination time of your seeds.

If the flame touches the thick bark of a tree it does no harm unless held there. This protection allows leafy weeds to be killed beneath and right up to tough, shrubby plants. It is even possible to kill small weeds with a rapid pass without harming herbaceous plants like cabbages.

Small blow-torches are very handy for spot-weeding rockeries, cracks in paths and patios. Simply cook every green leaf for a fraction of a second once a week till no more appear. Be careful near anything inflammable, including heathers, conifers and other evergreens.

If a weed manages to scatter seeds – such as might be discovered when pea haulm is removed – then an immediate slow pass with the flame-gun will kill them before they are incorporated in the topsoil. Similarly treat gravelled paths and drives where seed is shed on them.

WEED CONTROL AMONG OTHER PLANTS AND ON PATHS

With badly overrun borders it is simplest to write everything off and grass it all down for a while, as suggested above (page 241). If valued plants in the border are to be saved *in situ*, however, much weeding has to be done by hand. Where there are mainly annual weeds a weekly hoeing will soon restore clean conditions between the plants, but hand-weeding is always needed to pluck out any remnants hiding among stems.

It is much more difficult to remove established weeds. Hoeing can be arduous as the root systems fill much of the ground, and digging the weeds out is detrimental as they hide among plant roots. If the ground between plants is mulched with strips of impenetrable material such as carpet or plastic the weeds are forced to grow up through gaps where they can be cut or pulled more easily, and this reduces the area to be treated.

Once the initial weeds are cleared by weekly sessions, maintenance is needed fortnightly with regular hoeing and hand-weeding. Mulches make this much easier but can be expensive for large areas; so can ground cover plants. See pages 48 and 187 for types.

Shrubs and hedges seem to invite weeds that climb up the stems. Some of these climbers choke woody plants, but ecologically they are valuable, especially ivy, as they provide useful nest sites for birds, insects and small animals as well as great quantities of nectar and pollen. Do not worry about removing all the weed's top-growth from the shrubs or hedge: sever it regularly at ground level and it will wither away.

As mature shrubs and trees are little inconvenienced by low ground cover, this is excellent for keeping weeds out. But before eradicating established weeds only to plant ground cover, consider regulating them. Mow high or use a strimmer and cut the top-growth back regularly so that the cuttings feed the soil as for a sward. With a strimmer it is easy to cut close up to and under valuable plants, cutting deeply into the weeds. Low-growing plants such as violets and primroses can be encouraged by cutting around and over them leaving them untouched. A strimmer is even more useful when bulbs are combined with shrubs or planted along the hedge base. After flowering and before the leaves die back, bulbs in bare soil are hard to weed and look tatty in grass. Grown among shrubs or against hedge bases they can be kept tidy by strimming grass and/or weeds around them until the leaves die back, when a neater job can be done.

In herbaceous borders it is easier to see weeds than in mixed or shrub borders, as the plants are dormant for part of the year . The application of a thick mulch over the whole area will suppress annual weeds and improve the appearance. Ground cover is not as effective as it competes with herbaceous plants, to their detriment.

Weeding among herbaceous plants must be done by hand or carefully with a hoe, as they have easily damaged root systems and shoots. When the plants are dormant, however, it is possible to use a flame-gun. This will cook seeds dropped on the surface and any emergent weeds through the winter months until the plants start again in spring. Many weeds start growth before herbaceous plants, but flame-gunning can still be done if early plant buds are protected with a mound of sharp sand. Asparagus is perfect for this sort of control: the beds are made up in autumn, and any weeds that emerge can be burnt till the shoots appear, but as these are cut and eaten flame-gunning can continue intermittently till early summer, when few more weeds germinate.

Ground cover is good at keeping down weeds when it is established, but there are few plants that will choke out existing established weeds – any that do are usually just worse weeds. Any ground cover must be planted into clean ground and kept clean until it totally dominates the area. Even then some weeds will always appear. If weeds become established among ground cover they can be controlled only by a strimmer cutting off those that emerge above the plants, or laboriously hand-weeded, which is only practical in small areas.

Grass is the commonest ground cover, so we tend to overlook it. If any area is cut close and

regularly it selects grasses, as they are able to grow from the base whereas most plants grow from the tips. This is why grass can be continuously grazed by animals, mown or strimmed. Short-cut grass does compete very strongly, which is little problem to most established trees and shrubs, but in their early life grass competition is crippling. Good preparation, then hoeing, hand-weeding or flame-gunning and mulches are necessary for at least the first two years or the plant will not perform well. For best results a clear, weedfree circle at least 5 to 6 ft (1·5–2 m) across is necessary for a standard tree, a little less for smaller plants. Less than 3 ft (1 m) across will not protect a tree from competition for its first years. It is also important to control the weeds at the perimeter: if these are left unchecked they will invade, particularly under mulches. Short-cut sward is worse than natural weed cover; the weeds produce growth later in the spring than the cut sward, which is competing with the tree from late winter. Trees growing in cut sward or lawns therefore benefit all the more from a large weed-free area.

Controlling grass in orchards with geese or other organic 'lawnmowers' may change the fertility significantly enough to offset the competition. The aesthetic appearance, utility and other benefits of grass sward mean that most orchards are grassed down and weed-free conditions confined to circles or along the rows. Thick straw mulches are often used for this.

The maximum offset to competition is obtained if the grass is cut regularly, with the clippings returned, when it is 5–6 in (12·5–15 cm) long and cut by half. Depending on many

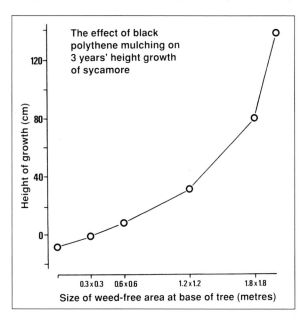

The effect of black polythene mulching on 3 years' height growth of sycamore

Weed competition (From *Trees and Weeds*, R.J.Davies, The Forestry Commission)(*Rob Dalton*)

Rosette weeds such as this dandelion put out leaves that flourish close to the surface, enabling them to escape mower blades (*Chris Algar*)

variables, this means about once a week to once a fortnight throughout the year.

The weeds in a grass sward can be controlled by changing the conditions to suit grasses more. Vigorous grass will outgrow weeds, so feeding is necessary (see *Lawns*, page 231). Longer grass competes more successfully than shorter; grass 2–3 in (5–7.5 cm) high excludes most weeds but makes your feet wet. Grass cut too short has daisies, but these disappear from longer grass, as do many other low-growing weeds of the 'rosette' type. Thistles are the most annoying of these but are easily eradicated by hand with a sharp knife; special lever-pronged tools have also been designed for pulling them up. Plantains and other rosette weeds can be cut out the same way. Sowing grass seed in the holes will help the sward re-establish more quickly.

The specialist grasses for bowling-green swards like acid conditions, while the tougher, more useful grasses prefer limey soils. Changing the pH with lime gets rid of most acid-loving weeds at the same time as helping these commoner grasses. Since most swards tend to become acid as the thatch thickens, regular scarifying and liming every few years are necessary to keep the soil suitable.

Cold heavy soils with bad drainage suit mosses. Here you must encourage the grasses with drainage, aeration, the incorporation of sharp sand and extra liming, as these soils tend naturally to acidity. Long sward encourages clover and this in turn aids the sward; rather than trying to eliminate the clover, get rid of the light green patches between by sowing more clover and the sward will be much healthier.

Where grass gets worn away weeds tend to step in, especially annuals that grow over winter. These then seed on to the sward and surrounding beds. Prevent this by replacing worn patches with stepping-stones or putting in a solid or gravel path.

Gravel paths and drives are kept weed-free by regular raking, flame-gunning or hand-weeding. Thick gravel is easy to keep clean, thin gravel more difficult; if there are any bald patches it is nearly impossible. The use of plastic membranes under gravel will prevent weeds emerging, but care must be taken to provide a slope, to prevent drainage problems.

Solid paths, drives and patios usually have cracks in which weeds gain a foothold and damage the fabric. Cleaning out all the gaps with a knife and pointing with cement is a permanent solution. Filling the cracks with sand or weed-free compost and low-growing plants like thymes leaves less room for weeds, but these plants need looking after themselves.

Regular flame-gunning is the easiest and most effective way of controlling weeds in cracks. Do not keep the flame on any spot for long, as the surface may flake. A strimmer can be used instead to pare back the top growth.

Ammonium sulphamate is not organic, but is a relatively safe herbicide sometimes used on paths, to remove tree stumps, or to clear vacant overgrown ground. It is non-selective; 1 lb to a gallon of water (450 gm to 5 l) will kill almost every species in an area of 100 sq ft (10 sq m), including woody plants and *Equisetum*. It should only be used in spring and summer, and crops can usually be safely planted after eight weeks, when it breaks down into harmless ammonium sulphate.

COMPOSTING WEEDS

The greatest return from weeding with the least loss is when the material is immediately incorporated into the topsoil. Some moisture is lost, but most of the material rapidly decomposes and can be absorbed by the crops. However, any trace elements and other valuable nutrients accumulated are then spread thinly. Removing the weeds and composting them concentrates the resource for later use with the most needy plants.

Small annual weeds are probably best just hoed in. Any that are larger and likely to reroot or set seed are better gathered up and removed after hoeing. Where mechanical cultivators are used the material is chopped *in situ*, so they must be used before any weeds reach an advanced stage.

Any weed can be safely composted, but it is essential to wither the most pernicious ones first and compost-making must be done perfectly (see *Composts*, page 30, for all the details). To wither weeds, just leave them spread out fully exposed for a week or two on a hard surface such as a concrete path before putting them in the compost bin. Weed seeds may be destroyed in composting, but many survive. It is probably best to burn the worst seed-bearing material along with any diseased material and thorny weeds, for hygiene and safety.

19 DISEASE PREVENTION

The presence of diseases in plants has been known for many centuries. The Greeks and Romans made reference to them in their various writings and even noticed that certain varieties of the same crop showed resistance to a particular disease. It was not, however, until the eighteenth century with the development of the microscope that there is evidence of detailed studies into the causes, effects and methods of treatment.

The major advances have really all been made in this century, because the economic importance of food production has prompted agriculturists to invest in research programmes to be able to recognize the symptoms, identify the history and distribution of the disease, the range of plants affected and the ability of plants to develop resistance to attack.

The definition of a disease is not always easy. Sometimes there are conditions when the difference between a healthy and an unhealthy plant is not sharply defined. Plant health is also related to more than just disease, for pest and nutritional disorders will also greatly affect the growth system. Once a plant's biological or physiological activities have been disrupted, the plant is vulnerable to disease.

TYPES OF DISEASE

The cause of a disease can be an attack by a disease-transmitting living organism, called a pathogen; the result of poor cultural conditions such as an excess or lack of heat, water, light, nutrients and so on, called a physiological disease; or a combination of these.

Pathogens can be subdivided into bacteria, fungi and viruses as the three main causes of disease; nematodes (tiny eelworms as small as $\frac{1}{125}$ in (0·02 mm) which include both parasitic root-feeders and their predators) and parasitic plants can be added to this classification. Diseases of fungal origin are also known by the term 'parasitic diseases'.

OPPOSITE: Bean chocolate spot (*Botrytis fabae*) (*Holt Studios*)

Bacterial diseases enter a plant through a wound resulting from mechanical damage or insect bites, or through natural sources such as leaf pores or leaf scars. They are transmitted by insects, wind, rain or the gardener through general cultivation of the soil or carrying diseased material. Bacterial diseases are influenced by atmospheric conditions. Hot, cold, wet or dry conditions can either encourage or limit the extent of an attack. Bacteria are the cause of diseases such as fire blight, bacterial wilts, leaf spots, vegetable soft rots and crown gall.

Fungal diseases can be very infectious, being transmitted by spores landing on the outer surface which germinate to enter the plant through a wound, natural opening or even penetration of the plant's external protective barriers. Fungi are also greatly influenced by weather conditions and are more prevalent in wet seasons. Fungal diseases include slime moulds such as club root, rusts, downy and powdery mildews, and smuts. Fungal diseases can be so severe as to cause economic disasters. The most far-reaching incidence was the potato blight that caused the Irish potato famine in the mid-1840s, with its consequential migration of the Irish people throughout the world. In recent years we have seen the destructive effect of Dutch elm disease.

Virus diseases can also be very infectious and are easily spread by contact with affected plants, either by surfaces or roots coming into contact or by grafting on to diseased stock. They are more serious on plants that are produced by propagation than those grown from seed. Viruses are the cause of discoloration, distortion, stunting and cell death. They include mosaics and spotted wilts.

SYMPTOMS

No matter what the cause, the first step in tackling a disease problem is its identification by the symptoms. Look up your plant in the list beginning on page 262, check the symptoms and identify the disease; then turn to the detailed information beginning on page 266 for methods of control and treatment.

Some symptoms may be peculiar to a particular disease, but there are others which have a multitude of causes. For example, plants wilting can be a common occurrence in the garden, especially due to lack of water in hot dry weather, but wilting can also be the result of a root pest, mechanical damage and other factors. In such circumstances it is necessary to study the plant and its environment carefully for all possible causes before looking for a specific disease.

Mineral deficiencies can sometimes be confused with diseases. Before concluding that there is a disease problem, first check for tell-tale signs of nutrient deficiency (see *Soil*, page 15).

In general, the main symptoms of diseases can be grouped as follows:

1. Death of the whole or part of the plant, which can be coupled with decay, rot or cankers.
2. Stunted and deformed growth, development of growths, distortion of buds or leaves.
3. Abnormal colouring of parts, including the development of spots or mosaics.
4. Wilting.
5. Development of fungal spores.
6. Premature fall of leaves or fruit; premature flowering and seed production.
7. Production of exudations such as gums.

PREVENTION

Many diseases have no cure and many can persist in the garden for a number of years, either by a build-up in the soil or through the harbouring of disease by bad cultural methods. Consequently, prevention must be uppermost in our efforts. This is best achieved by the adoption of good gardening practices.

Healthy soil grows healthy plants and healthy plants have a greater resistance to attack from pests and disease. A healthy soil is one which is rich in organic matter and contains all the nutrients to ensure good growth. The correct acid/alkaline relationship must be maintained, for if there is an excess one way or the other it is possible to 'lock up' nutrients in the soil so that although they are present they are not available to the plants. The condition of the soil is important; it must be well drained yet capable of retaining sufficient moisture for all the plants' needs.

Good steady growth is also essential. A check at any time during the growing period can leave the plant vulnerable to attack. Although this is closely related to the health of the soil, the environmental conditions play a considerable role. Sowing or planting out in cold, wet soil, subjecting young seedlings and tender plants to cold, frosty or windy weather or allowing plants to be scorched or dried out by the heat of the sun all contribute to weak plants and the possibility of their succumbing to disease problems. Optimum growing conditions are the main defence against disease.

CROP ROTATION

In the growing of vegetables, crop rotation plans are a very important factor in providing the crops with the optimum growing conditions as well as preventing disease. If the crop families are divided into groups requiring similar growing conditions, the soil can be prepared to suit their needs, adjusting the levels of specific nutrients and the soil pH level.

As many vegetable diseases are specific to one family, the use of a monocultural system (growing the same family in the same land every year) will quickly see a build-up in the soil of diseases which are destructive to this family. Once the soil is infected they can be very difficult to eradicate, as they can remain dormant for many years waiting for an opportunity to attack the crop the next time it is grown in the soil. Club root is said to be able to remain dormant in the soil for up to twenty years.

The pH level also plays an important role in the control of disease, for plants are sensitive to even quite small changes in it. In general plant growth will not occur outside the range of pH 3·5 to pH 8 (there are exceptions, such as some aquatic plants). Inside this band each family has a smaller specific range, usually about 3·5 units, in which it will grow. However, for optimum growth the range is even further reduced, to between about 0·5 and 1·5 units of pH.

The soil is extremely sensitive to pH and the solubility and availability of plant nutrients is greatly influenced by any changes. Nutrients become more or less available as the pH changes, to the extent that they can either be locked up in the soil and totally unavailable to the plants, or made so readily available that there are toxicity problems. These conditions are not conducive to optimum growth, and leave the plants open to attack.

The pH level also has an influence on the incidence and severity of disease. The best-known examples of this are the brassica family disease club root, which is very persistent in acid soils (pH less than 7) though not so frequent in alkaline soils (pH greater than 7), and potato wart and scab, which are more of a problem in alkaline than in acid soils.

Another way to avoid disease is to grow your own plants from good-quality seeds or by propagating from disease-free stock. Disease can be transmitted through seeds, and therefore it is important to ensure that the source is free from contamination. If keeping your own seed, do so only from unaffected plants. In fact, if there are any signs of disease the safest approach is not to keep seed, even from healthy plants.

Beware of accepting seed and plants from colleagues unless the source is known to be disease-free. This applies especially to brassicas, for club root is easily transmitted in this manner. The symptoms do not show themselves on seedling roots, and by the time they are apparent the ground is infected for many years to come. With potatoes buy certified seed, as potatoes suffer from many seed-transmitted diseases and it is not worth the risk of cutting corners and using poor-quality tubers.

RESISTANT VARIETIES

In recent years the importance of the development of resistant varieties has been recognized in combating disease. Although the use of these varieties does not guarantee immunity, it does enable plants to be grown which otherwise would be difficult to keep free from disease.

There are many varieties which have an inbuilt resistance to attack from specific diseases and, by cross-breeding, this attribute can be widened to produce resistance in other varieties of the same family.

However, work on breeding resistant strains is now reaching into the field of genetic engineering. This raises important questions: there is the risk of man-made genetic modifications escaping his control, with unpredictable consequences. Moreover, modified genes can be re-engineered back to the original variety without any change in outward appearance, removing from the individual any knowledge of the changes and hence the ability to choose. Fortunately not too much of this is going on at the moment, and much of the work is in the field of breeding resistance to the herbicides used on the crops.

A biological seed dressing has recently been introduced on to the market. Although it is not primarily aimed at disease control, the fact that germination is enhanced does mean that common disease problems encountered during this period have been reduced. Research is being undertaken to examine the use of *Trichoderma* to stimulate growth, both in vegetables and ornamentals. The mechanism suggested is that the fungus detoxifies the naturally occurring toxic products in the soil, allowing the plants to grow steadily in the early days of their life. There are claims from European research that *Trichoderma* will also control such pathogens as botrytis. See also page 156.

FUNGICIDES

Many fungal diseases are transmitted by airborne spores landing on the foliage and the best treatment for such diseases is preventive spraying of susceptible plants with an organically acceptable fungicide. These come in two forms under various brand names: copper based, such as a Bordeaux mixture, and sulphur, which is available as a fine powder or a liquid suspension. Both products could technically be classified as chemicals, for they contain materials obtained from chemical processes. Bordeaux mixture, which can be made at home, is a combination of copper sulphate and lime. Older text-books term sulphur as 'flowers of sulphur'; nowadays it is commonly sold as 'yellow sulphur'. Both products have been in use for many generations and time has proved them to be safe to use (with some exceptions), with no long-term toxic residues. Consequently they are acceptable products for the organic gardener. For brands and availability consult the catalogues of organic sundries suppliers.

The object in the use of preventive spraying is to deposit a thin layer of the fungicide so that when airborne spores land on the foliage they are prevented from entering the plant. It is therefore important to ensure that all surfaces are covered with the spray, for once the disease is established such preventive action becomes less effective. Unfortunately some fruits dislike both copper and sulphur and care must be used in these cases to avoid secondary damage.

Soil-borne diseases are best countered by ensuring that they do not come into contact with the plants they require to survive on. As we have seen, this needs a system of crop rotation. For those diseases capable of remaining dormant in the soil for longer than the three to four years of the normal crop rotation cycle, other means of combating them will have to be found, and as a last resort it may be necessary to avoid growing susceptible crops for the lifespan of the disease in the soil.

SOIL STERILIZATION

This is not practical on the large scale of the garden, but can be considered within the greenhouse, cold frame or seed bed. However, sterilization will not only kill off the disease but also much of the essential soil life in the treated areas. This will reduce the effectiveness of the breakdown of organic matter and the release of nutrients until the soil life has built up to the level required to maintain the soil in a highly fertile condition. If possible it is better to remove the contaminated soil from these areas and replace it with disease-free material.

Should preventive measures prove not to be totally successful and disease becomes evident within the garden, the identification of the disease as soon as possible is important in order that the appropriate corrective action can be taken. The amount of diseased material must be reduced to a minimum by cutting out and destroying affected parts, to ensure that the disease does not have the opportunity to spread to adjacent plants or to overwinter and initiate attacks the following year. The most effective way to destroy infected parts is by burning.

Weeds can play host to a number of diseases, so it is important to maintain a good level of weed control. Examine weeds to ensure that there are no signs of disease before adding them to the compost heap. Even if the heap is likely to develop enough heat to kill off any disease, it is safer not to add them deliberately to the compost system just in case it becomes a source of infection.

THE DISEASES

The information starting on page 266 is arranged as follows. The diseases are divided into:

Cankers	Rots	Spots
Club root	Rust	Viruses
Crown gall	Scab	Wilts
Leaf curl	Silver leaf	
Mildews	Sooty mould	

Within each group the individual diseases are listed in alphabetical order (for instance, under Cankers are Apple canker, Fire blight, Raspberry cane blight, Rose canker, Spur blight). Each disease is described and its causes given; then control and prevention are outlined, followed by notes on treatment. This may be repetitious (there is rarely a cure, and very often the plant or part of it must be destroyed), but it was felt easier for the gardener to find this information under the specific disease.

Identification of diseases by plant
(each disease is classified as a rot, virus, etc. if this is not clear from the name)

Plant and disease	Key symptoms
ANTIRRHINUM	
Leaf spot	Brown spots on leaves, often with a darker band around the edge, sometimes running into each other to cover the leaf which then dies. Black dot-like spores can appear on the flowers and stems
Rust	Brown spots with a yellow surround on the underside of the leaves. Corresponding yellowish spots appear on upper sides of leaves
ASPARAGUS	
Rust	Brown spots turning to black streaks on the stems and leaves. Whole plant turns black and dies
Violet root rot	Violet mould growth on the roots, interior of the roots rotting and hollow
BEANS (broad, French, runner)	
Chocolate spot	Small chocolate-coloured spots on the leaves of broad beans
Halo blight (spot)	Small brown spots on the leaves surrounded by a yellow 'halo'
Stem and root rot	Leaves turn yellow and die, roots and base of stem turn black and rot
BEETROOT	
Common scab	Cork-like spots on the skin; eating quality unharmed
Downy mildew	Yellow patches on the upper side of the leaves with a greyish mould on the underside
Leaf spot	Brown spots on the leaves, later forming holes in the leaves which can become disfigured

Identification of diseases by plant
(each disease is classified as a rot, virus, etc. if this is not clear from the name)

Plant and disease	Key symptoms
BRASSICAS (broccoli, Brussels sprouts, cabbage, cauliflower, swede, turnips)	
Club root	Leaves wilt in warm weather; when lifted, the roots are badly distorted and gnarled
Crown gall	Tumour-like swellings on roots
Damping off (rot)	Stems of seedlings rot just above soil level
Downy mildew	Yellow patches on upper side of leaves, white mould on underneath
Leaf spot	Brown spots, mainly on older leaves which may turn yellow and die
Soft rot	Cabbage heads rot, often with an unpleasant smell
BUSH FRUITS (blackberries, blackcurrants, gooseberries, loganberries, raspberries, red currants, strawberries, white currants)	
American gooseberry mildew	White powdery coating on leaves, turning brown and spreading to the fruits
Cane spot	White/purple spots on the berry canes
Coral spot	Coral-pink pimples on the leaves and shoots
Currant leaf spot	Brown spots first on the older leaves, spreading to the whole plant
Powdery mildew	White powdery coating on leaves and fruit
Reversion (virus)	Blackcurrant leaves look lopsided, plant flowers early but fails to set
Spur blight (canker)	Canes develop large purple patch at or near a leaf joint which grows to encircle the cane, turns silver and is covered with small black spots in the winter
Strawberry red core (rot)	Plants appear stunted in late spring/early summer, showing hard brown outer leaves with small reddish inner leaves. When lifted roots have turned dark brown or black and decayed
Wilt	Sudden drooping of leaves, plant dies
CARNATION	
Rust	Clusters of reddish-brown spots develop on leaves. The symptoms may also appear on the stems starting from soil level and travelling upwards
CARROT	
Bacterial soft rot	Roots become watery and slimy in storage
Sclerotinia rot	White mould on roots in storage
Violet root rot	Foliage stunted and yellow; roots covered with purple-coloured thread
CELERY	
Heart rot	Heart of plant is black, often turning into a rot
Leaf spot	Brown spots on the leaves, spreading to the stalks
CHRYSANTHEMUM	
Grey mould (rot)	Fluffy grey mould covers the plant
Petal blight (spot)	Brown spots on the flower petals
Rust	Rust-coloured spots on the undersides of the leaves which eventually die

Identification of diseases by plant
(each disease is classified as a rot, virus, etc. if this is not clear from the name)

Plant and disease	Key symptoms
CUCURBITS (courgettes, cucumbers, marrows, melons)	
Cucumber mosaic (virus)	Yellow/green mottling of leaves; fruit misshapen, bearing green blisters
Grey mould (rot)	Grey furry mould on leaves, stem and fruit; fruit begins to rot
Leaf spot	Brown spots on the leaves, growing in size until the leaf dies
Powdery mildew	White powdery coating on leaves and stems
Stem rot	Base of stem rots and the plant collapses
GRAPE-VINE	
Grey mould (rot)	Grey mould on leaves and young shoots, spreading to the fruit
Powdery mildew	White powdery coating on the leaves, stems and fruit
LETTUCE	
Downy mildew	Yellowing of upper side of leaves, off-white mould on the underside
Grey mould (rot)	Heads covered with grey mould. Heads rot beneath mould layer
Mosaic (virus)	Yellow mottling of leaves; plant's growth is stunted
Soft rot	Leaves become soft and slimy
ONIONS (including leeks and shallots)	
Downy mildew	Yellowing of the leaves followed by a white mould in damp weather
Neck rot	Grey mould around the neck when in storage; bulb begins to rot
Rust	Rust-coloured blisters on leaves
White rot	Leaves turn yellow and die; white mould around bulb, which starts to rot
PARSNIP	
Canker	Shoulder of the root starts to decay
PEAS	
Leaf spot	Brown spots on the leaves and pods
Powdery mildew	White powdery coating on the leaves and stems
POTATO	
Black leg (rot)	Blackening of stem both above and below the ground
Blight (rot)	Brown patches on the leaves with a white mould on the underside
Common scab	Skin is covered with rough blisters, but there is no damage to the flesh underneath
Dry rot	Depressions develop in the skin in storage; the flesh underneath turns brown
Leaf roll (virus)	Leaves roll upwards, becoming hard and brittle
Mosaic (virus)	Pale green/yellow mottling of the leaves
Powdery scab	Powdery pimples form on the skin
RHUBARB	
Crown rot	Tissue just below the crown rots
ROCK PLANTS	
Leaf spot	Greyish patches with dark spots appear on the leaves. The spots may run into each other and a grey mould may develop. The stems may also be affected
Powdery mildew	White powdery coating covers the leaves and stems
Rust	Yellowish spots appear on the leaves which may turn red or brown

Identification of diseases by plant

(each disease is classified as a rot, virus, etc. if this is not clear from the name)

Plant and disease	Key symptoms
ROSE	
Black spot	Black spots on the leaves
Powdery mildew	Leaves, shoots and buds covered with a white mould
Rust	Orange pimples on the twigs and underside of the leaves, turning darker later in the season
SPINACH	
Cucumber mosaic (spinach blight) (virus)	Leaves roll inwards and turn yellow, especially on late summer/autumn sowings
Damping off (rot)	Stem rots, plant topples over and dies
Downy mildew	Upper surface of leaves turns yellow, with an off-white mould on the underside
TOMATO	
Blight (rot)	Brown patches on the leaves which spread until the leaf dies; ripening fruit turns brown and rotting
Blossom end rot	Dark hard patch develops on the bottom of the tomato
Ghost spot	Brown spots on the skin surrounded by pale rings
Grey mould (rot)	Grey mould on the stems starting at a point of damage
Leaf mould (rot)	Upper surface of leaves turns yellow; a brown mould develops on underside
Stem and root rot	On young seedlings stem rots at soil level; roots system has rotted away. On older plants brown cankers develop just above soil level
Virus	Leaves mottled and distorted, plant stunted, fruit mottled or covered with dark patches
TREE FRUIT (apples, cherries, peaches, pears, plums)	
Apple canker	Deep gaping wounds with gnarled edges on the branches and trunk of the tree
Bacterial canker	Wounds with gnarled edges on branches and trunk, exuding an amber-coloured gum
Bitter pit (rot)	Small dark depressions on skin; when fruit is peeled, flesh is brown beneath the pits
Brown rot	Soft brown patches on the fruit, often starting from a wound while the fruit is still on the tree; later white pimples arranged in concentric rings appear
Cherry leaf scorch (spot)	Leaves develop yellow patches early in spring, leaves wither but fail to drop off branches
Fire blight (canker)	Blossom and leaves have the appearance of having been scorched by fire
Honey fungus (rot)	Toadstools grow on the bark at the base of the tree
Peach-leaf curl	Young leaves curl and twist, later turning brown and dropping prematurely
Powdery mildew	White powdery coating on leaves and young stems
Scab	Olive-green patches on leaves; young fruit are deformed and fall prematurely; older fruit have unsightly cracks in the skin
Silver leaf	Leaves turn an unhealthy silver colour

CANKERS

Canker is a term used to describe a disease caused by fungi or bacteria entering the plant through a dead twig or an open wound in the stem. Although true cankers occur only on woody plants, the term is used also with a number of vegetables where the death of plant tissues causes gnarling of the flesh and eventual rotting. These are really rots and are discussed in that section. Cankers can be the starting point for other organisms to attack the plant, such as toadstools.

APPLE CANKER (*Nectria galligena f. sp. Mali*)

A very destructive disease of the apple tree which in extreme cases can lead to its death. Pears are also affected, but to a lesser extent. As the bark shrinks and cracks, often in the form of concentric rings, it dies and peels away from the affected area. Deep gaping wounds with gnarled edges develop. The loss of bark can continue until a band is formed round the branch. This results in the death of the branch beyond the band as the flow of sap past it is checked. Should this occur on the trunk of the tree the tree will die. Cankers are more common on the older wood.

Prevention. Canker is encouraged by poorly drained, heavy soils, so corrective action is needed in such conditions. Grow resistant varieties.

Treatment. Cankered twigs must be pruned off and on the larger branches the affected area cut out, provided the tree is vigorous and bearing good crops of fruit. If not, it pays to cut off the whole branch. Ensure all cuts are made cleanly with sharp tools to prevent damage to surrounding bark, and paint all cut surfaces with a wood sealer. In severe cases spray with copper just before leaf fall in the autumn and again when the buds start to swell in the spring. A copper wire wound round the canker is said to be an effective control measure.

Should the canker continue to develop it may be necessary to cut down the whole tree, in which case a top graft with an immune variety can be made. All diseased wood must be destroyed.

FIRE BLIGHT (*Erwinia amylovora*)

A very serious disease on apples, pears, hawthorn, cotoneaster, pyracantha, sorbus and a number of other rosaceous trees. On pears the blossom and leaves die, looking as if they have been scorched by a fire, but remain on the tree. Dark green-brown cankerous wounds develop and in warm damp conditions a glistening white slime is exuded from the affected parts. The disease spreads rapidly throughout the

Fire blight (*Erwinia amylovora*) (Holt Studios)

tree, causing the death of the shoots and branches. A mature tree can be killed off completely within a few months. On apple trees there is a golden-brown slime from the affected parts. Quite often the tips of the shoots show the symptoms first.

Other trees affected show similar symptoms but there can be a yellowing of the leaves before the scorched appearance and it may only be the blossom which is affected on pyracantha.

The disease is spread by insects such as bees moving from infected to uninfected trees, and also by rain splashes. It was once a notifiable disease throughout the UK but is now so widespread in the south and midlands that it is notifiable in Cumbria, Northumberland and Scotland only.

Treatment. There is no cure. All infected wood must be cut out. Cut back far enough into the healthy wood to ensure that no diseased tissue remains.

RASPBERRY CANE BLIGHT (*Leptosphaeria coniothyrium*)

A damaging disease of raspberries which attacks the canes at or near ground level. The leaves shrivel and die and dark areas develop on the canes which then wither and die. The canes become brittle and easily broken off at the point of the canker.

Prevention. The infection can start through a wound in the cane caused by the raspberry cane midge, which must be controlled. Spray the newly developing canes with Bordeaux mixture. Do not transplant canes from an infected bed to clean sites. Disinfect secateurs after cutting out the canes to prevent affecting others. Handling canes carefully to avoid damage and giving the disease an entry point is the best prevention.

Treatment. Diseased canes must be cut back to below soil level and destroyed. Do not just break off the infected canes.

ROSE CANKER (*Leptosphaeria coniothyrium*)

The bark on the rose stem or branch cracks and develops gaping wounds, often brown in colour with a reddish-brown edge. These wounds can increase in size until the cracking encircles the affected part. This causes the death of the plant beyond the damage and, if on the main stem, the death of the bush.

Prevention. Remove all dead flowerheads and shoots and prune correctly to avoid leaving shoots that will die back and increase the chances of infection.

Treatment. There is no cure. Cut out and destroy diseased branches, and the entire bush if seriously affected.

SPUR BLIGHT (*Didymella applanata*)

A fungal disease of cane fruit – raspberries, loganberries, blackberries – which although it severely disfigures, very seldom kills the bush. Large purple patches develop on the canes adjacent to a leaf joint which spread to encircle the cane. The bud at the affected leaf fails to grow. In the winter the patch turns a silvery colour and is covered in small black spots (the fungal spores). These spores overwinter to be spread by the wind to new canes in the spring.

Prevention. New canes should be thinned out to allow plenty of air and light into them.

Treatment. All infected canes should be cut out and destroyed. If the disease is persistent, spray with Bordeaux mixture in early spring and then at three fortnightly intervals.

CLUB ROOT (*Plasmodiophora brassicae*)

This is the most serious and persistent disease of the cabbage family. The soil-borne organism invades the roots, causing them to swell rapidly to several times their normal size. The irregular swellings on the roots can look like fingers, giving it the name 'finger and toe disease'. Infected parts of the roots can disintegrate, releasing spores into the soil which can lie dormant for many years: soils which have not grown brassicas for ten years or longer have been found to be still infected. In the advanced stage of the disease the swellings start to rot, with a very unpleasant smell. Seriously affected plants will wilt and die.

The disease on turnips and swedes can be confused with the galls produced by the turnip gall weevil. These are hollow when cut and contain a weevil larva.

Prevention. The spores are less active in alkaline soils and where brassicas are to be grown the soil should be maintained between pH 6·5 and pH 7. Beware of importing the disease by buying plants. The only safe method is to grow your own from seed in sterile compost. Brassicas can be grown in infected soil by trenching out and filling the trench with sterile compost. This will keep the roots away from the infected soil (see page 97).

When harvesting do not leave root stumps in the ground: lift them immediately using a garden fork, making sure all parts of the root are removed. Examine for signs of the disease. It is safer to destroy this root material even though there may be no evidence of attack. Hygiene is important, for boots and tools can spread the spores. If working on infected land these need to be washed in hot soapy water before being used on other parts of the garden.

Avoid growing other brassicas such as wallflowers and the green manure mustard.

Raspberry spur blight (*Didymella applanata*) (*Holt Studios*)

Club root (*Plasmodiophora brassicae*) (*Jim Hay*)

Treatment. There is no cure, and apart from swedes no resistant varieties are available to date. Crop rotation is of little value as a control due to the long dormancy of the spores in the soil.

CROWN GALL (*Agrobacterium tumefaciens*)

A disease which attacks a variety of plants including fruit trees, bush fruits, ornamentals, flowers, trees and shrubs, roses and beetroot. Irregular swellings appear on the plants, quite often at the junction point of the root and the stem. On trees they can be quite large (several feet in diameter) and are usually very hard. On herbaceous plants the galls tend to be soft to the touch and may rot at the end of the season. On beetroot the root develops large rough tumour-like swellings.

Prevention. Avoid wounding by careless use of tools. If cutting out wood always use sharp tools to make a clean cut. Galls can be cut out and destroyed.

Treatment. There is no cure. Affected beetroot should be lifted and destroyed. Dress the contaminated soil with sulphur powder and avoid growing in the same soil for at least three years. Trees and shrubs do not appear to suffer significantly from attack, there being little or no deterioration in their vigour or condition apart from the unsightly swellings.

LEAF CURL (*Taphrina deformans*)

Leaf curl affects a number of trees – oak, alder, cherry, pear, almond – as a minor disease, but is one of the commonest and most serious on peaches and nectarines.

The symptoms first appear as the buds burst in the spring. The young leaves develop reddish,

Peach-leaf curl (*Taphrina deformans*) (*Holt Studios*)

curled patches. As these spread the leaves thicken, become puckered and twisted until they turn brown, die and drop prematurely. Young shoots can be affected and die back. Severe cases will cause defoliation and loss of the crop. If repeatedly attacked the tree will lose vigour and its ability to produce fruit.

The disease is at its worst following a cold wet spring, especially if the tree itself is growing in wet ground in a shaded area which tends to remain cool and damp.

Prevention. In damp areas, which tend to be deficient in the essential minerals, especially the trace minerals, a foliar spray of seaweed extract is beneficial.

Treatment. The best remedy is to spray with Bordeaux mixture at the end of winter or early spring just as the buds start to swell, and repeat in the autumn after the leaves have fallen. If the tree is trained against a wall ensure that the spray penetrates to the wall, as it is in this area that the spores will seek protection.

All affected leaves and twigs should be removed and destroyed as soon as noticed early in the season to prevent the disease developing.

MILDEWS

There are two diseases under this heading, downy mildew and powdery mildew. Although the symptoms are often confused the diseases are totally unrelated. Powdery mildew is the more common but both affect a wide range of vegetables, fruit and herbaceous plants. Some varieties can be attacked by both mildews.

Unlike most parasitic fungi the powdery mildew fungus filaments are external to the host plant, only pushing minute suckers into the sap to extract food. With downy mildew the fungus filaments are found inside the plant. Both do considerable damage.

To the naked eye the general difference is that powdery mildew displays a white powdery coating on the affected plants, whereas downy mildew shows as a yellowing of the leaves with an off-white/grey mould developing on the underside of the leaf. Downy mildew species are particular to one plant, while the same powdery mildew species will attack many varieties. It is also possible to find more than one species of powdery mildew attacking the same host plant.

Prevention. Powdery mildews are more prevalent in a warm dry season, particularly on plants growing in a light soil with insufficient spacing between. Downy mildew is more common in cool, damp, overcrowded conditions. It is related to the potato blight fungus. The spores can overwinter in the soil or remain on infected debris, so good hygiene practices are required to minimize future attacks.

Treatment is generally by cutting out and destroying affected parts. Treat downy mildews with a copper fungicide such as Bordeaux mixture, and powdery mildews with sulphur.

AMERICAN GOOSEBERRY MILDEW (*Sphaerotheca mors-uvae*)

A powdery mildew, this is a serious disease of the gooseberry and in recent years has also severely affected blackcurrants.

A white powdery mould growth appears on the young shoots, starting about mid-spring, quickly spreading to cover all the new growth and the developing fruit. The coating becomes denser and later in the season turns to a brown felt-like covering containing small black dot-like bodies which remain over the winter period. The plant's growth is checked and the fruit is deformed and tasteless.

Blackcurrants develop identical symptoms. However, the leaves are more severely affected and the symptoms do not usually show until late spring.

Prevention. Avoid establishing a fruit bed in damp shady conditions. Plant bushes at the recommended spacings. Correct pruning should be carried out to allow the circulation of air through the bush and keep the base clear of weeds. There is a link between the disease and the excess use of nitrogen fertilizers which produce lush, soft growth, so use the well-balanced seaweed organic fertilizers. Preventive action can be taken by treating gooseberries with sulphur just before the flowers open, and again when the fruit has set; repeat fortnightly up to four weeks before harvesting. Some gooseberry cultivars can be damaged by sulphur, in which case use a washing soda solution (1½ oz/40 gm household washing soda to 4 pts/2 l of water) at the same times as the sulphur applications.

On blackcurrants start treatment as the flowers open, repeating every two weeks until mid-summer.

Treatment. Any affected shoots must be cut out in the early autumn and destroyed.

APPLE POWDERY MILDEW (*Phodosphaera leucotricha*)

A very serious disease attacking the leaves, shoots and flowerbuds causing severe damage. The fungus overwinters in dormant buds which on opening in the spring release the disease to affect new growth. A white powdery coating appears on the leaves, spreading first to the shoots, then the

American gooseberry mildew (*Sphaerotheca mors-uvae*). TOP: early stage; ABOVE: late stage (*Holt Studios*)

flowers. The blossom withers and drops off. The symptoms spread rapidly to all parts of the tree. The leaves curl up and fall prematurely but a few are left at the growing tips of the branch.

Prevention. The disease is widespread in poor soils lacking in organic matter and basic food nutrients. Prevention is undertaken by building up the soil to an organically rich fertile condition.

Treatment. Once trees are affected the disease can be contained by pruning. All infected shoots are cut out in the autumn at a point well below the signs of the mildew. In the spring any buds showing traces of mildew must be removed, taking care not to disturb the powdery mould and so contaminate unaffected parts. Affected buds are distorted, usually thin and pointed. All infected parts must be destroyed.

Powdery mildew (*Sphaerotheca fuliginea*), common to cucurbits (*Holt Studios*)

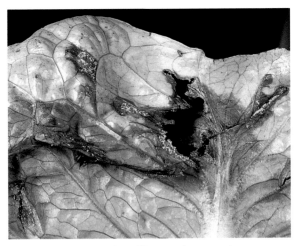

Lettuce downy mildew (*Bremia lactucae*) (*Holt Studios*)

If pruning fails to contain further development of the disease, treat with sulphur immediately the blossom has fallen and repeat at two-week intervals until mid-summer. Some varieties are damaged by sulphur, so check before applying. Bordeaux mixture can be used but again some varieties are susceptible to copper, so check.

BRASSICA MILDEW (*Peronospora parasitica*)

A very damaging downy mildew disease, attacking both seedlings and the mature crops. It is worst on seedlings raised in cool damp weather – the seedlings may be killed. On older plants spots appear on the upperside of the leaves which turn the leaves yellow, with a white fluffy mould growth on the underside. If mature heads of cabbage are affected purplish spots can appear with or without the mould and the head rots. Cauliflower curds can also be affected.

Prevention. The disease is at its worst in cold wet weather when the plants are slow-growing. The crops must not be planted out too early in the season when the growing conditions do not promote steady healthy growth. Do not leave decaying debris around the base of plants, as this can host the spores. Grow resistant varieties.

Treatment. Remove and destroy infected plants and spray with Bordeaux mixture to prevent the disease spreading through the crop.

CUCUMBER MILDEW (*Sphaerotheca fuliginea*)

Occurring on both outdoor and greenhouse varieties, this powdery mildew can cause serious losses. The leaves and stems are covered in a white powdery growth, particularly in the autumn. The first symptoms are small white spots which become powdery as they grow. In severe cases premature leaf fall can occur.

Prevention. The disease is encouraged by growing in dry soil in moist, cool conditions. The soil must be watered to keep it moist. Under glass, ensure that there is adequate ventilation, particularly around the base of the plants. Grow mildew-resistant varieties.

Treatment. A cautious application of sulphur can be used to contain the disease if it is applied immediately the first signs are noticed and repeated every seven to ten days. Many varieties are susceptible to sulphur, so preventive methods should be adopted throughout the growing season.

LETTUCE DOWNY MILDEW (*Bremia lactucae*)

The disease attacks lettuce outdoors, in frames or the greenhouse, seedlings in the spring and mature plants later in the season. The leaves develop pale green spots on the upper side, with the off-white mould on the underside opposite the spots. Later the affected areas turn brown and die off. Grey mould rot can develop which leads to the eventual death of the plant. When conditions favour the disease it spreads rapidly through the crop.

Prevention. The disease is most serious in cool damp weather outdoors and low temperatures with cold, wet soil in frames and greenhouses. Crowding plants too closely together also aids the spread of the fungus. Water the beds well before planting out, to minimize having to water during the growing season. If further watering is required avoid wetting the leaves. Do not water in the late evening; it is better early in the morning. Under glass ensure that there is adequate ventilation. Adopt good hygiene practices, not leaving decaying leaves lying on the soil surface. Practise crop rotation to avoid growing lettuce in the same bed for at least two years. Grow resistant varieties if the disease persists.

ONION DOWNY MILDEW (*Peronospora destructor*)

A common disease appearing in early summer as a yellowing of the leaves which develop a greyish-white mould and start to die from the tip downwards. The bulb fails to mature. In damp weather the disease spreads rapidly and the greyish-white mould can turn purple on the dying leaves. The disease travels down the stem into the bulb, which turns soft when stored. Often a mould growth appears around the neck which can be mistaken for neck rot. The disease is particularly severe in wet seasons when onions are grown in wet or poorly drained land.

Prevention. Good hygiene is needed, keeping the bed free from weeds and decaying debris. Do not leave onion debris on the bed once the crop has been lifted. Autumn-sown onions often start the disease; this crop must be avoided if mildew is a persistent problem. Grow resistant varieties.

Treatment. Once plants are affected control is difficult. Spraying the crop with Bordeaux mixture as soon as the first signs are seen and repeating every two weeks may help to prevent it spreading, but this is not always successful. Remove and destroy all affected plants as soon as possible. Do not grow onions in the same soil for at least five years.

PEA MILDEW (*Erysiphe pisi, Peronospora viciae*)

The pea can be attacked by both downy and powdery mildew. The downy type shows as a yellowing of the leaves with white/pale blue mould on the leaves and haulm. If young plants are affected growth is stunted. Infected pods are distorted, with brown blotches. The disease is common in cold wet weather. Powdery mildew shows as white powdery mould on both sides of the leaves, with white patches on the pods. In severe attacks the plants will wilt and die.

Prevention. This disease is more common on late crops grown in a dry season on light soils. Building up the soil fertility with mulches of organic matter will help to keep the plants growing at a steady rate and keep the soil moist in dry weather. Rotation of the crop is essential.

Treatment. Once the first signs appear dust the plants with sulphur while the dew is still on the leaves. If this fails to contain the spread, spraying with Bordeaux mixture can be tried. All infected haulms must be collected and destroyed once the crop has been harvested.

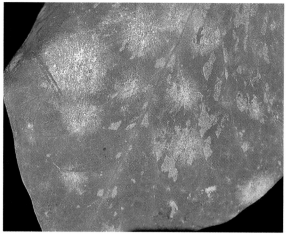

Pea powdery mildew (*Erysiphe pisi*) (*Holt Studios*)

Pea downy mildew (*Peronospora viciae*) (*Holt Studios*)

ROCK PLANT MILDEW (*Oidium et al.*)

Although each variety may have its own species of mildew, in general the symptoms and treatment are similar. A white powdery coating develops on the leaves, stems and flower parts. The leaves may discolour, often turning a pale yellow, or die and the plant may lose vigour and show signs of wilting.

Prevention. Growing under the optimum conditions of a rich organic soil and not allowing the plants to dry out in hot weather, together with good cultural practices, will in most cases offer resistance to attack. Grow resistant varieties.

Treatment. Once the first signs show a spraying of an organically acceptable fungicide will help to contain and prevent spreading of the spores. In severe cases the affected areas should be cut out and destroyed.

ROTS

Rots are the commonest disease in the garden. A part of the plant, which can be either above or below ground, decays; in the case of storage-related rots, this is after the crop has been harvested and stored. This means the symptoms are not necessarily seen during the growing period; it may take several weeks after harvesting before the indications show.

Rots are often divided into fruit and vegetable rot, stem and leaf rot, and foot and root rot, depending upon the part of the plant infected. Sometimes the difference between them is difficult to distinguish, for it can be the same organism which causes more than one rot. All have the same result, the devastation of the plants and the loss of stored produce.

Prevention. The fungi and bacteria which cause the rots can be airborne or soil-borne. In some cases a wound is needed for the disease to enter so care is required in handling plants, particularly young seedlings. This aspect is also important when crops are harvested for storing to ensure that 'storage' rots are not given any opportunity to enter via mechanical damage due to careless handling.

In the greenhouse environmental conditions play an important role in the prevention of rot diseases. Humidity and temperature must be regulated by ventilation, not draughts which can stress the plants making them even more vulnerable to attack.

Rots are also closely linked with lack of good hygiene practice. Do not leave vegetable debris around the plant stems.

Treatment. In general terms there is no cure once the disease is present. Remove and destroy diseased parts promptly before they have time to affect adjacent plants.

BACTERIAL SOFT ROT (*Erwinia carotovora*)

A very common disease in the garden on ornamentals and widespread on vegetables both in the garden and in storage. The first sign is a watery stain which grows rapidly, and the infected areas turn to a slimy brown mess, usually accompanied by an offensive smell. Vegetables in store may rot while the skin remains intact. It usually follows bruising or injury when being harvested as the result of damage by insects or slugs.

Prevention. As moisture is essential for the disease to invade, it is more active in wet, poorly drained soils. In storage, high humidity will

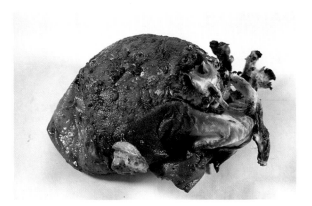

Bacterial soft rot (*Erwinia carotovora*) (*Holt Studios*)

encourage rapid spread of the disease. If caught at an early stage, roots in storage may be saved by keeping them in a dry atmosphere, for the rot may dry up and its spread be checked.

The disease is also linked with an over-application of farmyard manures on wet soils and a potassium deficiency in the soil. Correct any deficiency and avoid over-application of nitrogen – use the balanced organic fertilizers. Examine root crops being lifted for storing and remove any which are damaged. Lay these aside for immediate use. Check stores regularly, with both eyes and nose. Remove any signs of rot. Do not compost rotted material.

Treatment. There is no cure once the disease has invaded.

BITTER PIT (*Glomerella cingulata, Pezicula alba, P. malicorticis*)

This is a common disease on apples and is occasionally found on pears. It can develop while the fruit is still on the tree but more often while it is in storage. Round, dark depressions appear on the skin, and underneath each depression or 'pit' the flesh turns brown. There can also be brown spots scattered throughout the flesh. These spots are bitter-tasting, making the fruit inedible. The depressions may develop pink pimples. Cherries can also be attacked, but only the pimple symptoms occur.

Prevention. The real cause is unknown, but there is a suspected link with over-pruning on certain varieties. However, the disease is more troublesome when there has been dry weather during the growing season and is more common on soils which dry out rapidly. It is also linked with calcium-deficient soils. These factors can be corrected by the application of ground limestone or dolomite, regular mulching with organic matter to improve the moisture-retentive ability of the soil and watering the trees in dry weather. Examination of fruit in store at frequent intervals is important.

Treatment. There is no cure; any infected fruit must be removed and destroyed.

BLOSSOM END ROT

A tomato disease which can cause considerable loss of crop. Only the fruits are attacked, always starting at the end of the truss furthest from the stem. A small black spot appears at the bottom of the fruit at the point where the flower was attached. As the fruit swells the spot grows in size into a hard blackish patch which is slightly sunken, giving the fruit a flat bottom. This hard patch can extend well into the flesh, making the fruit inedible. The disease can be troublesome if tomatoes are being grown in peat-based growbags.

Prevention. The disease is caused by allowing the soil to dry out during the period when the fruits are swelling, coupled with a soil calcium deficiency. Good watering techniques are essential. Water regularly, applying sufficient water to keep the soil moist enough to ensure good steady growth. Do not overwater then allow the soil to dry out before watering again. Apply ground limestone or dolomite to correct calcium deficiency and check calcium is not 'locked up' in the soil by the over-application of other fertilizers.

Treatment. There is no cure, and all affected fruit must be removed, not only to prevent secondary infective penetration through the rot but also to allow the plant to channel its energy into the unaffected fruit.

BROWN ROT (*Sclerotinia fructigena, S. laxa*)

A very serious and common disease affecting apples, pears, plums, cherries and peaches, both while the fruit is on the tree and in store. Soft brown patches develop on the flesh, often starting at a wound, spreading rapidly through the fruit. Later off-white coloured mould pimples develop, arranged in a series of concentric rings around the fruit. If still on the tree the fruits will shrivel into a mummified state and remain on the tree throughout the winter. Shoots supporting the fruit can become affected, the bark withers and the shoot dies.

The fungi can overwinter on the mummified fruit to start the disease the following season. Spores on affected fruit will spread rapidly, either by rain splashes, wind or insects.

Prevention. Mummified fruit must be removed from the tree and any diseased wood cut out well below the infected area. Seal the cuts with a wound sealer. Do not store any suspect fruit; avoid damaging fruit when harvesting and preparing for storage. Examine fruit in store regularly and remove any showing signs of rotting. Some varieties are less susceptible than others. Protect fruit on the tree from damage, either accidental or by insect and animal attack. Keep the tree free from pests. The disease can also be transmitted via hands, so wash them thoroughly after harvesting affected fruits.

Treatment. There is no cure; all affected fruit must be collected and destroyed.

CHRYSANTHEMUM PETAL BLIGHT (*Itersonilia Perplexans*)

Common on chrysanthemums in the greenhouse or under cover outside. This disease shows as small brownish spots on the petals, spreading rapidly until the petal turns brown. Eventually the whole bloom is affected. First appearing in the autumn, the effects are at their worst by mid-season, especially if the weather is mild and damp and there are extremes in temperature between day and night.

Prevention. Keep the greenhouse well ventilated and apply a little heat at night if extreme day/night temperatures are likely. At the first showing of colour on the flowerhead spray with Bordeaux mixture and repeat at fortnightly intervals.

Blossom end rot (*Jim Hay*)

Brown rot (*Sclerotinia fructigena*) (*Natural Image*)

Treatment. There is no cure. All affected petals must be removed at the first sign of attack. Severely affected blooms must also be removed.

CROWN ROT (*Erwinia rhapontici*)

Affecting rhubarb, the leaves become discoloured, the terminal bud and the tissues just beneath the crown develop a soft brown rot and the crown itself begins to decay. The sticks are thin and spindly, discoloured and may also show signs of rot. This disease is widespread.
Prevention. As it is often caused by wet soils, plant new roots in a fresh, well-drained area.

Treatment. Affected crowns must be lifted and destroyed.

DAMPING OFF (*Pythium spp.*)

A very destructive disease which is the commonest cause of death of seedlings. Though most frequently found in the greenhouse it can also be troublesome outside. It is caused by fungi which persist in the soil and germinate when the conditions are right. The plants are attacked at soil level and can show various symptoms before they

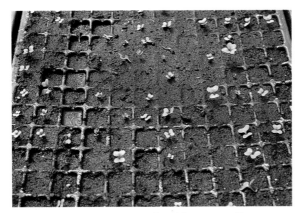

Damping off (*Pythium spp.*), cabbage seedlings (*Holt Studios*)

Damping off (*Pythium spp.*), young peas (*Holt Studios*)

wilt and die. There can be yellow, unhealthy-looking deformed leaves; thinning of the stems, which turn brown and become hard; the stems can be blackened and show signs of rotting; sometimes the root may rot, leaving only a blackened stump. A grey mould may also appear, which is caused by botrytis. In all cases the plant will fall over at soil level as if attacked by cutworm.

Prevention. The disease spreads rapidly in damp, stuffy conditions and in wet, dull weather, and is the result of neglect and bad cultural practices, overcrowding of the plants, growing in damp, shady situations, bad watering and poor ventilation in the greenhouse.

Preventive procedures must be adopted. Sow the seed thinly on the ground or germinate in pots and prick out with adequate space between seedlings. Use clean compost for seed-sowing and potting on. Give the maximum of light and sunshine, with adequate ventilation in the greenhouse, and adopt good hygiene by washing all pots and trays at the end of the season. Do not over-water plants in dull weather, particularly those in the greenhouse which are susceptible to the disease, such as lettuce. Do not handle young seedlings by their stem – the pressure of the fingers is sufficient to damage the stem tissue and give an entry point for the disease. Always handle by the seed leaves.

Treatment. At the first signs remove affected plants and the soil around the roots to reduce the chance of neighbouring plants being infected.

GREY MOULD ROT (*Botrytis cinerea*)

A very common and destructive disease affecting all plants. The symptoms vary from plant to plant, but generally there is a grey mould stage associated with rotting of affected parts. It is often simply referred to as botrytis. It is common in the greenhouse, affecting the vegetable and fruit crops as well as many pot plants. It will attack plants from the early seedling stage through to maturity. At the seedling stage it is closely linked with damping-off disease. The first signs are associated with the characteristic fluffy grey mould. Quite often there are watery patches on the stems, leaves and side shoots, and on pot plants brown spots appear on the flower petals just before the mould shows. If disturbed, clouds of the grey spores are released into the air. In the later stages rot sets in.

It is probably the most common of the tomato and cucumber diseases, starting at a wound caused by mechanical damage or the careless removal of side shoots or leaves. There is the secondary feature of 'ghost spots' on the fruit, which is discussed on page 286. Planting cucumbers too deep will increase the chance of attack. On lettuce the young seedling leaves show watery patches, turning into a brown rot which

Grey mould rot (Botrytis cinerea), tomato plant (Holt Studios)

Grey mould rot (Botrytis cinerea) on cucmber (Jim Hay)

rapidly spreads until the whole plant collapses. Older plants show a red-brown rotting at the base of the stem and on the leaves which progresses through the plant. The stem can rot off completely, severing the head from the root. This is a particularly bad disease on the cold greenhouse winter varieties of lettuce. Strawberries are particularly susceptible, the fluffy grey mould appearing in the fruit and flowers and turning into a soft brown rot.

Brown spots appear on the petals of roses, followed by rotting of the blooms when the weather is damp and humid. Herbaceous plants and shrubs also produce spots on the leaves which turn to rot, or the rot and the grey mould of the disease can start immediately. Other plants especially affected are azaleas (grey mould/ flower rot), begonias (grey mould/rot on leaves, stem and flowers), cyclamen (spots on the flowers), fuchsias, hydrangeas, pelargoniums (rotting of the flowers), carnations (rotting of the stem, leaves and flowerheads; cuttings can also be affected). Bulbs can also be attacked, when it shows as a brown or black rot.

Prevention. Preventive measures are the only control. Hygiene is important, for the spores can rest on decaying debris ready to germinate when the right conditions prevail. The disease is also spread by the winds. Usually a wound is needed for entry, so it is important not to damage the plants by careless handling or when working around the base of plants with tools. Do not

handle seedlings by their stem. The disease is encouraged by damp, cool conditions and is at its worst outdoors in the autumn. In the greenhouse the worst period is the winter and early spring. Ensure that there is always adequate ventilation and avoid planting too closely. Do not over-water and make the soil sodden. Apply only enough water to keep it moist, even if it means not watering for long periods over the winter, but do not allow the plants to wilt. Avoid checks in the growth of the plants resulting from planting out when the conditions are against a good steady growth. Using Bordeaux mixture or sulphur will help to prevent the spread of the disease to unaffected plants. A resistant variety of strawberry is available (see page 169).

Treatment. There is no cure once affected. At the first signs remove infected parts or in severe cases the whole plant, taking care not to disturb the spores which can be carried on the air to infect adjacent plants.

HONEY FUNGUS (*Armillaria mellea*)

An extremely serious 'disease of woody plants. Honey-coloured toadstools appear in the autumn on stems, trunks of trees or root stumps. The affected wood can develop a brown rot which turns into a white stringy form. The toadstools are killed off by the frost but the disease lives on in the roots as a mass of black bootlace-like strings. This root damage can leave the plants open to attack from other diseases.

Prevention. The disease can be transmitted by

Honey fungus (*Armillaria mellea*) (*Natural Image*)

root contact, so do not plant too close together. There are trees and shrubs which show resistance to the disease.

Treatment. The entire plant, with as much of the roots as possible, should be removed from the site. No woody plant should be replanted for at least a year.

ONION NECK ROT (*Botrytis allii*)

Probably the commonest disease among onions, it only appears after the bulbs have been in store for several weeks. It attacks shallots and garlic but to a much lesser extent. As the name implies it is a rotting of the neck, first showing as a softening, and when the outer skin is removed there is a grey mould rot. This rot spreads rapidly through the flesh.

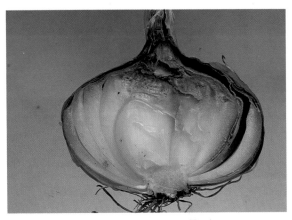

Onion neck rot (*Botrytis allii*) (*Jim Hay*)

Research work has shown that the extent of neck rot is proportional to the amount of rainfall in late summer, the period when the onions are being dried off for storing. Only those with dry, ripened necks should be stored, and kept in a cool, airy place. The disease can be spread by the seed. Much conventional seed is treated against the disease, whereas organically raised seed is not. Bulbs with a thick fleshy stem are more susceptible, so it is essential to ensure that the bulbs are well ripened before putting them into store.

Prevention. If the disease is persistent grow a coloured variety such as 'Southport Red Globe' (it has been found that coloured varieties are less susceptible than white-fleshed ones), or grow from sets. Rotate the crop on a three- to four-year cycle.

Treatment. None.

ONION WHITE ROT (*Sclerotium cepivorum*)

A very destructive disease of the growing bulb, affecting leeks, garlic and shallots as well as the onion. It can persist in the soil for many years. Both young and old bulbs are attacked. The leaves turn yellow and die back and in the seedling stage the plant falls over as the roots decay. There is a white fluffy mould around the root area. The fungus later produces small black fruiting bodies which live on in the soil to reproduce. Once a plant is infected the disease can spread along the row by root contact or the fungus moving through the soil.

Prevention. Once the soil is infected it takes many years to die out. Take care when lifting diseased bulbs not to spread infected soil to other parts of the garden. Do not grow any of the onion family on the bed for at least eight years. Prevent the build-up of the disease by rotating the crop. Do not compost any affected bulbs.

It is possible to grow in infected soil by using the 'compost trench' method. Dig out a trench and fill it with compost. Grow the onions in the compost to ensure that the roots do not come in contact with the soil.

POTATO BLACK LEG (*Erwinia carotovora var. atroseptica*)

A very common disease transmitted by planting diseased seed potatoes. It shows early in the season, starting in early summer, and usually only one or two plants are affected. The symptoms first show on the upper foliage which curls inwards, the leaves turning a yellow-green colour; the growth of the plant is stunted. The stem turns black just above soil level and begins to rot, but not all the stems on a plant are affected. Although rotting tubers may be found

Potato black leg (*Erwinia carotovora var. atroseptica*) (*Jim Hay*)

on affected plants, they may also produce healthy-looking tubers which in fact contain disease bacteria.

Prevention. Any tubers from affected plants must not be put into store, as they will infect clean tubers and cause them to rot. Tubers rotting in the soil leave the infection there for the next season.

It is better to use only certified seed potatoes. Keep seed in a well-ventilated place until planted out. Avoid damaging the tubers when harvesting and leave them on the surface for an hour or two to dry the skins before bagging.

Treatment. All infected plants must be lifted along with any tubers and destroyed. Ensure that there are no small tubers left in the soil.

POTATO AND TOMATO BLIGHT (*Phytophthora infestans*)

The same fungus causes both diseases and in the case of tomatoes both indoor and outdoor crops can be infected. It is the most serious of the potato diseases: a severe attack can destroy the whole crop. Dark green patches appear on the leaves, starting at the edge and spreading to cover the whole leaf. The lower leaves may be affected first. In damp conditions a white mould appears on the underside of the leaf. The wind and rain spread the disease spores to the stem and other parts of the plants as well as on to neighbouring foliage. The stems die off and rot. The rain washes the spores into the soil to infect the tubers, which develop brownish sunken patches that can grow to cover them entirely. The flesh inside is brown and decaying.

Indoor tomato crops can be infected if the potato crop is grown close by, usually between late summer and mid-autumn. Outdoor crops are affected as the spores are transmitted from the potatoes. Although the symptoms on the leaves are similar, tomatoes are not so severely affected. Brownish streaks appear on the stem, spots develop on the green fruits, which are often hard,

and as they ripen rots develop and the fruits decay. Apparently healthy fruit may develop the symptoms a few days after being picked.

The disease is spread by bad cultural practices, allowing infected tubers to decay in the soil or putting them into storage, and not destroying infected foliage. It often starts on the early crops, but as these are lifted before the main symptoms appear the disease may be missed until it shows on the main crop.

Prevention. It is very important to take immediate action to prevent the spread of the disease to the tubers and unaffected plants. Both upper and lower surfaces of the leaves must be sprayed with Bordeaux mixture at two-week intervals. If the disease has been troublesome in the past, as a precautionary measure spray the crop with Bordeaux mixture, starting in mid-summer before any symptoms appear. Again, spray both sides of the leaves every two weeks. Keep the rows well earthed up to prevent the spores contacting the tubers; do not lift any tubers for at least two weeks

Potato blight (*Phytophthora infestans*) (*Holt Studios*)

Tomato blight (*Phytophthora infestans*) (*Holt Studios*)

after the foliage has been cut off, to allow time for the spores to be washed off the furrows. Make sure no chits (small tubers) are left in the soil when harvesting the crop. Check all tubers lifted and do not store any suspected of being diseased.

There are varieties which show resistance to the disease.

Treatment. There is no cure once infected. If the disease continues to spread the foliage must be cut off and destroyed.

POTATO DRY ROT (*Fusarium spp.*)

A serious disease which shows only when the potatoes have been in storage for some time. Small, dark brown, sunken areas appear on the skin. When stored under dry conditions such as if bagged and kept in a shed, the sunken areas rapidly grow with white, blue or pinkish mould pimples developing on the skin. When the tubers are cut the flesh is brown under the sunken areas. Eventually the tuber dries up and shrivels.

When stored under a clamp the shrivelling of the tuber is not so severe and the dried-up stage is replaced by the flesh developing a soft wet rot which turns the tubers into a slimy mess.

Prevention. The infection penetrates the tuber through a wound, so care is needed when lifting the crop not to damage the tubers. Keep clamps cool and well ventilated. Grow resistant varieties.

Treatment. There is no cure once the disease has infected the tuber, so do not store any damaged tubers and at the first signs of any in store showing infection remove and destroy.

SCLEROTINIA ROT (*Sclerotinia sclerotiorum*)

This affects carrots in store. The roots turn soft, rot and develop a white fluffy mould. The disease can occasionally attack the growing crop, with the lower part of the leaves and the top of the root turning black. Any affected must be lifted and destroyed and those in store checked regularly for the symptoms.

The disease also attacks beans, cucumbers and the cabbage family, affecting the stem starting just above soil level. A brown rot develops along with a white fluffy mould (similar to grey mould). The flow of sap up the plant is restricted, the plant wilts and collapses and the crop is lost. With cauliflower the rot of the curd may not appear until after it has been cropped and kept for a few days.

Prevention. Keep weeds down at the base of growing plants. Store roots in a dry, airy place and do not grow susceptible crops in infected land for at least two years. Work on a three-year crop rotation cycle.

Treatment. There is no cure. Remove infected plants immediately the symptoms appear.

STEM AND ROOT ROTS (*Botrytis spp.*)

The symptoms and fungi that cause disease on both the stems and roots of plants are probably among the commonest in the garden. They are caused by a wide range of fungi, and the symptoms can be so similar that without expert examination it is not always possible to identify the correct cause. However, the end result is usually the same – the death of the plant. As the names imply, stem rots occur above the soil, whereas root rots affect the plants below the soil level. There are diseases which affect the plant both above and below the soil, and these are often referred to as 'foot' rots.

Some of the rots discussed under other headings are themselves stem and root rots, such as damping off or potato black leg. These have been identified as serious enough to merit individual treatment.

In all cases, once the basic lifeline of the plant is infected the life and success of the plant are

Potato dry rot (*Fusarium solani*) (*Holt Studios*)

Sclerotinia rot (*Sclerotinia sclerotiorum*) (*Holt Studios*)

Root rot (*Fusarium solani* sp. *viciae*) *(Holt Studios)*

limited, as the roots and stem are needed to enable it to feed and hold itself in position.

Beans. The foliage turns yellow and dies, starting at the bottom of the plant and progressing to the top. The stem turns brown at its base and shrivels.

Cucumber. Pale green spots later turning brown on the leaves, soft grey/green mould at the flower end of the fruit or rotting of the stem and roots. The plant wilts and dies.

Tomato. Collapse of seedlings or young plants at soil level. The roots may have rotted away or the plants look unhealthy and wilt in warm weather. The lower leaves yellow and wither, the base of the stem rots, the roots have rotted away. On older plants, there is black or grey rot at the base which travels up the stem. There may be black scars at the flower point on the fruit.

Other plants which can be severely affected are aster, begonia, cacti, calceolaria, chrysanthemum, gloxinia, pelargonium, primula, poinsettia.

Prevention. Always ensure healthy plants are grown in clean soil. With greenhouse crops remove the plant supports and destroy them. Wash down the glass and framework thoroughly. Check plants regularly during the season, taking care not to damage any, since a wound is the point of entry, as with many of the rot diseases. Remove all debris. Keep the house adequately ventilated, do not over-water and maintain the

border in a healthy fertile condition. Watering the roots with Bordeaux mixture will contain the disease to a limited level but if the attack is severe the border soil must be changed.

Hygiene is important outdoors. Remove all infected plants immediately – do not leave them to decay and infect neighbours. Maintain the soil fertility with the application of organic matter and well-balanced organic fertilizers. Crop rotation must be employed to prevent the build-up of the fungi in the soil.

Treatment. All infected plants must be lifted and destroyed. Do not replant in the same soil for at least two years – essential in the case of beans.

STRAWBERRY RED CORE (*Phytophthora fragariae*)

This serious and persistent soil-borne disease shows in late spring/early summer: plants are stunted with the outer leaves brown and hard and an inner cluster of small reddish leaves. When lifted in the winter the roots are dark brown or black in colour; the outer tissue is easily peeled off leaving a red core. In the summer this core is not easily seen and the disease can be confused with other root rots.

Prevention. Prevent by crop rotation. A strawberry bed should be cropped for no more than three years, when the plants should be lifted and a new bed made in a different area using potted-on runners from healthy plants or new crowns from a reputable source. The disease spreads easily to healthy crowns in wet soil. Ensure that the bed is well drained and not liable to waterlogging. The disease can also be spread by transplanting infected crowns, as well as by transferring contaminated soil on tools and footwear.

Treatment. The disease can be dormant in the

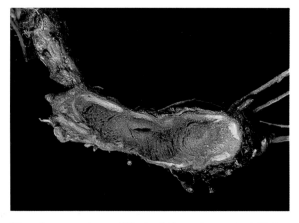

Strawberry red core (*Phytophthora fragariae*) *(Holt Studios)*

soil for up to twelve years, so it is difficult to eradicate once the land is contaminated. In Britain it is a notifiable disease: by law the Ministry of Agriculture, Fisheries and Food must be notified of its presence.

TOMATO LEAF MOULD (*Fulvia fulva syn. Cladosporum fulvum*)

Common on tomatoes grown under glass, but rare on the outdoor crop. Although the disease can appear from mid-spring onwards, in the majority of cases it does not show until early or mid-summer. Yellow patches develop on the upper surface of the leaves while correspondingly on the underside there is a brown velvety mould growth. This mould can occur on the upper surface as well. Later the yellow patches turn a reddish brown and the mould may turn purple. The leaves wither and die but do not always fall. The lower leaves are attacked initially, the disease spreading up the plant. Growth is checked, with a poor yield. Occasionally the flowers and fruit can also show the mould growth. This disease can spread rapidly through the greenhouse.

Prevention. Avoid humid conditions in the greenhouse by ensuring adequate ventilation, particularly at the base of the plants. The removal of the lower leaves if the foliage becomes too dense will help to keep the air circulating at the base. Do not plant out too closely. Spraying with Bordeaux mixture will act as a preventive if the weather is humid and there are extreme day/night temperatures. Immediately the first signs are seen, remove and destroy all affected leaves and dust the remaining ones with fine sulphur powder. In the case of a severe attack encourage one or two side shoots to grow to produce enough foliage to develop fully and ripen the fruit. Do not leave decaying debris at the base of the plants. If leaf mould is a persistent problem burn sulphur in the greenhouse before the old tomato plants have been removed, but empty the house of all other plants before doing so. Grow resistant varieties.

Treatment. Once affected, there is no cure.

VIOLET ROOT ROT (caused by *Helicobasidium purpureum*)

Seriously affecting asparagus, this disease can also attack beetroot, carrots, parsnips, potatoes, swedes, turnips as well as many ornamentals. The symptoms are similar for most plants. The growth is stunted, the leaves turn yellow and die while the roots are covered with a purple thread-like mould. The disease is most severe in acid soils and when the weather is cold.

Prevention. Prevention is helped by keeping the soil healthy and fertile by the application of ample organic matter and well-balanced organic fertilizers. Maintain the soil in a neutral state by dressing with ground limestone or dolomite. Keep the beds free from weeds, in particular docks and dandelions which are also prone to attack. There are resistant varieties of carrots.

To protect healthy asparagus crowns, tubes made from a stiff waterproof material, such as plastic sheet, are placed over the crown and pushed into the soil to about a spade depth. This prevents the spread of the disease to the unaffected plants.

Treatment. Once the symptoms appear, lift and destroy all affected plants. Take care not to spread infected soil to other parts of the garden. In severe cases a new bed must be made for asparagus and the old bed used for the brassicas and legume families. Do not store roots affected with the disease.

As the fungus is soil-borne, root crops should not be grown in affected soil for at least three to four years.

RUST (*Puchinia*)

Rust is a general name to cover a number of fungal diseases all producing the same symptoms, rust-coloured spots on the underside of leaves, often accompanied by pale yellow spots on the upper surface. Severe attacks can cover the whole leaf area, causing the premature death of the leaves. Stems can show spots or streaks while flowers can be distorted or fail to develop.

Prevention. There is a link with excessive nitrogen and a potash deficiency in the soil. Spray with Bordeaux mixture and repeat two or three weeks later. Do not leave diseased leaves at the base of plants or leave plants to overwinter in the ground. Control weeds, especially groundsel, as they are host to the disease. Grow resistant varieties. Plants susceptible to rust are:

Antirrhinum. Do not overwinter in the ground; do not grow in the same ground for at least two years.

Asparagus. Do not grow in wet soils; cut out shoots at first sign of rust; do not leave decaying debris on the bed. Dust with sulphur after the crop has been harvested.

Carnation. More severe on greenhouse varieties. Maintain adequate ventilation to prevent the humidity rising to high levels.

Rose rust (*Phragmidium mucronatum*) (Holt Studios)

Apple scab (*Venturia inaequalis*) (Jim Hay)

Avoid splashing the leaves when watering to prevent spreading spores from affected plants. Take cuttings from healthy plants only.

Chrysanthemum   More common under glass. Reduce humidity by increased ventilation. Take cuttings from healthy plants only. Immerse roots in hot water at 115°F (46°C) for ten minutes to check the disease.

Leek.   Can also affect other members of the allium family. Adopt crop rotation of at least four years.

Mint.   Replant in clean soil. Hot-water treatment as for chrysanthemums will check the disease.
Plum.   Can also affect peaches, nectarines and apricots. Not a serious disease – linked with rust on anemones.

Rock plants.   Keep the beds free from rust host weeds such as groundsel.

Rose.   Destroy winter prunings, as disease hibernates on twigs over winter. Beware of Bordeaux mixture disfiguring certain varieties.

Treatment (for all types).   None; affected parts must be removed and destroyed at the first sign of the disease.

SCAB

Scab is the name given to the dry, hard, crust-like growths on the skins of root vegetables and cracked patches on the skins of fruit. It is caused by various species of fungi.

APPLE AND PEAR SCAB (*Venturia inaequalis, V. pirina*)

Although the scabs are different species of fungi the symptoms and control are very similar in each case. With pears the fruit is often affected before the leaves and the damage to the fruit is more severe.

Olive green blotches appear in the spring on the leaves, which turn grey in the centre and develop rough dry scabs. The blotches spread to cover the leaf, which dies prematurely. As the disease spreads to the fruits they show small dark patches which later turn hard. As the fruit swells this area is unable to expand and the skin forms unsightly cracks. The flesh is undamaged. Young fruit can fail to mature and fall prematurely. Young shoots can also be attacked, which can lead to them becoming infected with canker bacteria.

The disease overwinters on fallen debris at the base of the tree and young wood just below the bark, producing rough blisters on the bark. It is encouraged by growing on poorly drained soils, the excessive use of nitrogen fertilizers and cold, wet weather at blossom time. It is worst in wet summers.

Prevention.   Improve the soil conditions by laying drains if necessary and use only balanced organic fertilizers. No variety is immune, but some are more susceptible than others.

Treatment.   Collect all diseased fruit and fallen debris from the base of the tree and cut out all diseased wood. All these should be destroyed by burning. Spray the tree with Bordeaux mixture just before flowering (at the green bud stage), at the pink bud stage, soon after petal fall and again four weeks later. If the wood is affected continue to spray every four weeks until the crop is harvested.

Bordeaux mixture can cause 'russeting' on the more delicate apple varieties, in which case a sulphur-based fungicide should be used. However, there are a number of varieties which dislike sulphur, and these should not be sprayed after the blossom has developed.

Common scab (*Streptomyces scabies*) (*Jim Hay*)

Powdery scab (*Sponogospora subterranea*) (*Jim Hay*)

COMMON SCAB (*Streptomyces scabies*)

This is a very common disease on potatoes, but is also found on beetroot, radishes and swedes. Although it is not serious in that it does not affect the yield or flavour, it is unsightly and, on potatoes, causes considerable wastage when preparing for eating.

There are no signs of the disease on the foliage, but when the tubers or roots are lifted they have crusty spots on the skin. Although many are only on the surface, some may penetrate into the flesh. Cracking caused by the scab can be the starting point for secondary attacks from soil pests which can lead to significant losses.

The disease is more severe in dry, sandy soils, gritty soils where materials such as fire ashes have been added, alkaline soils or those heavily limed for a previous crop and on newly broken-in grassland. It is more common in dry seasons.

Prevention. The only way to prevent it is by growing scab-resistant varieties, buying certified seed and not adding lime to the soil where potatoes are to be grown. The condition of the soil needs to be improved by the application of organic matter or the growing of green manures and the soil pH must be reduced to a level of about 5. In badly affected soils, when planting out cover the seed potatoes with an ample layer of well-rotted manure to allow the potatoes to grow up into this and not in the soil. Practise crop rotation methods.

POWDERY SCAB (*Sponogospora subterranea*)

This disease affects the tubers of potatoes, although it is not as widespread as common scab. It can also attack the roots of tomatoes. In the mild form it is very similar in appearance to common scab, but a brown powder can be seen inside each scab. In severe cases the scabs can grow to form large cankerous wounds.

Prevention. The disease is at its worst in poorly drained alkaline soils and the growing of potatoes in these conditions must be avoided.

Silver leaf (*Chondrostereum purpureum*) (*Holt Studios*)

Buy certified seed with resistance to the disease, avoiding planting any showing signs of scab. Practise crop rotation, working on as long a cycle as possible if the disease has been troublesome. Do not recycle diseased tubers or peelings through the compost system, but burn them.

SILVER LEAF (*Chondrostereum purpureum syn. Stereum purpureum*)

A disease affecting apples and stone fruit, most destructive on plums. It can affect currants, gooseberries, hawthorns and willow. It is not easy to identify initially, even though the symptoms are the leaves developing a metallic silvery sheen. Quite often only one branch is affected at first but it soon spreads through the tree. By mid-summer the symptoms are very obvious. Later the affected branches die and develop a purple fungus growth on the bark. This growth is highly infectious and is easily spread to unaffected trees. When the dead branch is cut off the exposed wood shows a brown staining.

Prevention. The fungus enters through wounds such as pruning cuts, so seal all cuts with a wound sealer. See also page 156.

Treatment. The leaf stage is not a source of the disease, so affected branches should be cut off and destroyed before the appearance of the mould growth. Cut the branch back into healthy wood which does not show signs of the brown stain.

If the main stem is affected the entire tree will need to be felled. Look for signs in the roots and if infected these will need to be removed as well. Do not leave dead wood to rot in orchards or debris at the bottom of the trees.

It is recommended that all affected wood is destroyed by the middle of summer.

SOOTY MOULD (*Cladosporium spp.*)

Sooty moulds are common on plants which are infested with sap-feeding pests, aphids, scale insects, mealy-bugs, etc. These pests produce a sticky substance, honeydew, which covers the leaves of the infected plants. Fungi grow on the affected parts to produce a sooty mould.

Although the fungi do not cause any damage to the plant, the build-up of the mould reduces the light available to the leaf, affecting the photosynthesis process, which eventually causes the death of the leaf. The moulds also contaminate the fruit of a plant as well as making it look unsightly.

Prevention. Control of pests will keep the plant free from attack.

Treatment. Affected leaves can be washed to clean off the mould, as can fruit before eating, for there is seldom any damage to the flesh.

SPOTS

Disfiguration of the leaves and other parts of plants by spots, blotches or mottles are symptomatic of many diseases. These are caused by a large variety of fungi, bacteria and viruses, making it difficult at times to identify the real cause. Often blotches can be a warning that parts of the plant are being affected by a disease and these are discussed under the appropriate section. Spots tend to be much smaller and more uniform in shape than blotches.

Not all spots are the results of disease. Environmental conditions such as air pollution or watering in the direct heat of the sun will mark the leaves of plants. Often with these causes the spots will not be limited to one species but will be found on neighbouring plants. However, it is not always the case, as some varieties are more sensitive to the environment than others.

Prevention. The wide variety of causes and the severity of the diseases make it difficult to generalize. Copper-containing fungicides such as Bordeaux mixture can be effective in suppressing certain of the diseases, but Bordeaux mixture can cause spots and other damage on some species and even different varieties of the same species. Sulphur can also be used to contain the disease in some cases. The following should be singled out for individual discussion.

ANTIRRHINUM LEAF SPOT (*Phillosticta antirrhini*)

A common fungal disease in humid weather, especially in the spring, when the leaves develop brownish spots with a darker edge. These may run together causing the leaves to die off. The flowerheads and stems can develop black dot-like spores which may cause the death of the whole plant. The disease is spread from adjacent plants or transmitted through affected seed.

Treatment. Spray with Bordeaux mixture at the first signs of attack. Badly affected plants should be lifted and destroyed.

BEAN CHOCOLATE SPOT (*Botrytis fabae*)

A common disease of the broad bean. As the name implies, the leaves, stems and pods are covered with dark chocolate-coloured spots. The spots may merge together, resulting in the death of the affected part and eventually the whole plant. In mild attacks it is possible to produce a crop of edible beans, even though the crop will be very much reduced.

Prevention. The disease flourishes in overcrowded conditions and when plants are grown in badly drained soils. There is a link with potassium deficiency. It is also more prevalent in a wet, mild spring following severe weather in the earlier part of the year.

Early crops should be given as much shelter as possible. Ensure the correct spacing between the plants when the seed is sown. Correct any deficiency with the addition of rock potash when the bed is being prepared.

Treatment. Once the disease symptoms appear there is no cure, so prevention is the only defence. Badly infected plants should be destroyed by burning and not composted.

BEETROOT LEAF SPOT (*Cercospora beticola*)

The leaves develop brown spots with a lighter centre which may die off and drop out. If the spots are numerous the whole leaf may die prematurely. The older leaves are the most readily affected and it is common to see these dying while the young leaves continue to grow. This damage to the leaves gives a reduction in root growth, resulting in a much lower crop yield. If plants are grown for seed the seeds can be affected.

Prevention. The disease appears to be more predominant in wet weather and when the crop is grown in overcrowded conditions on poor soils. Build up the level of fertility in the soil by generous applications of organic matter and the use of balanced organic fertilizers. Thin out seedlings to the correct spacing.

Treatment. All affected leaves must be removed and destroyed immediately at the first signs of the symptoms, to prevent the spores being windblown to other plants. There is no cure, nor are there any resistant varieties available.

BRASSICA RING SPOT (*Mycosphaerella brassicicola*)

Cabbages, cauliflower and Brussels sprouts are the main varieties attacked, but it can appear on other members of the brassica family. Small, dark brown spots appear, mainly on the older leaves, but can also appear on the stems and the buttons of the sprouts. The spots will grow in size up to about 1 in (2·5 cm) in diameter. With time the brown spots turn grey in the centre, with a large number of small black dots forming a number of concentric rings. Badly affected foliage turns yellow and dies.

Prevention. Cool, moist weather with rain encourages the disease (it is more prevalent in the south-west of the UK). Collect all leaf litter from around the plants which may become a source for spreading the spores. Do not grow seedlings in the brassica bed and practise crop rotation so as not to grow the same crops two years running on the same land.

Treatment. Once the plants are affected, cut off and destroy all affected parts.

CANE SPOT (*Elsinoe veneta*)

A very common disease on raspberries, this can

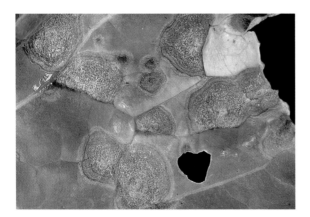

Brassica ring spot (*Mycosphaerella brassicicola*) (*Holt Studios*)

Celery leaf spot (*Septoria apicola*) (*Holt Studios*)

also affect blackberries and loganberries. The canes, leaves and flower-stalks develop purple spots in the early summer which turn to a greyish-white colour in the centre and produce spores. On the canes the spots eventually turn into cankers. The fruit, especially loganberries, can be affected and deformed. The canes are weakened and the fruit yield is much reduced. In severe cases the canes can be killed off.

Prevention. The disease is at its worst in wet weather, as it is spread by rain splashes containing the spores. Do not grow susceptible varieties. Spray adjacent canes with Bordeaux mixture or treat with sulphur in early spring when the buds are just about to open. Repeat when the flowerbuds are just open enough to show colour. Repeat every two weeks until the end of flowering.

With sulphur, use at the full strength for the first application, but further sprays need to be diluted to half-strength solutions.

Treatment. At the first sign of the disease all affected canes must be cut out and destroyed by burning.

CELERY LEAF SPOT (*Septoria apicola*)

This can cause considerable damage. Action must be taken immediately the symptoms are seen, for this seed-transmitted disease can kill off the plants if left unchecked. Small brown spots develop on the leaves, usually starting on the older ones, quickly spreading to the other foliage and shoots. The spots rapidly increase in size until they merge together, resulting in the death of the leaf. Once the stalks are affected the whole plant dies.

Prevention. The only safeguard is to buy good-quality seed and not to keep your own seed if the infection is present in the crop. The seed can be sterilized by soaking in hot water, 122°F (50°C), for half an hour, but it is not a guaranteed method of avoiding the disease.

In the autumn any diseased leaves or stalks must be removed and destroyed, not left lying about to contaminate the soil.

Treatment. Spray the whole crop with Bordeaux mixture at the first signs of attack and repeat as necessary at two- to three-week intervals. If the disease has been troublesome in past seasons then spray two or three times in the early summer as a precautionary measure.

CHERRY LEAF SCORCH (*Gnomonia erythrostoma*)

A very common complaint, this is easily recognized in the winter by the dead leaves hanging on the tree over the winter period into the early spring. The fungus overwinters in these leaves, ready to attack the young foliage and fruit. In the spring these leaves develop yellow spots which gradually grow in size and turn brown. The leaves eventually wither but remain on the tree. Affected fruit have dark spots in the flesh.

Prevention. Grow varieties which show resistance to the disease. For further protection spray thoroughly with Bordeaux mixture when the leaf buds are about to burst open, just before the flowers open and again once the petals have fallen.

Treatment. Remove all diseased leaves in the winter and destroy by burning.

CORAL SPOT (*Nectria cinnabrina*)

This is commonly seen on dead wood lying in damp areas, such as piles of logs or stakes, or on

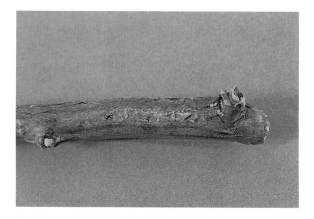

Coral spot (*Nectria cinnatrina*) on dead wood (Jim Hay)

fence-posts surrounded by long grass which is not cut back regularly. The fungal spores show as coral-coloured pimples on the wood at any time of the year.

Prevention. Although the disease will live only on dead wood, it can attack living wood either through affecting a dying twig on the plant or through wounds caused by bad pruning or mechanical damage in the early spring. This affected new wood wilts, dies and eventually becomes covered with the coral-coloured pimples.

There is no cure, but good hygiene in the garden will help prevent an attack. Do not stack old wood where it is likely to become damp and rot. Trim the grass around the bottom of fence-posts and apply a coat of preservative.

Do not leave dead wood on trees or bushes. Any pruning cuts or mechanical damage should be treated with a wound sealer.

Treatment. Any affected wood should be destroyed by burning. Any diseased bush fruits are better lifted and destroyed.

CUCUMBER LEAF SPOT (*Colletotrichum lagenarium*)

Sometimes called cucumber anthracnose, this disease shows as small pale green spots on the leaves, often starting on a vein, which turn brown in the centres with a yellowish edge. The spots can grow until the whole leaf is covered, when it will wither and die. A pink mould develops on the stem and leaf-stalks, which later turn black. Damage to the fruit does not appear until it is reaching maturity, when rough, sunken, watery areas appear. These can also develop pinkish spores in damp weather. The fruit eventually dies.

Prevention. The spores are spread by the hands and by adhering to the framework of the greenhouse. Do not touch the plants more than necessary and wash down the greenhouse in the spring before the cucumbers are planted out. Make sure the greenhouse is well ventilated, avoiding large fluctuations in temperature. The following year grow the cucumbers in sterile soil. Grow resistant varieties.

Treatment. At the first signs of attack remove and destroy affected leaves. Treat the plants every week with sulphur (cucumbers are damaged by copper fungicides).

CURRANT LEAF SPOT (*Pseudopeziza ribis*)

Starting in late spring, small, irregular brown spots develop on the leaves, and gradually merge, causing the leaf to die and fall prematurely. The spots on the underside of the leaves are lighter in colour. The disease spreads quickly over the plant, the loss of leaf area weakening the bushes and giving a reduced crop the following season. The disease attacks both currants and gooseberries. Red currants can be attacked on the stems and fruit.

Prevention. There are no resistant varieties but some are less susceptible than others.

Treatment. The disease is prevalent in wet seasons. At the first signs of attack spray with Bordeaux mixture and repeat fortnightly throughout the damp weather. Remove all affected leaves, collect any which have fallen and destroy by burning.

GHOST SPOT (*Botrytis cinerea*)

Small raised dark spots surrounded by a yellowish halo appear on the skins of tomato fruits, both green and ripe. It is more common towards the end of the season, especially when the weather is cold and damp. There are signs of grey mould rot on the plant.

Prevention. It is caused by grey mould spores landing on the fruit, either falling off affected plants when they are being handled or splashed by water. Prevent attacks by ensuring that there is adequate ventilation around the plants. Take care not to disturb any mould spores and do not splash water on the developing fruit if there is grey mould rot in the greenhouse.

Treatment. There is no cure. Although the fruit are unsightly, the eating quality is not too seriously affected. However, if the damp conditions are present in the greenhouse for long periods the grey mould rot can set in on the fruit.

HALO BLIGHT (*Pseudomonas phaseolicola*)

This is a disease of the runner bean, both the dwarf and standard varieties. The symptoms show as small brown spots on the leaves and are surrounded by a yellow halo. The pods develop round greasy-looking spots, the seeds being blistered and misshapen. Brown scars may also appear on the stems. The plant's growth is stunted and the yield greatly reduced. Plants affected at the seedling stage are unable to survive. The disease is more severe in hot weather.

Prevention. As the disease is transmitted through the seed, do not keep your own if the disease is in the garden. Buy good-quality seed. Do not chit (pre-germinate) by soaking the seed in water, for any infection present will be passed on to all the seeds in the water. Instead, soak the seed between sheets of damp newspaper.

Practise crop rotation principles and grow resistant varieties.

Treatment. At the first signs of attack, spraying with Bordeaux mixture will help to contain the disease. However if it starts to spread to adjacent plants it is safer to lift those affected and destroy by burning.

PEA LEAF SPOT (*Ascochyta pisi*)

Large brown sunken spots, sometimes with a darker edge, appear on the leaves, stems and pods. If the stems of young plants are infected the plants will die. It is worse in wet seasons.

Prevention. This is a seed-transmitted disease, so do not keep your own seed if the plants have been affected. Do not chit seed by soaking them in water, but by putting between sheets of damp newspaper.

Treatment. Lift and destroy all infected plants in severe cases, and practise crop rotation procedures.

PETAL BLIGHT (*Itersonilia perplexans*)

Common on chrysanthemums in the greenhouse,

Ghost spot (*Botrytis cinerea*) (*Jim Hay*)

Halo blight (*Pseudomonas syringae phaseolicola*) (*Holt Studios*)

Pea leaf spot (*Ascochyta pisi*) (*Holt Studios*)

Rose black spot (*Diplocarpon rosae*) (*Holt Studios*)

this fungal disease causes small brown spots on the petals which spread rapidly until the whole petal is covered. Eventually the whole flower is affected.

Prevention. The disease is more severe in mild, damp weather, the symptoms first appearing in the autumn and building up in severity. Extreme differences between day and night temperatures will also encourage the disease.

Spraying with Bordeaux mixture when the bud just begins to open will help to prevent it. Repeat the sprays at two-week intervals. Ensure that the greenhouse is well ventilated, and if there are extremes between night and day temperatures shade during the day and switch on a little heat at night.

Treatment. All affected petals and blooms must be removed and destroyed at the first signs of attack.

ROSE BLACK SPOT (*Diplocarpon rosae*)

Starting in mid-summer, black spots appear on both sides of the leaves, spreading rapidly from the lower leaves up through the bush. The spots can increase in size until the whole leaf is covered, when it dies and falls prematurely. The defoliation can cause dormant buds to produce young leaves, and this weakens the bush for the coming season. Extensive defoliation can weaken the bush even further and in extreme cases leads to its death. On some varieties the disease can extend into the wood, which is a

source of infection the following year if not pruned out.

Prevention. The disease is prevalent in a warm wet season and on bushes growing on badly drained soils or soils in poor condition.

Spray or dust with sulphur starting in mid-summer and continue every two weeks until early autumn. When all the leaves have fallen give a further spray with Bordeaux mixture. Bordeaux mixture should not be used during the summer period as it will disfigure the bush. As the disease can be washed off the bush into the soil and overwinter, a mulch of dry grass cuttings laid down in early spring and maintained through the year will prevent the spores rising from the soil. In a serious infection it pays to remove the top layer of soil from beneath the bush and replace it with fresh soil, not out of the rose bed.

Some varieties can provide resistance.

Treatment. In the winter prune out all diseased wood and all weak shoots. Collect all affected leaves and destroy by burning. The disease can be contained by removing all affected leaves immediately the symptoms show.

VIRUSES

This classification covers a large number of different microscopic organisms, which produce a wide range of symptoms. Viruses vary from other diseases in that they are of an infectious or contagious nature, being easily transmitted by the inoculation of sap from a diseased plant to a healthy one, often by sap-sucking pests such as aphids or thrips. Infection of a healthy plant can also arise by grafting onto it a diseased shoot. Many of the symptoms are very similar to those of fungal and bacterial diseases, which can make them difficult to identify. However, as a rule of thumb, if the symptoms cannot be related to a recognized disease or a nutritional or environmental cause, and if not all the plants are affected, just one here and there, the cause is more than likely to be a virus.

Viruses are not in general the direct cause of death, as with other diseases. However, they do considerably weaken the plant, leaving it vulnerable to other ailments. The symptoms tend to be confined to the shoot portions and can take the following forms : mottling (mosaic); bronzing and yellowing of the leaves, often with a certain amount of distortion; crinkling; rolling. Flower petals are also distorted and stay green; flowers fail to open or are malformed. The plants are stunted in their growth, distorted and yield greatly reduced. The number of crops known to show virus disease symptoms is very large and includes common vegetable crops.

Prevention. Control pests in the effort to limit the spread of the disease, acting promptly to deal with aphid attacks. As the virus can be transmitted on tools, sterilize pruning equipment after cutting out diseased wood. Viruses are also transmitted by the hands, so always wash after touching diseased tissue.

Weed control is important, as weeds can be host to disease. The removal of old plant stumps and roots and the general maintenance of good hygiene within the garden all help to minimize attacks. Buy virus-free stock and use resistant varieties where available.

Treatment. At the first signs of infection, plants should be lifted and destroyed. As this is drastic action, be sure the problem is being caused by a virus.

MOSAICS

Although many plants show mosaic symptoms which are similar, they can be caused by a number of different viruses. Common symptoms are pale green or yellow mottling of the leaves, often accompanied by curling or distortion. One or two strains of the virus can kill off the leaf and stem and there is distortion of fruits. Plants are stunted and may show signs of wilt. Yields of fruit are much reduced.

A magnesium shortage can cause yellow

Cucumber mosaic virus (*Holt Studios*)

mottling on the leaves, which can be confused with mosaics. The most important mosaics are tomato tobacco mosaic, and the cucumber mosaic which, despite its name, affects a wide range of plants including tobacco, tomato, celery, spinach, beans, peas, beet, vegetable marrow and begonia. There is a brassica mosaic which affects the brassica vegetables and docks. Raspberries are also prone to attack.

Prevention. Do not grow in infected soil. Do not let tomatoes come into contact with any tobacco plants or tobacco-based products. Wash hands thoroughly if tobacco has been handled. Grow resistant varieties.

Treatment. Destroy all affected plants.

REVERSION

This is a serious virus disease of blackcurrants, transmitted by a pest, the big bud mite. The symptoms are easily recognized in early or mid-summer by the misshapen leaves. The bush produces large numbers of very small leaves which are 'bunched', making it look more like a nettle than a blackcurrant. Close examination of the affected leaves shows that they are sharply pointed and narrow with no basal cleft. Instead of the normal five or six subsidiary veins on each side of the main leaf vein there are only four or fewer. The bush flowers earlier in the season than normal, the flowers being more highly coloured; they fail to set, so there are few or no berries produced.

Prevention. Action must be taken to eliminate the big bud mite from the bed. New bushes should be of certified stock.

Treatment. Once the infection has been confirmed the bush must be lifted and destroyed immediately to avoid any further infection.

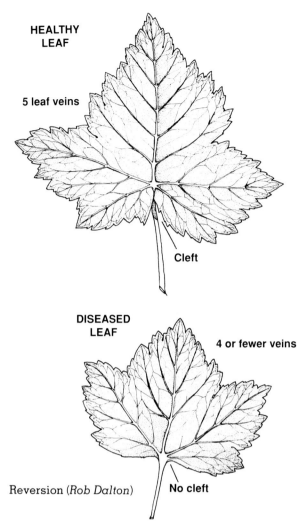

HEALTHY LEAF

5 leaf veins

Cleft

DISEASED LEAF

4 or fewer veins

Reversion (Rob Dalton)

No cleft

WILTS

The symptoms tend to be similar for all plants: the leaves bend down, turn yellow and shrivel, starting with the lower leaves and working progressively up the plant. The effect may be on one side only. The wilting may occur suddenly, especially in hot weather, the plants then recovering slightly in the evenings. When the stem is cut there are reddish-brown streaks running up it. Severely affected plants may die.

Wilting of the foliage can be caused by a number of bad cultural practices, such as under- or over-watering, mechanical damage to the plant and the effects of other diseases. However, there are a number of viruses which cause true wilt disease, which can be soil- or seed-borne.

ASTER WILT (*Phialophora asteris*)

This affects the annual variety and can easily be confused with damping off, except that the stem is attacked well above soil level.

RASPBERRY BLUE STRIPE WILT (*Verticilium spp.*)

A soil-borne disease which causes sudden wilting, especially in hot weather. Close examination of the canes shows a blue stripe on one side only. The cane will eventually die.

Prevention. Do not use contaminated land for at least six years.

Treatment. There is no cure. Remove and destroy the affected plant before the disease spreads along the row. Should this occur, remove the whole row and replace with healthy canes in new ground.

SPOTTED WILT

This affects many greenhouse plants such as tomatoes and gloxinias. It can cause considerable damage, often resulting in the death of the plant. The first symptoms appear as ring spots on the leaves. The heads of the plants become bunched and have a bronze appearance. The growth of the plant is stunted.

Prevention. Do not grow other susceptible plants alongside tomatoes, such as arum lily, cinerarias and solanum. Change the greenhouse soil and wash down the glass and framework. Grow resistant tomato varieties and do not plant out too early in cold soil.

Treatment. This is a very infectious disease, transmitted by greenhouse thrips. There is no cure. Infected plants must be lifted and destroyed.

STRAWBERRY VERTICILIUM WILT (*Verticilium spp.*)

This causes the outer leaves to wilt, with black/brown streaks appearing on the stalks of the inner leaves.

Treatment. There is no cure for this soil-borne disease. All diseased plants must be lifted and destroyed, removing as much of the contaminated soil with the plant as possible. If the disease persists, destroy all the plants and replant a new bed in another part of the garden.

20 PEST CONTROL

This chapter, on organic pest control, begins by detailing the effect of chemical pesticides on life in a fruit tree. This should illustrate some of the key principles of pest management, and explain why and how organic methods can be best.

THE EFFECTS OF CHEMICAL CONTROL

If a scientist wishes to study red spider mites or aphids on fruit trees, and needs to ensure that he has large and devastating colonies of the insects to work with, all he needs to do is to soak the tree with broad-spectrum insecticides, sit back and wait. Within a surprisingly short time, the tree will usually become smothered with these pests, most satisfactorily from the scientist's point of view. When the non-organic gardener does the same thing, having spotted a few aphids, perhaps, and concerned to nip in the bud a possible problem, he feels somewhat aggrieved at the result, and complains what a terrible year it is for red spider mites or aphids. He then goes to buy some more spray, maybe even more powerful than the last.

Why does this happen? And why is it that red spider mites are rarely a problem on organically grown trees, even in old, neglected orchards?

There are two main reasons. The first, and most important, is simply that both red spider mites and aphids are normally kept in check by the large number of predators and parasites that live in fruit trees. These include predatory bugs, beetles, flies, fly larvae, lacewings, parasitic wasps and spiders, not to mention blue tits and great tits. For a rough, though fluctuating, balance is achieved between predators and prey. The prey will always be present, but not normally in numbers that will significantly reduce the vigour or cropping ability of the fruit tree. If, however, you use a spray to try to eradicate this low-level pest population, you will certainly kill most of them off, but you will also kill most of the helpful predators and parasites. It is an unfortunate fact that aphids and

mites (in common with almost all other pests) can breed many times faster than can their natural enemies. For example, aphid numbers can increase ten- to twentyfold within a week during the summer months, whereas important aphid predators, such as hover-flies and ladybirds, have generation intervals of a month or more, while many spiders and carabid beetles have only one generation a year. In a few weeks, therefore, the surviving pests, freed from the natural control of their predators and parasites, will undergo a population explosion. But beware – this process applies equally when the more powerful organic pesticides, such as nicotine, are used.

The second reason is to do with the fact that aphids and red spider mites have been subjected to chemical assaults for so long, with such a broad range of chemicals, that they have evolved some resistance to whole classes of pesticides. The more effective a chemical is, in terms of the percentage of the target pest killed, and the more persistent it is, the greater the natural selection pressure will be, increasing the likelihood of resistant strains developing. Resistance by common pests, such as aphids, scale insects and glasshouse whiteflies, to the more powerful and persistent organochlorides, was followed by similar resistance to the more toxic but less persistent organophosphates, carbamates and, more recently, pyrethroids. This development of resistance takes place most swiftly in species that can multiply quickly – the pests. The slower-breeding predators, by contrast, take much longer to develop it, and indeed most, therefore, show little if any tolerance of modern pesticides. Spraying with insecticides, therefore, frequently allows a higher percentage of pests than predators to survive, and starting from this higher base level, the pest population explosion is even more rapid and destructive.

There is now some movement towards selective insecticides, aimed at particular pest species, that allow non-target species, including predators and parasites, to survive. And although the organic gardener will have nothing to do with these for other reasons (such as

OPPOSITE: Black slug (*Arion ater*), the biggest, come in many colours, despite their name (*D.H.Thomas*)

chemical residues on food), such developments are certainly an improvement. Unfortunately, chemicals like these tend to be much more expensive, and in practice are often not used by commercial growers. This may be because more than one pest is being targeted, and one cheap spray that will kill everything is seen as a better bet than several expensive but selective pesticides. Worse still, resistance to the selective chemicals soon appears, and as an accelerating need for new formulations arises, costs escalate.

All this sounds like, and is, something of a nightmare. But growing food organically is a practical and logical alternative , at least in the UK, where there are comparatively few serious pests.

PEST MANAGEMENT

While the conventional grower has to use the metaphorical equivalent of tear-gas and baton charges to control unruly mobs of caterpillars and scale insects, the organic gardener tries to avoid incitement to riot in the first place. Certainly there are 'organic' pesticides, just as there are concentrated 'organic' fertilizers, and these can be very useful in an emergency (see table). However, their use can indicate a failure of proper pest management.

THE PREVENTIVE APPROACH

Vegetable gardens tend to be laid out in regimental style, with straight rows of single crops laid out at standard spacings. The usual reason given is that this system makes hoeing, harvesting and so on easier, and the individual needs of each crop can most easily be met. This is a good argument where large supplies of vegetables are required, or time is severely limited, but it often means that aesthetically, and in terms of pest control, this part of the garden suffers. The vegetable garden is often consigned to a site at the end of the garden, screened from view, or is even exiled altogether to an allotment. This is a pity, because the organic gardener needs to have his crops constantly under his watchful eye. Blocks and rows of closely related vegetables are a pests' paradise, in which they can quickly and simply locate large patches of food plant, and spread rapidly from one plant to the next.

Many studies have now shown that diverse stands of mixed crops support more species of insects than monocultures. As relatively few insects are in fact pests, more species can be taken to mean more wildlife (which is good in its own right), and, most importantly, more predators and parasites.

The simplest way of achieving diversity is to bring the flower and vegetable gardens together, producing a cottage or ornamental kitchen-garden style informality that can have both

Commonly available organic pesticides for

Pesticide

Bacillus thuringiensis
Bacterial pesticide spray that is specific to the caterpillars of butterflies and moths – see Commercially available biological control agents, page 315

Derris
A spray or powder derived from derris roots

Pyrethrum
A spray of powder derived from the flowers of *Chrysanthemum cinerariaefolium*

Quassia
A spray derived from the wood of *Balanites*, *Picrasma* and Quassia

Soft soap
A soap of vegetable origin, used in the past for cleaning

Insecticidal soap
Soaps of vegetable origin, based upon salts of fatty acids, that have been selected for their insecticidal properties

Aluminium sulphate
A simple chemical that is not really 'organic', but which is sometimes used in place of synthetic chemicals

Copper sulphate
Another simple chemical, as above

emergency treatments

Pests controlled	Dangers, qualifying comments
Butterfly and moth caterpillars	Will not be effective against sawfly larvae, such as the gooseberry sawfly, which look very similar to caterpillars. Indiscriminate use would threaten harmless species of butterflies and moths. Completely safe to all predators, pets, and gardeners, and therefore the best spray to use against these pests
Aphids, beetles, caterpillars, mites (including red spider mites), sawfly grubs, thrips, whitefly and most other insects	An indiscriminate insecticide, that is toxic to ladybird larvae, parasitic wasps, anthocorid bugs, predatory mites, green lacewings and honey-bees. Less toxic to hover-fly and lacewing larvae. Poisonous to fish, so should be kept away from ponds and streams. On the other hand it breaks down very quickly to harmless products, and has low toxicity to warm-blooded animals
As above, but particularly flying insects, including aphids, flies, thrips and whiteflies	Toxic to ladybirds, predatory flies, bugs, parasitic wasps and other beneficial insects. Toxic to fish as for derris. Breaks down quickly in sunlight, but is a very rapid contact killer. Safe near warm-blooded animals. Often mixed with piperonyl butoxide, an extract of sassafras, which increases its toxicity but which, when predators are taken into consideration, is not necessarily a good thing. Avoid using pyrethroids, as these are not natural products, but synthetic chemicals that are more toxic and persistent than pyrethrum. Always try to find pure pyrethrum
Aphids, small caterpillars, sawfly grubs, mites and other small insect pests	Toxic to predator bugs, mites and lacewings. Said to be harmless to adult ladybirds and bees. Sometimes included with other organic pesticides
Aphids	Although mildly insecticidal against aphids, soft soap is more frequently added to other insecticides as a wetting agent, to get the spray to stick to foliage. Harmless to most predators
Aphids, mealybugs, red spider mites, sawfly grubs, soft scales, whiteflies and other small insects and mites	This is a contact spray that acts partly by damaging the cuticle of small insects, and disrupting respiration. Larger beneficial insects can tolerate this action, but smaller predators, such as anthocorid bugs and hover-fly larvae, may be killed. Best used therefore as a spot treatment for concentrated colonies of pests such as aphids, in an emergency. Can also damage a few sensitive plants (if in doubt do a small test spray)
Small slugs and snails	Kills small slugs and snails by direct contact, and best applied following a cultivation, or the clearing of a crop when the slugs will be active on the surface. Should not be used on seedlings or lettuces, which can be damaged. Aluminium may be more toxic to humans than was previously thought, so if used, this chemical must be applied with caution (see section on Slugs, page 303)
Small slugs and snails	Similar application and action to aluminium sulphate. This chemical can accumulate in the soil, and become toxic to earthworms

practical and aesthetic benefits. Merely from the pest control point of view, the advantages are considerable (other benefits, such as garden wildlife and plant nutrition, are dealt with in other chapters, pages 64, 196 and 212). Where such a radical change is not practical, the introduction of rows of flowers to the vegetable garden, and even the inter-planting of two or more different species of vegetable within the same row or block, can be a considerable gain.

Pest numbers and damage to plants will be reduced, both through the action of predators and through slowing the spread of pests. Where mixed planting schemes are used, pests find it harder to locate their food plant among others with competing scent and architecture. Even once it has found its host plant, there is a further delay in the spread of the pest to the rest of that particular crop. For example, a cabbage white butterfly (*Pieris brassicae*) might lay her eggs on a cauliflower plant. The resulting caterpillars can, in a conventional planting, simply crawl from plant to plant along the row. If, however, the cauliflowers are not adjoining, but inter-planted with beans, for example, the caterpillars will be effectively isolated. Such hold-ups in the spread of many pests may be sufficient in themselves to provide effective crop protection, where harvesting may occur before the spread has become significant.

PREDATORS AND PARASITES

Why should a diversity of plants increase the diversity and numbers of predators and parasites – after all, these creatures prey upon pests, not plants?

Take carabids, or ground beetles, for example. These valuable nocturnal predators live, as their name implies, mainly on the soil beneath plants, feeding on things like cabbage root fly eggs, aphids and slugs. Different species, however, require different microclimatic conditions – humidity, temperature and light levels can affect where they choose to live. Beneath an 'open' crop, such as onions or sweetcorn, conditions at ground level will be drier, hotter and with higher light levels than under a 'closed' crop such as French beans or potatoes. The range of beetle species that likes to live under the 'closed' crops will be different from that under the 'open' crops. As one carabid species has different food preferences from another, the aim must be to encourage as many species of beetle as possible to exist under all crop plants. In that way all pests will, with luck, be kept in check.

Then there are the parasitic wasps that help control caterpillars, whitefly, aphids, scale insects and many other pests. These tiny ant-like creatures are generally unnoticed by gardeners, and yet are enormously beneficial. They lay their eggs in the eggs, larvae, pupae or adults of their

The lacewing (*Chrysopa*) is a voracious aphid predator, especially in its larval stage (*Holt Studios*)

host species, which are then consumed by the wasp larvae, destroying the pest, and leading to a new generation of wasps. The adult wasps, however, feed upon nectar. Growing flowers between vegetables will therefore attract and sustain the wasps, which are then on hand to parasitize any pests on neighbouring food plants.

Flowers will also attract hover-flies, which feed on both the nectar and the pollen. These flies are now widely recognized as important predators of aphids. The pollen provides the flies with the protein necessary for egg production; the eggs will hatch among colonies of aphids into larvae that can each consume as many as 1,000 aphids during the course of their development.

Lacewings follow a similar pattern: they are attracted initially by nectar from flowers, but will go on to leave eggs that will hatch into excellent aphid predators (for a summary of the important invertebrate predators, see chart overleaf).

All these predators and parasites are therefore attracted by the more varied environments of mixed planting and cropping systems. Many of these beneficial insects can subsist on alternative prey when pest numbers are low, or at different stages of their development. Such alternative prey is more readily available within inter-planted crop systems, and predators can thus perform a lying-in-wait strategy, ready and waiting to control any pest invasions.

But apart from these essentially short-term advantages, whereby predatory insects are attracted into the cropping area by annual flowers, even greater benefits can be derived from the long-term stability conferred by perennials, including small trees and shrubs. Annual flowers and vegetables, particularly when rotated (as they should be) from year to year, offer only a temporary refuge to the more mobile of beneficial insects. Such systems rely upon surrounding hedgerows and wild patches as source areas, in which, for example, adult queen social wasps can hibernate, spider eggs can overwinter under stones or bark, and carabid beetle larvae develop in undisturbed soil. The inclusion of perennials, whether food-producing or ornamental, among your crops, can offer such refuges within the garden, under your own personal control and protection.

These might be plants such as raspberries, blackcurrants, rhubarb, herbs and strawberries, traditionally grown next to the vegetables. They are better located within the vegetable plots, perhaps as 'hedges' between the sub-plots of a rotated system, offering small islands of relative stability, and environmental diversity. Even these plants must be pruned, divided or mulched each year, and should be kept clean and open to minimize disease. A far better refuge can be provided by the thickets and tangled growths of many informally grown decorative plants. Think of the sheltered heart of a pampas grass plant, the dense cover of an ivy-smothered bank, or even the base of a hedgerow composed of native species, deep with old twigs, dead leaves and humus. Such places are the winter retreats not just of useful insects, but of many larger animals too.

ATTRACTING LARGER PREDATORS

With surprisingly few exceptions, such as rabbits, mice and squirrels, attracting birds, mammals, reptiles and amphibians to the garden does a lot more good than harm. Granted, mice may dig up your newly sown peas, and blackbirds may raid the red currants, but these problems are relatively easily avoided with netting. Wildlife and organic gardening are complementary, and both greatly improve the interest and beauty of your surroundings.

Once again, the more diverse and stable you can make the garden environment, the more species of animal can thrive in such surroundings. Birds are the most important of these larger natural biological control agents. They are also the easiest to attract.

Provide them with secure nesting sites, shelter and food, and they will come. The informal garden, with its dense evergreens and hedgerows, will provide many species with all of these. Nest-boxes can be put up to increase the population of tits, for example, whose numbers are limited more by the availability of nest sites than by shortage of food. A family of tits or wrens, with a dozen or so chicks to feed, will require thousands of small caterpillars and aphids, all of which will be collected as near to the nest site as possible. Blackbirds, thrushes and starlings will all help to control the largest and nastiest pests, such as slugs and leatherjackets. In winter these birds can be further assisted, and encouraged to stay, by providing them with fruiting shrubs such as holly, crab apple and rowan (see *The Wildlife Garden*, page 218).

Hedgehogs, as everyone knows, eat slugs, and

Slow-worm, to be found in rockeries, especially under large flat stones (*Bill Symondson*)

can be easily attracted with the odd dish of cat-food, and thickets in which to hibernate and raise their young. They also eat earthworms and carabids, unfortunately, but on balance they probably do more good than harm. A pond in the garden will allow frogs and toads to multiply, and populate the borders with more slug-eaters. The frogs will lie in wait in the damper areas, ambushing anything edible that passes, while the toads love dry stone walls and rockeries where ants, their favourite food, tend to nest. Slow-worms too may be found in such sites, particularly under large flat stones where they find slugs hiding during the day.

All these larger animals will benefit from a garden in which vegetables, flowers, trees and shrubs are mixed together. By encouraging these predators, you help to keep your plants pest-free.

PLANT NUTRITION AND PESTS

The subject of organic fertilizers is dealt with elsewhere in this book (see *Soil*, page 24; *Composts*, page 26), as is the whole question of rotations that take advantage of the different nutrient requirement of various crops (see pages 57 and 88). An important aspect of organic principles and pest management is involved here, however.

High levels of nitrogen, whether from artificial sources such as sulphate of ammonia, or of organic origin, such as dried blood or poultry manure, are not naturally encountered by plants. Indeed, their physiology is geared to compete for available supplies in an environment that usually provides sub-optimal levels. Many vegetables therefore respond to a sudden surge in nitrogen levels by putting on rapid, sappy growth. Weight for weight, the dry-matter content of the vegetables, and their food value, declines, while the nitrogen itself is thought to be a hazard to our health. What is more, the cell walls become distended and thin, allowing both pests and diseases to enter more easily. The outer cuticle of both leaves and stems can no longer resist the

Important garden predators

Predator	Recognition	Main pests attacked
Amphibians Toads	Easily distinguished from frogs by the warty dull grey-brown skin	Ants, woodlice, slugs, snails and almost any other invertebrate that is small enough to swallow
Frogs	Smooth skin, often brightly marked with browns, greens and yellows	Slugs, caterpillars, flies and almost anything else that can be ambushed and subdued
Beetles Carabid beetles (or Ground beetles)	Fast-moving mainly black nocturnal beetles, although some of the day-active species have bright metallic colours. Simple thread-like antennae, attached between eye and jaw, with eleven segments. There are around 300 species in the UK alone, ranging in size from a few millimetres to over 2·5 cm (1 in) long. Most species are predatory in both adult and larval stages	Aphids, caterpillars and pupae of many moths, eggs, larvae and pupae of cabbage and carrot root flies, slugs and many others
Staphilinid beetles (or rove beetles)	Mainly black or black and orange beetles, with long slender bodies, on which the wing-covers are much shorter than the abdomen. A very large group of predators (plus a few parasites), with over a thousand species in Europe. Many of the smaller species are day-active, although most of the larger ones, such as the well-known Devil's Coach-horse, are nocturnal	Similar host range to that of Carabids above, feeding opportunistically on insects, slugs, etc.
Ladybirds	The familiar black and red or orange seven-spot and two-spot are the commonest and most important species	Aphids are consumed in vast numbers by both adults and larvae
Birds Tits, warblers, robins, fly-catchers, wrens, tree creepers, blackbirds, thrushes, starlings, owls, crows, swallows and many others		All pests are exploited by birds, from aphids and caterpillars to rabbits and mice
Bugs Anthocorid bugs (under ¼ in/5 mm)	Common species have a chequered appearance, with white, brown and black markings on wings, legs and antennae. Have the usual identifying mark of a bug – a long piercing beak, or rostrum, for sucking the juices from their victims	Aphids, capsid bugs, scale insects, red spider mites, small caterpillars and many others, particularly in trees and shrubs
Assassin bugs – such as *Empicoris* *vagabundus* (Approx ¾ in/15 mm)	*E. vagabundus* looks like a gnat at rest, but can be distinguished by the long curved beak and short front legs, which are less than half the length of the middle and hind pairs. Legs and antennae flecked with black against the insect's generally fawn background	A general predator of aphids, mites, bugs and small caterpillars in trees

How to encourage

Install a pond that is free from fish, has sides that slope gradually, to allow easy access and egress, and which is densely planted with weeds, lilies, and marginal plants, to allow escape from cats and herons, and to encourage insects

Frogs are highly effective slug predators, and of almost anything else that can be ambushed and subdued (*Natural Image*)

As above. Whereas toads like to live in drier parts of the garden, frogs like dense, damp vegetation, which is also where they are most needed to control slugs

Most carabid larvae live in the soil, and therefore require undisturbed ground in which to develop – such as land supporting perennials, hedgerows, and lawns. Controlled refuges (see slug section) allow ground beetles to live within plots. Use of collars of roofing felt to discourage cabbage root flies from laying eggs has the same effect, increasing predation upon the eggs of these pests

As for carabids above. May well take advantage of insects living in your manure and compost heaps

Rove beetle (*Staphylinus olens*) (D.H.Thomas)

A nettle patch will frequently help to build up ladybird numbers early in the season, when they exploit nettle aphids. Adults overwinter in dead vegetation, under bark, in walls and under stones, sometimes congregating in huge numbers within favoured sites. These should be left undisturbed

Put up nest boxes, to increase the density of birds in your garden. Provide trees and shrubs in which they can nest and shelter. Provide food and water in winter. Hang fat or nuts in fruit trees in winter, to encourage tits to search for overwintering eggs, larvae and pupae of insect pests (see pages 194 and 218)

Avoid using even organic pesticides, and certainly not tar oil winter washes on trees and shrubs

As above

Assassin bug (*Empicoris vagabundus*) (D.H.Thomas)

Important garden predators

Predator	Recognition	Main pests attacked
Bugs		
Black-kneed capsid bugs *Blepharidopterus angulatus* (Approx ⅓ in/8 mm)	Distinguishable from many similar capsids (many of which are pests) by black knee-joints on a generally green insect	Particularly useful as a control for fruit tree red spider mites in apple trees
Centipedes (Up to 2 in/50 mm)	One pair of legs per body segment as compared with two pairs for millipedes. Fast-moving nocturnal hunters	Many insects taken, but also slugs and snails
Flies Marsh flies (Sciomyzids) (Many species around ¼ in/6 mm)	A group of about sixty-five British flies, many with dark patches on the wings, but which require expert identification to distinguish them from other anonymous-looking species	Slugs and snails – the whole family are specialists at parasitizing molluscs
Hover-flies (Syrphids) (Many species around ½ in/10 mm)	Familiar, mainly black and gold flies, that hang in the air making a high-pitched whine. A diagnostic feature is the vein running parallel with the hind margin of the wing	Aphids (see section on aphid control). The species *Episyrphus balteatus* is particularly useful, in that it often enters glasshouses to lay its eggs
Harvestmen (Up to 2½ in/60 mm)	Spider-like Arachnids, with a small body and eight very long legs (second pair is the longest). The body is not, unlike spiders, divided into two parts, and there is no distinct abdomen. They have no silk or venom	General predators of many insects, including aphids and caterpillars
Lacewings Green lacewing *Chrysopa carnea* (¾ in/20 mm)	Uniformly green insects, with four long lacy green wings of roughly the same size, and with long antennae	Mainly aphids, which are attacked by larval lacewings, and also to a lesser extent by the adults. Many other small insects taken, including scale insects and small caterpillars
Mammals Hedgehogs		Slugs, beetles, grubs, leatherjackets and caterpillars. Will also eat baby mice and rats
Shrews (1–2 in/30–50 mm)	Mouse-like insectivorous mammals related more closely to moles. Long snout, with small sharp teeth, lacking the incisors of rodents. Dark slate-coloured fur	Slugs, beetles, caterpillars, millipedes and many other invertebrates
Bats (Wing-span up to 11 in/28 cm)	Nocturnal flying mammals	Flying insects, including moths, beetles, aphids and gnats

How to encourage

s anthocorid bugs

Black-kneed capsid bug
(*Blepharidopterus angulatus*)
(*D.H.Thomas*)

eed daytime refuges, in the form of stones and logs to hide
nder, and undisturbed thick vegetation

row plenty of flowers among your crops to encourage the adults.
he damp conditions around a pond will bring in some species

he flies feed on pollen and nectar, the former being required
or the development of eggs in the female. Interplant aphid-
usceptible crops with a succession of flowers

eed undisturbed areas in which to find daytime refuges,
nd in which to breed

he adults are mainly nectar feeders, and are therefore attracted
y flowers. Experimentally, it has been found that spraying a
op with sugar and water can attract the adults, which then lay
ggs that hatch into larvae that will control resident aphid
olonies

Harvestman, notable for its eight
very long legs – a useful
predator of aphids and
caterpillars (*Holt Studios*)

rovide nesting and overwintering boxes (see *The Wildlife Garden*,
age 214). Can be fed with cat-food and bread, although
ilk should be avoided as they cannot digest this properly

equire dense vegetation, particularly hedgerows, with accumulated
af-mould in which to burrow and nest

ut up bat boxes. Avoid blocking access points to your attic, where they may
ell be living, and take advice from your local bat group if woodworm treat-
ent has to be contemplated. Harming bats or their roosts is unlawful in
e UK

Horseshoe bat (*Holt Studios*)

Important garden predators

Predator	Recognition	Main pests attacked
Mites Predatory mites, especially *Eutrombidium rostratus,* the Velvet mite (1/10 in/2-3 mm)	No easy way to recognize predatory species amongst the pests. Velvet mites are bright red, and frequently seen moving around on the paths, walls and tree trunks. Usually eight legs	Other mites, including fruit tree and glasshouse red spider mites
Reptiles Slow-worms (up to 10 in/25 cm)	Unmistakable legless lizards, either uniformly grey-brown, or a rich fawn along the back with dark brown sides	Slugs, particularly Grey Field slugs
Slugs Testacella slugs (up to 5 in/12 cm)	Pinkish brown body, graduating to a bright orange-pink underside. Main diagnostic feature is an external mussel-shaped shell on the back, near the hind end, with a network of darker veins radiating out from under this	Other slugs, particularly subterranean species such as the Garden slugs and Keeled slugs. Found particularly in soil with high organic matter, in leaf-mould and in old compost heaps. Also eat earthworms, but will not damage plants
Spiders (From microscopic to 2½ in/60 mm)	Body with a distinct abdomen and eight legs. They produce silk, which is mainly used for the capture of insects in a variety of webs and snares. Many hunt or ambush their prey, subduing it with the aid of poison fangs	Mainly flying insects, notabl flies, aphids, and other bugs Useful in the garden, the gla house and the home. All Brit species are harmless to hum
Wasps Social wasps (¾ in/20 mm)	The familiar yellow and black wasps that feed around dustbins	Crane-flies, caterpillars and many other insects are captured and taken back to their nests, to be fed to the wasp grubs
Digger, Potter and Mason wasps (Size varies with species, many around ½ in/10 mm)	Like all wasps, these have four wings and a pronounced waist. Many are black and yellow like social wasps, but generally smaller and more lightly built	Caterpillars and many other insects are paralysed with the sting, and taken back to feed individual grubs in chambers within the ground, or in specially constructed clay pots or cells
Ichneumon flies (up to 1 in/25 mm)	Long thin parasitic wasps, with four wings and long antennae, with 16+ segments	Mainly moth larvae, but notably also Large White caterpillars. Single eggs are laid in the larvae, which pupate normally, but hatch into wasps
Braconids and Chalcids (Most less than ¼ in/ 5 mm)	Tiny ant-like wasps with four wings. There are thousands of species, most specific to a particular host	Caterpillars, whitefly, aphids, scale insects, beetles and most other pests

How to encourage

Avoid using even mild organic pesticides, such as soft soap, except in emergencies

Like to live under paving slabs and in rockeries. Slabs can be provided near susceptible crops

Regular incorporation of organic matter is standard organic practice, and will encourage these predators. Use of beer traps, beetle pitfall plots, controlled refuges or search and destroy techniques for pest slug species will not harm these, as they are rarely to be found on the surface

Testacella slug – a predator of Garden and Keeled slugs (*D.H.Thomas*)

Many lay eggs in autumn, under stones and in undergrowth, which hatch the following spring. Such sites should be preserved. Avoid using organic pesticides wherever possible

Adults feed upon nectar and will come to flowers. They also go for other sweet things, such as apples and jam: the anti-social aspect of social wasps

Adults feed upon nectar and will come to flowers. Leave undisturbed wildlife areas in your garden in which such creatures can nest

Potter wasps (*Bill Symondson*)

Commonly found among dense vegetation, especially hedgerows

Attracted particularly to umbelliferous plants, the flat open flowers and nectaries of which can be reached by these insects. Many of the *Compositae* are also utilized, and can be used for interplanting

probing mouth parts of the sap-sucking bugs, particularly aphids and scale insects. Many of these pests carry bacteria, fungi and viruses from one plant to another. In the end, high nitrogen levels bring about increases in both pest and disease attacks.

Good organic practice, therefore, which avoids concentrated sources of plant nutrients, will provide plants that are healthier for us to eat. What is more, they will be healthier plants in their own right, better able to resist attacks by pests and diseases.

RESISTANT PLANT VARIETIES

All gardeners, whatever their methods, benefit from the development of pest-resistant plants. Resistance, however, is rarely the same as immunity, and may sometimes only work where the pests are offered a choice. For example slugs, given the opportunity to attack two different varieties of potato, may go for one rather than the other. If only the less-preferred variety is on offer, that may well be attacked, although the amount of damage will be less.

The mechanisms of resistance vary, and may involve chemical repellents in the tissues, as in lettuces (see below) and potatoes (see page 307), or more simply a difference in the hairiness or thickness of the plant cuticle. Such characteristics may have been lost during the domestication of crop plants, but may still be available in wild relatives. A good example is the hairiness of wild potato leaves and stems, which effectively resist aphid attacks. As aphids carry blight and other diseases between potato plants, considerable effort has gone into attempts to cross-breed domestic and wild strains, in an attempt to produce a hairy-leaved potato that will give a good yield. Unfortunately, none is yet available on the market, but considerable progress has been made.

These physical and chemical characteristics may work by discouraging feeding by the pests upon such plants. Alternatively, the pests themselves, feeding on resistant varieties, may grow less well, or produce fewer, less vigorous offspring. Such resistance will often be to one type of pest only, and in time these pests may evolve to overcome such challenges. Meanwhile, however, slug-resistant potatoes, root-aphid-resistant lettuces and root-fly-resistant carrots are of great benefit to organic gardeners.

Unfortunately, there are all too few such plant varieties. This is not so much because resistant varieties cannot be produced – many cultivated vegetables have wild relatives that contain the necessary genes for pest resistance. There are two main problems, however.

First, it is often the case, particularly with chemical resistance, that resistant varieties simply taste unpleasant to us and presumably to the pests. For example, the sweetest varieties of cabbage, such as Hispi, attract slugs from all directions, which is not surprising – Hispi is a tender and delicious salad variety. On the other hand, a spring cabbage such as April, which is good cooked but far too bitter to eat raw, has considerable resistance to slug attack during the winter. The same is true of lettuces – varieties that taste almost as bitter as dandelion, such as the reddish Continuity, have considerably more resistance than sweet types such as Webbs Wonderful or Little Gem. In extreme cases, such as with the glucosinolates that offer natural protection to certain brassicas, such compounds can be damaging to health, causing goitre in humans. Fortunately this is not usually the case. Resistance of Avoncrisp lettuce to root aphids (*Pemphigus bursarius*), and partial resistance of Sytan carrots to carrot root fly (*Psila rosae*) have been achieved with varieties that are of good culinary quality. Such vegetables are, however, like gold dust, and there are all too few of them.

Secondly, there is the whole question of legal requirements, the costs involved with registering seed varieties, and restrictions upon individuals or organizations maintaining and selling varieties that have particular qualities, such as pest resistance, benefiting a minority market, such as organic gardeners. Varieties that, in the past, were considered distinct, perhaps for their ability to thrive in a particular soil, or resist a particular pest or disease, are now lumped together, often simply on the basis of their appearance. This is a direct result of the introduction of registration and maintenance costs for seed varieties. Many of the so-called new varieties that are offered in place of older ones are in fact F1 hybrids. Although such varieties have their advantages, in terms of producing a strongly growing and uniform crop, they offer no new genetic material, being simply a recombination of genes from existing varieties. Genetic diversity is being lost as seed companies 'rationalize' their lists, a diversity that was fostered by past communities, who selected plants over the centuries that would do well in their particular locality. It is not too late to salvage some of this heritage, thanks to the work of a few dedicated individuals and organizations, who have created seed banks and libraries to preserve what is left.

An important additional benefit of resistant varieties is that they provide protection against the vectors of disease. Raspberries have been produced that are resistant to all four of the known races of raspberry aphid (*Amphorophora idaei*). These aphids carry viruses that drastically reduce the productivity of the canes. By controlling the aphid you control the spread of the virus.

As a final point, it must be borne in mind that

the degree of resistance of any particular variety is influenced to some extent by environmental factors. Of these, the most important is probably the level of fertility. High levels of potassium, phosphorus and, particularly, nitrogen, increase susceptibility to pest attack. Organic systems, therefore, with their lower input levels, are suited to take advantage of mechanisms of resistance that operate most efficiently under such conditions. Where partial resistance exists, as in crops such as potatoes (to slugs) and carrots (to root fly), other control measures, such as manipulation of sowing and harvesting times, and the use of protective barriers, will augment this inbuilt varietal advantage, and lead to an acceptable level of clean, damage-free crops. It seems to be the case that partial resistance is widespread, even among modern vegetable varieties. Routine use of insecticides by growers and seedsmen over the years has hidden such differences from view. In the face therefore of limited financial backing for research in this area, organic gardeners must help themselves. Apart from choosing known resistant varieties wherever possible, avoid growing just one variety: by splitting your options, you are most likely to find one that will evade pest attack in your particular garden and growing conditions.

Genetic engineering provides a means of greatly speeding up the process whereby genes for resistance may be introduced to crops. This is still a controversial subject among organic growers – many feel that the dangers of this technology may outweigh the benefits. Plans exist, for example, to transfer the *Bacillus thuringiensis* (BT) endotoxin genes into plants that are attacked by caterpillars, giving them in-built protection. If it is acceptable to eat vegetables sprayed with this highly specific and useful organic insecticide, would it not be also acceptable to eat vegetables that contain the same chemicals in their tissues? Personally, I have my doubts. A spray with BT, and all other organic sprays, should be an emergency measure, used only when other techniques fail. Although the natural toxins produced by BT have been tested and are thought to be safe to humans, and almost certainly are so in the sort of quantities used in a well-run organic garden, that is no reason to be complacent. Routine doses of toxins from food plants that make their own supplies would be much higher, and may have unforeseen long-term effects.

THE BIG FOUR

Four pests stand out as being of principal concern to gardeners, namely slugs, aphids, cabbage white caterpillars and the root flies (cabbage and carrot). These cause the vast majority of pest damage in gardens, and therefore merit particular attention. Other pests are covered by the extensive charts at the end of this chapter. Many of the principles and control techniques discussed in relation to these primary species can be applied to the control of many other pests.

SLUGS

The generally cool, wet summers and mild winters in the UK are ideal for these molluscs, of which there are about thirty British species. Most countries have either a hot, dry period in summer, or a very cold interval in winter, severely limiting mollusc numbers. We have introduced our adaptable Grey Field Slug from North America to Australia, and from Finland to Brazil. For most gardeners in the UK they are the number one headache, and frequently the cause of lapses in organic integrity. Farmers lose millions of pounds annually to slug damage, with almost every crop grown (including grass) suffering. Much of this damage happens despite chemical protection in the form of pellets, which are far less effective than imagined. A major problem with slug pellets is that they tend to poison only the larger, more mobile slugs, and many of these recover unless weather conditions are right. Indeed, on most nights only a proportion of the slug population will be active in any case. Even intensive use of pellets is unlikely to reduce the slug population in a garden by more than 10%. Unfortunately, recent studies have shown that carabid beetles, predators of slugs and other pests, are significantly reduced through poisoning by pellets, which removes an important natural check upon slug numbers.

Slugs are simply snails that have evolved away their shells. The reasons for this are unclear, although it was possibly an adaptation that allowed them to exploit calcium-poor environments. Only one snail, the Garden Snail, *Helix aspersa*, is much of a problem in Britain, and can cause considerable damage, particularly in gardens surrounded by old walls. Most of what is said below about slugs applies equally to snails.

The Problem. If you are a gardener, you will have been troubled by slugs. They attack all the commonly grown vegetables and most ornamentals, at least as seedlings, including such unlikely plants as trees and cacti. All parts of plants are attacked, from the roots and tubers to the leaves and fruits. The most severe damage is probably done in the spring, when vulnerable seedlings can be wiped out overnight. In autumn, too, especially after a moist summer during which the slugs can build up their numbers (densities of 200 slugs per sq m and more are common), attacks may be intense. Unfortunately for organic gardeners, slug numbers

European grey field slug (*Deroceras reticulatum*), which has spread across the continents (*D.H.Thomas*)

Keeled slug (*Milax budapestensis*), a specialist at root destruction (*Holt Studios*)

Garden slug (*Arion hortensis*) (*Holt Studios*)

are generally higher in soils with high organic content, whether from manure or compost.

Not all slugs are pests by any means, and many feed principally on fungi and dead organic matter. However, most of the slugs actually in your vegetable garden will be pest species, probably one of the four main villains: the Grey Field Slug (*Deroceras reticulatum*), the Garden Slug (*Arion hortensis*), the Keeled Slug (*Milax budapestensis*), and the Black Slug (*Arion ater*).

Grey Field Slugs eat everything, and are probably the worst of all. They feed on the soil surface and within plants, but will also attack roots, such as potatoes, that are within a few inches of the surface. They come in a range of attractive shades, from creamy white to purple, but are usually a fawn-grey, less than 1½ in (4 cm) long. They can have three successive generations in a bad year.

The Garden Slugs eat almost everything, not only consuming all the above-surface parts of plants, but burrowing down to get at the roots too. They have a nasty trick of gnawing off marrow and bean plants at ground level. They will riddle potatoes with holes. They are usually black, with a watery orange underside, generally less than 1¼ in (3 cm) long.

The Keeled Slugs are specialists at root destruction, attacking crops such as potatoes, carrots and beetroots. They are particularly difficult to deal with as they spend almost all their lives underground. They are black or dark grey-brown, with a thin pale orange line down the centre of the back, and are generally less than 2½ in (6 cm) long.

The Black Slugs are the biggest. They come in many colours, including white, brick red, brown, yellow, cream and fawn but most frequently black, with an orange fringe and underside, and can grow to as long as 8 in (20 cm). They sometimes hump up and rock from side to side when disturbed. Fortunately they do little damage for most of the year, mainly eating rotting material, but in spring, when there is less food available to them, they may well attack seedlings.

Life cycle. This varies between species, but generally eggs are laid in spring and autumn, most hatching in spring. The eggs are creamy white or translucent, and can often be found under large stones. Most are laid in soil crevices, in moist soils. Slugs take from a few months to a year to mature, with the smaller species growing more rapidly than the larger. The young slugs are simply

Eggs of the black slug (*Arion ater*)
(*Bill Symondson*)

Seedlings can be given slug protection using
recycled plastic bottles (*Joy Larkcom*)

miniatures of the adults, and start doing damage
immediately. Adults overwinter in the soil,
burrowing deep to avoid the frost which, in a hard
winter, destroys many of them. Burrowing also
helps them to avoid hot dry weather, which again
causes high mortality. Conditions that are best for
plant growth (warm and humid) are also best for
the slugs. In a mild winter, however, slug damage
may occur at any time, with feeding taking place at
temperatures only just above freezing. They are
particularly troublesome following a shower of
rain, when the extra humidity, and drop in
temperature, stimulates them into activity.

Avoiding trouble – cultural methods.   Avoid
using un-rotted mulches around susceptible
crops as these, unlike well-rotted manure or
compost, are particularly attractive to slugs.
Plants grown through polythene are also severely
attacked.

Slugs prefer wet, sticky, poorly drained clay
soils, with a rough surface, offering plenty of soil
crevices in which they can find ideal refuges and
egg-laying sites. Avoid these conditions by
improving drainage and soil structure.
Construction of raised beds helps on heavy soils.
Incorporation of compost and, in severe cases,
coarse grit, will help considerably. A fine surface
tilth destroys the soil-crack refuges.

Thorough cultivation before planting and
sowing, preferably with a rotovator, is probably
the best of all direct control measures. Many
slugs will be destroyed, while others, particularly
the eggs and smaller slugs, will be exposed to
desiccation and predation. Cultivations during
very cold or hot weather are most effective.

Weedy ground attracts slugs. Although the
presence of weeds can reduce damage to
adjoining crops, by offering them an alternative
food source, this can be a risky strategy. Whereas,

for example, potatoes grown in weedy ground
may benefit from reduced attacks by surface-
feeding slugs, lettuces grown under similar
conditions are likely to be preferred to the weeds,
and severely damaged. Weeds offer improved
breeding sites to slugs, and will encourage a
build-up in numbers which, when the weeds are
cleared, will attack any subsequent crop.

Slug preferences can be exploited for crop
protection. Chrysanthemums grown on their own
are attacked by slugs, but if lettuces are grown
among the chrysanthemums, the slugs will attack
those instead. This principle can be adapted to
many situations.

Clear potatoes and other crops as early as
possible in the autumn, as soon as they are ripe
for storage. As a potato ripens, sugars in the roots
are converted to starch. It is thought that the high
sugar levels in unripened potatoes (which make
early potatoes so delicious) are in fact repellent to
slugs, and offer considerable protection at this
stage. Mature potatoes lose this protection as they
ripen, and must therefore be harvested before the
slugs move in.

Vegetable gardens are often surrounded by
mown grass paths. Slug numbers on the grass are
frequently greater than on the soil. Mowing the
grass at night, when the slugs are crawling about
on the surface, offers an eccentric but practical
means of destroying them in such source areas.

Slugs will not move far as long as they have a
food supply. Clearing the remains of a crop will
result in the movement of the slugs away to
adjoining plants, or on to a subsequent crop.
Precautions are therefore necessary, such as
rotovation and/or intensive trapping.

Plastic barriers will inhibit the spread of slugs.
These can be in the form of semi-rigid sheets, on
edge, surrounding plots, or more locally in the
form of bottle cloches. Regular inspection is

needed to ensure slugs are not trapped *inside* such barriers.

Various materials have been used to surround plants and can, under certain circumstances, offer temporary protection. These include coarse scratchy materials, such as ashes, broken eggshells and sharp sand, and other substances, such as soot and lime, that act both chemically and as desiccants. All such materials need constant maintenance, as they are easily blown or washed away, but can, in combination with other techniques, reduce slug activity.

Night-time searches by torchlight can catch slugs by the thousand, and are certainly more productive, in terms of time, than beer traps. Combined with the more defensive methods described above, such forays can significantly reduce the numbers of larger slugs in a given area, and thus damage to plants. However, recruitment to the slug population from hatching eggs and growing young, and some limited movement into the area from outside, means that perseverance is needed.

Trapping, natural enemies and biological control. Traps containing either milk or beer have been used for decades to catch slugs. However, they must be used very intensively to have any real effect on reducing damage, requiring at least one trap every yard/metre in all directions; even then only the larger, more mobile slugs may be significantly reduced in numbers. These traps are labour-intensive and costly in milk and beer. They must be set with their rims at least ½ in (1 cm) above the soil level to avoid catching predatory beetles, which may well be doing more good than the beer traps. Roofs of slate or tile are needed to keep out the rain, or alternatively plastic pots with lids can be used, with access slits cut in the sides.

'Controlled refuges' may be used, as an alternative or in addition. These are simply pieces of wood, tile or carpet placed on the soil among

Carabid beetle (*Bill Symondson*)

crops; they act in two ways. They offer within-plot refuges for predatory beetles, which help to control slugs and many other pests. They also attract slugs, which use them as daytime refuges and sites for egg-laying. Regular weekly inspection, and collection of any slugs or their eggs found, offers a quick and effective means of control.

The larger carabid beetles, the best slug predators, can be concentrated within susceptible crops by the construction of pitfall plots. These can be simply made with corrugated lawn edging, with the soil outside the plot flush with the top of the plastic, and a drop of at least 1¼ in (3 cm) on the inside. Beetles will fall in and, because most of them cannot fly or climb the plastic, they will increase in number. The more beetles you have, the more effectively the slugs (and other pests) will be controlled. It is important to let the beetles out of the plots as soon as they are no longer needed, in order to allow them to find suitable breeding sites elsewhere in the garden.

Marsh flies (*Schiomizidae*) are parasites of slugs and snails, and are attracted by the wildlife garden, with its ponds and flowers. Although most marsh flies parasitize snails, two species, *Tentanocera elata* and *Euthycera cribrata*, have been found to be more or less specific to slugs, and have been investigated in detail as potential biological control agents. These flies can lay up to 600 eggs in a season, while each fly larva may kill from nine to twenty-five slugs. The newly hatched larva waits for a slug to pass by, then grabs hold of it with special mouth hooks, and burrows straight inside. At this stage it is a parasite, consuming the living slug tissue. Eventually the slug will die, and the larva then leads more of a predatory existence, waiting to ambush passing slugs, or following them along their slime trails.

Carabid beetles have also been shown to be effective as biological control agents, and practical means of harnessing them are under

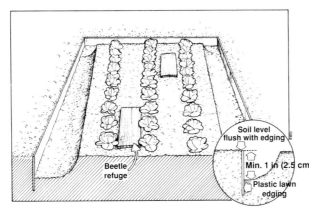

Experimental pitfall plot encloses carabid beetles for slug control (*Rob Dalton*)

Soil level flush with edging

Beetle refuge

Min. 1 in (2.5 cm)

Plastic lawn edging

investigation. Although many carabids will eat slugs, certain species, such as *Pterostichus niger* and *Abax parallelepipedus*, have been shown to be particularly important slug predators. *A. parallelepipedus* will lay up to 300 eggs in a season, may live for several years and, like several other useful species, is commonly found in gardens. Several micro-organisms, including nematode worms, a microsporidium, and certain strains of *Bacillus thuringiensis* (BT) all show promise, and may one day make organic slug control much simpler. (See also the section on commercially available biological control agents, page 315.)

Many birds will feed on slugs, including thrushes, blackbirds, robins, starlings, crows, jackdaws, gulls and even owls. Encourage these in the garden with shrubberies to nest in and provide winter berries, plus nest-boxes where appropriate. The shrubs will also provide cover for hedgehogs, shrews and badgers, while a pond will encourage frogs and toads to take up residence (see page 295). If you are really lucky you might encourage rare mollusc-eaters such as slow-worms, glow-worms and the extraordinary testacella slugs, which prey upon subsoil species in their burrows.

If you have space and opportunity, you can use chickens or ducks as biological control agents. The hens must be confined to a patch of ground that needs to be cultivated in any case, which they will clear of weeds, fertilize and thoroughly search for slugs and anything else that moves. Ducks can be given more freedom, and, as long as they have plenty of space, will do little damage to plants, although seedlings need protection from their big feet. Ducks are particularly fond of slugs.

Various natural products, including plant extracts from the tropical *Phytolacca dodecardra* and the temperate *Phytolacca americana*, plus a chemical extracted and subsequently synthesized from the common ragworm, offer the possibility of organic slug pellets in the near future. Some interesting new work involves the slug-repellent and killing

Thrush anvil: many birds rank high among slug predators (*D.H.Thomas*)

Slug resistance of potato varieties
Highly resistant: Pentland Dell, Pentland Ivory, Pentland Falcon, Stourmont Enterprise
Intermediate resistance: Majestic, Desiree, King Edward, Pentland Crown, Pentland Hawk, Record, Romano
Most susceptible: Maris Piper, Cara, Kingston, Ulster Glade

properties of propolis from beehives – the active ingredient(s) are being identified and isolated as potential molluscicides. As long as these do not harm other organisms, they will be a great improvement upon the existing formulations.

Aluminium sulphate and copper sulphate have in the past been considered acceptable for organic gardening. Both are contact molluscicides which can be used when the slugs are active on the surface. Applications should therefore be made on warm humid evenings, particularly following the clearing of a crop or recent cultivation, when the slugs will be seeking new food sources and refuges. Aluminium sulphate should not be applied to seedlings or lettuces, which can be damaged. Personally I would avoid using either of these chemicals – neither is very effective. A link has been established between Alzheimer's disease and aluminium in some susceptible individuals. Repeated use of copper sulphate, which can accumulate in the soil, can kill earthworms.

Resistant varieties. Although resistance to slug damage in potatoes has been shown in comparative trials, any variety, even the most resistant, may be attacked where no alternative food is on offer. Resistance, where it occurs, is in the skin of potatoes, and is due to the presence of two chemical compounds. When a slug bites the potato, these two chemicals come together to form quinones, which are highly reactive and highly unpleasant for the slug. However, where damage has already been caused by some other pest, wire-worms or spotted millipedes for example, this provides an entry point for the slugs that by-passes the defences in the skin.

The winter brassicas – kale, sprouting broccoli and spring cabbage – are more resistant to slug attack than, for example, summer cabbage, cauliflowers or Brussels sprouts. All are susceptible as seedlings.

The Continuity lettuce, and other 'red' varieties, are supposed to have greater resistance. In the ornamental garden some varieties are more resistant than others. For example *Lilium henryi* and *Lilium tigrinum* have roots that are more resistant to slug attack than *Lilium davidii* or *Lilium regale*. As many lilies are hybrids, their resistance will depend upon their ancestry. In hostas the blue-leaved types are less prone to slug damage than others. Discretion may be the better part of valour when it comes to slugs, and changing the variety is sometimes simpler than controlling the slugs.

APHIDS

Aphids, often referred to as greenfly or blackfly, are a very large group of homopteran bugs, with over 500 species in Britain alone, a few of which can be serious pests. While some species, such as the Peach-potato aphid (*Myzus persicae*), are general pests, feeding upon a wide range of host plants, others are specialists, and, like the Lettuce root aphid (*Pemphigus bursarius*), are really only a problem on one or a few particular types of plant. The damage they do, directly and indirectly, is enormous. Their small size has a considerable advantage in that they can frequently be carried for hundreds of miles by the wind, to found new colonies. Like all the most successful pests their main advantage is their phenomenal reproductive capacity, with single aphids having the theoretical potential to give rise to millions of tons of descendants in a few months. The strategies used to achieve these rates of increase vary between species, and can sometimes be quite complex. Most overwinter as eggs, following sexual fertilization, but then increase in summer by parthenogenesis, where females give birth to nymphs that are genetic clones of themselves, without any need for males. The nymphs come into the world with their own offspring already partially developed inside them. Colonies may increase in summer ten- to twentyfold in a week.

The problem. Aphids feed by inserting their mouthparts (stylets) into the stems, leaves or roots of plants, allowing the sap to flow up minute channels into their bodies. Vast amounts of this fluid have to be processed by the aphids in order to trawl out the small quantities of protein contained in it; this can stunt and distort plant growth.

Most of the sap leaves the other end of an aphid little changed, forming a sticky mess on the leaves. Although this has some advantage to the aphid, in that it deters some predators, it damages the leaves by restricting gaseous exchange through the leaf pores. It also frequently leads to secondary growths of sooty moulds, contaminating vegetables and disfiguring ornamentals.

Worse of all, in many cases, aphids spread diseases between plants, carrying viruses and other pathogens in their saliva.

Life cycles. As these vary from species to species, a chart has been constructed to show, in outline, the life cycles of some of the more important pest species. Often, as with the Black bean aphid, different host plants are used in summer and winter, offering additional opportunities for control.

Avoiding trouble – cultural methods. Interplanting slows down the spread of aphids from one plant to the next and encourages predators. Flowers will attract predators and parasites.

Avoid growing the winter host plants of troublesome species: Lombardy poplars for Lettuce root aphid, viburnum, euonymus and philadelphus for Black bean aphid.

Avoid feeding plants with excess nitrogen, which encourages soft sappy growth that is particularly prone to aphid attack. Cabbage aphid cycles can be broken by destroying all remaining overwintering plants before putting out new transplants, although admittedly this is often impractical. Bury all infested material in the compost heap or bean trenches.

Removal of the soft tips of broad bean plants when mature will help to limit the damage. Autumn-sown plants are tougher, and less often attacked.

The use of grease bands on trees and shrubs will prevent ants from protecting the aphids from their predators. Rub off woolly aphid colonies with methylated spirit. Sometimes, simply a strong jet of water will solve the problem. If all else fails, a spray with one of the soft soaps will kill aphids effectively, without the need to resort to the non-selective derris and pyrethrum. Soft soaps are made from plant extracts, and should not be confused with ordinary 'hard' soaps, derived from fossil fuels, the latter being far too harsh for use on the garden. 'Insecticidal soaps' are simply types of soft soap that have been selected as being particularly effective at killing small insects, the soap acting chemically upon their thin exoskeletons, and drowning them by disrupting the surface tension of the spray water. Larger insects, such as bees and ladybirds, being much more robust, are not killed by the soft soaps (although the insecticidal variety can also harm some of the smaller predators), but they can be killed by derris and pyrethrum. The timing of sprays can be very important. Leaf-curling plum aphids (*Brachycaudus helichrysi*), for example, have hatched on plums and damsons by mid-winter, and proceed to feed on the dormant buds, damaging the leaves both before and after they open. Spraying these in early spring will avoid harming the beneficial bees and predators.

Natural enemies and biological control. Ladybirds (adults and larvae), hover-flies (larvae) and lacewings (larvae) are the most important

Aphid life-cycle

Species	Overwinter	Summer	Autumn
Peach-potato aphid *Myzus persicae* (green or yellow)	Eggs on peaches and nectarines, or as actively breeding adults in glasshouses or outdoors in mild winters	Nymphs grow into winged adults, which migrate in late spring to many plants including potatoes, peas, tomatoes, beans, cucumbers, plus a great many ornamentals	Return to lay eggs on peach trees
Black bean aphid *Aphis fabae* (black)	Eggs on viburnum and euonymus, or as adults in a mild season	Nymphs grow into winged adults, which migrate in late spring to broad, French and runner beans, plus several ornamentals. Many summer generations of wingless females reproduce by parthenogenesis, i.e. non-sexually	A winged generation appears and returns to the winter host where a sexual generation lays eggs
Cabbage aphid *Brevicoryne brassica* (mealy grey green)	Eggs on brassica plants, also some adults in a mild season	Nymphs mature and produce a winged generation that spreads to new plants in the middle of the summer. However, colonies on all plants increase rapidly by parthenogenic reproduction of wingless females	A sexual generation appears and lays eggs
Lettuce root aphid *Pemphigus bursarius* (yellowish grey)	Eggs in leaf stalk galls on Lombardy poplars, although some wingless adults survive on the roots of lettuce plants, particularly in glasshouses	Populations build up on the poplars until early summer, when the winged adults migrate to lettuce and sow-thistle roots. Wingless females then reproduce and build up numbers	A winged generation is produced that returns to poplar trees
Woolly aphid *Eriosoma lanigerum* (brown aphid covered in fluffy wax tufts)	Young aphids on apples, rowans, other ornamentals, in galls and bark fissures	Reproduce mainly as wingless females – winged adults spread to new hosts nearby	Seek sheltered sites in which to overwinter

Woolly aphids on apple tree (*Chris Algar*)

aphid predators, and everything should be done to attract these and the many parasitic wasps.

The two- and the seven-spot kinds are the commonest and most important ladybird species, found early in the year breeding mainly on nettle aphids. Each larva and adult needs to eat several hundred aphids.

Hover-flies are attracted by the smell of the aphid colonies, and will lay their eggs among them. Each hover-fly larva requires up to 1,000 aphids to develop properly, and there are many beautiful species, found in gardens, that feed exclusively on aphids.

Parasitic wasps are frequently responsible for

Ladybird larva needs several hundred aphids to reach adulthood (*Natural Image*)

Hover-fly (*Episyrphus balteatus*), together with the lacewing and ladybird, one of the main aphid predators (*Natural Image*)

Parasitic wasp (*Mark Jervis*)

the collapse of aphid colonies. Careful examination will often reveal brown 'mummies' among the aphids, which are parasitized individuals. Where these are seen no treatment is necessary – the colony is collapsing in any case. Several species of wasp are under investigation as biological control agents for glasshouse crops, including *Aphidius matricariae*, which is now available. Also on offer is the nocturnal predatory

midge, *Aphidoletes aphidimyza*, which lays up to a hundred eggs near aphid colonies. The aphids are initially paralysed by a toxin, after which they are consumed by the larvae. Development rate depends upon temperature, and can take from four to sixteen days. Other control agents that can be purchased include green lacewings, *Chrysopa carnea*, and the fungal spray, *Verticilium lecanii* (see Commercially Available Biological Control Agents, page 315), which can be used in glasshouses on crops requiring a high humidity (it is not effective outside).

Hanging fat or peanuts in trees will encourage tits in the winter which, while waiting their turn, will try to balance their diets with a little protein in the form of aphids and their eggs.

Woolly aphids are being controlled by an American parasitic wasp, which is now widespread in orchards in southern England. Many other predators make their contribution, including other small birds (wrens, warblers, flycatchers), spiders, carabid and staphilinid beetles, predatory bugs and many more.

Resistant varieties. Varieties of lettuce resistant to lettuce root aphid exist, and can completely overcome this problem. Choose Avondefiance, Avoncrisp or Sabine.

Raspberry aphid-resistant varieties include Malling Orion, Malling Delight and Malling Leo. The broad bean variety Bolero is resistant to black bean aphids. Partial resistance to cabbage aphid has been reported in Red Drumhead and Yates Giant Red. Resistance declines as the season progresses.

CABBAGE WHITE CATERPILLARS

The term 'cabbage white' is normally applied to two species of butterfly, namely the Large White (*Pieris brassicae*) and the Small White (*Artogeia rapae*). These are in fact the only species of butterfly that cause significant crop damage in the UK.

The problem. Both species attack the leaves of garden brassicas including cauliflowers, kales, cabbages, broccoli, kohl rabi, Brussels sprouts and turnips. Many wild and ornamental plants may also be attacked, including mignonette, nasturtium and horse-radish. Holes are eaten in the leaves, while the centre of the plant becomes contaminated with droppings. In severe cases, the plant may be reduced to a skeleton. Secondary infection with disease frequently follows, although by this time it is somewhat academic, as the plant is probably ruined.

Life cycle. The Large White butterflies hatch from overwintering pupae in late spring, laying eggs in batches of six to a hundred on either side of brassica leaves. The female looking for plants on which to lay her eggs first 'tastes' the leaves to check their mustard content. This mustard, found in all the host plants utilized, is in fact a chemical defence by the plant against insect attack, which the cabbage whites have managed to overcome. Indeed, the mustard is particularly important to the Large Whites, which store this substance in their tissues, and use it as a chemical defence of their own, particularly against birds. The eggs hatch in about a week, and the larvae feed gregariously and in synchrony, protected by a web which they spin over the leaf. Later they disperse, often on to adjacent food plants. The larvae smell unpleasant, and produce droplets of green fluid if disturbed. The first generation usually pupates on or near the brassicas themselves after about a month. A second generation hatches in mid- to late summer, followed by a third, in a good summer, in early autumn. Larvae from these later generations seek pupation sites on trees, fences and walls, where they pass the winter.

The Small White has a very similar life cycle, but the first generation is generally around a month or so earlier in the year. The eggs are laid singly, hatching into well camouflaged velvety-green caterpillars. As these do not have the same degree of chemical protection as the Large White larvae, the green caterpillars are often found hiding in the heart of brassica plants, where they are protected from predators, and cause great damage.

Small White (*Artogeia rapae*) (*Bill Symondson*)

Avoiding trouble – cultural methods. Scattering your plants, or at least reducing contact between adjacent plants by interplanting, will help to prevent the spread of Large White caterpillar colonies. It also makes it more difficult for the females to find the plants.

Do not leave infested or unwanted cabbages in the garden. For example, always remove cauliflower plants once you have harvested the curd, to avoid providing the butterflies with another breeding site. Heavily infested plants may be buried in the compost heap – if some of the caterpillars do get out they can do no more damage as long as they are not yet mature enough to pupate, nor able to crawl to other food plants.

Simple examination of the leaves, and destruction by hand of the egg batches and caterpillar colonies, can be an effective control where small numbers of plants are involved.

Covering plants with netting (½ in/1 cm maximum holes) will prevent egg-laying in the first place.

Natural enemies and biological control. Several parasitic wasps attack Large and Small White larvae, in particular an Ichneumon fly (*Pimpla sp.*), and the Braconid (*Apanteles glomeratus*). Whereas the Ichneumon flies generally hatch from the pupae, the Braconid is a far more visible and familiar sight. Up to 150 grubs of this wasp hatch from a single caterpillar, pupating to form bright yellow silk cocoons which may completely smother the empty husk of the host larva.

Many birds, spiders, anthocorid bugs, ground beetles and hover-fly larvae will feed upon one stage or another of these butterflies.

Bacillus thuringiensis (BT) is now widely available as a microbial spray that kills only caterpillars, and spares all the natural enemies. It can be sprayed onto the foliage in the normal way, and must be eaten by the larvae to be effective. With this available, there is no need to resort even to the organic sprays, pyrethrum and

Large White caterpillar (*Pieris brassicae*) (*D.H.Thomas*)

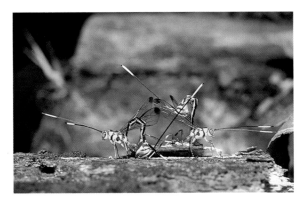

Ichneumon fly (*Holt Studios*)

Carrot root fly (*Psila rosae*) larva (*Holt Studios*)

derris, which, although non-persistent, are also non-selective, and may well kill beneficial insects and damage pond life.

Resistant varieties.   Partial resistance is found in Red Drumhead, Super Red, Yates Giant Red and Resistant Danish cabbage varieties .

CARROT ROOT FLY

The problem.   The carrot root fly (*Psila rosae*) is a very small black insect (⅓ in/8 mm long) that is likely to escape notice in the garden, but which can do damage, in its larval form, out of all proportion to its size. As all gardeners know to their cost, the white larvae burrow into carrot roots in late summer and autumn, contaminating and discolouring what they do not eat, and affecting the flavour of even lightly attacked roots. Less well known is the fact that these larvae may be feeding on the root hairs of the growing carrots from spring onwards, stunting growth and turning the leaves reddish-coloured. Parsnips, parsley, celery and several umbelliferous herbs are also attacked, as are indeed related hedgerow flowers, such as hemlock and hedge parsley. The galleries mined by these grubs allow other pests, such as slugs, wire-worms and millipedes, easy access to the inside of the roots, causing further damage. Diseases too may enter through such lesions, such as the parsnip cankers.

Life cycle.   Larvae from the previous season pupate during the autumn, winter or early spring, either in roots left in the ground, or in the surrounding soil. The pupae then start to hatch in late spring, and the females seek out carrots and other food plants, next to which they lay their eggs in the soil. These hatch in about a week, and feed, mainly on the root hairs, for a month, before they in turn pupate. The second generation then start to hatch in late summer, but these larvae grow more slowly, as temperatures drop. They feed more on the main root, burrowing inside for protection against frost and predators. The fly itself may be found

however at any time between late spring and early autumn.

Avoiding trouble – cultural methods.   Sowing your first crop of carrots in late spring or early summer avoids the first generation of grubs. A late spring, however, may catch you out, because then a late fly hatch, due to the lower temperatures, may still be around to attack the carrot seedlings. Other precautions are therefore necessary.

Sowing sparsely circumvents the dangers of thinning. The female fly homes in on the host mainly by following the scent. Thinning involves the bruising of young leaves, which liberate a strong and easily detected scent. If it has to be done, remove all thinnings, firm in the remaining seedlings, and water well to damp down the smell.

Varieties such as Early Nantes can be sown in early summer and harvested early, avoiding the worst of both fly generations, and providing sweet, quickly grown salad carrots for summer use. Maincrop carrots can also be sown late, but must not be allowed to remain in the soil into the autumn and winter. Such carrots should be lifted and stored in sand as soon as they are mature. Many of the grubs will be left behind in the soil, and if damaged roots, which may contain grubs, are used first, the remainder should keep well.

Interplanting carrots with onions and other strongly scented plants helps to disguise the carrot smell from the flies. Such a disguise may, in addition, be introduced artificially. In the past, a string soaked in creosote was stretched along the row, but as this is rather unpleasant to handle and not very organic, a better solution is to use a scattering of fresh sawdust, which is more adaptable to interplanting systems. Ensure, however, that the sawdust is not from timber treated with insecticide. A mulch of fresh lawn mowings has a similar effect, with the additional benefit of maintaining soil moisture in dry weather, although you may attract slugs.

Crop rotation is essential – you do not want

flies hatching in spring among your new crop of carrots. Remember that parsnips, parsley, celery and some herbs are attacked by the fly too, and must therefore be in the same rotation as the carrots (see page 84).

Old woody carrot or parsnip roots should never be left in the ground or even on the compost heap, where the fly can hatch out in spring. Burial in a well-made heap, capable of generating high temperatures, will destroy them, or you can entomb them deep in the ground (2ft/60 cm down). Otherwise they can be tied up and stored in plastic bags until mid-summer, by which time the flies should have hatched and died, and the contents can be tipped on to the compost heap. For small numbers of roots, submerge them for twenty-four hours in a bucket of water, to drown the grubs.

Lightweight spun polyester material is now available that can physically deny searching females access to the plants. This can either be used as a conventional cloche, stretched over wire hoops, or as a floating mulch, supported simply by the growing plants. The holes in the material are too small for the flies to get through, but allow rain-water to penetrate and air to circulate freely. It must be well anchored all round, but not so tightly stretched as to restrict plant growth. It must also, of course, be applied soon after sowing, before the flies can lay their

Carrot root fly barrier (*Roy Lacey*)

eggs. Such materials have the additional benefit of 'bringing on' the plants more quickly, which may allow them to reach maturity before the late-summer generation of fly is about.

The female carrot fly seeks carrots by flying close to the ground, following the scent plume upwind. Polythene or fine netting barriers may be constructed on frames to surround the plants, the theory being that this will thwart most of the flies, some of which will simply go around the patch, while others, trying to fly over the top, will overshoot. The barriers should be at least 2 ft 4 in (70 cm) high (the higher the better), and not more than about 3 ft (1 m) across from one side to the other. Again, plants will benefit from the warmth and shelter of such barriers, and grow more quickly.

A simpler solution is to grow carrots under polythene cloches until the middle of summer. Fly damage will be minimal, and yields can easily double.

Increased sowing density results in reduced fly damage per root, and higher yields.

Natural enemies. Carrot root fly eggs will be attacked by predatory carabid and staphilinid beetles. The use of within-bed refuges, in the form of pieces of slate, tile or wood, will help to encourage these insects (see under Slugs, controlled refuges, page 306), as will interplanting.

Several parasitic wasps attack the grubs. Flowers grown nearby will help to attract these nectar-feeding insects. Larvae and pupae overwintering in the soil should be exposed by thorough cultivation. They will be snapped up by robins, dunnocks and many other birds.

Resistant varieties. Attempts are being made to produce good-quality carrot varieties from crosses with the highly resistant Libyan species, *Daucus capillifolius*. Low levels of phenolic acids in this species, required by the grubs to complete their development, deter adults looking for suitable host plants. This is a white-rooted species, without culinary merit, but crosses with ordinary orange carrots have produced new varieties with both fly resistance and good eating quality. None of these new varieties is yet available, unfortunately. Meanwhile some partial resistance has been found in existing commercial carrots.

Partially resistant varieties: Bridge, Early Scarlet Horn, Empire, Fancy, French Forcing Horn, Ideal, James Intermediate, Prima, Sytan, Tantal, Tiptop, Touchon, Vertou. If none of these is available, go for a 'Nantes' type carrot, as most resistance has been found in this group.

Susceptible varieties: Danvers Half Long 126.

CABBAGE ROOT FLY

The problem. The cabbage root fly (*Delia radicum*) is not related to the carrot root fly: it is in fact closer to the common house-fly. The adults may be found from early spring right through to late autumn, while the ⅓ in (8 mm) white grubs may attack plants throughout this period. Any of the brassicas may be attacked – cabbages, cauliflowers, Brussels sprouts, broccoli, kohl rabi, turnips, radishes, oil-seed rape and swedes, plus some wild plants, wallflowers and stocks. The root crops among these, such as turnips and radishes, are mined in the same way as carrots by the carrot root fly, and with similar consequences. Most of the worst damage takes place between mid-spring and mid-summer, when transplanted brassicas of all types are most susceptible and are frequently killed. As the plants mature, later in the season, they can tolerate root fly attacks, although they may suffer from loss of vigour, or succumb to secondary diseases. The grubs frequently migrate up inside the stems of the plants, and can sometimes be found inside Brussels sprouts.

Life cycle. There are three generations a year. Pupae overwinter in the soil, and most hatch in mid-spring. Eggs are laid on or near the base of the host plants, each female laying about forty

Cabbage root fly (*Delia radicum*) (*Holt Studios*)

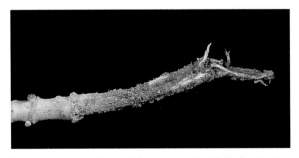

Damage caused by cabbage root fly (*Holt Studios*)

Protective felt square fitted round young brassicas can protect against root fly attack (*Chris Algar*)

to eighty eggs, which hatch and feed on the roots for about a month before pupation. The second generation appears in early to mid-summer, and a third in early or mid-autumn. As a good general indicator, the first generation of flies usually hatches at the time when hedge parsley comes into flower, which of course varies with latitude, altitude, and seasonal temperatures.

Avoiding trouble – cultural methods. Lightweight spun polyester used as a floating cloche or mulch can be used to control this pest in exactly the same way as for carrot root fly protection (see page 313).

Interplanting will disguise the appearance and smell of the brassicas from the cabbage root fly females looking for laying sites, as well as from other brassica pests. Undersowing with a ground cover plant such as white clover has been shown to reduce fly attacks, possibly by disrupting the egg-laying behaviour of the females, and by encouraging predators. Interplanting with broad and French beans has proven successful where the plants are approximately the same size at planting out.

Protective squares (6 x 6 in/15 x 15 cm) of roofing felt or carpet underlay can be most effective at reducing damage. These are fitted round young brassicas, which prevents the flies laying near the base of the plant. What is more, the material acts as a mulch, conserving moisture around the roots of the young plant and promoting growth. The larger the plant gets, the better it can withstand fly attack.

Rotation with non-host plants is essential – you should not make it too easy for the hatching flies. Raising transplants to a larger than normal size in pots will ensure that a good root system exists, better able to withstand attack. This practice may already be used as a means of growing brassicas in land infected with club root.

This can be followed by progressive earthing up of the stems, allowing adventitious root development.

Natural enemies. Where squares of roofing felt are used, some eggs will inevitably still be laid by the female cabbage root fly. However, these are preyed upon by several species of small carabid beetles, which use the squares as refuges.

Winter cultivation will expose pupae to the birds, and again infected plant material must be disposed of in a way that prevents the grubs completing their life cycle. This is a stronger flier than the carrot root fly, and may travel considerable distances to reach your garden.

The organic garden will contain thousands of spiders, which have in the past been sadly neglected as natural control agents, but which are probably the prime predators of the adult root flies and many other pests.

Additional refuges for carabid and staphilinid beetles within brassica beds may be counter-productive where protective squares are used. The latter attract the predators to precisely where they are needed, at the base of the plants.

Resistant varieties. Partial resistance is shown by Persista, Golden Acre, Red Drumhead, Super Red, Drumhead Late, Late Purple Flat Poll, Yates Giant Red, Little Rock.

COMMERCIALLY AVAILABLE BIOLOGICAL CONTROL AGENTS

Unless otherwise stated, all these control agents are for use in glasshouses only. Full details of how to use these predators will be provided on request from most suppliers, while the costs are often less than those for a chemical alternative. The growing of a few flowers in the glasshouse (particularly umbellifers) will help sustain many predators and parasites for longer. Eradication of ants, that protect pests such as aphids, scale insects and mealybugs from predators, may be necessary, and can best be achieved by pouring boiling water on the nests. Access by ants to staging can be prevented with fruit-tree grease.

The numbers at the end of each entry refer to the suppliers listed in the Appendix (page 394).

APHIDS

Aphidius matricariae: parasitic wasp, ⅟₁₆ in (2 mm) long, lays eggs in aphids, lives for up to two weeks. Unusually, more than 60% of the wasps are females. Generation intervals of two to three weeks. Large numbers of eggs are laid, resulting in up to a hundred adult offspring per female wasp. This is a native parasite, that may become established by itself. Supplied as adults. (2,3,4,5,6,11)

Aphidoletes aphidimyza: nocturnal predatory midge, ⅟₁₆ in (2 mm) long, lays up to a hundred eggs. Larvae feed on aphids, and each generation takes approximately three weeks to complete development. Supplied as pupae. (2,3,4,5,6,8, 9,10,11)

Chrysopa carnea: the green lacewing, whose active red and yellow larvae, up to ½ in (1 cm) long, crawl about the plants consuming aphids, thrips, small caterpillars and other pests. The beautiful green adults, with their lacy green wings, feed on aphids too, sucking out the body fluids. However, they also need pollen to develop their eggs, so flowers in the glasshouse are particularly important. Supplied as eggs or pupae. (2,4)

Verticilium lecanii: a fungus that kills aphids, but which will only work in glasshouses that maintain a high humidity (85-90%), for the growing of cucumbers for example. Spray on to infested plants. Will also kill whiteflies, thrips and scale insects, and a single application may eliminate these pests for several months. Unfortunately, the conditions that suit this fungus are also ideal for destructive pathogenic fungi that attack plants, such as *Botrytis sp.* Parasitic wasps are little affected, however, and are thought to help spread the fungus to pest colonies. Supplied as a powder. (7,10)

CATERPILLARS

Bacillus thuringiensis: a bacterium that can be sprayed onto infested crops, which will kill only lepidopterous larvae that feed upon treated foliage. Caterpillars are killed by a toxin released by the bacterium, but which is harmless to everything (and everybody) else. Can be used outdoors as well as in the greenhouse. Supplied as a powder to mix with water, and now widely available, even from better garden centres. Sold in the UK under trade names such as Dipel, Bactospeine, and Thuricide. (2,3,4,5,6,7,8,11)

Chrysopa carnea: see Aphids

LEAF MINERS

Dacnusa sibirica: a parasitic wasp. The adult wasp locates the larva within the leaf mine, and lays an egg in it, piercing both leaf and larva with her ovipositor. The adult lives for about two weeks, during which she lays up to ninety eggs, which mature into new adults in approximately three weeks. Supplied as adults. (2,3,4,5,8,11)

Verticilium lecanii can be introduced into greenhouses to control aphids, whiteflies, thrips and scale insects (*Holt Studios*)

Cryptolaemus montrouzieri, a ladybird that can control mealybugs (*Holt Studios*)

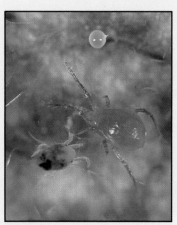

Red spider mite predator, *Phytoseiulus persimilis* (*Holt Studios*)

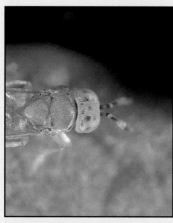

Metaphycus helvolus which parasitizes scale insects (*Holt Studios*)

Encarsia formosa emerging from parasitized whitefly scale (*Holt Studios*)

Some of the growing number of biological control agents

Diglyphus isaea: a parasitic wasp. A British species that may find its own way into the glasshouse from mid–summer onwards. The leaf miner is first killed or paralysed by the adult wasp, which then lays eggs next to the grub. Around sixty eggs are laid per female, which take two and a half to three weeks to develop. An indication of the degree of parasitism is afforded by the 'pit props' the wasp larva constructs in the mine with its droppings. Has the advantage of immediately immobilizing the leaf miners and preventing further damage. Adult wasps also feed directly on leaf miners. Supplied as adults. (2,3,4,5,8)

MEALYBUGS

Cryptolaemus montrouzieri: a black and orange/brown ¼ in (4 mm) long Australian ladybird, with larvae that resemble mealybugs. Both adults and larvae are excellent mealybug predators, one larva requiring approximately 250 mealybugs to complete development. Life cycle takes twenty-five to fifty days (86-68°F/30-20°C). About ten eggs a day will be laid in mealybug colonies, each female laying up to 500 eggs in total. Not suitable for tomato mealybugs. Fix net curtains over vents to prevent predators escaping. Supplied as adults. (2,3,4,5,6,9,10,11)

Leptomastix dactylopii, Leptomastiidea abnormis and *Anagyrus pseudococci:* parasitic wasps, lay eggs in immature mealybugs which become mummified. At 68°F (20°C) the life cycle takes about four weeks. *L. abnormis* is more useful at lower temperatures (68-77°F/20-25°C) than the other two species (77°F/25°C+). Supplied as adults. (2,3,5,11)

RED SPIDER MITES

Phytoseiulus persimilis: a predatory mite, originally from Chile, that is similar in appearance to the pest. Feeds upon mites and their eggs, adults eating around seven mites a day. Can increase very rapidly under warm (72°F/22°C+) humid conditions, much more quickly than the pest, which may be exterminated, causing the predator to die out. Supplied on leaves or mixed with bran. A widely used and highly successful control agent. (2,3,4,5,6,7,8,9,10,11)

SOFT SCALES

Metaphyccus helvolus: parasitic wasp, that both lays its eggs in these pests and also, like many other parasitoids, makes holes in other scales with its ovipositor, simply to feed upon the contents. Parasitizes about six scales a day, but

may kill up to twenty-four scales in the same interval to feed on them. Life cycle eleven to thirty days (86-68°F/30-20°C). Adults live much longer than most parasitoids, up to two months. Supplied as adults. (2,3,4,5,6,11)

THRIPS

Amblyseius mackenziei and *Amblyseius cucumeris:* predatory mites that attack thrips. Unlike *Phytoseiulus persimilis*, the red spider mite predator, the mite can survive on alternative prey (such as red spider mites) once it has eliminated the thrips, performing a useful lying-in-wait strategy that prevents re-infestation. Can co-exist with the red spider mite predator. Supplied in shaker bottles, or in dispensers containing wheatgerm and grain mites. The thrip predators breed in the dispensers, feeding upon the grain mites, while a slow but constant stream of thrip predators escapes from the dispensers into the crop. (2,3,4,5,8,11)

Verticilium lecanii: see Aphids

Chrysopa carnea: see Aphids

VINE WEEVILS

Steinernema carpocapsae and *Heterorhabditis bacteriophora:* nematode worms that kill vine weevil grubs within the glasshouse soil or growing medium. Will also kill the larvae of Sciarids (mushroom flies or fungus gnats) and other soil pests. The nematodes release a bacterium that kills the grubs, usually within forty-eight hours of treatment, and then proliferate in the corpse. Simply watered onto beds and pots. Found to be more effective than the now banned organochloride chemicals that this biological control agent has replaced. Supplied as liquid concentrate held in a synthetic sponge. (1,2,3,4,11)

WHITEFLY

Encarsia formosa: parasitic wasp, which lays its eggs in the larval whiteflies that resemble scale insects, turning them black. Adults live about two weeks, laying up to a hundred eggs. Life cycle takes twenty-four to twenty-eight days (86-68°F/30-20°C). Also kills immature scales by probing with the ovipositor, and feeding. As with most of these parasites, early establishment is essential, or the whiteflies may simply out-breed the wasps. One of the most successful and widely used control agents. Supplied as parasitized scales. (2,3,4,5,6,7,8,9,10,11)

Verticilium lecanii: see Aphids

Pests chart

Pest	Plants affected	The problem
Ants Common Black *Lasius niger* Yellow Meadow *Lasius flavus* Pharaoh's *Monomorium* *pharaonis* Argentine *Iridomyrmex humilis* and many others	Little direct damage to plants. Oily seeds, such as those of primulas and rhododendron, often taken as a food source. Indirect damage to almost any plant	Ant nests may physically undermine small plants, especially in rockeries. The mounds constructed by meadow ants can cause problems in lawns. Apart from seeds, some plant material may be taken by certain species for the growing of fungi in their nests, but this is rarely a serious problem. The protection of aphids (which are 'milked' by *L. niger* and other species for honeydew) from predators and parasites is sometimes an important problem. Ladybirds, lacewings (and their larvae) and parasitic wasps may be driven away. Scale insects and mealybugs may be similarly attended and protected
Beetles Asparagus beetle *Crioceris asparagi* (adults black and yellow, up to ½ in/6 mm, larvae dark grey)	Asparagus	Adults and larvae feed on foliage throughout the summer. In extreme cases plants may be completely defoliated. Adults hibernate under plant debris, etc. close to the soil. There are three generations per annum
Blossom beetles *Meligethes aeneus* (like small black ladybirds, up to 1/16 in/2mm)	On many flowers, but in the garden particularly noticeable on sweet peas, runner beans, chrysanthemums etc. Also on calabrese	Enter gardens in early summer. This is a recent phenomenon, caused by the spread in cultivation of oilseed rape. Mainly a cosmetic problem however
Cockchafers *Melolontha melolontha* (the largest of several chafers – enormous crescent-shaped white grubs up to 1 ½ in/40mm, huge beetles with brown wing cases and white triangles along the sides)	Almost all plants can be affected by the grubs, which can be particularly troublesome in lawns, on soft fruit such as strawberries and raspberries, on young trees, and in herbaceous borders	Roots, tubers, corms and stems attacked, killing or weakening plants, and rendering them susceptible to secondary diseases. Eggs laid in the soil in summer can take up to five years to grow into adults. The adults can damage leaves, flowers and fruit of several trees and shrubs, notably apples and roses
Flea beetles *Phyllotreta sp.* (several species, tiny flea-like beetles in several colours, mainly black, some striped with yellow, up to 1/10 in/3 mm)	Crucifers, including cabbages, kale, turnips, radishes and swedes, plus wallflowers, and many ornamentals such as godetias, irises, stocks and nasturtiums	Holes eaten in the leaves of seedlings in the spring, which, particularly in dry weather, will seriously weaken or kill the young plants. The main damage is done by the adults following hibernation. Later, in late spring/early summer, eggs are laid in the soil, and the emerging larvae attack the roots or (in some species) enter the leaves as leaf miners. These become adults by autumn, when further damage can occur before they go into winter hibernation. They can transmit viruses between plants
Lily beetles *Lilioceris lilii* (bright red beetle, up to ¼ in/6 mm, slimy orange larvae)	Lilies, Solomon's seal, fritillarias, *nomocharis*	Adults and larvae feed upon the leaves, often causing extensive damage in early summer

Control measures	Natural enemies and biological control (* see pages 296 and 315)	

No action should be contemplated against ants unless an immediate problem is seen to be developing, as ants are also important garden predators, taking huge numbers of pest insects such as caterpillars and grubs. They can be prevented from protecting aphids, scale insects and mealybugs in trees and shrubs by grease banding (see Winter Moths). Nests in inconvenient places may be destroyed with boiling water. Derris will also kill ants.

Lizards, toads, birds and predatory beetles

Aphids being 'herded' by ants (Chris Algar)

Pick off by hand, clear plant debris where beetles are known to be hibernating. Derris dust as a last resort

Larvae attacked by the parasitic wasp *Tetrastichus asparagi*

If cut flowers are placed for a short time in a dark shed, the beetles will leave them and fly towards the light. They will occasionally damage calabrese – fine netting used for cabbage root fly will exclude these too

General predators, mainly birds and spiders

Asparagus beetles (*Criocerus asparagi*) (D.H.Thomas)

Rarely a problem in cultivated ground, but can, like wire-worms, be found in newly converted lawn or pasture. In lawns use of a heavy roller in late spring/early summer will crush pupae and emerging adults beneath the surface. Thorough cultivation will rapidly eliminate this problem, where practicable

Birds, including the crow family, starlings, black-birds and thrushes

Cockchafer (*Melolontha melolontha*) (Holt Studios)

Water plants well in dry weather. Clear plant debris in winter, under which flea beetles are known to be hibernating. Vigorously growing young seedlings can withstand attacks better. Later sowings, in early summer, escape the worst attacks. Floating mulches of polypropylene will exclude most beetles flying onto the site. Boards coated with grease can be held over infested plants – the beetles jump when disturbed and can be caught. Use derris if all else fails

Several parasitic wasps attack the larvae, as do carabid and staphilinid beetles. Adults caught by general predators, such as birds and toads

Pick off by hand, clear plant debris on which they are overwintering. As a last resort apply derris dust

Red warning coloration indicates that they are probably distasteful to many predators

Pests chart

Pest	Plants affected	The problem
Beetles		
Pea and Bean weevils *Sitonia lineatus* and others (inconspicuous brown short-snouted weevils, up to ¼ in/5 mm)	Peas and beans, plus roses, carnations, lupins and several other ornamentals	Semi-circular sections removed from the edges of the leaves, particularly of seedling peas and beans. Larva feed on root nodules. Overwintering adults lay eggs in spring, which become adult by mid-summer, when further damage can occur. One generation per year
Raspberry beetles *Byturus tomentosus* (creamy-brown larvae with dark heads, up to ⅓ in/8 mm)	Raspberries, blackberries, loganberries and related hybrids	Although the adults cause some damage to developing buds in spring, it is mainly the unpleasant presence of the grubs in ripe fruit that is the problem. Eggs laid by overwintering adults in spring on the flowers. These hatch in about two weeks, and immediately tunnel into the fruit. If not picked and inadvertently eaten, the grubs pupate in the soil beneath the canes. One generation per year
Strawberry beetles *Harpalus rufipes* *Pterostichus madidus* *Pterostichus melanarius* (black ground beetles up to 1 in/20 mm)	Strawberries	Ground beetles are the most valuable general insect predators we have in the garden, but they will nibble at strawberries, particularly after dry weather. They are to be found throughout the summer months. *H rufipes* goes for the seeds, whereas the other species eat the flesh
Vine weevils *Otiorhynchus sulcatus* (large, grey-brown weevils up to ½ in/10 mm white grubs, up to ⅓ in/8 mm)	Many pot plants attacked, including cyclamen, begonias and primulas. Rhododendrons and other outdoor plants also attacked	Mainly a glasshouse problem, where roots, bulbs and corms are eaten by the grubs. Adults can cause mainly cosmetic damage to leaves and stems upon which they feed. Under glass grubs and adults may be found at all times of year. Almost all vine weevils are female, which can reproduce by parthogenesis, without males. As each vine weevil can lay 1,000 eggs, this pest can quickly become a major problem
Wire-worms *Athous haemorrhoidalis* and *Agriotes lineatus* (yellow to golden brown, with six legs near the head, tough-skinned and leathery, up to 1 in/25 mm)	Can attack the roots of almost any vegetable, and many herbaceous ornamentals	Eat plant roots, burrowing into root crops such as potatoes, and into bulbs. Such holes frequently allow secondary infestations of millipedes or slugs to cause further damage, or allow the entry of pathogens. The adults are click beetles, which flick themselves into the air when touched. Eggs laid in early to mid-summer the larvae taking up to five years to reach pupation
Birds		
Blackbirds, thrushes, bullfinches, sparrows, pigeons, blue tits and others	Soft fruit, fruit trees, peas and beans, brassicas, flowers of many kinds	Fruit of all sorts are eaten by many birds. Bullfinches are particularly annoying in that they feed upon fruit and leaf buds. Sparrows and other birds will pull off the flowers of primulas, crocuses and other plants for no very good reason. Red-flowered runner beans are particularly prone to this too. Many birds will peck at apples, pears and plums, causing damage that is further extended by wasps and earwigs. Pigeons will shred brassicas in winter, especially when snow is on the ground

Control measures	Natural enemies and biological control (* see pages 296 and 315)	

Only seedlings are at serious risk, and if these are growing strongly they can resist most attacks. Clear plant debris where adults are known to overwinter

Birds, predatory beetles

Pea and bean weevil (*Sitona lineatus*) (*Holt Studios*)

Light cultivation of the soil around the canes in winter will expose the hibernating adults to predators and the weather. Derris can be applied as soon as flowering has finished, in the hope that at least some of the grubs will be caught as they hatch, and before they have time to burrow out of reach into the fruit. Applying derris too early risks killing pollinators, so to be safe apply only in the late evening

General predators, including birds, spiders and predatory beetles. Many in fact eaten by humans

Do not attempt to kill these insects: they are far too valuable. Catch them among strawberries in jars, sunk to their rims in the soil, and transfer them to pitfall plots to protect other crops from slug damage (see section on slug control, page 306)

Birds, hedgehogs, toads

Vine weevils cannot fly. Grease bands can therefore be used as barriers to prevent entry to the glasshouse, or to staging, or on individual pots. Staging can also stand on bricks in bowls of water to which detergent is added, again preventing access to the plants. Avoid introducing the pest on plant material brought into the glasshouse. Discard infested pot plants

General predators outdoors, especially birds and ground beetles. A nematode is now sold commercially that controls these grubs more effectively than the old persistent chemicals that have now been banned. Soon to be made available to the amateur market*. A fungus, *Metarhizium anisopliae*, has also been found to provide effective control, and may soon become available

Mainly a problem in newly cleared ground, particularly old pasture. Weed control will make the site unattractive to egg-laying females, and the problem will diminish in time. Avoid using infested compost, especially if made from old turf. Cultivation between crops exposes the larvae to predators. Lift root crops early in infested ground

Birds and, probably, ground beetles

Wire-worm (*Agriotes* species) in potato tuber (*Holt Studios*)

Netting is the best answer. However, modern mono-filament netting is difficult for birds to see, and they can easily become entangled in it. Ensure that it is tightly stretched. Threads of wool can be woven into the netting to make it more visible. Check frequently to release trapped birds. Seedlings can be protected by pea guards. A single strand of black cotton stretched along the row above the seedlings appears to discourage birds. Flashing strips of foil and vibrating tapes can also work. Scarecrows may work for a while. Grow white-flowered beans

Birds are better discouraged from feeding on particular crops, rather than controlled. Apart from pigeons and bullfinches, all the other 'pest' species are important garden predators

Pests chart

Pest	Plants affected	The problem
Capsid Bugs Common green capsid *Lygocoris pabulinus* (⅜ in/12 mm, several similar species. Mostly green, some yellow or brown. Bugs can be distinguished by their 'sucking' mouthparts)	Fruit trees, soft fruit bushes, potatoes, beans and many ornamentals	Irregular holes eaten in leaves, attacks on developing buds and shoots lead to distorted growths and skin blemishes on fruit. Can transmit viruses. Eggs over-winter on plants or leaf litter, hatching into nymphs in spring. These develop through to adults that lay the eggs of a second generation in early/mid-summer
Earwigs Common earwig *Forficula auricularia* (Fast-moving, brown, long body, ending in pincers, up to 1 in/25 mm)	Many flowers, notably chrysanthemums and dahlias. Apples and other fruit	Holes eaten in petals causing cosmetic damage. In fruit, may extend and further contaminate holes made by other pests.
Eelworms Many species *Nematode* (Microscopic worm-like creatures, up to ¹⁄₁₆ in/2 mm)	Potatoes, onions, parsnips, beans, brassicas, carrots, strawberries, chrysanthemums, daffodils, and many other vegetables and ornamentals	Feed parasitically inside the roots, stems and leaves of plants, consuming the fluid contents of cells. This leads to a variety of symptoms, often including distortion of growth, discoloration of leaves, stunting or death. In moist conditions there is a rapid turnover of successive generations. In dry soil, eggs can remain viable for many years
Flies Cabbage root fly (see page 314) *Delia brassicae* Carrot root fly (see page 312) *Psila rosae*		
Crane-flies (leatherjackets) *Tipula sp.* (large dark grey leathery grubs of the Daddy-long-legs, up to 2 in/5 cm)	Lawns, vegetables, ornamentals	The grubs eat the roots of many plants, causing them to wilt and turn yellow. Adults lay eggs in late summer which feed through the autumn, spring and following summer
Leaf miners Many species (up to ¼ in/6 mm)	Beetroot, celery, holly, chrysanthemums, carnations, sweet williams and many more	The larvae of many species of fly live within leaves, burrowing between the upper and lower layers, well protected from most predators
Mushroom flies *Sciara sp.* and others (tiny midge-like flies, with equally small white grubs, although some species grow to 1 in/25 mm)	Seedling plants in glasshouses, and in mushrooms	The grubs live in potting composts, both on fungi and also on the roots of many seedlings. Under glass there is no respite, with continuous successive generations

Control measures	Natural enemies and biological control (* see pages 296 and 315)
As many bugs are in fact predatory, control of just those species that cause damage is difficult. Liquid derris or derris dust can be used for spot treatment in an emergency. Most attacks cause simply cosmetic damage and are not likely seriously to affect plant health or yield	Birds, spiders, wasps and other general predators
Grow susceptible flowers away from source areas of rotting plant debris. As earwigs are predators of aphids and pests they should not be killed. Limited trapping in upturned flower pots stuffed with straw, on the ground or on top of poles, can remove earwigs from among valuable flowers	Birds, frogs and toads, shrews
Avoid plant material from doubtful sources, as plants, cuttings, tubers, bulbs and even seeds can introduce eelworms to the garden. Strict four-course rotation of crops will avoid the worst attacks. A few species can be controlled by interplanting with French or African marigolds. Certain potato varieties are resistant to particular eelworm species, e.g. Maris Piper and Pentland Javelin resist yellow potato cyst eelworm	No information
Mainly a problem of ground recently brought into cultivation. Thorough cultivation and control of weeds will soon eliminate this pest. In lawns, affected areas can be watered, covered with polythene, and left overnight. By morning most grubs will have come to the surface, and can be brushed up	Birds, particularly starlings and members of the crow family
Crush the larvae or pick off affected leaves. Winter cultivation exposes overwintering pupae to the weather and predators	Several parasitic wasps attack these grubs. In glass-houses the parasitic wasps Dacnusa sibirica and Diglyphus isaea can be used*
Ensure that plants are correctly watered, as stressed plants will be particularly vulnerable. Yellow sticky traps, as used for whitefly, will help control the adults. No action is needed unless plants are suffering, as many species are harmless	Taken by birds and predatory beetle larvae. Nematodes available for the control of vine weevils will also kill these fly larvae*

Common green capsid (*Lygocoris pabulinus*) on raspberry fruit (*Holt Studios*)

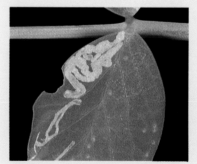

Leaf miner in pea leaf (*Holt Studios*)

Pests chart

Pest	Plants affected	The problem
Flies		
Onion fly *Delia antiqua* (white grubs up to ⅓ in/8 mm)	Onions, shallots and leeks	Grubs burrow into the bulbs and stems, often killing young plants, contaminating others, and allowing diseases access to the flesh. Life cycle very similar to that of its relative, the Cabbage root fly
Thrips, 'Thunder flies' (primitive insects, ⅒ in/3-4 mm long, dark bodies and four leathery wings. Many species)	Several vegetables, including peas, beans, brassicas, tomatoes and onions. Also very many flowers, outdoors and in the glasshouse, including gladioli, roses, carnations, chrysanthemums and sweet peas	Feed upon leaves, piercing surface cells and consuming contents. This disfigures plants, causing surface flecking, a silvery sheen and frequently distorted growth. Can transmit plant viruses. The larvae are similar to the adults, but wingless. Breeding only limited by temperature with adults and larvae overwintering in the soil. Adults carried long distances by the wind
Mammals		
Mice *Apodemus sylvaticus* Several other species	Peas and beans, bulbs of daffodils, tulips, lilies and others	Peas and beans are frequently eaten almost as soon as they are sown, while bulbs and corms may be attacked at any time, although mice tend to move into sheds and garages in winter, where stored fruit and seeds may be consumed
Moles *Talpa europaea*	Lawns, vegetables and herbaceous plants	Mole damage is indirect, the result of disturbance caused to plants during the mole's burrowing activities. There is also the cosmetic damage to lawns, which look less attractive if covered in molehills
Rabbits *Oryctolagus cuniculus*	Most vegetables, many ornamentals, fruit and other trees	Most garden vegetables can be stripped of their leaves by rabbits, particularly in winter when other natural food is scarce. Root crops are also vulnerable, such as carrots, beetroot and even parsnips. Bark may be stripped from young fruit trees, especially when snow is on the ground. Rabbits can breed at any time of the year, although most are born in late winter and early summer
Squirrels *Sciurus carolinensis*	Fruit and nut trees, bulbs	Generally the main problem is damage to the bark, buds and shoots of trees. In the garden they will often make the growing of nut trees almost impossible, and will take plums and many other fruits too, including soft fruit. Will also dig up and eat many bulbs and corms

Control measures	Natural enemies and biological control (* see pages 296 and 315)	
Winter cultivation will expose pupae to the weather and to predators. Remove all infested material. Rotate crops. Intercropping may help 'hide' the onions from the flies. Onions grown from sets usually unaffected by this pest	Birds and ground beetles	 Onion fly (*Delia antiqua*) (*Holt Studios*)
Mainly a problem in hot dry conditions where the plants are stressed, so try to ameliorate and avoid this situation. The best spray to use is insecticidal soap, otherwise derris or pyrethrum	Introduce *Amblyseuis cucumeris* or *A. mackenzieri* early in the season, as biological control agents in the greenhouse*. Attacked by general predators, such as spiders, birds etc.	 'Thunder fly' – rose thrip (*Thrips fuscipennis*) (*Holt Studios*)
Spring traps are the only real answer. If used outdoors, confine them to cloches, cold frames and pea guards, as there are few sights more heart-rending than a robin caught by a mousetrap	Foxes, birds of prey, stoats, weasels. The best biological control is a healthy young cat	
Moles can be trapped, although personally I would rather put up with the damage. Various chemical and acoustic repellents have been used without great success, but they may be worth a try	Most predators find moles distasteful	
Apart from shooting and trapping, netting of one sort or another is the best answer. Chicken-wire fences must be dug well into the soil, to prevent them burrowing underneath. Electrified sheep netting can also be used – although more expensive this provides a flexible system that is quicker and easier to install. None of the repellents that are available is entirely reliable. Spiral tree guards can prevent damage to bark	Foxes, birds of prey, stoats, weasels, pole cats, mink. A strong young cat will take many young rabbits, while a dog will chase them away. Ferrets can be used to catch rabbits if they are living in burrows. Myxomatosis was also introduced as a biological control, spreading via fleas and mosquitoes. Considerable resistance has built up in rabbit populations, which are now on the increase	 Electrified netting provides a flexible rabbit deterrent (*Bill Symondson*)
Netting is the only answer, but it will be a battle of wits between you and the squirrels	Birds of prey, stoats, weasels and pine martens. Cats will sometimes surprise a squirrel on the ground	

Pests chart

Pest	Plants affected	The problem
Mealybugs Glasshouse mealybugs, especially *Pseudococcus obscurus* (Homopteran bugs, up to ⅒ in/ 4 mm, soft bodied and covered in white waxy material)	Attack a wide range of glasshouse plants, including vines, cacti, ferns, figs and African violets	Feed on sap, debilitating the plant, and contaminating it with honeydew and sooty moulds. Mainly disperse as young nymphs, adult colonies being largely immobile. Can breed throughout the year in heated glasshouses
Millipedes Spotted millipede *Blaniulus guttulatus* (cream millipedes with a row of red spots down each side, up to ¼ in/ 20 mm) Also several other species (Millipedes have two pairs of legs per segment, and are slow-moving. Centipedes, which are beneficial predators, have one pair of legs per segment, and move more rapidly. Up to 2 in/50 mm)	Spotted millipedes mainly a problem in potatoes. Other species will attack root crops, pea, bean and other seedlings, bulbs and corms, strawberries	Spotted millipedes can be a serious pest of potatoes burrowing into them and allowing secondary pests and diseases access to the tubers. Other millipedes will extend damage caused by pests such as slugs and wire-worms. Particularly a problem where high levels of organic matter are used and in association with mulches
Mites Glasshouse Red Spider mite *Tetranychus urticae* (red, yellow or green at different times of year, less than 1mm, spherical spider-like creatures with eight legs)	Outdoor and glasshouse plants attacked, including cucumbers, tomatoes, peppers, strawberries, vines, fuchsias, chrysanthemums and many others	Typical bronzing of the leaves caused by feeding upon the surface. Colonies of mites found on the undersides. Growth frequently distorted; in the later stages the whole plant may be covered in web. Plants may be killed. Generation intervals of as little as a week in summer. Overwinter as adults in soil crevices
Fruit Tree Red Spider mites *Panonychus ulmi* As above	Apples, pears, plums and related ornamentals, such as hawthorns and rowans	Similar damage to glasshouse species. Weakens and disfigures the trees, and may severely reduce yields. Overwinter as reddish egg masses on twigs. Several summer generations
Blackcurrant Gall mites *Cecidophyopsis ribis* (less than 0·25 mm)	Blackcurrants	Known as 'big bud'. Infested buds become round and swollen, leading to distorted growth. The mites transmit the virus that causes 'reversion' disease. As the buds burst in spring the mites spread to new dormant buds
Pear Leaf Blister mites *Eriophyes pyri* (less than 0·25 mm)	Mainly pears, but also sometimes rowans, apples, cotoneasters and related species	Mites in overwintering buds damage the developing young leaves, within the tissues of which they feed during the summer. This causes yellowish blisters, that blacken later in the year. Towards the end of summer the mites invade new buds

Control measures	Natural enemies and biological control (* see pages 296 and 315)	

Can be brushed off with soapy water or methylated spirit. Avoid introducing infested material in the first place

Introduce *Cryptolaemus montrouzieri*, a ladybird that feeds on these bugs in the greenhouse. Both adults and larvae are excellent predators. Also in the glasshouse, several commercially available parasitic wasps can be tried*

Strict rotation of root crops will avoid the worst problems. Winter and between-crops cultivation will expose them to predators. Identify and deal with the primary pests that are initiating the damage

Birds, predatory beetles, hedgehogs

Mealybugs (*Pseudococcus obscurus*) (*Holt Studios*)

Good glasshouse hygiene destroys overwintering opportunities. As for thrips, it is mainly hot dry conditions that favour the mites, which attack less vigorous and stressed plants. Spray foliage with water during hot conditions, to raise humidity levels, and ensure good ventilation. Avoid importing infested material. Destroy badly affected plants. Spray with derris or insecticidal soap

Introduce *Phytoseiulus persimilis* as a biological control agent: a predatory mite from South America, very effective in glasshouses. It is not particularly mobile, so must be widely distributed. It may eliminate red spider mites entirely, then die out itself*

Spotted millipedes (*Blaniulus guttulatus*) attacking potato (*Holt Studios*)

Less of a problem for organic gardeners, as this is a classic pest that is promoted by the use of sprays that kill their natural enemies. Spot applications with liquid derris or insecticidal soap can be used with care, in an emergency

Black-kneed capsid and anthocorid bugs, birds and other general predators

Pick off swollen buds during the winter. In severe cases, or where reversion appears, burn all the bushes and replace with clean stock, preferably on a new site

As above, but probably less likely to be limited by predation, as the mites are well protected within the buds

Pick off affected leaves in the spring

No information

Big bud on blackcurrant bush caused by microscopic gall mite (*Cecidophyopsis ribis*), leading sometimes to reversion disease (see page 288) (*Chris Algar*)

Pests chart

Pest	Plants affected	The problem
Moths Cutworms Several species including: Large Yellow Underwing *Noctua pronuba* Turnip moth *Agrotis segetum* (large fat brown, green or greyish larvae up to 2 in/50 mm)	Brassicas, carrots, beetroots, potatoes, marrows, strawberries, lettuces and many others	Roots, stems and leaves of plants, particularly young transplants, attacked at ground level from early summer onwards. Plants frequently completely severed. Two generations a year, with larvae pupating in the soil. Largely nocturnal feeders
Cabbage moth *Mamestra brassicae* (green, brown or black, up to 2 in/50 mm) Diamond back moth *Plutella* *xylostella* (small and green, up to ⅝ in/12 mm)	*Mamestra* attacks brassicas, plus many other plants including lettuces, sweetcorn and tomatoes *Plutella* is a problem only on brassicas	Both species feed on leaves and contaminate plants with frass. *Mamestra* burrows into the hearts of brassicas, rendering them inedible
Codling moths *Cydia pomonella* (white maggot-like larvae, up to ¾ in/20 mm)	Mainly apples, sometimes other fruit	Burrow into young fruitlets, then eat them as they grow, contaminating the fruit with frass-filled galleries, and rendering it inedible. Eggs laid in early/mid-summer. Hatching larvae immediately tunnel into the fruit, from which they emerge a month later to pupate within cocoons in cracks and fissures within the bark, or often under tree ties. There is sometimes a partial second generation
Pea moth *Cydia nigricana* (small yellow larvae up to ¼ in/6 mm with black heads)	Peas	Caterpillars burrow into young pea pods, destroying the developing peas. Moths hatch from overwintering pupae in early summer, laying eggs which hatch into larvae that feed during mid-summer. A single generation
Swift moth *Hepialus lupulinus* *Hepialus humuli* (white and grub-like, up to 3 in/70 mm)	Lettuces, strawberries and many ornamental plants affected, notably bulbs, corms and tubers of, for example, daffodils, gladioli and lilies	Larvae attack roots, bulbs and tubers below ground, at all times of year. These primitive moths scatter their eggs among plants from the air, where plants are densely packed or the ground is weedy – not on to open soil. Feeding continues through the winter and larvae may take two years to pupate

Control measures	Natural enemies and biological control (* see pages 296 and 315)
earch the soil beneath affected plants y day, or go out to look for feeding rvae at night. Thoroughly cultivate the oil between crops to expose larvae and upae to predators. Plastic bottles ushed into the soil over individual lants as a protection against slugs will lso help prevent cutworm attacks	Spray *Bacillus thuringiensis* where attacks are on to leaves*. Many general predators, including birds, ground beetles, shrews, and frogs. Adult moths caught by birds, bats and spiders
ick off larvae when found. Rotate rops. Thoroughly cultivate between rops. (For additional advice see ection on Large and Small White aterpillars, pages 310–312)	Spray with *Bacillus thuringiensis**. Encourage general predators, such as birds, predatory beetles and social wasps

arvae can be persuaded to pupate under ieces of corrugated cardboard tied to runks. Organic sprays will not be very ffective, as the larvae are out of reach vithin the fruit. By monitoring emergence of gg-laying females – can spray with liquid erris from one week after moths begin o appear. Use of pheromone traps an help. Hang traps from late spring. he traps are readily available and may, y catching males, provide some limited ontrol in their own right

Most pupae are found by birds during the winter, particularly tits, but also wrens, tree creepers, robins, etc. Their effectiveness can be maximized by locating nest boxes in the trees or nearby in summer, and hanging peanuts/fat from the branches in winter. Many other predatory insects will contribute to control

Codling moth (*Cydia pomonella*) caterpillar in apple: pheremone traps, synthetic sex hormones which divert the male moth, can sometimes help avert attacks (*Holt Studios*)

ime the sowing of peas to avoid this est if it causes problems. Therefore void sowing in early/mid-spring – sow arlier under cloches, or later in the pen. Winter cultivations expose upae to predators and the weather

Bacillus thuringiensis is not effective, as the larvae, feeding within the pods, cannot take up a lethal dose. Encourage general predators (see Cabbage moth)

argely a problem of newly cleared or veedy ground, which will solve itself f the ground is kept clear. Winter igging exposes larvae to the weather, redators and pathogens

General predators, especially birds and predatory ground beetles

Pests chart

Pest	Plants affected	The problem
Moths		
Winter moth *Operophtera brumata* March moth *Alsophila aescularia* Mottled umber *Erannis defoliaria* (green or brown 'looper' caterpillars. Winter moth larvae up to 1 in/25 mm)	Apples, pears, plums, cherries and a great many other trees	Developing leaf and flower buds eaten in spring, followed by leaves and shoots. Growths distorted and crops reduced. Wingless females crawl up trunks of trees, and lay eggs from mid-autumn to the following spring, depending upon species. Full-grown larvae return to the soil to pupate
Other moths	All garden plants	Consume leaves, shoots, roots, tubers and even the wood of trees
Sawflies Gooseberry sawfly *Nematus ribesii* (caterpillar-like green larvae with black spots and a black head, up to 1½ in/40 mm)	Gooseberries	Bushes may be entirely stripped of leaves in a bad attack, in spring and summer, with damage often starting unseen in the centre of the bush. The inconspicuous black and orange adults (which have four wings and are more closely related to wasps and ants than flies) hatch from pupae in spring, to lay eggs on the leaves. Pupation takes place in the soil beneath the bushes. There are three generations a year
Sawflies on other trees and shrubs Many species (generally look like lepidopterous larvae, but with more legs, or slug-like, particularly the ½ in/15 mm black Pear and Cherry Slugworm)	Apples, pears, plums, cherries, roses, poplars, willows, pines, spiraea and many more	On fruit trees developing fruitlets attacked, causing them to drop off. Leaves reduced to skeletons in many instances, and/or rolled up to form refuges for the larvae (roses), or gall-forming (willow)
Scale Insects Homopteran bugs up to ¼ in/5 mm. Many species (white, yellow or brown scales on leaves and stems)	Mainly ornamental plants, especially in glasshouses and indoors	Sap-feeding insects that reduce plant vigour, and disfigure plants with honeydew and secondary sooty moulds. Mainly parthenogenic reproduction. Only young nymphs have legs for dispersal, older nymphs and adults are static

Control measures	Natural enemies and biological control (* see pages 296 and 315)
Grease bands provide a fool-proof method of eliminating this problem, if properly maintained. Apply either directly to the trunk, below the first branches, or tie on greased paper bands. Make sure they are in place by mid-autumn. A derris spray can be used	*Bacillus thuringiensis** can be used if you forgot to put on the grease bands. General predators, particularly birds, but also predatory bugs, beetles, parasitic flies and wasps
Many attacks can be removed by hand picking, and whole colonies may simply be removed by cutting out an infested branch. Derris, pyrethrum or quassia can be used as contact insecticides as a last resort, but not where BT can be better applied	*Bacillus thuringiensis* will control all moth larvae feeding on exposed parts of the plants that can be coated with this bacterium*. However minor attacks are best left to natural predators and parasites to deal with whenever possible

Mild attacks can be picked off by hand. Otherwise, spray with derris, pyrethrum or quassia

Attacked by general predators, e.g. birds, beetles, spiders and social wasps

Some fruit varieties more vulnerable than others, with the apples Charles Ross, Ellison's Orange, James Grieve and Worcester Pearmain, and the plums Belle de Louvain, Czar and Victoria proving highly susceptible to attack. Pick off affected fruitlets, rolled leaves and larvae where seen. Running poultry under the trees will destroy most of the pupating larvae, otherwise cultivate to expose them to predators. Spray as for Gooseberry sawfly

As for Gooseberry sawfly

First signs of attack by gooseberry sawfly (*Nematus ribesii*) – eggs on underside of leaves (*Holt Studios*)

Avoid importing infested material into the garden or glasshouse. Sprays with derris or pyrethrum have only limited value against young mobile nymphs. Can be brushed off the leaves of pot plants with soapy water

Attacked by parasitic wasps outdoors. Species suitable as biological controls in glasshouses under investigation, including the commercially available *Metaphyccus helvolus**. Attacked by general predators, including anthocorid bugs, beetles and birds

Scale insects (*Coccus hesperidum*): see page 317 for biological control (*Holt Studios*)

Pests chart

Pest	Plants affected	The problem
Wasps Social wasps *Paravespula* *vulgaris* *Paravespula* *germanica* and others (the familiar yellow and black wasps that like jam sandwiches and dustbins; up to ¾ in/20 mm)	Apples, pears, plums and other fruit	Feed on the fruit, usually just as it has ripened, creating large cavities or extending existing bird damage. Overwintering queens slowly build up new colonies over the summer, so that peak populations coincide with the ripening of autumn fruit
Whiteflies Glasshouse whitefly *Trialeurodes* *vaporarium* (tiny homopteran bugs resembling white moths, wing-span ⅒ in/3 mm)	Tomatoes, cucumbers, peppers, fuchsias, primulas, etc.	An accidentally introduced tropical pest. Sap feeding reduces the plant's vigour, and encourages sooty moulds. Rarely a problem outside glasshouses. Will breed continuously in heated greenhouses, taking about three weeks to develop from eggs to adults
Cabbage whitefly *Aleyrodes* *proletella* As above	Brassicas, i.e. cabbages, cauliflowers, Brussels sprouts, etc.	Sap-feeding insects that reduce plant vigour, and contaminate food crops with honeydew and secondary sooty moulds. Adults may be found at any time of the year, breeding only limited by cold weather
Woodlice Several species including *Oniscus asellus* *Porcellio scaber* *Armadillidium* *vulgare* (up to ¾ in/20 mm)	Mainly glasshouse plants, especially seedlings	Although these crustaceans eat mainly decomposing material, they can gnaw at seedlings and established plants

Control measures	Natural enemies and biological control (* see pages 296 and 315)
Wasps also perform a useful function in the garden, in that they collect large numbers of caterpillars and other insects to feed to their larvae. Nests can be destroyed by the introduction of derris dust at dusk, but should really only be considered where the location of the nest is causing problems. Netting of fruit trees to prevent bird damage will also reduce wasp damage. Hanging jars containing a small amount of jam plus half a jar of water with a little detergent in it in fruit trees is an old but effective means of exercising localized control	Birds and spiders

| Hang up yellow sticky traps that catch both these and greenfly. Use derris, pyrethrum, or insecticidal soap sprays. Companion planting with French marigolds (*Tagetes*) or nasturtiums claimed to be beneficial. Avoid introducing the pests on new plants. Can be sucked up with a vacuum cleaner | Introduce *Encarsia formosa*, a parasitic wasp that controls whitefly nymphs*. *Verticilium lecanii*, a fungus that will kill aphids, can be effective under hot humid conditions against whitefly too. Another fungus, *Cephalosporium leconii*, is sold specifically for whitefly control* |

Glasshouse whitefly (*Trialeurodes vaporarium*) and eggs: see page 317 for biological control (*Holt Studios*)

| Remove old brassica plants as soon as they are no longer needed. Break the cycle – try to avoid the spread of whitefly from overwintering plants to new seedlings. Floating mulches offer some protection (see Cabbage Root Fly, page 314). Pick off leaves covered with the scale-like larvae. Spray with derris, pyrethrum, or insecticidal soap | Encourage the whole range of enemies by interplanting with flowers, particularly umbellifers and *compositae*. Enemies include parasitic wasps, spiders, beetles, fly larvae, etc. *E. formosa** cannot be used outdoors |

| In the glasshouse they can be easily controlled by good hygiene, and the removal of night-time resting sites, e.g. under old pots and trays. If a problem outside, this is usually where plants are growing near rotting wood or other decomposing material, and will therefore be localized. Often attracted by plastic mulches and bark chips. Removal of such source areas or the growing of seedlings elsewhere is usually all that is required | Frogs, toads, shrews, birds, predatory beetles, spiders and others |

21
GROWING UNDER COVER

THE UNHEATED GREENHOUSE

The unheated greenhouse will grow a wide range of flowers, pot plants and vegetables successfully without the use of artificial heat. Any plant which needs to be kept at a temperature in excess of the normal outside conditions is dealt with in the 'Heated greenhouse' section, page 357.

Almost anything which can be grown outdoors can be grown in an unheated greenhouse or polytunnel. However, always ensure that the greenhouse variety of plant is selected, because not all outside varieties enjoy growing inside.

Pests and Diseases. The greenhouse environment means that pests and diseases can be particularly destructive once established, the most common pests being red spider mite and whitefly. See the chapters on pests and diseases (pages 258,290). Slugs, which can be particularly devastating, can mostly be kept out with a copper strip, which they will not cross, nailed across the doorstep and a few inches up the door frame. Of the diseases botrytis is the most serious. Good practices will keep the greenhouse free from attack. It should be kept well ventilated to avoid excessively damp conditions.

THE VEGETABLE GREENHOUSE

As with the garden, the greenhouse can be used in spring, summer and autumn/winter seasons. The greenhouse offers protection during the bad weather period, allowing a wide range of crops to be grown – so much so that unless a large house is available there will be insufficient growing space for the complete range of varieties available.

Remember, though, the temperature in an unheated greenhouse can also drop below freezing. On cold nights, plants may need protecting with newspaper or other insulating material.

OPPOSITE: **Greenhouse interior** (*Photos Horticultural*)

Tomatoes and cucumbers in growing bags (*Photos Horticultural*)

To be successful the greenhouse requires glass down to ground level and the crops to be grown directly in the border soil. Soil from the garden is not suitable. It is recommended that everything be grown in compost. Well rotted, weed-free garden compost, supplemented with mulches, is best for borders. (See *Propagation*, page 73 for seed and potting composts.)

The borders need to be dressed twice, once in the spring and again in the autumn. In a fully utilized house there may not be a single period when all borders are empty, in which case each can be treated in turn. Dress the borders with calcified seaweed at a rate of 8 oz/sq yd (225 g/sq m), then lay down a 1–2 in (2·5–5 cm) layer of well-rotted compost. Unless seeds are to be sown shortly afterwards it can remain as a surface mulch.

The continual addition of compost will raise the soil level with time. However, it can be maintained at a constant height by removing the rootball of tomatoes, cucumbers, etc. with a spadeful of soil around them. It is not good practice to pull out these plants leaving a mass of roots in the border.

The question of changing or sterilizing the greenhouse soil is often raised. In an organic greenhouse there is no need for either if good husbandry has been practised to maintain a balanced soil. Sterilization with heat or washes kills off the soil micro-organisms, each of which is essential in the relationship between the plants and the soil. To kill them off means the link is broken and the health and vitality of the plants impaired. If you feel that the soil needs a rest then such plants as tomatoes and cucumbers can be grown in pots or growing bags. Dispose of the growing medium in the open garden, not in the greenhouse border. If, however, problems do arise and the soil does need to be changed, replace it with well-rotted sterile compost.

It has been known for healthy crops to be grown for over twenty years in the same soil simply by adhering to good cultural techniques.

Just as in any other section of the garden, planning is essential to produce crops throughout the year. Possibly even more planning is needed in the greenhouse, for space is limited. The best approach is to draw up a year-plan based on the three seasons (see table).

It is best to start off with a plan of the greenhouse drawn to scale. Three are needed, one for each season. Decide which crops are to be grown and how many plants or rows of each are expected to be planted, and lay these on the plan in as much detail as possible. Put a cross for each plant, with the correct spacing between plants and rows. This will give a complete picture, showing whether or not everything can be fitted in.

All three plans must be drawn up at the same time, for it will be very surprising if there is not an overlap at some point. To avoid this, plant spacing or positioning in the house may have to be altered to allow one crop to be harvested before the next is planted: new plants can be put between existing ones, or the crop can be harvested in such a manner that spaces are created for the following crop.

The main clash is normally at the time of planting out tomatoes and cucumbers, but fortunately these do not mind sharing the bed with other crops such as beetroot and carrots. In fact, tomatoes and carrots are a good companion planting combination.

The plan should also make allowance for another companion combination: the growing of a

> **Typical year-plan**
>
> **Late winter/spring** Aubergines, beetroot, carrots, lettuces, potatoes, radishes
>
> **Summer** Celery (self-blanching), courgettes, cucumbers, French beans (dwarf and climbing), sweetcorn, sweet peppers, tomatoes, turnips
>
> **Autumn/winter** Carrots, cress, lettuces, potatoes, radishes, spring cabbage

pungent-smelling *Tagetes* variety and nasturtiums in the greenhouse is recommended to keep the house free from whitefly. If not controlled, the nasturtiums would eventually take over the greenhouse. Two plants in a 10 x 8 ft (3 x 2·5 m) house are sufficient, and must be cut back severely and frequently.

INDIVIDUAL CROPS

This section examines the cultivation of many favourite vegetables. Where sowing and planting requirements are the same as for outside, please refer for details to *The Vegetable Garden* (page 82).

Aubergines. Although these may be grown with reasonable success outdoors in a sheltered position in warmer districts, they are more generally regarded as a greenhouse plant.

Seeds are sown in late winter or early spring in a temperature of 60–65°F (15·5–18°C). As the

Aubergines respond well to a base dressing of worm compost when the fruits begin to swell (*Photos Horticultural*)

greenhouse is too cold at this time of the year the best method is to sow the seeds singly in 3 in (7·5 cm) pots on a south-facing windowsill in the house. They can be moved into the greenhouse as the weather warms up, but there must be a minimum inside the greenhouse of 50°F (10°C). If the seedlings outgrow the pots due to delays in planting on as a result of the weather they will need to be potted on. If this is the case, as aubergines will grow happily in pots, it is best to transplant the seedlings into 6 or 7 in (15 or 17·5 cm) pots as their final growing positions. The pots can either stand on the soil or be buried up to the lip for more stability, spaced 18 in (45 cm) apart. However, they do produce a better-quality crop if grown in the border.

Pinch out the growing tips when the plants are about 6 in (15 cm) tall. Four fruits are enough for a plant to support, all others being pinched out, as well as lateral growths being stopped.

The plants need to be kept well watered. Once the fruits begin to swell apply a liquid feed at regular intervals and dress the base of the plants with worm compost. If the temperature in the greenhouse rises above 80°F (26°C) syringe with a fine spray of water.This will not only help the fruit to set and mature but will minimize attacks from the red spider mite.

Pick the fruits when they are fully coloured, shiny and still soft to the touch. If left too long on the plant they will become dry, tough and unpalatable.

Apart from the red spider mite, the only other real problem is mildew if the weather is damp in the autumn.

Beetroot. A very easy crop to grow in the greenhouse, the method being similar to that for an outside crop. Prepare the soil about midwinter and cover it with protective netting or similar to assist the soil to warm up. Starting a month later, sow the seed, one every inch (2·5 cm), ½ in (1·25 cm) deep with 6 in (15 cm) between rows. Water well and replace the protective covering. Remove the covering on warm days and replace if the night temperatures are forecast to drop.

The crop needs very little further attention apart from removing the protective cover once the first true pair of leaves are fully developed. Keep the soil just moist, not wet.

The seedlings can be thinned or left to grow as 'baby' beet. When the size of a golf ball these can be eaten. Pick to leave a root every 3 in (7·5 cm), which are left to grow to normal beetroot size.

As the roots will be ready to pick from three months later, there can be a clash with the planting out of tomatoes and cucumbers. Again space can be made for these by cropping the beetroot to leave a 10 in (25 cm) gap for the summer crops to go in.

A good variety for the greenhouse crop is 'Boltardy'. These are at their best when young, eaten raw as part of a salad.

Carrots. An early crop of carrots can be grown by sowing in the greenhouse soil in late winter or a late crop of early-variety carrots in late summer. A summer crop can also be grown if carrot fly is a persistent problem in the area.

The treatment is as for growing beetroot, except that for the late sowing the ground cover is not needed. Seeds are sown thinly in rows 6 in (15 cm) apart and can either be thinned out to 2 in (5 cm) apart as soon as the seedlings are large enough to handle or thinned when large enough to eat.

The carrots need little further attention, but do not allow the soil to dry out, or the greenhouse temperature to rise in excess of 80°F (26°C); ventilate well and spray the atmosphere with water using a fine nozzle on the syringe to keep the house cool.

Carrots will grow happily with tomatoes, so again the roots can be picked to leave a space about 10 in (25 cm) in diameter to plant the tomatoes into.

Carrots inside are not normally bothered with carrot fly, but should an attack occur it will be necessary to change the greenhouse soil, as the maggots will overwinter to attack next year's crops. As the fly can survive in temperatures down to 25°F (-4°C) it is only outside that it will be killed off by cold weather.

Varieties worth growing are 'Amsterdam Forcing', 'Nantes Express' or the ball type 'Rondo'.

Celery. The best for a greenhouse crop is the self-blanching or American Green variety, as there is normally insufficient space available to allow earthing up.

Seeds are sown in early to mid-spring in a seed-raiser or 3 in (7·5 cm) pot on a south-facing windowsill. As the seeds are fine it is best not to cover them, but press them firmly into the compost, then moisten either by the capillary action of the 'wick' in the seed-raiser or by standing the pot in water. Do not water from the top as this tends to wash the seed over to one spot. Transplant when the seedlings are large enough to handle, into individual pots or cellular trays. Transfer into the greenhouse.

The seedlings can be planted into the border in late spring, when space becomes available as the spring crops are lifted. Plant in blocks so that adjacent plants will blanch each other, with 9 in (23 cm) between plants. Do not allow the plants to dry out but keep well watered, especially in warm weather.

Celery are hungry feeders so, along with the

standard soil preparation between crops, when the plants are about 6 in (15 cm) tall lay down a ½ in (1 cm) mulch of worm compost or finely sieved garden compost and hoe into the top surface of the bed. Apply a foliar feed of seaweed extract and repeat every three to four weeks.

The sticks will be ready from late summer onwards and can be used into the winter period. This type is not very hardy and will be killed off by the frost, even in the greenhouse. As a result the crop will need to be protected if frost is forecast. Should it be damaged there is no need to lift the plants; cut off the damaged foliage and leave the roots in the soil over the winter. These will grow again in the spring.

Courgettes. One of the easiest vegetables to grow under glass, but – a word of warning – the leaves do grow very large under cover and will smother adjacent plants unless they are given plenty of room.

Sow the seeds individually in pots in late spring. Push seed into the soil and cover the pot with a polythene bag. Plant in the border when the roots have filled the pot, leaving 24 in (60 cm) between plants. Water well after planting and repeat every two to three days until the plants are well established. Little further attention is required apart from making sure they do not dry out in warm weather.

Harvest the courgettes when they are about 4 in (10 cm) long. Do not leave them to grow into marrows, as this will reduce the production of young fruits. If the leaves grow too large one or two may be thinned out, but remember that loss of leaf area will reduce the vigour of the plants.

There are two diseases to look out for: grey mould, which can be troublesome in wet weather, causing the flowers, fruit and leaves to rot – lift and destroy affected plants; and mildew, which can be a problem towards the end of the season. At the first sign dust the plants with sulphur.

Cress. Either cress or salad rape can be sown to give a salad crop in the winter. Rake the border into a fine tilth then broadcast the seed at about ½ oz/sq yd (15 gm/sq m). Water the soil thoroughly, then cover the seed with a two- to three-sheet thickness of newspaper until the seeds begin to germinate. Do not cover the seed with soil.

Cut the cress when large enough to eat, about 2–3 in (5–7.5 cm) tall, about two weeks after sowing. If the bed is kept moist a second growth will appear.

Cucumber. Next to tomatoes this is the most popular greenhouse-grown vegetable, a very productive plant, capable of producing forty or more high-quality fruits each. This means that only one or maybe two plants will supply the average household with sufficient fruit to meet their needs with possibly some to spare.

The 'frame' cucumber is the variety which needs the protection of the greenhouse to succeed. Seeds are sown individually in 3 in (7.5 cm) pots from early to mid-spring. To ensure good germination and minimize the chances of the seed rotting, it is best pushed end-on into the compost with just the tip showing. Make sure the end the root grows from is the one in the compost, that is, push the pointed end into the compost. If planted the wrong way the root will soon show, in which case, turn the seed round, making sure the root is in contact with the compost.

Cover the pot with a plastic propagator lid or a blown-up polythene bag held in place by an elastic band around the rim, to retain the moisture in the compost. A temperature of 65–70°F (18–21°C) is required for germination, which takes place within two to three days. Immediately the seeds have germinated remove the covering from the pot to give the plant maximum light.

If the weather is cold and the minimum temperature cannot be maintained the seeds can be germinated on a south-facing window sill in the house. However, remember a minimum temperature of 60°F (15.5°C) is needed before you transfer them to the greenhouse. If in doubt delay sowing until the weather is warmer. No benefit will be gained by starting too early, only to lose the plants by allowing them to get too cold.

The seedlings must not be allowed to become pot-bound, otherwise their growth will be checked. It is advisable to pot them on into a 4½–5 in (11.5–12.5 cm) pot when they have produced four or five true leaves. This could be after as short a period as ten to fourteen days if the day/night temperatures are holding at 70/65°F (21/18°C). On repotting a short stake should be used to keep the plant upright. If horizontal strings are to be used to support the plant when it is mature, the stake should be long enough to reach the bottom string.

Take care when handling the seedlings not to damage the tender stem. To remove from the smallest pot, turn it upside down on the palm of the hand with the stem hanging down between the second and third fingers. A sharp tap of the rim of the pot on the bench will release the root ball so that it rests on the hand. The plant is turned over, putting the root ball in the other hand, from where it can be gently inserted into the larger pot. By this method the stem is not touched.

Do not press the compost too firmly when potting on. Remove any flowers or tendrils, the

A raised mound of fertile compost supports a flourishing crop of cucumbers (*Chris Algar*)

thin leafless shoots which curl around stakes, which may have appeared at this stage.

Cucumbers do best in fertile organic soil, and as they do not like their roots to sit in wet conditions it should be well drained and aerated. Consequently it is common to grow the plants on a raised bed in the border, consisting of a mound of compost about 6–9 in (15–23 cm) high on top of the soil. If a number of plants are to be grown the mound is 12–15 in (30–37·5 cm) wide and long enough to accommodate the plants spaced 30 in (75 cm) apart. For one or two plants it is easier to build a mound for each one, 12–15 in in diameter with again 30 in between. Prepare the beds about two weeks before planting, watering well to soak the compost thoroughly.

When the greenhouse temperature can be guaranteed, place the plants in their pots on top of the mound for a day or two to acclimatize them to their growing position. The plants should be showing about eight to ten leaves at this point. Plant out with the top of the root ball level with the top of the mound. This allows surplus water to drain away from the root ball.

One disadvantage of the mound method is that in hot weather the compost, with a larger surface area exposed to the sun, will dry out much more quickly than the border soil. It will need daily attention, so if the greenhouse is not frequently visited, as can be the case on an allotment, it is safer to grow the cucumbers directly in the border soil.

If cucumbers have been grown in the same border for a number of years, or if there have been signs of root rot the previous year, it is best to rest the soil by growing the plants on in 12 in (30 cm) diameter pots, or growbags. If pots are used, half-bury them in the border, surrounding the top of the pot with soil to prevent it drying out too quickly with the heat of the sun.

Good steady growth is essential during the early period. Keep the plants well watered but do not allow the soil to become sodden. Maintain a high humidity around them by spraying with a fine-nozzled syringe on the leaves and damping down the greenhouse by pouring water on the floor.

As the plant starts to grow it will need support and can be trained up stakes or strings suspended from the roof. If using stakes or canes, push them into the soil before planting out, otherwise there is a possibility of damaging the young roots if a stake is pushed through them. If the string method is preferred, the string should be long enough to lie in the bottom of the planting-out hole so that the root ball sits on it, keeping it taut. As the cucumber grows it is tied to the stake or the stem is gently twisted around the string to keep it upright. Pinch out the growing tip when it reaches the top of the support. Also pinch out any tendrils produced, so that the plant's energy is channelled into producing fruit.

It is important that the supports do not collapse when the plant is loaded with fruit, so strings should be fixed on a stout frame securely fastened to the greenhouse frame. Stakes can be linked to the greenhouse by hanging a horizontal stake a few inches from the roof and tying each stake to it. Side shoots, the growth from the leaf joint with the stem, will also need to be pinched out, but in a manner that maximizes the crop.

There are two types of greenhouse cucumber, the standard, which produces both male and female flowers, and the all-female. There is a slight difference in the training methods for each.

On the standard cucumber the fruits develop on the side shoots, so these are allowed to grow until a fruit (female) flower is produced, normally after four to six leaves, when the shoots are pinched out two leaves beyond the fruit. Further side shoots will grow and again these are pinched out two leaves beyond the fruit. To keep the fruit off the soil and to ease the weight from the main stem the side shoots can be tied to horizontal strings tied to the vertical support. Horizontal strings are run 9 in (23 cm) apart. No fruit is allowed to develop on the main stem. Late in the season some of the older shoots can be cut out, allowing new shoots to develop to keep the plant fruiting.

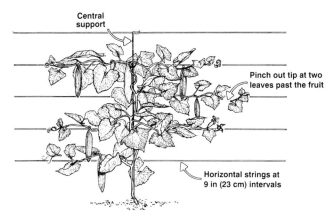

Central
support

Pinch out tip at two
leaves past the fruit

Horizontal strings at
9 in (23 cm) intervals

Training a cucumber plant (*Rob Dalton*)

With the all-female cucumber the fruit is formed at a leaf joint with the main stem, so it is necessary to pinch out the side shoots as they are formed. However, as this restricts the plant to a main stem the height of the greenhouse, two side shoots are allowed to develop from the bottom and are staked and trained similarly to the main stem to give a good supply of fruit.

On the standard varieties the female flowers must not be fertilized by the male as they will produce seed and become bitter-tasting. The male flowers are removed as soon as they appear to prevent this happening. They are easily recognized, the male being attached to the plant by a thin stalk while the female has a bulbous one, in fact a baby cucumber.

Throughout the growing period the plants should be kept well watered, but, to stress the point again, do *not* allow the roots to become waterlogged. The atmosphere should be kept humid to prevent foliage being scorched by the sun, but the greenhouse must be well ventilated once the temperature exceeds 80°F (26°C). If the weather remains hot it is best to apply shading to the glass. In the small greenhouse a cucumber can be grown behind a row of tomatoes, which will give adequate shading.

To maintain good growth apply a liquid feed every two weeks. Cucumbers are surface-rooting plants and it is not uncommon to see a mass of roots on the surface of the soil. This is the time to lay down a mulch of compost or chopped wilted comfrey leaves covered by a 1 in (2·5 cm) layer of worm compost. Repeat this mulch every time the roots appear – a minimum of three mulches over the season.

Pick the fruits before they grow too large or turn yellow. Cut regularly, as this encourages more fruit to develop. Either cut the stem with a sharp knife or twist the fruit until the stalk is severed. Do not pull the fruit off the plant.

Cucumbers are susceptible to several pests and diseases. Red spider mite is controlled by moisture: the spraying of the foliage three or four times a day and the damping down of the greenhouse is the best preventive method.

Mildew is a fairly common disease at the end of the season as the weather becomes colder, and mildew-resistant varieties such as 'Cordoba' and female varieties of 'Carmen' and 'Mildana' should be grown if it is troublesome. At the first sign of an attack immediate action to contain the disease must be taken.

Young fruits wilting from the flower end usually indicate a weakened plant, caused either by inadequate watering, feeding, poor root structure or overcropping of the plants.

French beans. Both the dwarf and climbing varieties produce an early crop of tender beans from a greenhouse. The cultivation is as for an outdoor crop, but the house provides protection against frost. The seeds can be sown a little earlier, dwarf from early spring in milder areas to mid-spring in harder climates, climbers from late spring onwards.

Seeds can be sown directly in the border soil or individually in 4 in (10 cm) pots for transplanting later in the season. Dwarf French beans are very successful in a pot, four plants to an 8 in (20 cm) pot, either sown direct or transferred from the smaller individual pots. If sowing directly in the soil plant out 6 in (15 cm) apart.

The climbing varieties need to be supported and can be grown up canes or strings spaced 15 in (37·5 cm) apart. The plants will wind themselves around the supports like runner beans. When the plants are 6 in (15 cm) tall mulch the bed with a thick layer of compost.

The plants like a humid atmosphere but do not like to be overwatered. The best approach is to spray frequently with water from a fine-nozzled syringe. Keep warm but ventilate freely when the greenhouse temperature exceeds 85°F (29°C). To maximize the crop pinch out the primary and secondary lateral growths at the third leaf joint.

The beans are at their best when young – do not leave them too long on the plant, for they will turn tough and stringy.

Lettuces. There is little point in trying to grow lettuces in the greenhouse during the summer months as they are a relatively easy crop to grow outside, with a wide variety to choose from. However, over the winter, when green salad material is scarce and imported organically-grown lettuce expensive, a greenhouse crop is worth its weight in gold. The introduction of short-day varieties has made it possible to grow lettuces over the coldest months of the year to a standard of superb quality and flavour.

Winter lettuces, unlike their summer counterpart, are not the easiest of crops to grow.

Marmer lettuce can be picked in early winter from the cold greenhouse (*Harry Smith*)

To achieve any reasonable level of success there are a few basic rules to abide by.

Varieties specifically bred for the cold winter greenhouse must be used. An outside variety, even one such as 'Winter Density', will not give the solid rich green heads required. Different varieties have different sowing dates, and it is important that seeds are sown at the right time. Most failures result from not abiding by these simple rules and the seed catalogues should be studied to make sure the correct choice is made.

Seeds are sown thinly in a 3 in (7·5 cm) pot on a south-facing windowsill in the house. The seeds do best if they are not covered with compost but gently pressed into the surface with a flat object after the compost has been thoroughly watered. Cover the pot with a plastic propagator lid or a blown-up polythene bag held in place with an elastic band around the rim. Put the pot in a dark cool cupboard and examine every twelve hours, for germination takes place very quickly. Immediately the fine roots show, move into the light. Once the seed leaves start to develop remove the pot covering.

Lettuces do not like having their roots disturbed, so transplant the seedlings into cellular trays or individual pots as soon as the seed leaves are large enough to grip between the fingers. At no time must the stem be touched, as this can damage the delicate tissue and be a source of botrytis. The same applies with planting into their final growing positions, which should be done as soon as the young seedlings are large enough to survive in the border soil. This can be a problem with the early autumn-sown varieties, for there may still be tomatoes and cucumbers in the border. Although lettuces can be planted between these crops, and no doubt their bottom leaves could be removed to allow as much light to the lettuce as possible, there is always the danger of damage to the lettuce roots when the summer crops are lifted.

If the roots begin to fill the cellular trays, when they can be seen protruding from the drainage holes, the plants can be potted on into plant pots, or better still paper pots. Make these by wrapping an open sheet of tabloid-size newspaper around a bottle of about 3 in (7·5 cm) diameter to form an open-ended tube. A spot of wood glue along the edge of the newspaper holds the tube together. Remove the bottle and cut the tube into three 3 in (7·5 cm) lengths. These

Lettuce varieties suitable for cold greenhouse winter growing

Variety	Seed sown	Crop
Columbus	Late summer–late winter	Mid autumn–late-spring
Cynthia	Late autumn–mid-winter	Late winter–mid-spring
Dandie	Late summer–late autumn	Late autumn–mid-spring
Kellys	Late autumn–mid-winter	Mid- to late spring
Klock	Late autumn on	Mid-spring on
Kwick	Late summer	Late autumn–early winter
Marmer	Mid late summer	Late autumn–early winter
	Late autumn–mid-winter	Mid- to late spring
May King	Mid autumn–early spring	Early spring–early summer
Novita	Early autumn–late winter	Early spring–late spring
Ravel	Mid-autumn	Early spring
	Mid-winter	Mid- to late spring

Recycled newspaper makes biodegradable paper pots including larger sizes for potting on, avoiding root damage (Jim Hay)

short tubes are placed end-on in a seed tray, twenty-four to a 14 x 9 in (35 x 23 cm) tray, and filled half-full of compost. Transplant the lettuce seedlings into the paper tubes and fill with compost. When the border is ready, plant out the whole pot; the paper soon rots in the soil, which causes the least disturbance to the roots. Do not plant too deeply, as lettuces do not like having their leaves covered with soil.

Remember, plants started off inside will need to be gently hardened off for the cold conditions of the greenhouse. Put them in the greenhouse during the day for a day or so before leaving them overnight, then leave for several nights before planting into the border.

After the greenhouse border has been prepared, water thoroughly a day or two before the lettuces are planted out. Greenhouse lettuces are very susceptible to fungal diseases, particularly botrytis, which are encouraged by bad watering. It is therefore important that the border soil contains sufficient moisture to minimize the amount of watering. In fact, it is preferable if further watering can be avoided during the growing period. If the soil does look dried out, check by scraping the surface to see how far down it is dry; if there are signs of wilting further watering may be needed. Water in the early morning so that the foliage will be dry

by night-time. Try not to wet the leaves, only the soil and root ball area.

Ventilation is important if the greenhouse temperature rises above 65°F (18°C), particularly if it follows a cold night. Rapid temperature fluctuations should be avoided as they cause 'tip burn'.

Plant the lettuces in a 9 in (23 cm) square formation, which – and this is important – will allow them to grow to a good size without being overcrowded. After cutting do not leave roots in the soil to rot and possibly contaminate the remaining plants.

Peppers. A crop grown in a similar manner to tomatoes, these have become very popular, for modern varieties give an excellent crop in an unheated greenhouse. There is also the advantage that the fruits do not need to ripen before being harvested, as green peppers are almost as delicious as the ripened red or yellow ones.

For a good crop seeds need to be sown as early as possible – from mid-winter onwards, although in an unheated greenhouse it is usually early spring before the temperatures are suitable. The seed can be sown in a 3 in (7·5 cm) pot on a south-facing window sill in the house at a temperature of 65°F (18°C), then transplanted into 4½ in (11·5 cm) pots.

Sow peppers early for a good late summer crop
(*Photos Horticultural*)

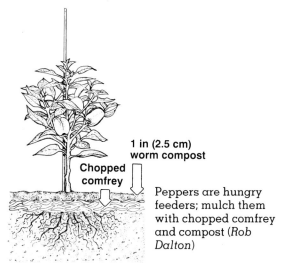

1 in (2.5 cm)
worm compost

Chopped
comfrey

Peppers are hungry
feeders; mulch them
with chopped comfrey
and compost (*Rob
Dalton*)

The plants can be grown directly in the border soil or further potted on into 10 in (25 cm) pots. Supports of canes or strings will be needed, for the plants will grow up to 5 ft (150 cm) tall. They are hungry feeders and will need to be mulched with chopped, wilted comfrey topped with a 1 in (2.5 cm) layer of worm compost once they start to produce fruit. It may be difficult to provide the full feeding necessary for pot-grown plants and a liquid foliar feed should be applied weekly.

For reasonable-sized fruits it may be necessary to thin them out if they are formed too closely together. This should be carried out at an early stage of growth to allow the plant to channel its energy into the remaining fruits. A good plant can produce up to twenty-five fruit.

Potatoes. A very easy crop to grow in the green-

house. Their cultivation is identical to that for an outside crop, the seed being selected as early in the new year as possible, but no later than the end of winter (a further sowing in early autumn will provide new potatoes in December).

Choose an early variety for greenhouse growing. Stand the seed on end with the eyes uppermost to sprout in a room where the temperature can be held at 55–65°F (13–18°C). They are best kept in the light, for short firm shoots are preferable to the long spindly ones produced if sprouted in the dark. Once the shoots are about ½ in (1 cm) long, spray them with water at room temperature twice a day. Give them a good soaking but do not allow the tubers to sit in water because they may rot. In about two weeks the seeds will begin to produce roots. They are now ready to plant out in the greenhouse, where they should be treated as for outdoors but spaced more closely at 9 in (23 cm).

As the potato and the tomato are members of the same family, do not grow potatoes in the soil which will be used for tomatoes later in the season. If the same area of soil is to be used it is safer to grow the potatoes in pots. These can either sit on top of the soil or be sunk into it. The latter helps to stop the pot drying out too quickly.

Place a 2 in (5 cm) layer of compost in the pot, then the seed potato on top, and half fill the pot with compost. As the foliage shows through continue to fill the pot, either with compost or, if the pot is sunk into the border, the soil which has been dug out.

The plants require little further attention apart from keeping the soil moist, an important factor if pots are used. A regular feed of comfrey liquid will maintain a good steady growth. The foliage may grow a little leggy and can interfere with other early crops if allowed to fall over. It can be held upright by placing two canes either side of the rows (or pots) at each end and tying strings at about 9 in (23 cm) intervals as a support.

When the potatoes are large enough to eat, either the plants can be lifted or the hand pushed

Potatoes in pots (*John Walker*)

into the soil to 'feel' for the potatoes, only picking the quantity needed at any one time.

Although plants under cover are well protected from frost damage, severe weather early in the growing period can damage the young leaves. If they are affected, draw a little soil around the damaged area to encourage new growth. Once this has grown to about 4–6 in (10–15 cm) high, cut out the weakest shoots to leave only the three or four strongest. Make a clean cut with a sharp knife. This will ensure a good crop, although it may not be as heavy as from the unfrosted plants.

If pots are being used because a tomato crop is to follow, do not empty the pot contents on to the greenhouse border.

Radishes. A fast-growing crop taking up very little space, these can be grown at any time of the year and are useful for filling in between plants and rows.

A spring sowing of a summer variety can be made from late winter through to mid-spring; or an autumn sowing can be made. Over the summer months radishes can still be grown under cover but it is better to grow them outside.

It is best to grow a variety bred for growing under cover, but if the preferred variety is not one of these a reasonable crop will still be obtained. There is a 'winter varieties' group in the catalogues which are sown from mid-autumn through to late winter.

Radishes are sown in rows or broadcast in the soil. They need no attention apart from being well watered after sowing. Harvest when large enough to eat, before they turn woody or run to seed.

Radishes are attacked by the carrot fly, so rotate them if carrots are also being grown in the greenhouse.

Spring cabbage. An early crop of spring cabbage can be cut from the greenhouse up to four weeks before the outside crop, depending upon the winter weather.

The seeds are sown as for the winter crop, and can be planted out in the border soil. Space 9 in (23cm) apart with 15 in (37·5 cm) between rows, burying the plants up to their first pair of seed leaves. They need little attention apart from ensuring that they do not dry out. If water is needed, water the soil and not the foliage, for they are susceptible to botrytis if the leaves are left wet, especially if the weather is cold. Whitefly can be a problem in the early spring.

Pick when the hearts are large enough to eat. If left they will hearten up to the quality of the outside plants.

Sweetcorn. Sweetcorn is not the easiest of crops to grow in the colder climates, and in these areas it is best grown under cover. Sow the seeds individually in 3 in (7·5 cm) pots in mid- to late spring, planting in the border in very late spring. As the plants need to be pollinated plant in squares with 18 in (45 cm) between each.

Keep well watered in dry weather. The roots develop very close to the surface and need to be covered as they appear, to prevent them drying out. Water the area thoroughly then cover the roots with a 2 in (5 cm) layer of compost. To sustain a steady growth feed regularly with a liquid foliar feed.

Sweetcorn do not like competition from weeds, so control these by hand-picking. Do not use the hoe because the roots grow near the surface and are easily damaged.

When the plants come into flower shake the tassels at the top of the stems to release the pollen on to the flowers. Although the plants may start to form a number of cobs it is best to restrict them to three, to ensure good-sized cobs.

The failure of the plant to produce cobs is caused by failure to pollinate the flowers, allowing the soil to dry out, or sowing and planting too late in the season. The only pest to worry about is the fruit fly, which causes the plants to be stunted, even die in severe attacks. The cobs are small and deformed in attacked plants. Examine the plants in mid-summer for the maggot, and hand-pick.

The other problem for sweetcorn is 'smut', producing swollen distorted plants and later dark powdery spores. Lift and destroy the plants immediately and do not grow sweetcorn in the greenhouse for at least five years. Some varieties are resistant.

Tomatoes. The most popular greenhouse-grown vegetables, but one which can be very troublesome. If not treated with sufficient care, the plants can prove susceptible to disease, physiological disorders and soil sickness caused by poor soil management. As a result a number of cultural methods other than growing directly into the soil have been developed over the years, such as ring culture, straw bale culture, use of pots and grow bags, and planting grafted stock. Grafting standard varieties of tomatoes on to root-stocks which have inherent resistance to disease helps the gardener to overcome the weaknesses of the variety chosen, particularly wilt diseases.

There is a wide range of tomato varieties to choose from. Some are very old but still considered by many to have the finest flavour, whereas some are recent heavy-cropping F1 hybrids. There are the small 'cherry' tomatoes and the very large, often misshapen 'beefsteak' varieties.There are yellow tomatoes, which have lost a little of their popularity in recent years but which do add colour to the salad bowl.The choice of what is to be grown will depend on personal taste.

Tomatoes

Variety	Resistance to disease	Comments
Standard		
Ailsa Craig		Heavy cropper, good flavour
Alicante	Resistant to mildew; free from greenback	Excellent flavour, high yield, uniform shape; grows well in low greenhouse temperatures
Gardener's Delight		Cherry-sized, very sweet-tasting, heavy cropper
Golden Sunrise		Golden-yellow colour, medium-sized, good flavour
Harbinger		Old favourite, heavy cropper, good flavour
Moneymaker		Reliable, heavy cropper; large trusses of medium-sized smooth red fruit, excellent flavour
F1 hybrids		
Beefmaster (beefsteak type)		Extremely large fruit
Big Boy (beefsteak type)		Tall plants, carrying fruit weighing 1 lb (450 g) each; scarlet colour, fine flavour
Counter	Highly resistant	Commercial variety, high yield, good flavour; grows well in low greenhouse temperatures
Dombello	Highly resistant	Early, good flavour, no centre (beefsteak type) core
Estrella	Highly resistant	Used widely commercially; early; large-sized fruit
Pixie		Dwarf variety; good flavour, medium-sized; also good outside
Shirley	Highly resistant	Large trusses of medium-sized fruit; uniform shape
Sweet 100		Cherry-sized; crops over long period; very sweet-tasting
Totem		Bush variety, good in pots; heavy crop, fine flavour

Seeds are sown in trays on a south-facing windowsill from early spring; a temperature of 60–65°F (15·5–18°C) must be maintained. Although sowing can start in mid-winter this is too early for the cold greenhouse, and keeping the plants indoors for an extended period with the shortage of light will result in the plants growing leggy. Sprinkle a few seeds on top of the compost. (Count the number of plants needed and add 25% more seed as spares.) Cover the seed with compost to a depth the thickness of a seed by shaking an ⅛ in (3 mm) mesh riddle containing compost *once* over the pot. Stand the pot in a dish of water until the capillary action brings water up to the surface, allow the excess water to drain off then place a plastic propagator lid on the pot or cover it with a blown-up polythene bag held in place by an elastic band around the rim (see page 359).

Germination takes about seven to ten days; remove the cover from the pot as soon as the seed leaves appear. When they are large enough to handle prick out the seedlings individually into 3 in (7·5 cm) pots to allow them to develop a good root structure. It is important that the roots do not become pot-bound or starved, so cellular trays are too small without another transplanting stage.

Care must be taken when pricking out to handle the plants only by the leaves. The pressure of the fingers on the stem can damage it enough to provide an entry point for botrytis. Use a dibber to make the hole for the transplant, pressing the soil firmly against the roots. Bury the seedlings deep into the compost, up to ¼ in (0·5 cm) from the seed leaves.

Water well with water at room temperature, then no more for a week. Overwatering at this stage can cause damping off.

Keep the seedlings indoors for a day to allow them to recover from the shock of transplanting, then, provided the minimum temperature of 50°F (10°C) can be guaranteed, they can be put on the greenhouse soil or staging. If the weather is too cold the leaves will turn blue, the plant is checked and the results will be disappointing if it is unable to recover fully. In an extended period of cold weather it is safer to take the plants back indoors.

After about three weeks they will need to be potted on into 4 in (10 cm) pots. Water well on

Tomato care	
Install supports	
Stakes	Put stakes in place before putting plants into final position
String	Suspend strings from supports and place ends under root-ball when putting plants into final position
Ties	Tie plant to supports at frequent intervals to prevent stalk bending under weight of fruit
Water	Apply 1 pt (0·5 l) to each plant, increasing to 8 pt (4·5 l) a day when plant supports 4-5 trusses, depending on soil condition
Remove side shoots	As they appear
Pinch growing point	As it reaches greenhouse roof, or after 5-6 trusses appear
First feed	As first truss sets – liquid feed plus mulch
Subsequent feeds	
Liquid	Twice a week, comfrey liquid; reduce to once a week towards end of season, stopping in mid-autumn; plus, once every two weeks, liquid seaweed extract mixed with comfrey
Mulch	Twice in season, say at third and fifth truss setting
Pollinate	As first flowers open; continue throughout season
Ventilate	Freely when temperature reaches 65°F (18°C)
Stop watering	In early autumn

repotting but from then on only if the compost is dry. The day before planting into their final growing positions water to ensure that the plants have a moist root ball. The border needs to be prepared at the same time.

If plants are to be bought be very careful selecting them, for it is easy to inherit problems. Plants must be of good colour, still carry their seed leaves and be short-jointed.

Plant out with 15 in (37·5 cm) between, making sure the hole is deep enough to plant up to the first pair of seed leaves. Do not compress the soil too firmly around the root ball; water well. It is important that the first truss is as near the ground level as possible, otherwise the number of trusses before the plant reaches the roof may be reduced. If the plant has been too long indoors and has grown too leggy for a deep enough hole to be made, a rectangular hole about 6 in (15 cm) deep and in length from the bottom of the pot to the first pair of seed leaves can be made. Lay the plant sideways in the hole with the stem resting on the top edge. Fill in the trench, making sure the whole stem is surrounded by compost. It will

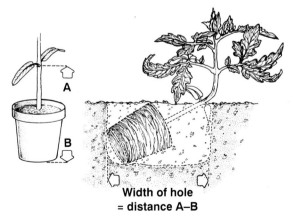

Width of hole = distance A–B

Settling a leggy tomato plant (Rob Dalton)

Do not buy plants if they have:		
No seed leaves	–	plants have been checked by poor watering or affected by the cold
Pale colouring	–	insufficient light, subjected to high temperatures
Blueish-coloured leaves	–	affected by the cold
Leggy growth	–	insufficient light, excessive feeding
Yellowing of leaves	–	overwatering

RIGHT: Tomatoes interplanted with French marigolds to deter whitefly (*Joy Larkcom*)

String supporting tomato plants (*C.T.Marshall*)

Remove tomato side-shoots (*Rob Dalton*)

very quickly turn and start to grow vertically. If other crops are to be grown in the border at the same time mark the position of the root ball, as it is now not directly beneath the stem.

As the plants grow they will need to be supported. If stakes are used these are best put into position before the tomato is planted out to avoid damage to the roots. If strings are used these should be long enough to have a small portion lying in the bottom of the hole so that the root ball sits on top, holding the string tightly in place. As the weight of fruit can be considerable (15–20 lb/7–9 kg per plant) the supports need to be strong enough to carry this load. Stakes should be tied back to the greenhouse frame by hanging a horizontal support from the roof and tying each vertical stake to it. The plants are tied to the stake or twisted around the string as they grow. When tying allow for the thickening of the stem as it grows.

Tomatoes grow quickly after planting out. Careful watering is needed at this stage, for too much can lead to flower-setting problems later. Start with about a pint (0·5 l) of water per plant per day, increasing as the plant grows to about 8 pints (4·5 l) per plant per day when carrying four to five trusses. Use your judgement, however, for if the soil is still wet from a previous application do not add any more at that stage. Be regular; never let the plants dry out then overwater, for this too can be the cause of many problems as the season progresses, in particular 'blossom end rot'.The fruit may also split.

Always use water at greenhouse temperature – keep a few gallons in buckets or a watering can standing in the greenhouse. Water from the spout of the can, not the rose, but do not hold it in one place for too long otherwise it will wash the soil away from the roots.

Each plant is restricted to a single stem, unless it is a bush variety, to direct all its strength into producing fruit. Side shoots will form at the joint between the stem and the leaf and these are removed as soon as they appear. Break off cleanly so as not to tear the skin of the stem, as wounds are an inlet for infection. When the

Gardener's Delight, growing up string (*Photos Horticultural*)

plant reaches the greenhouse roof, usually after five or six trusses, the growing tip is pinched out.

Feeding is just as important as watering, for tomatoes are very greedy plants. Feeding should not start until the first fruits have set. Then a mulch of chopped, wilted comfrey leaves covered by 1 in (2·5 cm) layer of worm compost is applied to the soil. Mulching also helps to retain the soil moisture. Repeat this mulch twice more during the season.

Liquid feeding starts at the same time. Spray twice a week with comfrey liquid, diluted in the ratio of twenty parts water to one part comfrey. Every fourteen days seaweed extract, diluted to the manufacturer's recommendation, can be mixed with the comfrey liquid. This will balance the nitrogen and potash the plants need. Towards the end of the season reduce the feed to once a week, as the plants now require less potash. Do not liquid feed if the soil is dry or when the sun is hot on the leaves.

To ensure good setting the flowers need to be pollinated, especially important when the flowers of the first truss are developed, as there is little or no pollen in the air. Setting, as the process is called, is helped by spraying the plants daily with water at greenhouse temperature, preferably around midday. The flowers should also be hand-pollinated by touching each flower in turn with the bristles of a small camel-hair paint-brush. The pollen sticks to the hairs and is transferred from plant to plant. As the number of trusses increases this procedure becomes less important; gentle tapping of the supports will

release sufficient pollen into the atmosphere to fertilize the flowers. The first truss can be the heaviest and therefore needs special care if disappointment is to be avoided.

As the summer temperatures rise ventilation becomes very important. Start to ventilate as the temperature reaches 65°F (18°C). Excessive temperatures will cause uneven ripening of the fruit as well as leaf scorch. Avoid rapid increases in temperature in the mornings after a cold night.

In long periods of hot weather shade the greenhouse to reduce air temperature. Do not allow the atmosphere to dry out; frequent spraying of water into the air along with damping down by pouring water on the path will create the required humidity as well as reducing air temperature.

It is not good practice to start removing the bottom leaves when the first truss starts to ripen, as many gardeners believe. The leaf is part of the growing system of the plant and should be left on the stem as long as possible, preferably to die off naturally. However, the lower leaves may need to be thinned out to improve the ventilation around the base of the plants. Care is needed when removing them so as not to damage the stem. Lift the leaf upwards until it breaks cleanly away from the stem. Tearing the stem tissue can be an entry point for disease.

When to pick the tomatoes is a matter of personal preference. Some people like their tomatoes when they are half-coloured and firm, whereas others prefer them fully ripe and a little softer to the touch. Pick with care, breaking the fruit stem off at the knuckle, leaving the calyx on the tomato. The fruit keep better if removed in this manner.

As the cooler weather of early autumn arrives the ripening process slows down. To encourage the ripening of the remaining fruit start reducing the amount of water given and stop feeding the plants. Stop watering altogether about mid-autumn. Leave the fruits on the plants as long as possible, but once the chance of frosts arrives the plants should be stripped and the fruit ripened indoors. If the border is needed for a following crop the plants can be cut off at soil level and hung up in the greenhouse for the fruit to ripen.

Do not pull the old plants out by their roots but use a spade, taking out a spadeful of soil with the root ball. This not only helps to remove any possible soil problems with the old plant but also maintains a constant soil level.

Tomatoes are a very sensitive crop, susceptible to a number of pest and disease problems. Greenfly and whitefly are the commonest pests, with damping off, grey mould, stem rot, leaf mould, blight and blossom end rot as well as a number of viruses all common in the badly maintained greenhouse.

Vegetables – summary

Crop	When to sow	When to plant	Ready to eat	Varieties
Aubergine	Late winter–early spring	Late spring–early summer	Mid–late summer	Black Prince Long Purple
Beetroot	mid- to late winter		Late spring	Boltardy
Carrot	mid- to late winter		Late spring	Nantes Express Amsterdam Forcing
	Late summer		Early autumn	Rondo
Celery	Early–mid-spring	Late spring	Late summer	American Green
Courgette	Early spring	Late spring	Early–mid-summer	Zucchini Gold Rush
Cress	Late summer–mid-autumn		Early autumn	Salad Rape Fine Curled
Cucumber	Early spring	Late spring	Early summer	Diana Monique
French bean	Early spring		Early summer	Tendergreen
Lettuce	Late summer–late winter	Early autumn–early spring	Late autumn late spring	(see Lettuce table, page 341)
Pepper	Mid-winter–early spring		Late summer–early autumn	Ace F1
Potato	Late summer Late winter		Early winter Early summer	Early variety
Radish	Late winter–mid-spring		Mid-spring	French Breakfast
Sweetcorn	Mid-to late spring	Late spring–early summer	Late summer	Sunrise F1
Tomato	Early spring	Late spring	Mid-summer	(see Tomato table, page 345)
Turnip	Early spring Late summer		Late spring Mid-autumn	Snowball

Turnip. Choosing a fast-growing variety of turnip will give a catch crop between seasons. Sow thinly in rows 6 in (15 cm) apart, thinning the seedlings out to 2 in (5 cm) apart. They need little attention apart from keeping the soil moist.

Start to crop when the roots are about the size of a golf ball, pulling every second plant to increase the spacing to 4 in (10 cm). This allows some of the roots to develop to a larger diameter. However, do not let them grow too large – they are much sweeter when small.

FRUITS

The majority of fruit trees and bushes can be grown under glass, but as they tend to take up a considerable amount of space there is little point in growing the hardy varieties which do well outside. However, a large greenhouse sited in a sunny position will offer the conditions to grow fruit which would otherwise be difficult to grow in coolish temperate climates.

When choosing a variety ensure that it is suitable for growing inside, as some do not respond well to such conditions. Consider its growth habit and what training will be needed. Will it grow as a bush or trained against a wall? The lean-to greenhouse with its solid wall is ideal for supporting trees.

All fruits need well-drained soil; none enjoys its roots sitting in wet soil.

Apricots. Grow well in the unheated greenhouse, provided the soil is rich in organic matter. Although they prefer an alkaline soil this is not essential for a successful crop.

It is best to start with a young tree, preferably a maiden but no older than four years. Plant out when the tree is dormant, any time between late autumn and early spring, although the best time is late autumn. Give the border a good soaking before planting. The top of the roots should be just below the soil surface. Take care not to damage the root ball, as this can lead to the production of suckers. After planting the tree should be severely pruned, cutting the laterals back to about two-thirds their length. All weak shoots are also cut out. Do not allow fruit to form in the first year after planting.

Give the border a good watering in late winter to encourage new growth. Keep the soil well watered once the growth appears and continue throughout the early part of the summer to ensure that the fruit swells to a good size. Once it does, reduce the amount of water.

In spring apply a potash-rich fertilizer. A mulch of wilted comfrey leaves covered with a layer of well-rotted compost is ideal. A comfrey liquid foliar feed applied at frequent intervals with a liquid seaweed extract added to the comfrey every second feed will suffice throughout the growing season.

Apricots are self-pollinated, so one tree alone can be successful. However, as they tend to flower early in the year, when the greenhouse door is probably closed, preventing the bees from entering, it is best to hand-pollinate. Use a fine camel-hair paint-brush and choose a dry warm day when the flowers are fully open.

Thinning is not normally necessary, as the plant can carry all the fruit set, but occasionally if the tree is overloaded some removal of fruit may be needed for good-sized fruit to be grown.

Wait until the stones are starting to form, easily seen when a fruit is cut open, and leave about 4 in (10 cm) between each fruit. Sometimes there can be a fruit-fall early in the season, and leaving the thinning until after this period safeguards against ending up with too little fruit.

Apricots grow best when fan-trained against a wall. Pruning should be kept to a minimum, just enough to keep the tree well shaped, prevent overcrowding and remove any dead shoots. Side shoots are shortened back to six leaves.

Pick the fruits when they are fully coloured and come away easily from the tree. If left too long they tend to dry out and become tasteless.

The main pest is the red spider mite, easily controlled by maintaining a moist atmosphere in the greenhouse and carefully ventilating, holding the temperature down to 65–70°F (18–21°C).

Figs. Are really grown successfully only under glass in cool climates like Britain. They do not require a very rich soil, but it must be well drained.

Planting is best carried out in late autumn, but can be carried over into early spring. It is preferable to purchase pot-grown two- to three-year-old trees, because figs tend to produce a considerable amount of weak growth if left to develop naturally. In the border the roots are easily curtailed by lining the hole with wood or slate. After planting the tree is pruned severely,

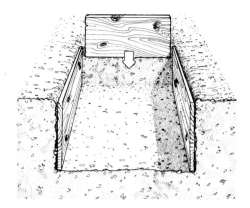

Planting a fig: line hole with wood or slate to curtail root growth (*Rob Dalton*)

and no fruit is allowed to develop during the first year.

In the spring the soil is dressed with a well-balanced organic fertilizer followed by a mulch of well-rotted compost. As the new growth shows the soil needs to be kept moist until the tree has produced several leaves; then water freely right through until the fruit has been harvested.

A frequent foliar feed of comfrey liquid will help the fruit develop. Dress the soil with seaweed meal in mid-autumn when the plant is preparing for dormancy. Pollination of the flowers is not necessary. If the figs drop off the cause is likely to be insufficient water rather than bad setting.

The figs will start to ripen from late summer and will continue through to mid-autumn. Pick when ripe, easily judged by squeezing the fruits. If they are soft and easily removed from the tree they are ready to eat.

Brown Turkey, an old, hardy fig variety (*Harry Smith*)

Pruning a fig tree (*Rob Dalton*)

**Prune severely
after planting**

**Following autumn, cut out weak or
overcrowded shoots and some of the old
wood. Leave strong growing shoots**

At the end of the season the leaves will turn yellow, die and fall. At the first sign reduce the quantity of water until watering has stopped altogether by the time all the leaves have fallen. The plant is now kept dry over the winter dormancy period.

If the tree has produced a great amount of new, weak wood, or failed to produce a good crop of fruit, the roots could be further restricted by pruning them in mid-autumn after the leaves have fallen. The tree is also pruned at this period. Cut out weak or overcrowded shoots as well as some of the old wood, leaving strongly growing shoots. If some of the side shoots produce too much growth they can be cut back to six leaves in the summer.

Figs respond best to being grown in a fan shape.

Grapes. Grow very successfully in a cold greenhouse, so much so that one vine can take up the whole house. Drainage is of the utmost importance in their cultivation. If necessary, lay drains to draw off any excess water.

The bed, which can be either inside the greenhouse or outside, needs to be well prepared about two months before planting. Plenty of organic matter, compost or well-rotted manure must be incorporated into the soil down to two spades' depth. To ensure good drainage mix in a spadeful or two of rubble. A 6 in (15 cm) layer of chopped turf can be laid on the surface if available.

When buying vines make sure they are a suitable variety for growing in an unheated greenhouse (see *Fruit*, page 170). One vine is normally sufficient for the amateur greenhouse, and can be planted out between mid-autumn and late winter. In the northern hemisphere, if the greenhouse runs north to south it is best planted at the north end, while in an east/west orientated house, plant at the end opposite the door, training the vine along the northerly roof span. In a lean-to it is usual to train along the glass side. Training should be along transverse wires suspended about 9 in (23 cm) below the glass.

When planting out, if the roots have formed a tight ball this should be gently opened out and spread over the bottom of the hole. Do not plant too deeply: the uppermost roots should be covered with only about 3 in (7·5 cm) of soil. Water well, firm, then mulch the surface with compost or well-rotted manure.

If the root is planted outside the greenhouse a section of the end wall will need to be removed. Keep the opening to a minimum and fill the gaps around the vine with sacking or straw.

When growth starts the plant needs to be well watered and the leaves and stems sprayed with water to create a humid atmosphere. The vine needs to be trained to suit the greenhouse, working on the principle of allowing one shoot to grow towards

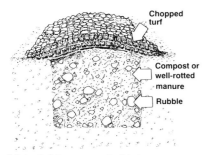

Chopped
turf

Compost or
well-rotted
manure

Rubble

Material incorporated into
growing hole of vine (*Rob Dalton*)

Foster's Seedling, suitable for unheated greenhouse (*Harry Smith*)

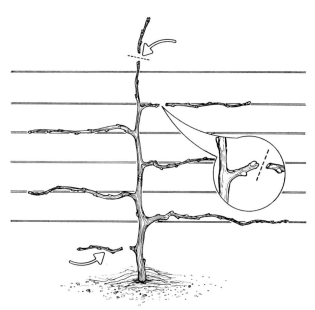

Pruning a vine (*Rob Dalton*)

the apex of the house, the laterals being thinned out, selecting the strongest for training along the wires. The laterals are stopped at the second leaf past the fruit or, in the first year, when no fruit is allowed to form, after the sixth or seventh leaf.

When the flowers appear keep the greenhouse atmosphere dry. Tap the stems or use a camel-hair paint-brush to help pollination. The soil should be kept moist: at no time allow it to dry out. Apply a liquid feed at regular intervals. Maintain a temperature of around 75°F (24°C) by

ventilating as much as possible and avoid sudden fluctuations in temperature. Once the flowers have set the humidity should be increased again by spraying the vines daily with water at greenhouse temperature.

Thinning of the bunches should start about two weeks after the fruit has set and can continue until it is the size of peas. Using vine scissors, cut out about half the fruits so that they are spaced about ½ in (1 cm) apart. This is a skilled job, and it will take a little practice to become proficient. It is important not to try to grow too many bunches of grapes – do not allow more than one on each lateral.

Pruning is carried out after all the leaves have fallen, but must be completed by late winter. All laterals are cut back to two buds, the weakest one being cut out in the spring once growth has started. Summer pinching of the laterals to leave one every 15 in (38 cm) is required as the vine is trained along the house.

Melons. Are closely related to cucumbers and are treated in a very similar manner. Seeds are sown in mid- or late spring in a minimum temperature of 65°F (18°C), and raised in the same way as cucumber. Select a variety suitable for a greenhouse.

Prepare mounds, and when the melon has about four true leaves it is planted in the mound with the top of the root ball still visible. Water well, then no more until the plant produces new growth. Plants should be spaced about 24 in (60 cm) apart.

The plants can be allowed to spread over the soil or trained up stakes or wires. Lying on the soil leaves the fruit vulnerable to attack from slugs or rot, so it is best to train them up supports, like cucumbers.

Flowers are produced on the side shoots, which are stopped two leaves past the fruit. Both male and female flowers are produced, the female requiring fertilizing by the male. To ensure good fertilization, remove the fully

Melons	
Variety	*Characteristics*
Blenheim Orange	Old variety, medium-sized, scarlet-fleshed fruit with good flavour; reliable, high yield
Ogen	Round, medium-sized fruit with pale green flesh; sweet-tasting, heavy cropper
F1 Sweet Heart	Small, oval fruit, very firm pink flesh with a very sweet taste. Easy to grow, the best in a poor season. Recommended for colder areas such as northern UK

Melons need to be supported with special melon nets (*Photos Horticultural*)

opened male flower, remove its petals and push it into the female flowers. This needs to be done two or three times on successive days to ensure good setting. It is best done at midday if possible, when the flowers are fully opened. Fertilized fruits will begin to swell within a few days.

Water the plants fully, as if the soil dries out the fruits will drop prematurely. Do not allow the stem to become wet, for this will increase the incidence of stem disease. If the roots begin to show on the soil surface cover with a 1 in (2·5 cm) layer of compost. A regular feed with a weak solution of seaweed extract will maintain steady, healthy growth. The number of fruits should be limited to four or five per plant. As they swell they will need to be supported. Special melon nets can be used, one for each fruit, tied to the support framework. Stop watering when the melons have reached the size wanted.

Pick when fully ripe from late summer, when they begin to change colour and the end of the fruit feels slightly soft. It should also come away easily from the plant. As the weather cools down the fruit can be removed and ripened off indoors.

Red spider mite can cause considerable damage. Prevent attacks by maintaining a moist soil. Mildew can also be troublesome.

Peaches and nectarines. The nectarine is a smooth-skinned variety of peach and is treated in precisely the same way. One interesting point is that they can both be raised from each other's stones; however, seedlings seldom follow the parent in quality and are disappointing in many respects. It is best therefore to purchase plants from a reputable supplier. For suitable varieties see *Fruit*, page 159. As they take up considerable room they are not recommended for a small greenhouse. The trees are planted at least 15 ft (4·5 m) apart if fan-trained. They are at their best grown as a fan against the wall of a south-facing lean-to. The soil needs to be well prepared. Good drainage is essential and if the soil tends to stay wet, drains will need to be laid to run off excess water. However, the soil must be capable of retaining sufficient moisture to ensure good steady growth. The best soil is one of chopped turf containing about a quarter its volume of well-rotted compost, to a depth of two spades. A spadeful or two of rubble should be added to keep the soil porous. If turf is unobtainable dig plenty of compost or well-rotted manure into the border, again incorporating the compost.

Trees should be maidens or two years old, as they transplant more easily. They should be planted in mid-autumn with the base of the tree at least 9 in (23 cm) away from any wall. Spread the roots out into a shallow hole of large diameter. Do not plant too deeply – no more than 2–3 in (5–7·5 cm) of soil should cover the top roots. Water thoroughly. Cut the stems of maidens back to about 24 in (60 cm) above soil level to encourage the development of new shoots to train to the correct shape. On two-year-olds, cut the branches back to half their length.

As soon as new growth appears the plant must be well watered, for the soil must not be allowed to dry out or die-back can occur. Remove all the buds except for two, one on either side of the main stem. Train the two side shoots out at an angle of 45° when about 18 in (45 cm) long, along canes tied to horizontal wires attached to the wall. In early spring dress the soil well with a 2 in (5 cm) mulch of well-rotted compost or manure and repeat in early summer.

In the second winter cut the laterals back to about 18 in (45 cm). The following summer select two strong buds on the upper side of the branch and one on the lower, removing all the others. Never select buds pointing towards the wall. These six new shoots are tied to canes when about 18 in (45 cm) long.

In the third winter cut each new shoot back to, again, 18 in (45 cm) at a triple bud cluster (two fruit buds, fat ones, and one growth bud, slender one), for by the third summer the wall space will be full. The tree is now ready to be encouraged to produce fruit. Allow shoots to grow on the laterals at 6 in (15 cm) apart, rubbing out all the others. When about 18 in (45 cm) long the tips are pinched out.

Peaches and nectarines fruit on year-old side growth, so there must always be sufficient growth allowed. Do not, however, allow the tree to become overcrowded.

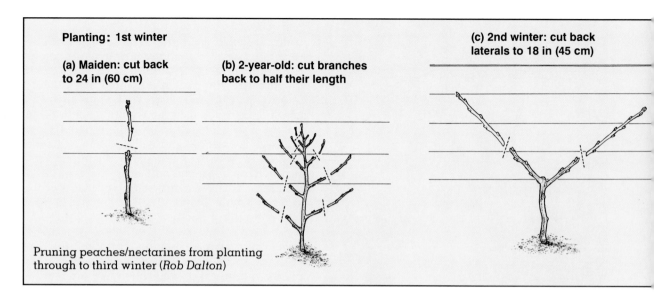

Planting: 1st winter

(a) Maiden: cut back to 24 in (60 cm)

(b) 2-year-old: cut branches back to half their length

(c) 2nd winter: cut back laterals to 18 in (45 cm)

Pruning peaches/nectarines from planting through to third winter (*Rob Dalton*)

Feeding consists of a dressing of seaweed fertilizer in mid-winter and a mulch of compost or well-rotted manure in early spring. If an old tree does not produce enough side shoots, dress with blood, fish and bone before the mulch. Give the tree a thorough soaking before the growth starts in the late winter, and keep the soil moist during the summer period, otherwise fruit drop may occur.

The trees are self-pollinating, but to ensure a good set hand-pollinate by tapping the shoots and brushing the flowers with a small camel-hair paintbrush. Do not allow the tree to produce too many fruit. To secure good-sized fruits thin out when

As peaches ripen, pull back foliage to expose to as much sun as possible (*Photos Horticultural*)

about the size of a hazelnut and again, if necessary, when the size of a walnut. Use scissors to avoid damaging the bark.

Good ventilation is essential, but avoid draughts or sudden changes in temperature. A very hot, dry atmosphere can lead to an attack by the red spider mite. Try to restrict the temperature in the greenhouse to no more than 80°F (26°C).

As the fruit begins to ripen, pull back the foliage to allow as much sun on to it as possible. Pick when the fruit feels slightly soft and comes away easily from the tree. By selecting the correct varieties a succession of fruit can be pulled from mid- to late summer.

As the leaves begin to die at the end of the season, give as much ventilation as possible and soak the roots to simulate the autumn weather outdoors. As with grapes, peaches and nectarines must be fully dormant over the winter.

Leaf curl can be troublesome, but is easily avoided by keeping the leaves as dry as possible.

Strawberries. Under glass the strawberry season is sufficiently early for you to enjoy the crop and have them out of the way to make room for other summer crops. For suitable varieties see *Fruit*, page 169.

The plants are potted into 6 in (15 m) pots in late summer and left outside. Stand them on several sheets of newspaper to avoid the roots growing through the bottom of the pot into the soil. As the winter rains begin the pots are laid on their sides to prevent the compost becoming too wet. (They can also be placed in a cold frame.)

In late winter transfer them into the greenhouse, and once the new growth begins to develop moisten the compost. At this stage a temperature of no more than 50°F (10°C) is needed, so ventilate freely on warm days.

When the flowers open they will need to be

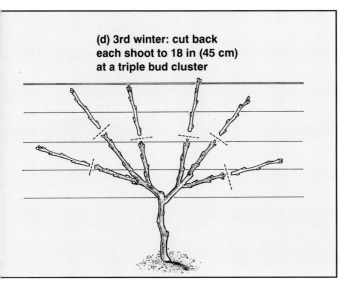

(d) 3rd winter: cut back each shoot to 18 in (45 cm) at a triple bud cluster

Alpines are suited to a cold greenhouse but still require climate control (*Photos Horticultural*)

A 50:50 mix of potting compost and grit is ideal for alpines (*Chris Algar*)

fertilized by hand, using the camel-hair paint-brush technique. Once the flowers have set the house temperature can be allowed to rise to between 60 and 70°F (15·5–21°C), but once the fruits begin to ripen drop the temperature to nearer the 60°F (15·5°C) mark. Keep well watered and out of the direct rays of the sun. A liquid seaweed extract feed will encourage fruiting over a long period.

When the crop has finished remove the plants from the greenhouse and put in an outside strawberry bed. Do not use the same plants for next year's greenhouse crop, for they will not do so well a second season under glass.

ORNAMENTALS

A wide range of plants can be grown in a cold greenhouse to promote a dazzling display of colour, either through the flowers or decorative foliage. Although the majority are pot grown there are a number which do better if grown in the border soil: for instance, universal pansies (excellent over the winter period), primroses, polyanthus, passion-flower and plumbago. As pot plants need to be stood on a bench or staging, part of the house should be given over to this, as it is difficult to mix pot plants with the tomatoes and cucumbers. The management of the greenhouse is slightly different in that an area is needed for mixing composts and potting plants, the storage of pots and seed trays. Depending upon the choice of varieties, a propagating frame may also be required. Organic products, plant foods and pest and disease control are as appropriate for ornamental plants as for food crops.

Alpines. Alpines are grown in a totally cold greenhouse. It is a misconception that they are hardy plants capable of withstanding extremely

cold weather because they survive high up on snow-covered mountains. It must be remembered that for a large part of the year they are under an insulating blanket of snow, which keeps them at a constant temperature. Alpines do not like damp weather, cold winds and extremes of temperature, and under such conditions they struggle to survive.

The greenhouse must be well ventilated to provide uniform temperature conditions. The alpines are best grown on benches covered with 2 in (5 cm) of gravel to ensure that excess water from the pots drains away. The compost itself needs to be gritty, as much as 50:50 potting compost to grit. Put a layer of crocks in the bottom of the pot, for good drainage is essential.

The plants can stand outside during the summer months, buried in the soil up to the rim to keep them cool and ensure that they do not dry out too quickly. They are brought into the greenhouse around mid-autumn, where they need to be kept cool by opening up the house to give maximum ventilation. Water sparingly, just enough to keep the compost moist. To prevent it drying out, it can be covered with a layer of grit,

Hardy annuals, sown in late summer, overwinter to provide a splash of colour in early spring (*Photos Horticultural*)

Begonias provide an excellent display in the flower greenhouse, many at home without heat. (*Photos Horticultural*)

multi-coloured if you like for a decorative effect. The greenhouse can remain open except in very cold frosty weather.

Annuals. Many of the plants we grow as bedding can be raised in a cold greenhouse and will continue to grow successfully under glass to give an impressive display of colour over a long period. Sown to the supplier's instructions, the plants are transplanted into pots. The size of the pot depends greatly upon the height of the plant, not only to accommodate the root ball but also for stability. As a rough guide a plant 6–9 in (15–23 cm) tall needs a 4–5 in (10–12·5) pot, 12–18 in (30–45 cm) tall a 5–6 in (12·5–15 cm) pot and 18–24 in (45–60 cm) tall a 6–8 in (15–20 cm) pot.

Although the half-hardy annuals will give a display over the summer months, the hardy varieties can be sown in late summer and overwintered to give a splash of colour in early spring.

Begonias. These plants, with their many varieties, ornamental leaves and showy flowers, give an excellent display and are an essential addition to the flower greenhouse. Some of the winter-flowering varieties require a little heat and are therefore not suitable for the cold greenhouse.

They are either tuberous-rooted or fibrous-rooted, the latter grown from seed. Seeds are sown in late winter and as a temperature of 65°F (18°C) is needed the seeds are germinated in a propagating frame. As the seeds are very fine they are sprinkled over the surface of damp compost and gently pressed into the surface with a flat object. Do not cover with compost, only with a plastic propagating lid. Prick out into trays when large enough to handle, watering just

enough to keep the compost moist. In late spring pot on into 3 in (7·5 cm) pots, using a coarse compost. Two parts each of compost and leaf-mould passed through a ½ in (1 cm) riddle with one part of coarse sand is ideal. In a further four weeks transfer to a 5 in (12·5 cm) pot.

The tuberous varieties are brought to life in early spring by placing them in a seed box and just covering with damp peat. When the foliage is about 2 in (5 cm) high the tubers are potted into 6 in (15 cm) pots using the potting compost described.

Do not overwater at any time: the compost should be just moist. The plants also need to be kept cool – a temperature of around 60°F (15·5°C) is all that is needed. Maintain a slightly humid atmosphere by spraying and damping down the house. Shade the glass in hot weather.

The first flower buds should be removed to allow the plant to become well established. This technique gives bigger and better blooms. When in flower feed weekly with a 20:1 comfrey liquid feed or other high-potash feed until the plant stops flowering. At this point watering should be reduced and, when the stems fall away from the tuber, stopped altogether. Any leaves still on the plant can be snapped off to encourage dormancy, but it must not be forced by breaking the main stem.

The tubers are cleaned and dried then stored in sand or coconut fibre (coir) in a frost-proof place until the following season.

Chrysanthemums. These are probably the most written-up flower in the garden.

The greenhouse varieties, often called 'indoor' or 'late flowering', are in bloom from mid- to late autumn. Cultivation in a cold greenhouse is

All the year round chrysanthemum, Yellow Princess Anne, likes plenty of light and air. (*Harry Smith*)

generally the same as for heated greenhouse varieties, the first potting into 9 in (23 cm) pots being no later than early summer. They are transferred into the greenhouse by mid-autumn, when the buds are beginning to show and before there are any frosts.

Do not overcrowd in the greenhouse: space them about 18 in (45 cm) apart, giving the plants plenty of light and air, otherwise they will be prone to mildew and botrytis.

Regular watering and feeding with a high-potash feed such as comfrey liquid is essential to maintain good healthy growth.

THE HEATED GREENHOUSE

The use of artificial heat in a greenhouse, either just sufficient to keep it frost-free, or to maintain it at elevated temperatures, offers a new aspect of growing to gardeners. Although the use of heat has many advantages, it does have the one major

The heated greenhouse opens up a new dimension (*Photos Horticultural*)

Mist propagators

When rooting cuttings, it is often important to keep them moist. Once removed from the plant the cutting soon wilts, due to loss of moisture from its leaves. As there is no root to absorb moisture from the soil the plant must obtain it from the air. Mist propagators keep the environment constantly damp by injecting into it a fine water mist at frequent intervals. This not only provides the water required by the plant but also keeps it cool in hot weather.

Mist propagator (*Two Wests and Elliott Ltd*)

For the propagator to be effective, bottom heat is used to hold the atmospheric temperature to about 75°F (24°C). Good drainage on the bench is important, to prevent the base medium on which the pots and trays stand from becoming too wet. The bed should be at least 3 in (7·5 cm) deep, the bottom half of coarse grit and the top coarse sand.

Once rooted, the cuttings must be hardened off by reducing the temperature and frequency of the mist.

drawback of cost. This is a factor the grower must take into account before setting out to grow plants that require it.

Heated greenhouses are 'cool houses' where the minimum overnight temperature is 45°F (7°C) and a day temperature of not less than 55°F (13°C) is necessary at any part of the year; 'warm houses' where the night and day temperatures are not less than 55°F (13°C) and 65°F (18°C) respectively; and 'hothouses' where the minimum night temperature is 60°F (15·5°C), while the day temperatures can reach 75 to 85°F (24–29°C). To operate warm and hothouses needs a heating system of the correct capacity and the finance to maintain it.

Winter can be a dull, miserable time of the year. A little heat can turn the greenhouse into a blaze of colour. Although the number of plants in flower is far fewer than during the summer, there is still plenty to keep the greenhouse attractive.

One important point to remember over the winter period is that, should the heating fail and the temperature drop even to below freezing, do not rush to raise it back to the original setting. To do this will kill anything which has survived. Cover the plants with newspaper or similar to cut out as much light as possible, and raise the temperature gradually over the space of an hour or two. Once the minimum temperature is reached remove the newspaper. Even the most delicate of plants can be saved by this method.

Ventilation and watering are very important, especially during the winter months. Excessive moisture both in the air and the soil will encourage mildew and fungal disease. Use ventilators on the side opposite the prevailing wind in the winter to prevent gusts of cold air chilling the plants. Close them before the sun goes down and the air temperature begins to fall.

Water is most needed in the spring or early summer. Over the winter the rule in the greenhouse is: *water only when the plant needs it.* Just because the soil or compost looks dry is not the reason to soak it. On the other hand, if the compost in the pot does dry out it shrinks away from the sides and any water added from the top runs straight out at the bottom.

Judging the right time and the right amount of water is not always easy, one reason why many gardeners still favour the clay pot. Tapping with a stick soon indicates the condition of the compost inside: pots needing water have a ring to them, whereas those still moist have a dull sound. With plants grown in the border soil it is an easy matter to dig down an inch or two to see how far down the soil is moist.

VEGETABLES

Generally vegetables do better in the unheated greenhouse, except for tomatoes and cucumbers where low temperatures can check the plants. However, the use of a little heat in the early months of the year can allow early sowings to be made for both inside and outside planting.

To germinate most seeds a temperature of 60°F (15·5°C) is needed, and unless there are other plants in the greenhouse it is not worth holding it at this temperature for a few trays of seeds. An electric propagator can be used for this purpose, and will be essential for those seeds requiring higher germination temperatures (sometimes up to 75 or 80°F/24 or 26°C). They are available in several sizes and heating capacities. They are covered with clear plastic lids which are ventilated to minimize condensation.

An alternative to the propagator is to use buried soil-heating cables, using part of the border or a prepared bed on the benching. This form of bottom heating is particularly useful when propagating cuttings, or for the growing on of pot plants.

Variable thermostatic controls can provide temperatures within the range of 45–85°F (7–29°C) with this electric propagator (*Humex, Geeco Ltd*)

Soil-heating cables to heat borders offer an alternative to propagators (*Humex, Geeco Ltd*)

To induce the maximum heat into the growing medium it is best to sink the pots or trays slightly into the bed, or, if they are placed on the surface, to fill the spaces between with moist peat or sand. This local application of heat allows the seedlings, cuttings and plants to grow at a steady rate even when the greenhouse air temperatures are quite low, and is very economical.

As soil-warming cables have very little or no influence over the greenhouse air temperature, they are no protection against air frost.

If you do not wish to use an electric propagator you can sow on a south-facing windowsill. You can use 3 in (7·5 cm) pots or half or whole seed trays, covering them with purpose-made plastic propagator lids. Holes in the top allow an exchange of air so that the atmosphere is kept fresh and the compost is able to breathe. The lids are a good fit on the rim of the pot and tray, so they are not easily knocked off. Although the clear plastic allows the lids to be left in place until the seed leaves develop, it is best to remove them at the first opportunity, for all coverings do reduce light transmission and the seedlings will become leggy.

Clear polythene bags are an alternative, blown up, the neck placed over the pot or tray and held in place with an elastic band. For general seed germination, the corners of the bag should be snipped off with a pair of scissors to allow some air circulation inside, otherwise it will sweat, and the condensation will reduce the light transmission. Another possibility is that of the seeds rotting or the seedlings damping off if the atmosphere is too damp.

For users of polystyrene cellular trays, a propagating system is available where the tray sits on a piece of capillary mat having one end in a water reservoir, the tray being covered with a clear plastic top. The capillary matting maintains the correct moisture level in the compost, the top providing the atmosphere for good germination and growing on. This system will also fit a standard seed tray.

These propagating lids do have the disadvantage that high temperatures are built up inside them if they are left in the heat of the sun. Although the humidity level inside will give the plants a limited amount of protection, it is safer to shade them from direct sunlight on hot days.

If in trays, the seedlings need to be transplanted into cellular trays or individual pots as soon as they are large enough to handle. Remember always to handle by the seed leaves. If the seedlings are a little leggy do not be afraid to plant them deep, almost up to the seed leaves.

Using bubble polythene, divide off a section of the greenhouse just large enough to hold the trays of seedlings, to minimize the volume of air needing to be heated. Set the heater thermostat to hold this section at 45–55°F (7–13°C). As more trays are filled the heated part of the greenhouse will need to be extended. The seedlings will stay inside until the soil and weather conditions are fit for them to be planted outside. Remember that the young plants need to be hardened off before being put in their final growing position.

In exceptionally cold springs there can be a delay before setting outside the very early sowings. It must be borne in mind that all the effort of an early start is lost if the plants are put outside when the conditions are not conducive for good growing. One problem with this is that if they are left too long in pots or trays they will become pot-bound. It is not always easy to transfer them into a larger container, and every time they are moved there is the possibility of damaging the roots and checking the plants. One method of avoiding this is to prick out the sowings into paper pots (see page 342).

Tomatoes can be cropped in late spring from a late summer sowing. For this, a minimum night temperature of 55°F (13°C) must be maintained. During the day the ideal temperature is around 65°F (18°C), but once 70°F (21°C) is reached the ventilator will need to be opened. Avoid excessive daytime temperatures. Watering will vary with the type of day; on dull days the plants may require as little as ½ pt (0·3 l) each while on a bright sunny day the quantity can increase to ½ gal (2 l) each. 'Red Alert' is a good variety for autumn sowing.

FRUITS

Like vegetables, many fruits produce good crops from the unheated greenhouse; however, citrus fruits are really only suitable for the heated greenhouse or conservatory except in a warm climate.

Citrus fruits. Growing oranges and lemons from pips is something almost every child has done, but the results are unreliable and the trees do not come true. It is doubtful if any fruit would ever be produced. Cuttings or grafted plants are needed to make them worth growing. As with other fruits in the greenhouse, citrus trees can be grown either in the border soil or in a pot. Pots are preferable, for they can be put outside between late spring and early autumn to leave space in the greenhouse for other plants, and they are easier to control.

The pot needs to be well drained, as the roots

Meyer's lemon (*Photos Horticultural*)

will not tolerate standing in wet compost. Start off with a pot the right size for the root ball, increasing it as the tree grows until a final size of 15–18 in (38–45 cm) is reached. Disturb the root ball as little as possible when potting on.

Citrus trees need a minimum temperature of 45°F (7°C), so must be taken inside before there is any chance of frosts. They will need very little water over the dormant winter period, just an occasional drink to keep the compost moist and prevent the leaves dying off.

The tree starts to grow again in early spring when the quantity of water should be increased. If the trees are left in the greenhouse they need to be sprayed with water at greenhouse temperature and the house damped down on hot days to keep the atmosphere moist. However, this procedure must stop once the flowers begin to open, as the sun on the water droplets will scorch the petals.

The plants need to be fed at two-week intervals with a liquid seaweed extract starting as soon as good growth develops. A mulch of worm compost will help to keep the pot compost fertile.

A little pruning is needed to keep the trees under control. Cut out any weak or damaged shoots and trim the remainder back to hold the shape. Over-pruning can result in the tree producing a great deal of weak growth. Pruning can be carried out at almost any time of the year, but is preferable in the early spring or autumn.

Trees kept indoors over the summer will need to be fertilized. Use a fine camel-hair paint-brush to transfer the pollen from the male to the female flowers. The young fruits will overwinter on the tree. Pick them in spring when they develop a deep colour. There is no need to pick them all at once – they will remain on the tree in perfect

Oranges and other citrus fruits can be grown in a sufficiently heated greenhouse – minimum 45°F (7°C) (*Harry Smith*)

condition for several weeks. Some varieties will turn green again as the weather starts to warm up.

Scale insects can be a problem, so examine the underside of the leaves regularly for signs of the black sooty mould which so often accompanies them. Root rot is also troublesome if the plants are grown in waterlogged conditions.

Figs. Although figs grow very well in the cold greenhouse the use of a little heat in early spring will allow two crops of fruit to be harvested in a year. A temperature of 55–60°F (13–18°C) is needed to start the plants into early growth, and they must be given as much light as possible.

Once growth begins keep well watered and apply a foliar feed of liquid comfrey every two to three weeks. This crop will be ready to harvest in the early summer with the second crop in early autumn.

Peaches and nectarines. Grow as for the cold greenhouse, except that in late winter increase the house temperature to 50°F (10°C) to produce an early crop of fruit.

ORNAMENTALS

The range of ornamental plants that can be grown in a heated greenhouse is almost endless; here, a few of the more popular varieties are discussed in detail. Much of what was said in the unheated greenhouse section still applies to the heated house.

Cacti and succulents. Although 'cacti' and 'succulents' are often used interchangeably they do not mean the same thing. Succulents are fleshy-leaved plants that store up water and food to enable them to survive in long periods of drought, while cacti are simply a popular variety of succulent. Not all spiny succulents are cacti: a true cactus is one which has several spines growing in a bunch from points on the ribs. Both survive in the same growing conditions; in the outside world this can be in desert regions, where they have to face the extreme heat of the sun with the minimum amount of water. Cacti and succulents will therefore thrive in the warm, dry atmosphere of a greenhouse. Not all varieties need the protection of the greenhouse; some are hardy enough to survive the whole year outdoors, but only in milder areas.

Their fascination is their variety of shapes and sizes, from a plant the size of a thimble up to those 7 or 8 ft (2-2·5 m) tall. They are attractive plants throughout the year. The range of varieties is wide enough to give an almost continual display of brilliant flowers, and there are also some kinds with brightly coloured spines. Cacti and succulents are also popular because they will survive no matter what their treatment, even

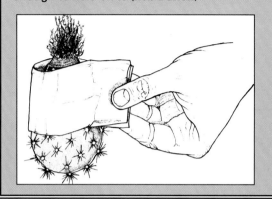

Handling cacti

Repotting cacti may appear a daunting task, as the sharp spines do not make them the easiest plants to handle. Fold a piece of paper several times to form a strip 1–2 in (2·5–5 cm) wide, depending upon the size of the plant, and long enough to wrap around the body, still leaving enough to hold on to (*Rob Dalton*)

near-neglect. However, to get the best out of them they do need care and attention, the right amount of sunshine, water and the right compost mix.

There are many fallacies about cacti flowering. Tales such as only once every twenty years are myths. Once a plant has reached the maturity to start flowering it will do so every year provided it is kept in the correct conditions.

The simplest way to start off cacti and succulents is to buy plants from a garden centre. All too often they will be in pots too small for good root development and they will need to be repotted into 3½ in (8 cm) pots. This is best done between the end of summer and early spring, when the plants are dormant.

The potting mix is important, for cacti and succulents do not like wet soil. A good mix is equal parts of well-rotted compost and coarse sharp sand, with a layer of crocks in the bottom of the pot. Do not overfirm the compost around the roots. As the plant develops it may need to be repotted, not because it is outgrowing the pot but simply to replace the exhausted compost. In the majority of cases the plant will be put back in the same pot; the use of too large a pot does not encourage the plant to give of its best.

Watering begins in early spring when the plant begins to show growth after the winter rest period. As the root ball will be dry the best method for this first watering is to stand the pots in water up to the rim and allow them to soak for four to five hours. Drain off and do not water again for at least a week.

Continue to water freely over the summer, giving them a good soaking and then allowing the compost to dry out between applications. Do

The fascination of cacti and succulents is in their variety of shapes and sizes (*Harry Smith*)

not water a little every day, as with other plants in the greenhouse; remember their natural environment is a desert where they would be subjected to heavy periods of rain followed by hot, dry periods.

At the end of the summer reduce the amount of water until mid-autumn, when no water is given again until early spring, unless it is an exceptionally warm winter. If in doubt always give too little water rather than too much, as the plants have a tendency to rot.

Little or no shading is needed, for the majority enjoy hot sunshine, but ventilate adequately as they do like fresh air.

Provided the compost in the pot is changed occasionally there will be no need to feed, except for a dilute comfrey liquid or half-strength seaweed extract, given to help revitalize the plant after flowering and again when it starts to show growth in the spring.

Over the winter period cacti and succulents need to be kept at a minimum temperature of 45°F (7°C), with some varieties needing as much as 60°F (15·5°C). They are easily damaged by frost, as the water inside the plants freezes.

These plants are easily propagated. Some produce offsets, which can be gently pulled off in early to mid-spring and pushed into moist sharp sand. Sometimes globular leaves will fall off, and can be treated in the same way.

Varieties which produce shoots or stems are best propagated by cuttings taken in mid- to late summer and pushed into sand; the pot is covered in the usual way.

They can also be grown easily from seed. The

Flowering cacti: *Aporocactus, Epiphyllum, Rhipsalidopsis* and *Chamaecereus* (*Photos Horticultural*)

seeds are extremely fine and should be sown in a seed tray in a fine sandy compost mix, but do not cover with compost. Stand the tray in water until the surface of the compost is just moist, then cover with a sheet of glass. Germination will take about a month if a temperature of 65–70°F (18–21°C) is maintained. Keep the compost moist until the seedlings gain some size, for in essence they are initially little more than globules of water which easily dry up in the heat of the sun.

Cacti are little troubled by pests, although on the varieties covered with hair the mealybug can be difficult to dislodge if it is allowed to gain a foothold.

Calceolarias.   There are two varieties, the half-hardy shrub and the herbaceous perennial, the latter being held by many growers to give the finest display of colour in a greenhouse from mid-spring to early summer. Both varieties are grown from seed, although the shrub variety can be propagated from cuttings taken in the autumn from summer-flowering plants and in the spring from winter-flowering varieties.

Calceolaria seeds are very fine and are sown in a pot from late spring to mid-summer on the surface of very fine compost. Do not cover the seed with compost. Stand the pot in water until the surface of the compost is just moist, then cover the pot as usual. Keep it in an unheated, shady spot until the seeds germinate.

As soon as the seedlings are large enough to handle prick out into cellular trays, again keeping them in an unheated, shady spot with plenty of ventilation on hot days. Do not allow the plants to dry out at any time, for the secret of success is to keep a good steady growth rate. When the seedlings have developed four or five leaves, transplant into 3 in (7·5 cm) pots. Keep the plants shaded from the direct rays of the sun. Spray the foliage and damp down the greenhouse on hot, dry days.

In early to mid-autumn the plants need to be repotted again into 5 in (12·5 cm) pots. If they have been kept outside in a cold frame they now need to be taken into the greenhouse. Keep them well ventilated, at a temperature between 45 and 55°F (7–13°C). Be careful with the watering: keep only the compost moist, and if possible avoid wetting the crown or foliage. It is best to stand the pots in water rather than watering from the top with a can.

In late winter or early spring, before the flower buds begin to show, repot into 7 or 8 in (17–20 cm) pots and try to maintain the greenhouse at the above temperatures, avoiding great fluctuations. Once the flower buds begin to appear, water with half-strength liquid seaweed extract every ten to fourteen days.

Once the herbaceous plants have flowered

Calceolaria *herbeohybrida* mixed *(Photos Horticultural)*

they can be put on the compost heap, as new seed should be sown for next year. With the half-hardy shrubs, cuttings should be taken in late summer to early autumn, using the young, non-flowering basal shoots. Root them in a 50:50 compost/coarse sand mix, and pinch out the growing tips in late winter.

Greenfly can be troublesome, and botrytis can attack the plants in the winter period if the humidity is too high.

Chrysanthemums.   The heated greenhouse varieties flower from late autumn through to mid-winter, at a time when other sources of colour can be scarce. There is nothing nicer than a display of chrysanthemum blooms at Christmas. They are propagated by cuttings.

After flowering the stems are cut back to 4–6 in (10–15 cm) above soil level, any dead leaves, suckers or side shoots being removed. Take the stools from the pot and shake off as much of the old compost as possible, then wash the pot and re-pot the stools with fresh compost. Give the plants a good watering and place in the light in a cool greenhouse. No further watering should be necessary, but do not allow them to dry out. Fresh air and plenty of light will encourage the growth of sturdy basal shoots.

Only basal shoots should be used for cuttings – stem shoots do not produce good plants. One theory put forward for this is that they are the off-shoots from dying tissue, while basal shoots are from the living.

Cuttings are taken when the shoots are 2–3 in (5–7·5 cm) long, usually in mid- to late winter, but they can still be taken into early spring. Select a short, jointed shoot and using a sharp knife cut off just below soil level, then trim the shoot back to just below the nearest joint. Remove the lower leaves up to about 1 in (2·5 cm) from the tip of the shoot. Using a sandy compost, with one part of coarse sand, dibber the shoots in to about 1 in (2·5 cm) deep. Water well and keep at a temperature of 45–50°F (7–10°C). A number of shoots can be rooted in a single large pot, or they can be individually rooted in 3 in (7·5 cm) pots. Do not throw away the stools, for in a few days more shoots will appear which can also be rooted.

No further attention is needed – except to prevent the compost drying out – until the roots have developed, usually signalled by the appearance of new growth. If a number have been rooted in one pot now is the time to transplant them into 3 in (7·5 cm) pots. Do not allow the plants to become pot-bound. After a further four weeks pot on into a 5 or 6 in (12·5–15 cm) pot and then in early summer into the final 9 in (23 cm) pot. Do not disturb the root ball any more than necessary during potting on. For these stages add one part of leaf-mould to the compost mix.

Once the greenhouse temperature starts to rise above 60°F (15·5°C), from mid-spring onwards, move the plants to cooler conditions outside (preferably in a cold frame). Harden them off before removing from the warm greenhouse and beware of frosts, protecting if necessary. If they have grown tall the plants may need to be staked before being moved outside. Water to keep the compost moist, in the early morning in preference to the evening.

Starting in late summer a well-balanced organic feed can be given at regular intervals to keep the plants growing at a good steady rate.

Stopping and disbudding can be very confusing for the beginner, because what needs

Disbudding chrysanthemums (*Photos Horticultural*)

to be done depends upon the variety grown and the form of display required. Stopping also controls the moment when the flowers come into bloom, and the expert grower will work his schedules out exactly to make sure the blooms are at their best when they are wanted, particularly important if they are to be shown.

As a general rule, when the plants are about 6 in (15 cm) tall the centre growing bud is pinched out. If there is no bud the growing tip is removed. Lateral growth (breaks) will soon appear, which is thinned out to leave three or four shoots of about equal strength. Although one stopping is normally sufficient for the average grower, some will make a second stopping when these shoots are about 6 in (15 cm) long.

The plant needs to be disbudded. As the shoots grow, buds will appear at the leaf joints, and if they are left a number of small flowers will develop, so some of them need to be removed if good-sized flowers are wanted. Where large blooms are to be grown all the buds are removed except the centre one.

The plants are taken into the greenhouse in early autumn before there is any chance of frost. The house needs to be adequately ventilated to prevent mildew, but needs to be kept at a fairly uniform temperature of 45–50°F (7–10°C). Do not allow the pots to dry out, especially when the blooms begin to open.

The most common pests and diseases to attack the plants are greenfly, earwigs, leaf miner, rust and mildew.

Cineraria. An excellent greenhouse plant, which will give a show of colour from late autumn through till late spring. It is best treated as an annual and raised from seed each year. Two to three sowings are needed, in mid- and late spring and in mid-summer to give the longest period of flowering.

Late flowering chrysanthemum, Mavis Shoosmith (*Harry Smith*)

Cineraria, *Senecio cruentus* (*Photos Horticultural*)

Sow thinly in a tray of moist compost. Do not cover the seeds with compost, but just press them gently into it with a flat object. Cover the tray with glass or a propagator lid and hold at a temperature of 55–60°F (13–15·5°C) in the shade. Germination will take up to three weeks. When the seedlings have three leaves prick out into 3 in (7·5 cm) pots and as they grow pot them on into 5 in (12·5 cm) and finally 8 in (20 cm) pots towards mid-autumn.

Put the plants outside over the summer months, keeping them moist and cool in hot weather with an overhead spray. Towards the middle of autumn move the plants into the greenhouse and start to give a weak liquid seaweed feed every two weeks. Ventilate freely but hold the greenhouse temperature at a minimum of 40–45°F (4·5–7°C). Give as much light as possible. Water just sufficiently to keep the compost moist.

Beware of attacks from greenfly, leaf miner and botrytis.

Cyclamen. Can be grown from seed or corms, both sown or planted in late summer; corms will flower the same winter whereas plants from seed will flower the following year.

Sow the seed 2 in (5 cm) apart in a seed tray and only just cover with compost. Sowing like this means they do not need to be pricked out after germination. If sown in a pot they need to be transferred to 2 in (5 cm) square cellular trays as soon as they are large enough to handle. When they have three or four leaves they are transferred into 3 in (7·5 cm) pots. Keep at an average temperature of 50°F (10°C) over the winter.

In early spring pot on into 4 in (10 cm) pots and finally around mid-summer into 6 in (15 cm) pots. Throughout the summer keep well watered and shade in very hot weather, not allowing the atmosphere to become too dry as this can encourage red spider mite. Ventilate the greenhouse freely.

Corms are planted in 6 in (15 cm) pots 1½–2 in (4–5 cm) deep and kept at a temperature of 50–60°F (10–15·5°C). From the late summer of the first year with corms and the second year with seed the treatment is the same. They like plenty of light but not direct sun and an average temperature of 55°F (13°C).

The plants will flower freely between late autumn and early spring, giving an impressive display of colour. When flowering has finished, gradually decrease the watering until all the leaves die off, leaving just the dormant corm in the pot. Remove to a cold frame or store under the greenhouse staging, laying the pots on their sides to prevent the corms getting wet and rotting.

The best display is given by one-year plants, and therefore it is recommended that fresh seed be sown every year. Corms should not be used after two years of flowering.

Freesias. One of the most fragrant flowers for the winter greenhouse, being in flower from early winter to mid-spring from a succession of sowings. They are grown from both seed and corms, either flowering in the first season.

Both are sown in a 5 in (12·5 cm) pot; about six seeds or corms are evenly spaced in the pot. The seeds are sown on the surface, then covered with a light layer of compost. The corms need to be sown about 2 in (5 cm) deep. Seeds are sown from early spring to early summer and corms planted from mid-summer to early autumn. Keep the compost moist, standing the pots in an airy

Freesia are synonymous with fragrance in the winter greenhouse (*Harry Smith*)

frame. As the plants grow they need to be staked.

In early autumn move the pots into the greenhouse with a minimum temperature of 45°F (7°C). Give a liquid feed at weekly intervals when the flower stems begin to show. This is continued until the foliage starts to die off, when the amount of water is reduced until all the foliage dies. The pots with the corms are stored to rest over the summer period. If stored under the staging lay the pots on their sides to prevent the compost being moistened by water dripping down. In mid-summer the pots are emptied and the corms separated from the old compost, split and re-potted for the coming winter.

Primulas. Seeds are sown from late winter to late spring, depending on the variety grown, to give a display of flowers from late autumn to mid-spring. Sow thinly in moist compost and do not cover, just gently pressing the seed into the compost with a flat object. Hold at a temperature of 60°F (15·5°C).

As soon as the seedlings are large enough to handle prick out into cellular trays. Keep out of the direct heat of the sun. About three to four weeks later transfer into 3 in (7·5 cm) pots and, once these become full of roots, into 5 in (12·5 cm) pots. If needed a further potting into a 6 in (15 cm) pot can be done in early to mid-autumn. Over the flowering period keep well ventilated and keep the compost moist at all times, although when watering avoid wetting the leaves. Any leaves showing signs of rotting should be removed. A minimum temperature of 50°F (10°C) should be maintained.

Once flowering has finished the plants are put on the compost heap, as they produce the best show grown from seed each year.

CONSERVATORIES

Heating the conservatory can be done as in the greenhouse, or by extending the domestic central heating system. The temperature depends upon the use. For a living room most people like a temperature of about 70°F (21°C). There is a wide range of plants for this temperature, but the dry atmosphere associated with living areas does not encourage good growth for many of them. The humidity can be raised locally without having to damp down the whole atmosphere of the conservatory. In too dry an atmosphere the leaf edges of the plants become crinkly and turn brown.

The foliage needs to be sprayed at frequent intervals with water at room temperature, using a fine mist spray, and rainwater whenever possible.

Leave water in containers among the plants so that as it evaporates it forms a micro-climate. For pots a tray can be filled with grit or gravel and

with water to just below the level of the grit. Do not allow the bottom of the pot to come into contact with the water, otherwise the compost will become sodden.

Feeding will depend upon whether the plants are in pots or a bed. Those in a bed do not need such frequent feeding, as the compost is not exhausted so quickly. Foliar feeds are the easiest to apply and should be used frequently throughout the growing season. The best to use are the seaweed extracts and liquid comfrey solutions. Ensure the compost is moist before feeding.

In beds a powder feed can be applied, along with a mulch of compost in the spring. If there is room in the pots a mulch can also be added to supplement the foliar feeding.

Be on a constant lookout for pests, in particular aphids. In the warm atmosphere of a conservatory these can multiply at an alarming rate, so at the first signs take remedial action. Ensure that the undersides of the leaves are treated, as this is where most of them hide. Provided the plant is not too large the most effective method is to submerge it totally in the control solution. Fill a bucket with the solution, and, holding the root ball firmly in the pot with one hand, turn the plant upside down and dip all the foliage into the solution for a few seconds. Remove and let the plant drip dry.

The variety of plants that can be grown is nearly endless, as the conditions within the conservatory can be controlled to grow whatever is liked. A few of the more popular plants not previously discussed are coleus, ferns, ficus, palms and plumbago.

Coleus. Their multi-coloured perennial foliage makes them very attractive plants, kept in shape by pinching back the shoots. They are easily germinated from seed sown in late winter or early spring at a temperature of 70°F (21°C), or can be propagated from cuttings taken from non-flowering shoots at almost any time. Pot on the plants as they grow, up to a maximum 5 in (12·5 cm) pot. Protect from strong sunlight.

Feed regularly with a weak liquid feed and keep well watered during hot weather. Pinch out any flowerheads to keep the leaves in full colour, unless they are a variety grown for its flowers.

Ferns. Probably one of the oldest species of plant. Worldwide it is estimated that there are something in the region of 10,000 fern species. Some are evergreen, others deciduous. There is a range of 'tropical' ferns which need minimum temperatures around 68–70°F (20–21°C) and a high humidity level. However, there is a good selection that enjoy the lower levels of a living area.

Ferns are grown for their fronds. They require an open compost mix with good drainage. A

A mid-spring conservatory (*Pat Brindley*)

Problems to be aware of

Leaves turning yellow or curling with the plant beginning to wilt – too near a source of heat, e.g. a radiator

Stem rotting and leaves curling – too much water

Old leaves beginning to curl, new ones undersized – too much light

Collecting fern spores (*Rob Dalton*)

(a) Spore cases on the undersides of fronds produce dust-like particles

(b) Before cases burst, collect into a bag and leave until dried off

(c) Agitate bag to release spores

suitable compost could consist of equal parts of garden compost, leaf-mould and coarse sand.

They are propagated in a number of ways. Some produce new growth from the fronds, which are pegged down into the compost to take root; some can be divided; but the commonest method is by sowing the spores. As the fern does not produce flowers it does not seed, but dust-like particles are produced on the underside of the fronds inside little flat cases (sporangia). When these cases dry out they burst, releasing the spores into the air. The cases need to be collected before this happens and dried off so that the spores can be collected.

Moist compost in a 5 in (12·5 cm) pot is given a thin dusting of the spores any time between early spring and mid-summer. The pot is covered with a plastic propagating cover or a sheet of glass. Shade and moisture are needed to encourage growth, which will take a few weeks at temperatures of 70°F (21°C). The first tiny growth is called a prothallus and is a flat, heart-shaped green body. On its underside are male cells and a female egg. Provided the moisture levels are right the males swim over to the female to fertilize it, and a fern is born. Hygiene is very important in this process and pots and compost must be sterile.

When large enough to handle, transplant the young ferns into a 2 in (5 cm) pot. Ferns do not like being over-potted and it is advisable to pot on frequently into one size larger pots until finally reaching a 5 in (12·5 cm) pot for a standard-sized fern. Tree ferns will obviously need larger sizes.

Keep the compost moist and the atmosphere humid by spraying the foliage with water at room temperature. Shade from the direct glare of the sun. The plants need to be fed regularly over the summer months. Less water is required over the winter, but the compost should not be allowed to dry out.

Scale insects and aphids can be troublesome and botrytis can develop if the plants are crowded together in stagnant air conditions.

Ficus. The fig family includes a number of species which grow well in conservatory conditions. There are shrubs, trees, climbers and trailing plants. The most popular is the rubber plant, with its adaptability to centrally heated conditions, producing large glossy leaves with an impressive range of colours. It will eventually grow into a tree if allowed to, so it needs to be kept to acceptable proportions by limiting the size of the pot to 6 in (15 cm).

The leaves need to be washed regularly in the summer months to keep them shiny and to reduce the chance of attack from scale insects. A regular feed in the summer will develop nice-sized, well coloured leaves. Keep the compost moist. In extremely hot weather shade from the rays of the sun and spray the leaves overhead with tepid water.

Reduce the water over the winter months but do not allow the compost to dry out, and maintain a minimum temperature of 60°F (15·5°C).

Palms. A considerable number of species are classified under the name 'palm', and no self-respecting conservatory would be complete without one. There are about 1,500 species, all evergreen; many can grow too large and need to be kept under control by growing them in relatively small pots to restrict root growth. There are also varieties which are of more compact size.

Plants are commonly bought from garden centres, but can also be grown from seed. Sow the seeds in a 5 in (12·5 cm) pot and cover to the depth of the seed with compost. Keep the

1,500 species of palm to choose from (*Harry Smith*)

compost moist and hold at 70°F (21°C) until they germinate. When two leaves form prick out into individual 2 in (5 cm) pots, keeping them in a moist atmosphere held at 65°F (18°C). Give plenty of light but shade from strong sunlight. Pot on as the plant grows, using a compost mix as for ferns with good drainage at the bottom of the pot. Do not over-pot; work gradually up in pot size. A sign that the plant is ready for the next size is when the roots start to lift the compost out of the pot.

Water well all the year round, sponging the leaves with tepid water in the morning and evening during the spring and summer months. Give a liquid feed at two-weekly intervals during the growing period and if there is room top-dress with worm compost in the spring to encourage strong growth.

Palms can be subject to attack from scale insects and red spider mite, which can seriously distort the leaves. The daily sponge will help to prevent such attacks.

Plumbago. Leadwort is one of the most useful flowering plants for the conservatory, with its clusters of sky-blue flowers. It is easy to grow, needing only frost protection over the winter and temperatures below 75°F (24°C) in the summer.

Plants can be obtained from seed or cuttings. Seeds are sown in early spring in temperatures of 65–70°F (18–21°C) and a humid atmosphere. Moisten the compost by standing it in a tray of water until the surface is wet, drain, then place in a polythene bag until germination occurs in about two to three weeks. Prick out when large enough to handle and pot on into 6–8 in (15–20 cm) pots. Plants grown from seed flower in their second season. Cuttings are taken in late spring or early summer from a non-flowering shoot and rooted in a sandy compost.

Water the plants freely over the summer months, keeping the compost just moist over the winter period. After flowering cut back to keep the plant under control to within 10 in (25 cm) of the previous year's growth. Feed frequently with comfrey liquid throughout the summer and spray the foliage with tepid water during hot weather to encourage a continual display of flowers.

COLD FRAMES AND CLOCHES

One of the most important features of growing under cover is the extra three to four weeks of growing time it offers at both the beginning and the end of the season. This can be achieved by use of the greenhouse or walk-in polythene tunnel for both flowers and fruit. There is, however, a wide range of plants which enjoy protection in the early part of the season but prefer the cover to be removed once the conditions are favourable. A cloche or cold frame provides the right answer.

Hygiene under cold frames and cloches

Growing is in many ways no different from growing outside or in a greenhouse or polythene tunnel. Good cultural techniques, including adequate ventilation, must still be used and care is needed to keep pests and diseases under control. Although growing under this sort of cover does give protection against such pests as carrot and onion fly and flea beetle, others can be attracted into the area, and the cover can give them the ideal conditions in which to multiply and devastate the plants. As with the greenhouse, once soil becomes badly infected the only solution may be to change it.

Traditional cold frame (*Harry Smith*)

Lightweight aluminium/polycarbonate cold frame (*Harry Smith*)

The undercover environment is ideal for the protection of pests over the winter period. Mice can be particularly troublesome if they decide to use the frame or cloche as a home in severe weather.

Slugs find frames and cloches ideal places to live and breed. Provided the rain can be kept out, a ring of calcified seaweed about 1 in (2·5 cm) thick completely surrounding the plants will be very effective.

COLD FRAMES

Conventional frames are generally not used for covering crops growing directly in the soil, mainly because the methods of construction do not make them portable. Commonly, side walls are of brick or thick wooden boards, and the lights (the removable glass lids) must be sufficiently heavy not to blow off in the wind. They are looked upon more as an extension to the greenhouse. They have many uses: to house relatively hardy plants to allow more space in the greenhouse for more delicate varieties over the winter, to harden off plants reared in the warmth of the greenhouse before planting outside, and as a growing area.

The use of aluminium framework glazed with plastic or polycarbonates has slightly changed the traditional image of the frame, for these lightweight models can be portable. They do have a disadvantage in that plastic or polycarbonate side walls are not as warm as the brick- or wooden-sided frames, but if portability is important, these are easier to handle.

Frames can be of almost any length, but unless there is access all round, the width should be no more than can be easily crossed with an outstretched arm – about 4 ft (120 cm).

The size of the lights should be such that they will remain in place in windy weather, yet not be too heavy to be lifted off. Probably the largest

practical size is 6 x 4 ft (180 x 120 cm). The back wall of the frame is higher than the front to allow the rain to run off the lights and to give maximum daylight to the plants. The angle of the lights can vary between 5° and 15°. The shallower the angle the closer the plants are to the glass at the back of the frame. The side walls need to be solid to prevent cold draughts entering the frame, and not too high otherwise they will cut off the light and the plants will grow leggy. An 8 in (20 cm) front wall rising to a 10 in (25 cm) back wall is a reasonable size.

Plastic or polycarbonate can be used in place of glass in the covering lights, with the advantages that less heat is lost than with glass, it is not so easily broken and, being light, is easier to handle.

Seedlings and cuttings are often given an early start by growing them in the warmth of the greenhouse, maybe using artificial heat, giving conditions warmer than the plants would find outside. Before they are transferred outside into

Rotation of vegetable crops

A year-cycle could comprise the following vegetable crops:

Winter lettuce – set out from mid-autumn through to early spring. In the warmer months the seed can be sown in the frame, but when it turns colder more reliable germination comes from sowing indoors and transplanting into the frame

Spring onions – sow in mid- to late summer to stand over the winter, or in late winter/early spring for an early crop

Japanese onions – although they are hardy enough to stand the cold winter weather a short row in the frame sown in late summer helps to fill the gap which can arise between the last of the stored summer crop and the first of the outside Japanese in early summer

Carrots – sow in late winter for an early crop, with another sowing a month later

Beetroot – treat as for carrots

Courgettes/marrows – sow in mid-spring, either in pots for transplanting to another bed in the garden or directly in the frame

Beans – both runners and French can be sown from early spring. French beans will grow well in the frame but runners will need transplanting once the threat of frosts has passed

Bush tomatoes – sow indoors or in the greenhouse in late winter/early spring for planting out in the frame in mid-spring

Ridge cucumber – sow indoors or in the greenhouse in early spring for planting out in the frame in mid- to late spring

Spring cabbage – a few plants planted in early to mid-autumn will bring forward the harvest by a few weeks the following spring

Potatoes – plant an early variety in early autumn for new potatoes for Christmas Day

Lettuce – a mid- to late summer sowing of Winter Density will see this cos variety cropping up to mid-winter, but do not cover unless the weather is severe

Cauliflowers – an early autumn sowing can be kept over the winter for planting out the following spring

the open air it is important that they become gradually accustomed to cooler conditions. This is an ideal job for the frame, for the lights can be removed in stages, first of all during the day and later on at night as well.

A cold frame should be in use all the year round, either with plants in pots or trays passing through the frame at the appropriate stage in their growing cycle, or with plants growing to maturity in the soil of the frame.

When growing in the frame it must be remembered that the same principles apply to that soil as to any other part of the garden: it should be even more organic, rich and fertile, if anything, for that small area may be more productive than any other section. Two or even three crops may be grown in the frame in one season.

Crop rotation principles also apply when vegetable growing, for under-soil pests and diseases can multiply quickly.

Despite the protection of the frame the outside weather can still do considerable damage, especially severe overnight frosts which will easily penetrate the glass or polythene. (The frame does, however, protect against wind and limits the frost penetration of the soil.) Additional protection can be given by covering with hessian sacking, old carpet or blanket, or even straw. Remember that the framework must be capable of supporting the extra weight. Use dry materials, otherwise they too will freeze, making it difficult to remove them in the mornings. Always remove the

covering during the day to allow the maximum amount of light to the plants to prevent them becoming drawn and leggy.

Hot-beds. The cold frame can be turned into a hot-bed, starting in mid-winter. Again, this is used mainly to give an early season. Fresh horse

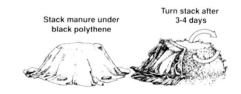

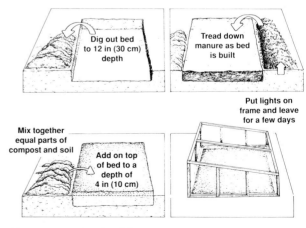

Preparing a hot-bed (*Rob Dalton*)

manure, preferably that which has the straw well wetted with urine, is stacked under a sheet of black polythene about seven to ten days before the hot-bed is made, to start the heating process in the manure. After three to four days turn over the stack to get the cold edges into the centre to warm up.

The soil in the frame is dug out to a depth of 12 in (30 cm) and the hole is filled with the horse manure. Continue building until the manure is at the old soil level. Tread it down firmly every few inches as the bed is built. Mix an equal part of the extracted soil with well-rotted garden compost and add on top of the bed to a depth of 4 in (10 cm). Put the lights on the frame to keep in the heat and leave for a few days.

If only a small frame is used and if it is of portable material, the bed can be built on the soil surface and the frame put on the top.

Strawy horse manure is not so readily available these days, as many stables now use wood shavings to bed down the horses. However, a hot-bed can still be made using under-soil heating cables.

Once the soil begins to warm up, seeds can be sown such as radish, carrot, beetroot, lettuce, cauliflower and turnip. Keep the lights in place until the seed germinates, then give a little air in the early morning, closing down the lights again in the early afternoon. If the weather is frosty keep the lights closed; the frame can be surrounded with more horse manure to act as an insulating blanket.

From a hot-bed, radishes will be ready by the end of winter, lettuce in early spring, carrots, beetroot and cauliflowers in late spring. Once the cauliflowers are cut the bed can be used for courgettes or cucumbers. Pots and trays can be placed on the bed for a source of bottom heat.

With a little experience the cold frame will be found to be a most valuable asset in the garden.

CLOCHES

Cloches are believed to have been devised by the French. They were made of glass in the shape of a bell, one bell being placed over each plant. In some areas this type of cloche is still in use. As their importance grew so did their size, until now the conventional cloche is segmented to make a continuous cloche to cover a whole row.

Originally cloches were made from sheets of glass held in place by wire clips, but in recent years plastics, polycarbonates and man-made fabrics have become available. The range is wide and may be confusing for beginners. Before rushing out to buy, carefully consider what the cloche is to be used for, how much it will be moved around the garden, how complicated is the method of construction and dismantling and where it will be stored when not in use.

The chief types of cloche are:

Glass. The conventional design of cloche has glass side and roof panels held together with wires. They are available in two basic designs, the 'tent', with two pieces leaning together to form an A-shape, and the 'barn' with vertical or sloping sides and a sloping roof on top. The type of design determines the width of the rows covered. The tent has a width of about 12 in (30 cm), while the barn will extend up to about 30 in (75 cm). Each design is about 24 in (60 cm) long and open-ended so that they can be put together to build up a continuous row of the required length. To prevent the wind blowing through the run and causing a draught the ends are blocked by a sheet of glass held in place with a cane.

Glass cloches are very portable, easily picked up by a lifting lug provided as part of the glass and wire retaining system. They are heavy enough to be simply placed on top of the soil without further anchoring against the winds. There are sufficient gaps between the sheets of glass to provide adequate ventilation, and the end pieces can always be removed if necessary. However, if the soil dries out and the plants need to be watered the cloches need to be lifted off to allow the watering can in. Their main disadvantage is that, unless you have a great deal of safe storage space, they need first to be stripped down and stored safely when not in use. Whichever way they are stored, the glass should be thoroughly washed before it is put away.

Tent cloches are easily made without the use of complicated and often expensive wires. Canes can be pushed into the soil at an angle to cross just above the top of the glass, and tied in place with string. The glass is held in place by one set of canes on the outside, another on the inside.

Glass allows more light to the crops than any other cloche material.

Polycarbonate. This can be used in place of glass with the same designs. Although it is not as easily broken as glass it is more vulnerable to scratching. If the sheets become badly scratched the amount of light transmitted through them is greatly reduced and can cause the plants to become leggy.

Plastics. These cloches can be bought as kits, with pegs and hooks to hold the material in place, or made at home using rigid or pliable PVC and other plastic materials (see overleaf). Some of the bought models are of an intricate design, with movable/sliding sides to give easy access to the plants for watering, weeding, increased ventilation and removal. The average

Victorian lantern-shaped cloche
(*Harry Smith*)
RIGHT: Cloche styles (*Rob Dalton*)

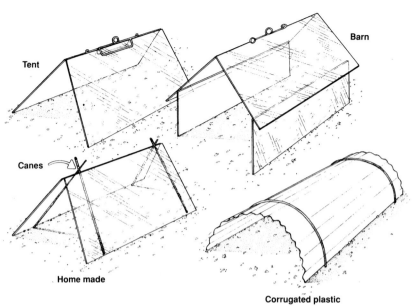

Tent

Canes

Home made

Barn

Corrugated plastic

Making plastic cloches

Corrugated, clear roofing sheets can be used to make your own cloche. Simply push one edge into the soil and bend the sheet into a semi-circular shape, pushing the other edge also into the soil. Canes are pushed into the soil at the edges for extra support, but if this is insufficient against the wind, ⅛ in (3 mm) diameter fencing wire can be bent into the correct semi-circular shape with about 12 in (30 cm) straight ends to push into the soil. Place the wire hoops over the outside of the cloche once it is in position. The ends are covered with pieces of sheeting cut to size. This construction is light and easy to handle and store away when not in use. Always wash down the sheeting before putting it away.

life of the sheeting is about three years before scratching and deterioration of the plastic cut down the light transmission to unacceptable levels.

Polythene. A miniature polythene tunnel will provide one of the cheapest forms of cloche. Again it can be a DIY job, using clear 200-gauge polythene sheeting (thicker material will cut out too much light) and fencing wire. This design has the advantage that the length of the cloche can be formed from one piece of material. However, it does need a little care when you erect it to ensure that the polythene stays in place. Mark out a straight line with a string, and push the wire hoops into the soil about 5 ft (150 cm) apart. Dig out two trenches to about 3 in (7·5 cm) deep along the line of the hoops. Bunch one end of the polythene sheeting and tie it to a stake firmly held in the ground at about 12 to 18 in (30–45 cm) from the first hoop. Pull the sheet of polythene tightly over the hoops with the edges sitting in the trenches, bunch the other end and tie it to a second stake. Now fill in the trenches to hold the sheeting firmly in place. It is important to do this, for should the sheeting come loose and flap about, considerable damage can be done to the plants under the cloche. Again, this type of construction can be bought in kit form, some designs having provision for the hoops to be threaded into the polythene to ensure that they are spaced at the correct distance and to help hold everything in place.

The disadvantages of this type are the limited life of the polythene (about two years) and its poor heat-retaining properties. The inside temperature of the cloche can quickly drop to the outside temperature. The light properties are not as good as many of the other cloche materials, and if it is left in place too long the plants can become soft and leggy. As the cloche can be totally sealed, ventilation and condensation problems can be encountered. Lifting part of the buried edge out of the soil and putting blocks underneath will form air gaps to reduce this problem. Some gardeners punch holes or make slits in the polythene, but this does reduce the life of the material. However, material with pre-punched holes can now be obtained.

Plan view of polythene cloche construction

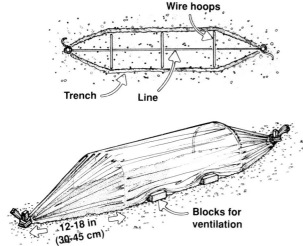

DIY miniature polytunnel (*Rob Dalton*)

Floating cloche over carrots (*Chris Algar*)

Other man-made fabrics. The disadvantages of polythene sheeting can be avoided by using one of the clear porous fabric materials that are now widely available. There are two main types, made of a porous woven polyethylene and a porous non-woven 'floating' polypropylene material. These come in rolls which are laid over the crop and which allow in fresh air, light (up to 70% of ambient light) and rain, while also providing pest protection. When not in use, the covering can be easily folded up and stored.

The merit of the woven material is its strength and tear-resistance. Its disadvantage is that it is a 'hard' fibre and is heavier than the non-woven fabric. If left in contact with plants it can be very abrasive on young, tender leaves. Accordingly, the woven material is best used in the manner of a mini-polythene tunnel. It can be purchased as a kit complete with hoops for erection into a cloche.

The non-woven polypropylene type of material has the properties of a light fleece and its distinguishing characteristic is that it 'floats' over the plants, easily lifting with them as they grow. Accordingly, no superstructure is required, the material simply being laid on top of the plants, without harm. It is also available in

Covering a trench

An alternative way of using woven material is to lay it flat on the ground, over a trench. This gives it some of the advantages of the floating, non-woven cloches.

At the seedling stage, the row is marked and a trench drawn out about 6 in (15 cm) deep. The seedlings are planted in the bottom of the trench and the woven fabric is laid across the trench at ground level so as not to come in contact with the plants. This is an ideal technique for members of the cabbage family for, as they grow, the trench can be filled in. This encourages a good root structure to anchor the plants in the soil, and is especially important with Brussels sprouts. In a no-dig garden, it is not prudent to firm down the soil with the feet around the plants, as is common practice with many gardeners.

As the plants grow, the covering is lifted and supported on a framework made from canes or small-bore aluminium tubing, the edges of the material being held in place by burying them in

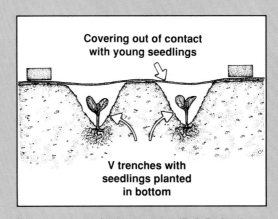

Porous woven cloche variant (*Rob Dalton*)

the soil or using weights, in the same manner as with a non-woven floating cloche. The framework can be raised in several stages.

Suggested cloche calendar for the vegetable grower

Season	Vegetable	Variety	Use of cloche (sow or plant unless otherwise indicated)
Mid–winter	broad beans	Aquadulce, Sutton	
	Brussels sprouts	Achilles, Peer Gynt	
	cabbage	Hispi	
	carrots	Nantes Express	
	cauliflowers	All the Year Round	
	leeks	Musselborough	
	lettuce	Columbus, Cynthia, Ravel	
	onions	Bedfordshire Champion	
	peas	Kelvedon Wonder	
	radishes	French Breakfast	
Late winter	beetroot	Boltardy	
	Brussels sprouts	Achilles, Peer Gynt	
	cabbage	Hispi	
	carrots	Nantes Express	
	cauliflowers	All the Year Round	
	leeks	Musselborough	
	lettuce	Columbus, Novita	
	onions	Ailsa Craig, Southport Red Globe	
	potatoes	early variety	
	radishes	French Breakfast	
Early spring	dwarf French beans	Masterpiece, The Prince	
	runner beans	Hammond's Dwarf Scarlet	
	beetroot	Boltardy	
	courgette	Zucchini	
	lettuce	Winter Density	
	peas	Kelvedon Wonder	
	turnips	Milan White Forcing	
Mid–spring	dwarf French beans	Tendergreen	
	runner beans	Kelvedon Marvel	
	cucumbers	Telegraph	
	sweetcorn	Sunrise	
	tomatoes	Red Alert	
	turnips	Snowball Early White	
Late spring	beans		keep cloches in place until all chances of frost have passed
	cucumbers		
	tomatoes		
	potatoes		remove cloche from first planting
	peppers		keep covered until harvested in autumn

wide, 7 ft (2·2 m) rolls and, in commercial quantities, up to 13 ft (4 m) wide. Amateur gardeners can secure considerable cost savings by clubbing together to purchase these larger quantities. The disadvantage of the non-woven fleece is that it is not as strong as the woven fabric. It needs careful handling and is not likely to outlast two seasons.

It is widely used in the early part of the year to extend the season by promoting good germination at a time when it would otherwise be nearly impossible, and to allow earlier transplanting of seedlings by increasing the air and soil temperatures under the covering. It can also provide effective summer protection against carrot root fly and other pests.

Suggested cloche calendar for the vegetable grower

Season	Vegetable	Variety	Use of cloche (sow or plant unless otherwise indicated)
Early summer	beans cucumbers tomatoes		cloches can be removed
	onions		place cloches over autumn-sown varieties to help them ripen off
Mid–summer	dwarf French beans Japanese onions shallots	The Prince Express Yellow	cover to assist ripening
Late summer	carrots lettuce	Nantes Express Winter Density	sow for covering later sow for covering later
Early autumn	carrots lettuce cauliflower potatoes tomatoes (See also The Vegetable Garden page 127)	Nantes Express Winter Density Marmer, All the Year Round early variety for Christmas	cover late summer sowing cover late summer sowing remove stakes, lay them down on straw/newspaper on the soil and cover to assist ripening
Mid–autumn	broad beans herbs lettuce peas spinach beet	Aquadulce Winter Density, Columbus Meteor	cover cover
Late autumn	broad beans peas (mild climates)	Aquadulce Meteor	
Early winter	leeks swedes		cover in frosty weather to keep soil soft enough to lift them protect any plants susceptible to damage from cold weather

The material is laid loosely over the area to be protected and is held down by burying the edges in the soil, or using weights such as bricks or, preferably, polythene bags filled with sand or earth, which are less likely to tear the fleece. Sufficient slack must be left to allow the material to 'float' with the plants as they grow.

The design of cloches is constantly changing, with new concepts and materials appearing on the market every year. Before buying, study carefully what is available and look at what other gardeners use to ensure you choose what is appropriate for your purpose.

PREPARATION AND PLANTING

To grow successfully under cloches a little

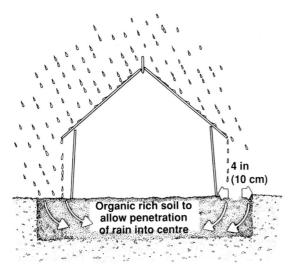

Under-cloche irrigation (*Rob Dalton*)

planning is required. Before you erect the cloches the soil needs to be thoroughly prepared. If they are to be of the rigid construction which will be left in position for a considerable period, the soil will need to absorb its moisture from water running off the cloche. It therefore needs to be organically rich so that the moisture can penetrate sideways, keeping the soil inside the cloche moist. The use of the mulching technique of the no-dig method (see page 59) will provide these conditions. If mulching is not used, it is best to dig plenty of compost into a strip about 4 in (10 cm) wider than the cloche, repeating for all the parts of the garden where the cloche could be moved to next. The best time to prepare the soil by either method is in the autumn, to allow time for the organic matter to be taken into the top layers of the soil by the microlife, and, for a dug area, to settle down after being disturbed.

If the soil is not able to absorb this moisture, or where the plants are seedlings which have not yet developed a root system, watering will be needed at some time, with the cloche having to be either moved or dismantled. Alternatively, irrigation can be put in place before the erection of the cloche for connection to a water supply

when required. The best method is to use the porous hose which allows the water to 'weep' out along its length (see *Garden Irrigation*, page 382).

Before you erect the cloche a dressing of a general organic fertilizer will supply the plants with the nutrition needed to give good growth over the period under cover. Cold, wet or frozen soil is totally unsuitable for seed-sowing or planting young seedlings, and so the cloche should be put into position at least ten to fourteen days beforehand to allow the soil time to warm up. Seal up the ends and reduce the gaps to a minimum to keep the inside as warm as possible.

The basic principles of seed-sowing and transplanting apply to cloches, but one point of importance is that the rows must be straight and parallel to each other, and correctly spaced. Use a line to mark out the rows and measure accurately between them. If the cloche is to cover several rows and each one is slightly further apart than planned the cloche may not cover the last row.

Cloches are most effective when rotated around the garden, a practice known as strip cropping. It is better if their sequence can be planned to move to adjacent rows rather than from one part of the garden to the opposite end.

Intercropping may also be undertaken within the cloche, combining quick-maturing plants such as radishes and salad materials with peas, French beans, and so on.

In gardens where space is limited it may be necessary to group together plants that require the same treatment, such as covering and uncovering at the same times, or needing the same moisture/atmosphere conditions. Remember also to leave sufficient space in the garden for crops sown in the early summer, which will not be covered.

FRUIT AND FLOWERS

Cloches and cold frames also play a part in the fruit and ornamental gardens. Plants grown in pots can be placed in the frames, and the cloches used to cover plants growing in the ground for strategic periods to give an early or extended

Strip cropping
(*Rob Dalton*)

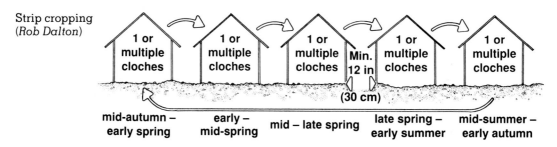

Cloches moved to adjacent rows across
land for seasonal protection

Harden off annual seedlings in cold frame (*Photos Horticultural*)

Cloche as windbreak (*Rob Dalton*)

season for the fruit crop or flower display. For early strawberries some plants can be covered or potted up for putting into frames in mid-autumn. If you cover more plants in early spring and grow the remainder of the bed conventionally, a continuous supply of the fruit can be harvested over an extended period. Ventilate well during warm weather from early spring onwards. Water freely once the plants start to produce flowers. The flowers may need to be hand-pollinated, using a fine camel-hair paint-brush. Fruit should be available from late spring onwards.

Melons are another fruit which will grow successfully under cover. Seedlings can be planted out in late spring/early summer in pots or at 36 in (90 cm) intervals in the soil. Pinch out the growing tip when the plants are about 6 in (15 cm) high and subsequently all laterals produced except the two strongest, training these along the cloche to either side of the plant.These laterals are stopped again when about 24 in (60 cm) long. Fruit will be produced either on these laterals or on sub-laterals.

The flower garden can benefit from the use of cloches, especially in the early part of the season. Many gardeners start off their half-hardy annuals in the greenhouse; however, there is an advantage at times to sowing in their final growing positions, when the check from transplanting and the change from greenhouse to outside conditions can be avoided. Sow thinly in mid-spring and thin out to the required spacing.

Hardy annuals can be sown in the spring or autumn. Certain regions have weather conditions too severe for an autumn sowing to succeed unless this is protected over the winter by cloches or frames. In a mild late autumn or early winter the plants can be allowed to grow uncovered, but once the cold sets in they must be covered immediately. If in doubt about the weather erect the cloches once the seeds are sown. The same applies to a spring sowing.

Bulbs can also be brought on quickly with the use of a covering. Plant the bulbs in early to mid-autumn, cover and leave until flowering, which will be as much as four weeks ahead of an outdoor bulb. As some bulbs are tall, allowance for this will need to be made in the design of the cloche or frame used.

INDIVIDUAL CLOCHES

If individual plants need to be covered a miniature cloche can be made by cutting the bottom off a clear plastic bottle, pushing the cut edge into the soil. This offers double protection from both the weather and slugs (see page 305).

The rigid material cloches made of glass or plastic can be used as a wind-break to protect tall plants such as tomatoes. Stand the cloche on end as close to the plant as possible, holding it in position with a cane pushed into the soil to prevent it being blown over on to the plant. For added protection two cloches can be placed together to encircle the plant.

GARDEN IRRIGATION

Every spring and summer will have periods during which your plants can run short of water. A brief spell of sunshine, a few windy days, and your soil will start to dry out. In dry summers water, or rather the lack of it, can become much more serious for your plants and irrigation can become essential for the survival of your garden.

When to apply water is often as important as the amount of water that you use. Selected watering of your fruit and vegetables, for example, even during a wet summer, can greatly increase yields and crop quality and be well worth the effort involved.

The methods you use to water your garden are vital. Watering incorrectly will encourage the formation of shallow roots and plants that have little or no resistance to drought.

WHY DO PLANTS NEED WATER?

The answer to this question is complex. To manufacture food plants need sunlight, carbon dioxide and water. This process is called photosynthesis, and without it no growing plant could survive for more than a week or two. Even on a cloudy day sunlight is always available, and carbon dioxide is in the air all around us, but the lack of water inhibits the process.

Plants have tiny pores in their leaves, called stomata. These open during the day to allow carbon dioxide into the plant; at the same time, however, they also allow water to escape into the air. The stomata will close when the plant is losing more water from its leaves than it can take up through its roots. By this method the plant can protect itself from some of the early effects of dry conditions; but, of course, with these tiny valves shut the plant cannot get enough carbon dioxide and so is not able to manufacture enough food for itself. Growth slows or stops; plants become stunted; yields drop; poor flower formation may follow. If a dry spell develops into a drought this

Microscopic 30 μm long, 10 μm wide valves (stomata) on plant leaves open and shut to regulate water loss (Gene Cox)

lack of water may eventually kill the plant.

WHEN TO WATER

There is usually no point in watering your garden if plenty of soil water is still available. But how will you know when this soil water starts to run out? Waiting until your plants show signs of distress is not the best idea. So what is the alternative? Experts can detect very subtle changes in the leaf colour and posture of some plants, which are the earliest indications that soil water is just starting to dry up. However, very few of us are such experts. A much more reliable guide is to dig out a spade's depth of soil from beside the plants that you are concerned about. Feel the soil at the bottom of the hole. If it feels moist then there is no need to irrigate, but if it feels dry this strongly indicates that watering is needed.

SOIL TYPES

Different soil types and locations can significantly affect the garden's watering requirements. An understanding of these different factors can make the gardener's job much easier.

CLAY SOILS

These retain much more water than do soils of a more sandy type, and it can take months of hot

OPPOSITE: To the parched garden, the arrival of water spells a moment of dazzling regeneration (*Photos Horticultural*)

Cracks and hard, crusted surface characterize clay soil response to drought (*Chris Algar*)

dry weather before plants growing on clayey soils are affected. Once a clay soil does begin to dry out, however, it will hold onto its remaining moisture very tightly, so much so that the roots cannot take it up into the plant. Cracks start to appear in the clay. This has four serious effects: first, the cracks allow dry air to penetrate deep into the soil, to carry on the drying process and increase the depth of the cracks. Secondly, the cracks themselves can literally tear the plant roots apart, making a plant more vulnerable to drought. Thirdly, a hard crust can form on the surface, making it difficult for any seedlings to germinate, and accelerating the loss of water from the soil. Finally, and perhaps most importantly, the formation of cracks in the soil makes watering extremely difficult: any water applied to the surface will tend to run down the cracks and percolate deep into the soil, where it will be locked away from the roots of your plants.

To prevent the formation of cracks on a clay soil, hoe the surface to form a fine tilth about ½ in (1 cm) deep, which forms a barrier to water loss. Seed beds can be helped by raking in well rotted leaf-mould before sowing. As clay soils hold a lot of water, you can apply large amounts of water at fairly infrequent intervals. The actual amount you apply is of course dependent on weather conditions but a rule of thumb is 1½ gal (7 l) per sq ft (30 sq cm) applied every three weeks.

If, nevertheless, cracks do start to appear, mix leaf-mould and water into a thick paste and pour this down the cracks. Allow the mixture to dry and shrink and then repeat the process three or four days later.

SANDY SOILS

The particles in these soils are larger than those in clay, which means that sandy soils are free-draining and can dry out very quickly. The gardener with a sandy soil should always be alert for drought. During a dry spell, watering little and

often has to be the rule, perhaps ½ gal (2·5 l) per sq ft (30 sq cm) every few days in hot dry weather. Newly planted or shallow-rooted plants can begin to suffer after only four or five days into a dry spell. If you want to sow seeds on a sandy soil, incorporate leaf-mould into the seed drill prior to sowing and cover the seeds with dry soil.

BADLY DRAINED OR SHALLOW SOILS

Badly drained soils of any description, clay or sand, are the first to suffer during a drought. If your soil is well drained to a depth of only 8 in (20 cm) or so, this greatly restricts the development of root systems. Every time the roots try to establish themselves deeper down, they are killed by the hard pan below.

Before planting anything on such a poor soil, dig out a much deeper and wider hole than normal, break up the subsoil with a pick or crowbar, and increase the depth of soil available for rooting by mixing in a large amount of compost.

REDUCING WATER LOSS

The more water you can keep in the soil by preventing its escape into the atmosphere, the less you will have to water your garden in times of shortage. It is possible to reduce the amount of water loss from the surface by using a mulch of shredded bark, or garden compost. A black plastic sheet hidden from sight with a layer of gravel can also be of great assistance in preserving soil moisture. The use of these is described in more detail in *Mulches*, page 47.

The wind is a major cause of water loss from both soil and plants. If your garden is on an exposed site, your problems can be magnified by just a few dry, breezy days. Under these conditions, plants have to take more water from the soil to compensate for the increased loss from their leaves. A temporary windbreak about 3 ft (90 cm) high could reduce the water loss from your garden by up to 60%.

HOW TO WATER

There is a right and a wrong way to go about watering your garden. Do it inefficiently and you could waste a lot of effort and leave your plants worse off than they were in the first place. It is important thoroughly to wet the whole root depth of the soil – if you wet only the surface you can encourage the formation of shallow root systems, which can have disastrous consequences, making your plants more susceptible to drought. Check by digging a hole about three hours after you have finished watering. Do not give your plants a daily light sprinkling of water; most of this will be lost by evaporation.

Another useful tip is to concentrate your

watering efforts around the bases of the plants, leaving the rest of the soil dry. For instance, if you have rows of crops, just water the narrow strip of plants, leaving the soil between rows dry.

If your soil is sandy or prone to drought, but only if, it is well worth while spacing your plants more widely, as this gives each plant access to a greater volume of soil and therefore water. For these soils do not grow 'catch' crops in your vegetable garden, as too many plants could end up competing for the scarce moisture.

WATER QUALITY

Usually tap water is safe enough to use on your plants, but never forget that it contains aluminium and chlorine as well as possible traces of pesticides, herbicides and pharmaceutical residues. Mains water from a chalky or limestone catchment area will be alkaline and may be harmful to lime-hating plants. Without a doubt the best thing for irrigation is rainwater. The only exceptions may be when you are taking cuttings or trying to get delicate seedlings to grow, when sterile water may be a great help. Rainwater is safe for all plants, including lime-haters. The only problem is how to collect enough of it. In times of drought most waterbutts empty very quickly. In hot windy weather each square yard of soil may require 6 gallons of water (27 l per sq m) to replace what is lost. For even a small garden of about 120 sq yd (100 sq m) this means the application of at least 600 gallons (2,700 l) of water every week or so, whereas the average waterbutt holds about 50 gallons (230 l). This leaves the gardener with no alternative but to use tap water. In times of water shortage, kitchen, bathroom or washing-machine waste water can be used. Over the short term this will do no harm, but avoid any water that has had household bleach in it, which can be fatal for most plants in your garden.

IRRIGATION SYSTEMS

These do not have to be complicated. They are simply an aid to getting water exactly where you want it. A length of old guttering with small holes drilled in it can be a really effective aid to efficient watering. The guttering is simply laid against the crop you wish to water and filled with water from a hose. The only potential problem with this is that slugs tend to like the damp, dark environment,

A computer-operated system can monitor and control volume of water delivery when you are absent

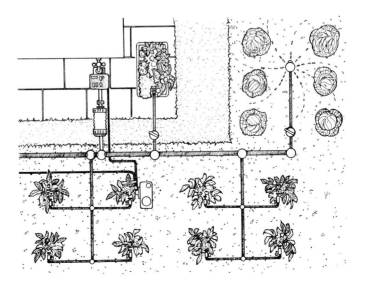

Automated irrigation system
(*Rob Dalton*)

Perforated plastic seep hose
concentrates watering effort
(Fred McPherson)

particularly when the weather is dry, so keep a regular check on the underside of the guttering. If you cannot lay your hands on guttering, a shallow trench drawn alongside the row of crops that you want to water will help to concentrate your watering effort. Plastic tubing with holes in it (known as a seep hose) is now readily available and is very effective. You can make your own, by drilling or melting small holes in a hosepipe, if you have one spare, and blocking up the end with a cork or bung. If you decide to use a seep hose, hammer wooden stakes into the end of each row of plants requiring irrigation. This stops the hose from damaging plants when it is moved to the next row. To water the row of plants is simply a matter of connecting the hose to a tap and then adjusting the water pressure so that the roots are watered but the soil between rows remains dry. This discourages the germination of weed seeds, so preserving some of the soil moisture.

For individual plants that may need a lot of water such as tomatoes, sink a large flowerpot into the soil alongside the plant stem. Do this at planting-out time. Water poured into the pot is directed to the root system, there is no surface run-off, and root systems close to the surface of the soil are not damaged by the erosive effect of the water falling on the soil's surface.

You can save yourself a great deal of trouble, of course, if you use a more automated watering system. These systems vary in sophistication. Perhaps the simplest is a series of trickle hoses laid out with bends and branches as required, connected to a central tap. This tap can be fitted with a timing device that switches on the water, so that your garden is watered each day without your having to think about it. An alternative to an electrically controlled timer is a system based on the principle of osmosis, where water is drawn from the filled trickle hose only as the adjacent soil dries out. More sophisticated still, and of particular value in the greenhouse, is capillary matting, a thick, felt-like material that soaks up moisture and is laid beneath the pots and so on. Used in conjunction with a timing device which keeps it regularly supplied with moisture, this is the ideal answer for the greenhouse owner who wants to go on holiday.

Overhead systems are also available, particularly for use in the greenhouse. Such systems consist of a number of pipes fitted with nozzles to spray water down on to the plants. The spray can be turned on and off by hand, or automatically using a time switch.

Although all these automated systems can save you a good deal of effort, they do have a few drawbacks. First and most obviously, they are quite expensive to buy and set up. Secondly, they deliver the same amount of water to each plant, so if, like most amateurs, you are growing a number of different species together, your watering will always be a compromise between the requirements of one plant and another. A third problem can also arise with overhead sprays: in cold weather they can produce extremely high humidity, while in hot weather they can give rise to leaf scorch.

HOW MUCH WATER

It is possible to calculate the water requirements for each of your plants. As discussed, to some extent this depends on your soil type - sandy, clay or whatever. As a guide, assume that a fully wetted sandy soil holds less than 1 in (2·5 cm) of water per 12 in (30 cm) of depth, a clayey soil 3½ in (8·5 cm) for the same depth, while a loam may hold about 2 in (5 cm) for the same depth.

Roughly speaking, you can assume that the root volume of a plant is the same as the volume of the plant above the soil's surface. The roots of a fully grown cauliflower will therefore have access to about

Water poured into the plant pot goes direct to the root system, avoiding surface run-off

Individual plant care (Rob
Dalton)

How to calculate water loss (*Rob Dalton*)

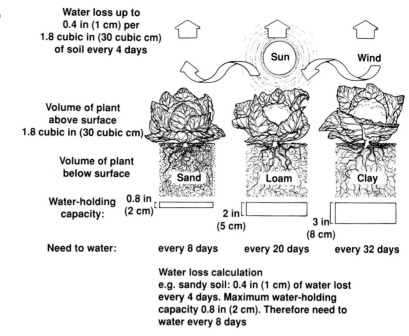

Water loss up to 0.4 in (1 cm) per 1.8 cubic in (30 cubic cm) of soil every 4 days

Volume of plant above surface 1.8 cubic in (30 cubic cm)

Volume of plant below surface

Water-holding capacity: 0.8 in (2 cm)   2 in (5 cm)   3 in (8 cm)

Sand   Loam   Clay

Need to water: every 8 days   every 20 days   every 32 days

Water loss calculation e.g. sandy soil: 0.4 in (1 cm) of water lost every 4 days. Maximum water-holding capacity 0.8 in (2 cm). Therefore need to water every 8 days

a cubic foot (0·028 cu m) of earth which, if it is fairly average loam, could hold about 2 in (5 cm) of water or about a gallon (5 l). During hot and sunny weather, loss from one plant and its surrounding soil will usually amount to at least a gallon every twenty days. If the soil is sandy rather than average loam, less water needs to be applied but more frequently; if a clayey soil, more water less frequently. This is only a rough guide – if your plants are beginning to wilt, give them water and ignore what the calculator says.

WHICH PLANTS TO WATER

As watering requires both commitment and effort, it is better to concentrate on plants that really need it, leaving the other plants to look after themselves. However, the drier the soil conditions the greater will be your list of plants that need water.

Trees and shrubs. Trees and shrubs that have been established for

Critical watering times for flowers and trees		
Species	*When to water*	*Effect*
Azaleas	Regular watering essential	Plants will not survive prolonged dry spell
Conifers, particularly species of *Chamaecyparis, Cryptomaria, Juniperus, Picea, Pinus, Taxus, Thujia, Tsuga*	During first year after transplanting	Prevents loss of many new transplants
Dahlias	When leaves show signs of wilting	Improved flowers
Hydrangeas	Regular watering essential	Plants will die back if not provided with water
Rhododendrons	Regular watering essential	Plants will die if not watered during drought

Critical watering times for fruit

Crop	When to water	Effect
Apples	Late spring to early summer	Increased yields the next year
Blackcurrants	Late spring to late summer	Higher yields
Raspberries	When fruit starts to turn red	Higher yields
Strawberries	After flowering	Bigger fruit

a number of years will have extensive root systems going deep into the subsoil. These will cope with any foreseeable drought conditions and can safely be left to their own devices. There are a few exceptions to this rule, however: rhododendrons, azaleas and hydrangeas will need special attention, as their root systems are near the soil's surface. Scoop out a hollow, with minimal root disturbance, around the base of the stem. This hollow can then be flooded with water at regular intervals.

Newly planted trees and shrubs will be at risk during dry conditions, especially if they are in an exposed position and subject to the added stress of wind removing water from their leaves and the soil. A plastic sheet spread around the base after flooding the area may help, as will a thick mulch, if it is applied in the spring while the soil moisture content is still high. A temporary windbreak may also be useful.

Lawns. A long dry spell will make your lawns appear brown and dead, but established lawns are rarely killed by drought. You have just to be patient and wait for the following year, when they will recover. If you have a newly laid lawn, or want to maintain your lawn, large quantities of water are needed, and the best way to apply this is with a sprinkler system. If you start this irrigation procedure you have to keep it up until significant amounts of rain fall. Irregular watering can cause more damage than none at all.

Herbaceous plants. Mature, well-established plants should survive long dry spells without too many problems. Growth may be retarded and flowering may be restricted, but the plants should survive. If you wish to irrigate a prize specimen, scoop out a shallow trench around it, and flood the trench regularly.

Bedding plants. Some bedding plants will withstand dry conditions better than others. Nicotiana, gazanias, geraniums, French marigolds and zinnias will survive a dry period fairly well, but if they show signs of stress regular irrigation will be needed. Others such as begonias, chlorophytum, cinerarias and petunias will die

back without regular watering of their roots, and it is best to concentrate your efforts here.

Fruit and vegetables. These require considerably more attention than flowering plants. Because they are grown for their yields and not their looks, you are requiring them to manufacture and store considerable amounts of food. This, of course, needs large amounts of water for the process of photosynthesis. If water is restricted the plants may survive, but yields will be greatly reduced or even non-existent.

The needs of vegetables and fruit for water are complicated by the fact that water is beneficial only at certain times of the life-cycle, and the requirement can vary from species to species. In some cases watering can be positively harmful to yields if carried out at the wrong time. Vegetables that never go short of water will produce a vast amount of foliage. This is fine if they are leaf crops such as cabbage and lettuce, but is counterproductive if it reduces the number of flowers, as in the case of peas or French beans.

Copious watering can also reduce the flavour of some crops such as carrot and parsnip. To help you water your fruit and vegetables in the most efficient manner, saving you time and ensuring maximum yields, see the watering charts for fruit and vegetables.

A DROUGHT-RESISTANT GARDEN

As a final thought, it is possible to do away with all or most watering by planning a drought-resistant garden. This means giving up growing bedding plants, reducing the size of your lawn and concentrating your efforts on growing plants that are resistant to drought conditions and also look attractive. Most established trees and shrubs are, as mentioned, able to withstand almost any drought. Examples of small drought-resistant plants are cistus, spurges (*Euphorbia*) and genista. Almost all plants with silver or grey leaves such as cotton lavender (*Santolina*), pinks and artemisia are also drought-resistant. In the vegetable garden choice is rather more restricted, but once they have germinated, carrots, beetroot and sweetcorn can survive a dry spell.

Critical watering times for vegetables

Crop	When to water	Effect
Artichoke (Jerusalem)	Never	Water would lower yield
Bean (broad)	When in flower	Increases crop
Bean (French)	Water only to help germination	Watering can lower yields
Bean (runner)	Before sowing, then at least weekly; in very hot weather daily	Much bigger yields
Beetroot	Water to help germination	
Brussels sprout	Puddle plants in if soil is dry	
Cabbage (Chinese)	Water daily in dry weather	Without regular water, plants go to seed
Cabbage (spring)	Puddle plants in if soil is dry	
Cabbage (summer)	Puddle plants in, water regularly in drought	Increased yield prevents plants going to seed
Calabrese	Water every 2–3 days in drought	Maintains yield
Carrot	Water only to help germination	Watering at any other time lowers yield
Cauliflower (summer)	Puddle in; never allow to go short of water	Any shortage of water will cause plant to go to seed
Celery	Water daily	Any lack of water could cause the crop to fail completely
Courgette	Water only when fruits start to swell, unless weather is very dry	Watering at other times encourages leaf formation
Cucumber (ridge)	Water as often as you can	Gives better texture and increased yield
Kohl rabi	Water when the root starts to swell	Watering before this time encourages leaf formation
Leek	Puddle in new plants, then water as often as you can	The more you give the bigger your crop
Lettuce	Regular water is essential	Encourages good heart formation and tenderness
Marrow	Water when fruits start to swell	Watering before this encourages leaf formation
Onion (from sets)	In a dry year flood ground before planting	Aids establishment
Onion (spring)	Once you start to water you must not stop	Will do badly without water
Parsnip	Never water	
Potato (early)	Water regularly	Increased yield; can save a crop in a dry year
Potato (maincrop)	Water when flowers start to form	Increased yield; prevents potato scab
Radish	Water every few days	More tender crop
Spinach	Water during drought	Will extend the harvest season
Swede	Never water	Watering only encourages leaf formation
Sweetcorn	Water when plants are young	
Tomato (outdoor)	Regular watering needed	Irregular watering causes fruit to split, and can cause blossom end rot
Turnip	Water only in a very dry year, about a month before harvest	

23 TOOLS

Given just one tool to take as a castaway on to a desert island, I would probably choose the versatile hoe. You can use it for digging, weeding, drilling seeds and earthing up. No wonder the hoe is man's oldest gardening tool, still in use after more than 42,000 years. Although there are now various types, it is fairly certain that Stone Age man would recognize the modern hoe and know how to use it.

The earliest versions were of wood or bone, the wooden ones being a forked branch, possibly fire-hardened at the business end. Even when iron appeared on the scene to revolutionize the crafting of tools, the wooden hoe was still widely used.

Another very early tool was the digging stick, found among different cultures worldwide and still in use in the twentieth century. The Romans brought both variety and sophistication to gardening tools, but in Europe there was no divergence of design between gardening and agricultural implements until the Middle Ages, when a genre of farming tools, drawn by animals, was slowly evolved. At that point, says the gardening historian Anthony Huxley, 'the tools of the garden became gradually more refined and more specialized'.

Types of hoe.   In my armoury of tools I have a draw hoe, used mainly for earthing up potato, leek and celery plants, a Dutch hoe for general weeding, and an onion hoe that has been handed down through several generations of the family and now has a blade honed to surgical sharpness. Variants of these basic designs include the Wilkinson 'swoe', a beautifully balanced tool with a working shape like a golf putter which cuts through weeds at just the right level with a minimum of effort; and the scuffle hoe, which has sharpened edges both front and back and can therefore be pushed or pulled.

OPPOSITE: Hoeing tools for mechanical weeding: (clockwise from top), four-tine muck rake or crome, garden rook, Dutch hoe, flat-bladed draw hoe, draw hoe, onion hoe, three-prong cultivator, swoe (*Roy Lacey*)

Hand-held paraffin flame gun (*Roy Lacey*)

For organic gardeners who, of course, shun the use of herbicides in weed control, the hoe is vitally important, but it must be used correctly. The cutting edge of the hoe should sever the roots of the weed from the stem. This means operating with the blade about 1 in (2·5 cm) below the surface. This was a major consideration in the design of the swoe.

Flame-gunning   as a method of weed control in an organic environment (see *Weeds*, page 254) also calls for precision in operation. I have used a hooded, wheeled flame-gun, powered by liquefied petroleum gas, on a smallholding, and now use a hand-held paraffin-powered gun for eradicating weeds in paths and driveways in a town garden, but the technique is the same. The secret is not to try to burn off established weeds in one sweep. Two stages are needed. The first involves using the gun like a scythe, walking

Ecologically helpful mulch mowers shred grass finely for leaving on lawn (*Al-Ko*)

Spring-tined rake to clear thatch and leaves from lawn (*Roy Lacey*)

slowly forward and holding the gun with the flame just about 4 in (10 cm) above the surface. The intense heat causes the plant cells to collapse, and the plants will wither. A second sweep will complete the task. Obviously, a flame-gun is potentially dangerous, on a par with a bonfire, and suitable safety precautions should be observed.

In the Netherlands this type of weed-control technique is even further advanced: machines have been developed especially for use in commercial greenhouses in which infra-red radiation is the operating principle, and this technique is gaining wide acceptance.

Lawn tools. Grass is a crop the British gardener grows remarkably well – too well, perhaps, because of the vast expenditure of effort and energy involved in keeping it manicured. According to trade sources, more money is spent on the lawn than on any other part of the garden. Yet, to keep a lawn in reasonably good condition, the only essential tools are a garden fork to admit air to the roots of the grass, a lawn rake, and a mower.

In seeking the velvety striped effect coveted by many, the least expensive hand-mower will do as good a job as the most expensive ride-on machine with electric ignition and a battery of accessories. About 90% of all garden mowers in the UK are powered ones, the majority driven by mains electricity.

Most lawn owners prefer to have a machine that collects the clippings, even though their disposal may present a problem. Leaving clippings on the lawn as a mulch, however, is far better for the health of the grass than collecting them, even for compost-making. Experiments by the Department of Agriculture and Horticulture at Reading University proved that clippings left on the lawn do not build up thatch or increase the weed population. The nutrients, particularly nitrogen, are recycled in as little as fourteen days. Mulch mowers, designed for this purpose, already popular in the USA and the Continent, are now available in the UK. These automatically shred the clippings into a fine mulch before ejecting them. Recycling the grass in this way, rather than adding it to the household waste for landfill sites (now banned in parts of the USA), is good ecological practice.

Choosing the right type of mower for the organic garden involves basically the same criteria as those for the inorganic garden, with additions. The mower should be large enough for the lawn or lawns; safe to use; within budget both to buy and maintain, and with a good servicing and spares back-up; and should give the finish to the lawn that is required. In addition it should be energy-efficient and environmentally sound. This means taking other factors into account, such as quietness in operation and longevity; if petrol-driven, it should be with lead-free fuel.

For small lawns of up to about 1,000 sq ft (93 sq m – about half the lawns in Britain) a hand-driven cylinder mower is still the best type for the green gardener to choose because it does not use fuel, is quiet and gives the best possible cut. For larger lawns requiring a powered machine, the market is dominated by the electric mowers; for lawns of 4,000 sq ft and over (370 sq m), the petrol-driven machines take over.

Although a garden fork is ideal for aerating small lawns on light soil, larger lawns and heavy soil, particularly where there is waterlogging, may call for mechanical aid, such as a wheeled solid-tine aerator or its powered version, or a slitter aerator that can be attached to the lawn-mower. However, even the owner of a large lawn may feel that expenditure on a powered spiker is scarcely warranted and, happily, such machines can be hired by the day.

Raking to remove the overwintered thatch and the autumn's

fallen leaves is simple enough with a spring-tine rake, but even this task has been mechanized with the multi-purpose lawnraker, used for spiking, raking and collecting the leaves.

For trimming long grass at the edges of the lawn and in places where the mower cannot reach, long-handled shears are cheap to buy, easy to maintain and environmentally welcome. Grass trimming can also be undertaken with powered strimmers or brush-cutters.

Shredders. One of the problems about making compost in the average small garden is that there is never enough material of the right sort to recycle. Indeed, quite a lot of organic material that could be used for composting is wasted, usually being consigned to the anti-social bonfire, because it is so tough that it would take an inordinate time to rot down: woody prunings, hedge trimmings and the stems of cabbages and Brussels sprouts. Happily, garden machine manufacturers have realized that this problem is relatively easy to solve with a large-scale version of the kitchen mincing machine, and have produced the compost shredder. You feed the woody material and fibrous items into the inlet hopper of the machine, and motor-operated blades then shred it into fine chippings, which can be used as an organic mulch, or added to the compost bin where they will decompose much more quickly than if left in their original condition.

There are some important aspects of shredders to bear in mind. Some are very noisy in operation, particularly in an urban location. Even the smallest of those available in the UK costs the equivalent of a powered lawn-mower, but might only be used for a few days of the year. So before buying a shredder it might be well worth while saving your prunings, sprout stems and the like, and hiring a machine for a day.

Modern technology such as shredders assist the organic gardener, rescuing valuable mulching material from the old-style bonfire (*Al-Ko*)

Two other points to remember are that a shredder is a bulky piece of equipment and will need to be stored under cover for much of the year. It is also heavy: at 22–40 lb (10–18 kg) too heavy to move easily unless fitted with wheels. A final point is that even the largest of the garden shredders cannot cope with branches thicker than about 1⅘ in (45 mm) in diameter. A wide range is available to suit all sizes of garden.

I have said that hiring a shredder for a day makes sense for a small garden. The same is true for other machines and tools that are used infrequently, such as a flame-gun, hedge trimmer, chainsaw, rotovator or powered scarifier, but be sure to read the small print on the conditions of hire. If you finish the job sooner than expected and let a friend or neighbour borrow the machine, you may be liable for any damage to the machine or third-party claim.

Pruners. There must be very few gardens where a pruning tool is not needed, even if the prunings are not destined for a shredder. There are two main types: secateurs for light pruning of roses, shrubs and cane fruit, and long-handled loppers for heavy-duty work.

As with so many other tools, it is good sense to buy the best quality that you can afford, because a pair of secateurs double the price of another model will invariably give far more than double the length of satisfactory service.

There are two types of secateurs, anvil and bypass, according to the cutting action. With carbon steel blades common to both types, there is little to choose between the two in terms of efficiency and durability. Points to look for when buying secateurs are ease of action, comfortable grip, preferably with contoured handles, and the

Garden version of kitchen mincing machine converts woody materials into mulch or material for compost bin (*Al-Ko*)

Safety first

All garden machinery is potentially hazardous and should be used according to manufacturers' instructions. Here are some basic safety rules:

* Do not use electric tools when it is wet and always protect them with a residual current-breaker device

* Always disconnect a machine from the power source before cleaning it or leaving it unattended

* Keep children and pets away from the work area

* Wear protective gloves, ear protectors and eye shields when using hedge trimmers, shredders and chainsaws

* Wear safety boots or shoes when using brush-cutters and cultivators

facility to adjust the blades according to the pruning job being tackled.

Although the organic gardener shuns the expediency of chemical weedkillers and the swift kill of insecticides, there is no reason why he or she should be denied the benefits of modern technology. I have no doubt that the introduction of stainless steel to the manufacture of garden tools has been a major benefit to the gardener and not just to the makers and merchants. Although a stainless steel spade, for example, might not outlast a carbon steel one, it does make digging easier because moist soil does not cling to the blade. Cleaning, too, is a simple matter of brushing off surplus soil.

Another type of spade that has many devotees is the Wolf-Terrex Autospade, enabling the gardener to dig without bending. It has a spring and lever action that eliminates the physical lifting of the spade and soil, so you dig in an upright position. It is particularly valuable for those with back problems or other disabilities. The same manufacturers came up with the ingenious idea of producing a wide range of tool-

The widger, a tool for pricking out (*Roy Lacey*)

Pruning tools: choose between anvil (orange handle) and bypass secateurs to taste, but go for top quality, and use long-handled lopper for heavy-duty work on bigger shrubs (*Roy Lacey*)

The inexpensive but indispensable dibber. Here it is being used for planting out leeks. The shaft is marked in inches (*Roy Lacey*)

heads to fit just one handle, using a patented snap-lock system. The thirty-eight tools in the system include several types of hoe, a soil miller for seed bed preparation, grubber, crumbler and adjustable cultivator, three types of rake and trowel. As well as saving money, the multi-change tool system saves storage space. Most of the tools are designed to be pulled through the soil, so there is minimum strain on the gardener's spine.

Two tools that I would not be without are also the least expensive ones in my tool shed. One is a dibber for, among other things, planting leeks; the other is a widger, a little spatula-like tool that is just the job for the delicate task of pricking out seedlings, winkling out weeds from the lawn and gently stirring the compost of the house plants.

One surprising bonus of converting my vegetable garden to deep-bed production (see *Methods of Cultivation*, page 59) has been a decreasing dependence on tools. The soil structure of the beds has improved over the years to the point where it is now quite unnecessary to dig out root crops; they are easy to harvest by hand. The spade is still used for other areas of the garden and for preparing for crops, such as peas and runner beans, that I prefer to grow away from the beds, while the fork is mainly used for transferring well-made compost to a wheelbarrow and then to the parts of the garden where it is to be used.

FURTHER READING

Algar, Chris, *The Chase Organics Gardening Manual*, Ian Allen, 1989.

Baines, Chris, *How to Make a Wildlife Garden*, Elm Tree Books, 1985.

Balfour, E.B., *The Living Earth*, Universe Books, 1976.

Bleasdale, J., Salter, P., *et al.*, *The Complete Know and Grow Vegetables*, Oxford University Press, 1991.

Brickell, Christopher (Ed.), *The Royal Horticultural Society Gardeners' Encyclopedia of Plants & Flowers*, Dorling Kindersley, 1989.

Brooks, Audrey, *et al.*, *Garden Pests and Diseases*, Mitchell Beazley, 1988.

Buczacki, Stefan and Harris, Keith, *Collins Guide to the Pests, Diseases and Disorders of Garden Plants*, Collins, 1981.

Carr, Anna, *et al.* (Eds), *The Encyclopedia of Organic Gardening*, Rodale Press, 1978.

Carson, Rachel, *Silent Spring*, Houghton Mifflin, 1962 (US), Hamish Hamilton, 1963 (UK).

Chambers, John, *Wildflower Garden*, Elm Tree Books, 1987.

Chancellor, R. J., *The Identification of Weed Seedlings of Farm and Garden*, Blackwell Scientific Publications, 1966.

Chinery, Michael, *Collins Guide to the Insects of Britain and Western Europe*, Collins, 1986.

Chinery, Michael, *The Living Garden*, Dorling Kindersley, 1986.

Coleman, Eliot, *The New Organic Grower*, Cassell, 1990.

Darwin, Charles, *Darwin on Humus and the Earthworm: The Formation of Vegetable Mould*, Faber and Faber, 1945.

Elphinstone, Margaret and Langley, Julia, *The Green Gardener's Handbook*, Thorsons 1990.

Fish, Margery, *Cottage Garden Flowers*, Faber and Faber, 1961.

Franck, Gertrud, *Companion Planting*, Thorsons, 1983.

Gibbons, Bob and Liz, *Creating a Wildlife Garden*, Hamlyn, 1988.

Hamilton, Geoff, *The Ornamental Kitchen Garden*, BBC Books, 1990.

Hamilton, Geoff, *Successful Organic Gardening*, Dorling Kindersley, 1987.

Hart, Robert A. de J., *Forest Gardening*, Green Books, 1991.

Hay, Jim, *Natural Pest and Disease Control*, Century, 1987.

Hay, Jim, *Vegetables Naturally*, Century, 1986.

Hillier, Harold G., *The Manual of Trees and Shrubs*, David and Charles, 1991.

Hills, Lawrence D., *Grow Your Own Fruit and Vegetables*, Faber and Faber, 1975.

Hills, Lawrence D., *Organic Gardening*, Penguin, 1977.

Hussey, N.W., *et al.* (Ed.), *Biological Pest Control, The Glasshouse Experience*, Blandford Press, 1985.

Jeavons, John, *How to Grow More Vegetables*, Ten Speed Press, 1979.

Kitto, Dick, *Composting*, Thorsons, 1988.

Lacey, Roy, *Organic Gardening*, David and Charles, 1988.

Lacey, Roy, *The Green Gardener*, David and Charles, 1990.

Lacey, Roy, *The Organic Greenhouse*, David and Charles, 1992.

Larkcom, Joy, *Oriental Vegetables*, John Murray, 1991.

Larkcom, Joy, *The Salad Garden*, Frances Lincoln, 1984.

Larkcom, Joy, *Vegetables From Small Gardens*, Faber and Faber, 1986.

Larkcom, Joy, *The Vegetable Garden Displayed*, The Royal Horticultural Society, 1992

Mabey, Richard (Ed.), *The Complete New Herbal*, Penguin, 1991.

Mollison, Bill and Holmgren, D., *Permaculture One*, Transworld, 1978.

Mollison, Bill, *et al.*, *Permaculture Two*, Tagari, 1979.

Owen, Jennifer, *Garden Life*, Chatto and Windus, 1983.

Owen, Jennifer, *The Ecology of a Garden*, Cambridge University Press, 1991.

Philbrick, H. and Gregg, R., *Companion Plants*, Robinson and Watkins, 1967.

Philip, Chris, *The Plant Finder*, Moorland, 1992.

Phillips, Roger, *Wild Flowers of Britain*, Pan Books, 1977.

Poincelot, Raymond P., *Organic No-dig, No-Weed Gardening*, Rodale Press, 1986 (US), Thorsons, 1988 (UK)

Soper, John, *Bio-dynamic Gardening*, Bio-dynamic Agricultural Association, 1983.

Stephens, John, *The National Trust Book of Wildflower Gardening*, Dorling Kindersley, 1987.

Stickland, Sue, *Planning The Organic Flower Garden*, Thorsons, 1986.

Stickland, Sue, *Planning The Organic Herb Garden*, Thorsons, 1986.

Stickland, Sue, *The Organic Garden*, Hamlyn, 1987.

Yamaguchi, Mas, *World Vegetables*, Van Nostrand Reinhold, 1983.

BOOKLETS

HDRA/Search Press: *How to Control Fruit and Vegetable Pests* (Pauline Pears and Bob Sherman); *Healthy Fruit and Vegetables* (Pauline Pears and Bob Sherman); *Soil Care and Management* (Jo Readman); *Weeds* (Jo Readman); *How to Make your Garden Fertile* (Pauline Pears). HDRA miscellaneous handbooks and leaflets.

National Institute of Agricultural Botany handbooks.

Royal Horticultural Society: Wisley handbooks.

ORGANIC MAGAZINES

Les Quatre Saisons (bi-monthly), 6 rue Saulnier, 75009, Paris, France.

Organic Gardening (monthly), P. 0. Box 4, Wiveliscombe, Taunton, Somerset TA4 2QY.

Organic Gardening (9 issues p.a.), 33 E. Minor Street, Emmaus PA 18098, USA.

ASSOCIATIONS

(research and advice)

Bio-dynamic Agricultural Association, Woodman Lane, Clent, Stourbridge, W. Midlands DY9 9PX.

Brogdale Horticultural Trust, Brogdale Farm, Brogdale Road, Faversham, Kent ME13 8XZ. Maintains national fruit collection.

Cottage Garden Association, 15 Faenol Avenue, Abergele, Clwyd LL22 7HT.

Elm Farm Research Centre, Hamstead Marshall, Newbury, Berks. RG15 0HR. Operates an organic farm and advisory service.

Friends of the Earth (environmental issues), 26–28 Underwood Street, London N1 7JQ.

Henry Doubleday Research Association, Ryton-on-Dunsmore, Coventry CV8 3LG. Demonstration organic gardens and information at the National Centre for Organic Gardening, Coventry.

Herb Society, P. 0. Box 599, London SW1 4RW.

Horticulture Research International, Wellesbourne, Warwick CV35 9EF.

National Insititute for Agricultural Botany, Huntingdon Road, Cambridge CB3 0LE.

Permaculture Association, 4 Red Lake, Dartington, Totnes, Devon TQ9 6HF.

Permaculture Institute, P. 0. Box 1, Tyalgum, NSW 2484, Australia.

Rodale Institute, Box J10, 222 Main Street, Emmaus, PA, 18098, USA.

Royal Horticultural Society, Vincent Square, London SW1P 2PE.

Royal Society for Nature Conservation, The Green, Nettleham, Lincoln LN2 2NR.

Soil Association, 86–88 Colston Street, Bristol BS1 5BB. Operates its symbol system certifying organic standards.

Wild Flower Society, 86 Outwoods Road, Loughborough, Leics. LE11 3LY.

SUPPLIERS

COMPOSTS, MANURES, ORGANIC FERTILIZERS, MULCHES, GENERAL ORGANIC SUPPLIERS*

Camland Products (bark mulch), Fordham House, Fordham, Cambs. CB7 5LN.

Chase/HDRA*, Coombelands Lane, Addlestone, Weybridge, Surrey KT15 1HY.

Cowpact (manure), P. O. Box 595, Adstock, Bucks. MK18 2RE.

Cumulus*, Phinetum Lodge, Churcham, Glos. GL2 8AD.

Dig and Delve Organics* (derris, pyrethrum, quassia), Fen Road, Blo' Norton, Diss, Norfolk IP22 2JH.

Greenvale Organic (fertilizer/manure), Greenvale Farm, Clapham Lodge, Northallerton, N. Yorks. DL7 9LY.

Hydrocut (plastic mulch), Sudbury, Suffolk CO10 6HB.

Maxicrop (liquid seaweed), Cavendish House, 10 Eversley Park, Chester CH2 2AJ.

The Mealworm Co, Unit 1, Universal Crescent, North Anston Trading Estate, Sheffield S31 7JJ,

Melcourt Industries (bark mulch), Three Cups House, Tetbury, Glos. GL8 8JG.

Norfolk Farm Composts, Docking Farm, Oulton, Norwich NR11 6BR.

Organic Concentrates, 3 Broadway Court, Chesham, Bucks. HP5 1EN.

Organic Garden Centre*, P. O. Box 14, Kingsbridge, Devon TQ7 1YA.

Papronet (plastic mulch), Wyke Works, Hedon Road, Hull HU9 5NL.

Pelco, Five Hills, High Bannerdown, Bath BA1 7JY.

Polythena (plastic mulch), 76 Oaklands Avenue, Watford WD1 4LW.

West Riding Organics, 147 Brights Buildings, New Mill Road, Honley, Huddersfield HD7 2QE.

BIOLOGICAL CONTROLS (Numbers relate to specific pest controls, see pages 315–17)

1. Agricultural genetics, MicroBio Divison, 126 Science Park, Milton Road, Cambridge CB4 4FZ.

2. Applied Horticulture, Fargro Ltd, Toddington Lane, Littlehampton BN17 7PP.

3. Bunting Biological Control, Great Horkesley, Colchester, Essex CO6 4AJ.

4. Biological Crop Protection, Occupation Road, Wye, Ashford, Kent TN25 5AH.

5. Brinkman Biological Control, Spur Road, Quarry Lane, Chichester, W. Sussex PO19 2RP.

6. English Woodlands, Grower Services Division, Hoyle Depot, Graffham, Petworth GU28 0LR.

7. Chase/HDRA, Coombelands Lane, Addlestone, Weybridge, Surrey KT15 1HY.

8. Koppert, 1 Wadhurst Business Park, Faircrouch Lane, Wadhurst, E. Sussex TN5 6PT.

9. Natural Pest Control, Yapton Road, Barnham, Bognor Regis PO22 0BQ.

10. The Plant Sales Centre, Royal Horticultural Society Garden, Wisley, Woking GU23 6QB.

11. WyeBugs, Biological Sciences, Wye College, Ashford, Kent TN25 5AH.

Agralan (codling moth), The Old Brockyard, Ashton Keynes, Swindon, Wilts. SN6 6QR.

ORGANIC INSECTICIDES

Ad Chem (soft soap), P.O. Box 161, Grassy Lane, Wolverhampton WV10 6BR.

Koppert, (Savona soft soap), 1 Wadhurst Business Park, Faircrouch Lane, Wadhurst, E. Sussex TN5 6PT.

Pan Britannica Industries (derris, pyrethrum, quassia), Waltham Cross, Herts. EN8 7DY.

Phostrogen (Safers insecticidal soap), Corwen, Clwyd LL21 0EE.

EQUIPMENT, SUNDRIES

Access Frames (cold frames and irrigation systems), Crick, Northampton NN6 7XS

Agriframes (cages), Charlwoods Road, East Grinstead, Sussex RH19 2HG.

Al-Ko (shredders, mulch lawnmowers), Number One Industrial Estate, Medomsley Road, Consett, Co. Durham DH8 6SZ.

Blackwall Products (compost tumbler), Unit 4, Riverside Industrial Estate, 150 River Way, London SE10 0BH.

C and C Tunnels (polytunnels), P. O. Box 37, Newtown, Powys SY17 5ZZ.

Citadel Products (polytunnels), 10 Castle Road, Kineton, Warks. CV35 0BR.

Daisy Distribution (Hotterotter compost bin), P.O. Box 595, Adstock, Buckingham MK18 2RE.

Early Bird Worms, 17 Hill Cottages, Flag Hill, Great Bentley, Essex CO7 8RG.

Ferryman (polytunnels), Edgerley Cottage, Lapford, Crediton, Devon EX17 6AH.

Gardena (irrigation system), 7 Dunhams Court, Letchworth Garden City, Hertfordshire SG6 1BD.

Globe Garden Services (Kemp shredders and compost tumbler), 163A Warwick Road, Solihull, W. Midlands, B92 7AR.

Hydrocut (floating cloche), Sudbury, Suffolk CO10 6HB.

Knowle Nets, East Road, Bridport, Dorset DT6 4NX.

J. P. Lamb (cultivator), 2 Croft Lane, Liverpool L9 9DL.

Mylan Products (cloches), Squirrels Wood, Reigate Road, Leatherhead, Surrey KT22 8QY.

Organibox (compost bins), The Halifax Wireform Co., Calder Mill, Hebdon Bridge, W. Yorks. HX7 6LJ.

Original Organics (Rotol compost bin, worm composting system), Organic House, P. O. Box 6, Tiverton, Devon EX16 7SL.

Papronet (cloches), Wyke Works, Hedon Road, Hull HU9 5NL.

Propapack (cellular trays), Hi-Po Marketing, Southbank Nurseries, Vines Cross, nr. Heathfield, E. Sussex TN21 9HG.

Solardome (greenhouse), 9 Bridlington Road, Hunmanby, Filey, Yorks. YO14 0LR.

Spear and Jackson (tools), Handsworth Road, Sheffield S13 9BR.

G. W. Thornton (Mantis cultivator),Grether House, Cranwell Industrial Park, Shawcross Street, Stockport, Cheshire SK1 3HB.

C. H. Whitehouse (greenhouses), Buckhurst Works, Bells Yew Green, Frant, Tunbridge Wells TN3 9BN.

Wiggly Wigglers (worm composting system), The Bank, Preston-on-Wye, Herefordshire. HR2 9JU

Wolf Tools, Alton Road, Ross-on-Wye, Herefordshire HR9 5NE.

SEED

Robert Bolton (sweet pea), Birdbrook, Halstead, Essex CO9 4BQ.

J. W. Boyce, Lower Carter Street, Fordham, Ely, Cambs. CB7 5JU.

John Chambers (wildflower), 15 Westleigh Road, Barton Seagrave, Kettering, Northants. NN15 5AJ.

Chase HDRA, Coombelands Lane, Addlestone, Weybridge, Surrey KT15 1HY.

Chiltern Seeds, Bortree Stile. Ulverston, Cumbria LA12 7PB.

Samuel Dobie, Broomhill Way, Torquay, Devon TQ2 7QW.

Emorsgate Seeds (wildflower), Terrington Court, Popes Lane, Terrington Street, Clement, Kings Lynn, Norfolk PE34 4NT.

Mr Fothergill's, Gazeley Road, Kentford, Newmarket, Suffolk CB8 7QB.

W. W. Johnson, Boston, Lincs. PE21 8AD.

King's of Kelvedon, Monks Farm, Pantlings Lane, Coggeshall Road, Kelvedon, Essex CO5 9PG.

S. E. Marshall, Wisbech, Cambs. PE13 2RF.

M.A.S. (grass), 9 Brevel Terrace, Charlton Kings, Cheltenham, Glos. GL53 8JZ.

W. Robinson (onion, tomato), Sunny Bank, Forton nr. Preston, Lancs. PR3 0BN.

Suffolk Herbs, Pantlings Lane, Coggeshall Road, Kelvedon, Essex CO5 9PG.

Suttons Seeds, Hele Road, Torquay, Devon TQ2 7QJ.

Thompson and Morgan, London Road, Ipswich, Suffolk IP2 0BA.

Unwins Seeds, Histon, Cambridge CB4 4ZZ.

INDEX